# Lecture Notes in Computer Science    1154

Edited by G. Goos, J. Hartmanis and J. van Leeuwen

**Springer**
*Berlin*
*Heidelberg*
*New York*
*Barcelona*
*Budapest*
*Hong Kong*
*London*
*Milan*
*Paris*
*Santa Clara*
*Singapore*
*Tokyo*

Dino Pedreschi   Carlo Zaniolo   (Eds.)

# Logic in Databases

International Workshop LID '96
San Miniato, Italy, July 1-2, 1996
Proceedings

 Springer

Series Editors

Gerhard Goos, Karlsruhe University, Germany

Juris Hartmanis, Cornell University, NY, USA

Jan van Leeuwen, Utrecht University, The Netherlands

Volume Editors

Dino Pedreschi
Dipartimento di Informatica, Università degli Studi di Pisa
Corso Italia 40, I-56125 Pisa, Italy
E-mail: pedre@di.unipi.it

Carlo Zaniolo
Department of Computer Science, University of California at Los Angeles
Los Angeles, CA 90024, USA
E-mail: zaniolo@cs.ucla.edu

Cataloging-in-Publication data applied for


Die Deutsche Bibliothek - CIP-Einheitsaufnahme

**Logic in databases** : proceedings / International Workshop LID
'96, San Miniato, Italy, July 1 - 2, 1996. Dino Pedreschi ; Carlo
Zaniolo (ed.). - Berlin ; Heidelberg ; New York ; Barcelona ;
Budapest ; Hong Kong ; London ; Milan ; Paris ; Santa Clara ;
Singapore ; Tokyo : Springer, 1996
  (Lecture notes in computer science ; Vol. 1154)
  ISBN 3-540-61814-7
NE: Pedreschi, Dino [Hrsg.]; LID <1996, San Miniato>; GT




CR Subject Classification (1991): H.2, H.3.3,F.4.1, I.2.3

ISSN 0302-9743
ISBN 3-540-61814-7 Springer-Verlag Berlin Heidelberg New York

© Springer-Verlag Berlin Heidelberg 1996
Printed in Germany

Typesetting: Camera-ready by author
SPIN 10525557    06/3142 – 5 4 3 2 1 0    Printed on acid-free paper

# Foreword

This volume contains the papers presented at the International Workshop on *Logic in Databases*, LID'96, held at San Miniato, Italy, July 1-2, 1996. The aim of the workshop is to identify and promote logic-based methods and techniques most relevant to the design and development of the next generation of information systems. In the call for papers, contributions were solicited that stress the usability, simplicity, and efficiency of logic-based solutions to relevant problems in the area of databases and information systems.

In response to the call for papers, 49 manuscripts were submitted. While the quality of submissions was generally high, only 21 papers could be accepted for presentation within the limited time allowed by the workshop format.

In addition to the contributed papers, this volume contains the papers by Jack Minker (Univ. of Maryland), who delivered the keynote lecture, and by Robert A. Kowalski (Imperial College), and Shalom Tsur (Argonne Nat. Lab.), who presented invited lectures.

Finally, the volume contains position statements for the panel discussion on "Deductive Databases: Challenges, Opportunities and Future Directions."

The LID'96 workshop is the result of the efforts of many, whom we would like to recognize and thank. In addition to authors of invited papers and contributed papers, the success of LID'96 must be credited to the distinguished program committee. A very special acknowledgment is also owed to the organizing committee. Besides the members of the program and organizing committees, the following researchers served as reviewers, and their effort is gratefully acknowledged:

| | |
|---|---|
| A. Brogi | M. Gabbrielli |
| N. Heintze | S. Greco |
| K. Shim | A. Siebes |
| D. Seipel | V. Vassalos |
| P. Breche | Z. Lacroix |
| N. Shiri | T. Eiter |
| A. Raffaetà | F. Gire |
| D. Boulanger | H.M. Jamil |
| P. Mancarella | U. Straccia |
| K.S. Candan | B. Adelberg |
| J. Simeon | M. Fugini |
| F. Buccafurri | W. Slany |
| M. Stumptner | G. Ghelli |
| S. Adali | L. Palopoli |
| D. Aquilino | I.N. Subramanian |

The workshop was made possible by the financial support of the Commission of the European Communities under the EC-US Cooperative Activity ECUS033— *Non-Determinism in Deductive Databases*. LID'96 is in fact the final workshop of this project.

We also acknowledge support from the NSF IRI program, Consiglio Nazionale delle Ricerche (CNR), Gruppo Nazionale per l'Informatica Matematica (GNIM) of CNR, Università di Pisa, CNUCE-Institute of CNR, Area di Ricerca di Pisa del CNR, Area "Logic-Based Databases" of Compulog-Net. We owe special thanks to Cassa di Risparmio di San Miniato, who provided the "Centro Studi I Cappuccini" where the workshop was held.

The paper by A. Bonner and M. Kifer, *Concurrency and Communication in Transaction Logic*, is not included in this volume since it is already published elsewhere.

Pisa, August 1996                                      Dino Pedreschi, Pisa, Italy
                                                    Carlo Zaniolo, Los Angeles, USA

# Program Committee

P. Asirelli (IEI-CNR, Italy)
M. Boehlen (Aalborg U., Denmark)
A. Bonner (U. Toronto, CA)
J. Chomicki (Monmouth U., USA)
H. Decker (Siemens, Germany)
U. Geske (GMD, Germany)
M. Gelfond (UTEP, USA)
F. Giannotti (CNUCE-CNR, Italy)
G. Gottlob (TU Wien, Austria)
S. Grumbach (INRIA, France)
R. Kowalski (Imperial College, UK)
L.V.S. Lakshmanan (Concordia U., CA)
I.S. Mumick (AT&T Research, USA)
K. Ross (Columbia U., USA)

D. Saccà (U. Calabria, Italy)
F. Sadri (Imperial College, UK)
F. Sadri (U. North Carolina, USA)
O. Shmueli (Technion, Israel)
S. Sripada (ECRC, Germany)
D. Srivastava (AT&T Bell L., USA)
V.S. Subrahmanian (U. MD, USA)
L. Tanca (U. Verona, Italy)
S. Tsur (Argonne Nat. Labs, USA)
F. Turini (U. Pisa, Italy)
J. Ullman (Stanford U., USA)
V. Vianu (UCSD, USA)
J. Widom (Stanford U., USA)

# Organizing Committee

M. Carboni (CNUCE-CNR, Italy)
S. Contiero (Univ. Pisa, Italy)
G. Manco (CNUCE-CNR, Italy)

C. Renso (Univ. Pisa, Italy)
E. Ricciardi (IEI-CNR, Italy)
S. Ruggieri (Univ. Pisa, Italy)

# Table of Contents

# Invited Lecture

# Logic and Databases: A 20 Year Retrospective*

Jack Minker

Department of Computer Science,
Institute for Advanced Computer Studies,
University of Maryland, College Park, MD 20742 U.S.A.
minker@cs.umd.edu
http://www.cs.umd.edu~minker

*Dedicated in Honor of Jerrold Gallaire and Jean-Marie Nicolas**

Abstract. As a workshop held in Toulouse, France in 1977, Gallaire,
Minker and Nicolas stated that logic and databases were a field in its own
right (see [151]). This was the first time that this designation was made.
The impetus for this started approximately twenty years ago in 1976
when I visited Gallaire and Nicolas in Toulouse, France, whose culminated in a workshop held in Toulouse, France in 1977. It is appropriate,
then to provide an assessment as to what has been achieved in the twenty
years since the field started as a distinct discipline. In this retrospective
I shall review developments that have taken place in the field, assess the
contributions that have been making, consider the state of in phenoma-
tions of deductive databases and discuss the nature of work in the area.

## 1   Introduction

As described in [224] the logic and databases started in
the late 1960s. Prominent among the developments was the work by Levien and
Maron [230, 232, 208, 190, 200, 201] and Kuhns [130, 182, 188] at the Rand Corporation (Green and Raphael [151, 152] were the first to realize the importance

* I would like to thank the Organizing Committee of the Workshop on Logic in
  Databases, San Miniato, Italy, 1996 for inviting me to present a lecture at the Workshop. I would like to thank many of my colleagues for their thoughts on the significant developments in the field, including Robert Demolombe, Hervé Gallaire, Georg
  Gottlob, Tom Green, Larry Henschen, Bob Kowalski, Jean-Marie Nicolas, Raghu
  Ramakrishnan, Kotagiri Ramamohanarao, Ray Reiter and Carlo Zaniolo. Many of
  my former and current students and Ph.D. students also contributed thoughts, in-
  cluding Sergio Alvarez, Chitta Baral, José Alberto Fernández, Terry Gaasterland,
  Jorge Lobo, and Carolina Ruiz. Although many of the
  views reflected in the paper may be shared by those who made suggestions, I take
  full responsibility for them. Support for this paper was received from the National
  Science Foundation under grant number IRI 9300691.
** This paper is dedicated in honor of my co-authors, co-authors, colleague and friends
  Hervé Gallaire and Jean-Marie Nicolas who have helped to make the field of deduc-
  tive databases a reality.

# Logic and Databases: A 20 Year Retrospective*

Jack Minker[1]

Department of Computer Science
Institute for Advanced Computer Studies
University of Maryland. College Park, MD 20742 U. S. A.
minker@cs.umd.edu
http://www.cs.umd.edu/~minker

*Dedicated in Honor of Hervé Gallaire and Jean-Marie Nicolas***

**Abstract.** At a workshop held in Toulouse, France in 1977, Gallaire, Minker and Nicolas stated that *logic and databases* was a field in its own right (see [131]). This was the first time that this designation was made. The impetus for this started approximately twenty years ago in 1976 when I visited Gallaire and Nicolas in Toulouse, France, which culminated in a workshop held in Toulouse, France in 1977. It is appropriate, then to provide an assessment as to what has been achieved in the twenty years since the field started as a distinct discipline. In this retrospective I shall review developments that have taken place in the field, assess the contributions that have been made, consider the status of implementations of deductive databases and discuss the future of work in this area.

## 1  Introduction

As described in [234], the use of logic and deduction in databases started in the late 1960s. Prominent among the developments was the work by Levien and Maron [202, 203, 199, 200, 201] and Kuhns [186, 187, 188] at the Rand Corporation. Green and Raphael [151, 152] were the first to realize the importance

---

* I would like to thank the Organizing Committee of the *Workshop on Logic in Databases*, San Miniato, Italy, 1996 for inviting me to present a lecture at the Workshop. I would like to thank many of my colleagues for their thoughts on the significant developments in the field, including: Robert Demolombe, Hervé Gallaire, Georg Gottlob, John Grant, Larry Henschen, Bob Kowalski, Jean-Marie Nicolas, Raghu Ramakrishnan, Kotagiri Ramamohanarao, Ray Reiter and Carlo Zaniolo. Many of my former and current students and Ph.D. students also contributed thoughts, including Sergio Alvarez, Chitta Baral, José Alberto Fernández, Terry Gaasterland, Parke Godfrey, Jarek Gryz, Jorge Lobo, and Carolina Ruiz. Although many of the views reflected in the paper may be shared by those who made suggestions, I take full responsibility for them. Support for this paper was received from the National Science Foundation under grant number IRI 9300691.
** This paper is dedicated in honor of my co-authors, co-editors, colleagues and friends, Hervé Gallaire and Jean-Marie Nicolas, who have helped to make the field of deductive databases a reality.

of the Robinson Resolution Principle [294] for databases. Early uses of logic in databases are reported upon in [235] and are not covered here. Detailed descriptions of many of the accomplishments made in the 1960s can be found in [247].

A major influence of the use of logic in databases was the development of the field of logic programming through the work of Kowalski [180], who promulgated the concept of logic as a programming language, and by Colmerauer and his students who developed the first *Prolog* interpreter [79]. Throughout the paper I will refer to logic programs that are function-free as *deductive databases (DDBs)*. I do so since databases are finite structures. Most of the results discussed can be extended to include logic programming.

The impetus for the use of logic in databases came about through meetings in 1976 in Toulouse, France, when I visited Hervé Gallaire and Jean-Marie Nicolas while on sabbatical leave. The idea of a workshop on "Logic and Data Bases" was conceived at that time. It is clear that a number of individuals had the idea of using logic as a mechanism to handle databases and deduction at around that time and they were invited to participate in the workshop. The appearance of the book, edited by Gallaire and Minker, *Logic and Data Bases*[3], [131], was highly influential in the development of the field, as were the books [132, 133] that were a result of two subsequent workshops held in Toulouse. Another influential development was the article by Gallaire, Minker and Nicolas [134], which surveyed work in the field up to the date of the article.

The use of logic in databases was received by the database community with a great deal of skepticism. It is reported that one of the key researchers at the time stated that, "...logic and databases had little to do either with the theory or the practice of databases." It might also be well to recall some of the comments made in the review of the book *Logic and Data Bases*, [155]. The reviewer took issue with the statement in the Foreword to the book, where Gallaire and I called *logic and databases* a *field*. The reviewer believed that a *field* had to satisfy criteria that he set forth and that these criteria were not met by the book. He stated,

> More significant are the conscious efforts of the editors and most of the authors to promote the work in the volume as representing a field – a well-defined area of research, complete with important past achievements and stimulating areas for future work.

At the time the review came out, and in retrospect, I believe that Gallaire and I were correct in our assessment that *logic and databases* is, indeed, a *field*. In [235] 'important past achievements and stimulating areas for future work' are described. The accomplishments I cite in this article, and the papers that appear in this workshop, are testaments to the accuracy of our remarks.

The reviewer also stated,

> The present volume is a collection of papers on a topic, some more interesting than others but none really outstanding...

---

[3] Nicolas was not one of the editors of the book by his choice. He played a key role in organizing the workshop.

While each individual may have different criteria for what is outstanding, it should be noted that there were several papers in the book that have now become *classics* in our field. I refer to the article by Reiter on the *Closed World Assumption (CWA)* [288] and by Clark on *Negation-as-Failure (NAF)* [75]. Indeed, several other important papers appeared in the book, such as those by Nicolas and Gallaire [257] on theory vs. interpretation, by Kowalski [181] on logic for data description, by Nicolas and Yazdenian [259] on integrity constraints, and several early implementations [64, 172, 231] of *DDBs*.

It is clear that logic has everything to do with the theory of databases, and many of those who were then critical of the field have changed their position. In the remainder of this paper I shall describe what I believe to be the major intellectual developments in the field, the status of commercial implementations and future trends. As will be seen, the field of logic and databases has been very prolific. I apologize in advance to any author whose work I have inadvertently not covered or referenced.

## 2  Intellectual Contributions of Deductive Databases

In describing the contributions of logic to databases, it is necessary to take note of work in relational databases as specified by Codd [77]. Codd formalized databases in terms of the relational calculus and the relational algebra. He provided a logic language, the relational calculus, and described how to compute answers to questions in the relational algebra and the relational calculus. Both the relational calculus and the relational algebra provide declarative formalisms to specify queries. This was a significant advance over network [76] and hierarchic systems [335], which only provided procedural languages for databases. The relational algebra and the relational calculus permitted individuals who were not computer specialists to write declarative queries, and to have the computer answer the queries. The development of syntactic optimization techniques (see [84, 337, 338] for references on this topic) permitted relational database systems to retrieve answers to queries efficiently and to compete with network and hierarchic implementations. Relational systems have been enhanced to include "views". A view as has been used in relational databases is, essentially, a non-recursive procedure. There are, today, numerous commercial implementations of relational database systems for large database manipulation and for personal computers. Relational databases may be considered a forerunner of logic in databases.

Although relational databases used the language of logic in the relational calculus, it was not formalized in terms of logic. The formalization of relational databases in terms of logic and the extensions that have been developed are the focus of this paper. Indeed, *formalizing databases through logic has played a significant role in our understanding of what constitutes a database, what is meant by a query, what is meant by an answer to a query, and how databases may be generalized for knowledge bases*. It has also provided tools and answers to problems that would have been extremely difficult without the use of logic.

In the remainder of the paper I will focus on some of the more significant aspects that have been contributed by logic in databases. I shall discuss the following contributions:

1. A formalization of what constitutes a database, a query, and an answer to a query.
2. A realization that logic programming extends relational databases.
3. A clear understanding of the semantics of large classes of databases that include alternative forms of negation, and disjunction.
4. An understanding of relationships between model theory, fixpoint theory and proof procedures.
5. An understanding of the properties that alternative semantics may have and their complexity.
6. An understanding of what is meant by integrity constraints and how they may be used to perform updates, semantic query optimization, cooperative answering and database merging.
7. A formalization and solutions to the update and view update problems.
8. An understanding of bounded recursion and recursion, and how they may be implemented in a practical manner.
9. An understanding of the relationship between logic based systems and knowledge base systems.
10. A formalization of how to handle incomplete information in knowledge bases.
11. A correspondence that relates alternative formalisms of nonmonotonic reasoning to databases and knowledge bases.

I will address the area of implementations of *DDBs* in section 3, where commercial developments have not progressed as rapidly as the intellectual developments. I will then discuss some trends and future directions in section 4.

## 2.1 Formalizing Database Theory

The first formalization of databases in terms of logic was due to Reiter [290] who noted that underlying relational databases there were a number of assumptions that were not made explicit. In particular, he noted that with respect to negation, an assumption was being made that facts not known to be *true* in a relational database, are assumed to be *false*. This assumption is the well-known *closed world assumption (CWA)*, expounded earlier by Reiter in 1978 [288]. A second assumption is the *unique name assumption*, which states that any item in a database has a unique name, and that individuals with different names are not the same. The last assumption is the *domain closure assumption*, which states that there are no other individuals than those in the database.

Having recognized these assumptions, Reiter then formalized relational databases as follows. He stated that a relational database is a set of ground assertions over a language $\mathcal{L}$ together with a set of axioms. The language $\mathcal{L}$ does not contain function symbols. These assertions and axioms are of the following form:

- **Assertions:** $R(a_1, \cdots, a_n)$, where $R$ is an n-ary relational symbol in $\mathcal{L}$, and $a_1 \cdots, a_n$ are constant symbols in $\mathcal{L}$.

- **Unique Names Axiom:** If $a_1, \cdots, a_p$ are all the constant symbols of $\mathcal{L}$, then

$$(a_1 \neq a_2), \cdots, (a_1 \neq a_p), (a_2 \neq a_3), \cdots, (a_{p-1} \neq a_p)$$

- **Domain Closure:** If $a_1, \cdots, a_p$ are all the constant symbols of $\mathcal{L}$, then

$$\forall X((X = a_1) \vee \cdots \vee (X = a_p))$$

- **Completion Axioms:** For each relational symbol R, if $R(a_1^1, \cdots a_n^1), \cdots, R(a_1^m, \cdots, a_n^m)$ denote all facts under R, the completion axiom for R

$$\forall X_1 \cdots \forall X_n (R(X_1, \cdots, X_n) \rightarrow$$
$$(X_1 = a_1^1 \wedge \cdots \wedge X_n = a_n^1) \vee \cdots \vee (X_1 = a_1^m \wedge \cdots \wedge X_n = a_n^m))$$

- **Equality Axioms:**
$$\forall X \ (X = X)$$
$$\forall X \forall Y \ ((X = Y) \rightarrow (Y = X))$$
$$\forall X \forall Y \forall Z ((X = Y) \wedge (Y = Z) \rightarrow (X = Z))$$
$$\forall X_1 \cdots \forall X_n (P(X_1, \cdots, X_n) \wedge$$
$$(X_1 = Y_1) \wedge \cdots \wedge (X_n = Y_n) \rightarrow P(Y_1, \cdots Y_n))$$

The *completion axiom* is what Clark had proposed as the basis for his Negation-as-Failure rule [75]. Another contribution of logic programs and databases is that:

*The formalization of relational databases in terms of logic now permits the definition of a query and an answer to a query to be defined precisely. A query is a statement in the first-order logic language $\mathcal{L}$. Q(a) is an answer to a query, Q(X), over a database DB if Q(a) is a logical consequence of DB.*

## 2.2   Deductive Databases (DDBs)

Relational databases have been shown to be a special case of deductive databases. A deductive database may be considered as a theory, *DDB*, in which the database consists of a set of ground assertions, referred to as the *extensional database (EDB)*, and a set of axioms, referred to as the *intensional database (IDB)*, of the form:

$$P \leftarrow Q_1, \ldots, Q_n, \tag{1}$$

where $P, Q_1, \ldots, Q_n$ are atomic formulae in the language $\mathcal{L}$. Databases of this form are termed *Datalog* databases [337, 338]. The name *Datalog* comes from those in the database community. A *Datalog* database is a particular instance of a more general Horn logic program that permits function symbols in clauses given by Formula (1). The recognition that logic programs are significant for databases was understood by a number of individuals in 1976. Many of them have articles in the book [131]. The generalization permits views to be defined that are recursive.

*The recognition that logic programming and databases are fundamentally related has led to more expressive and powerful databases than is possible with relational databases defined in terms of the relational algebra.*

That logic programming and *DDBs* are fundamentally related is a consequence of the fact that databases are function-free logic programs. As shown in many papers and in particular, in Gottlob [146], the expressive power of logic programming extends that of relational databases.

Integrity constraints play an important role in database systems. In addition to defining a database in terms of an *EDB* and an *IDB*, it is also necessary to formalize what is meant by an *integrity constraint (IC)*. There are a number of definitions as to what constitutes an *IC*. Kowalski [306, 181] suggests that an integrity constraint is a formula that is *consistent* with the *DDB*, while for Reiter, and Lloyd and Topor [290, 215], an *IC* is a theorem of the *DDB*. Reiter has proposed other possible definitions of integrity constraints in [292, 293]. He states that *ICs* should be statements about the content of a database. *ICs* can be written in a modal logic to use a belief operator to express beliefs that the database must satisfy. He explores Levesque's KFOPCE [198], an epistemic modal logic, as a suitable framework.

In [91], Demolombe and Jones revisit the basic notion of *ICs* in deductive databases. Their view is that *ICs* are statements *true* about the world, whereas a database is a collection of *beliefs* about the world. *ICs* then can be used to qualify certain information in the database as *valid* or *complete*. They define these properties formally in the framework of doxatic logic.

The major use that has been made of integrity constraints in the database community has been in updating to assure that the database is consistent. Nicolas [256] has shown how, using techniques from *DDBs*, improvements can be made to the speed of update. Blaustein [33] has also made contributions to this problem. It has been shown by Reiter [288] that one can query a Horn database with or without integrity constraints and the answer to the query is the same. However, this does not preclude the use of integrity constraints in the query process. While *ICs* do not affect the result of a query, they may affect the efficiency with which this result may be computed. Integrity constraints provide *semantic* information about the data in the database. If a query requests a join for which there will never be an answer because of the system constraints, this can be used to advantage by not performing the query and returning an empty answer set. This avoids performing an unnecessary join on two potentially large relational tables in a relational database system, or performing a long deduction in a *DDB* system. The process of using integrity constraints to constrain a search has been referred to as *semantic query optimization (SQO)* [57, 58]. McSkimin and Minker [227] were the first to use integrity constraints for *SQO* in *DDBs*. Hammer and Zdonik [154] and King [177] were the first to apply *SQO* to relational databases. Chakravarthy, Grant and Minker [57, 58] formalized *SQO* and developed the *partial subsumption algorithm* and method of *residues*. These provide a general technique applicable to any relational or *DDB* that is able to perform *SQO*. Godfrey, Gryz and Minker, [144], show how to apply the technique in a bottom-up approach. Gaasterland and Lobo [128] extended the work to include databases with negation in the body of clauses, and Levy and Sagiv [206] showed how to handle recursive *IDB* rules in *SQO*. The early work on semantic query optimization by [227] may be a forerunner of the work that has been developed on constraint logic programming by Jaffar and Lassez [167]. See Jaffar and Maher for a comprehensive survey of constraint logic programming [166].

A topic related to semantic query optimization is that of *cooperative answering systems*. The objective in a cooperative answering system is to provide information to a user as to why a particular query succeeded or failed. When a query fails, the user, in general, cannot tell why the failure occurred. There may be several reasons: the database currently does not contain information to respond to the user, or there will never be an answer to the query. The distinction could be important to the user. Another aspect related to integrity constraints is that of *user constraints (UCs)*. A user constraint is a formula, that models a user's preferences. It may constrain providing answers to queries in which the user may have no interest (e.g., stating that in developing a route of travel, the user does not want to pass through a particular city), or provide other constraints that may restrict the search. As shown by [130, 129, 122, 125], user constraints, which are identical in form to integrity constraints, can be used for this purpose. While integrity constraints provide the semantics of the entire database, user constraints provide the semantics of the user. User constraints may be inconsistent with the database and hence, a separation of these two semantics is essential. To maintain the consistency of the database, only integrity constraints are relevant. A query may be thought of as the conjunction of the query and the user constraints. Hence, a query can be semantically optimized based both on *ICs* and *UCs*.

With user and integrity constraints, it is possible to develop a system that provides responses to users that inform them as to the reasons why queries succeed or fail [126, 145]. Other features may be built into a system, such as the ability to relax a query given that it fails, so that an answer to a related request may be found. This has been termed *query relaxation* [125]. A survey of work in cooperative answering systems may be found in [123].

*Semantic query optimization, user constraints and cooperative answering systems are important contributions both for relational and DDB systems. I believe that they will eventually be incorporated into commercial relational and DDB systems.*

Indeed, I cannot imagine a *DDB* developed for commercial systems to be successful if it does not contain both semantic query optimization and cooperative answering capabilities. How can one expect users to understand why deductions succeed or fail if such information is not provided? How can queries doomed to fail because they violate integrity or user constraints be allowed to take up a significant amount of search time if the query cannot possibly succeed? I also believe that these techniques must be incorporated into relational technology. As discussed in section 3, this is beginning to happen. Practical considerations of performing semantic query optimization in a bottom-up approach have been addressed by [144].

## 2.3 Extended Deductive Database Semantics

The first generalization of relational databases was to permit Horn rules that could be recursive. A Horn rule is one in which the head of a rule is an atom and the body of a rule is a conjunction of atoms. These databases are referred to as deductive databases. Subsequently, other *DDBs* that may contain negated atoms in the body of rules were permitted. In the following sections I discuss the alternative extensions that have been made to *DDBs* and describe why they are significant.

**Horn Semantics and Datalog** One of the early developments was due to van Emden and Kowalski [340] who wrote a seminal paper that discussed the semantics of Horn theories. I believe that a significant contribution to logic programming and *DDBs* was *the recognition by van Emden and Kowalski that the semantics of Horn databases can be characterized in three distinct ways by model, fixpoint or proof theory. These three characterizations lead to the same semantics.*

Model theory deals with the definition of a collection of models of a database that captures the intended meaning of the database. Fixpoint theory deals with the definition of a fixpoint operator that constructs the collection of all atoms that can be inferred to be *true* from the database. Proof theory deals with the definition of a procedure that finds answers to queries with respect to the database. van Emden and Kowalski [340] also showed that if one considers all Herbrand models of a Horn *DDB*, the intersection is a unique minimal model. The unique minimal model is the same as all of the atoms in the fixpoint, and are the only atoms provable from the theory.

To find if the negation of a ground atom is *true*, one can subtract, from the Herbrand base (the set of all atoms that can be constructed from the constants and the predicates in the database), the minimal Herbrand model. If the atom is in this set then it is assumed to be *false* and its negation is *true*. Alternatively, answering queries that consist of negated atoms that are ground may be achieved using negation-as-finite failure as described by [288, 75].

The first approaches to answering queries in *DDBs* did not handle recursion and were primarily top-down (or backward reasoning) or top-down using sets [131]. The approach to answering queries in relational database systems was a bottom-up (or forward reasoning) approach, since all answers are usually required and it is more efficient to do so in a bottom-up approach. Pioneering work in handling recursion in *DDBs* was done by Chang [64, 65], McKay and Shapiro [317] and Henschen and Naqvi [156]. Both Chang, and McKay and Shapiro used a bottom-up approach to handle recursion, while Henschen and Naqvi used an iterated top-down approach. This work was followed by a large number of papers on computing recursion including the *naive* and *semi-naive evaluation methods* [11]. These methods are based on primitive deduction techniques and are generally inefficient. They perform bottom-up reasoning proceeding from the database. Hence, they do not use constants that may appear in a query to guide the search. Top down reasoning takes into account constants that appear in a query. The *QSQ* method introduced by Vieille [344, 346] and the extension tables method defined by Dietrich and Warren [92] are key representatives of this approach. On the other hand, the renaming of the Alexander [295] and *magic set* [12, 24] methods make use of the constants for bottom-up reasoning. Bry [48] reconciles the bottom-up and top-down methods to compute recursive queries. He shows that the Alexander and magic set methods based on rewriting and the methods based on resolution implement the same top-down evaluation of the original database rules by means of auxiliary rules processed bottom-up. Based on the work by Bry, Brass [43] developed a rewriting method for *Datalog-programs* which simulates *SLD-resolution* more closely than the usual magic set method. It improves upon the method of Ross [299], can save joins and simulates *SLD-resolution* closely. In addition, it was also first shown by Minker and Nicolas [239] that there are forms of rules that lead to *bounded recursion*. That is, the deduction process using these rules must terminate in a finite number of steps. This work has been extended by Naughton and Sagiv [254].

*The efficient handling of recursion and the recognition that some recursive cases may inherently be bounded contributes to the practical implementation of deductive databases. An understanding of the relationship between resolution-based (top-down) and fixpoint-based (bottom-up) techniques and how the search space of the latter can be made identical to top-down resolution with program transformation is another contribution of DDBs.*

**Extended Deductive Databases and Knowledge Bases** The ability to develop a semantics for theories in which there are rules with a literal (i.e., an atomic formula or the negation of an atomic formula) in the head and literals with possibly negated-by-default literals in the body of a clause, has significantly expanded the ability to write and understand the semantics of complex applications. Such clauses, referred to as *extended clauses*, are given by:

$$L \leftarrow M_1, \cdots, M_n, not\ M_{n+1}, \cdots not\ M_{n+k}, \tag{2}$$

where $L$ and the $M_j$, $j = 1, \cdots, (n + k)$ are literals. Databases with such clauses combine both *classical negation* and *default negation* (represented by *not* immediately preceding a literal), and are referred to as *extended deductive databases*. The combining of classical and default negation provides users with greater expressive power.

The development of logic programs where default negation may appear in the body of a clause first appeared in the proceedings of a workshop, held in 1986 [233]. Selected papers from the workshop were published in 1988 [234]. The concept of stratification was discussed first by Chandra and Harel [62] and introduced to logic programs by Apt, Blair and Walker [7], and by Van Gelder [341] who considered stratified theories in which $L$ and the $M_j$ in Formula (2) are atomic formulas and there is no recursion through negation. For such theories they show that there is a unique preferred minimal model, computed from strata to strata. Przymusinski [271] has termed this minimal model to be the *perfect model*. He also extends the concept to *locally stratified* theories.

The theory of stratified databases was followed by that permitting recursion through negation in Formula (2) where the $L$ and $M_j$ are atomic formulae. In the context of *DDBs* they are called *normal deductive databases*. There have been a large number of papers devoted to defining the semantics of these databases. These semantics, drawn from [245], are summarized in the second and third columns of Table 1. The most prominent of these for the Horn case, are the *well-founded semantics* of Van Gelder, Ross and Schlipf [137], and the *stable semantics* of Gelfond and Lifschitz [139]. The well-founded semantics leads to a unique three-valued model. Stable semantics may lead to a collection of minimal models. For some *DDBs* this collection may be empty. Fitting [119] has also defined a three-valued model to capture the semantics of normal logic programs.

There have been a number of normal deductive database semantics that have been developed that have been shown to be equivalent. You and Yuan [352], show that a number of extensions to the stable model semantics coincide: the regular model semantics of You and Yuan [350], the partial stable model of Saccà and Zaniolo [305], the preferential semantics of Dung [103], and a stronger version of the stable class semantics of Baral and Subrahmanian [22]. R-stable models have been proposed by Jakobovits and Vermier [168].

There have been several implementations of the well-founded semantics. Chen and Warren [67] have developed a top-down approach to answer queries in this semantics, while Leone and Rullo [194] have developed a bottom-up method for *Datalog* databases. Sagonas, Swift and Warren [307] show that a fixed order of computation does not suffice for answering queries in the well-founded semantics. They introduce a variant of *SLG* resolution [332], $SLG_{strat}$ which uses a fixed computation rule to evaluate ground left-to-right dynamically stratified programs. There have been several methods developed for computing answers to queries in stable model semantics. Fernández et al. [117] develop a bottom-up approach based on the concept of *model trees*. Every branch of a model tree is a model of the database, where a node in a tree is an atom that is shared by each branch below that node. Nerode et al. [25] have developed a method based on linear programming. Also, Inoue, Koshimura and Hasigawa [163] have developed a method to compute stable model semantics. Ruiz and Minker, [301], devised a procedure to construct the collection of partial (3–valued) stable models of a *DDB*. Baggai and Sunderraman [10] have developed a bottom-up method to compute the Fitting model.

A further extension of normal deductive databases, proposed by Gelfond and Lifschitz [140] and by Pearce and Wagner [260], permits clauses in Formula (2) where $L$ and $M_j$ are literals and therefore combines classical and default negation in one database. Blair and Subrahmanian [32] use the same idea as in [140, 260] to handle literals in paraconsistent logic programs. The semantics for for normal deductive databases has been described by [244, 245].

| Semantics | Horn | | Disjunctive | |
|---|---|---|---|---|
| | Theory | Reference | Theory | Reference |
| **Positive Consequences** | | | | |
| Fixpoint | $T_P$ | [340] | $T_P^I$ | [243] |
| Model | Least | [340] | Min. Models | [232] |
| | Model | | Model-State | [276] |
| Procedure | SLD | [158] | SLI/SLO | [248, 276] |
| | | | Case Based | [286] |
| **Negation** | | | | |
| Theory | CWA | [288] | GCWA | [232, 243] |
| | | | WGCWA | [300, 277] |
| Rule | NAF | [75] | SN-rule | [241] |
| | | | NAFFD-rule | [277] |
| Procedure | SLDNF | [75] | SLONF | [276] |
| **Stratified Programs** | | | | |
| Fixpoint | $T_P$ | [7] | $T_P^C$ | [243] |
| | | | $T_P^I$ | [300, 242] |
| Model | Standard | [7] | Stable State | [242] |
| | Perfect | [267] | Perfect | [271] |
| Procedure | SLS | [272] | SLP | [115] |
| **Normal Programs** | | | | |
| | Well-Founded | | Strong/Weak Well-F/Stationary | |
| Fixpoint | $I^\infty$ | [138] | | |
| Model | $M_{WF}(P)$ | [138] | $M_{WF}^{S/W}(P)$ | [297] |
| | | | $M_P$ | [269] |
| Procedure | SLS | [296, 268] | | |
| | General Well-Founded | | General Disj. Well-Founded | |
| Fixpoint | $I^E$ | [19] | $S^{ED}$ | [20] |
| Model | $M_P^E$ | [21] | $MS_P^{ED}$ | [21] |
| Procedure | SLIS | [20] | SLIS | [269] |
| | Stable Models | | Stable Models | |
| Fixpoint | $T_P^M$ | [117, 163] | $T_P^M$ | [117, 163] |
| Model | Stable | [139] | Stable | [273, 274] |
| Procedure | SLP | [115] | SLP | [115] |
| **Extended Programs** | | | | |
| | Stable Models | | Stable Models | |
| Fixpoint | | | | |
| Model | Stable | [140, 141] | Stable | [273, 274] |
| Procedure | | | | |
| | Stationary | | Stationary | |
| Fixpoint | $S^{SE}$ | [244] | $S^{SE}$ | [244] |
| Model | Stationary | [3] | | |
| Procedure | | | | |
| | Arbitrary Semantics SEM | | Arbitrary Semantics SEM | |
| Fixpoint | $T_P^E$ | [244, 245] | $T_P^E$ | [244, 245] |
| Model | $\mathcal{M}_P^{SEM}$ | [244, 245] | $\mathcal{M}_P^{SEM}$ | [244, 245] |
| Procedure | $EPP_{SEM}$ | [244, 245] | $EPP_{SEM}$ | [244, 245] |

**Table 1.** (Taken from [245]) Semantics of Horn and Disjunctive Logic Programs

These notions of default negation have been used as separate ways to interpret and to deduce default information. That is, each application has chosen one of these notions of negation and has applied it to every piece of data in the domain of the application. In [246], Minker and Ruiz define a new class of more expressive DDBs that allow for the combination of several forms of default negation in the same database. In this way different pieces of information in the domain may be treated appropriately. They introduce a new semantics called the *well–founded stable* semantics that characterizes the meaning of DDBs that combine the well–founded and the stable semantics.

Many complexity results have been obtained for deductive databases. Schlipf [313] has written a comprehensive survey article that summarizes the results. Some of these results, taken from [313], are listed in Table 2. A user may wish to determine which semantics to be used based upon the complexity expected to find answers to queries.

*The development of the semantics of extended deductive databases that permit a combination of classical negation and multiple default negations in the same deductive database are important contributions. The study of and the development of results in the computational complexity of these databases are important contributions to database theory. They permit wider classes of applications to be developed.*

Knowledge bases are important for artificial intelligence and expert system developments. A general way in which one can represent knowledge bases is through logic. All of the work developed for extended deductive databases concerning semantics and complexity apply directly to knowledge bases. Baral and Gelfond [13] have written an article which describes how extended deductive databases may be used to represent knowledge bases. Extended deductive databases, together with integrity constraints permit a wide range of *knowledge bases* to be implemented. Many papers devoted to knowledge bases consider them to consist of facts and rules. Certainly, this is one aspect of a knowledge base, as is the ability to extract proofs. However, integrity constraints supply another aspect of knowledge and differentiates knowledge bases which may have the same rules, but different integrity constraints. I believe that one should *define a knowledge base to consist of an extended deductive database plus integrity constraints.*

Since alternative extended deductive semantics have been implemented, the knowledge base expert should focus on the particular knowledge base problem that is to be developed. His focus should be upon writing the rules and integrity constraints that characterize the database, selecting the particular semantics that meets the needs of the problem and employing a *DDB* system that uses the required semantics.

*The field of deductive databases has contributed to providing an understanding of knowledge bases and their implementation.*

## 2.4 Extended Disjunctive Deductive Database Semantics

In databases that have been discussed above, information is definite. However, there are many situations where our knowledge of the world is incomplete. For example, when a null value appears as an argument of an attribute of a relation, the value of the attribute is unknown. Uncertainty in databases may be represented by probabilistic information. See [190, 330, 255]. Another area of incompleteness arises when it is unknown as to which among several facts are *true*, but it is known that one or more are *true*. It is therefore necessary to be able to represent and understand the semantics of theories that include incomplete data. A natural way to extend databases to include incomplete data is to permit disjunctive statements as part of the language. This leads to deductive databases which permit clauses to have disjunctions in their heads. These clauses are represented as,

$$L_1 \vee L_2 \vee \ldots \vee L_m \leftarrow M_1, \ldots, M_n, not\ M_{n+1}, \ldots not\ M_{n+k}, \qquad (3)$$

and are referred to as *extended disjunctive clauses*. A database that consists of such clauses is referred to as an *extended disjunctive deductive database (ED-DDB)*. The book by Lobo, Minker and Rajasekar [216] describes the theory of disjunctive logic programs and includes several chapters devoted towards disjunctive deductive databases.

In section 2.4, I discuss the semantics of *DDDBs*, where clauses are given by Formula (3), where the literals are restricted to atoms and there is no default negation in the body of a clause. In section 2.4, I discuss the semantics of *EDDDBs*, where there are no restrictions on clauses in Formula (3).

**Disjunctive Deductive Databases (DDDBs)** As I noted in [236], work in disjunctive theories was pursued seriously after a workshop I organized in 1986 [233]. The field of *disjunctive deductive databases (DDDBs)* started approximately in 1982 with the appearance of the paper by Minker [232], who described how one can answer both positive and negated queries in such databases. For a historical perspective of disjunctive logic programming and *DDDBs*, see [235]. There is a major difference between the semantics of deductive databases and those for *DDDBs*. Whereas *DDBs* usually have a unique minimal model that describes the meaning of the database, *DDDBs* generally have multiple minimal models.

As shown in [232] it is sufficient to answer positive queries over *DDDBs* by showing that the query is satisfied in every minimal model of the database. Thus, in the *DDDB*, {a ∨ b}, there are two minimal models, {{a}, {b}}. The query, a?, is not satisfied in the model {b}, and hence, it cannot be concluded that a is *true*. However, the query, (a ∨ b) is satisfied in both minimal models and hence the answer to the query {a ∨ b} is *yes*. To answer negated queries, it is not sufficient to use Reiter's *CWA* [288] since, as he noted, from the theory DB = {a ∨ b}, it is not possible to prove a, and it is not possible to prove b. Hence, by the *CWA*, *not a* and *not b* follow. But, {a ∨ b, not a, not b} is not consistent. The

*Generalized Closed World Assumption (GCWA)*, [232] resolves this problem by specifying that a negated atom be considered *true* if the atom does not appear in any minimal model of the database. This provides a model theoretic definition of negation. An equivalent proof theoretic definition, also presented in [232], is that an atom $a$ may be considered to be *false* if, whenever $a \vee C$ may be proven from the database, then also $C$ may be proven from the database, where $C$ is an arbitrary positive clause.

For related work on negation in disjunctive theories see Yahya and Henschen [349], Gelfond, Przymusinski and Przymusinska [143], Chan [59, 60], Sakama [308], Suchenek [331], Bossu and Siegel [38], Ross and Topor [300], and Lobo, Rajasekar and Minker [277]. For surveys on negation see the articles by Shepherdson [318], by Apt and Bol [8], by [99] and by Minker [237].

In deductive databases, it is natural for the fixpoint operator to map atoms to atoms. However, for *DDDBs*, it is natural to map positive disjunctions to positive disjunctions. A set of positive disjunctions is referred to as a *state*. A *model state* is a state all of whose minimal models satisfy the *DDDB*. The concept of a state was defined by Minker and Rajasekar [240, 243] as the domain of a fixpoint operator $T_P$ whose least fixpoint characterizes the semantics of a disjunctive logic program $P$. The operator is shown to be monotonic and continuous, and hence converges in $\omega$ iterations. The fixpoint computation operates bottom-up and yields a minimal model state that is logically equivalent to the set of minimal models of the program. The Minker/Rajasekar fixpoint operator is an extension of the van Emden/Kowalski fixpoint operator. If one considers all model states of a *DDDB* and intersects them, then the resultant is a model state, and among all model states it is minimal. Hence, one obtains a unique minimal model in a Horn database, while one obtains a unique model state in a *DDDB*.

Decker [86, 87] develops a fixpoint operator for *DDDBs*. His fixpoint operator reduces to the Minker/Rajasekar fixpoint operator [240, 243]. At each iteration of his operator, Decker finds partial models of the database. In the limit, he obtains the set of minimal models of the database. If one were to take an atom from each minimal model and form a disjunction, the resulting set of all such disjunctions is equivalent to the minimal model state of the *DDDBs*.

Answering queries in *DDDBs* has been studied by a number of individuals. Grant and Minker [238] were among the first to address the problem of computing answers to queries in *DDDBs*. They investigated the case where the database consists exclusively of ground positive disjuncts. Yahya and Henschen [349] developed a deductive method to determine whether or not a conjunction of ground atoms can be assumed *false* in a *DDDB* under the *EGCWA*. The *EGCWA* is an extension of the *GCWA*. Bossu and Siegel [38] developed a deductive method to answer a query by subimplication (a generalization of the *GCWA* that handles databases that have no minimal models). Henschen and Park [157] provide a method to answer *yes/no* questions is a database that consists of an *EDB*, an *IDB* and *ICs* that are all function-free. In addition, they allow negated unit clauses to be part of the database. The axioms in the *IDB* may be recursive. Liu and Sunderraman [212] generalize the relational model to represent disjunctive data. For this purpose they develop a data-structure, called *M-table* to represent the data. The relational algebra is then generalized to operate on *M-tables*. Although their extended algebra is sound, it is not complete. They answer some types of queries with a *maybe*, which may in fact be *true*. Yuan and Chiang [354] have developed a sound and complete query evaluation algorithm for disjunctive databases, that is, for databases that do not contain recursive *IDB* rules. They define an extended algebra in terms of an *extended union, extended intersection, extended projection, extended selection, extended cartesian product* and *extended division* operators.

Fernández and Minker [118] developed the concept of a *model tree*. They show how one can incrementally compute sound and complete answers to queries in *hierarchical DDDBs*. A *DDDBs* is hierarchical if it contains no recursion. In [116] they show how one can develop a fixpoint operator over trees to capture the meaning of a *DDDB* that includes recursion. The tree representation of the fixpoint is equivalent to the Minker/Rajasekar fixpoint [240, 243].

The above approaches to answering queries in disjunctive databases have the following limitations. Grant and Minker [238] can only compute answers to queries that contain a disjunctive extensional database. Henschen and his students [349, 157, 68] can only answer *yes/no* questions. Liu and Sunderraman [211, 212] provide sound, but not complete answers to queries. To be able to compute sound and complete answers, Yuan and Chiang [354] essentially have to compute the fixpoint of the entire *DDB* to answer each query. Fernández and Minker compute the model tree of the extensional *DDDB* once. To answer queries *IDB* rules may be invoked. However, the models of the extensional disjunctive part of the database do not have to be generated for each query. The approach by Fernández and Minker to compute answers generalizes both to stratified and normal *DDDB*.

Loveland and his students [214, 218, 321, 287, 286] have developed a top-down approach when the database is *near Horn*. They have developed a case-based reasoner that uses *Prolog* to perform the reasoning. This is one of the few efforts that have implemented disjunctive deductive databases. Loveland, Reed and Wilson [219] have introduced a relevancy detection algorithm to be used with *SATCHMO*, developed by Manthey and Bry, for automated theorem proving. Their system, termed *SATCHMORE (SATCHMO with RElevancy)*, improves on *SATCHMO* by limiting the uncontrolled use of forward chaining. Another approach using theorem proving is the work by Stickel on a theorem prover *PTTP (Prolog Technology Theorem Prover)* [327].

A number of individuals have investigated the complexity of answering queries in disjunctive logic programs. For example, Imielinski and Vadaparty [162], Vardi [342] and Imielinski [160]. Chomicki and Subrahmanian [71] discuss the complexity of the Generalized Closed World Assumption. There are some disjunctive theories that are tractable. See Borgida and Etherington [37], and Lobo, Yu and Wong [217] for such cases. See Dalal [82] for a discussion of an algorithm to detect if a disjunctive theory is tractable. A comprehensive description of complexity results for propositional logic programs is given by Eiter and Gottlob

[106]. A summary of complexity results, drawn from [106], is given in Table 3.

*The development of model theoretic, fixpoint and proof procedures has placed the semantics of DDDBs on a firm foundation. Methods to handle DDDBs have started to be developed and should eventually enhance implementations. The GCWA and alternative theories of negation have enhanced our understanding of default negation in DDDBs. Complexity results provide an understanding of the difficulties to find answers to queries in such systems.*

**Extended Disjunctive Deductive Databases** Fernández and Minker [114] present a new fixpoint characterization of the minimal models of disjunctive and stratified disjunctive deductive databases. They prove that by applying the operator iteratively, in the limit, it constructs the perfect models semantics (Przymusinski [271]) of stratified disjunctive deductive databases. Given the equivalence between the *perfect models semantics of stratified programs* and *prioritized circumscription* [271] their fixpoint characterization captures the meaning of the corresponding circumscribed theory. Based on these results they present a bottom-up evaluation algorithm for stratified *DDDBs*. This algorithm uses the *model-tree* data structure to represent the information contained in the database and to compute answers to queries. In [112, 113], Fernández and Minker develop the theory of *DDDBs* using the concept of model trees. Work on updates in *DDDBs* is described in [148, 149, 111].

Four alternative semantics were developed for non-stratifiable normal *DDDBs* at approximately the same time: Ross [297], Baral, Lobo and Minker [21, 20] and two other semantics by Przymusinski [269, 273]. Ross termed his semantics the *strong well founded semantics*, Baral, Lobo and Minker defined their semantics to be the *Generalized Disjunctive Well-Founded Semantics (GDWFS)*. They defined a fixpoint operator, and gave a model theoretic and proof theoretic semantics for such *DDDBs*. Przymusinski [273, pag. 466] defines an extension of the *stable model semantics* for normal disjunctive databases. He also defined in [269] the *stationary semantics*. As in the case of normal deductive databases it will be necessary to develop effective bottom-up computing techniques to answer queries in these theories. Some results already exist in this area for some classes of disjunctive databases as noted above.

In addition to the above semantics, a number of other important semantics have been developed. Przymusinski [270] describes a new *semantic framework* for disjunctive logic programs and introduces the *static expansions* of disjunctive programs. The class of static expansions extends both the classes of stable, well-founded and stationary models of normal programs and the class of minimal models of disjunctive programs. Any static expansion of a program $P$ provides the corresponding semantics for $P$ consisting of the set of all sentences logically implied by the expansion. The stable model semantics has also been extended to disjunctive programs [141, 274]. Leone, Rullo and Saccà [195], develop an efficient algorithm for solving the (co-NP-hard decision) problem of checking if a model is stable. The algorithm runs in polynomial space and single exponential time (in the worst case). The algorithm runs in polynomial time on the class of *head-*

*cycle free programs* (discussed below), and in the case of general disjunctive logic programs limits the inefficient part of the computation only to the components of the program which are not head-cycle free. The D-WFS semantics of Brass and Dix [45] is also of considerable interest as it permits a general approach to bottom-up computation in disjunctive programs.

The last two columns of Table 1 summarize work accomplished in the semantics of *DDDBs*, and is drawn from [245]. See, also, the paper by Eiter, Leone and Saccà [108], in this collection, that summarizes complexity results for partial models for disjunctive databases. They summarize results for partial stable models [274]; maximum stable models (M-stable) which are partial stable models under set inclusion [108, 302]; regular models [351] which are similar in spirit to M-stable models, but based on a weaker concept; and least undefined stable models [108, 302] which are the partial stable models with the minimal degree of undefinedness.

As noted in this and previous sections, there are a large number of different semantics both for extended deductive and extended disjunctive deductive databases. A user who wishes to use such a system is faced with the problem of selecting the appropriate semantics for his needs. Which semantics should be used, and under what circumstances? There have been no guidelines that have been developed. However, many complexity results have been obtained for these semantics. Schlipf [313] and Eiter and Gottlob [106] have written comprehensive survey articles that summarize the complexity results that are known for alternative semantics. Some of these results, taken from [104, 106], are listed in Table 2. A user may wish to determine the semantics to be used based upon the complexity expected to find answers to queries.

In addition to the results for extended disjunctive theories, there is work in investigating tractable cases of disjunctive theories. Ben-Eliyahu and Dechter [26] introduced the concept of a *head-cycle free (HCF)* clause. Let a clause consist of a disjunction of literals. A *dependency graph* $G_P$ is associated with each program $P$ as follows:

- each clause of the form, Formula (2) and each predicate in $P$ is a node.
- there is a positive (negative) arc from a predicate node $p$ to a rule node $\delta$ iff $p$ appears positive (negative) in the body of $\delta$, and an arc from $\delta$ to $p$ (resp., and also an arc from $p$ to $\delta$) if $p$ appears in the head of $\delta$.

The *positive dependency graph* of $P$ is a subgraph of $G_P$ containing only positive arcs. A directed cycle in $G_P$ is called *negative* if it contains at least one negative arc. A deductive database $P$ is *head-cycle free* if for every two predicate names $p$ and $q$, if $p$ and $q$ are on a positive directed cycle in the dependency graph $G_P$ then there is no rule in $P$ in which both $p$ and $q$ appear in the head. It is shown in [28] that answers to queries expressed in this language can be computed in polynomial time. Furthermore, the language is sufficiently powerful to express all polynomial time queries. It is further shown in [27] that there is an algorithm that performs, in polynomial time, minimal model finding and minimal model checking if the theory is *HCF*. An efficient algorithm for solving the (co-NP-hard decision) problem of checking if a model is stable in function-free disjunctive logic programs is developed in [195]. They show that the algorithm runs in polynomial time on the class of *head-cycle free programs* and in the case of general disjunctive logic programs, it limits the inefficient part of the computation only to the components of the program which are not head-cycle free.

In addition to work on tractable databases, consideration has been given to approximate reasoning. In such reasoning, one may give up soundness or completeness of answers. Efforts have been developed both for deductive and disjunctive deductive databases by Selman and Kautz [314, 171, 315], who developed lower and upper bounds for Horn (Datalog) databases and compilation methods, by Cadoli [51], who developed computational and semantical approximations, and by del Val [88, 89], who developed techniques for approximating and compiling databases. See also Cadoli [52] for additional references concerning compilation, approximation and tractability of knowledge bases.

A second way to determine the semantics to be used is through their properties. Dix in [93, 94] proposed a large number of criteria that are useful to consider in determining the appropriate semantics to be used. Indeed, Dix developed semantics both for normal [96, 97] and normal disjunctive [95, 44] deductive databases that satisfy some of the properties that he describes. While some of these properties are adaptations and extensions to those developed by Kraus, Lehmann and Magidor [185] to compare nonmonotonic theories, others were newly developed, such as, *relevance, partial evaluation* and *modularity*.

One property an arbitrary semantics, *SEM*, might have is that if a tautology is eliminated from a database, then the semantics of *SEM* should not be changed. Table 4 summarizes other useful properties of semantics of deductive databases and specifies for some alternative semantics the properties that they satisfy. This table is adapted from similar tables in [98, 99, 47, 46]. Although complexity results and properties that a semantics satisfy are extremely useful, no generally accepted criteria yet exist as to why one semantics should be used over another. A semantics may have all the properties that one may desire, and be computationally tractable and yet not provide answers that a user expected. Perhaps the best that can be expected is to provide users with complexity results and criteria by which they may decide as to which semantics meets the needs of their problems.

Understanding the semantics of disjunctive theories is related to nonmonotonic reasoning. The field of nonmonotonic reasoning has resulted in several alternative approaches to perform default reasoning [225, 289, 226, 249, 250]. The survey article by Minker [237] and papers by [106, 54] cite results where alternative theories of nonmonotonic reasoning can be mapped into extended disjunctive logic programs and databases. Hence, *DDDBs* may be used to compute answers to queries in such theories. See Cadoli and Lenzerini for complexity results concerning circumscription and closed world reasoning [50, 53]. See also Yuan and You [353] for a description of the relationships between autoepistemic circumscription and logic programming. They use two different belief constraints to

| Semantics | Propositional | | First Order over Herbrand models | | First Order no function symb. over Herbrand models | |
|---|---|---|---|---|---|---|
| | Complexity | Ref. | Complexity | Ref. | Data Complexity | Ref. |
| **Positive Consequences** | | | | | | |
| Minimal Model | $\mathcal{O}(|P|)$ | [101, 165] | r.e.–complete | [323, 322, 5] | polynomial in $|E|$ | [61] |
| **Negation** | | | | | | |
| CWA | $\mathcal{O}(|P|)$ | [101, 165] | co–r.e.–complete | [323, 322, 5] | co–r.e.–complete | [61] |
| **Stratified Programs** | | | | | | |
| Perfect | $\mathcal{O}(|P|)$ | | complete arithmetic | [6] | polynomial in $|E|$ | [62] |
| **Locally Stratified Programs** | | | | | | |
| Perfect | $\mathcal{O}(|P|)$ | | $\Delta_1^1$–complete over $\omega$ | [31] | N/A | |
| **Normal Programs** | | | | | | |
| 2–valued completion | co–NP–complete | [178] | $\Pi_1^1$–complete over $\omega$ | [178] | co–NP–complete | [178] |
| 3–valued completion | $\mathcal{O}(|P|)$ | folklore | $\Pi_1^1$–complete over $\omega$ | [119] | polynomial in $|E|$ | [119] |
| Stable | co–NP–complete | [223] | $\Pi_1^1$–complete over $\omega$ | [222, 312] | co–NP–complete | [223] |
| Well–Founded | $\mathcal{O}(|A||P|)$ | folklore | $\Pi_1^1$–complete over $\omega$ | [136, 312] | polynomial in $|E|$ | [138, 136] |
| **Extended Programs** | | | | | | |
| Stable | co–NP–complete | [245] | $\Pi_1^1$–complete over $\omega$ | [245] | co–NP–complete | [245] |
| Well–Founded | $\mathcal{O}(|A||P|)$ | [245] | $\Pi_1^1$–complete over $\omega$ | [245] | polynomial in $|E|$ | [245] |

**Table 2.** (Adapted from [313]) Complexity of Horn Logic Programs

**Notation:** The complexity results in the above table refer to worst case analysis for skeptical reasoning, i.e. to determining if a given literal is *true* in every canonical model (with respect to a particular semantics) of the program. For logic programs with no function symbols, the data complexity over an *EDB E* is presented. The notation used is the following: $|P|$ denotes the length of the program $P$; $|A|$ denotes the number of propositional letters in $P$; $|E|$ denotes the total number of symbols that occur in the *EDB E*.

| Semantics | Propositional | | First Order over Herbrand models | | First Order no function symb. over Herbrand models | |
|---|---|---|---|---|---|---|
| | Complexity | Ref. | Complexity | Ref. | Data Complexity | Ref. |
| **Positive Consequences** | | | | | | |
| Minimal Models | $\Pi_2^P$–complete | [104] | | | $\Pi_2^P$–complete | [107] |
| **Negation** | | | | | | |
| GCWA | $\Pi_2^P$–complete | [104] | $\Pi_2^0$–complete | [71] | $\Pi_2^P$–complete | [107] |
| WGCWA | co–NP–complete | [60] | | | | |
| **Stratified Programs** | | | | | | |
| Perfect | $\Pi_2^P$–complete | [104] | | | $\Pi_2^P$–complete | [107] |
| **Locally Stratified Programs** | | | | | | |
| Perfect | $\Pi_2^P$–complete | [104] | | | $\Pi_2^P$–complete | [107] |
| **Normal Programs** | | | | | | |
| Stable | $\Pi_2^P$–complete | [104] | | | $\Pi_2^P$–complete | [107] |
| Partial Stable | $\Pi_2^P$–complete | [104] | | | $\Pi_2^P$–complete | [107] |
| **Extended Programs** | | | | | | |
| Stable | $\Pi_2^P$–complete | [105] | | | $\Pi_2^P$–complete | [107] |
| Partial Stable | $\Pi_2^P$–complete | [245] | | | $\Pi_2^P$–complete | [107] |

**Table 3.** (Taken from [104, 106]) Complexity of Disjunctive Logic Programs (with Integrity Constraints)

define two semantics, the *stable circumscriptive semantics* and *the well-founded circumscriptive semantics*, for autoepistemic theories. The work in [353] and on *static semantics* developed by Przymusinski [270] appear to be related.

Another area to which *DDDBs* have contributed is to the null value problem. If an attribute of a relation may have a null value, where this value is part of a known set, then one can represent this as a disjunction of relations, where, in each disjunction a different value is given to the argument. For papers on the null value problem both in relational and deductive databases, see [29, 30, 78, 147, 150, 161, 210, 213, 291, 343, 355].

There are several significant contributions of *DDDBs*:

1. *Greater expressive power is provided to the user to develop knowledge base systems.*
2. *Alternative concepts of negation have been developed.*

| Property | Condition on a Semantics SEM to satisfy the Property | | | | | | | |
|---|---|---|---|---|---|---|---|---|
| | Clark's Compl. | GCWA | WGCWA | Perfect | Stable | WFS | D-WFS | Static |
| **Elimination of Tautologies** | If a rule $A \leftarrow B, \text{not } C$ with $A \cap B \neq \emptyset$ is eliminated from a program $P$, then the resulting program is SEM–equivalent to $P$. | | | | | | | |
| | No | Yes | No | Yes | Yes | Yes | Yes | Yes |
| **Generalized Principle of Partial Evaluation (GPPE)** | If a rule $A \leftarrow B, \text{not } C$, where $B$ contains an atom $B$, is replaced in a program $P$ by the $n$ rules $A \cup (A^i - \{B\}) \leftarrow ((B - \{B\}) \cup B^i), \text{not } (C \cup C^i)$ where $A^i \leftarrow B^i, \text{not } C^i$ $(i = 1, \ldots, n)$ are all rules for which $B \in A^i$, then the resulting program is SEM–equivalent to $P$. | | | | | | | |
| | Yes | Yes | Yes | Yes | Yes | Yes | Yes | Yes |
| **Positive/ Negative Reduction** | If (1) a rule $A \leftarrow B, \text{not } C$ is replaced in a program $P$ by $A \leftarrow B, \text{not } (C - C)$ where $C$ appears in no rule head, and (2) a rule $A \leftarrow B, \text{not } C$ is deleted from $P$ if there is a fact $A' \leftarrow$ in $P$ such that $A' \subseteq C$, then the resulting program is SEM–equivalent to $P$. | | | | | | | |
| | Yes | N/A | N/A | Yes | Yes | Yes | Yes | Yes |
| **Elimination of Non-Minimal Rules** | If a rule $A \leftarrow B, \text{not } C$ is deleted from a program $P$ if there is another rule $A' \leftarrow B', \text{not } C'$ such that $A' \subseteq A$, $B' \subseteq B$, and $C' \subseteq C$, where at least one $\subseteq$ is proper, then the resulting program is SEM–equivalent to $P$. | | | | | | | |
| | Yes | Yes | No | Yes | Yes | Yes | Yes | Yes |
| **Consistency** | If $\text{SEM}(P) \neq \emptyset$ for all disjunctive deductive database $P$. | | | | | | | |
| | No | Yes | Yes | Yes | No | Yes | Yes | Yes |
| **Independence** | If for every literal $l$, $l$ is *true* in every $M \in \text{SEM}(P)$ iff $l$ is *true* in every $M \in \text{SEM}(P \cup P')$ provided that the language of $P$ and $P'$ are disjoint and $l$ belongs to the language of $P$. | | | | | | | |
| | No | Yes | Yes | Yes | No | Yes | Yes | Yes |

**Table 4.** (Adapted from [98]) Properties of the semantics of disjunctive deductive databases.

3. *Complexity results have been found for alternative semantics of disjunctive databases including alternative theories of negation.*
4. *Methods have been developed to permit prototype systems to be implemented.*
5. *Disjunctive databases can be used as the computational vehicle for a wide class of nonmonotonic reasoning theories.*

# 3  Implementation Status of Deductive Databases

The field of deductive databases has made significant intellectual contributions during the past 20 years. However, these have not been matched by implementations that are available in the commercial market. In the early 1970's, when Codd introduced the relational model [77], there were numerous debates in the database community as to the efficacy of such systems relative to network [84] and hierarchic systems [84]. These debates ended when an effective relational system was implemented and shown to be comparable to these systems. Now, some of those individuals who are prominent in relational databases claim that deductive databases are not effective and are not needed. Although I believe otherwise, these comments can be addressed better either when a full commercial implementation of a deductive database is available, or when many of the techniques introduced in deductive databases find their way into relational databases. I believe that both of these are beginning to happen.

In the following subsection I discuss the stages through which implementations of deductive databases have progressed. I describe some of the contributions made during each stage. Following this, I discuss the reasons why I believe that no current systems are commercially marketed and speculate on how this might change.

## 3.1  Deductive Database Systems

There have been three stages of implementations of deductive database systems. The first stage is pre-1970, the second is 1970-1980 and the third is 1980-present. Each of these stages has contributed towards understanding the problems inherent in developing a deductive database system.

**First Stage: Pre 1970s.** The work that stands out during this period was that of Levien, Maron and Kuhn [202, 203, 199, 200, 201, 186, 187, 188] at the Rand Corporation who developed a prototype system that demonstrated the feasibility of performing deduction in databases. The second was by Green and Raphael [151, 152] who recognized that the resolution method of Robinson [294] was a uniform procedure based on a single rule of inference that could be used for deductive databases. This was the first general approach to deductive databases. The work at the Rand Corporation was termed *Relational Data File (RDF)* and was started in 1963. A procedural language, *INFEREX*, was used to execute inference routines. Plausible and formal inferencing were both possible in *RDF*. Temporal reasoning was also permitted. The system was implemented on a file consisting of some 55,000 statements. The work by Green and Raphael resulted in a system termed *Question Answering System (QA-3.5)*. It was an outgrowth of Raphael's thesis on *Semantic Information Retrieval (SIR)* [282] that performed deduction. *QA-3.5* was a generalization of this work and included a natural language component. Another system, *Relational Store Structure (RSS)*, was started in 1966. The system performed deduction and was developed by Marrill [80, 81]. The system had twelve deductive rules built into the program. It was also possible to incorporate other deductive rules into the system. The *Association Store Processor (ASP)* developed by Savitt, Love and Troop [311] also performed deduction over binary relational data. The inference rules, specified as relational statements were handled by breadth-first, followed by a depth-first search. These efforts, as well as those cited in [247], were important pre-cursors to deductive databases. In Table 5, adapted from [247], I list some of the capabilities of systems developed in the first stage.

**Second Stage: 1970-1980.** The *SYNTEX* system built by Nicolas and Syre [258] used logic as the basis for deduction. It was when I heard Nicolas lecture at the IFIP Congress in 1974 that I decided to visit him in Toulouse on my sabbatical leave the following year. It was there that Nicolas, Gallaire and I conceived of holding our "Workshop on Logic and Data Bases." The work by Chang [64], Kellogg, Klahr and Travis [172], and by Minker [231] represent work during the second stage of development of deductive databases. These papers appear in the book by Gallaire and Minker [131]. Table 6 provides a brief summary of some of the features of these systems.

Kellogg, Klahr and Travis developed a system termed *Deductively Augmented Data Management (DADM)*. The system precomputed unifications among premises so as to not have to recompute them during deduction. Variables were typed. Inference plans and database access strategies were created from a premise file without requiring access to database values.

Minker described the *Maryland Refutation Proof Procedure System (MRPPS 3.0)* that performed top-down searches for large databases. It permitted arguments of predicates to contain function symbols and had a knowledge base index to access the data. The system performed deduction and used a typed unification algorithm and a semantic network. The semantic query optimization method described in [227] was incorporated in the system. An answer extraction, natural language mechanism that also provided voice output was part of the system.

Chang described the *DEDUCE 2* system. The system performed deduction over databases. Horn rules were used. These rules were not recursive and were compiled in terms of base relations. Integrity constraints were used to perform semantic query optimization on queries. He also discussed the problems that arise with respect to recursive rules and termination [65].

**Third Stage: 1980-Present.** A large number of prototype *DDBs* were developed during this period and most of them are described in [280]. I shall briefly discuss several major efforts during this period: work at ECRC led by Jean-Marie Nicolas, work at MCC led by Shalom Tsur and Carlo Zaniolo, work at the University of Wisconsin led by Raghu Ramakrishnan, and work at Stanford led by Jeff Ullman. Each of these efforts were attempts to develop operational and

| Name | QA–3.5 [151, 152] Question– Answering System | ASP [311] Association Stor- ing Processor | RDF [202, 200] Relational Data File | RSS [80, 81] Relational Struc- tures System |
|------|------|------|------|------|
| Organization | Stanford Research Inst. | Hughes Aircraft Corp. | RAND Corp. | Computer Corp. of America |
| Designers | Raphael, Green & Coles | Savitt, Love & Troop | Levien & Maron | Marill |
| Computer | PDP 10 | IBM 360/65 | IBM 7044 & 360/65 | IBM 360/75 |
| Pgmg. Lang. | LISP 1.5 | Assembly Language | Assembly Language | Assembly Language |
| Input Lan- guage Model | "Near– natural" language model based on simple trans- formations and context–free grammar | Stylized input form & a procedu- ral language | Stylized input forms ana- lyzed by FORE- MAN Language | "Near– natural" language model based on matching sen- tence templates |
| Syntactic Analysis Technique | Earley algo- rithm for context– free grammar | N/A | N/A | Match of sentence against stored templates |
| Semantics Analysis Technique | Semantics stack built during syn- tax analysis phase | N/A | N/A | "Pattern $\Rightarrow$ action" opera- tion invoked as a result of template match |
| Intermediate Language | First–order predi- cate calculus | Binary relations | Binary relations | $n$–ary re- lations ($n \leq 7$ as implemented) |
| Data Structures | LISP chained list structures | Relational state- ment elements random- ized (coded) and replicated state- ments stored un- der each element | Files quadru- plicated and or- dered by state- ment number and three elements | Statement el- ements are hash- coded and "open" statements linked to corre- sponding "closed" statements |
| Inference Procedures | Formal the- orem proving by Robinson Resolu- tion Procedure | Inference rules specified as rela- tional statements are han- dled by "breath– first–followed– by–depth" | "Plausible" inference rules are specified in a pro- cedural language called INFEREX | Twelve general rules of deductive logic are used |
| Output Language | "Near–natural" language gener- ated in a synthesis phase | Relational statements | Relational statements | "Near– natural" language generated from $n$– ary relational statements |

Table 5. (Adapted from [247]) First Stage DDB Implementations

| Name | MRPPS 3.0 [231] | DADM [172] | Deduce 2 [64] |
|---|---|---|---|
| | Maryland Refutation Proof Procedure System | Deductively Augmented Data Management | |
| Organization | University of Maryland | System Development Corp. | IBM San Jose |
| Designers | Minker, McSkimin, Wilson & Aronson | Kellogg, Klahr, & Travis | Chang |
| Computer | UNIVAC 1108 | | |
| Pgmg. Lang. | SIMPL | | |
| Input Language Model | Multi–sorted Well–Formed formulae | Primitive Conditional Statements and Natural Language | DEDUCE [63] (based on Symbolic Logic) |
| Intermediate Language | Clausal Form | Primitive Conditional Statements | DEDUCE |
| Data Structures | Semantic Networks, Knowledge Base Index | Predicate Array, Premise Array, Semantic Network, Predicate Connection Graph [183, 319] | Connection Graph |
| Inference Procedures | SL–resolution [184] and LUSH–resolution [159] | Connection Graph | Connection Graph |
| Output Language | Natural Language Voice and English [263] | Primitive Condition Statements | DEDUCE |
| Features | Semantic Query Optimization, Multi–Sorted Variables, No Recursion, Non–Horn Clauses, Clauses need not be Function–Free, Relations not in First Normal Form | Semantic Query Optimization, Multi–Sorted Variables, No Recursion | Semantic Query Optimization |

Table 6. Second Stage DDB Implementations

possibly commercial *DDBs*. They contributed significantly to both the theory and implementation of *DDBs*. Detailed descriptions of contributions made by these systems and others may be found in [280]. I briefly describe some highlights here. In Table 7, I list some of the capabilities of systems developed in the third stage. Those listed are taken from [280].

*Implementation efforts at ECRC* on *DDBs* started in 1984 and led to the study of algorithms and prototypes: deductive query evaluation methods (QSQ/SLD and others) [344, 345, 346, 192]; integrity checking (Soundcheck) [85]; the deductive database system EKS(-V1) by Vieille and his team [347]; hypothetical reasoning and integrity constraints checking [348]; and aggregation through recursion [193]. The EKS system used a top-down evaluation method and was released to ECRC shareholder companies in 1990. ECRC was also engaged in research on the development of a deductive object-oriented deductive database.

*Implementation efforts at MCC* on a *DDB* started in 1984 and emphasized bottom-up evaluation methods [336] and query evaluation using such methods as seminaive evaluation, magic sets and counting [12, 24, 303, 304], semantics for stratified negation and set-grouping [23], investigation of safety, the finiteness of answer sets, and join order optimization. A system, termed *LDL* was implemented in 1988, and released with refinements during the period 1989-1991. It was among the first operational *DDBs* that was widely available. It was distributed to universities and shareholder companies of MCC.

*Implementation efforts at the University of Wisconsin* on the *Coral DDBs* started in the late 1980s. Bottom-up and magic set methods were implemented. The system, written in *C* and *C++*, is extensible and provides aggregation modularly stratified databases. *Coral* supports a declarative language, and an interface to C++ which allows for a combination of declarative and imperative programming. The declarative query language supports general Horn clauses augmented with complex terms, set-grouping, aggregation, negation, and relations with tuples that contain universally quantified variables. CORAL supports a wide range of evaluation strategies, and automatically chooses an efficient evaluation strategy. Users are permitted to guide query optimization by selecting from among alternative control choices. *Coral* provides imperative constructs such as update, insert and delete rules. Disk-resident data is supported using the *EXODUS* storage manager, which also provides transaction management in a client-server environment. *Coral* is available over the net and has been disseminated widely in the academic community.

*Implementation at Stanford University* on a *DDBs* started in 1985 on a system called *NAIL! (Not Another Implementation of Logic!)*. The results of this work led to the first paper on recursion using the Magic Sets method [12], done in collaboration with the group at MCC. Other contributions were aggregation in logical rules, and theoretical contributions to negation: stratified negation by Van Gelder [341], well-founded negation [138] and modularly stratified negation [298]. A language, called *GLUE* [261, 251] was developed. *GLUE* is a language for logical rules that has the power of *SQL* statements, together with a conventional language that permits the construction of loops, procedures and modules.

*Implementations of DDBs in the first, second and third stages of their development have demonstrated the feasibility and practicality of the technology. Tools and techniques have been developed to produce efficient DDBs.*

## 3.2 Prospects for Commercial Implementation of DDBs [4]

One might address why, after 20 years that theoretical research was started in deductive datases, no commercial systems exist. To place this statement in perspective, it is well to recall that it required approximately twelve years for relational systems to become a reality. Additionally, as Jeff Ullman has stated on a number of occasions, deductive database theory is more more subtle than relational database theory. Nevertheless, there have been many prototypes, starting from the 1960s until the present, as described in section 3.1. However, none of the systems in [280] are likely to become commercial products with possibly two exceptions, *Aditi* [281] and *VALIDITY* [120, 209], developed at the Bull Corporation. According to a personal communication from Ramamohanarao, the leader of the *Aditi* effort, *Aditi* is perhaps one year from being a commercial product. Whether or not it will become a product remains to be seen. I believe that it will depend upon moving the system from a university setting to industry. Implementors and applications specialists will be required, rather than university researchers.

At the Bull Corporation, Jean-Marie Nicolas has headed up an effort with Laurent Vieille and their colleagues, to develop a deductive database system that integrates object-oriented features. The effort has been on-going for about 4 years and appears to be entering the market place. There are indications that the effort will be moved from the Bull Corporation to a new company that will be responsible for its maintenance, marketing and improvements. They have been developing a system called *VALIDITY*, which is an outgrowth of the work at *ECRC*, and may be less than one year away from being a commercial product. Indeed, in a personal communication with Jean-Marie Nicolas, there are indications that *VALIDITY* is already in use by some selected applications partners. The *VALIDITY* team has written a summary state of the art report on deductive and deductive object-oriented databases [333].

There are several reasons why we may not have had commercial systems earlier. Most of the prototype systems that have been developed have been at universities. Unless there is commercial backing for the venture, universities are not in a position either to develop or to support the maintenance that is required for large system developments. Those systems that have been developed in research

---

[4] Revisions made to this section subsequent to the Workshop on Logic in Databases, held in San Miniato, Italy, July 1-2, 1996, incorporate comments made in the panel session, *Deductive Databases: Challenges, opportunities and Future Directions*, by Arno Siebes, Shalom Tsur, Jeff Ullman, Laurent Vieille and Carlo Zaniolo, and in a personal communication by Jean-Marie Nicolas. I am responsible for any views expressed here.

| Name | Developed | Recurs. | Negation | Aggregat. | Upd. | ICs | Optimizat. | Storage | Interfaces |
|---|---|---|---|---|---|---|---|---|---|
| Aditi [339] | U. Melbourne | General | Stratified | Stratified | No | No | Magic Sets, Seminaive | EDB, IDB | Prolog |
| COL [1] | INRIA | ? | Stratified | Stratified | No | No | None | Main memory | ML |
| Concept-Base [169] | U. Aachen | General | Locally Stratified | No | Yes | No | Magic sets, Seminaive | EDB only | C, Prolog |
| CORAL [279] | U. Wisconsin | General | Modular Stratified | Modular Stratified | No | No | Magic sets, Seminaive, Context factoring, Projection pushing | EDB, IDB | C,C++, Extensible |
| EKS–V1 [347] | ECRC | General | Stratified | General | Yes | Yes | Query–subquery, left/right linear | EDB, IDB | Persistent Prolog |
| DECLARE [174] | MAD Intelligent Systems | General | Locally Stratified | General | No | No | Magic sets, Seminaive, Projection pushing | EDB only | C, Common Lisp |
| LDL, LDL++, Salad [69] | MCC | General | Stratified | Stratified | Yes | No | Magic sets, Seminaive, left/right linear, Projection pushing, "Bushy depth–first" | EDB only | C, C++, SQL |
| LOGRES [49] | Polytech. of Milan | Linear | Inflation. Semant. | Stratified | Yes | Yes | Seminaive Algebraic Xforms | EDB, IDB | INFORMIX |
| NAIL/ GLUE [251] | Stanford U. | General | Well–Founded | Glue only | Glue only | No | Magic sets, Seminaive, Right–linear | EDB only | None |
| Starburst [253] | IBM Almaden | General | Stratified | Stratified | No | No | Magic sets, Seminaive (variant) | EDB, IDB | Extensible |

Table 7. (Taken from [280]) Existing Implementations of DDBs

organizations controlled by consortia (ECRC and MCC) have not had the full backing of the consortia members. Second, the implementation effort to develop a commercial product was vastly underestimated by some of the organizations. There is a large investment that must be made to develop a deductive database that will both compete with relational technology and extend it. It should be emphasized that according to industry standards, an investment in the order of $30 to $50 million dollars is required to develop and place in the market a database system, whatever technology it relies upon. Furthermore, researchers tend to change their interests rather than to consolidate their work and invest into technology transfer towards industry to favor development of commercial software. Third, until recently, there has not been a convincing demonstration of a large commercial problem that requires a deductive database. This may have been a reason why the *LDL* system at *MCC*, and the *ECRC* developments were terminated. However, today, there appear to be a large number of applications that could take advantage of this technology as evidenced by the book edited by Ramakrishnan, "Applications of Logic Databases," [278]. In addition, Levy, Mendelzon, Sagiv and Srivastava [204] study the problem of computing answers to queries using materialized views and note that this work is related to applications such as Global Information Systems, Mobile Computing, view adaptation and maintaining physical data independence. In [205] they describe how deductive databases can be used to provide uniform access to a heterogeneous collection of more than 100 information sources on the World Wide Web. The work by Pulido [275] on *STARBASE*, an automatic method that reorders literals in the body of a rule so that the next literal to be processed is guaranteed to be the most instantiated, might be useful to consider in conjunction with this work. Fourth, none of the university researchers tried to obtain venture capital to permit them to build a product outside of the university. Efforts by some from MCC to obtain venture capital did not succeed. The *VALIDITY* effort to develop a system in an industrial setting is a prospect as described above.

Does lack of a commercial system at this date forebode the end of logic and databases? I believe that such a view would be naive. First, there still is the prospect, as noted above, that we will have a commercial deductive database system. Second, when one considers the fact that it took a good twelve years before relational database technology entered the market place from the late 1960s, when research into relational systems started (see [77]), there is no need to be alarmed. Third, as the following developments portend, relational databases are starting to incorporate techniques stemming from research in deductive databases.

Indeed, many of the techniques introduced within *DDBs* are finding their way into relational technology. The new SQL standards for relational databases are beginning to adopt many of the powerful features of deductive databases. Although there are always delays and discrepancies between specifications of SQL standards and their effective support by commercial systems, this is a good sign. In the SQL-2 standards (also known as SQL-92) [229], a general class of integrity constraints called *asserts* allow for arbitrary relationships between tables and views to be declared. These constraints exist as separate statements in the database, and are not attached to a particular table or view. This extension is powerful enough to express the types of integrity constraints generally associated with deductive databases. However, it should be noted that only the full SQL-2 standard includes assert specifications. The intermediate SQL-2 standard, which is the basis for most current commercial implementations, does not include asserts. For most current commercial implementations, asserts are not included. At the present time, the relational language for the next generation *SQL, SQL3* will provide an operation called *recursive union* that directly supports recursive processing of tables [228]. As noted in [228],

> The use of the recursive union operator allows both linear (single-parent, or tree) recursion and non-linear (multi-parent, or general directed graph) recursion. This solution will allow easy solutions to bill-of-material and similar applications.

Linear recursion is currently a part of the client server of *IBM's DB2* system. It appears that they are using the *magic sets* method to perform linear recursion. There are indications that the *ORACLE* database system will also support some form of recursion.

A further development is that some form of *semantic query optimization* is beginning to be incorporated in relational databases. In some instances, such as *DB2*, cases are recognized when only one answer is to be found and the search is terminated. In other systems, it appears that equalities and other arithmetic constraints are being added to optimize the search. It will not be too long, in my view, before join elimination will be considered and introduced to relational technology. One can now estimate when it will be useful to eliminate a join [144]. The tools and techniques already exist and it is merely a matter of time before the users and the system implementers have them as part of their database systems.

Another technology that is available for commercial use is that of cooperative databases. The tools and techniques exist, as evidenced by the *COBASE* [73, 74] and *CARMIN* [127] work. With the introduction of recursion and semantic query optimization techniques into relational database technology, it will be necessary to provide users with cooperative responses so they understand why certain queries fail or succeed, as may be the case. It will also permit queries to be relaxed when the original query fails. This will permit reasonable, if not logically correct answers to be provided to users. Since user constraints may be handled in the same way that integrity constraints are handled, we will see relational systems that incorporate the needs of individual users into a query, as represented by their constraints.

Although the relational database community may ignore that the features that they are adding to their systems are outgrowths of developments in deductive databases, we should not be concerned. We should be pleased that our work in developing logic-based theories is now coming to fruition and has also helped in traditional relational database systems.

*Two significant developments have taken place in the implementation of commercial DDBs. The first is the incorporation of techniques developed in DDDBs into relational technology. Recursive views that use the magic set technique for implementation are being permitted and methods developed for semantic query optimization are being applied. The second is the development of a deductive object–oriented DBs, VALIDITY, that appears to be in commercial use; and the development of the Aditi DDBs that is scheduled for commercial use in approximately one year. It remains to be seen how long one can make patches to relational technology to simulate the capabilities of deductive databases systems.*

# 4    Emerging Areas and Trends

In the previous sections we have shown that there are many theories for negation both in extended deductive databases and in disjunctive deductive databases. There have been many different semantics proposed based on these theories. We understand a great deal about negation, except for how and when one should use a given theory. This will be a major area of confusion when users become cognizant of what is available for them to use. Much more work has to be done if the areas of implementation and application are to catch up to the intellectual developments that have taken place over the past 20 years. We have saturated the market for alternative theories of semantics and should move to more fertile topics. Unless we do so, funding for logic and databases will start to wane, as I believe that it has in the United States. That does not mean that we should abandon all research in theories of negation and alternative semantics, but we have to take stock of what we have accomplished and make it more accessible for users.

The role of logic will be of increasing importance due to the need to handle highly complex data (partly due to the advances in networking technology and the reduction of cost in both processing time and primary, secondary and tertiary memory). This data will require more complex models of data access and representation. Advances will require formal models of logic rather than ad-hoc solutions. Below, I shall briefly mention a number of fertile areas for further exploration. This is not intended to be an exhaustive listing of important areas to investigate.

*Temporal databases*, which deal with time, needs additional research. It is important for historical databases, real-time databases and other aspects of databases. Work in this area has been done by Snodgrass [326, 324, 325], Chomicki [70], and Wolfson and Sistla [320]. A paper on applying transition rules to such databases for integrity constraint checking appears in this collection [224].

*Transactions and updates* have not had sufficient attention. There exist semantic models of updates [109, 149, 111] that assure that views and data are updated correctly. Considerably more work is required in the area of transactions which require sequences of updates. Long duration transaction models and workflow management are areas that require work. In emerging applications of database systems, transactions are viewed as sequences of nested, and most probably interactive sub-transactions that may sparsely occur over long periods of time. In this scenario new complex transaction systems must be designed. Logic-based transaction systems will be essential to assure that an appropriate and correct transaction is achieved. Work in this area is being done by Bonner and Kifer [34, 35], Lin and Reiter [208, 207], and others [179, 4, 72, 110, 135, 220].

*Active databases* consist of data that protects its own integrity and describes the database semantics. Active rules are represented by the formalism, *Event-Condition-Action (ECA)* [334] and denote that whenever an event E occurs, if condition C holds, then trigger action A. It has a behavior of its own beyond passively accepting statements from users or applications. Upon recognition of certain events, it invokes commands and monitors and manages itself. It may invoke external actions that interact with systems outside the database. Indeed, it may activate a potentially infinite set of triggers. Although declarative constraints are provided for such systems, the *ECA* formalism is essentially procedural in nature. Zaniolo has noted the need for declarative semantics of triggers [356, 357]. He has developed a unified semantics for active and deductive databases and has shown how active database rules relate to transaction-conscious stable model semantics. Work reported upon in this collection by [18] proposes a first step towards characterizing active databases. Additional work is required to develop a clear semantics, sound implementations and a better understanding of complexity issues in active databases. Work in the situation calculus and Datalog extensions apply here.

*Data mining and inductive inference* deal with finding generalizations that may be extracted from a database or a logic program. Such generalizations may be integrity constraints that must be *true* with respect to the database, or generalizations that may be *true* of the current state, but may change if there are updates. It will be up to the database administrator to determine which of the generalizations are integrity constraints, and which are applicable only to the current state and must be checked at update time. Semantic query optimization can handle either of these two cases, and inform the user as to which constraint may be applicable to a query. As demonstrated in the work of Muggleton and De Raedt [252], logic programming may be used to find inductive inferences. The book edited by Piatetsky-Shapiro and Frawley [262] covers work on knowledge data mining. Laurent and Vrain [191], in this collection, discuss how to couple deductive databases and inductive logic programming to learn query rules for optimizing databases with update rules.

*Integrating production systems with deductive databases* is future work that is needed. A formal approach to performing such an integration and to developing the semantics of rule-based systems will result. Since rule-based systems have played a role in active systems, work in this area will benefit active database efforts. Related work in this area is described in [153, 221, 284, 285, 283]

*Logical foundations of object-oriented deductive databases* is needed. In many ways object-oriented databases relate to hierarchic and network systems. It is essential that such systems have a formal theory and a semantics. This is difficult as there does not appear to be a formal definition of an object-oriented database.

Efforts have been undertaken by Kifer and his co-workers [175] to develop a formal foundation for object-oriented databases. Extensive work is required to develop semantic query optimization techniques, a formal theory of updating and all of the tools and techniques developed for deductive databases.

*Description logics* are concerned with restricting knowledge representation so that deduction over a knowledge base is tractable, but is still powerful enough to represent the knowledge in a natural manner. KRYPTON was an early such hybrid knowledge representation system which combined a functional knowledge representation with a specialized connection graph theorem prover [40, 41]. KL-ONE is perhaps the best known knowledge representation system based on a description logic [42]. CLASSIC is a modern successor of KL-ONE which allows for the definition of complex objects and moves towards database support [36, 39]. In deductive databases, representational power is also limited to allow for more tractable deduction (via specific proof procedures). Some of these limits are a restriction to Horn clauses, no logical terms, no existential quantification, and so forth. Research in deductive databases has sought to extend the representational power some, yet preserve tractability to the greatest extent possible: for example, disjunctive deductive databases allow for general clauses and the addition of null values allow for a type of existential quantification. The topics of deductive databases and description logics have remained somewhat distinct. However, their goals are quite similar. As the representation power improve in each, and better more efficient proof procedures are developed, we should see a convergence of these areas.

*Heterogeneous databases* are of considerable interest. The objective here is to integrate into one system multiple databases that do not necessarily share the same data models. There is the need for a common logic-based language for mediation and a formal semantics of such databases. Work on the *Hermes* system by Subrahmanian [328], the *Tsimmis* system by Garcia-Molina and his colleagues [66], and the work by Ramakrishnan on [230] are illustrative of work on this subject. It is not unlikely that heterogeneous databases will also be required to handle textual data. Kero and Tsur [173], in this collection, describe the $\mathcal{IQ}$ system that uses a deductive database $\mathcal{LDL} + +$ to reason about textual information. Language extensions for the semantic integration of deductive databases is proposed by [9] in this collection. The language allows *mediators* to be constructed, using a set of operators for composing programs and message passing features.

*Multi-media databases* [329] is an emerging area for which new data models are needed. These databases have special problems such as manipulating geographic databases; picture retrieval where a concept orthogonal to time may appear in the database: space; and video databases, where space and time are combined. Temporal and spatial reasoning will be needed. Logic will play a major role in the development of query languages for these new data models, will permit deductive reasoning, and a formal semantics will provide a firm theoretical basis for them.

*Combining databases* is a topic related to both heterogeneous and multimedia systems. Here one is trying to combine databases that share the same integrity constraints and schema. Such databases arise in distributed systems work and in combining knowledge bases. In addition to handling problems that arise because the combined databases may be inconsistent, one has to handle priorities that may exist among individual facts. A formal treatment of this subject started with Minker and his co-workers [15, 16, 17, 266, 265, 264].

*Integrity constraints, semantic query optimization and constraint logic programming* are related topics. Semantic query optimization uses constraints in the form of integrity constraints to prune the search space. These integrity constraints introduce equalities, inequalities, and relations into a query to help optimize the search [58]. Constraint logic programming introduces domain constraints. These constraints may be equalities, inequalities, and may even be relations [167, 166]. Constraint databases and constraint-intensive queries are required in many advanced applications. In constraint databases, constraints can capture spatial and temporal behavior which is not possible in existing databases. The relationships between these areas need to be explored further and applied to deductive databases. Spatial databases defined in terms of polynomial inequalities are investigated by [189], who consider termination properties of *Datalog* programs.

*Abductive reasoning* is the process of finding explanations for observations in a given theory. Selman and Levesque [316] developed an approach using logic, which is described in Kakas, Kowalski and Toni [170]. Given a set of sentences T (a theory), and a sentence G (an observation), the abductive task can be characterized as the problem of finding a set of sentences $\Delta$ (abductive explanation for G) such that

(1) $T \cup \Delta \models G$,
(2) $T \cup \Delta$ is consistent.
(3) $\Delta$ is minimal with respect to set inclusion [316, 170, 54].

A comprehensive survey and critical overview of the extension of logic programming to perform abductive reasoning (abductive logic programming) is given in [170]. They outline the framework of abduction and its applications to default reasoning; and introduce an augmentation theoretic approach to the use of abduction as an interpretation for negation-as-failure. They show that abduction has strong links to extended disjunctive logic programming. Abduction is shown to generalize negation-as-failure to include not only negative but also positive hypotheses, and to include general integrity constraints. They show that abductive logic programming is related to the justification based truth maintenance system of Doyle [102]. Inoue and Sakama [164] develop a fixpoint semantics for abductive logic programs in which the belief models are characterized as the fixpoint of a disjunctive program obtained by a suitable program transformation. For a summary of complexity results on abductive reasoning and nonmonotonic reasoning see the excellent survey by Cadoli and Schaerf [54].

*High-level robotics* is an area of active research. In approaches taken to this problem, logic has played a significant role. Knowledge bases are used in high level robotics to solve problems in cognition required to plan actions for robots and to deal with multiple agents in complicated environments. Work in deductive and disjunctive databases relates to this problem. In some instances a robot may have several options that can be represented by disjunctions. Additional information derived either by alternative information derived from sensors may serve to disambiguate the possibilities. There are several groups engaged in this research: the University of Toronto [196, 197], the University of Texas at El Paso [14], the University of Texas at Austin [142] and the University of Linkoping [309, 310]. Kowalski and Sadri [182], discuss a unified agent architecture that combines rationality with reactivity in this collection, and relates to this topic.

*Applications of deductive database techniques* will be important. Greater emphasis is required to apply deductive database technology to realistic problems. Deductive databases have been shown to be important both for relational and deductive systems on such topics as semantic query optimization [56], cooperative answering [124], Global Information Systems and Mobile Computing [204, 83].

*Implement Deductive (DDB) and Object-Oriented Deductive Databases (DOOD).* It is important to develop a commercial *DDB* or *DOOD* system. The deductive model of databases is beginning to take hold as evidenced by the textbook, "Foundations of Databases," by Abiteboul, Hull and Vianu [2]. The prospect that the *Aditi* [281] system may be available in a year is indication that progress is being made in developing a commercial *DDBS*. The merger of object-oriented and deductive formalisms is taking place as illustrated by the proceedings of the DOOD conference series [176, 90, 55, 209]. This series was established in 1989 at the initiative of Shojiro Nishio, together with Serge Abiteboul, Jack Minker and Jean-Marie Nicolas. That the *VALIDITY* [121, 120], system is probably in use by customers at the present time is an indication that the object-oriented and deductive formalisms are soon to be available commercially. Additional features will be required for commercial systems such as cooperative answering [123] and arithmetic and aggregate operators, as described in this collection by Dobbie and Topor [100].

*It is clear from the above, that logic and databases can contribute significantly to a large number of exciting new topics. Hence, the field of logic and databases will continue to be a productive area of research and implementation.*

## 5 Summary

In section 1, I discussed the significant pre-history of the field of *logic and databases*. I noted the work by Levien, Maron and Kuhns [202, 203, 199, 200, 201, 186, 187, 188], by Green and Raphael [151, 152], and referred to my paper [234], where the pre-history of the field is discussed. In sections 2 and 3, I discussed the major accomplishments that have taken place in this field in the 20 years since 1976. Among these accomplishments are the extension of relational databases, the development of the semantics and complexity of these alternative databases, permit knowledge base systems to be represented and developed, and nonmonotonic reasoning systems to be implemented. In section 4,

I discussed many exciting new areas that will be important in the near and long-term future. *It is clear that the field of logic and databases has had a significant pre-history before 1970, and a well-defined area of research, complete with past achievements and continued future areas of work.*

In these past twenty years we have seen logic and databases progress from a fledgling field, to a fully developed, mature field. The new areas that I have cited that need further investigation show that we have not nearly exhausted the work in this field. I envision that many more workshops will be held on this topic. *Logic and databases has contributed to the field of databases being a scientific endeavor rather than an ad-hoc collection of techniques. We understand what constitutes a database, a query, an answer to a query, and where knowledge has its place.* I look forward to the next twenty years of this field. I hope that I will have an opportunity, then, to look back and see a field that has accomplished much, and is still vibrant. To remain vibrant, we will have to take on some of the new challenges, rather than to be mired in the semantics of more exotic databases. We will have to address implementation issues and we will have to be able to provide guidance to practitioners who will need to use the significant developments in logic and databases.

# References

1. S. Abiteboul and S. Grumback. A rule-based language with functions and sets. *ACM Transactions on Database Systems*, 16(1):1–30, 1991.
2. S. Abiteboul, R. Hull, and V. Vianu. *Foundations of Databases*. Addison-Wesley Publishing Comp, 1995.
3. J. Alferes and L. Pereira. On logic program semantics with two kinds of negation. In K. Apt, editor, *Proceedings of the Joint International Conference and Symposium on Logic Programming*, pages 574–588, Washington, D.C. USA, Nov 1992. The MIT Press.
4. P. Ammann, S. Jajodia, and I. Ray. Using formal methods to reason about semantics-based decompositions of transactions. In *Proc. of 21st VLDB Conference*, pages 218–227, 1995.
5. H. Andreka and I. Nemeti. The generalized completeness of horn predicate logic as a programming language. *Acta Cybernetica*, 4(1):3–10, 1978.
6. K. Apt and H. Blair. Arithmetic classification of perfect models of stratified programs. *Fundamenta Informaticae*, XIII:1–18, 1990. With addendum in vol. XIV: 339-343. 1991.
7. K. Apt, H. Blair, and A. Walker. Towards a theory of declarative knowledge. In J. Minker, editor, *Foundations of Deductive Databases and Logic Programming*, pages 89–148. Morgan Kaufmann Pub., Los Altos, California, 1988.
8. K. Apt and R. Bol. Logic programming and negation: a survey. *Journal of Logic Programming*, 19/20:9–71, May/June 1994.
9. P. Asirelli, C. Renso, and F. Turini. Language extensions for semantic integration of deductive databases. In D. Pedreschi and C. Zaniolo, editors, *Logic in Databases (LID'96)*, pages 425–444, July 1-2 1996. Also in this collection.
10. R. Bagai and R. Sunderraman. Bottom-up computation of the fitting model for general deductive databases. *Intelligent Information Systems*, 6(1):59–75, Jan. 1996.

11. F. Bancilhon. Naive evaluation of recursively defined relations. In M. Brodie and J. Mylopoulos, editors, *On Knowledge Base Management Systems–Integrating Database and AI Systems*, pages 165–178. Springer-Verlag, 1986.

12. F. Bancilhon, D. Maier, Y. Sagiv, and J. Ullman. Magic sets and other strange ways to implement logic programs. In *Proc. ACM Symp. on Principles of Database Systems*, March 1986.

13. C. Baral and M. Gelfond. Logic programming and knowledge representation. *Journal of Logic Programming*, 19/20:73–148, July 1994.

14. C. Baral, M. Gelfond, and A. Provetti. Representing Actions: Laws, Observations and Hypothesis. *Journal of Logic Programming (to appear)*, 1996.

15. C. Baral, S. Kraus, and J. Minker. Combining multiple knowledge bases. *IEEE Transactions on Knowledge and Data Engineering*, 3(2):208–220, July 1991.

16. C. Baral, S. Kraus, J. Minker, and V. Subrahmanian. Combining knowledge bases consisting of first order theories. Technical Report CS-2531, Dept of Computer Science, University of Maryland, College Park Md 20742, 1990.

17. C. Baral, S. Kraus, J. Minker, and V. Subrahmanian. Combining default logic databases. *Journal of International Information Systems*, 1994. To appear.

18. C. Baral and J. Lobo. Formal characterization of active databases. In D. Pedreschi and C. Zaniolo, editors, *Logic in Databases (LID'96)*, pages 195–215, July 1-2 1996. Also in this collection.

19. C. Baral, J. Lobo, and J. Minker. Generalized well-founded semantics for logic programs. In M. E. Stickel, editor, *Proc. of Tenth Internatinal Conference on Automated Deduction*, pages 102–116, Kaiserslautern, Germany, July 1989. Springer-Verlag.

20. C. Baral, J. Lobo, and J. Minker. Generalized disjunctive well-founded semantics for logic programs: Procedural semantics. In *Proceedings of the Fifth International Symposium on Methodologies for Intelligent Systems*, pages 456–464, Knoxville TN, USA, 1990.

21. C. Baral, J. Lobo, and J. Minker. Generalized disjunctive well-founded semantics for logic programs: Declarative semantics. In *Proceedings of the Fifth International Symposium on Methodologies for Intelligent Systems*, pages 465–473, Knoxville TN, USA, 1990.

22. C. Baral and V. Subrahmanian. Stable and extension class theory for logic programs and default theory. *Journal of Automated Reasoning*, pages 345–366, 1992.

23. C. Beeri, S. Naqvi, O. Shmueli, and S. Tsur. Set constructors in a logic database language. *Journal of Logic Programming*, 10 (3&4), 1991.

24. C. Beeri and R. Ramakrishnan. On the power of magic. *Journal of Logic Programming*, 10(3/4):255–300, 1991.

25. C. Bell, A. Nerode, R. Ng, and V. Subrahmanian. Implementing stable model semantics by linear programming. In *Proceedings of the 1993 International Workshop on Logic Programming and Non-monotonic Reasoning*, June 1993.

26. R. Ben-Eliyahu and R. Dichter. Propositional semantics for disjunctive logic programs. *Annals of Mathematics and Artificial intelligence*, 12:53–87, 1994.

27. R. Ben-Eliyahu and L. Palopoli. Reasoning with minimal models: efficient algorithms and applications. In *Proc. of the Fourth International Conference on Principles of Knowledge Representation and Reasoning*, pages 39–50, 1994. Full paper submitted for journal publication.

28. R. Ben-Eliyahu, L. Palopoli, and V. Zemlyanker. The expressive power of tractable disjunction. In W. Wahlster, editor, *ECAI96. 12th European Conference on Artificial Intelligence*, pages 345–349, 1996.

29. J. Biskup. A formal approach to null values in database relations. In H. Gallaire, J. Minker and J.M. Nicolas, editors, *Advances in Data Base Theory*, volume 1, pages 299–341. Plenum Press, New York, 1981.

30. J. Biskup. A foundation of Codd's relational maybe-operations. University Park, 1981. Pennsylvania State Univ.

31. H. Blair, W. Marek, and J. Schlipf. The expressiveness of locally stratified programs. Technical report, Mathematical Sciences Institute, Cornell University, 1992. Available as technical report 92-8.

32. H. Blair and V. Subrahmanian. Paraconsistent logic.

33. B. Blaustein. *Enforcing database assertions: techniques and applications*. PhD thesis, Harvard University, Computer Science Dept., Cambridge, Mass., Aug. 1981. Ph.D. dissertation.

34. A. Bonner and M. Kifer. Transaction logic programming. In D. S. Warren, editor, *Logic Programming: Proc. of the 10th International Conf.*, pages 257–279, 1993.

35. A. Bonner and M. Kifer. Concurrency and communication in transaction logic. In D. Pedreschi and C. Zaniolo, editors, *Logic in Databases (LID'96)*, pages 153–172, July 1-2 1996. Also in this collection.

36. A. Borgida, R. J. Brachman, D. L. McGuiness, and L. A. Resnick. CLASSIC: A structural data model for objects. *ACM SIGMOD Record*, 18(2):58, June 1989. Also published in/as: 19 ACM SIGMOD Conf. on the Management of Data, (Portland OR), May–Jun 1989.

37. A. Borgida and D. Etherington. Hierarchical knowledge bases and efficient disjunction. In *Proceedings of the First International Conference on Principle of Knowledge Representation and Reasoning (KR-89)*, pages 33–43, Toronto, Ontario, CANADA, 1989.

38. G. Bossu and P. Siegel. Saturation, nonmonotonic reasoning and the closed-world assumption. *Artificial Intelligence*, 25(1):13–63, Jan. 1985.

39. R. Brachman, A. Borgida, D. McGuinness, P. Patel-Schneider, and L. Resnick. The Classic knowledge representation system of KL-ONE: The next generation. In *International Conference on Fifth Generation Computer Systems*, pages 1036–1043, ICOT, Japan, 1992.

40. R. J. Brachman, R. E. Fikes, and H. J. Levesque. KRYPTON: A functional approach to knowledge representation. *IEEE Computer*, 16(10):67–73, Oct. 1983.

41. R. J. Brachman, V. P. Gilbert, and H. J. Levesque. An essential hybrid reasoning system: Knowledge and symbol level accounts of KRYPTON. In *International Joint Conference on Artificial Intelligence*, pages 532–539, Aug. 1985.

42. R. J. Brachman and J. G. Schmolze. An overview of the KL-ONE knowledge representation system. *Cognitive Science*, pages 171–216, Aug. 1985.

43. S. Brass. Sldmagic — an improved magic set technique. In B. Novikov and J. Schmidt, editors, *Advances in Database and Information Systems - ADBIS'96*, Sept 1996.

44. S. Brass and J. Dix. Disjunctive Semantics based upon Partial and Bottom-Up Evaluation. In L. Sterling, editor, *Proceedings of the 12th Int. Conf. on Logic Programming, Tokyo*, pages 199–213. MIT Press, June 1995.

45. S. Brass and J. Dix. A general approach to bottom–up computation of disjunctive semantics. In J. Dix, L. Pereira, and T. Przymusinski, editors, *Nonmonotonic Extensions of Logic Programming*, pages 127–155. Lecture Notes in Computer Science 927. Springer-Verlag, 1995.

46. S. Brass and J. Dix. Characterizations of the Disjunctive Stable Semantics by Partial Evaluation. *Journal of Logic Programming*, forthcoming, 1996.

47. S. Brass and J. Dix. Characterizing D-WFS: Confluence and Iterated GCWA. In L. Pereira and E. Orlowska, editors, *JELIA '96*, LNCS 1111, Berlin, 1996. Springer.

48. F. Bry. Query evaluation in recursive databases: bottom-up and top-down reconciled. *Data and Knowledge Engineering*, 5:289–312, 1990.

49. F. Cacace, S. Ceri, S. Crespi-Reghizzi, and R. Zicari. Integrating object-oriented data modeling with a rule-based programming paradigm. In *Proc. of ACM SIGMOD Conference on Management of Data*, May 1990.

50. M. Cadoli. The complexity for model checking for circumscrioptive formulae. *Information Processing Letters*, 44:113–118, Oct 1992.

51. M. Cadoli. Semantical and computational aspects of Horn approximations. In *Proc. of IJCAI-93*, pages 39–44, 1993.

52. M. Cadoli. Panel on "Knowledge compilation and approximation": terminology, questions, references. In *Proc. of the Fourth Int. Symp. on Artificial Intelligence and Mathematics, AI/Math-96*, pages 183–186, January 3-5 1996.

53. M. Cadoli and M. Lenzerini. The complexity of closed world reasoning and circumscription. *J. Comp. and Syst. Sci.*, 43:165–211, 1994.

54. M. Cadoli and M. Schaerf. A survey of complexity results for non-monotonic logics. *Journal of Logic Programming*, 13:127–160, 1993.

55. S. Ceri, K. Tanaka, and S. Tsur, editors. *Proc. of the 3rd Int. Conf. on Deductive and Object-Oriented Databases - DOOD'93*, December 1993. In LNCS 760, Springer-Verlag, Heidelberg, Germany.

56. U. Chakravarthy, J. Grant, and J. Minker. Logic-based approach to semantic query optimization. *ACM Transactions on Database Systems*, 15(2):162–207, June 1990.

57. U. S. Chakravarthy, J. Grant, and J. Minker. Foundations of semantic query optimization for deductive databases. In J. Minker, editor, *Proc. Workshop on Foundations of Deductive Databases and Logic Programming*, pages 67–101, Washington, D.C., Aug. 1986.

58. U. S. Chakravarthy, J. Grant, and J. Minker. Logic based approach to semantic query optimization. *ACM Transactions on Database Systems*, 15(2):162–207, June 1990.

59. E. Chan. A possible world semantics for non-Horn databases, 1989. University of Waterloo, Canada.

60. E. Chan. A possible world semantics for disjunctive databases. *IEEE Trans. Data and Knowledge Eng.*, 5(2):282–292, 1993.

61. A. Chandra and D. Harel. Structure and complexity of relational queries. *Journal of Computer System Sciences*, 25:99–128, 1982.

62. A. Chandra and D. Harel. Horn clause queries and generalizations. *Journal of Logic Programming*, 2(1):1–15, Apr. 1985.

63. C. Chang. DEDUCE—a deductive query language for relational databases. In C. Chen, editor, *Pattern Recognition and Artificial Intelligence*, pages 108–134. Academic Press, New York, 1976.

64. C. Chang. Deduce 2: Further investigations of deduction in relational databases. In H. G. J. Minker, editor, *Logic and Databases*, pages 201–236. Plenum, New York, 1978.

65. C. Chang. On evaluation of queries containing derived relations. In H. G. J. M. J.-M. Nicolas, editor, *Advances in Database Theory, Volume 1*, pages 235–260. Plenum Press, New York, 1981.

66. S. Chawathe, H. Garcia-Molina, J. Hammer, K. Ireland, Y. Papakonstantinou, J. Ullman, and J. Widom. The TSIMMIS project: Integration of heterogeneous information sources. In *Proceedings of IPSJ Conference, Tokyo, Japan,* October 1994. Available via anonymous FTP from host db.stanford.edu, file /pub/chawathe/1994/tsimmis-overview.ps.

67. W. Chen and D. Warren. A goal-oriented approach to computing well founded semantics. In K. Apt, editor, *Proceedings of the joint international conference and symposium on logic programming,* Washington, D.C., Nov. 1992.

68. S. Chi and L. Henschen. Recursive query answering with non-Horn clauses. In E. Lusk and R. Overbeek, editors, *Proc. $9^{th}$ International Conference on Automated Deduction,* pages 294–312, Argonne, IL, May 1988.

69. D. Chimenti, R. Gamboa, R. Krishnamurthy, S. Naqvi, S. Tsur, and C. Zaniolo. The LDL system prototype. *IEEE Transactions on Knowledge and Data Engineering,* 2(1):76–90, 1990.

70. J. Chomicki. Efficient checking of temporal integrity constraints using bounded history encoding. *ACM Transactions on Database Systems,* 20(2):111–148, May 1995.

71. J. Chomicki and V. Subrahmanian. Generalized closed world assumption is $\pi_2^0$–complete. *Information Processing Letters,* 34:289–291, May 1990.

72. P. Chrysanthis and K. Ramamritham. Synthesis of extended transaction models using ACTA. *ACM, TODS,* 19(3):450–491, 1994.

73. W. W. Chu, Q. Chen, and A. Hwang. Query answering via cooperative data inference. *Journal of Intelligent Information Systems,* 3:57–87, 1994.

74. W. W. Chu, Q. Chen, and M. A. Merzbacher. CoBase: A cooperative database system. Studies in Logic and Computation 3, chapter 2, pages 41–73. Clarendon Press, Oxford, 1994.

75. K. L. Clark. Negation as Failure. In H. Gallaire and J. Minker, editors, *Logic and Data Bases,* pages 293–322. Plenum Press, New York, 1978.

76. CODASYL. *CODASYL Data Base Task Group April 71 Report.* ACM, New York, 1971.

77. E. Codd. A relational model of data for large shared data banks. *Comm. ACM,* 13(6):377–387, June 1970.

78. E. F. Codd. Extending the database relational model to capture more meaning. *ACM Trans. Database Syst.,* 4(4):397–434, 1979.

79. A. Colmerauer, H. Kanoui, R. Pasero, and P. Roussel. Un systeme de communication homme-machine en francais. Technical report, Groupe de Intelligence Artificielle Universitae de Aix-Marseille II, Marseille, 1973.

80. Computer Corporation of America. Relational structures research. Technical report, Computer Corporation of America, August 5 1967. For Contract Period April 6, 1966-July 5, 1967.

81. Computer Corporation of America. Relational structures applications research. Technical report, Computer Corporation of America, July 11 1969. For Contract Period May 5, 1967-March 31, 1969.

82. M. Dalal. Some tractable classes of disjunctive logic programs. Technical report, Rutgers University, 1992.

83. S. Dar, H. Jagadish, A. Levy, and D. Srivastava. Answering queries with aggregation using views. In *Proceedings of the 22nd International Conference on Very Large Databases, VLDB-96,* Sept 1996. To appear.

84. C. Date. *An Introduction to Database Systems, Sixth Edition.* Addison-Wesley Publishing Comp, 1995.

85. H. Decker. Integrity enforcement on deductive databases. In *Proc. 1st Int. Conf. on Expert Database Systems*, April 1986.

86. H. Decker. On alternative models, fixpoints and consistency of disjunctive databases, May 1991.

87. H. Decker. On the declarative, operational and procedural semantics of disjunctive computational theories. In *Proceedings of the $2^{th}$ International Workshop on the Deductive Approach to Information Systems and Databases*, Aiguablava, Spain, Sept. 1991. Invited paper.

88. A. del Val. Tractable databases: how to make propositional unit resolution complete through compilation. In *Proc. of KR-94*, pages 551–561, 1994.

89. A. del Val. An analysis of approximate knowledge compilation. In *Proc. of IJCAI-95*, 1995.

90. C. Delobel, M. Kifer, and Y. Masunaga, editors. *Proc. 2nd Int. Conf. on Deductive and Object-Oriented Databases - DOOD'91*. Springer-Verlag, Heidelberg, Germany, December 1991.

91. R. Demolombe and A. J. Jones. Integrity constraints revisited. *Journal of the IGPL (Interest Group in Pure and Applied Logics): An Electronic Journal on Pure and Applied Logic*, 4(3):369–383, 1996.

92. S. Dietrich and D. S. Warren. Extension tables: memo relations in logic programming. In *Proc. Symp. on Logic Programming*, pages 264–273, San Francisco, Ca, 1987.

93. J. Dix. Classifying Semantics of Logic Programs. In A. Nerode, W. Marek, and V. S. Subrahmanian, editors, *Logic Programming and Non-Monotonic Reasoning, Proceedings of the first International Workshop*, pages 166–180, Cambridge, Mass., July 1991. Washington D.C, MIT Press.

94. J. Dix. A Framework for Representing and Characterizing Semantics of Logic Programs. In B. Nebel, C. Rich, and W. Swartout, editors, *Principles of Knowledge Representation and Reasoning: Proceedings of the Third International Conference (KR '92)*, pages 591–602. San Mateo, CA, Morgan Kaufmann, 1992.

95. J. Dix. Classifying Semantics of Disjunctive Logic Programs. In K. R. Apt, editor, *LOGIC PROGRAMMING: Proceedings of the 1992 Joint International Conference and Symposium*, pages 798–812, Cambridge, Mass., November 1992. MIT Press.

96. J. Dix. A Classification-Theory of Semantics of Normal Logic Programs: I. Strong Properties. *Fundamenta Informaticae*, XXII(3):227–255, 1995.

97. J. Dix. A Classification-Theory of Semantics of Normal Logic Programs: II. Weak Properties. *Fundamenta Informaticae*, XXII(3):257–288, 1995.

98. J. Dix. *Disjunctive deductive databases: theoretical foundations and operational semantics*. PhD thesis, Institut für informationssysteme abteilung wissensbasierte systeme, Technische Universität Wien, Sept 1995. Habilitation Thesis.

99. J. Dix. Semantics of Logic Programs: Their Intuitions and Formal Properties. An Overview. In A. Fuhrmann and H. Rott, editors, *Logic, Action and Information - Essays on Logic in Philosophy and Artificial Intelligence*, pages 241–327. DeGruyter, 1995.

100. G. Dobbie and R. Topor. Arithmetic and aggregate operators in deductive object-oriented databases. In D. Pedreschi and C. Zaniolo, editors, *Logic in Databases (LID'96)*, pages 399–407, July 1-2 1996. Also in this collection.

101. W. Dowling and J. H. Gallier. Linear time algorithms for testing the satisfiability of propositional horn formulae. *Journal of Logic Programming*, 1:267–284, 1984.

102. J. Doyle. Truth Maintenance System. *Artificial Intelligence*, 13, 1980.

103. P. Dung. Negations as hypothesis: an abductive foundation for logic programming. In *Proc. of the 8th International Conference on Logic Programming*, 1991.
104. T. Eiter and G. Gottlob. Complexity aspects of various semantics for disjunctive databases. In *Proceedings of the Twelfth ACM SIGART-SIGMOD-SIGART Symposium on Principles of Database Systems (PODS-93)*, pages 158–167. ACM Press, May 1993.
105. T. Eiter and G. Gottlob. Complexity results for disjunctive logic programming and application to nonmonotonic logics. In D. Miller, editor, *Proceedings of the International Logic Programming Symposium ILPS'93*, pages 266–278, Vancouver, Canada, October 1993. MIT Press.
106. T. Eiter and G. Gottlob. On the computation cost of disjunctive logic programming: Propositional case. *Annals of Mathematics and Artificial Intelligence*, 15(3-4):289–323, Dec. 1995.
107. T. Eiter, G. Gottlob, and H. Mannila. Adding Disjunction to Datalog. In *Proceedings of the Thirteenth ACM SIGACT SIGMOD-SIGART Symposium on Principles of Database Systems (PODS '94)*, pages 267–278, May 1994.
108. T. Eiter, N. Leone, and D. Saccà. The expressive power of partial models for disjunctive databases. In D. Pedreschi and C. Zaniolo, editors, *Logic in Databases (LID'96)*, pages 261–280, July 1-2 1996. Also in this collection.
109. R. Fagin, J. Ullman, and M. Vardi. On the semantics of updates in databases. In *Proc. Senth ACM SIGACT/SIGMOD Symposium on Principles of Database Systems*, pages 352–365, 1983.
110. A. Farrag and M. Ozsu. Using semantic knowledge of transactions to increase concurrency. *ACM, TODS*, 14(4):503–525, 1989.
111. J. Fernández, J. Grant, and J. Minker. Model theoretic approach to view updates in deductive databases. *Journal of Automated Reasoning*, 1996. To appear.
112. J. Fernández and J. Minker. Semantics of disjunctive deductive databases. In *Proceedings of the International Conference on Database Theory*, pages 332–356, 1992. (Invited Paper).
113. J. Fernández and J. Minker. Theory and algorithms for disjunctive deductive databases. *Programmirovanie*, N 3:5–39, 1993. (also appears as University of Maryland Technical Report,CS-TR-3223, UMIACS-TR-94-17,1994. Invited Paper in Russian).
114. J. Fernández and J. Minker. Bottom-up computation of perfect models for disjunctive theories. *Journal of Logic Programming*, 25(1):33–51, October, 1995.
115. J. A. Fernández and J. Lobo. A proof procedure for stable theories. Submitted to the Journal of Logic Programming, 1993.
116. J. A. Fernández, J. Lobo, J. Minker, and V. Subrahmanian. Disjunctive LP + integrity constraints = stable models semantics. In L. Lakshmanan, editor, *Proceedings of the ILPS'91 Workshop on Deductive Databases*, pages 110–117, San Diego, California, Oct. 1991. Extended Version presented at the Second International Symposium on Artificial Intelligence.
117. J. A. Fernández, J. Lobo, J. Minker, and V. Subrahmanian. Disjunctive LP + integrity constraints = stable model semantics. *Annals of Mathematics and Artificial Intelligence*, 8(3-4):449–474, 1993.
118. J. A. Fernández and J. Minker. Bottom-up evaluation of Hierarchical Disjunctive Deductive Databases. In K. Furukawa, editor, *Logic Programming Proceedings of the Eighth International Conference*, pages 660–675. MIT Press, 1991.
119. M. Fitting. A Kripke-Kleene semantics for logic programs. *Journal of Logic Programming*, 2:295–312, 1985.

120. O. Friesen, G. Gauthier-Villars, A. Lefebvre, and L. Vieille. Applications of deductive object-oriented databases using del. In R. Ramakrishnan, editor, *Applications of Logic Databases*. Kluwer Academic Publishers, 1995.

121. O. Friesen, A. Lefebvre, and L. Vieille. VALIDITY: Applications of a dood system. In *Proc. 5th Int. Conf. on Extending Database Technology - EDBT'96 (LNCS 1057)*, Avignon, France, March 1996. Springer Verlag.

122. T. Gaasterland. *Cooperative Answers for Database Queries*. PhD thesis, University of Maryland, Department of Computer Science, College Park, 1992.

123. T. Gaasterland, P. Godfrey, and J. Minker. An overview of cooperative answering. *Journal of Intelligent Information Systems*, 1(2):123–157, 1992. Invited paper.

124. T. Gaasterland, P. Godfrey, and J. Minker. An overview of cooperative answering. *Journal of Intelligent Information Systems*, 1(2), 1992.

125. T. Gaasterland, P. Godfrey, and J. Minker. Relaxation as a platform for cooperative answering. *Journal of Intelligent Information Systems*, 1:293–321, 1992.

126. T. Gaasterland, P. Godfrey, J. Minker, and L. Novik. A cooperative answering system. In A. Voronkov, editor, *Proceedings of the Logic Programming and Automated Reasoning Conference*, Lecture Notes in Artificial Intelligence 624, pages 478–480. Springer-Verlag, St. Petersburg, Russia, July 1992.

127. T. Gaasterland, P. Godfrey, J. Minker, and L. Novik. A cooperative answering system. In *Proceedings of the Logic Programming and Automated Reasoning Conference*, St. Petersburg, Russia, July 1992.

128. T. Gaasterland and J. Lobo. Processing negation and disjunction in logic programs through integrity constraints. *Journal of Intelligent Information Systems*, 2(3), 1993.

129. T. Gaasterland and J. Minker. User needs and language generation issues in a cooperative answering system. In P. Saint-Dizier, editor, *ICLP'91 Workshop: Advanced Logic Programming Tools and Formalisms for Language Processing*, pages 1–14, INRIA, Paris, France, June 1991.

130. T. Gaasterland, J. Minker, and A. Rajasekar. Deductive database systems and knowledge base systems. In *Proceedings of VIA 90*, Barcelona, Spain, Oct. 1990.

131. H. Gallaire and J. Minker, editors. *Logic and Databases*. Plenum Press, New York, Apr. 1978.

132. H. Gallaire, J. Minker, and J.-M. Nicolas, editors. *Advances in Database Theory*, volume 1. Plenum Press, 1981.

133. H. Gallaire, J. Minker, and J.-M. Nicolas, editors. *Advances in Database Theory*, volume 2. Plenum Press, 1984.

134. H. Gallaire, J. Minker, and J.-M. Nicolas. Logic and databases: A deductive approach. *ACM Computing Surveys*, 16(2):153–185, June 1984.

135. H. Garcia-Molina. Using semantic knowledge for transaction processing in a distributed database. *ACM, TODS*, 8(2):186–213, 1983.

136. A. V. Gelder. The alternating fixpoint of logic programs with negation. In *In Eighth ACM Symposium on Principles of Database Systems*, pages 1–10, 1989. Available from UC Santa Cruz as UCSC-CRL-88-17.

137. A. V. Gelder, K. Ross, and J. Schlipf. Unfounded Sets and Well-founded Semantics for General Logic Programs. In *Proc. 7$^{th}$ Symposium on Principles of Database Systems*, pages 221–230, 1988.

138. A. V. Gelder, K. Ross, and J. Schlipf. The well-founded semantics for general logic programs. *Journal of The association for Computing Machinery*, 38(3):620–650, July 1991.

139. M. Gelfond and V. Lifschitz. The stable model semantics for logic programming. In R. Kowalski and K. Bowen, editors, *Proceedings of the Fifth International Conference and Symposium on Logic Programming*, pages 1070–1080, Seattle, WA. USA, Aug. 1988. The MIT Press.

140. M. Gelfond and V. Lifschitz. Logic programs with classical negation. In D. Warren and P. Szeredi, editors, *Proceedings of the Seventh International Conference on Logic Programming*, pages 579–597, Jerusalem, Israel, June 1990. The MIT Press.

141. M. Gelfond and V. Lifschitz. Classical negation in logic programs and disjunctive databases. *New Generation Computing*, 9:365–385, 1991.

142. M. Gelfond and V. Lifschitz. Representing actions and change by logic programs. *Journal of Logic Programming*, 17(2,3,4):301–323, 1993.

143. M. Gelfond, H. Przymusinska, and T. Przymusinski. The extended closed world assumption and its relation to parallel circumscription. *Proc. Fifth ACM SIGACT-SIGMOD Symposium on Principles of Database Systems*, pages 133–139, 1986.

144. P. Godfrey, J. Gryz, and J. Minker. Semantic query evaluation for bottom-up evaluation. In *Proc. ISMIS96*, June 1996. University of Maryland Technical Report, CS-TR-3558, UMIACS-TR-95-109.

145. P. Godfrey, J. Minker, and L. Novik. An architecture for a cooperative database system. In W. Litwin and T. Risch, editors, *Proceedings of the First International Conference on Applications of Databases*, Lecture Notes in Computer Science 819, pages 3–24. Springer Verlag, Vadstena, Sweden, June 1994.

146. G. Gottlob. Complexity and expressive power of disjunctive logic programming (research overview). In M. Bruynooghe, editor, *International Logic Programming Symposium ILPS'94*, pages 23–42, Ithaca, NY, USA, Nov 1994. The MIT Press.

147. J. Grant. Incomplete information in a relational database. In *Proc. Fund Inf III*, pages 363–378, 1980.

148. J. Grant, J. Gryz, and J. Minker. Updating disjunctive databases via model trees. Technical Report CS-TR-3407, UMIACS-TR-95-11, Department of Computer Science, University of Maryland, College Park, MD 20742, Feb. 1995.

149. J. Grant, J. Horty, J. Lobo, and J. Minker. View updates in stratified disjunctive databases. *Journal Automated Reasoning*, 11:249–267, March 1993.

150. J. Grant and J. Minker. Answering queries in indefinite databases and the null value problem. In P. Kanellakis, editor, *Advances in Computing Research: The Theory of Databases*, pages 247–267. 1986.

151. C. Green and B. Raphael. Research in intelligent question answering systems. *Proc. ACM 23rd National Conference*, pages 169–181, 1968.

152. C. Green and B. Raphael. The use of theorem-proving techniques in question-answering systems. *Proc. 23rd National Conference ACM*, 1968.

153. H. Groiss. A formal semantics for a rule-based language. In *IJCAI Workshop on Production Systems and their Innovative Applications*, 1993.

154. M. Hammer and S. Zdonik. Knowledge-based query processing. *Proc. 6th International Conference on Very Large Data Bases*, pages 137–147, Oct. 1980.

155. D. Harel. Review number 36,671 of Logic and Data Bases by H. Gallaire and J. Minker. *Computing Reviews*, 21(8):367–369, August 1980.

156. L. Henschen and S. Naqvi. On compiling queries in recursive first-order databases. *J.ACM*, 31(1):47–85, Jan. 1984.

157. L. Henschen and H. Park. Compiling the GCWA in Indefinite Databases. In J. Minker, editor, *Foundations of Deductive Databases and Logic Programming*, pages 395–438. Morgan Kaufmann Pub., Washington, D.C., 1988.

158. R. Hill. Lush resolution and its completeness. Technical Report DCL Memo 78, Department of Artificial Intelligence, University of Edinburgh, August 1974.

159. R. Hill. Lush resolution and its completeness. Technical Report DCL Memo 78, Department of Artificial Intelligence, University of Edinburgh, August 1974.

160. T. Imielinski. Incomplete deductive databases. *Annals of Mathematics and Artificial Intelligence*, 3:259–293, 1991.

161. T. Imielinski and W. Lipski. Incomplete information in relational databases. *J. ACM*, 31(4):761–791, 1984.

162. T. Imielinski and K. Vadaparty. Complexity of query processing in databases with OR-objects. In *Proc. 7$^{th}$ ACM SIGACT/SIGMOD Symposium on Principles of Database Systems*, pages 51–65, Philadelphia, Pennsylvania, March 29-31 1989.

163. K. Inoue, M. Koshimura, and R. Hasegawa. Embedding negation as failure into a model generation theorem prover. In D. Kapur, editor, *Proceedings of the Eleventh International Conference on Automated Deduction*, pages 400–415, Saratoga Springs NY, USA, June 1992. Springer-Verlag.

164. K. Inoue and C. Sakama. A fixpoint characterization of abductive logic programs. *Journal of Logic Programming*, 27(2):107–136, May 1996.

165. A. Itai and J. A. Makowsky. On the complexity of Herbrand's theorem. Technical report, Dept. of Computer Science, Israel Institute of Technology, Haifa, 1982.

166. J. Jaffar and M. Maher. Constraint logic programming:a survey. *Journal of Logic Programming*, 19-20:503–581, May-July 1994.

167. J. Jafffar and J.-L. Lassez. Constraint logic programming. In *Proc. of the 14$^{th}$ ACM Symposium on Principles of Programming Languages*, pages 111–119, Münich, Germany, Jan 1987.

168. H. Jakobovits and D. Vermier. R-stable models for logic programs. In D. Pedreschi and C. Zaniolo, editors, *Logic in Databases (LID'96)*, pages 251–259, July 1-2 1996. Also in this collection.

169. M. Jeusfeld and M. Staudt. Query optimization in deductive object bases. In G. Vossen, J. C. Feytag, and D. Maier, editors, *Query Processing for Advanced Database Applications*. Morgan-Kaufmann, 1993.

170. A. C. Kakas, R. A. Kowalski, and F. Toni. Abductive logic programming. *Journal of Logic and Computation*, 6(2):719–770, 1993.

171. H. Kautz and B. Selman. Forming concepts for fast inference. In *Proc. of AAAI-92*, pages 786–793, 1992.

172. C. Kellogg, P. Klahr, and L. Travis. Deductive planning and pathfinding for relational data bases. In H. Gallaire and J. Minker, editors, *Logic and Data Bases*, pages 179–200. Plenum Press, New York, 1978.

173. B. Kero and S. Tsur. The $\mathcal{IQ}$ system: a deductive database information lens for reasoning about textual information. In D. Pedreschi and C. Zaniolo, editors, *Logic in Databases (LID'96)*, pages 377–395, July 1-2 1996. Also in this collection.

174. W. Kiebling and H. Schmidt. DECLARE and SDS: Early efforts to commercialize deductive database technology. 1993.

175. M. Kifer, G. Lausen, and J. Wu. Logical Foundations of Object-Oriented and Frame-Based Languages. *Journal of ACM- to appear*, 1993.

176. W. Kim, J.-M. Nicolas, and S. Nishio, editors. *Proc. 1st Int. Conf. on Deductive and Object-Oriented Databases - DOOD'89*. North-Holland Publishing Co., Amsterdam, The Netherlands, 1990, December 1990.

177. J. King. Quist: A system for semantic query optimization in relational databases. *Proc. 7th International Conference on Very Large Data Bases*, pages 510–517, Sept. 1981.

178. P. Kolaitis and C. Papadimitriou. Why not negation by fixpoint? *JCSS*, 43:125, 1991.

179. H. Korth and G. Speegle. Formal aspects of concurrency control in long duration transaction systems using the NT/PV model. *ACM, TODS*, 19(3):492–535, 1994.

180. R. Kowalski. Predicate logic as a programming language. *Proc. IFIP 4*, pages 569–574, 1974.

181. R. Kowalski. Logic for data description. In H. G. J. Minker, editor, *Logic and Data Bases*, pages 77–102. Plenum Press, New York, 1978.

182. R. Kowalski and F. Sadri. Towards a unified agent architecture that combines rationality with reactivity. In D. Pedreschi and C. Zaniolo, editors, *Logic in Databases (LID'96)*, pages 131–150, July 1-2 1996. Also in this collection.

183. R. A. Kowalski. A proof procedure using connection graphs. *Journal of the ACM*, 22(4):572–595, Oct. 1975.

184. R. A. Kowalski and D. Kuehner. Linear Resolution with Selection Function. *Artificial Intelligence*, 2:227–260, 1971.

185. S. Kraus, D. Lehmann, and M. Magidor. Nonmonotonic Reasoning, Preferential Models and Cumulative Logics. *Artificial Intelligence*, 44(1):167–207, 1990.

186. J. Kuhns. Answering questions by computer: A logical study. Technical report, The Rand Corporation, Dec. 1967.

187. J. Kuhns. Logical aspects of questions answering by computer. *Third International Symposium on Computer and Information Sciences*, Dec. 1969.

188. J. Kuhns. Interrogating a relational data file: Remarks on the admissibility of input queries. Technical report, The Rand Corporation, Nov. 1970.

189. B. Kuipers, J. Paredaens, M. Smits, and J. V. den Bussche. Termination properties of spatial Datalog programs. In D. Pedreschi and C. Zaniolo, editors, *Logic in Databases (LID'96)*, pages 95–109, July 1-2 1996. Also in this collection.

190. L. Laksmanan and N. Shiri. A parametric approach to deductive databases with uncertainty. In D. Pedreschi and C. Zaniolo, editors, *Logic in Databases (LID'96)*, pages 55–73, July 1-2 1996. Also in this collection.

191. D. Laurent and C. Vrain. Learning query rules for optimizing databases with update rules. In D. Pedreschi and C. Zaniolo, editors, *Logic in Databases (LID'96)*, pages 173–192, July 1-2 1996. Also in this collection.

192. A. Lefebvre and L. Vieille. On deductive query evaluation in the DedGin* system. In W. Kim, J.-M. Nicolas, and S. Nishio, editors, *1st Int. Conf. on Deductive and Object-Oriented Databases*, December 1989.

193. L. Lefebvre. Towards and efficient evaluation of recursive aggregates in deductive databases. In *Proc. 4th Int. Conf. on Fifth Generation Computer Systems (FGCS)*, June 1992. extended version in. New Generation Computing 12, Ohmsha Ltd. & Springer-Verlag, 1994.

194. N. Leone and P. Rullo. The safe computation of the well-founded semantics for logic programming. *Information Systems*, 17(1):17–31, Jan. 1992.

195. N. Leone, P. Rullo, and F. Scarcello. Stable model checking for disjunctive programs. In D. Pedreschi and C. Zaniolo, editors, *Logic in Databases (LID'96)*, pages 281–294, July 1-2 1996. Also in this collection.

196. Y. Lesperancè, H. Levesque, F. Lin, D. Marcu, R. Reiter, and R. Scherl. A logical approach to high level robot programming – a progress report. In *Working notes*

*of the 1994 AAAI fall symposium on Control of the Physical World by Intelligent Systems, New Orleans, LA*, November 1994.

197. H. Levesque, R. Reiter, Y. Lesperance, F. Lin, and R. Scherl. Golog: A logic programming language for dynamic domains. *Journal of Logic Programming*, 1996. To appear.

198. H. J. Levesque. Foundations of a functional approach to knowledge representation. *Artificial Intelligence*, 23:155–212, Mar. 1984.

199. R. Levien. A computer system for inference execution and data retrieval. *Comm. ACM*, 10:715–721, 1967.

200. R. Levien. Relational data file ii: Implementation. *Proc. Third Annual National Colloquium on Information Retrieval*, pages 225–241, May 1967.

201. R. Levien. Relational data file: Experience with a system for propositional data storage and inference execution. Technical report, The Rand Corporation, Apr. 1969.

202. R. Levien and M. Maron. *Relational Data File: A Tool for Mechanized Inference Execution and Data Retrieval*. The Rand Corporation, Dec. 1965.

203. R. Levien and M. Maron. A computer system for inference execution and data retrieval. 10(11):715–721, Nov. 1967. Received September, 1966.

204. A. Levy, A. Mendelzon, Y. Sagiv, and D. Srivastava. Answering queries using views. In *Proceedings of the 14th ACM SIGACT-SIGMOD-SIGART Symposium on Principles of Database Systems, PODS-95*, May 1995.

205. A. Levy, A. Rajaraman, and J. Ordille. Querying heterogeneous information sources using source descriptions. In *Proc. of the 22nd VLDB Conference*, 1996.

206. A. Levy and Y. Sagiv. Semantic query optimization in datalog programs. In *Principles of Database Systems 1995 (PODS95)*, pages 163–173, 1995.

207. F. Lin and R. Reiter. How to progress a database II: The STRIPS connection. Technical report, Dept of Computer Science, University of Toronto, 1993.

208. F. Lin and R. Reiter. How to progress a database (and Why) I: Logical foundations. In *KR94*, pages 425–436, 1994.

209. T.-W. Ling, A. Mendelzon, and L. Vieille, editors. *Proc. 4th Int. Conf. on Deductive and Object-Oriented Databases - DOOD'95*. Springer-Verlang, December 1995. LNCS 1013, Heidelberg, Germany.

210. W. Lipski. On databases with incomplete information. volume 28, pages 41–70. ACM, New York, 1981.

211. K.-C. Liu and R. Sunderraman. Indefinite and maybe information in relational databases. *ACM Transactions on Database Systems*, 15(1):1–39, 1990.

212. K.-C. Liu and R. Sunderraman. On representing indefinite and maybe information in relational databases: A generalization. In *Proceedings of IEEE Data Engineering*, pages 495–502, Los Angeles, Feb. 1990.

213. Y. Liu. Null values in definite programs. In S. Debray and M. Hermenegildo, editors, *Proceedings of North American Conference on Logic Programming*, pages 273–288, Austin, Texas, Oct. 1990. MIT Press.

214. J. Lloyd. *Foundations of Logic Programming*. Springer–Verlag, second edition, 1987.

215. J. W. Lloyd and R. W. Topor. A basis for deductive database systems. *Journal of Logic Programming*, 2(2):93–109, July 1985.

216. J. Lobo, J. Minker, and A. Rajasekar. *Foundations of Disjunctive Logic Programming*. MIT Press, 1992.

217. J. Lobo, C. Yu, and G. Wang. Computing the transitive closure in disjunctive databases. Technical report, Department of Electrical Engineering and Computer Science, University of Illinois at Chicago, 1992.

218. D. Loveland. Near-Horn prolog. In J. Lassez, editor, *Proc. 4$^{th}$ International Conference on Logic Programming*, pages 456–459, 1987.

219. D. Loveland, D. Reed, and D. Wilson. Satchmore: Satchmo with relevancy. Technical report, Duke University, Durham, North Carolina, USA, April 1993.

220. B. Ludascher, W. May, and G. Lausen. Nested transactions in a logical language for active rules. In D. Pedreschi and C. Zaniolo, editors, *Logic in Databases (LID'96)*, pages 217–242, July 1-2 1996. Also in this collection.

221. C. Maindreville and E. Simon. Modeling non-deterministic queries and updates in deductive databases. In *Proc. of VLDB*, 1988.

222. V. W. Marek, A. Nerode, and J. Remmel. The stable models of a predicate logic program. In K. Apt, editor, *Proceedings of the Joint International Conference and Symposium on Logic Programming*, pages 446–460, Washington D.C., USA, Nov 1992. The MIT Press.

223. V. W. Marek and Truszczyński. Autoepistemic logic. *Journal of the ACM*, 38(3):588–619, 1991.

224. C. Martin and J. Sistac. Applying transition rules to bitemporal deductive databases for integrity constraint checking. In D. Pedreschi and C. Zaniolo, editors, *Logic in Databases (LID'96)*, pages 111–128, July 1-2 1996. Also in this collection.

225. J. McCarthy. Circumscription - a form of non-monotonic reasoning. *Artificial Intelligence Journal*, 13:27–39, 1980.

226. McDermott and J. Doyle. Non-monotonic logic i. *Artificial Intelligence Journal*, 13:41–72, 1980.

227. J. McSkimin and J. Minker. The use of a semantic network in deductive question-answering systems. *Proc. IJCAI 5*, pages 50–58, 1977.

228. J. Melton. An SQL3 snapshot. In *Twelfth International Conference on Data Engineering*, pages 666–672, 1996.

229. J. Melton and A. R. Simon. *Understanding the New SQL: A Complete Guide.* Morgan Kaufmann, San Mateo, California, 1993.

230. R. Miller, Y. Ioannidis, and R. Ramakrishnan. Translation and integration of heterogeneous schemas: Bridging the gap between theory and practice. *Information Systems*, 19(1):3–31, Jan. 1994.

231. J. Minker. Search strategy and selection function for an inferential relational system. *Transactions on Data Base Systems*, 3(1):1–31, Mar. 1978.

232. J. Minker. On indefinite databases and the closed world assumption. In *Proceedings of the Sixth Conference on Automated Deduction*, pages 292–308, 1982. Also in: *Lecture Notes in Computer Science 138*, pages 292-308. Springer Verlag, 1982.

233. J. Minker, editor. *Proceedings of Workshop on Foundations of Deductive Databases and Logic Programming*, Aug. 1986.

234. J. Minker, editor. *Foundations of Deductive Databases and Logic Programming*. Morgan-Kaufmann, 1988.

235. J. Minker. Perspectives in deductive databases. *Journal of Logic Programming*, 5:33–60, 1988.

236. J. Minker. Toward a foundation of disjunctive logic programming. In *Proceedings of the North American Conference on Logic Programming*, pages 121–125. MIT Press, 1989. Invited Banquet Address.

237. J. Minker. An overview of nonmonotonic reasoning and logic programming. *Journal of Logic Programming*, 17(2, 3 and 4):95–126, November 1993.

238. J. Minker and J. Grant. Answering queries in indefinite databases and the null value problem. In P. Kanellakis, editor, *Advances in Computing Research*, pages 247–267. JAI Press, 1986.

239. J. Minker and J.-M. Nicolas. On recursive axioms in deductive databases. *Information Systems*, 7(4):1–15, 1982.

240. J. Minker and A. Rajasekar. A Fixpoint Semantics for Non-Horn Logic Programs. Technical Report CS-TR-1869, Department of Computer Science University of Maryland, College Park, 1987.

241. J. Minker and A. Rajasekar. Procedural interpretation of non-Horn logic programs. In E. Lusk and R. Overbeek, editors, *Proceedings of the Ninth International Conference on Automated Deduction*, pages 278–293, Argonne, IL. USA, May 1988.

242. J. Minker and A. Rajasekar. Disjunctive logic programming. In *Proceedings of the International Symposium on Methodologies for Intelligent Systems*, pages 381–394, 1989. (Invited Lecture).

243. J. Minker and A. Rajasekar. A fixpoint semantics for disjunctive logic programs. *Journal of Logic Programming*, 9(1):45–74, July 1990.

244. J. Minker and C. Ruiz. On extended disjunctive logic programs. In J. Komorowski and Z. Raś, editors, *Proceedings of the Seventh International Symposium on Methodologies for Intelligent Systems*, pages 1–18. Lecture Notes in AI. Springer-Verlag, June 1993. (Invited Paper).

245. J. Minker and C. Ruiz. Semantics for disjunctive logic programs with explicit and default negation. *Fundamenta Informaticae*, 20(3/4):145–192, 1994. Anniversary Issue edited by H. Rasiowa.

246. J. Minker and C. Ruiz. Mixing a default rule with stable negation. In *Proceedings of the Fourth International Symposium on Artificial Intelligence and Mathematics*, pages 122–125, Jan. 1996.

247. J. Minker and J. Sable. Relational data system study. Technical Report RADC-TR-70-180, Rome Air Development Center, Air Force Systems Command, Griffiss Air Force Base, New York, September 1970. Auerbach Corporation Report AD 720-263.

248. J. Minker and G. Zanon. An Extension to Linear Resolution with Selection Function. *Information Processing Letters*, 14(3):191–194, June 1982.

249. R. Moore. Possible-world semantics for autoepistemic logic. In *Proceedings of AAAI Workshop on Non-Monotonic Reasoning*, pages 396–401, New Paltz, 1984.

250. R. Moore. Semantical considerations on nonmonotonic logic. *Artificial Intelligence 25*, pages 75–94, 1985.

251. S. Morishita, M. Derr, and G. Phipps. Design and implementation of the Glue-Nail database system. In *Proc. ACM-SIGMOD'93 Conf.*, pages 147–167, May 1993.

252. S. Muggleton and L. D. Raedt. Inductive logic programming: theory and methods. *Journal of Logic Programming*, 19/20:629–679, May/July 1994.

253. I. Mumick, S. Finkelstein, H. Pirahesh, and R. Ramakrishnan. Magic is relevant. In *Proc. of the ACM SIGMOD Intl. Conf. on Management of Data*, May 1990.

254. J. Naughton and Y. Sagiv. A decidable class of bounded recursions. *Proc. of the Sixth ACM SIGACT-SIGMOD-SIGART Symposium on Principles of Database Systems*, pages 227–236, Mar. 1987.

255. R. Ng and V. Subrahmanian. Probabilistic logic programming. *Information and Computation*, 101(2):150–201, 1993.

256. J.-M. Nicolas. Logic for improving integrity checking in relational databases. *Acta Informatica*, 18(3):227–253, Dec. 1979.

257. J.-M. Nicolas and H. Gallaire. Data base: Theory vs. interpretation. In H. Gallaire and J. Minker, editors, *Logic and Data Bases*, pages 33–54. Plenum Press, New York, 1978.

258. J.-M. Nicolas and J.-C. Syre. Natural question - answering and automatic deduction in system syntex. *Proc. IFIP Congress 1974*, pages 595–599, 1974.

259. J.-M. Nicolas and K. Yazdanian. Integrity checking in deductive databases. In H. Gallaire and J. Minker, editors, *Logic and Data Bases*, pages 325–599. Plenum, New York, 1978.

260. P. Pearce and G. Wagner. Logic programming with strong negation. In P. Schroeder-Heister, editor, *Proceedings of the International Workshop on Extensions of Logic Programming*, pages 311–326, Tübingen, FRG, Dec. 1989. Lecture Notes in Artificial Intelligence, Springer -Verlag.

261. G. Phipps, M. Derr, and K. Ross. Glue-Nail: A deductive database system. In *Proc. ACM-SIGMOD'91 Conf.*, May 1991.

262. G. Piatetsky-Shapiro and W. J. Frawley, editors. *Knowledge Discovery in Databases*. AAAI Press and MIT Press, Menlo Park, California, 1991.

263. P. Powell. Answer-Reason extraction in a parallel relatioanal data base system. Master's thesis, Department of Computer Science, University of Maryland, College Park, MD 20742, 1977.

264. S. Pradhan. Combining datalog databases using priorities. In *Advances in Data Management '94*, pages 355–375. Tata-McGraw Hill, India, 1995.

265. S. Pradhan and J. Minker. Combining datalog databases using priorities. *Journal of Intelligent & Cooperative Information Systems*, 1995.

266. S. Pradhan, J. Minker, and V. Subrahmanian. Combining databases with prioritized information. *Journal of Intelligent Information Systems*, 4(3):231–260, May 1995.

267. T. Przymusinski. Perfect model semantics. In R. Kowalski and K. Bowen, editors, *Proceedings of the Fifth International Conference and Symposium on Logic Programming*, pages 1081–1096, Seattle, WA. USA, Aug. 1988. The MIT Press.

268. T. Przymusinski. Every logic program has a natural stratification and an iterated fixed point model. In *Proceedings of the Eighth ACM SIGACT-SIGMOD-SIGART Symposium on Principle of Database Systems*, pages 11–21, Philadelphia, PA. USA, 1989.

269. T. Przymusinski. Stationary semantics for disjunctive logic programs and deductive databases. In S. Debray and M. Hermenegildo, editors, *Proc. of the North American Conference on Logic Programming*, pages 40–62, Austin, Texas, Oct. 1990.

270. T. Przymusinski. Static semantics for normal and disjunctive logic programs. *Annals of Mathematics and Artificial Intelligence*, 14:323–357, 1995. Festschrift in honor of Jack Minker.

271. T. C. Przymusinski. On the declarative semantics of deductive databases and logic programming. In J. Minker, editor, *Foundations of Deductive Databases and Logic Programming*, chapter 5, pages 193–216. Morgan Kaufmann Pub., Washington, D.C., 1988.

272. T. C. Przymusinski. On the Declarative and Procedural Semantics of Logic Programs. *Journal of Automated Reasoning*, 5:167–205, 1989.

273. T. C. Przymusinski. Extended stable semantics for normal and disjunctive programs. In D. Warren and P. Szeredi, editors, *Proceedings of the 7<sup>th</sup> International Logic Programming Conference*, pages 459–477, Jerusalem, 1990. MIT Press. Extended Abstract.

274. T. C. Przymusinski. Stable semantics for disjunctive programs. *New Generation Computing*, 9:401–424, 1991.

275. E. Pudilo. Database query evaluation with the STARBASE method. In D. Pedreschi and C. Zaniolo, editors, *Logic in Databases (LID'96)*, pages 335–354, July 1-2 1996. Also in this collection.

276. A. Rajasekar, J. Lobo, and J. Minker. Skeptical reasoning and disjunctive programs. In *Proceedings of First International Conference on Knowledge Representation and Reasoning*, pages 349–357. Morgan-Kaufmann, 1989.

277. A. Rajasekar, J. Lobo, and J. Minker. Weak generalized closed world assumption. *Journal of Automated Reasonig*, pages 293–307, 1989.

278. R. Ramakrishnan. *Applications of Logic Databases*. Kluwer Academic Publishers, 1995.

279. R. Ramakrishnan, D. Srivastava, and S. Sudarshan. CORAL—control, relations and logic. In L.-Y. Yuan, editor, *Proceedings of the 18th International Conference on Very Large Databases*, pages 238–250, Vancouver, Canada, Aug. 1992.

280. R. Ramakrishnan and J. Ullman. A survey of research on deductive database systems. *Journal of Logic Programming*, 23(2):125–149, May 1995.

281. K. Ramamohanarao. An implementation overview of the Aditi deductive database system. In *Lecture Notes in Computer Science 760, Third International Conference, DOOD'93*, pages 184–203, Phoenix, AZ, December 1993. Springer-Verlag.

282. B. Raphael. A computer program for semantic information retrieval. In M. Minsky, editor, *Semantic Information Processing*, pages 33–134. MIT Press, 1968.

283. L. Raschid. A semantics for a class of stratified production system programs. *Journal of Logic Programming*, 21(1):31–57, 1994.

284. L. Raschid and J. Lobo. A semantics for a class of non-deterministic and causal production system programs. *Journal of Automated Reasoning*, 12:305–349, 1994.

285. L. Raschid and J. Lobo. Semantics for update rule programs and implementation in a relational database management system. *ACM Transactions on Database Systems*, 1996. To appear.

286. D. Reed, D. Loveland, and B. Smith. An alternative characterization of disjunctive logic programs. In *Proceedings of the International Logic Programming Symposium*, Cambridge, Massachusetts, 1991. MIT Press. Also: Technical Report, CS-1991-11. Dept. of Computer Science. Duke University.

287. D. W. Reed and D. W. Loveland. A comparison of three prolog extensions. Technical Report CS-1989-8, Department of Conputer Science, Duke University, Durham, North Carolina 27706, March 1990. To appear in Journal of Logic Programming.

288. R. Reiter. On closed world data bases. In H. Gallaire and J. Minker, editors, *Logic and Data Bases*, pages 55–76. Plenum, New York, 1978.

289. R. Reiter. A logic for default reasoning. *Artificial Intelligence Journal*, 13:81–132, 1980.

290. R. Reiter. Towards A Logical Reconstruction of Relational Database Theory. In M. Brodie, J. Mylopoulos, and J. Schmit, editors, *On Conceptual Modelling*, pages 163–189. Springer-Verlag Pub., New York, 1984.

291. R. Reiter. A sound and sometimes complete query evaluation algorithm for relational databases with null values. *J.ACM*, 33(2):349–370, Apr. 1986.

292. R. Reiter. On integrity constraints. In M. Y. Vardi, editor, *Proceedings of the Second Conference on the Theoretical Aspects of Reasoning about Knowledge*, pages 97–111, San Francisco, California, Mar. 1988. Morgan Kaufmann Publishers, Inc.

293. R. Reiter. On asking what a database knows. In J. Lloyd, editor, *Computational Logic*, Basic research Series. Springer-Verlag Publishers, 1990. DG XIII Commission of the European Communities.

294. J. Robinson. A machine-oriented logic based on the resolution principle. *J.ACM*, 12(1), Jan. 1965.

295. J. Rohmer, R. Lescoeur, and J.-M. Kerisit. The Alexander method: a technique for the processing of recusive axioms in deductive databases. *New Generation Computing*, 4(3), 1986.

296. K. Ross. A procedural semantics for well-founded negation in logic programs. In *Proceedings of the Eighth ACM SIGACT-SIGMOD-SIGART Symposium on Principle of Database Systems*, Philadelphia, PA. USA, 1989.

297. K. Ross. Well-founded semantics for disjunctive logic programs. In *Proc. of the first International Conference on Deductive and Object Oriented Databases*, pages 352–369, Kyoto, Japan, Dec. 1989.

298. K. Ross. Modular stratification and magic sets for datalog programs with negation. In *Proc. ACM Symp. on Principles of Database Systems*, April 1990.

299. K. Ross. Modular acylicity and tail recursion in logic programs. In *Proc. of the Tenth ACM SIGACT-SIGMOD-SIGART Symp. on Principles of Database Systems (PODS'91)*, pages 92–101, 1991.

300. K. Ross and R. Topor. Inferring negative information from disjunctive databases. *Journal of Automated Reasoning*, 4(2):397–424, December 1988.

301. C. Ruiz and J. Minker. Computing stable and partial stable models of extended disjunctive logic programs. In J. Dix, L. Pereira, and T. Przymusinski, editors, *Nonmonotonic Extensions of Logic Programming*, pages 205–229. Lecture Notes in Computer Science 927. Springer-Verlag, 1995.

302. D. Saccà. The expressive power of stable models for bound and unbound DATA-LOG queries. *The Journal of Computer and System Sciences*, 1996. To appear.

303. D. Sacca and C. Zaniolo. On the implementation of a simple class of logic queries. In *Proc. ACM Symp. on Principles of Database Systems*, March 1986.

304. D. Sacca and C. Zaniolo. The generalized counting method for recursive logic queries. *Theoretical Computer Science*, 62, 1988.

305. D. Saccà and C. Zaniolo. Stable models and non-determinism to logic with negation. In *Proc. Workshop on Logic Programming and Nonmonotonic Reasoning*, pages 87–101, 1991.

306. F. Sadri and R. Kowalski. Database integrity. chapter 9, pages 313–362. Morgan Kaufmann Publishers, 1988.

307. K. Sagonas, T. Swift, and D. Warren. The limits of fixed-order computation. In D. Pedreschi and C. Zaniolo, editors, *Logic in Databases (LID'96)*, pages 355–374, July 1-2 1996. Also in this collection.

308. C. Sakama. Possible model semantics for disjunctive databases. In *Proc. First International Conference on Deductive and Object Oriented Databases*, pages 337–351, 1989.

309. E. Sandewall. Features and fluents: A systemetic approach to the representation of knowledge about dynamical systems. Technical report, Institutionen for datavetenskap, Universitet och Tekniska hogskolan i Linkoping, Sweden, 1992.

310. E. Sandewall. The range of applicability of some non-monotonic logics for strict inertia. *Journal of Logic and Computation*, 4(5):581–616, Oct. 1994.

311. D. Savitt, H. Love, and R. Troop. ASP: A new concept in language and machine organization. In *1967 Spring Joint Computer Conference*, pages 87–102, 1967.

312. J. Schlipf. The expressive powers of the logic programming semantics. *JCSS*, 1990. A preliminary version appeared in Ninth ACM Symposium on Principles on Database Systems, pages 196-204, 1990.

313. J. Schlipf. Complexity and undecideability results for logic programming. *Annals of Mathematics and Artificial Intelligence*, 15(3-4):257–288, Dec 1995.

314. B. Selman and H. Kautz. Knowledge compilation using Horn approximations. In *Proc. of AAAI-91*, pages 904–909, 1991.

315. B. Selman and H. Kautz. Knowledge compilation and theory approximation. *Journal of the ACM*, 1996. To appear.

316. B. Selman and H. Levesque. Abductive and default reasoning: A computational core. In *Proceedings AAAI-90*, pages 343–348, Boston, MA, 1989.

317. S. Shapiro and D. McKay. Inferences with recursion. In *Proceedings of the 1st Annual National Conference on Artificial Intelligence*, 1980.

318. J. Shepherdson. Negation in Logic Programming. In J. Minker, editor, *Foundations of Deductive Databases and Logic Programming*, pages 19–88. Morgan Kaufman Pub., 1988.

319. S. Sickel. A search technique for clause interconnectivity graphs. *IEEE Transactions on Computers*, C-25(8):823–835, Aug. 1976.

320. P. Sistla and O. Wolfson. Temporal conditions and integrity constraint checking in active database systems. In *Proceedings of the 1995 ACM SIGMOD International Conferenece on Management of Data*, San Jose, CA, 1995. ACM Press.

321. B. Smith and D. Loveland. A simple near-Horn Prolog interpreter. In R. Kowalski and K. Bowen, editors, *Proc. $5^{th}$ International Conference and Symposium on Logic Programming*, pages 794–809, Seattle, Washington, Aug. 1988.

322. R. Smullyan. On definability by recursion (abstract). *Bull, AMS62*, page 601, 1956.

323. R. M. Smullyan. Elementary formal system (abstract). *Bull, AMS62*, page 600, 1956.

324. R. Snodgrass. The temporal query language TQuel. *ACM Trans. Database Syst.*, 12(2):247–298, June 1987.

325. R. Snodgrass, editor. *Data Engineering.* IEEE Computer Society, December 1988. Special issue on temporal databases.

326. R. Snodgrass and E. McKenzie. Research concerning time in databases. *SIGMOD Record*, 15(4):19–52, December 1986.

327. M. Stickel. A PROLOG technology theorem prover: Implementation by an extended PROLOG compiler. *Journal of Automated Reasoning*, 4(4):353–380, 1988.

328. V. Subrahmanian, S. Adali, A. Brink, R. Emery, J. Lu, A. Rajput, T. Rogers, and R. Ross. Hermes: A heterogeneous reasoning and mediator system, 1994. Available from (http://www.cs.umd.edu/projects/hermes/overview/paper.

329. V. Subrahmanian and S. Jajodia. *Multimedia Database Systems*. Springer Verlag, 1995.

330. V. Subrahmanian and C. Ward. A deductive database approach to planning in uncertain environments. In D. Pedreschi and C. Zaniolo, editors, *Logic in Databases (LID'96)*, pages 77–92, July 1-2 1996. Also in this collection.

331. M. A. Suchenek. Minimal models for closed world databases. In Z. Ras, editor, *Proc. of ISMIS 4*, pages 515–522. Elsvier Sience Publishing Co. Inc., 1989.

332. T. Swift and D. Warren. An abstract machine for SLG resolution: definite programs. In *Proc. of the 1994 ILPS*, pages 633–652. The MIT Press, 1994.

333. T. V. Team. Summary state of the art on deductive and deductive object-oriented databases - dood. Technical report, Bull Corporation, April 1996. Groupe Bull report (limited distribution).

334. X. A. I. Technologies. HIPAC: a research project in active, time-constrained databases. Technical Report 187, Xerox Advanced Information Technologies, 1989.

335. D. Tsichritzis and F. Lochovsky. Hierarchic data-base model: A survey. *ACM Computing Surveys*, 8(1):67–103, March 1976.

336. S. Tsur and C. Zaniolo. LDL: A logic-based data-language. In *Proceedings of the 12th VLDB Conf*, August 1986.

337. J. D. Ullman. *Principles of Database and Knowledge-Base Systems, Volume I*. Principles of Computer Science Series. Computer Science Press, Incorporated, Rockville, Maryland, 1988.

338. J. D. Ullman. *Principles of Database and Knowledge-Base Systems, Volume II: The New Technologies*. Principles of Computer Science Series. Computer Science Press, Incorporated, Rockville, Maryland, 1989.

339. J. Vaghani, K. Ramamohanarao, D. B. Kemp, and P. J. Stuckey. Design overview of the Aditi deductive database system. In *Proc. of the 7th Intl. Conf. on Data Engineering*, pages 240–247, April 1991.

340. M. van Emden and R. Kowalski. The Semantics of Predicate Logic as a Programming Language. *J.ACM*, 23(4):733–742, 1976.

341. A. Van Gelder. Negation as failure using tight derivations for general logic programs. In J. Minker, editor, *Foundations of Deductive Databases and Logic Programming*, pages 149–176. Morgan Kaufmann, 1988.

342. M. Vardi. The complexity of relational query languages. In *Proc. of the 14th ACM Symposium on Theory of Computing*, pages 137–146, May 1982.

343. Y. Vassiliou. Null values in data base management: A denotational semantics approach. In *Proceedings of the ACM SIGMOD International Symposium on Management of Data*, pages 162–169, Boston, MA, 1979. ACM, New York.

344. L. Vieille. Recursive axioms in deductive databases: the Query/SubQuery approach. In *Proc. 1st. Int. Conf. on Expert Database Systems*, April 1986.

345. L. Vieille. Database-complete proof procedures based on SLD-resolutions. In *Proc. 4th Int. Conf. on Logic Programming*, May 1987.

346. L. Vieille. Recursive query processing: The power of logic. *Theoretical Computer Science*, 69, 1989.

347. L. Vieille, P. Bayer, V. Kuechenhoff, and A. Lefebvre. EKS-V1, a short overview. *AAAI'90 Workshop on Knowledge Base Management Systems*, July 1990.

348. L. Vielle, P. Bayer, and V. Kuechenhoff. Integrity checking and materialized view handling by update propagation in the EKS-V1 system. Technical report, ECRC, 1991. to appear as a chapter in the book "Materialized Views", A. Gupta and I. Mumick (eds), MIT Press, Cambridge, MA, USA, 1996.

349. A. Yahya and L. Henschen. Deduction in Non-Horn Databases. *J. Automated Reasoning*, 1(2):141–160, 1985.

350. J.-H. You and L. Yuan. Three-valued formalization of logic programming. In *Proceedings of the 9th ACM PODS*, pages 172–182, 1990.

351. J.-H. You and L. Yuan. A three-valued semantics for deductive databases and logic programs. *Journal of Computer and System Sciences*, 49:334–361, 1994.

352. J.-H. You and L. Yuan. On the equivalence of semantics for normal logic programs. *Journal of Logic Programming*, pages 211–222, 1995.

353. L. Yuan and J.-H. You. Autoepistemic circumscription and logic programming. *Journal of Automated Reasoning*, 10:143–160, 1993.

354. L. Y. Yuan and D.-A. Chiang. A sound and complete query evaluation algorithm for relational databases with disjunctive information. In *Proceedings of the Eighth Symposium on Principles of Database Systems*, pages 66–74. ACM Press, Mar. 1989.

355. C. Zaniolo. Database relations with null values. *JCSS*, 28:142–166, 1984.

356. C. Zaniolo. A unified semantics for active and deductive databases. In *Proceedings of 1st international workshop on rules in database systems*, pages 271–287. Springer-Verlag, 1993.

357. C. Zaniolo. Active database rules with transaction-conscious stable models semantics. In *Proceedings of DOOD 1996*, pages 55–72, 1996.

# Uncertainty

# A Parametric Approach to Deductive Databases with Uncertainty

V.S. Lakshmanan and Nematollaah Shiri

Department of Computer Science, Concordia University, Montreal, Canada
{laks,shiri}@cs.concordia.ca

**Abstract.** Numerous frameworks have been proposed in recent years
for deductive databases with uncertainty. These frameworks differ in (i)
their underlying notion of uncertainty, (ii) the way in which uncertainties are manipulated, and (iii) the way in which uncertainty is associated
with the facts and rules of a program. On the basis of (iii), these frameworks can be classified into implication based (IB) and annotation based
(AB) frameworks. In this paper, we develop a generic framework, called
the parametric framework as a unifying umbrella for IB frameworks. We
develop the declarative, fixpoint, and proof-theoretic semantics of programs in the parametric framework and show their equivalence. Using
the as a basis, we study query optimization in programs of our framework
of component queries in the parametric, and establish necessary and sufficient conditions for containment for classes of parametric conjunctive
queries. Our results shed light on how the very optimization for large
classes of query programs in IB deductive databases with uncertainty.

## 1 Introduction

Most real-life applications require an ability to represent, manage, and reason with uncertain knowledge. Practical considerations dictate that the framework used for knowledge representation with uncertainty admit efficient implementation and efficient computation. Logic database programming, with
its advantages of modularity and its powerful top-down and bottom-up query
processing techniques, has attracted the attention of researchers and numerous frameworks for deductive databases with uncertainty have been proposed
[3,7,8,10,12,13,14,16,19,20,21,24,25,27]. Typically these proposals offer
a framework in which deduction can be combined with some form of uncertainty
(including, e.g., certainty values, fuzzy sets, probabilities, possibilities, etc.). As
in classical logic programming, these frameworks offer a declarative semantics of
programs. On the operational side, this is supported by a sound and complete
(or weakly complete) proof procedure and a corresponding fixpoint semantics.

While there have been numerous proposals for deductive databases with uncertainty, unfortunately there has been very little progress on the aspect of query
optimization. This is particularly relevant given the importance of query optimization in typical data intensive applications of deductive databases technology.

# A Parametric Approach to Deductive Databases with Uncertainty

Laks V.S. Lakshmanan and Nematollaah Shiri

Department of Computer Science, Concordia University, Montreal, Canada
{laks,shiri}@cs.concordia.ca

**Abstract.** Numerous frameworks have been proposed in recent years for deductive databases with uncertainty. These frameworks differ in (i) their underlying notion of uncertainty, (ii) the way in which uncertainties are manipulated, and (iii) the way in which uncertainty is associated with the facts and rules of a program. On the basis of (iii), these frameworks can be classified into implication based (IB) and annotation based (AB) frameworks. In this paper, we develop a generic framework called the *parametric framework* as a unifying umbrella for IB frameworks. We develop the declarative, fixpoint, and proof-theoretic semantics of programs in the parametric framework and show their equivalence. Using this as a basis, we study the query optimization problem of containment of conjunctive queries in this framework, and establish necessary and sufficient conditions for containment for classes of parametric conjunctive queries. Our results yield tools for use in the query optimization for large classes of query programs in IB deductive databases with uncertainty.

## 1 Introduction

Most real-life applications require an ability to represent, manage, and reason with uncertain knowledge. Practical considerations dictate that the framework used for knowledge representation with uncertainty admit efficient implementation and efficient computations. Logic database programming, with its advantages of modularity and its powerful top-down and bottom-up query processing techniques has attracted the attention of researchers, and numerous frameworks for deductive databases with uncertainty have been proposed [6, 7, 8, 10, 12, 13, 14, 15, 19, 20, 21, 24, 25, 27]. Typically these proposals offer a framework in which deduction can be combined with some form of uncertainty (including, e.g. certainty values, fuzzy sets, probabilities, possibilities, etc.). As in classical logic programming, these frameworks offer a declarative semantics of programs. On the operational side, this is supported by a sound and complete (or weakly complete) proof procedure and a corresponding fixpoint semantics.

*While there have been numerous proposals for deductive databases with uncertainty, unfortunately there has been very little progress on the aspect of query optimization.* This is particularly relevant given the importance of query optimization in typical data intensive applications of the deductive databases technology.

The underlying uncertainty formalisms in the proposed frameworks vary, and include, among others, probability theory [13, 14, 20, 21], fuzzy set theory [24, 27], multi-valued logic [7, 8, 10, 12], possibilistic logic [6], evidence theory [19], and hybrid (i.e., a combination of numerical and non-numerical methods) approaches [13, 15, 22]. Examples 1 – 6 illustrate these frameworks informally. We do not enter into a debate of which form of uncertainty is the best. Rather, our contention is that different forms may be appropriate for different applications. Furthermore, *different* ways of *manipulating* uncertainty may be required for *one* application (see Example 7, for an illustration). Thus the query optimization problem facing us is a challenging one; how do we study query optimization issues in such a way that our results and tools will be applicable over a spectrum of frameworks for deductive databases with uncertainty? Before we proceed to address these questions, we classify the proposed frameworks, on the basis of their approaches, into the *annotation based* and *implication based*, described as follows.

In the *annotation based* (AB) approach, a rule is of the form

$$A : f(\beta_1, \ldots, \beta_n) \leftarrow B_1 : \beta_1, \ldots, B_n : \beta_n$$

which asserts "the certainty of $A$ is at least (or is in) $f(\beta_1, \ldots, \beta_n)$, whenever the certainty of $B_i$ is at least (or is in) $\beta_i$, $1 \le i \le n$". Here $f$ is an $n$-ary computable function and $\beta_i$ is either a constant or a variable ranging over an appropriate certainty domain. Examples of AB frameworks include Subrahmanian [25], Kifer and Li [10], Ng and Subrahmanian [19, 20, 21], and Kifer and Subrahmanian [12].

In the *implication based* (IB) approach, a rule is of the form

$$A \xleftarrow{\alpha} B_1, \ldots, B_n$$

which says that the certainty associated with the implication $B_1 \wedge \ldots \wedge B_n \to A$ is $\alpha$. Computationally, given an assignment $v$ of certainties to the $B_i$s, the certainty of $A$ is computed by taking the "conjunction" of the certainties $v(B_i)$ and then somehow "propagating" it to the rule head. Examples of IB frameworks include van Emden [27], Fitting [7, 8], Lakshmanan and Sadri [14, 15], and Lakshmanan [13]. Some of these frameworks are illustrated informally in Examples 1 – 6.

Let us briefly compare the AB and IB approaches. While the way implication is treated in the AB approach is closer to classical logic, the way rules are fired in the IB approach has a definite intuitive appeal [12]. The AB approach is strictly more expressive than the IB. For instance, it is shown in [12] that the AB framework GAP proposed in [12] can simulate van Emden's IB framework. In fact, we note that any IB framework can be simulated within an appropriately defined AB framework which respects the multiset-based semantics. See [16] for the details on the expressive power of the IB and AB approaches. The down side is that query processing (particularly resolution and fixpoint evaluation) in the AB approach is more complicated than in the IB approach. E.g., unlike in the IB approach, unification is more involved in the AB approach, and resolution requires constraint solving. With respect to bottom-up fixpoint computation, our experience with a number of IB frameworks suggest that under many cases, this computation can be done in time polynomial in the size of the input database (e.g. see [13, 14, 15]). By contrast, the discontinuity of the $T_P$ operator in AB frameworks in general creates complications. These observations suggest that the IB approach may be more amenable to efficient implementation.

Returning to our previous question on query optimization, how can we attack this problem in such a way that the results apply to a wide variety of IB frameworks? Rather than study query optimization for individual frameworks, we believe that a unified study of this problem in a "framework independent" way would yield useful insights. Given the usefulness of manipulating uncertainty in more than one manner (e.g. see Example 7) for a given application, such a unified study is likely to be far more beneficial.

**Contributions of this paper:**

(1) We develop a generic framework for deduction with uncertainty, called the *parametric framework*. We show that by "tuning" the parameters of this framework appropriately, any of the previously known IB frameworks as well as new ones can be realized as a special case.

(2) We develop a declarative, proof-theoretic, and fixpoint semantics of (positive) programs in the parametric framework and establish their equivalence.

(3) We study the problem of containment for classes of conjunctive queries in the parametric framework and establish necessary and sufficient conditions for containment for classes of parametric conjunctive queries. Our results yield tools for query optimization for large classes of conjunctive queries in known IB frameworks. For lack of space, however, all the proofs and parts of our results on query optimization are omitted. The full paper [17] includes the details.

Section 2 motivates the parametric framework and shows how various IB frameworks can be realized as special cases of this framework. It also illustrates the power of the parametric framework by showing how it can be very naturally used for manipulating uncertainty in several different ways within one program. Section 3 collects together the relevant preliminary notions. Section 4 compares the work in this paper with previous work on similar unifying frameworks developed in different contexts, and: (i) brings out the novelty and unique features of our work, and (ii) shows why a new unifying framework was necessary for establishing the results of this paper. Section 5 presents the syntax and semantics of programs in the parametric framework, and establishes the equivalence of the declarative, fixpoint, and proof-theoretic semantics. Query optimization issues and results are presented in Section 6, and concluding remarks in Section 7.

## 2 A Motivation for the Parametric Framework

In this section, we motivate our parametric approach to unifying/generalizing IB frameworks with uncertainty. The task in the unification is (i) to permit various forms of uncertainty to be manipulated in different ways, and (ii) to allow for the fact that certain manipulations amount to treating different derivations of an atom as a set (e.g. [6, 7, 8, 15, 13, 27]) while others amount to treating it as a multiset (e.g. [14]).

Consider the following "generic" IB program $P$.

$r_1 : \quad A \xleftarrow{\alpha_1} B.$

$r_2 : \quad A \xleftarrow{\alpha_2} C.$

$r_3 : \quad B \xleftarrow{\alpha_3} .$

$r_4 : \quad C \xleftarrow{\alpha_4} .$

where $A, B, C$ are ground atoms, and $\alpha_i$ is the certainty associated with rule $r_i$, $1 \leq i \leq 4$. Examples 1 – 6 illustrate several IB frameworks using $P$.

*Example 1.* (Classical Logic) Let $V = \{0, 1\}$, and $\alpha_i = 1$, for $1 \leq i \leq 4$. Suppose the propagation and conjunction functions associated with $r_i$ are both *min*, and the disjunction function associated with each atom is *max*. Then, $P$ is a program in classical logic. ∎

*Example 2.* (Dubois et al. [6]) Let $V = [0, 1]$, i.e., the unit interval. Suppose $\alpha_1 = 0.8$, $\alpha_2 = \alpha_3 = 0.7$, and $\alpha_4 = 0.8$ are possibility/necessity degrees associated with the implications. Suppose the conjunction, propagation, and disjunction functions are as in the previous example. Then $P$ is a program in the framework proposed by Dubois et al. [6]. In a fixpoint evaluation of $P$, the possibility/necessity degrees derived for $A, B, C$ are $0.7, 0.7, 0.9$, respectively. ∎

*Example 3.* (van Emden [27]) Let $V = [0, 1]$, and suppose $\alpha_i$s are certainty values defined as in Example 2. Suppose the conjunction and disjunction functions are as before, but the propagation function is $*$. Then $P$ is a program in van Emden's framework [27], essentially founded on fuzzy set theory [29]. ∎

*Example 4.* (MYCIN [3]) Let $V = [0, 1]$, and suppose $\alpha_i$s are probabilities defined as in the previous example. Suppose $*$ is the propagation and conjunction functions associated with every rule in $P$, and $f_d(\alpha, \beta) = \alpha + \beta - \alpha * \beta$ is the disjunction function associated with every atom in $P$. Viewing an atom as an event, $f_d$ returns the probability of the occurrence, of any one of two independent events, in the probabilistic sense. Note that $f_d$ is the combination function used in MYCIN [3].

Let us consider a fixpoint evaluation of $P$. In the first step, we derive $B$ and $C$ with probabilities $0.7$ and $0.8$, respectively. In step 2, applying $r_1$ and $r_2$, we obtain two derivations of $A$, each with probability $0.56$, which when combined we get $f_d(0.56, 0.56) = 0.8064$. Note that in this example it is crucial that derivations be collected as a multiset, since otherwise collecting them as a set would yield $0.56$ as the certainty of $A$, which is incorrect. ∎

*Example 5.* (Lakshmanan and Sadri [15]) Suppose there are three sources contributing to the information in a database. Let each certainty in $V$ be a set of vectors of the form $(a_1\ a_2\ a_3)$, where $a_i \in \{\perp, -1, 1, \top\}$. The case $a_i = 1$ indicates source $i$ has confirmed the data. Similarly, if $a_i$ is $-1$, $\perp$, or $\top$, it means $a_i$s contribution to the particular data is negative, none, or contradictory. Suppose $\alpha_1 = (\perp\ 1\ \perp)$, $\alpha_2 = (1\ \perp\ \perp)$, $\alpha_3 = (\perp\ \perp\ 1)$, and $\alpha_4 = (1\ 1\ \perp)$ are the certainties associated with the rules in $P$. In this framework, the only propagation and conjunction function, $\overset{s}{\wedge}$, is defined as follows. Given the source vectors $u = (a_1\ a_2\ a_3)$ and $v = (b_1\ b_2\ b_3)$, $u \overset{s}{\wedge} v = (lub(a_1, b_1)\ lub(a_2, b_2)\ lub(a_3, b_3))$, and for any sets of source vectors $S_1$ and $S_2$, $S_1 \overset{s}{\wedge} S_2 = \{u \overset{s}{\wedge} v \mid u \in S_1 \text{ and } v \in S_2\}$. Here *lub* is the join operator corresponding to the partial order $\top \preceq 1 \preceq \perp$ and $\top \preceq -1 \preceq \perp$. The only disjunction function defined in this framework is $\overset{s}{\vee}$, which is essentially the set union operator. A fixpoint evaluation of $P$ delivers $A, B, C$ with certainties $\{(\perp 1\ 1),\ (1\ 1\ \perp)\}$, $\{(\perp \perp 1)\}$, $\{(1\ 1\ \perp)\}$, respectively. ∎

*Example 6.* (Lakshmanan and Sadri [14]) Let $\mathcal{V} = \mathcal{C}[0,1] \times \mathcal{C}[0,1]$. Each element in $\mathcal{V}$, called a confidence (level), is a pair of closed intervals in $[0,1]$. If $\alpha = \langle [a_1, a_2],\ [a_3, a_4] \rangle$ is the confidence associated with an atom, say $A$, it means it is *believed* that probability that $A$ is true lies in $[a_1, a_2]$, and the probability that $A$ is false lies in $[a_3, a_4]$.

Let $\alpha_1 = \alpha_4 = \langle [0.7, 0.8],\ [0.1, 0.2] \rangle$, $\alpha_2 = \langle [0.8, 0.95],\ [0.05, 0.15] \rangle$, and $\alpha_3 = \langle [0.9, 0.95],\ [0, 0.15] \rangle$. Suppose the conjunction function associated with $r_1$ and $r_2$ is $\wedge_{pc}$, and the disjunction function associated with $A$ is $\vee_{ind}$, where *pc* stands for positive correlation mode and *ind* for independence, in the probabilistic sense. These modes are defined as follows. (See [14] for full explanation of the modes.) Let $\alpha = \langle [a_1, a_2],\ [a_3, a_4] \rangle$ and $\beta = \langle [b_1, b_2],\ [b_3, b_4] \rangle$ be a pair of elements in $\mathcal{V}$. Then, $\wedge_{pc}(\alpha, \beta) = \langle [min\{a_1, a_2\}, min\{b_1, b_2\}],\ [max\{c_1, c_2\}, max\{d_1, d_2\}] \rangle$ and $\vee_{ind}(\alpha, \beta) = \langle [1 - (1 - a_1)(1 - a_2), 1 - (1 - b_1)(1 - b_2)],\ [c_1 c_2, d_1 d_2] \rangle$.

Let us consider a fixpoint evaluation of $P$. Initially, each atom is assigned the least confidence, $\langle [0, 0],\ [1, 1] \rangle$ in $\mathcal{V}$, which corresponds to the truth value *false* in standard logic. In step 1, we derive $B$ and $C$ with confidences $\langle [0.9, 0.95],\ [0, 0.15] \rangle$ and $\langle [0.7, 0.8],\ [0.1, 0.2] \rangle$, respectively. In step 2, we obtain two derivations of $A$ with confidence $\langle [0.7, 0.8],\ [0.1, 0.2] \rangle$, which when combined, using $\vee_{ind}$, yields $\langle [0.91, 0.96],\ [0.01, 0.04] \rangle$ as the confidence of $A$. In step 3, no new/better fact is derived, and hence the evaluation terminates. Note that, again, the role of multisets is crucial; if derivations were collected as sets, we would have obtained just one copy of $A$, resulting in an incorrect confidence level.

Note that this is not to suggest that a user in such a framework is forced to conceive of uncertainty as multisets. However, because of the way the fixpoint evaluation proceeds, using different derivations, we may deduce a fact with the same certainty more than once, which suggests that, in general, we need to collect the derived facts as multisets. ∎

The idea of a parametric framework inspired by observing that in an IB framework with uncertainty, a user specifies, implicitly or explicitly, the following notions, or *parameters*, as we call them.

1. The notion of uncertainty, which we denote by $\mathcal{V}$. It is usually assumed that $<\mathcal{V}, \preceq, \otimes, \oplus>$ is a complete lattice, where $\otimes$ is the meet operator and $\oplus$ is the join. We denote the partial ordering on $\mathcal{V}$ by $\preceq$. For concepts of lattice theory, see [1]. The elements of $\mathcal{V}$ could be certainty factors (e.g. [27]), probabilities, vectors of elements or sets of such vectors (e.g. [13, 15]), (pairs of) probability ranges (e.g. [14]), etc. Indeed, $\mathcal{V}$ could even be a bilattice [7, 8]. Independent of the structure and the semantics of the elements in $\mathcal{V}$, we refer to them as *certainty* or *truth* values, interchangeably. Once the

parameters in a system are fixed, the structure and the semantics of these elements would become known.

2. The family $\mathcal{F}_c = \{f_c^i\}_{i \in \mathcal{I}_1}$ of "conjunction" functions allowed, where $\mathcal{I}_1$ is an index set. Associated with each rule in a program is a function, $f_c^i$, in $\mathcal{F}_c$ which "combines" the certainties of the atoms in the rule body and returns the certainty of the rule body as a whole. Since rule bodies contain a number of atoms, we model conjunction functions as mappings from finite multisets over $\mathcal{V}$ to $\mathcal{V}$.

3. The family $\mathcal{F}_p = \{f_p^i\}_{i \in \mathcal{I}_2}$ of "propagation" functions allowed, where $\mathcal{I}_2$ is an index set. Associated with each rule in a program is a function, $f_p^i$, in $\mathcal{F}_p$ which combines the certainty of the rule body with the certainty of the rule itself and returns the certainty of the rule head. Thus, $f_p^i$ controls the propagation of truth from the rule body to the head.[1] Propagation functions are binary functions on $\mathcal{V}$.

4. The family $\mathcal{F}_d = \{f_d^i\}_{i \in \mathcal{I}_3}$ of "disjunction" functions allowed, where $\mathcal{I}_3$ is an index set. Associated with each predicate symbol $p$ in a user program is a function, $f_d^i$, in $\mathcal{F}_d$ which combines a number of certainties associated with a ground $p$-atom[2] (obtained e.g. by different derivations) and returns a single certainty of the $p$-atom. That is, disjunction functions are mappings from finite multisets over $\mathcal{V}$ to $\mathcal{V}$.

The following example illustrates the expressive power of the parametric framework. This program could not be expressed in any existing IB frameworks. The point here is that *different* ways of manipulating uncertainty are combined within *one* program.

*Example 7.* Consider the following program containing knowledge related to some health organization. Here, the certainty domain is $\mathcal{V} = \mathcal{C}[0, 1]$, the set of closed intervals in $[0, 1]$. In this example, we use $pc$, $ign$, and $ind$ modes of combination, denoting positive correlation, ignorance, and independence, respectively. (See [14] for a full explanation of these modes.) The various combination modes used in this program are defined as follows. Let $\alpha = [a_1, b_1]$ and $\beta = [a_2, b_2]$ be any intervals in $\mathcal{V}$. Then,

$$V_{ign}(\alpha, \beta) = [max\{a_1, a_2\}, \ min\{1, b_1 + b_2\}]$$
$$V_{pc}(\alpha, \beta) = [max\{a_1, a_2\}, \ max\{b_1, b_2\}]$$
$$\wedge_{pc}(\alpha, \beta) = [min\{a_1, a_2\}, \ min\{b_1, b_2\}]$$
$$\wedge_{ind}(\alpha, \beta) = [a_1 * a_2, \ b_1 * b_2]$$

When the rule body has one atom, we may use $i$, the *identity* function, defined as $i([a, b]) = [a, b]$, as the conjunction function.

The organization has information about the connectivity of the areas in a region along with the degrees of connectivity, expressed as follows. The triple

---

[1] In an AB framework, the role of conjunction and propagation functions is played by the so called *certainty* functions.

[2] An atom whose predicate symbol is $p$.

$\langle f_d, f_p, f_c \rangle$ associated with a rule in this program denotes, respectively, the disjunction, propagation, and conjunction functions.

$$r_1 : \quad close(a, b) \xleftarrow{\quad [0.9,1] \quad}; \qquad\qquad \langle \vee_{ign}, \wedge_{pc}, \_ \rangle$$

$$r_2 : \quad close(a, c) \xleftarrow{\quad [0.8,1] \quad}; \qquad\qquad \langle \vee_{ign}, \wedge_{pc}, \_ \rangle$$

$$r_3 : \quad close(b, c) \xleftarrow{\quad [0.7,1] \quad}; \qquad\qquad \langle \vee_{ign}, \wedge_{pc}, \_ \rangle$$

$$r_4 : \quad close(Y, X) \xleftarrow{\quad [1,1] \quad} close(X, Y); \qquad \langle \vee_{ign}, \wedge_{pc}, i \rangle$$

The first rule says that area $a$ is connected to area $b$ with degree at least 0.9. Rule $r_4$ says closeness is definitely a symmetric property. The next rule asserts that there is an outbreak of disease $d$ in area $a$.

$$r_5 : \quad outbreak(d, a) \xleftarrow{\quad [1,1] \quad}; \qquad\qquad \langle \vee_{pc}, \wedge_{pc}, \_ \rangle$$

An area $X$ is connected to $Y$, provided $X$ is close to $Y$, or there is some area $Z$ which is close to $X$ and is connected to $Y$. This is expressed as follows.

$$r_6 : \quad connected(X, Y) \xleftarrow{\quad [1,1] \quad} close(X, Y); \qquad\qquad \langle \vee_{pc}, \wedge_{ind}, i \rangle$$

$$r_7 : \quad connected(X, Y) \xleftarrow{\quad [0.8,0.9] \quad} close(X, Z), connected(Z, Y); \quad \langle \vee_{pc}, \wedge_{pc}, \wedge_{pc} \rangle$$

Finally, we define $affected(D, A)$ which asserts that area $A$ is affected by disease $D$.

$$r_8 : \quad affected(D, A) \xleftarrow{\quad [0.7,0.8] \quad} outbreak(D, A); \qquad\qquad \langle \vee_{pc}, \wedge_{pc}, \wedge_{ind} \rangle$$

$$r_9 : \quad affected(D, A) \xleftarrow{\quad [0.8,0.9] \quad} close(A, A_1), affected(D, A_1); \quad \langle \vee_{pc}, \wedge_{pc}, \wedge_{pc} \rangle$$

∎

## 3 Preliminaries and Notations

In this section, we provide some definitions and fix our notations. We begin with multisets. A *multiset*, also called a *bag*, is a collection of elements in which multiple occurrences of the elements are allowed. Let $B$ be any set. A *multiset* $X$ over $B$ is a mapping from $B$ to $\mathcal{N} = \{0, 1, 2, 3, \ldots\}$. We refer to $B$ as the *base* set of $X$. We use $\dot{\in}$ to denote membership for multisets, i.e., if $X$ is a multiset which contains $m$ occurrences of $b$, for any $b \in B$ and any $m \in \mathcal{N}$, then we write $(b : m) \in X$, or $b \dot{\in} X$. If $x = (b : m) \in X$, we call $b$ the *basic part* of $x$, and call $m$ the *multiplicity* of $b$ in $X$. By default, the multiplicity of every element in $B$ not present in $X$ is 0. To distinguish between multisets and sets, we use $\{\!\ldots\!\}$ for multisets. The empty multiset, denoted $\dot{\emptyset}$, is the multiset in which the multiplicity of every element (in $B$) is 0. Let $X, Y$ be any finite multisets over a base set $B$. We say $X$ is "multiset-contained" in $Y$, denoted $X \dot{\subseteq} Y$, provided $\forall b \in B$, if $X$ contains $m$ copies of $b$, then $Y$ contains at least $m$ copies of $b$.

In the context of logic programming and deductive databases with uncertainty, we consider multisets over $B = B_P \times \mathcal{V}$, where $B_P$ is the Herbrand base of a given logic program $P$, and $\mathcal{V}$ is the set of truth values employed. In this case, if $X$ is a multiset over $B$, then each element in $X$ is of the form $(A, \alpha) : m$, where $A \in B_P$ is a ground atom, $\alpha \in \mathcal{V}$ is a truth value associated with $A$, and $m \in \mathcal{N}$ is the multiplicity of the basic part $(A, \alpha)$ in $X$.

In this paper, we adopt the following conventions in using the various symbols. We use lower case letters to represent predicate symbols and constants, the upper case letters $A, B, \ldots$ from the beginning of the alphabet to represent ground atoms, and $X, Y, \ldots$ to represent multisets as well as variables in the predicate arguments. In this case, the type of the symbol used would be clear from the context. We use the lower case Greek letters $\alpha, \beta, \ldots$ to represent the truth values in $\mathcal{V}$. We will use $\preceq$ to denote the partial order on $\mathcal{V}$.

# 4 Related Work

In this section, we compare our parametric framework with previous work, notably Kifer and Li [10], Kifer and Subrahmanian [12], and Debray and Ramakrishnan [5], because, like this work, they generalize and/or unify specific frameworks. We will also consider the probabilistic framework of Lakshmanan and Sadri [14], because this work was inspired by it.

In the context of rule based systems with uncertainty, Kifer and Li [10] identified the main drawback in the earlier works on quantitative logics being their lack of enough support for various conjunction and disjunction functions required in such systems; only *max* and *min* were supported as the disjunction and conjunction functions. They discuss that, in practice, more general such functions are required, and propose a set of "reasonable" properties which should be satisfied by such functions. They also proposed an AB framework with generic combination functions, defined in terms of their properties. They essentially considered a "parametric" approach similar in spirit to ours. They developed a model and fixpoint semantics based on multisets. While their semantics does not rely on the various types of independence among the rules in a program, they assume supporting evidences for an atom should be absolutely independent of each other. The main problem with the proposed framework is that the $T_P$ operator defined is not continuous. Also, it is unclear under what condition one can expect finite termination. The recurrence based evaluation they proposed, although elegant, is a departure from the conventional (semi)-naive evaluation method, and the possibility of efficient implementation of their method is not clear. In the theory of Generalized Annotated logic Programming (GAP), discussed next, Kifer and Subrahmanian [12] solved several of these problems.

Kifer and Subrahmanian [12] proposed the GAP framework as a unifying framework which generalizes various results and treatments of temporal and multi-valued logic programming, e.g. [2, 8, 11, 24, 27]. A main difference between GAP and any IB framework, including ours, is clearly in the approach. The two approaches have their own advantages and disadvantages, as discussed in Section 1. In terms of expressive power, GAP can simulate the computation of some IB frameworks.[3] As the semantics developed for GAP is based on sets, it *cannot* simulate those IB frameworks which have multisets as the basis of their semantics. For instance, the probabilistic IB framework proposed in [14],

---

[3] This is done through the annotation variables allowed in GAP.

an instance which can be simulated within our parametric framework, cannot be simulated in GAP without changing its underlying semantics to be based on multisets. Although the GAP framework [12] allows an infinite family of disjunction functions $\sqcup_j$, $j \geq 0$, all these functions are based on the lattice join $\sqcup$. This is quite restricted compared to the infinite family $\mathcal{F}_d$ of disjunction functions (which need not be lattice based) allowed in the parametric framework.

Debray and Ramakrishnan [5] proposed an axiomatic basis for Horn clause logic programming. Their framework nicely simulates a variety of "Horn-clause-like" computations, arising, for instance, in deductive databases, quantitative deduction, and inheritance systems, in terms of two operators, instance ($\hat{\otimes}$) and join ($\hat{\oplus}$). In the context of uncertainty reasoning, they show how their framework captures the computation in van Emden's language [27]. In this context, it seems from their axioms that the proposed framework can also capture the fixpoint computation of IB frameworks which have sets as the basis for their semantical structures, e.g. [15]. However, as explained below, the proposed setting is incompatible with probabilistic frameworks, such as [13, 14, 21, 20].

First, in the formulation of the logic in [5], one of their axioms states that for any values $t$ and $t'$, the value $t\hat{\otimes}t'$ conveys no more information than does $t$.[4] In a probabilistic logic, this could be interpreted as saying in a weighted set of evidences, adding an evidence, $t\hat{\otimes}t'$, which is subsumed by another element in the set, $t$, does not increase the information "content" of the set. This may be inappropriate in a probabilistic setting. For, suppose, $e$ is an event with probability 0.5. Then, according to this axiom, if we add a lower probability value, 0.4, to a set of such values, $\{0.5\}$, the content of the result set, $\{0.4, 0.5\}$, does not increase, which may not always be true, e.g. when the combination mode is "independence".

The second limitation of the framework in [5] is the distributivity requirement of their lattice. This is not suitable, in general, for probabilistic inferencing. In fact, the appropriate probabilistic conjunction and disjunction used in an application are driven by the underlying assumptions about the nature of event interaction, and they need not distribute over one another, in general. For instance, if $\alpha_1, \alpha_2$ and $\alpha_3$ are confidences in the probabilistic framework of Lakshmanan and Sadri [14], with the disjunction mode $\bigvee_{ign}$ (i.e. ignorance) and the conjunction mode $\wedge_{pc}$ (i.e. positive correlation), then $(\alpha_1 \bigvee_{ign} \alpha_2)\wedge_{pc}\alpha_3 \neq (\alpha_1 \wedge_{pc}\alpha_3)\bigvee_{ign}(\alpha_2 \wedge_{pc}\alpha_3)$.

We now consider the probabilistic deductive databases of Lakshmanan and Sadri [14], which inspired our parametric language. In their framework, they considered "parameterized" conjunctions and disjunctions in the context of probabilistic deduction and developed a probabilistic calculus. Our framework differs from theirs in several ways. First, the uncertainty domain in our framework is itself parameterized. Also, we allow a family of propagation functions as yet another parameter. This allows in the same rule, to use a propagation function different from the conjunction function. We showed in Example 6 that their

---

[4] Axiom 4.1 in [5]. For any values $t, t' \in D$, (1) $\{t\}\hat{\oplus}\{t\hat{\otimes}t'\} \approx \{t\}$; and (2) $\{t\}\hat{\otimes}\{t\hat{\oplus}t'\}$. Note that $t\hat{\otimes}t'$ is an instance of $t$, denoted $t\hat{\otimes}t' \preceq t$.

framework fits into our framework by the appropriate choice of the parameters. Finally, unlike all the above works, we address query optimization and establish necessary and sufficient conditions for containment of conjunctive queries. We remark that Ioannidis and Ramakrishnan [9] considered the problem of query containment in a broad setting where relations may be interpreted as sets or as multisets. A comparison with their work appears in Section 6.

## 5  Parametric Deductive Databases

In this section, we introduce the parametric framework. First, we characterize the families of propagation, conjunction, and disjunction functions allowed in terms of their properties. Then we introduce the syntax of our language. We will then develop the declarative, fixpoint, and proof-theoretic semantics of programs in the language and establish their equivalence.

Let $\mathcal{L}$ be an arbitrary, but fixed, first order language that contains infinitely many variable symbols, finitely many constants and predicate symbols, but no function symbols.

While $\mathcal{L}$ does not contain function symbols, it contains symbols for families of propagation $(\mathcal{F}_p)$, conjunction $(\mathcal{F}_c)$, and disjunction $(\mathcal{F}_d)$ functions characterized as follows.

### 5.1  Properties of Combination Functions

Let $\mathcal{V}$ be a set of truth values and $\mathcal{B}(\mathcal{V})$ the set of finite multisets over $\mathcal{V}$. Then, a propagation function is a mapping from $\mathcal{V}^2$ to $\mathcal{V}$, and a conjunction or disjunction function is a mapping from $\mathcal{B}(\mathcal{V})$ to $\mathcal{V}$. For practical reasons, we assume every function in $\mathcal{F} = \mathcal{F}_c \cup \mathcal{F}_p \cup \mathcal{F}_d$ can be computed "efficiently".

In order that derivations in our parametric framework are meaningful, we impose some natural requirements on the functions in $\mathcal{F}$, as enumerated below. Let $f \in \mathcal{F}$ be any function. For simplicity, we state the following properties assuming $f$ is a binary function on $\mathcal{V}$. The properties have their obvious formulation when $f$ is a function from $\mathcal{B}(\mathcal{V})$ to $\mathcal{V}$. Since we require our conjunction and disjunction functions to be associative (property 6 below), the binary formulation is quite meaningful in all cases. Properties (7-9) are peculiar to functions $f : \mathcal{B}(\mathcal{V}) \to \mathcal{V}$.

(1) *Monotonicity:* $f(\alpha_1, \alpha_2) \preceq f(\beta_1, \beta_2)$, whenever $\alpha_i \preceq \beta_i$, for $i = 1, 2$.

(2) *Continuity:* $f$ is continuous w.r.t. each one of its arguments.

(3) *Bounded-Above:* $f(\alpha_1, \alpha_2) \preceq \alpha_i$, for $i = 1, 2$. That is, the result of $f$ is not "more" than any one of its arguments.

(4) *Bounded-Below:* $f(\alpha_1, \alpha_2) \succeq \alpha_i$, for $i = 1, 2$. That is, the result of $f$ is not "less" than any one of its arguments.

(5) *Commutativity:* $f(\alpha, \beta) = f(\beta, \alpha)$, $\forall \alpha, \beta \in \mathcal{V}$.

(6) *Associativity:* $f(\alpha, f(\beta, \gamma)) = f(f(\alpha, \beta), \gamma)$, $\forall \alpha, \beta, \gamma \in \mathcal{V}$.

(7) $f(\{\!|\alpha|\!\}) = \alpha$, $\forall \alpha \in \mathcal{V}$.

(8) $f(\emptyset) = \bot$, where $\bot$ is the least element in $\mathcal{V}$.

**(9)** $f(\emptyset) = \top$, where $\top$ is the greatest element in $\mathcal{V}$.

**(10)** $f(\alpha, \top) = \alpha, \forall \alpha \in \mathcal{V}$.

*We require that (i) conjunction functions satisfy properties 1, 2, 3, 5, 6, 7, 9, 10; (ii) propagation functions satisfy properties 1, 2, 3, 10; and (iii) disjunction functions satisfy properties 1, 2, 4, 5, 6, 7, 8.* Similar assumptions were made by Kifer and Li [10] in a different context. A detailed comparison with [10] appears in Section 4.

The continuity of functions in $\mathcal{F}$ is needed for proving continuity of the immediate consequence operator (Lemma 7). This assumption is not crucial for our results on query optimization in Section 6. The commutativity and associativity of the conjunction functions are required for allowing query optimization, e.g. performing subgoal reordering, if desired. The commutativity and associativity of the disjunction functions are needed so that, in evaluating a program, the truth value obtained for each ground atom is unique and is independent of the order in which the facts are derived and the truth values are combined. Boundedness assumptions are imposed in order that derivations make intuitive sense. Property 9 for a conjunction function together with property 10 for a propagation function allow derivation of $A$ with certainty $\alpha$ from a rule of the form $A \xleftarrow{\alpha}$ , i.e., with empty body. Property 8 has a similar rationale.

## 5.2   Syntax

**Definition 1.** A *parametric program* $P$ (p-program) is a 5-tuple $\langle \mathcal{V}, \mathcal{R}, \mathcal{C}, \mathcal{P}, \mathcal{D} \rangle$, whose components are defined as follows.

**(1)** $\mathcal{V}$ is a set of certainties partially ordered by $\preceq$. We require that $< \mathcal{V}, \preceq, \otimes, \oplus >$ be a complete lattice, where $\otimes$ is the meet operator and $\oplus$ is the join. We denote the least element of the lattice by $\bot$, and the greatest element by $\top$, which correspond, respectively, to the truth values *false* and *true* in classical logic.

**(2)** $\mathcal{R}$ is a finite set of *parametric rules* (p-rules), each of which is a statement of the form:

$$r : \quad A \xleftarrow{\alpha_r} B_1, \ldots, B_n; \ \langle f_d, f_p, f_c \rangle$$

where $A, B_1, \ldots, B_n$ are atomic formulas, $\alpha_r \in \mathcal{V} - \{\bot\}$ is the certainty value associated with the implication in $r$, $f_d \in \mathcal{F}_d$, $f_p \in \mathcal{F}_p$, and $f_c \in \mathcal{F}_c$.

**(3)** $\mathcal{C} : \mathcal{R} \to \mathcal{F}_c$ is a mapping which associates with each p-rule a conjunction function.

**(4)** $\mathcal{P} : \mathcal{R} \to \mathcal{F}_p$ is a mapping which associates with each p-rule a propagation function.

**(5)** $\mathcal{D} : Pred(P) \to \mathcal{F}_d$ is a mapping which associates with each predicate symbol in $P$ a disjunction function. $Pred(P)$ denotes the set of predicate symbols in $P$.

In rule $r$ above, $A$ is called the rule *head*, and $B_1, \ldots, B_n$ is called the rule *body*. A *fact* is a special case of a p-rule in which $n = 0$. We will use p-program and program interchangeably. The same remark holds about p-rule and rule. If a rule body is empty, then the conjunction function is not important (as every conjunction function must satisfy Property 9), in which case, the triple associated with the rule looks like $\langle f_d, f_p, \_ \rangle$.

## 5.3  Semantics

In this section, we present the semantics of p-programs. Without loss of generality, we restrict our study of the semantics to Herbrand structures. First, we develop the *declarative* semantics based on the notion of valuations, and show that any p-program has a least valuation, w.r.t. the ordering $\preceq$ on valuations. We will then develop a fixpoint semantics of p-programs and show that the least valuation of a p-program is equivalent to the least fixpoint semantics. Finally, we present a sound and complete proof-theoretic semantics for p-programs and establish its equivalence with the declarative semantics.

Let $P$ be a p-program, and $B_P$ the Herbrand base of $P$. A *valuation* $v$ of $P$ is a function from $B_P$ to $\mathcal{V}$. That is, $v$ associates with each ground atom in $B_P$, a truth value in $\mathcal{V}$. A *ground instance* of a p-rule $r$ in $P$ is a rule obtained from $r$ by replacing all occurrences of each variable in $r$ with an element of the Herbrand domain. Since p-programs are function free, this domain contains just the constants mentioned in $P$, and hence is finite. The *Herbrand instantiation* of $P$, denoted $P^*$, is the set of all ground instances of all the p-rules in $P$. The notion of satisfaction of p-programs by valuations is defined as follows.

**Definition 2.** (Satisfaction) Let $P$ be any p-program, $r$ be any p-rule in $P$, and $v$ be any valuation of $P$. Let $\rho \equiv (A \xleftarrow{\alpha_r} B_1, \ldots, B_n; \langle f_d, f_p, f_c \rangle) \in P^*$ be any ground instance of $r$. Then, we say that
(a) $v$ *satisfies* $\rho$, denoted $\models_v \rho$, $iff$ $f_p(\alpha_r, f_c(\{v(B_1), \ldots, v(B_n)\})) \preceq v(A)$.
(b) $\models_v r$ iff $v$ satisfies every ground instance $\rho$ of $r$.
(c) $v$ satisfies $P$, denoted $\models_v P$, iff (1) $\forall r \in P$: $\models_v r$, and (2) $\forall A \in B_P$ : $f_d(X) \preceq v(A)$, where $X = \{f_p(\alpha_r, f_c(\{v(B_1), \ldots, v(B_n)\})) \mid \rho \in P^*\}$.

Note that $f_d$ is the disjunction function associated with the predicate symbol of atom $A$, and $X$ is the multiset of truth values, each of which is obtained by applying a ground rule in $P^*$ with head $A$. Also note that it follows from Properties 9 and 10 that whenever $n = 0$, $f_p(\alpha_r, f_c(\emptyset)) = \alpha_r$. As noted in [10] and [14], although $v$ may satisfy every p-rule in $P$, in general, it may fail to satisfy $P$. For $v$ to also satisfy $P$, condition c(2) ensures that for each atom $A \in B_P$, the truth value assigned to $A$ by $v$ is not "less than" $f_d(X)$, i.e., we must ensure that $v(A) \succeq f_d(X)$. For every valuation $v$ of $P$, if $\models_v P$, we say that $v$ is a *model* of $P$.

The ordering $\preceq$ on $\mathcal{V}$ can be extended to valuations in the well-known manner; for any valuations $u$ and $v$ of a p-program $P$, $v \preceq u$ iff $v(A) \preceq u(A), \forall A \in B_P$. For all valuations $u, v$ of $P$ and $\forall A \in B_P$, we have (1) $(u \otimes v)(A) = u(A) \otimes v(A)$ and (2) $(u \oplus v)(A) = u(A) \oplus v(A)$. We then have the following lemma.

**Lemma 3.** *Let $P$ be any p-program, and $\Upsilon_P$ the set of valuations of $P$. Then $\langle \Upsilon_P, \otimes, \oplus \rangle$ is a complete lattice.*

The least element of $\langle \Upsilon_P, \otimes, \oplus \rangle$ is a valuation, $v_\perp$, which maps every atom $A \in B_P$ to $\perp$, and its greatest element is a valuation, $v_\top$, which maps $A$ to $\top$.

The following lemma is the counterpart of the model intersection property in standard logic programming.

**Lemma 4.** *Let $u$ and $v$ be any valuations satisfying a p-program $P$. Then $u \otimes v$ is also a valuation satisfying $P$.*

The notion of of least valuations, introduced next, corresponds to the notion of least models in standard logic programming.

**Theorem 5.** *Let $P$ be a p-program, and $\Upsilon_P$ the set of valuations of $P$. Then, $\otimes\{v \mid v \in \Upsilon_P, \models_v P\}$ is the least valuation satisfying $P$.*

Next, we develop a fixpoint theory for p-programs. To this end, as in standard logic programming, we associate an immediate consequence operator, $T_P$, with a p-program $P$. We will show that the least fixpoint of $T_P$ exists and is equivalent to the least valuation satisfying $P$.

**Definition 6.** Let $P$ be any p-program, and $P^*$ be the Herbrand instantiation of $P$. Also let $\Upsilon_P$ be the set of valuations of $P$. The *immediate consequence operator* is a mapping $T_P : \Upsilon_P \rightarrow \Upsilon_P$, defined as follows. For all $v \in \Upsilon_P$ and $\forall A \in B_P$, $T_P(v)(A) = f_d(X)$, where $f_d$ is the disjunction function associated with the predicate symbol of $A$, and $X = \{f_p(\alpha_r, f_c(\{\beta_1, \ldots, \beta_n\})) \mid (A \xleftarrow{\alpha_r} B_1, \ldots, B_n; \langle f_d, f_p, f_c \rangle) \in P^*, \beta_k = v(B_k), 1 \leq k \leq n\}$.

We define the bottom-up iterations of $T_P$, in the usual way, as follows.

$$T_P \uparrow k = \begin{cases} v_\perp & \text{if } k = 0 \\ T_P(T_P \uparrow k - 1) & \text{if } k \text{ is a successor ordinal} \\ \oplus\{T_P \uparrow \ell \mid \ell < k\} & \text{if } k \text{ is a limit ordinal} \end{cases}$$

**Lemma 7.** *The operator $T_P$ is monotone and continuous.*

The next result shows that a valuation satisfies a p-program iff it is a prefixpoint of $T_P$.

**Lemma 8.** *Let $P$ be any p-program, and $v$ be any valuation of $P$. Then, $\models_v P$ iff $T_P(v) \preceq v$.*

We denote the *least fixpoint* of $T_P$ by $lfp(T_P)$. The following theorem, analogous to the van Emden-Kowalski theorem in standard logic programming [28], establishes a connection between the fixpoint and the declarative semantics of p-programs.

**Theorem 9.** *Let $P$ be any p-program. Then $lfp(T_P) = \otimes\{v \mid \models_v P\}$.*

We have developed a proof theory for the parametric framework based on the notion of disjunctive derivation trees (DDT), adapted from [14]. Intuitively, a DDT for a ground atom $A$ w.r.t. a p-program $P$ is a collection of derivation trees each of which is an and/or tree encoding a proof of $A$ from $P$. We have the following results.

**Theorem 10.** (Soundness) *Let $P$ be any p-program, and $A \in B_P$ be any goal. If $T_A$ is a DDT for $A$ w.r.t. $P$ such that $\alpha \in \mathcal{V}$ is the truth value associated with the root of $T_A$, then $\alpha \preceq lfp(T_P)(A)$.*

**Theorem 11.** (Completeness) *Let $P$ be any p-program, and $A \in B_P$ be any goal such that $lfp(T_P)(A) = T_P \uparrow k(A)$, for some positive integer $k$. Then there exists a DDT, $T_A$, for $A$ w.r.t. $P$ such that $\alpha \in V$ is the certainty associated with the root of $T_A$ and $lfp(T_P)(A) \preceq \alpha$.*

## 6 Containment of Conjunctive Queries

In this section, we study containment of conjunctive queries in our framework. Containment and equivalence are the central notions used in query optimization in relational and deductive databases [26]. We quickly review some basic notions from classical database theory, which will be used in the rest of this section. A *conjunctive query* is a rule of the form

$$Q : \quad p(X_1, \ldots, X_n) \longleftarrow q_1(Y_1, \ldots, Y_m), \ldots, q_k(Z_1, \ldots, Z_\ell).$$

where the $q_i$s are predicates referring to relations in the database while $p$ can be thought of as the query predicate; all the variables $X_i$ in the head are assumed to appear in the body. Given a database $D$ which has relations corresponding to the predicates in the body of $Q$, we define *instantiation* of $Q$ w.r.t. $D$ as a ground substitution on the variables of $Q$. An instantiation $\theta$ of $Q$ w.r.t. $D$ is said to be *valid* provided the body of $Q$ is true w.r.t. $D$, under the instantiation $\theta$. In future, we mean only valid instantiation whenever we refer to instantiations. The set of all (valid) instantiations of $Q$ w.r.t. $D$ is denoted $inst(Q, D)$. The *evaluation* of $Q$ on $D$ is defined as $Q(D) = \{p(X_1, \ldots, X_n)\theta \mid \theta \in inst(Q, D)\}$ whenever $Q$ is viewed as a set, and as $\{p(X_1, \ldots, X_n)\theta \mid \theta \in inst(Q, D)\}$, whenever $Q(D)$ is viewed as a multiset. In both cases, notice that the input database $D$ is always a classical (i.e., set based) database. The context will make it clear how $Q(D)$ is viewed. Given two conjunctive queries $Q_1, Q_2$ defining the same query predicate $p(X_1, \ldots, X_n)$, we say that $Q_1$ is *contained* in $Q_2$, denoted $Q_1 \subseteq Q_2$, provided for every input database $D$, $Q_1(D) \subseteq Q_2(D)$. $Q_1$ and $Q_2$ are *equivalent*, denoted $Q_1 \equiv Q_2$, provided $Q_1 \subseteq Q_2$ and $Q_2 \subseteq Q_1$.

A simple and powerful tool for the study of conjunctive query containment in the classical case is the *containment mapping* [4]. Let $Q_1, Q_2$ be any pair of conjunctive queries as shown below in schematic form.

$$Q_1 : H \longleftarrow B_1, \ldots, B_k.$$
$$Q_2 : H' \longleftarrow C_1, \ldots, C_m.$$

Formally, a symbol mapping from $Q_2$ to $Q_1$ is a mapping $h$ from the variables occurring in $Q_2$ to those occurring in $Q_1$. Such a mapping $h$ induces a mapping from the predicates in $Q_2$ to those in $Q_1$. A symbol mapping $h$ is a *containment mapping* (c.m.) provided, $h(H') = H$, and for every $1 \leq i \leq m$, $h(C_i) = B_j$, for some $1 \leq j \leq k$. In the classical case, conjunctive query containment is completely characterized by the existence of containment mappings [4]. This has played a central role in the development of many query optimization algorithms. *An interesting question to ask is when the tools developed for classical query optimization can be applied for queries against deductive databases with any of the various uncertainty formalisms considered in this paper. It is important to* know this because for those cases where classical techniques continue to apply, queries can be processed quite efficiently. In this section, we focus on the problem of conjunctive query containment and answer the following question. *Exactly when does containment of conjunctive queries in IB deductive databases with uncertainty reduces to containment in the classical case? In other words, when is it completely characterized by containment mappings?*

Intuitively, we expect the answer to the above question will be positive exactly when the parameters (especially the combination functions) in our framework satisfy certain conditions. In a recent paper, Ioannidis and Ramakrishnan [9] considered the problem of query containment in a broad setting where relations may be interpreted as sets or as multisets (akin to the treatment of relations in commercial relational database management systems). This is particularly relevant to our work, given the importance of multisets in the context of deduction with uncertainty. They show that as long as a framework (for database querying) can be reduced to viewing relations as sets, containment is completely characterized by containment mappings. The following example shows that unfortunately simply classifying the combination functions as "set-based" and "multiset-based" is not meaningful w.r.t. the parametric framework.

*Example 8. Consider a p-rule of the form $A \xleftarrow{\alpha} B, C; \langle f_d, f_p, f_c \rangle$, where $A, B$, and $C$ are any ground atoms, $\alpha \in \mathcal{V}$ is the certainty of the rule, and $f_d, f_p, f_c$ are the disjunction, propagation, and conjunction functions in the rule, respectively. Let $\mathcal{V} = [0, 1]$ be the certainty lattice, and $v$ be a valuation such that $v(B) = v(C) = 0.5$. Then a "set-based" conjunction function would ignore the duplicate copies of $0.5$. However this is not logically correct, as the certainties are associated with different ground atoms. The problem is that such a conjunction function cannot distinguish between the above p-rule and the p-rule $A \xleftarrow{\alpha} B, B; \langle f_d, f_p, f_c \rangle$.* ∎

We argue that the classification of the functions used in the parametric framework that is appropriate for our purposes should be based on how the functions are related to the appropriate lattice operations. Specifically, we should look at how the conjunction functions compare with the meet $\otimes$ of the certainty lattice, and the disjunction functions with the lattice join $\oplus$.

In classical case, containment is based on set theory. When dealing with programs in deductive databases with uncertainty, we have to also take into account the certainty associated with atoms. We refer to conjunctive queries in the parametric framework as *parametric conjunctive queries* (PCQs, for short). A PCQ $\mathbf{Q}$ is a non-recursive p-rule of the form $H \xleftarrow{\alpha} B_1, \ldots, B_k; \langle f_d, f_p, f_c \rangle$. We use bold $\mathbf{Q}$s to denote PCQs, and $Q$s to denote classical conjunctive queries. When $\mathbf{Q}$ is a PCQ, we will also denote by $Q$ the underlying classical conjunctive query obtained from $\mathbf{Q}$ by stripping all the parameters.

We develop some notations. An *annotated tuple* is an expression of the form $t : \alpha$ where $t$ is an ordinary tuple, and $\alpha \in \mathcal{V}$ is a certainty value. An *annotated relation* is a finite set of annotated tuples. An *annotated database* is a finite set of annotated relations. Let $D$ be an annotated database and $A$ be a ground atom. Then we let $D(A)$ denote the certainty associated by $D$ with $A$. Computation in the parametric framework can be conveniently captured in terms of annotated relations and databases. Notice that an Herbrand structure is essentially an annotated database. We define the evaluation of $\mathbf{Q}$ on database $D$ as the annotated relation for the predicate defined by $\mathbf{Q}$. Formally, for any ground atom $A$, $\mathbf{Q}(D)(A) = f_d(\{\beta \mid \exists$ a ground substitution $\theta$ such that $A = H\theta$, and $\beta = f_p(\alpha, f_c(\{D(B_i\theta) \mid 1 \leq i \leq k\}))$. As in the classical case, we refer to a substitution such as $\theta$ above as an *instantiation*, and denote the set of such instantiations by $inst(\mathbf{Q}, D)$. Throughout this section, we assume that the input databases to parametric queries are annotated databases, while input databases to classical queries are conventional relational databases. It is important to note that in both cases, the input databases do *not* contain duplicates. The following lemma links computation of queries in terms of the operator $T_P$ to computation in terms of annotated databases.

**Lemma 12.** *Let* $\mathbf{Q}$ : $H \xleftarrow{\alpha} B_1, \ldots, B_k; \langle f_d, f_p, f_c \rangle$ *be a PCQ, and* $D$ *be any annotated database. Then for any ground atom* $A$ *defined by* $\mathbf{Q}$*, we have that* $\mathbf{Q}(D)(A) = lfp(T_{P \cup D})(A)$*, where* $P$ *is the p-program containing just* $\mathbf{Q}$*.*

The sole usefulness of this lemma is that it is more convenient to treat conjunctive query evaluation in terms of the notion of input/output (a la the definition $\mathbf{Q}(D)$) than in terms of the classical logic programming operator $T_P$. This lemma shows that the two treatments are equivalent as far as the predicate defined by the query is concerned.

In our study of containment of PCQs, we will find it useful to define containment between a pair of parametric queries based on several criteria. The following definitions make this precise.

**Definition 13.** *Let* $\mathbf{Q}$ : $H \xleftarrow{\alpha} B_1, \ldots, B_k; \langle f_d, f_p, f_c \rangle$ *be a PCQ,* $D$ *an input annotated database, and* $\theta$ *an instantiation of* $\mathbf{Q}$ *w.r.t.* $D$*. Then* $\mathbf{Q}^{\theta}(D) = H\theta : \beta$*, where* $\beta = f_p(\alpha, f_c(\{D(B_1\theta), \ldots, D(B_k\theta)\}))$*. Intuitively,* $\mathbf{Q}^{\theta}(D)$ *denotes the derivation by* $\mathbf{Q}$ *of an instance of* $H$ *(corresponding to* $\theta$*) from* $D$*.*

We extend the partial order on the certainty lattice $\langle \mathcal{V}, \preceq \rangle$ to annotated tuples in the obvious way; for any two annotated tuples $A : \alpha$ and $B : \beta$, $A : \alpha \preceq B : \beta$ iff $A$ and $B$ are identical ground atoms and $\alpha \preceq \beta$ according to the lattice ordering.

**Definition 14.** *Let* $\mathbf{Q}_1$ *and* $\mathbf{Q}_2$ *be any PCQs. We say that* $\mathbf{Q}_1 \subseteq \mathbf{Q}_2$*, provided for every input database* $D$ *and for every instantiation* $\theta_1 \in inst(\mathbf{Q}_1, D)$*, there exists an instantiation* $\theta_2 \in inst(\mathbf{Q}_2, D)$*, such that* $\mathbf{Q}_1^{\theta_1}(D) \preceq \mathbf{Q}_2^{\theta_2}(D)$*, where* $\preceq$ *denotes the partial order on annotated tuples defined above.*

The set-theoretic containment defined in Definition 14 captures the intuition that on any input database $D$, every derivation by $\mathbf{Q}_1$ is matched or bettered by some derivation by $\mathbf{Q}_2$.

**Definition 15.** Let $\mathbf{Q}_1$ and $\mathbf{Q}_2$ be as above. Then we say that $\mathbf{Q}_1 \dot{\subseteq} \mathbf{Q}_2$, provided for every input database $D$, there exists a 1-1 function $m$ from $inst(\mathbf{Q}_1, D)$ to $inst(\mathbf{Q}_2, D)$, such that for each instantiation $\theta \in inst(\mathbf{Q}_1, D)$, $\mathbf{Q}_1^\theta(D) \preceq \mathbf{Q}_2^{m(\theta)}(D)$.

The notion of *multiset based containment* defined above captures the intuition that on any input database $D$, every derivation by $\mathbf{Q}_1$ is matched or bettered by a distinct derivation by $\mathbf{Q}_2$. We will also find use for the following notions of containment on classical conjunctive queries.

**Definition 16.** Let $Q_1$ and $Q_2$ be classical conjunctive queries. Then $Q_1 \subseteq Q_2$, provided for every input database $D$, every tuple in $Q_1(D)$ is also in $Q_2(D)$. This is the conventional notion of containment.

**Definition 17.** Let $Q_1$ and $Q_2$ be classical conjunctive queries. Then $Q_1 \dot{\subseteq} Q_2$, provided for every input database $D$, every tuple in $Q_1(D)$ is also in $Q_2(D)$, and with no less multiplicity, i.e. $Q_1(D) \dot{\subseteq} Q_2(D)$. (Recall that $Q_i(D)$ may be viewed as a set or multiset. (See Section 3 for a definition of $\dot{\subseteq}$).

**Definition 18.** (Containment and Equivalence) Let $\mathbf{Q}_1$ and $\mathbf{Q}_2$ be any pair of PCQs, and $D$ any annotated database. We write $\mathbf{Q}_1(D) \preceq \mathbf{Q}_2(D)$, provided for every ground atom $A$ corresponding to the query predicate, $\mathbf{Q}_1(D)(A) \preceq \mathbf{Q}_2(D)(A)$, according to the lattice ordering. We say $\mathbf{Q}_1$ is contained in $\mathbf{Q}_2$, $\mathbf{Q}_1 \leq \mathbf{Q}_2$, provided for every annotated database $D$, we have $\mathbf{Q}_1(D) \preceq \mathbf{Q}_2(D)$. $\mathbf{Q}_1$ is equivalent to $\mathbf{Q}_2$, $\mathbf{Q}_1 \equiv \mathbf{Q}_2$, iff $\mathbf{Q}_1 \leq \mathbf{Q}_2$ and $\mathbf{Q}_2 \leq \mathbf{Q}_1$.

We write $f_p^1 \preceq f_p^2$, provided $\forall \alpha, \beta \in V, f_p^1(\alpha, \beta) \preceq f_p^2(\alpha, \beta)$; we write $f_c^1 \preceq f_c^2$ ($f_d^1 \preceq f_d^2$), provided for every (finite) multiset $X$ of certainty values, $f_c^1(X) \preceq f_c^2(X)$ (respectively, $f_d^1(X) \preceq f_d^2(X)$).

In order to characterize when $\mathbf{Q}_1 \leq \mathbf{Q}_2$, we need to make some reasonable assumptions on $\mathbf{Q}_1$ and $\mathbf{Q}_2$. This is formalized as follows.

**Definition 19.** Let $\mathbf{Q}_1$ and $\mathbf{Q}_2$ be any PCQs, shown below.

$\mathbf{Q}_1 : H \xleftarrow{\alpha_1} B_1, \ldots, B_k; \langle f_d^1, f_p^1, f_c^1 \rangle.$

$\mathbf{Q}_2 : H' \xleftarrow{\alpha_2} C_1, \ldots, C_m; \langle f_d^2, f_p^2, f_c^2 \rangle.$

We say that $(\mathbf{Q}_1, \mathbf{Q}_2)$ is an **admissible pair**, provided (i) $\perp \prec \alpha_1 \preceq \alpha_2$, (ii) $f_p^1 \preceq f_p^2$, (iii) $f_c^1 \preceq f_c^2$, and (iv) $f_d^1 \preceq f_d^2$. Sometimes we say that $\mathbf{Q}_1$ and $\mathbf{Q}_2$ are an admissible pair to mean that $(\mathbf{Q}_1, \mathbf{Q}_2)$ is an admissible pair.

Note that when $(\mathbf{Q}_1, \mathbf{Q}_2)$ is an admissible pair, $(\mathbf{Q}_2, \mathbf{Q}_1)$ need not be so. Also, by the above definition, any pair of PCQs with identical parameters is admissible. In the absence of such reasonable assumptions on $\mathbf{Q}_1$ and $\mathbf{Q}_2$, there may be no hope for a syntactic characterization of containment of conjunctive queries with uncertainty. By a c.m. from $\mathbf{Q}_2$ to $\mathbf{Q}_1$, we mean a c.m. from $Q_2$ to $Q_1$. The necessity of containment mapping for containment is established next.

**Lemma 20.** *Let $\mathbf{Q}_1$ and $\mathbf{Q}_2$ be any pair of admissible PCQs, shown below.*

$\mathbf{Q}_1 : H \xleftarrow{\alpha_1} B_1, \ldots, B_k; \langle f_d^1, f_p^1, f_c^1 \rangle.$

$\mathbf{Q}_2 : H' \xleftarrow{\alpha_2} C_1, \ldots, C_m; \langle f_d^2, f_p^2, f_c^2 \rangle.$

*Suppose that $\mathbf{Q}_1 \leq \mathbf{Q}_2$. Then there exists a c.m. from $\mathbf{Q}_2$ to $\mathbf{Q}_1$.*

In general, the mere existence of a containment mapping from $\mathbf{Q}_2$ to $\mathbf{Q}_1$ is *not* sufficient for $\mathbf{Q}_1 \leq \mathbf{Q}_2$. The following points explain this.

1. Intuitively, for $\mathbf{Q}_1 \leq \mathbf{Q}_2$, we need to ensure that on any input database $D$, for each derivation of a ground atom $A$ by $\mathbf{Q}_1$, there is a derivation of $A$ by $\mathbf{Q}_2$, with no less certainty. Sometimes, this is not enough. (See 3 below.)

2. When $f_c^2 \prec \otimes$, an *arbitrary* c.m. does not ensure that each derivation by $\mathbf{Q}_1$ will be matched or bettered by some derivation by $\mathbf{Q}_2$. (See Example 9 below.)

3. When the disjunction function $f_d^1 \succ \oplus$, i.e. it does not ignore duplicates, simply ensuring that each derivation by $\mathbf{Q}_1$ will be matched or bettered by some derivation by $\mathbf{Q}_2$ is *not* enough. Several derivations of the same atom by $\mathbf{Q}_1$ might be combined to beat the combined certainty of this atom computed from the derivations by $\mathbf{Q}_2$. (See Example 10 below.)

*Example 9.* To illustrate point 2 above, consider the following PCQs.

$$\mathbf{Q}_1 : p(X) \overset{1}{\longleftarrow} q(X); \qquad \langle f_d, *, f_c \rangle$$
$$\mathbf{Q}_2 : p(X) \overset{1}{\longleftarrow} q(X), q(X); \ \langle f_d, *, f_c \rangle$$

where $\mathcal{V} = [0,1]$ is the certainty lattice, $f_c \prec \otimes$, and $f_d = \oplus$. Note that in this example the corresponding parameters in $\mathbf{Q}_1$ and $\mathbf{Q}_2$ are identical. There is a c.m. from $\mathbf{Q}_2$ to $\mathbf{Q}_1$, namely the trivial one. Now, suppose $D$ is any input annotated database which contains $q(a) : \sigma$, where $\sigma$ can be any certainty in $(0,1)$. Let us take $\sigma = 0.5$. If we now evaluate these rules on $D$, we obtain $p(a)$ with certainty 0.5 from $\mathbf{Q}_1(D)$ and with certainty $\prec 0.5$ from $\mathbf{Q}_2(D)$. This is because $f_c^2(\{0.5, 0.5\}) \prec \oplus(\{0.5, 0.5\}) = 0.5$. ∎

*Example 10.* To illustrate point 3 above, consider the following pair of PCQs.

$$\mathbf{Q}_1 : p(X,Y) \overset{[0.8,0.9]}{\longleftarrow} q(X,Y), \ q(X,Z); \qquad\qquad \langle \vee_{ind}, \wedge_{pc}, \wedge_{pc} \rangle$$
$$\mathbf{Q}_2 : p(X,Y) \overset{[0,8,0.9]}{\longleftarrow} q(X,Y); \qquad\qquad\qquad\qquad \langle \vee_{ind}, \wedge_{pc}, \wedge_{pc} \rangle$$

where the parameters are as defined in Example 7. There exists a trivial c.m. from $\mathbf{Q}_2$ to $\mathbf{Q}_1$. Since $f_c^2 = \wedge_{pc} = \otimes$, this implies that each derivation of $\mathbf{Q}_1$ is matched or bettered by some derivation of $\mathbf{Q}_2$ (see below). But when $f_d^1 = \vee_{ind}$, (and hence $f_d^2 \succ \oplus$), the multiplicity of derivations matters. For instance, suppose $D = \{q(a,b) : [0.5, 0.5], q(a,c) : [0.6, 0.6]\}$ is the annotated input database. Then, there are two derivations of $p(a,b)$ by $\mathbf{Q}_1$ on $D$, corresponding to the instantiations: $X \mapsto a, Y \mapsto b, Z \mapsto b$, and $X \mapsto a, Y \mapsto b, Z \mapsto c$. The certainty associated with each of these two derivations of $p(a,b)$ is $[0.5, 0.5]$, which when combined yield $[0.75, 0.75]$. On the other hand, there is only one derivation of $p(a,b)$ by $\mathbf{Q}_2$ on $D$ and its associated certainty is $[0.5, 0.5]$. We may thus conclude that $\mathbf{Q}_1 \nleq \mathbf{Q}_2$. ∎

Our approach is thus to classify conjunctive queries based on the "behavior" of their underlying parameters, w.r.t. the above observations. Specifically, we will consider the cases where (1) the conjunction function $f_c^2$ associated with $\mathbf{Q}_2$ is $\otimes$, and (2) $f_c^2 \prec \otimes$. Under each of these cases, we distinguish between the cases in which the disjunction function $f_d^1$ associated with $\mathbf{Q}_1$ coincides with $\oplus$ and it does not. In the full paper [17], we develop precise characterization for containment under each of the various cases above. Our results yield characterizations of multiset containment of conjunctive queries when the input databases are classical (set based). (See Definitions 15 and 17). However, for lack of space, we only consider the case of lattice-theoretic conjunction and disjunction in this paper. The following result shows that in this case the existence of a containment mapping is necessary and sufficient for containment.

**Theorem 21.** *Let $\mathbf{Q}_1$ and $\mathbf{Q}_2$ be the following pair of admissible PCQs.*

$\quad \mathbf{Q}_1 : H \xleftarrow{\alpha_1} B_1, \ldots, B_k; \langle f_d^1, f_p^1, f_c^1 \rangle.$

$\quad \mathbf{Q}_2 : H' \xleftarrow{\alpha_2} C_1, \ldots, C_m; \langle f_d^2, f_p^2, f_c^2 \rangle.$

*Suppose $f_c^2 = \otimes$ and $\oplus = f_d^1$. Then, $\mathbf{Q}_1 \leq \mathbf{Q}_2$ iff there is a c.m. from $\mathbf{Q}_2$ to $\mathbf{Q}_1$.*

This characterization applies to frameworks proposed, e.g., by van Emden [27], Fitting [7, 8], and Lakshmanan and Sadri [15], to name a few. It should be pointed out that in a recent work, Lakshmanan and Sadri [18] study containment and uniform containment for deductive IST [15] and establish several results. By contrast, our results in this paper apply to various IB frameworks.

# 7   Summary and Future Research

Several frameworks for deduction with uncertainty have already been proposed, so the first question is, why yet another framework. Our work was motivated by the observation that progress on query optimization for deductive databases with uncertainty has been quite limited. We wanted to approach this problem from a "generic" point of view, without necessarily focusing on any one framework. To this end, it was necessary to abstract away the two main factors characterizing known IB frameworks for deduction with uncertainty: (i) the underlying notion of uncertainty (fuzzy sets, probabilities, etc.), (ii) the way in which uncertainty is manipulated (e.g. whether based on some lattice operations, some specific combination functions, etc.). Our choice of IB approach over AB approach was based on our belief, based on our experience with several IB frameworks, that they are in general more amenable to efficient computation. Abstraction of the two factors above has led to our parametric framework. With this as a basis, we were able to establish necessary and sufficient conditions for containment for various classes of PCQs. Two benefits of our generic approach to this study are: (i) we can trace which of the properties (see Section 5.1) on the families of functions are essential for our results on query optimization; (e.g. continuity is not a requirement); (ii) the parametric framework allows several different ways of uncertainty manipulation (e.g. some "set based" and some "multiset based") to be combined within one framework. As an illustration of the significance of our results, we showed in Section 6 that large classes of programs in known IB frameworks can be optimized using classical tools.

We are currently working on characterizing exactly when the "no teaming up" property exhibited by unions of classical conjunctive queries carries over to the parametric framework. Future work should address the central questions of containment and equivalence of programs. For instance, how can we lift the chase technique (e.g. see Sagiv [23]) to IB frameworks? Can we characterize exactly when program equivalence in IB frameworks reduces to classical equivalence? Another issue is regarding termination and data complexity. While datalog programs can be evaluated in PTIME, in the size of the input database, this is *not* always true in the presence of uncertainty. We believe the parametric framework proposed in this paper allows a systematic study of termination and data complexity properties of p-programs, at large. In [16], we report our preliminary results on this problem.

## Acknowledgments

This research was supported in part by grants from the NSERC (Canada) and FCAR (Quebec). Shiri's research was also supported by the Scholarship from the Ministry of Culture and Higher Education, Islamic Republic of Iran.

# References

1. Birkhof, Garrett. *Lattice Theory*. Providence, American Mathematical Society, 3rd edition, 1967.
2. Blair, H.A. and Subrahmanian, V.S. Paraconsistent logic programming. *Theoretical Computer Science*, 68:135–154, 1989.
3. Buchanan, B.G. and Shortliffe, E.D. A model of inexact reasoning in medicine. *Mathematical Biosciences*, 23:351–379, 1975.
4. Chandra, A.K. and Merlin, P.M. Optimal implementation of conjunctive queries in relational databases. In *Proc. 9th Annual ACM Symp. on the Theory of Computing*, pages 77–90, 1977.
5. Debray, S. and Ramakrishnan, R. Generalized Horn clause programs. manuscript, January 1994.
6. Dubois Didier, Lang Jérôme, and Prade Henri. Towards possibilistic logic programming. In *Proc. 8th Intl. Conference on Logic Programming*, pages 581–596, 1991.
7. Fitting, M.C. Logic programming on a topological bilattice. *Fundamenta Informaticae*, 11:209–218, 1988.
8. Fitting, M.C. Bilattices and the semantics of logic programming. *Journal of Logic Programming*, 11:91–116, 1991.
9. Ioannidis, Y.E. and Ramakrishnan, R. Containment of conjunctive queries: Beyond relations as sets. *ACM Transactions on Database Systems*, 20, 3:288–324, September 1995.
10. Kifer, M. and Li, A. On the semantics of rule-based expert systems with uncertainty. In M. Gyssens, J. Paradaens, and D. van Gucht, editors, *2nd Intl. Conf. on Database Theory*, pages 102–117, Bruges, Belgium, August 31-September 2 1988. Springer-Verlag LNCS-326.
11. Kifer, M. and Lozinskii, E.L. A logic for reasoning with inconsistency. In *Proc. 4th IEEE Symp. on Logic in Computer Science (LICS)*, pages 253–262, Asilomar, CA, 1989. IEEE Computer Press.

12. Kifer, Michael and Subrahmanian, V.S. Theory of generalized annotated logic programming and its applications. *Journal of Logic Programming*, 12:335–367, 1992.

13. Lakshmanan, Laks V.S. An epistemic foundation for logic programming with uncertainty. In *Proc. 14th Conf. on the Foundations of Software Technology and Theoretical Computer Science (FST and TCS'94)*. Springer-Verlag, LNCS-880, December 1994.

14. Lakshmanan, Laks V.S. and Sadri, F. Probabilistic deductive databases. In *Proc. Intl. Logic Programming Symposium*, pages 254–268, Ithaca, NY, November 1994. MIT Press.

15. Lakshmanan, Laks V.S. and Sadri, F. Modeling uncertainty in deductive databases. In *Proc. Intl. Conf. on Database Expert Systems and Applications (DEXA '94)*, Athens, Greece, September 1994. Springer-Verlag, LNCS-856.

16. Lakshmanan, Laks V.S. and Shiri, Nematollaah. On the termination and expressive power of deductive databases with uncertainty. Submitted for publication, June 1996.

17. Lakshmanan, Laks V.S. and Shiri, Nematollaah. A parametric approach to deductive databases with uncertainty. Tech. Report TR-DB-96-03, Concordia University, Montreal, Canada, March 1996.

18. Lakshmanan, L.V.S. and Sadri, F. Uncertain deductive databases: A hybrid approach, March 1996. Tech. Report TR-DB-96-02. Submitted for Publication.

19. Ng, R.T. and Subrahmanian, V.S. Relating Dempster-Shafer theory to stable semantics. Tech. Report UMIACS-TR-91-49, CS-TR-2647, Institute for Advanced Computer Studies and Department of Computer Science University of Maryland, College Park, MD 20742, April 1991.

20. Ng, R.T. and Subrahmanian, V.S. Probabilistic logic programming. *Information and Computation*, 101(2):150–201, December 1992.

21. Ng, R.T. and Subrahmanian, V.S. A semantical framework for supporting subjective and conditional probabilities in deductive databases. *Automated Reasoning*, 10(2):191–235, 1993.

22. Sadri, Fereidoon. Modeling uncertainty in databases. In *Proc. 7th IEEE Intl. Conf. on Data Eng.*, pages 122–131, April 1991.

23. Sagiv, Y. Optimizing datalog programs. In J. Minker, editor, *Foundations of Deductive Databases and Logic Programming*, pages 659–698. Morgan-Kaufmann, 1988. Extended abstract of this paper appears in Proceedings of the 1987 ACM Symposium on Principles of Database Systems, pp 237–249.

24. Shapiro, E. Logic programs with uncertainties: a tool for implementing expert systems. In *Proc. IJCAI'83*, pages 529–532. William Kauffman, 1983.

25. Subrahmanian, V.S. On the semantics of quantitative logic programs. In *Proc. 4th IEEE Symposium on Logic Programming*, pages 173–182, Computer Society Press, Washington DC, 1987.

26. Ullman, J.D. *Principles of Database and Knowledge-Base Systems*, volume II. Computer Science Press, Maryland, 1989.

27. van Emden, M.H. Quantitative deduction and its fixpoint theory. *Journal of Logic Programming*, 4(1):37–53, 1986.

28. van Emden, M.H. and Kowalski, R.A. The semantics of predicate logic as a programming language. *JACM*, 23(4):733–742, October 1976.

29. Zadeh, L.A. Fuzzy sets. *Information and Control* 8, pages 338–353, 1965.

# A Deductive Database Approach to Planning in Uncertain Environments

V. S. Subrahmanian and Charlie Ward

Department of Computer Science
and
Institute for Advanced Computer Studies
University of Maryland
College Park, Maryland 20742 U.S.A.

Abstract. We present a formal model for reasoning about probabilistic information in STRIPS-style planning. We has show that all probabilistic planning problems expressible in this model may be represented as equivalent probabilistic logic programs, yielding a sound and complete method for finding such plans.

## 1. Introduction

Over the last few years, there has been a great deal of interest in the relationship between logic programming and reasoning about actions and plans. Gelfond and Lifschitz [17] in particular, showed how we could reason about the effects of action sequences using logic programming techniques. However, Gelfond and Lifschitz's work addressed reasoning about fixed action sequences. Later, both Subrahmanian and Zaniolo [33] showed how to discover an action sequence (i.e. a plan) that accomplishes a given goal. They then showed how logic programs operating under the above semantics may then be used to solve planning problems. This approach was then extended by Brogi et. al [3] who showed how the "abstraction of a plan" problem may be extended to handle the construction of a "skeletal plan".

Recent research in AI planning systems has attempted to address the assumption that the agent constructing the plan has perfect knowledge of the world in which it operates. In practice, an agent rarely has perfect knowledge for two principle reasons. First, agents usually reason with beliefs about the world in which it is planning. Knowledge about the world is often incomplete or unreliable in many situations. Thus, there may be discrepancies between these beliefs and the actual state of the world. Second, external factors (e.g. other agents/human functioning in the same world, forces of nature, or inaccurately modeled actions and effects) may change the state of the world unbeknownst to the agent constructing the plan. The imperfection of knowledge which we encounter in most problem solving is a substantial barrier to the successful use of planning systems. For these problems because of this assumption. While solving the problem of reasoning with imperfect knowledge in its entirety is almost impossible, our aim in this paper is to take a step toward this goal of expanding the scope of AI planning systems by using logic programming/deductive database techniques.

# A Deductive Database Approach to Planning in Uncertain Environments

V.S. Subrahmanian and Charlie Ward

Department of Computer Science
and
Institute for Advanced Computer Studies
University of Maryland,
College Park, Maryland 20742, U.S.A

**Abstract.** We present a formal model for reasoning about probabilistic information in STRIPS style planning. We then show that all probabilistic planning problems expressible in this model may be represented as equivalent probabilistic logic programs, yielding a sound and complete method for finding such plans.

## 1 Introduction

Over the last few years, there has been a great deal of interest in the relationship between logic programming and reasoning about actions and plans. Gelfond and Lifschitz [11] in particular, showed how we could reason about the effects of action sequences using logic programming techniques. However, Gelfond and Lifschitz's work addressed reasoning about fixed action sequences. Later, Subrahmanian and Zaniolo [25] showed how to *discover* an action sequence (i.e. a plan) that accomplishes a given goal. They then showed how logic programs operating under the choice semantics may then be used to solve planning problems. This approach was then extended by Brogi et. al. [3] who showed how the Subrahmanian-Zaniolo approach may be extended to handle the construction of partial order plans [4].

Recent research in AI planning systems has attempted to address the assumption that the agent constructing the plan has perfect knowledge of the world in which it operates. In practice, an agent rarely has perfect knowledge for two principle reasons. First, agents usually reason with *beliefs* about the world in which it is planning. Knowledge about the world is often incomplete or unreliable in many situations. Thus, there may be discrepancies between these beliefs and the actual state of the world. Second, external factors (e.g. other agents/humans functioning in the same world, forces of nature, or inaccurately modeled actions and effects) may change the state of the world unbeknownst to the agent constructing the plan. The imperfection of knowledge which we encounter in most problem solving is a substantial barrier to the successful use of planning systems for these problems because of this assumption. While solving the problem of reasoning with imperfect knowledge in its entirety is almost impossible, our aim in this paper is to take a step toward this goal of expanding the scope of AI planning systems by using logic programming/deductive database techniques.

In particular we will allow planning agents to reason with *probabilistic data* (beliefs) about the world. We will define what it means to fire an action in such probabilistic worlds, and define what constitutes a plan in this framework. As what is true and what is false is only known with some degree of probability, plans may or may not achieve their intended goals with 100% certainty – rather, each plan achieves the desired goal with a certain probability. The planning problem then, in this situation, is the problem of finding a plan that *maximizes* the probability of accomplishing the desired goal. This constitutes the first major contribution of the paper.

Subsequently, we will show how probabilistic planning may be accomplished with the framework of probabilistic deductive databases with stable semantics as proposed by Ng and Subrahmanian [21]. In particular, we will show that given any probabilistic planning problem, we can convert it into an equivalent problem of answering a query to a probabilistic logic program under the semantics of Ng and Subrahmanian [21]. Specifically, this means that probabilistic logic programs may be used to construct probabilistic plans. This constitutes the second major contribution of this paper.

## 2 Standard STRIPS Style Planning

The syntax of STRIPS style planning is well established. We borrow the formal model presented below from Erol, Nau and Subrahmanian ([9]). This will become the foundation for our probabilistic model.

Let $\mathcal{L}$ be a first-order language with a possibly infinite number of variable symbols, finite number of predicate and constant symbols, and no function symbols. Then the Herbrand Base of $\mathcal{L}$, $B_{\mathcal{L}}$, is always finite. Throughout the following definitions, $\mathcal{L}$ always refers to a language which satisfies these properties.

**Definition 1.** A *state* is a finite set of ground atoms in $\mathcal{L}$.

**Definition 2.** An *operator*, $\alpha$, is a 4-tuple: (Name($\alpha$), Pre($\alpha$), Add($\alpha$), Del($\alpha$)), where

1. Name($\alpha$) is a syntactic expression of the form $\alpha(X_1, \ldots, X_n)$ where each $X_i$ is a variable symbol of $\mathcal{L}$;
2. Pre($\alpha$) is a finite set of literals, called the *precondition list* of $\alpha$, whose variables are all from the set $\{X_1, \ldots, X_n\}$;
3. Add($\alpha$) and Del($\alpha$) are both finite sets of atoms (possibly non-ground) whose variables are taken from the set $\{X_1, \ldots, X_n\}$. Add($\alpha$) is called the *add list* of $\alpha$, and Del($\alpha$) is called the *delete list* of $\alpha$.

Observe that negated atoms are allowed in the precondition list, but not in the add and delete lists.

**Definition 3.** A *first-order domain* (or simply a *domain*) is a pair $\mathbf{D} = (\mathbf{S_0}, \mathcal{O})$, where $\mathbf{S_0}$ is a state called the *initial state*, and $\mathcal{O}$ is a finite set of operators. The *language* of **D** is the first-order language $\mathcal{L}$ generated by the constant, predicate, and variable symbols appearing in **D**, along with an infinite number of additional variable symbols.

**Definition 4.** A *goal* is a conjunction of atoms which is existentially closed (i.e., the variables, if any, are existentially quantified).

**Definition 5.** A *planning problem* is a triple $\mathbf{P} = (\mathbf{S_0}, \mathcal{O}, \mathbf{G})$, where $(\mathbf{S_0}, \mathcal{O})$ is a domain and **G** is a goal.

**Definition 6.** Let $\mathbf{D} = (\mathbf{S_0}, \mathcal{O})$ be a domain, $\alpha$ be an operator in $\mathcal{O}$ whose name is $\alpha(\mathbf{X_1}, \ldots, \mathbf{X_n})$, and $\theta$ be a substitution that assigns ground terms to each $X_i$, $1 \le i \le n$. Suppose that the following conditions hold for states **S** and **S'**:

$$\{A\theta \mid A \text{ is an atom in } \mathrm{Pre}(\alpha)\} \subseteq \mathbf{S};$$
$$\{B\theta \mid \neg B \text{ is a negated literal in } \mathrm{Pre}(\alpha)\} \cap \mathbf{S} = \emptyset;$$
$$\mathbf{S'} = (\mathbf{S} - \mathrm{Del}(\alpha)\theta) \cup \mathrm{Add}(\alpha)\theta.$$

Then we say that $\alpha$ is $\theta$-*executable* in state **S** *resulting* in state **S'**. This is denoted symbolically as

$$\mathbf{S} \overset{\alpha, \theta}{\Longrightarrow} \mathbf{S'}.$$

**Definition 7.** Suppose $\mathbf{D} = (\mathbf{S_0}, \mathcal{O})$ is a domain and **G** is a goal. A *plan that achieves* **G** is a sequence $\mathbf{S_0}, \ldots, \mathbf{S_n}$ of states, a sequence $\alpha_1, \ldots, \alpha_n$ of operators, and a sequence $\theta_1, \ldots, \theta_n$ of substitutions such that:

$$\mathbf{S_0} \overset{\alpha_1, \theta_1}{\Longrightarrow} \mathbf{S_1} \overset{\alpha_2, \theta_2}{\Longrightarrow} \mathbf{S_2} \cdots \overset{\alpha_n, \theta_n}{\Longrightarrow} \mathbf{S_n} \tag{1}$$

and **G** is satisfied by $\mathbf{S_n}$, i.e. there exists a ground instance of **G** that is true in $\mathbf{S_n}$. We often say that (1) above is a plan of *length* $n$ that achieves **G**.

## 3 STRIPS Style Planning With Uncertainty

The STRIPS based planning model introduced thus far assumes that the planning agent has complete, correct knowledge of the initial state of the world. However, such an assumption is valid only in a restricted number of real world domains. More typically, the planner has definite knowledge of *some parts* of the initial state and only uncertain knowledge of the other parts of the initial state. We plan to use the concepts of planning state, operator, goal and $\theta$-executable to facilitate the construction of plans by planning agents having incomplete, imperfect information about the world. Thus, we begin by augmenting the definition of a state to incorporate probabilities.

**Definition 8.** If $A$ is an atom (not necessarily ground) in $\mathcal{L}$ and $\mu = [d_1, d_2]$ where $[d_1, d_2] \subseteq [0, 1]$, then $A : \mu$ is an *annotated atom*. $\mu$ is called the *annotation* of $A$ and represents the probability that $A$ is true.

Annotated atoms represent probability as a range of values: for $\mu$ above, $d_1$ is the minimum probability and $d_2$ is the maximum probability. The reason for defining probabilities of atoms in terms of a range of values is explained below. Note that this notation can be used to express single valued probabilities by letting $\mu = [d_1, d_1]$. Also notice that an annotated atom may express classical negation by setting $\mu = [0, 0]$. In general, the annotated atom, $A : [d_1, d_2]$, may be read as "the probability that $A$ is true lies in the range $[d_1, d_2]$."

**Definition 9.** A *p-state*, **S**, is a pair of sets $(U, C)$ where $U$ is a finite set of ground annotated atoms in $\mathcal{L}$ and $C$ is a finite set of ground atoms in $\mathcal{L}$ such that :

$$\forall i \neq j, A_i : \mu_i, A_j : \mu_j \in U \Rightarrow A_i \neq A_j$$
$$\{A \mid A : \mu \in U\} \cap C = \emptyset$$

We say that $U$ is the set of *uncertain* annotated atoms and that $C$ is the set of *certain* atoms of **S**. Furthermore, if $U$ is a set of annotated atoms, we will use $AT(U)$ to denote the set $\{A \mid \exists A : \mu \in U\}$.

Intuitively, in a p-state, $(U, C)$, $C$ represents a set of atoms (without annotations) that are *definitely known to be true* – in other words, the planning agent knows for sure that the atoms in $C$ are true. $U$ is a set of *annotated atoms* distinct from those in $C$. The atoms in $U$ are those about which the planning agent has probabilistic information. Note that technically it is possible to replace the pair $(U, C)$ by the equivalent pair $(U', \emptyset)$ where

$$U' = U \cup \{A : [1, 1] \mid A \in C\}.$$

However, from the point of view of *manipulating* p-states computationally (at the implementation level), it is convenient and useful to represent this as two distinct sets. We will return to this point later.

*Example 1.* The following example will be extended/modified throughout this paper. Suppose we wish to create a p-state representation of a world in which there are two rooms, the living room and the kitchen. In this world, our agent (a robot) is currently in the living room which contains a couch, television and lamp. The kitchen contains a refrigerator, counter, sandwich and lamp. The agent is certain about everything in the world except whether the lamp in the kitchen is on or off, and whether the sandwich is in the refrigerator or on the counter. One possible representation for this world is the following:

$U = \{$ on(lamp2) : $[0.5, 0.75]$,

   location(sandwich, refrigerator) : $[0.2, 0.4]$,

   location(sandwich, counter) : $[0.6, 0.8]$ $\}$

$C = \{$ location(couch, living-room),

   location(television, living-room), location(lamp1, living-room),

> on(television), on(lamp1), location(refrigerator, kitchen),
> location(counter, kitchen), location(lamp2, kitchen),
> location(agent, living-room) }

In this probabilistic model, we define *p-operators* and *p-goals* exactly as we did in the non-probabilistic model. *P-domains* and *p-problems* are also similarly defined except for the use of probabilistic p-states instead of standard states.

Suppose a planning agent is given a p-state, $(U, C)$, describing the world and wants to attempt to evaluate the effects of executing a operator, $\alpha$, in this p-state. The agent must first determine if the operator's pre-conditions are satisfied in the state. However, a p-state merely asserts the probabilities of ground atoms. This is the point at which we must clearly draw the distinction between plan generation and plan execution. At any given point in time during plan execution, an operator's pre-conditions can be tested with full certainty to determine whether or not it is executable. Conversely, during plan generation, an agent has uncertain knowledge about the world – the agent does not necessarily know which facts are absolutely true or false. Thus, given a p-state, it must assess the probability of being able to execute an operator $\alpha$ in that p-state, by evaluating the probability of the precondition, $Pre(\alpha)$, being true in the given p-state. To do this, we need to have the ability to associate a probability (range) with a conjunction of literals (i.e. the pre-conditions of the operator), given the individual probabilities of the atoms participating in the conjunction (i.e the annotations of the atoms in the p-state).

It is known from probability theory that it is not possible to precisely specify the probabilities of even simple formulas for atoms such as $(A \wedge B)$ when we do not know the nature of the dependencies between $A$ and $B$. However, it is still possible to precisely specify the *range* in which the probability of a formula must lie by using a system of linear constraints. For example, consider the probability of the formulas $(A \wedge B)$ and $(A \vee B)$ given the probabilities for $A \in [c_1, d_1]$ and $B \in [c_2, d_2]$. There are four possible "worlds" which could describe these two atoms:

1. $W_1$ : both $A$ and $B$ are true
2. $W_2$ : only $A$ is true
3. $W_3$ : only $B$ is true
4. $W_4$ : neither $A$ nor $B$ are true

Let $w_i$ represent the probability that world $W_i$ is the actual world. Then, we have the following set of linear constraints:

$$0 \leq c_1 \leq w_1 + w_2 \leq d_1 \leq 1,$$
$$0 \leq c_2 \leq w_1 + w_3 \leq d_2 \leq 1,$$
$$\sum_{j=1}^{4} w_j = 1,$$
$$w_1, \ldots, w_4 \geq 0.$$

¿From these constraints, we can calculate (as shown in [26, 20, 21]) the following :

$$\mathbf{min\ w_1} = \max(0, c_1 + c_2 - 1)$$
$$\mathbf{max\ w_1} = \min(d_1, d_2)$$
$$\mathbf{min\ (w_1 + w_2 + w_3)} = \max(c_1, c_2)$$
$$\mathbf{max\ (w_1 + w_2 + w_3)} = \min(1, d_1 + d_2)$$

Thus, the probability of $(A \wedge B) = w_1 = [\max(0, c_1 + c_2 - 1), \min(d_1, d_2)]$ and $(A \vee B) = (w_1 + w_2 + w_3) = [\max(c_1, c_2), \min(1, d_1 + d_2)]$. In general, we may recursively apply these calculations to determine a probability range for any conjunction or disjunction of annotated atoms:

**Definition 10.** Let $\mu_1 = [c_1, d_1]$ and $\mu_2 = [c_2, d_2]$ be annotations. Define:

$$\mu_1 \otimes \mu_2 = [\max(0, c_1 + c_2 - 1), \min(d_1, d_2)]$$
$$\mu_1 \oplus \mu_2 = [\max(c_1, c_2), \min(1, d_1 + d_2)]$$

*Example 2.* Borrowing from the previous example (1), let

$$A : \mu_a = \text{on(lamp2)} : [0.5, 0.75]$$
$$B : \mu_b = \text{location(sandwich, refrigerator)} : [0.2, 0.4]$$
$$C : \mu_c = \text{location(sandwich, counter)} : [0.6, 0.8].$$

We can calculate the probabilities of the following:

$$A \wedge B = \mu_a \otimes \mu_b = [0.0, 0.75]$$
$$A \wedge C = \mu_a \otimes \mu_c = [0.1, 0.8]$$
$$B \vee C = \mu_b \oplus \mu_c = [0.6, 1]$$

**Definition 11.** The *worlds representation* of a p-state, $\mathbf{S} = (\mathbf{U}, \mathbf{C})$, in $\mathcal{L}$ is a triple $(W, P, C)$, where $W = 2^{AT(U)}$ and $P$ is a function which assigns probability ranges to each member of $W$. $W$ and $P$ satisfy the following property:

if $W_i = \{A_1, A_2, \ldots, A_n\}$ then $P(W_i') = \bigotimes_{j=1}^{n} \{\mu_j \mid A_j : \mu_j \in U\}$.

Often, it will be notationally convenient to refer to the set $w = \{w_i \mid w_i = P(W_i)\}$ of probabilities for $W$. It is also important to note that each member of $W$ is a non-probabilistic state.

*Example 3.* Applying the above definitions to our example gives the following worlds representation:

$$W_1 = \{\text{on(lamp2)}, \text{location(sandwich, refrigerator)},$$
$$\text{location(sandwich, counter)}\}$$
$$W_2 = \{\text{on(lamp2)}, \text{location(sandwich, refrigerator)}\}$$
$$W_3 = \{\text{on(lamp2)}, \text{location(sandwich, counter)}\}$$

$W_4 = \{\text{on(lamp2)}\}$

$W_5 = \{\text{location(sandwich, refrigerator), location(sandwich, counter)}\}$

$W_6 = \{\text{location(sandwich, refrigerator)}\}$

$W_7 = \{\text{location(sandwich, counter)}\}$

$P(W_1) = [0.0, 0.4]$

$P(W_2) = [0.0, 0.75]$

$P(W_3) = [0.0, 0.8]$

$P(W_4) = [0.5, 0.75]$

$P(W_5) = [0.0, 0.8]$

$P(W_6) = [0.2, 0.4]$

$P(W_7) = [0.6, 0.8]$

$C = \{\text{location(couch, living-room)},$
$\text{location(television, living-room), location(lamp1, living-room)},$
$\text{on(television), on(lamp1), location(refrigerator, kitchen)},$
$\text{location(counter, kitchen), location(lamp2, kitchen)},$
$\text{location(agent, living-room)}\}$

Now we are prepared to create an analogue to the definition of $\theta$-executable to show how we apply an operator to a given p-state in the probabilistic model:

**Definition 12.** Let $(W, P, C)$ be the world representation of p-state $\mathbf{S} = (\mathbf{U}, \mathbf{C})$ and let $\alpha$ be a p-operator. $\alpha$ is *probabilistically $\theta$-executable* in $\mathbf{S}$ if and only if $\exists W_i \in W$ such that $\alpha$ is $\theta$-executable in $W_i \cup C$.

**Definition 13.** Let $\alpha$ be probabilistically $\theta$-executable in the worlds representation, $(W, P, C)$, of the p-state $S = (U, C)$. Let

$$W_{\text{unmapped}} = \{W_i \mid \alpha \text{ is NOT } \theta\text{-executable in } \mathbf{W_i}\}$$
$$W_{\text{mapped}} = \{W_i \mid \alpha \text{ is } \theta\text{-executable in } \mathbf{W_i}\}$$

Then *applying* $\alpha$ to the worlds representation of $S$ *results* in a new p-state $S'$ having the world representation, $(W', P', C')$ where:

$$W'_{\text{unmapped}} = W_{\text{unmapped}}$$
$$W'_{\text{mapped}} = \{W'_j \mid W_i \in W_{\text{mapped}} \text{ and } W_i \overset{\alpha,\theta}{\Longrightarrow} W'_j\}$$
$$W^* = W'_{\text{unmapped}} \cup W'_{\text{mapped}}$$
$$C' = \bigcap_{j=1}^{|W^*|} W_j^*$$
$$W' = \{W_j^* - C \mid W_j^* \in W^*\}$$
$$P'(W'_j) = \bigoplus\{P(W_i) \mid (W_i \in W_{\text{unmapped}} \text{ and } W_i = W'_j) \text{ or } W_i \overset{\alpha,\theta}{\Longrightarrow} W'_j\}$$

This is denoted symbolically as

$$S \overset{\alpha,\theta}{\hookrightarrow} S'.$$

*Example 4.* Let operator 'move' be the following:

1. Name(move) = move(X, SRC-LOC, DST-LOC);
2. Pre(move) = location(X, SRC-LOC) ;
3. Add(move) = location(X, DST-LOC) ;
4. Del(move) = location(X, SRC-LOC) .

Then applying move (substituting sandwich for X, refrigerator for SRC-LOC, and counter for DST-LOC) to the worlds representation of example 3 results in the following worlds representation:

$$W_1' = \{\text{on(lamp2), location(sandwich, counter)}\}$$
$$W_2' = \{\text{on(lamp2)}\}$$
$$W_3' = \{\text{location(sandwich, counter)}\}$$

$$P'(W_1') = [0.0, 1.0]$$
$$P'(W_2') = [0.5, 0.75]$$
$$P'(W_3') = [0.6, 1.0]$$

$$C' = \{\text{ location(couch, living-room),}$$
$$\text{location(television, living-room),}$$
$$\text{location(lamp1, living-room),}$$
$$\text{on(television), on(lamp1), location(refrigerator, kitchen),}$$
$$\text{location(counter, kitchen), location(lamp2, kitchen),}$$
$$\text{location(agent, living-room)}\}$$

Notice that from the original worlds representation, worlds $W_1$, $W_2$ and $W_3$ have collapsed into a single new world, $W_1'$. Likewise, worlds $W_5$, $W_6$, and $W_7$ have collapsed into the new world, $W_3'$. Their new probability distributions are:

$$P'(W_1') = \bigoplus\{P(W_1), P(W_2), P(W_3)\}$$
$$P'(W'_2) = \bigoplus\{P(W_4)\}$$
$$P'(W_3') = \bigoplus\{P(W_5), P(W_6), P(W_7)\}$$

**Definition 14.** Suppose $(W_0, P_0, C_0)$ is the worlds representation of a probabilistic (initial) state $S_0$, $\mathcal{O}$ is a set of planning operators, and **G** is a goal. A *probabilistic action sequence* is a sequence $\mathcal{P} =$

$$S_0 \overset{\alpha_1,\theta_1}{\hookrightarrow} S_1 \overset{\alpha_2,\theta_2}{\hookrightarrow} S_2 \cdots \overset{\alpha_n,\theta_n}{\hookrightarrow} S_n.$$

where $(W_i, P_i, C_i)$ is the worlds representation of $S_i$. The *probability that $\mathcal{P}$ achieves goal $G$* is given by

$$\bigoplus \{P_n(w_i) \mid (w_i \cup C_n) \text{ satisfies } G \,\&\, w_i \in W_n\}.$$

Given two real valued intervals $\mu = [d_1, d_2]$ and $\mu' = [d_1', d_2']$, we say that $\mu \gg \mu'$ iff $d_1 \geq d_1'$ and $d_2 \geq d_2'$.

In probabilistic planning, we are interested in finding a probabilistic action sequence $\mathcal{P}$ such that for all other planning sequences $\mathcal{P}'$, if the probability that $\mathcal{P}$ (resp. $\mathcal{P}'$) achieves $G$ is $\mu$ (resp. $\mu'$), then $\mu \gg \mu'$.

*Example 5.* If the robot were given the goal to make the location of the sandwich the counter, and generated the single step plan consisting of move(sandwich, refrigerator, counter) the probability that this plan would succeed is:
$$\bigoplus \{P'(W_1'), P'(W_3')\} = [0.6, 1.0].$$

## 4 From Probabilistic Planning to Probabilistic Logic Programming

In [20], Ng and Subrahmanian have proposed the notion of a probabilistic logic program. Subsequently, in [21], they extended this framework to handle non-monotonic modes of negation including both stable models of probabilistic logic programs as well as well founded semantics of such programs. In this section, we will show that all probabilistic planning problems may be uniformly translated into probabilistic logic programs. In particular, a probabilistic goal is achievable iff that goal is entailed by the associated probabilistic logic program.

The relationship between AI planning problems, and logic programming, has been extensively studied [11, 22]. However, most translations used the situation calculus. In contrast, Subrahmanian and Zaniolo [25] showed that AI planning problems can be captured within $\text{Datalog}_{1,s}$ which is a much more restrictive syntax than the situation calculus. Furthermore, very efficient algorithms to process $\text{Datalog}_{1,s}$ query processing problems have been developed [5]. The results in this section generalize those of Subrahmanian and Zaniolo [25]. First, we recall some definitions from Ng and Subrahmanian [20].

Ng and Subrahmanian [21] introduce the notion of an *annotation variable* – these variables range over $[0, 1]$. An *annotation function* of arity $n$ is a map from $[0, 1]^n$ to $[0, 1]$. An *annotation item* is inductively defined as follows:

- Each member of $[0, 1]$ is an annotation item.
- Each annotation variable is an annotation item.
- If $f$ is an $n$-ary annotation function, and $i_1, \ldots, i_n$ are annotation items, then $f(i_1, \ldots, i_n)$ is an annotation item.

If $A$ is an atom, and $ai_1, ai_2$ are annotation items, then $A : [ai_1, ai_2]$ are called *annotated items*. $[ai_1, ai_2]$ is called an *annotation*.

For instance, if $V$ is a variable ranging over $[0, 1]$, then an annotated atom of the form $A : [V, \frac{V+1}{2}]$ says that the probability of $A$ lies between $V$ and $\frac{V+1}{2}$. An annotated rule of the form $A : [\max(0, (V - 0.002)), \min(1, (V + 0.002))] \leftarrow B : [V, V]$ says that if the probability of $B$ is known to be $V$, then the probability of $A$ lies in the interval $[(V - 0.002), (V + 0.002)]$ (as long as both these expressions lie within $0, 1$).

**Definition 15.** If $A_1, \ldots, A_n, B_1, \ldots, B_m$ are atoms, then

$$(A_1 \& \ldots \& A_n \& \neg B_1 \& \ldots \& \neg B_m)$$

is called a *c-basic formula*[1].

If $F$ is a basic formula and $[d, e]$ is an annotation, then $F : [d, e]$ is an *annotated basic formula*.

Suppose $A_1, A_2$ are atoms and we know that $A_1$'s probability lies in the $[d_1, e_1]$ interval, while $A_2$'s probability lies in the $[d_2, e_2]$ interval. Then we can say that

1. $(A_1 \& A_2)$'s probability lies in the interval $[d_1, e_1] \otimes [d_2, e_2]$ and
2. $\neg A_1$'s probability lies in the interval $[1 - e_1, 1 - d_1]$.

Thus, if we have atom $A_1, \ldots, A_n, B_1, \ldots, B_m$ and we know the probability ranges of each of these atoms, then we can easily compute the probability range associated with the c-basic formula $(A_1 \& \ldots \& A_n \& \neg B_1 \& \ldots \& \neg B_m)$.

**Definition 16.** If $A_0 : [d_0, e_0]$ is an annotated atom, and $F_1 : [d_1, e_1], \ldots, F_n : [d_n, e_n]$, $G_1 : [v_1, w_1], \ldots, G_k : [v_k, w_k]$ are annotated basic formulas, then

$$A_0 : [d_0, e_0] \leftarrow F_1 : [d_1, e_1] \& \ldots \& F_n : [d_n, e_n] \&$$
$$NOT(G_1 : [v_1, w_1]) \& \ldots \& NOT(G_k : [v_k, w_k])$$

is called a *probabilistic clause*. All variables are universally quantified at the front of the clause. A *probabilistic logic program* is a finite set of probabilistic clauses.

It is important to note that in the above definition, the symbol $NOT$ is not the same as the symbol $\neg$ introduced earlier. The symbol $\neg$ is applied only to (un-annotated atoms), while the symbol $NOT$ is applied to annotated atoms/c-basic formulas. Intuitively, $NOT(G_i : [v_i, w_i])$ may be read as "It is not possible to prove that $G_i$'s probability lies in the interval $[v_i, w_i]$. Ng and Subrahmanian [21] have developed an extension of the stable model semantics and the well founded semantics to probabilistic logic programs of the above type.

Suppose $S_0 = (U, C)$ is a p-state, and $\mathcal{O}$ is a set of planning operators. We create a *probabilistic logic program*, $\mathcal{PLOP}(S_t, \mathcal{O})$ as follows:

---

[1] Basic formulas as defined in Ng and Subrahmanian [21] are somewhat broader and allow disjunctions as well. In this paper, the disjunctions are not necessary.

**(Step 1)** For each atom $p(t_1, \ldots, t_n) : [d, e] \in S_0$, the rule

$$p(t_1, \ldots, t_n, 0) : [d, e] \qquad \leftarrow$$

is in $\mathcal{PLOP}(S_\prime, \mathcal{O})$.

**(Step 2)** If $\alpha$ is an operator in $\mathcal{O}$, then for each atom $p(\mathbf{t_0}) \in \mathrm{Add}(\alpha)$ we have the rule

$$\mathrm{Add}(p_0(\mathbf{t_0}), \mathrm{J} + 1) : [V_1, V_2] \quad \leftarrow (p_1(\mathbf{t_1}, J) \,\&\, \ldots \,\&\, p_n(\mathbf{t_n}, J) \,\& $$
$$\neg q_1(\mathbf{s_1}, J) \,\&\, \ldots \,\& $$
$$\neg q_m(\mathbf{s_m}, J)) : [V_1, V_2] \,\& $$
$$fired(J, Name(\alpha(\mathbf{X}))) : [1, 1].$$

where $\mathrm{Pre}(\alpha) = \{p_1(\mathbf{t_1}), \ldots, p_n(\mathbf{t_n}), \neg q_1(\mathbf{s_1}), \ldots, \neg q_m(\mathbf{s_m})\}$.
Similarly, if $p(\mathbf{t_0}) \in \mathrm{Del}(\alpha)$ we have the rule

$$\mathrm{Del}(p_0(\mathbf{t_0}), \mathrm{J} + 1) : [V_1, V_2] \quad \leftarrow (p_1(\mathbf{t_1}, J) \&\, \ldots \,\& p_n(\mathbf{t_n}, J) \,\& $$
$$\neg q_1(\mathbf{s_1}, J) \,\&\, \ldots \,\& $$
$$\neg q_m(\mathbf{s_m}, J)) : [V_1, V_2] \,\& $$
$$fired(J, Name(\alpha(\mathbf{X}))) : [1, 1].$$

**(Step 3)** For each predicate symbol $p$, we have the rules

$$p(\mathbf{X}, J) : [V1, V2] \qquad \leftarrow \mathrm{Add}(p(\mathbf{X}), J) : [V1, V2].$$
$$p(\mathbf{X}, J) : [V1, V2] \qquad \leftarrow p(\mathbf{X}, J) : [V1, V2] \,\& $$
$$\mathrm{Del}(p(\mathbf{X}), J) : [0, 0].$$

**(Step 4)** If $\alpha$ is an operator in $\mathcal{O}$, then $\mathcal{PLOP}(S_\prime, \mathcal{O})$ contains the rules

$$firable(J, Name(\alpha)) : [1, 1] \quad \leftarrow (p_1(\mathbf{t_1}, J) \,\&\, \ldots \,\& p_n(\mathbf{t_n}, J) \,\& $$
$$\neg q_1(\mathbf{s_1}, J) \,\&\, \ldots \,\& $$
$$\neg q_m(\mathbf{s_m}, J)) : [V_1, V_2] \,\& V_1 > 0.$$
$$fired(J, Name(\alpha)) : [1, 1] \quad \leftarrow firable(J, Name(\alpha)) : [1, 1] \,\& $$
$$chosen(J, Name(\alpha)) : [1, 1].$$
$$chosen(J, Name(\alpha)) : [1, 1] \quad \leftarrow firable(J, Name(\alpha)) : [1, 1] \,\& $$
$$NOT(diffchoice(J, Name(\alpha)) : [1, 1]).$$
$$diffchoice(J, Name(\alpha)) : [1, 1] \leftarrow chosen(J, Name(\alpha_1)) : [1, 1] \,\& $$
$$Name(\alpha) \neq Name(\alpha_1).$$

where $\mathrm{Pre}(\alpha) = \{p_1(\mathbf{t_1}), \ldots, p_n(\mathbf{t_n}), \neg q_1(\mathbf{s_1}), \ldots, \neg q_m(\mathbf{s_m})\}$.

*Example 6.* Let operator turn-off be the following:

1. Name(turn-off) = turn-off(X);

2. Pre(turn-off) = on(X) ;
3. Add(turn-off) = off(X) ;
4. Del(turn-off) = on(X) .

Also, let operator turn-on be similarly defined. The probabilistic logic program representation of our example 3 augmented with these two operators is as follows (note: turn-on(X), is used for the purposes of demonstrating the *diffchoice* rule – i.e. the rules in steps 2 and 3 are not applied to turn-on(X)):

$$on(lamp2) : [0.5, 0.75] \leftarrow$$
$$location(sandwich, refrigerator) : [0.2, 0.4] \leftarrow$$
$$location(sandwich, counter) : [0.6, 0.8] \leftarrow$$
$$location(couch, living\text{-}room) : [1, 1] \leftarrow$$
$$location(television, living\text{-}room) : [1, 1] \leftarrow$$
$$location(lamp1, living\text{-}room) : [1, 1] \leftarrow$$
$$on(television) : [1, 1] \leftarrow$$
$$on(lamp1) : [1, 1] \leftarrow$$
$$location(refrigerator, kitchen) : [1, 1] \leftarrow$$
$$location(counter, kitchen) : [1, 1] \leftarrow$$
$$location(lamp2, kitchen) : [1, 1] \leftarrow$$
$$location(agent, living\text{-}room) : [1, 1] \leftarrow$$

$$Add(off(t_0), J+1) : [V_1, V_2] \leftarrow on(t_0, J) : [V_1, V_2] \,\&$$
$$fired(J, turn\text{-}off(\mathbf{X})) : [1, 1]$$
$$Del(on(t_0), J+1) : [V_1, V_2] \leftarrow off(t_0, J) : [V_1, V_2] \,\&$$
$$fired(J, turn\text{-}off(\mathbf{X})) : [1, 1]$$

$$on(\mathbf{X}, J) : [V_1, V_2] \leftarrow Add(on(\mathbf{X}), J) : [V_1, V_2]$$
$$off(\mathbf{X}, J) : [V_1, V_2] \leftarrow Add(off(\mathbf{X}), J) : [V_1, V_2]$$
$$location(\mathbf{X}_1, \mathbf{X}_2, J) : [V_1, V_2] \leftarrow Add(location(\mathbf{X}_1, \mathbf{X}_2), J) : [V_1, V_2]$$
$$on(\mathbf{X}, J) : [V_1, V_2] \leftarrow on(\mathbf{X}, J) : [V_1, V_2] \,\&$$
$$Del(on(\mathbf{X}), J) : [0, 0]$$
$$off(\mathbf{X}, J) : [V_1, V_2] \leftarrow off(\mathbf{X}, J) : [V_1, V_2] \,\&$$
$$Del(off(\mathbf{X}), J) : [0, 0]$$
$$location(\mathbf{X}_1, \mathbf{X}_2, J) : [V_1, V_2] \leftarrow location(\mathbf{X}_1, \mathbf{X}_2, J) : [V_1, V_2] \,\&$$
$$Del(location(\mathbf{X}_1, \mathbf{X}_2), J) : [0, 0]$$

$$firable(J, turn\text{-}off) : [1, 1] \leftarrow on(t_1, J) : [V_1, V_2] \,\& \, V_1 > 0$$

$$fired(J, \text{turn-off}) : [1,1] \leftarrow firable(J, \text{turn-off}) : [1,1] \,\&$$
$$chosen(J, \text{turn-off}) : [1,1]$$
$$chosen(J, \text{turn-off}) : [1,1] \leftarrow firable(J, \text{turn-off}) : [1,1] \,\&$$
$$NOT(diffchoice(J, \text{turn-off}) : [1,1])$$
$$diffchoice(J, \text{turn-off}) : [1,1] \leftarrow chosen(J, \text{turn-on}) : [1,1] \,\&$$
$$\text{turn-off}(\mathbf{X_1}) \neq \text{turn-on}(\mathbf{X_2})$$

It is easy to see that $\mathcal{PLOP}(\mathcal{S}_I, \mathcal{O})$ is a probabilistic logic program in the sense of Ng and Subrahmanian [21] and hence, it has a well defined stable model semantics. Due to space restrictions, we cannot recapitulate the stable model semantics of [21] here – the reader is referred to [21] for a detailed overview. The following result shows that probabilistic planning is neatly captured by the probabilistic logic program, $\mathcal{PLOP}(\mathcal{S}_I, \mathcal{O})$.

If $A = p(\mathbf{t})$ is an atom, then we use $A^\star$ to denote the atom $p(\mathbf{t}, J)$. Suppose $G = (A_1 \& \ldots \& A_m)$ is a goal. Then we use the notation $G^\star$ to denote the goal

$$(\exists J)(A_1^\star \& \ldots \& A_m^\star).$$

**Theorem 17.** *Suppose $(S_0, \mathcal{O})$ is a probabilistic planning domain, $G$ is a goal, and $0 \leq r \leq 1$ is a real number. Then:*

1. *If*

$$S_0 \overset{\alpha_1, \theta_1}{\hookrightarrow} S_1 \overset{\alpha_2, \theta_2}{\hookrightarrow} S_2 \cdots \overset{\alpha_n, \theta_n}{\hookrightarrow} S_n.$$

   *is a probabilistic plan that achieves goal $G$ with probability greater than or equal to $r$, then there exists a stable model $M$ of $\mathcal{PLOP}(\mathcal{S}_I, \mathcal{O})$ such that:*
   (a) *$M$ satisfies $G^\star : [r,1]$ and*
   (b) *The atoms $fired(\alpha_1, 0) : [1,1]$, $\mathbf{fired}(\alpha_2, 1) : [1,1]$, $\ldots$, $\mathbf{fired}(\alpha_n, (n-1)) : [1,1]$ are all true in $M$.*

2. *If $M$ is a stable model of $\mathcal{PLOP}(\mathcal{S}_I, \mathcal{O})$ such that $M$ satisfies $G^\star : [r,1]$ and the atoms $fired(\alpha_1, 0) : [1,1]$, $\mathbf{fired}(\alpha_2, 1) : [1,1]$, $\ldots$, $\mathbf{fired}(\alpha_n, (n-1)) : [1,1]$ are all true in $M$, then*

$$S_0 \overset{\alpha_1, \theta_1}{\hookrightarrow} S_1 \overset{\alpha_2, \theta_2}{\hookrightarrow} S_2 \cdots \overset{\alpha_n, \theta_n}{\hookrightarrow} S_n$$

   *is a probabilistic plan that achieves goal $G$ with probability greater than or equal to $r$.*

This is the most important result of this paper. In effect it says that probabilistic plans may be constructed in a sound and complete manner using probabilistic logic programs in the following way:

1. Given any probabilistic planning domain $(S_0, \mathcal{O})$, construct the probabilistic logic program $\mathcal{PLOP}(\mathcal{S}_I, \mathcal{O})$. This is a one-time step that can be accomplished in time linear in the size of $(S_0, \mathcal{O})$.

2. Whenever a goal $G$ and a threshold $r$ is presented, i.e. the user wants to find a plan that achieves goal $G$ with probability $r$ or more, try to find out if there is a stable model $M$ of $\mathcal{PLOP}(\mathcal{S}_I, \mathcal{O})$ in which the goal $G^* : [r, 1]$ is true. If so, then the set of $fired(-, -)$ atoms in $M$ constitutes a plan that achieves the desired goal. Otherwise, no such plan exists.

# 5  Related Work

Kiessling and his group [13, 23] have developed a framework called DUCK for reasoning with uncertainty in databases. This is an elegant framework which differs from that of Ng and Subrahmanian [20, 21] in that the latter assumes that we are completely ignorant about the relationship between events , while the former assumes independence of events. Lakshmanan and Sadri [18] have proposed a different foundation for probabilistic deductive databases. In principle, in every proposal for (probabilistic) deductive databases, there is an inherent (probabilistic) relational algebra underlying it, and it is interesting to compare such algebras with our proposal here. The main point is that Kiessling's proposals [13, 23] assume a fixed strategy (such as independence), as does Ng and Subrahmanian's [20, 21] (ignorance). The proposal in [18] supports a few explicitly stated strategies. Probabilistic databases with independence assumptions have also been studied by Cavallo and Pittarelli [6] and Barbara et al. [1].

In contrast, this paper first develops the notion of planning in probabilistic domains and subsequently shows how probabilistic planning may be captured within the framework of probabilistic logic programming.

Other authors, such as Kifer et. al. [14, 7] develop a *fuzzy* logic based approach to handling uncertainties. As probability theory is the best known way of reasoning with uncertainty and chance, and as the differences between fuzzy logic and probability theory are very well known, we do not address this work here. These works do not deal with planning.

In the planning literature, Kushmerick et. al. [16] study the problem of reasoning in uncertain domains. [16] develops a notion of planning with uncertainty where the probabilities of atoms are known precisely and then makes independence assumptions to assess the probabilities of conjuncts. Our probabilistic planning framework improves upon the work of Kushmerick et. al. by (1) removing the independence assumption, and (2) allowing atoms to have probability ranges rather than point probabilities – this is particularly useful in, for instance, reasoning about sensor data where a sensor could report that a sighted object is a Red Cross vehicle with, say, 65% certainty – but the certainty must be modified to account for sensor error $e$, thus leading to an interval probability $[0.65 - e, 0.65 + e]$. In addition, we have shown how our probabilistic plans may be realized through logic programming techniques, thus potentially bringing to bear, the entire body of work on query optimization to the AI planning arena.

# 6 Conclusions

Though AI planning has a long history, there has been relatively little work in the area of planning in the presence of uncertainty. Formal approaches to this problem have only just started to emerge [16], following upon rigorous formalizations of planning in certain domains [9].

In this paper, we have first presented a formal declarative semantics for planning in the presence of uncertain knowledge of the world. In particular, our definition of a p-state captures the "certain" knowledge of the world, as well as the "uncertain" knowledge that the planning agent has about the world. Based on this notion of a p-state, we have specified how actions affect or transform a p-state into a new p-state. A plan is a sequence of actions each of which are firable in their corresponding p-states with non-zero probability. Associated with any plan is a probability that the plan accomplishes the goal. We have then formally defined the planning problem in terms of maximizing this probability.

Subsequently, we have shown how planning problems of this kind may be neatly captured as probabilistic logic programs [20, 21] – this result implies that any algorithm for processing queries to probabilistic logic programs may be used to compute probabilistic plans in a sound and complete manner.

## Acknowledgements

Ward's work was supported in part by NSF grant IRI-9314905, and by ARO grant DAAH-04-G-0337. Subrahmanian's work was supported by the Army Research Office under grant DAAH-04-95-10174, by the Air Force Office of Scientific Research under grant F49620-93-1-0065, by ARPA/Rome Labs contract Nr. F30602-93-C-0241 (Order Nr. A716), and by an NSF Young Investigator award IRI-93-57756.

## References

1. D. Barbara, H. Garcia-Molina and D. Porter. (1991) *A Probabilistic Relational Data Model*, IEEE Trans. on Knowledge and Data Engineering.
2. Émile Borel. (1965) Elements of the Theory of Probability, Translated by John E. Freund. Prentice-Hall Inc.
3. A. Brogi, V.S.Subrahmanian and C. Zaniolo. The Logic of Total and Partial Order Plans: A Deductive Database Approach, accepted for publication in: ANNALS OF MATH AND ARTIFICIAL INTELLIGENCE.
4. D. Chapman. (1987) Planning for conjunctive goals, Artificial Intelligence, 32,3, pps 333-378.
5. J. Chomicki. (1990) Polynomial-time computable queries in Temporal Deductive Databases, PODS'90.
6. R. Cavallo and M. Pittarelli. (1987) *The Theory of Probabilistic Databases*, Proc. VLDB 1987.
7. D. Dubois and H. Prade. (1988) *Default Reasoning and Possibility Theory*, Artificial Intelligence, 35, pp 243-257.

8. R. Fagin, J. Y. Halpern and N. Megiddo. (1989) *A Logic for Reasoning About Probabilities*, Information and Computation.

9. K. Erol and D.S. Nau and V.S. Subrahmanian. (1995) Complexity, Decidability and Undecidability Results for Domain-Independent Planning. ARTIFICIAL INTELLIGENCE Journal, 76,1-2, pps 75–88, 1995.

10. Fenstad, J.E., *The structure of probabilities defined on first-order languages*, Studies in inductive logic and probabilities, volume 2, University of California Press, (Ed. R.C. Jeffrey), 1980, pp. 251–262.

11. M. Gelfond and V. Lifschitz. (1993) Representing action and change by logic programs, Journal of Logic programming, 17, pps 301-322.

12. U. Guntzer, W. Kiessling and H. Thone. (1991) *New Directions for Uncertainty Reasoning in Deductive Databases*, Proc. 1991 ACM SIGMOD, pp 178–187.

13. W. Kiessling, H. Thone and U. Guntzer. (1992) *Database Support for Problematic Knowledge*, Proc. EDBT-92, pps 421–436, Springer LNCS Vol. 580.

14. M. Kifer and A. Li. (1988) *On the Semantics of Rule-Based Expert Systems with Uncertainty*, 2-nd Intl. Conf. on Database Theory, Springer Verlag LNCS 326, (eds. M. Gyssens, J. Paredaens, D. Van Gucht), Bruges, Belgium, pp. 102–117.

15. M. Kifer and E. Lozinskii. (1989) *RI: A Logic for Reasoning with Inconsistency*, 4-th Symposium on Logic in Computer Science, Asilomar, CA, pp. 253-262.

16. N. Kushmerick, S. Hanks and D.S. Weld. (1995) An algorithm for probabilistic planning. ARTIFICIAL INTELLIGENCE Journal, 76,1-2, Special Volume on Planning and Scheduling, pp 239–286.

17. Lakshmanan, Laks V.S. An epistemic foundation for logic programming with uncertainty. Technical report, Concordia University, Montreal, Canada, 1994. Preliminary version to appear in 14th Conf. on the Foundations of Software Technology and Theoretical Computer Science, December 1994.

18. Lakshmanan, Laks V.S. and Sadri, F. Probabilistic deductive databases. In *Proc. International Logic Programming Symposium*, pages 254–268, Ithaca, NY, November 1994. MIT Press.

19. Lakshmanan, Laks V.S. and Sadri, F. Modeling uncertainty in deductive databases. In *Proc. Int. Conf. on Database Expert Systems and Applications (DEXA '94)*, Athens, Greece, September 1994. Springer Verlag. Lecture Notes in Computer Science, vol. 856.

20. R. Ng and V.S. Subrahmanian. (1993) Probabilistic Logic Programming, INFORMATION AND COMPUTATION, 101, 2, pps 150–201, 1993.

21. R. Ng and V.S. Subrahmanian. (1995) Stable Semantics for Probabilistic Deductive Databases, INFORMATION AND COMPUTATION, 110, 1, pps 42-83.

22. J. Pinto and R. Reiter. (1993) Temporal Reasoning in Logic Programming: A Case for the Situation Calculus, Proc. 1993 Intl. Conf. on Logic Programming, pps 203–221, MIT Press.

23. H. Schmidt, W. Kiessling, U. Guntzer and R. Bayer. (1987) *Combining Deduction by Uncertainty with the Power of Magic*, Proc. DOOD-89, pps 205–224, Kyoto, Japan.

24. V.S. Subrahmanian. (1995) *Invited Talk*, 1995 Intl. Conf. on Uncertainty in AI, Montreal, Canada, Aug. 1995.

25. V.S. Subrahmanian and C. Zaniolo. Relating Stable Models and AI Planning Domains, accepted for publication in: *Proc. 1995 Intl. Conf. on Logic Programming*, Tokyo, Japan.

26. Peter Walley. (1991) Statistical reasoning with imprecise probabilities. Chapman and Hall.

# Temporal and Spatial Reasoning

# Termination Properties
## of Spatial Datalog Programs

Bart Kuijpers, Jan Paredaens, Marc Smits, and Jan Van den Bussche

University of Antwerp*

**Abstract.** We consider spatial databases defined in terms of polynomial inequalities, and investigate the use of Datalog as a query language for such databases. Spatial Datalog programs are not guaranteed to terminate in this setting. Through a series of examples we show that useful restrictions on the databases under consideration, or on the syntax of allowed programs guaranteeing termination, are unlikely to exist. Rather, termination of particular recursive spatial queries must be established by ad-hoc arguments, if it can be established at all. As an illustration of the difficulties that can be encountered in this respect, we discuss the topological connectivity query.

## 1   Introduction

The framework of constraint databases, introduced by Kanellakis, Kuper and Revesz [5], provides an elegant and powerful model of spatial databases [11]. In this setting, a spatial database, viewed as a possibly infinite set of points in real space, is represented as a Boole in combination of polynomial inequalities. For example, the unit disk in the real plane except its upper-half quadrant would be presented as

$$(x^2 + y^2 \le 1) \wedge \neg(x \ge 0 \wedge y \ge 0)$$

By extending the relational calculus with polynomial inequalities, one obtains a simple spatial query language. For example, the query whether the database $S$ contains a circle as a subset can be expressed as

$$(\exists a_0)(\exists b_0)(\exists r)(\forall x)(\forall y)((x - a_0)^2 + (y - b_0)^2 = r^2 \Rightarrow S(x, y)).$$

Although variables now range over the whole of the real numbers, queries expressed in the calculus can still be effectively computed using methods from symbolic computation.

The expressiveness of this calculus is limited, however. For example, the combined results of Benedikt et al. [2] and Grumbach and Su [6] imply that one cannot express in the calculus that the database is topologically connected. The

---

* Postdoctoral research fellow of the Belgian National Fund for Scientific Research.
** Address: UIA, Informatica, Universiteitsplein 1, B-3610 Antwerpen, Belgium. Email: {kuijpers, pareda, msmits, vdbuss}@uia.ua.ac.be.

# Termination Properties
# of Spatial Datalog Programs

Bart Kuijpers, Jan Paredaens, Marc Smits and Jan Van den Bussche*

University of Antwerp**

**Abstract.** We consider spatial databases defined in terms of polynomial inequalities, and investigate the use of Datalog as a query language for such databases. Recursive programs are not guaranteed to terminate in this setting. Through a series of examples we show that useful restrictions on the databases under consideration or on the syntax of allowed programs, guaranteeing termination, are unlikely to exist. Hence, termination of particular recursive spatial queries must be established by ad-hoc arguments, if it can be established at all. As an illustration of the difficulties that can be encountered in this respect we discuss the topological connectivity query.

## 1  Introduction

The framework of *constraint databases*, introduced by Kanellakis, Kuper and Revesz [8], provides an elegant and powerful model of spatial databases [11]. In this setting, a spatial database, viewed as a possibly infinite set of points in real space, is represented as a Boolean combination of polynomial inequalities. For example, the unit disk in the real plane except its upper left quadrant would be represented as

$$\{(x,y) \mid x^2 + y^2 \le 1 \wedge \neg(x \ge 0 \wedge y \ge 0)\}.$$

By extending the relational calculus with polynomial inequalities one obtains a simple spatial query language. For example, the query whether the database $S$ contains a circle as a subset can be expressed as

$$(\exists x_0)(\exists y_0)(\exists r \ne 0)(\forall x)(\forall y)((x - x_0)^2 + (y - y_0)^2 = r^2 \Rightarrow S(x,y)).$$

Although variables now range over the whole of the real numbers, queries expressed in the calculus can still be effectively computed using methods from symbolic computation.

The expressiveness of the calculus is limited, however. For example, the combined results of Benedikt et al. [2] and Grumbach and Su [6] imply that one cannot express in the calculus that the database is topologically connected. The

---

\* Post-doctoral research fellow of the Belgian National Fund for Scientific Research.

\*\* Address: UIA, Informatica, Universiteitsplein 1, B-2610 Antwerpen, Belgium. Email: {kuijpers, pareda, msmits, vdbuss}@uia.ua.ac.be.

topological connectivity query can be viewed as the spatial analogue of the standard relational query of graph connectivity, which is also not expressible in the standard relational calculus. In order to be able to express queries such as graph connectivity, in the standard relational context, one typically uses a more powerful query language such as Datalog [17], an extension of the relational calculus with recursion.

It is therefore natural to likewise extend the calculus with recursion in the spatial context. However, we then face the well-known fact that recursion involving arithmetic over an unbounded domain, such as the polynomial inequalities over the reals in our setting, is no longer guaranteed to terminate. In other words, the property of effective computability of queries in the spatial calculus is lost when extending the calculus with recursion. For example, the following trivial program does not terminate:

$$R(0) \longleftarrow$$
$$R(y) \longleftarrow R(x), \ y = x + 1.$$

One approach to this problem could be to look for useful restrictions on the spatial databases under consideration, or on the syntax of allowed programs, guaranteeing termination. In the present paper we demonstrate through a series of examples that such restrictions are unlikely to exist. For example, we will see that even under severe restrictions such as the following, programs may still not terminate:

1. Only bounded spatial data are considered;
2. No arithmetic at all is allowed in programs;
3. Rules can only be of the form

$$R(x,y) \longleftarrow S(x,y), \ B,$$

where $S$ is the spatial database predicate and $B$ is the rest of the rule body. In other words, it is syntactically guaranteed that derived relations in the program can only contain points from the given bounded data set.

Our observations stand in contrast to results achieved by Revesz and others [8, 13, 14], which show that in other, non-spatial, instances of the constraint database framework (more specifically, databases and queries involving order constraints only), useful termination guarantees can be found.

We conclude that the termination of particular spatial recursive queries will have to be established by ad-hoc arguments, if it can be established at all. As a case study we investigate the topological connectivity query mentioned earlier. We give a program in the spatial version of Datalog that expresses the connectivity query in a natural way. It can be easily shown to terminate on *linear* spatial databases but the program may loop forever on non-linear spatial databases, even bounded ones. We can, however, give an effective characterization of the class of semi-algebraic sets for which termination is guaranteed. The proof of termination relies on Collins's Cylindrical Algebraic Decomposition method [4, 1].

This paper is organized as follows. Some definitions are given in Sect. 2. A series of examples of non-terminating programs is developed in Sect. 3. The topological connectivity query is discussed in Sect. 4. Conclusions are presented in Sect. 5.

## 2 Preliminaries

In the present paper, we consider a *spatial database* to be a geometrical figure in the real plane. A geometrical figure in the plane is a possibly infinite set $S$ of points in $\mathbf{R}^2$, where $\mathbf{R}$ stands for the real numbers. Equivalently, it is a binary relation on the infinite domain $\mathbf{R}$.

One wants almost always to represent a geometrical figure in some effective, finite manner. A rather general way of doing this is by using *real polynomial inequalities* of the form $p(x,y) > 0$, where $p(x,y)$ is a polynomial in the variables $x$ and $y$ with real coefficients. Such an inequality defines the figure $\{(x,y) \mid p(x,y) > 0\}$. By using Boolean combinations (union, intersection, and complement) of polynomial inequalities one can describe a rather general class of figures, known as the class of *semi-algebraic sets*. Note that $p(x,y) = 0$ can be expressed as $\neg(p(x,y) > 0) \wedge \neg(-p(x,y) > 0)$.

*Example.* As an example, the semi-algebraic set already mentioned in the Introduction is shown in Fig. 1. ☐

**Fig. 1.** Semi-algebraic set defined by $x^2 + y^2 \leq 1 \wedge \neg(x \geq 0 \wedge y \geq 0)$.

We assume familiarity with the language Datalog. We can turn Datalog into a spatial query language as follows:

- The underlying domain is the set of real numbers.

- The only EDB predicate is $S$, which is interpreted as the set of points in the spatial database, or equivalently, as a binary relation.
- Relations can be infinite.
- Polynomial inequalities are allowed in rule bodies.

Under the bottom-up semantics, the following fundamental closure property is satisfied by any Datalog program $P$ [8]:

> if the input relation $S$ is semi-algebraic, then every derived relation $R$ obtained by a finite number of iterations of $P$ is also semi-algebraic; moreover, a finite representation of $R$ can be effectively computed.

*Example.* As a simple example, the following program derives in $R$ the set of all points that either lie in the database or to the left of a point in the database:

$$R(x,y) \longleftarrow S(x,y)$$
$$R(x,y) \longleftarrow R(x',y), \ x < x'.$$

This program always terminates after two iterations and hence, by the above, when applied to a semi-algebraic set $S$, will produce a set $R$ that is also semi-algebraic. For example, if $S$ is the set of Fig. 1, then $R$ will be the set

$$\{(x,y) \mid S(x,y) \vee (\exists x')(S(x',y) \wedge x < x')\},$$

which can be defined by

$$-1 \leq y < 0 \wedge (x^2 + y^2 \leq 1 \vee x < 0) \quad \vee \quad 0 \leq y \leq 1 \wedge x < 0.$$

$\square$

The above example also illustrates that the effective computation of a semi-algebraic representation of the result involves the elimination of quantifiers; a classical theorem by Tarski [16] says that every logical description of a real figure with quantifiers can also be described without quantifiers. Good algorithms for quantifier elimination over the reals are known since the work of Collins [4, 1]; for an overview of the recent advances see Renegar's series of papers [12].

## 3  Non-terminating programs

In the Introduction we already mentioned the trivial program

$$R(0) \longleftarrow$$
$$R(y) \longleftarrow R(x), \ y = x + 1.$$

This program does not terminate, regardless of the input database (which is not used at all in the program), because the resulting set $R$ grows unboundedly. Let us therefore see what happens if a fixed bound is put on the result, by requiring that the result must stay within some fixed bounded region.

The following example shows that under this requirement programs may still loop forever:

$R(1) \longleftarrow$
$R(x) \longleftarrow R(x'), \; x = x'/2.$

Relation $R$ remains in the interval $[0,1]$ but the program does not terminate; the interval is repeatedly cut in half and this goes on indefinitely.

In search of termination guarantees, we therefore put the drastic restriction on programs that no arithmetic (polynomial inequalities) is allowed in rule bodies. In other words, we concentrate on pure Datalog programs. Clearly, under this restriction, programs that do not rely on the database, such as the two programs given above, can no longer loop forever.

The classical example in pure Datalog is the transitive closure program TC:

$R(x,y) \longleftarrow S(x,y)$
$R(x,y) \longleftarrow R(x,z), \; S(z,y).$

On finite inputs $S$, TC always terminates. On infinite inputs, however, this is of course no longer true. For example, TC will loop forever on the semi-algebraic set $S$ defined by $y = x + 1$; in the $n$-th iteration all points of the form $(x, x+n)$ are added.

It is a basic fact of standard relational database theory that on finite relations, pure Datalog programs always terminate [17]. One might hope that this property carries over to infinite but *bounded, semi-algebraic* sets. For example, by bounding the above-mentioned set $y = x + 1$ as

$$y = x + 1 \wedge 0 \leq x \leq 10,$$

TC will terminate after ten iterations. This hope is unjustified, however. On the bounded input

$$S = \{(x,y) \mid y = 2x \wedge 0 \leq x \leq 1/2\},$$

TC will loop forever; every iteration adds a line segment of increasing slope, as illustrated (for the first three iterations) in Fig. 2.

The previous example also shows that, even if we require not only the *input* set but also the *output* set to be bounded, programs still can loop forever. Indeed, the lines of increasing slope all remain in the unit square.

As a last resort in our search for termination guarantees, we therefore investigate the stronger requirement that the output set is always contained in the input set. In other words, we concentrate on *selection queries*. The output of a selection query on a bounded input is clearly also bounded.

Whether or not a program expresses a selection query is a semantic property, but we can put a strong syntactic range restriction on the rules so that only selection queries can be expressed: every rule has to be of the form

$$R(x,y) \longleftarrow S(x,y), \; B,$$

where $S$ is as always the EDB predicate denoting the database and $B$ is the rest of the rule body. A program in which every rule is of this form is called a *selection program*. The transitive-closure program is not a selection program.

The following program, a range-restricted variation of TC, is an example of a selection program:

**Fig. 2.** First three iterations of the transitive closure of $S = \{(x,y) \mid y = 2x \wedge 0 \le x \le 1/2\}$.

$$R(x,y) \longleftarrow S(x,y),\ S(x,x),\ S(y,y)$$
$$R(x,y) \longleftarrow S(x,y),\ R(z,x).$$

On unbounded semi-algebraic inputs, selection programs can loop forever, as witnessed by the set

$$S = \{(x,y) \mid y = x + 1 \wedge x \ge 0\} \cup \{(0,0)\}.$$

On this $S$, the above program will not terminate; in the first iteration the point $(0,0)$ is added, and in subsequent iterations subsequent points of the form $(n, n+1)$ are added. However, if we bound $S$, e.g., by adding the constraint $y \le 10$, the program will terminate.

Hence, our last hope is that

*selection programs on bounded semi-algebraic inputs always terminate.*

The following set destroys also this last hope:

$$S = \{(x,y) \mid y = x/2 \wedge 0 < x \le 1\} \cup \{(1,1)\}.$$

On this input, the above program does not terminate; in the first iteration the point $(1,1)$ is added, in the second iteration the endpoint of the line segment in the database is added, and in subsequent iterations the line segment is repeatedly cut in half, going on indefinitely. The first four iterations are illustrated in Fig. 3.

*Remark:* We point out that all spatial databases considered in the above discussion are *linear*, in the sense that they can be defined using linear polynomials only.

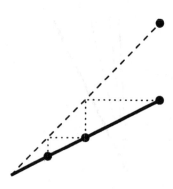

**Fig. 3.** First four iterations of a non-terminating selection program on a bounded semi-algebraic input.

# 4 Connectivity

A set $S$ of points in the plane is called *connected* (in the sense of Topology) if it cannot be partitioned by two disjoint open sets. If $S$ is semi-algebraic, $S$ is connected if and only if any pair of points in $S$ can be linked by a semi-algebraic curve lying entirely in $S$ [3].

In this section we will present a program for testing connectivity. The program is written in Datalog with polynomial inequalities and stratified negation.[3] The program works correctly (in particular, terminates) on any linear semi-algebraic set. It may, however, not work correctly (in particular, loop forever) on other spatial databases, even on bounded ones. The main theorem of this section gives an effective characterization of the class of semi-algebraic sets on which the proposed program is guaranteed to terminate and produce a correct result.

The program is shown in Fig. 4. The first pairs of points in $S$ that are derived by the program in relation *Path* are those that are connected by a straight line segment lying entirely in $S$. Then the transitive closure of *Path* is computed. After $n$ iterations of the transitive closure, *Path* contains all pairs of points in $S$ that can be connected by a piecewise linear curve consisting of $n$ line segments lying entirely in $S$.

To prove correctness of this program on a class $C$ of spatial databases we must establish two facts for every spatial database $S$ in $C$:

- *Soundness*: Two points in $S$ are in the same connected component of $S$ if and only if they can be connected by a piecewise linear curve lying entirely in $S$;
- *Termination*: The number of line segments needed to connect any such pair of points in $S$ is bounded.

---

[3] We will refer to this language simply as "Datalog".

$$Obstructed(x, y, x', y') \longleftarrow \neg S(\bar{x}, \bar{y}), \ \bar{x} = ax + a'x', \ \bar{y} = ay + a'y',$$
$$0 \le a \le 1, \ 0 \le a' \le 1, \ a + a' = 1$$
$$Path(x, y, x', y') \longleftarrow S(x, y), \ S(x', y'), \ \neg Obstructed(x, y, x', y')$$
$$Path(x, y, x', y') \longleftarrow Path(x, y, x'', y''), \ Path(x'', y'', x', y')$$
$$Disconnected \longleftarrow S(x, y), \ S(x', y'), \ \neg Path(x, y, x', y')$$
$$Connected \longleftarrow \neg Disconnected.$$

**Fig. 4.** A Datalog program for topological connectivity.

Termination guarantees that the transitive closure will terminate. Soundness then establishes the correctness of the test for connectivity performed by the program after the transitive closure is completed.

*Example.* Linear semi-algebraic sets always satisfy soundness and termination. This will be a corollary of our main theorem.

The set defined by $(y - x^2)(x^2 - y + 1/2) > 0$, shown in Fig. 5, does not satisfy termination. There is no upper bound on the number of line segment needed to connect the point at the origin to other points in the set; the higher the other point, the more line segments are needed.

Even on bounded semi-algebraic sets correctness cannot be guaranteed. Here we take as example the set defined by $y^3 - x^2 \ge 0 \land x \le 0 \land y \le 1$, depicted in Fig. 6. Indeed, since the tangent to the curve in the bottom point coincides with the vertical line, any straight line segment from the interior of the database (indicated as the shaded area) to the bottom point will leave the interior of the database. This implies that both soundness and termination fail in this case. □

**Fig. 5.** A database on which termination is not satisfied. The database consists of the points lying strictly between the parabola $y = x^2$ and the translated one $y = x^2 + 1/2$.

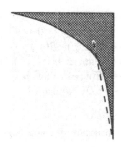

**Fig. 6.** Both soundness and termination fail on this bounded database.

We will actually demonstrate that the above examples of Figs. 5 and 6 illustrate essentially the only two cases on which the program of Fig. 4 will not work correctly. Our development will proceed in two steps:

1. First, we show how we can derive from a given semi-algebraic set $S$ another semi-algebraic set $S'$ in Datalog. The set $S'$ is special in that it will only contain "two-dimensional" points (defined precisely below). Furthermore, $S'$ is connected if and only if $S$ is.
2. By the first step, we can then in a second step restrict our attention to sets containing only two-dimensional points, and give a necessary and sufficient condition on these sets for correctness and termination of the Datalog program of Fig. 4.

The notion of 2-dimensional point depends on the notion of "observation" of a point with respect to some semi-algebraic set. This is formalized in the following definition. For a point $p$ and an $\varepsilon > 0$, let $C(p, \varepsilon)$ denote the circle with radius $\varepsilon$ and center $p$ and $D(p, \varepsilon)$ the closed disk with radius $\varepsilon$ and center $p$.

**Definition.** Let $S$ be a semi-algebraic set and let $p$ be a point.

- An $\varepsilon > 0$ is called an $S$-*observation radius* of $p$ if for each $\varepsilon'$ such that $0 < \varepsilon' < \varepsilon$, $S \cap C(p, \varepsilon)$ is isotopic to $S \cap C(p, \varepsilon')$.
- An $S$-*observation circle* of $p$ is a circle around $p$ whose radius is an $S$-observation radius of $p$.
- The minimum of 1 and the supremum of all $S$-observation radii of $p$ is denoted by $\varepsilon_{p,S}$.

Known properties of semi-algebraic sets [5] guarantee that these notions are well-defined.

Using the notion of observation we can introduce three classes of points with respect to $S$ as follows:

**Definition.** A point is

- 0-dimensional if its $S$-observation circles do not intersect $S$;
- 1-dimensional if each $S$-observation circle intersects $S$ in two points;
- 2-dimensional if each $S$-observation circle intersects $S$ in infinitely many points.

The points in $S$ that are 0-dimensional with respect to $S$ are the isolated points of $S$. The 1-dimensional points in $S$ are those lying locally on a curve of $S$. The 2-dimensional points with respect to $S$ are those for which the intersection of even the smallest of their neighborhoods with $S$ has a non-empty interior. Remark that there are points in the plane which do not belong to any of these classes.

For each semi-algebraic set in $\mathbf{R}^2$ we now define its "blown-up" version. An illustration is given in Fig. 7.

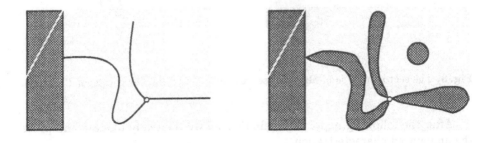

**Fig. 7.** A semi-algebraic set and an approximated picture of its blown-up version.

**Definition.** Let $S$ be a semi-algebraic set. The *blown-up version of $S$* equals

$$BU(S) = S \cup \bigcup_{p \in S_{01}} D(p, \varepsilon_{p,S}/3),$$

where $S_{01}$ is the set of 0- and 1-dimensional points of $S$.

The proof of the following proposition is straightforward.

**Proposition.** *(i) $BU(S)$ can be computed by a recursion-free Datalog program, and hence is semi-algebraic.*
*(ii) All points in $BU(S)$ are 2-dimensional with respect to $BU(S)$.*
*(iii) $BU(S)$ is connected if and only if $S$ is.*

A final technical concept we need is that a semi-algebraic set $S$ is "conical" locally around each of its points. More specifically, if $p \in S$, then $D(p, \varepsilon_{p,S}) \cap S$

is homeomorphic to a planar cone with top $p$ and base $C(p, \varepsilon_{p,S}) \cap S$. We will call the 2-dimensional regions of $D(p, \varepsilon_{p,S}) \cap S$ the *sectors of $S$ around $p$*. Fig. 8 gives an example of a point with three sectors.

Analogously, there exists a $\varepsilon_{\infty,S} > 0$ such that $\{(x,y) \mid x^2 + y^2 \geq \varepsilon_{\infty,S}\} \cap S$ is homeomorphic to the unbounded planar cone with top at infinity defined as

$$\{(\lambda x, \lambda y) \mid (x,y) \in S \wedge x^2 + y^2 = \varepsilon_{\infty,S} \wedge \lambda \geq 1\}.$$

Here, we call the 2-dimensional regions of $\{(x,y) \mid x^2 + y^2 \geq \varepsilon_{\infty,S}\} \cap S$ the *unbounded sectors of $S$*.

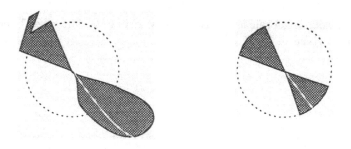

**Fig. 8.** The sectors of a semi-algebraic set around a point and the corresponding cone.

After the following important definition we will be ready to state and prove the announced characterization.

**Definition.** Let $S$ be a semi-algebraic set. A semi-algebraic set $S$ is called *border-visible* if

1. for each point $p$ on the border of $S$ and each sector of $S$ around $p$ there exists a interior point $q$ of $S$ in that sector such that the half open line segment $(p, q]$ is contained in the interior of $S$, and
2. for each unbounded sector of $S$ there exists an unbounded half line completely contained in that region.

*Example.* The set of Fig. 6 is not border-visible because it does not satisfy the first condition of the definition; the set of Fig. 5 is not border-visible because it does not satisfy the second condition. □

**Theorem.** *Let $S$ be a semi-algebraic set that contains only 2-dimensional points. The Datalog program of Fig. 4 tests correctly for topological connectivity of $S$ in finite time, if and only if $S$ is border-visible.*

*Proof.* First, assume $S$ is border-visible. According to the discussion in the beginning of this Section, we need to establish soundness and termination.

*A. Soundness.* It suffices to show soundness in the interior only, i.e., to show that two points in $S°$, the topological interior of $S$, are in the same connected component of $S°$ if and only if they can be connected by a piecewise linear curve lying entirely in $S°$. Indeed, because $S$ is two-dimensional, the points in $S$ on the border of $S$ are also on the border of $S°$, and thus soundness for points on the border of $S$ follows from soundness in the interior by border-visibility.

The if-implication is trivial. So we focus on the only-if implication. Two interior points that belong to the same connected component can be connected by a semi-algebraic curve lying entirely in the $S°$. It is well known that a uniformly continuous curve (such as a semi-algebraic one) can be arbitrarily closely approximated by a piecewise linear curve [9].

*B. Termination.* To establish termination we use a refined version of Collins's Cylindrical Algebraic Decomposition (CAD) [4, 1]. Collins's CAD, when applied to a semi-algebraic set $S$, shows the existence of a decomposition of $S$ in a finite number of cells, where each cell is either a *point*, a 1-dimensional *curve* or a 2-dimensional *region*. We can refine this decomposition in the extrema and points of inflection of the upper and lower borders of the cells, as illustrated for a bounded region in Fig. 9. This yields a cell decomposition in which each cell has an upper and lower border which is constant, monotonic concave or monotonic convex. We can further adapt the decomposition, by merging, wherever possible, any two adjacent cells where one lies above the other.

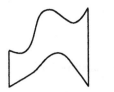 

**Fig. 9.** An example of a region in Collins's CAD and its refined version.

Since the decomposition is finite, it suffices to show for each cell $C$ that there exists an upper bound $\alpha(C)$ on the number of line segments needed in a piecewise linear path between any two points in $C$. This is trivial for those cells that are vertical line segments or single points.

The most difficult case is that where $C$ is a bounded region. This situation is illustrated in Fig. 10. Because of the merging of adjacent cells mentioned above, the left bottom point $p$ of the region is on the border of $S$. Let $T$ be the sector around $p$ that intersects $C$. Because $S$ is border-visible there exists a point $r$ in $T°$ such that the line segment $(p,r]$ is contained in $T°$. This point $r$ is not necessarily in $C°$. Therefore, we also choose a point $s$ in $C° \cap T°$.

We can perform a symmetric construction for the right upper point $p'$, leading to sector $T'$ and points $r'$ and $s'$. By the reasoning already employed in the soundness part of this proof, there is a piecewise linear curve going from $r$ to $s$ lying entirely in $T^\circ$, another going from $r'$ to $s'$ lying entirely in $(T')^\circ$, and another going from $s$ to $s'$ lying entirely in $C^\circ$. Hence, there is a piecewise linear curve $\gamma$ going from $p$ to $p'$ lying entirely in $C^\circ \cup T^\circ \cup (T')^\circ$.

Let $\beta(C)$ be the number of segments of $\gamma$. We can now take $\alpha(C) = \beta(C) + 2$. Indeed, let $q$ and $q'$ be points in $C$. Because $\gamma$ transverses $C$ completely, there are points on $\gamma$ with the same $x$-coordinate as $q$ and $q'$. We can connect $q$ and $q'$ with these points using a single vertical line segment lying in $C$ (indicated in Fig. 10 by dashed lines). So, $q$ and $q'$ can be connected by a piece-wise linear curve consisting of at most $\beta(C) + 2$ line segments.

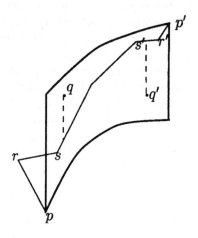

**Fig. 10.** The $\alpha$ of a bounded region.

The case where $C$ is an unbounded region is analogous. By border-visibility, we know that there exist unbounded lines starting in a point from the interior of $C$ and going into the direction where $C$ is of unbounded. One can think of the points $p$, $r$ and $s$ (or $p'$, $r'$ and $s'$) as all coinciding at infinity.

Finally, we prove the only-if implication of the theorem. Thereto, assume $S$ is not border-visible. So, at least one of the following two possibilities arises:

1. there exists a border-point $p$ of $S$ and a sector $T$ around $p$ such that there is no point in the interior of $T$ for which the line segment $(p, q]$ is contained in the interior of $S$,
2. there is an unbounded sector of $S$ in which no half line is contained.

Using the CAD of above, we see that these two possibilities are represented by the examples we have seen in Figs. 5 and 6. We already argued informally that in both cases, termination fails. It is a standard mathematical exercise to make these arguments formal. $\qquad\square$

**Corollary.** *The Datalog program of Fig. 4 tests correctly for topological connectivity of $S$ in finite time on every linear semi-algebraic set.*

*Proof.* Linear sets are clearly border-visible. The 2-dimensionality assumption in the theorem is only used in the soundness argument to deal with border points; in a linear set this is not necessary since its border is itself piecewise linear. In other words, blowing up is unnecessary in the linear case. □

We show that the class of semi-algebraic sets for which the Datalog program of Fig. 4 correctly tests connectivity is a decidable class.

**Theorem.** *It is decidable whether a given semi-algebraic set that consists of 2-dimensional points is border-visible.*

*Proof.* We briefly sketch a decision algorithm. Let $S$ be a semi-algebraic set that consists of 2-dimensional points. The border-points of $S$ can be classified according to the type of cone (i.e., the configuration of sectors around them) they have. The set of border-points of $S$ that have exactly one sector in their cone can be expressed in the relational calculus with polynomial inequalities by a formula that selects those border-points of $S$ for which even the smallest circle around it has one single (closed, open, or half-open/half-closed) arc segment in common with $S$. Although there is an uncountably infinite number of these points, the condition of border-visibility for these points can be translated into the relational calculus with polynomial inequalities, and we have noted in the Introduction that this calculus is effective.

It can be easily shown that the number of border-points of $S$ with more than one sector in their cone is finite. To check the condition of border-visibility for these points, we loop through all possible cone types with more than one sector and for each cone type we select the border-points of $S$ that have a cone of that type. There are symbolic algorithms for the first-order theory of the reals (e.g., Collins's algorithm [1, 4]) that can effectively enumerate these points.

Since we know, in this loop, the cone type for each such point $p$ it is possible to express $\varepsilon_{p,S}$ in the relational calculus with polynomial inequalities and thus to compute it. Without knowing the particular cone type the latter is not possible. We can also compute the sectors around $p$ by computing the connected components of $(D(p, \varepsilon_{p,S}) \cap S) \setminus \{p\}$. The computation of the connected components of a semi-algebraic set is explained in [15]. For each sector the condition of border-visibility can again be translated into the relational calculus with polynomial inequalities. We exit the loop when all border-points of $S$ are processed. Since the border-points of $S$ with more than one sector in their cone are finite in number, we exit the loop after a finite number of cone types have been considered.

Finally, for the unbounded sectors, we again have to loop through all possible cone types to determine the configuration of the unbounded sectors of $S$. Once we know this configuration, we can compute $\varepsilon_{\infty,S}$. We can compute the unbounded sectors by computing the connected components of $S \cap \{(\lambda x, \lambda y) \mid x^2 + y^2 = \varepsilon_{\infty,S} \wedge \lambda \geq 1\}$. The condition of border-visibility for the unbounded sectors can again be translated into the relational calculus with polynomial inequalities. □

# 5 Conclusion

It is not obvious how one can test for topological connectivity in the case of general semi-algebraic spatial databases by a program that always terminates. One may wonder whether topological connectivity is expressible at all in spatial Datalog. The query is certainly known to be algorithmically decidable in the general semi-algebraic case [15]. In this respect it should be noted that extending the relational calculus with polynomial constraints and while-loops yields a computationally complete query language for semi-algebraic spatial databases [7], and therefore connectivity is expressible in that language. It seems possible to simulate while-loops using an inflationary version of spatial Datalog. The problem remains however whether there exists a natural spatial query language in which connectivity is effectively expressible in a natural manner.

# Acknowledgment

We are indebted to Rudi Penne for most helpful discussions on the issue of termination.

# References

1. D.S. Arnon. Geometric reasoning with logic and algebra. *Artificial Intelligence*, 37:37–60, 1988.
2. M. Benedikt, G. Dong, L. Libkin, and L. Wong. Relational expressive power of constraint query languages. In *Proceedings 15th ACM Symposium on Principles of Database Systems*. ACM Press, 1996.
3. J. Bochnak, M. Coste, and M.-F. Roy. *Géométrie algébrique réelle*. Springer-Verlag, 1987.
4. G.E. Collins. Quantifier elimination for real closed fields by cylindrical algebraic decomposition. *Lecture Notes in Computer Science*, 33:134–183, 1975.
5. M. Coste. Ensembles semi-algébriques. In *Géometrie algébrique réelle et formes quadratiques*, volume 959 of *Lecture Notes in Mathematics*, pages 109–138. Springer, 1982.
6. S. Grumbach and J. Su. First-order definability over constraint databases. In Montanari and Rossi [10], pages 121–136.
7. M. Gyssens, J. Paredaens, J. Van den Bussche, and D. Van Gucht. Computable queries for spatial database systems. In preparation.
8. P.C. Kanellakis, G.M. Kuper, and P.Z. Revesz. Constraint query languages. *Journal of Computer and System Sciences*, 51(1):26–52, August 1995.
9. E.E. Moise. *Geometric topology in dimensions 2 and 3*, volume 47 of *Graduate Texts in Mathematics*. Springer, 1977.
10. U. Montanari and F. Rossi, editors. *Principles and practice of constraint programming*, volume 976 of *Lecture Notes in Computer Science*. Springer, 1995.
11. J. Paredaens, J. Van den Bussche, and D. Van Gucht. Towards a theory of spatial database queries. In *Proceedings 13th ACM Symposium on Principles of Database Systems*, pages 279–288. ACM Press, 1994.

12. J. Renegar. On the computational complexity and geometry of the first-order theory of the reals. *Journal of Symbolic Computation*, 13, 1992.

13. P.Z. Revesz. A closed-form evaluation for Datalog queries with integer (gap)-order constraints. *Theoretical Computer Science*, 116:117–149, 1993.

14. P.Z. Revesz. Safe stratified Datalog with integer order programs. In Montanari and Rossi [10], pages 154–169.

15. J.T. Schwartz and M. Sharir. On the piano movers' problem II. In J.T. Schwartz, M. Sharir, and J. Hopcroft, editors, *Planning, Geometry, and Complexity of Robot Motion*, pages 51–96. Ablex Publishing Corporation, Norwood, New Jersey, 1987.

16. A. Tarski. *A Decision Method for Elementary Algebra and Geometry.* University of California Press, 1951.

17. J. Ullman. *Principles of Database and Knowledge-Base Systems*, volume I. Computer Science Press, 1988.

# Applying Transition Rules to Bitemporal Deductive Databases for Integrity Constraint Checking

Carme Martín and Jaume Sistac

Universitat Politècnica de Catalunya
Departament de Llenguatges i Sistemes Informàtics
Pau Gargallo 5, 08028 Barcelona - Catalonia
e-mail:{martin,sistac}@lsi.upc.es

**Abstract.** A bitemporal deductive database is a deductive database that supports valid and transaction time. A set of facts to be inserted and/or deleted in a bitemporal deductive database can be done in a past, present or future valid time. This circumstance causes that the maintenance of database consistency becomes more hard. In this paper, we present a new approach to reduce the difficulty of this problem, based on applying transition and event rules, which explicitly define the insertions and deletions given by a database update. Transition rules range over all the possible cases in which an update could violate some integrity contraint. Although, we have a large amount of transition rules, for each one we argue its utility or we eliminate it. We augment a database with this set of transition and event rules and then standard SLDNF resolution can be used to check satisfaction of integrity constraints.

## 1 Introduction

Two measures of time were distinguished in [21], called valid time and transaction time. Valid time is the time when the fact is true in the modelled reality, while transaction time is the time when the fact is stored in the database. In a consensus glossary of temporal database concepts [8], a deductive database that supports valid time and transaction time is called a bitemporal deductive database and we denote it bt-ddb.

An integrity constraint is a condition that a database is required to satisfy at any time. We deal with static and dynamic constraints formulated in a first order language. A bt-ddb must be consistent, that is, when performing a past, present or future update, that happens at some valid time point, it is necessary to validate whether this update violates some integrity constraint, and if so the update must be rejected. The possibility of past, present and future updates in a bt-ddb causes that the maintenance of database consistency becomes more difficult.

Integrity constraint checking is an essential issue, which has been widely studied in relational and deductive databases (see for example [4] for a comprehensive state of the art survey), but not in the field of temporal deductive databases. The simplest solution to integrity checking would be to evaluate each constraint whenever the database is updated. However, it is usually too costly and highly redundant, since it does not take advantage of the fact that the database satisfies the constraints prior to the update. In this paper, we present a new approach for consistency maintenance in bt-ddb, that incorporates transaction time to our previous work (see [13] and [14]), based on applying transition and event rules, which explicitly define the insertions and deletions given by a database update. Transition rules range over all the possible cases in which an update could violate some integrity contraint. Although, we have a large amount of transition rules, for each one we argue its utility or we eliminate it. We augment a database with this set of simplified transition rules and event rules and then standard SLDNF resolution can be used to check satisfaction of integrity constraints.

The paper is organised as follows. The next section defines basic concepts of bt-ddbs and introduces a simple example that will be used throughout the paper. Section 3 presents the concepts of events, transition and event rules. Section 4 describes the application of transition rules for integrity constraint checking in bt-ddbs. Particularly, this part shows the utility of the transition rules for the example presented in section 2. Section 5 compares our approach with previous related work. Finally, section 6 gives the conclusions and points out future work.

## 2 Bitemporal Deductive Databases

A bt-ddb D consists of three finite sets: a set F of facts, a set R of deductive rules, and a set I of integrity constraints. The set of facts is called the extensional database (EDB), and the set of deductive rules is called the intensional database (IDB). A base predicate appears only in the extensional database and possibly in the body of deductive rules. A derived predicate appears only in the intensional database. Every bt-ddb can be defined in this form.

Facts, rules and integrity constraints are formulated in a first order language. We will use names beginning with a lower case letter for predicate symbols and constants and a capital letter for variables.

We consider a temporal domain $\tau$ isomorphic to the set of natural numbers, over which is defined the linear (total) order $<_\tau$, where $t_i <_\tau t_j$ means $t_i$ occurs before $t_j$. The set $\tau$ is used as the basis for incorporating the temporal dimensions into the database.

We assume that database predicates are either base or derived. For example, the base predicate $offered(C,T_v)$ and the derived predicate $some\_enrol(C,T_v)$ both contain a last term which is a valid time point ranging over the temporal domain $\tau$. Integrity constraints use the usual operators $=, >, <, \geq, \leq$ and $\neq$ to compare a valid time points and to express static and dynamic constraints. For example: $ic4 \leftarrow offered(C,T_v) \wedge \neg many\_students(C,T_v) \wedge many\_students(C,T1_v) \wedge T1_v < T_v$. The examples presented here are explained in detail in subsection 2.3.

We adopt a closed time interval model based in the valid time representation presented in [20], adding a transaction time dimension. Including transaction time we ensure that every old state is preserved. If we store only valid time one cannot remember if during a given period one knew another information different from the current one. We are interested in the history of the database and we willing to pay a high cost of the storage of old states. [20] uses two segments to representing current and history data, in which two valid time points are added, named FROM and TO (defining a valid time interval), valid time start and end in our case. We only use the equivalent to one segment and we add two more time points (transaction time start and end) to represent transaction time and to define a transaction time interval.

A fact is a ground atom. Last terms of any fact are four time points values ranging over the temporal domain $\tau$: valid time-start ($t_{vs}$), valid time-end ($t_{ve}$) corresponding to the lower and upper bounds of the valid time interval and transaction time-start ($t_{ts}$), transaction time-end ($t_{te}$) corresponding to the lower and upper bounds of the transaction time interval.

Each fact has a precise valid time-start $t_{vs}$ value stored from transaction time-start $t_{ts}$ to *now* (denoting the current time) or to transaction time-end $t_{te}$ when finally the fact cannot be accessible from current time anymore. However, the valid time-end value $t_{ve}$ may not be known. In this case, $t_{ve}$ is given the default value *forever* denoting an artificial time point for the end of time ready to handle future information, but that will change to precise value $t_{ve}$ when the user knows it (see subsection 3.1).

## 2.1 Deductive Rules

A deductive rule is a formula of the form:
$$p \leftarrow L_1 \wedge \dots \wedge L_n \quad \text{with } n \geq 1,$$
where $p$ is an atom, denoting the conclusion, $L_1 \wedge \dots \wedge L_n$ are literals representing conditions. Any variables in $p, L_1 \wedge \dots \wedge L_n$ are assumed to be universally quantified over the whole formula. A **derived predicate** $p$ may be defined by means of one or more deductive rules, but for the sake of simplicity, we only show the first case in this paper.

Condition predicates may be ordinary or evaluable. The former are base or derived predicates, while the latter are built-in predicates that can be evaluated without accessing the database.

In this paper we deal with stratified databases [2] and, as usual we require the bt-ddb before and after any updates to be allowed [11].

## 2.2 Integrity Constraints

An integrity constraint is a closed first order formula that the bt-ddb is required to satisfy. We deal with constraints that have the form of a denial:
$$\leftarrow L_1 \wedge \dots \wedge L_n \quad \text{with } n \geq 1,$$
where each $L_i$ is a literal. Any variables in $L_1 \wedge \dots \wedge L_n$ are assumed to be universally quantified over the whole formula.

For the sake of uniformity we associate with each integrity constraint an inconsistency predicate $Icn$, and thus it has the same form as a deductive rule. We call them integrity rules. Then, we rewrite the former denial as:
$$Icn \leftarrow L_1 \wedge \dots \wedge L_m \quad \text{with } m \geq 1.$$

The evolution through time of a deductive database can be described by valid and transaction time intervals for each predicate. According to this evolution scheme, static and dynamic constraints can be distinguished: the former restrict the validity to only one valid time of the bt-ddb, while the latter relate the validity to past and/or future valid times in addition to another one.

## 2.3 Example

*Base Predicates.*

*offered(C,T$_v$)* expresses that "course $C$ is offered at valid time $T_v$"
*takes(S,C,T$_v$)* expresses that "the student S is enrolled in course $C$ at valid time $T_v$".

*Deductive Rules.*

R.1    *some_enrol(C,T$_v$) ← takes(S,C,T$_v$).*
R.2    *many_students(C,T$_v$) ← takes(S1,C,T$_v$) ∧ takes(S2,C,T$_v$) ∧ S1 ≠ S2.*

    *some_enrol(C,T$_v$)* expresses that "the course $C$ has one or more students at valid time $T_v$", and *many_students(C,T$_v$)* expresses that "the course $C$ has two students at valid time $T_v$, at least".

*Static Integrity Constraints.*

IC.1    *ic1 ← takes(S,C,T$_v$) ∧ ¬offered(C,T$_v$)*
IC.2    *ic2 ← offered(C,T$_v$) ∧ ¬some_enrol(C,T$_v$).*

    *ic1* and *ic2* , respectively, enforce the properties that "a student $S$ can only be enrolled in course $C$ if course $C$ is offered" and "for course $C$ to be offered, it must have at least one student enrolled".

*Dynamic Integrity Constraints.*

IC.3    *ic3 ← takes(S,software engineering,T$_v$) ∧ takes(S,information systems,T1$_v$) ∧ T1$_v$≤T$_v$.*
IC.4    *ic4 ← offered(C,T$_v$) ∧ ¬many_students(C,T$_v$) ∧ many_students(C,T1$_v$) ∧ T1$_v$<T$_v$.*

    *ic3* and *ic4*, respectively, enforce the properties that "if a student $S$ is enrolled in the course *software engineering*, this student cannot be enrolled or cannot have been enrolled in the course *information systems*", "if two or more students were enrolled in a course $C$, this course cannot have less than two students in the future".

## 3  Events, Transition and Event Rules

In this section, we begin by adapting the concepts of event, transition and event rules that were formalised in [16] for the events model as an approach for the design of information systems from deductive conceptual models, and was applied in [22] to address database and transaction design decisions. In [16] and [22] valid and transaction time are equivalent and the database can only be updated in the current state. In our case, we explicitly distinguish between valid and transaction time and the updates can be done in a past, present or future valid time.

## 3.1 Events

Let $D$ be a deductive database at transaction time point $t_t$-$1$, $U$ an update and $D'$ the updated deductive database at transaction time point $t_t$ (*now*) as one can see in figure 3.1. We assume for the moment that $U$ consists of an unspecified set of facts to be inserted and/or deleted and the bt-ddb can only be updated in the transaction time point *now*.

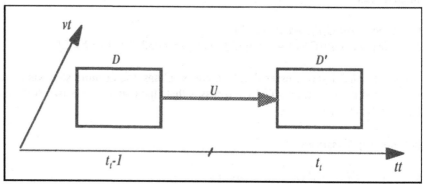

**Fig. 3.1.**

Let $p(x,t_v)$ be a predicate in $D$ and let $p'(x,t_v)$ denote the same predicate evaluated in $D'$. Assuming that $p(x,t_v)$ holds in $D$, where $x$ is a vector of constants, and $t_v$ is a valid time point, two cases are possible:

$p'(x,t_v)$ also holds in $D'$ (both $p(x,t_v)$ and $p'(x,t_v)$ are true). (1)

$p'(x,t_v)$ does not hold in $D'$ ($p(x,t_v)$ is true, but $p'(x,t_v)$ is false). (2)

And assuming that $p'(x,t_v)$ holds in $D'$, two cases are also possible:

$p(x,t_v)$ also holds in $D$ (both $p(x,t_v)$ and $p'(x,t_v)$ are true). (3)

$p(x,t_v)$ does not hold in $D$ ($p'(x,t_v)$ is true, but $p(x,t_v)$ is false). (4)

In case (2) we say that a **deletion event** occurs in the transition at valid time point $t_v$, we denote it by $\delta p(x,t_v)$ and we store it at transaction time point $t_t$ as shown in figure 3.2.

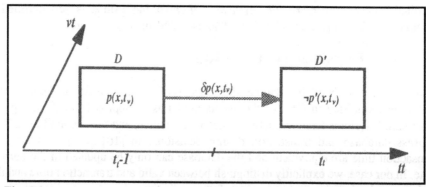

**Fig. 3.2.**

In case (4) we say that an **insertion event** occurs in the transition at valid time point $t_v$, we denote it by $\iota p(x,t_v)$ and we store it at transaction time point $t_t$ as shown in figure 3.3.

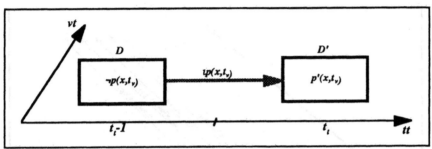

**Fig. 3.3.**

Formally, we associate an insertion event predicate $\iota p$ with each derived or inconsistency predicate $p$ and a deletion event predicate $\delta p$ with each derived predicate, defined as:

$$\forall X,T_v \, (\iota p(X,T_v) \leftrightarrow p'(X,T_v) \wedge \neg p(X,T_v)). \tag{5}$$
$$\forall X,T_v \, (\delta p(X,T_v) \leftrightarrow p(X,T_v) \wedge \neg p'(X,T_v)). \tag{6}$$

where $X$ is a vector of variables and $T$ is a valid time point variable.

From the above, we then have the equivalencies:

$$\forall X,T_v \, (p'(X,T_v) \leftrightarrow [p(X,T_v) \wedge \neg \delta p(X,T_v)] \vee \iota p(X,T_v)). \tag{7}$$
$$\forall X,T_v \, (\neg p'(X,T_v) \leftrightarrow [\neg p(X,T_v) \wedge \neg \iota p(X,T_v)] \vee \delta p(X,T_v)). \tag{8}$$

which relate the predicate $p'$ at transaction time point $t_t$ to the predicate $p$ at transaction time point $t_t$-$1$ and the events given by the transaction.

If $p$ is a derived predicate, then $\iota p$ and $\delta p$ represent induced insertions and deletions respectively.

If $p$ is an inconsistency predicate, then $\iota p$ that occur during the transition will correspond to violations of its integrity constraint. For example, if a given transition induces $\iota cn$, this will mean that such a transition leads to a violation of integrity constraint $icn$. Note that for inconsistency predicates $\delta p$ cannot happen in any transition, since we assume that the bt-ddb is consistent before the update, and thus $icn$ is always false.

We also use definitions (5) and (6) above for base predicates. In this case, $\iota p$ and $\delta p$ represent the events given by the update. Therefore, we assume from now on that $U$ consists of an unspecified set of insertion and/or deletion of events given by the update.

Note that an event happens at some time instant, while we require time intervals to express the changes produced by the transaction. Therefore, when an insertion event $\iota p(x,t_v)$ happens in a transaction time $t_t$ we really represent: $p_r(x,t_v,forever,t_t,now)$, and when a deletion event $\delta p(x,t_v)$ occurs in a transaction time $t_t$ we modify $p_r(x,t_{vs},t_{ve},t_{ts},now)$ by $p_r(x,t_{vs},t_v\text{-}1,t_t,now)$ and $p_r(x,t_{vs},t_{ve},t_{ts},t_t\text{-}1)$. When a deletion event occurs we do not really remove information; instead we store the fact that it has existed from one valid time to another valid time.

*Example.* Suppose the update *U* at transaction time 3:

{ι*offered(databases,2)*, ι*takes(ton,databases,2)*, δ*takes(maria,logic,2)*}

on the bt-ddb as shown in figure 3.4.

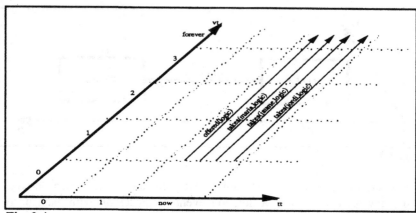

**Fig. 3.4.**

If this transaction does not violate any integrity constraint, at transaction time 3, we have the bt-ddb as shown in figure 3.5, and their facts will be, including the temporal information that appears in the figure 3.5 axis co-ordinates.

$$offered_r(logic,1,forever,2,now)$$
$$takes_r(jaume,logic,1,forever,2,now)$$
$$takes_r(jordi,logic,1,forever,2,now)$$
$$takes_r(maria,logic,1,forever,2,2)$$
$$takes_r(maria,logic,1,1,3,now)$$
$$offered_r(databases,2,forever,3,now)$$
$$takes_r(ton,databases,2,forever,3,now)$$

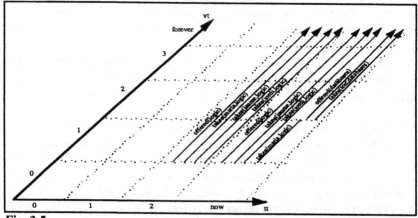

**Fig. 3.5.**

## 3.2 Transition Rules

Let $p \leftarrow L_1, ..., L_m$ be a deductive or inconsistency rule. When the rule is to be evaluated in the updated bt-ddb, its form is $p' \leftarrow L_1', ..., L_m'$, where $L_i'$ ($i = 1..m$) is obtained by replacing the predicate $Q$ of $L_i$ with $Q'$. Now if we rewrite each literal in the body by its equivalent definition, given in (7) or (8), we get a new rule called a **transition rule**, which defines predicate $p'$ in the updated bt-ddb in terms of transaction time point *now-1* of the predicates appearing in the body of the rule, and the events that occur at transaction time point *now*.

More precisely, if $L_i'$ is an ordinary positive literal $Q_i'(X_i, T_{vi})$ we apply (7) and replace it with:

$(Q_i(X_i, T_{vi}) \wedge \neg \delta Q_i(X_i, T_{vi})) \vee \iota Q_i(X_i, T_{vi})$

and if $L_i'$ is an ordinary negative literal $\neg Q_i'(X_i, T_i)$ we apply (8) and replace it with:

$(\neg Q_i(X_i, T_{vi}) \wedge \neg \iota Q_i(X_i, T_{vi})) \vee \delta Q_i(X_i, T_{vi})$

If $L_i$ is an evaluable predicate, we just replace $L_i'$(positive or negative) by its current $L_i$.

It will be easier to refer to the resulting expressions if we denote by:

$$
\begin{aligned}
O(L_i') \quad & = (Q_i(X_i, T_{vi}) \wedge \neg \delta Q_i(X_i, T_{vi})) && if\ L_i' = Q_i'(X_i, T_{vi}) \\
& = (\neg Q_i(X_i, T_{vi}) \wedge \neg \iota Q_i(X_i, T_{vi})) && if\ L_i' = \neg Q_i'(X_i, T_{vi}) \\
& = L_i && if\ L_i\ is\ evaluable \\
N(L_i') \quad & = \iota Q_i(X_i, T_{vi}) && if\ L_i' = Q_i'(X_i, T_{vi}) \\
& = \delta Q_i(X_i, T_{vi}) && if\ L_i' = \neg Q_i'(X_i, T_{vi})
\end{aligned}
$$

Both $O(L_i')$ and $N(L_i')$ express conditions for which $L_i'$ is true. $O(L_i')$ corresponds to the case that $L_i'$ holds because $L_i$ was already true in the Old transaction time point *now-1* and has not been deleted, while $N(L_i')$ corresponds to the case that $N(L_i')$ holds because it is New, induced in the transition, and false before. Note that $O(L_i') \rightarrow L_i$ and $N(L_i') \rightarrow L_i$.

With this notation, the equivalencies (7) and (8) become:

$$\forall X, T_v (p'(X, T_v) \leftrightarrow O(p'(X, T_v)) \vee N(p'(X, T_v))). \tag{9}$$
$$\forall X, T_v (\neg p'(X, T_v) \leftrightarrow O(\neg p'(X, T_v)) \vee N(\neg p'(X, T_v))). \tag{10}$$

and applying them to each of the $L_i'$ ($i = 1...n$) literals, we get:

$$p'(X, T_v) \leftarrow \bigwedge_{i=1}^{i=n} [O(L_i') \vee N(L_i') \,/\, O(L_i')] \tag{11}$$

where the first option is taken if $L_i'$ is an ordinary literal, and the second one if $L_i'$ is evaluable. After distributing $\wedge$ over $\vee$, we get an equivalent set of $2^k$ transition rules, each of them with the general form:

$$p_j'(X, T_v) \leftarrow \bigwedge_{i=1}^{i=n} [O(L_i') \,/\, N(L_i')] \qquad with\ j = 1, ..., 2^k \tag{12}$$

where $k$ is the number of ordinary literals in the $p'(X,T)$ rule, and

$$p'(X, T_v) \leftarrow p_j'(X, T_v) \qquad with\ j = 1, ..., 2^k. \tag{13}$$

We are conscious of the resulting amount of transition rules and we present afterwards in this paper some simplifications to drastically reduce them.

Note that in the case of integrity constraints, $\neg ici_1'$ always holds because the bt-ddb is assumed to be consistent at transaction time point $now\text{-}1$. For example, $takes(S,C,T_v)$ and $\neg offered(C,T_v)$ in:

$$ic1_1' \leftarrow takes(S,C,T_v) \wedge \neg \delta takes(S,C,T_v) \wedge \neg offered(C,T_v) \wedge \neg \iota offered(C,T_v),$$

are always false in a transaction time point $now\text{-}1$, and thus we can eliminate this transition rule.

## 3.3 Insertion Event Rules

Let $p$ be a derived or inconsistency predicate. Insertion events of $p$ were defined in (5) as:

$$\forall X,T_v\,(\iota p(X,T_v) \leftrightarrow p'(X,T_v) \wedge \neg p(X,T_v)).$$

And replacing $p'(X,T)$ by its equivalent definition given in (13) we get:

$$\iota p(X,T_v) \leftarrow p_i'(X,T_v) \wedge \neg p(X,T_v) \quad \text{with } i = 1, ..., 2^k. \tag{14}$$

By replacing $p_i'(X,T_v)$ with its equivalent definition given in (12), we get a set of **insertion events rules**. They allow us to deduce which $\iota p$ (induced insertions) happen in a transition. If $p$ is an inconsistency predicate, $\iota p$ facts correspond to a violation of the integrity constraint. Note that in the case of integrity constraints, $\neg ici$ always holds because the bt-ddb was consistent at transaction time point $now\text{-}1$, and we can simplify this literal:

$$\iota ici \leftarrow ici_i' \quad i=2, ..., 2^k \tag{15}$$

## 3.4 Deletion Event Rules

Let $p$ be a derived predicate. Deletion events of $p$ were defined in (6) as:
$$\forall X,T_v\,(\delta p(X,T_v) \leftrightarrow p(X,T_v) \wedge \neg p'(X,T_v)).$$
And replacing $p'(X,T)$ by its equivalent definition given in (13) we get:

$$\delta p(X,T_v) \leftarrow p(X,T_v) \wedge \neg p1'(X,T_v) \wedge ... \wedge \neg p_i'(X,T_v) \wedge ... \wedge \neg p2k'(X,T_v) \tag{16}$$

By replacing $p_i'(X,T_v)$ with its equivalent definition given in (12), we get a set of **deletion events rules**. They allow us to deduce which $\delta p$ (induced deletions) happen in a transition. Note that in the case of integrity constraints, $\delta icn$ cannot happen in any transition, since we assume that the bt-ddb is consistent before the update, and thus $icn$ is always false.

## 3.5 The Augmented Database

Let D be a bt-ddb. We denote the augmented bt-ddb by A(D), based in the concept of augmented deductive database defined in [17], to the bt-ddb consisting of D, its transition rules and its event rules.

If SLDNF resolution is complete for D, then it will also be complete for A(D). [17].

# 4 Applying Transition Rules for Integrity Constraint Checking in Bitemporal Deductive Databases

The augmented bt-ddb described in the previous section can be used directly to check if a transaction produces or not inconsistencies.

Let $D$ be a bt-ddb, $A(D)$ the augmented bt-ddb, and $TR$ a transaction consisting of a set of events at valid time point $T$. If $TR$ leads to an inconsistency then some of the $iicn$ will hold in the transition. Using SLDNF proof procedure, $TR$ violates integrity constraint $icn$ if the goal $\leftarrow iicn$ succeeds from input set $A(D) \cup TR$. If every branch of the SLDNF-search space for $A(D) \cup TR \cup \{\leftarrow iicn\}$ is a failure branch, then $TR$ does not violate $icn$, as show in figure 4.1.

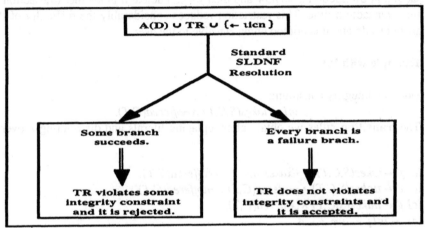

**Fig. 4.1.**

From the insertion event rule $iicn$ for (15), we then use the transition rules of $icn$ to proof the consistency of the bt-ddb. Following, we illustrate the utility of the transition rules for integrity constraints checking, but first we explain the simplifications applied to them. We show some updates that can violate some transition rules obtained for the constraints in the example presented in section 2. Specifically, we select the constraints where we can apply the different types of simplifications. Next subsections simulate (using a discontinuous line) what would happen if the transaction were applied in the bt-ddb. Note that we do not really apply the transaction, we only simulate.

## 4.1 Simplifications of Transition Rules.

In the following subsections we are going to show the following types of simplifications:

***Inconsistent Rules Simplification:*** When we find $\neg \psi(X,T) \wedge \psi(p,T1) \wedge T1 < T$ in a transition rule, we can eliminate it because $\psi(p,T1)$ is from $T1$ to *forever* and that includes $T$.

***Null Effect Rules Simplification***: When we find $\delta p(X,T) \wedge \iota p(X,T1) \wedge T1 < T$ in a transition rule, we can eliminate it because $\iota p(p,T1)$ is from $T1$ to *forever* and that includes $T$, it does not matter that $\delta p(X,T)$.

***Mutually Exclusive Rules Simplification***: When we find $\iota p(X,T) \wedge \delta q(X,T)$ in one transtion rule, and $\delta p(X,T) \wedge \iota q(X,T)$ in another transition rule we can eliminate both of them because if one of them holds then it means the other one happened in a previous transaction time and the database is already inconsistent.

Our simplifications consider an assumption concerning data manipulation: In a transaction we cannot insert and delete the same fact. We have to insert the fact in a transaction at transaction time *now* and then we can delete it in another transaction in a future transaction time. This restriction reduces considerably the difficulty of the update in bt-ddb and it is not too unmanageable to the user.

### 4.2 Example with Ic1

Consider the integrity constraint:
$$ic1 \leftarrow takes(S,C,T) \wedge \neg offered(C,T).$$
The **transition rules** we obtain after replacing literals and distributing $\wedge$ over $\vee$ are:

$$ic1_2' \leftarrow takes(S,C,T) \wedge \neg\delta takes(S,C,T) \wedge \delta offered(C,T).$$
$$ic1_3' \leftarrow \iota takes(S,C,T) \wedge \neg offered(C,T) \wedge \neg\iota offered(C,T).$$
$$ic1_4' \leftarrow \iota takes(S,C,T) \wedge \delta offered(C,T).$$
$$ic1' \leftarrow ic1_i' \quad i = 2,...,4$$

We show in figure 4.2 an example of a transaction that violates $ic1_2'$ at transaction time 3. And in figure 4.3 we show its derivation tree.

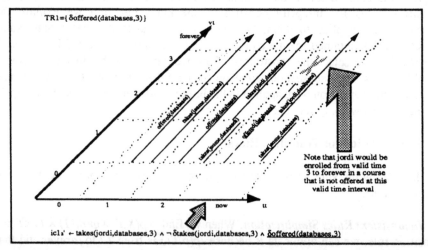

Fig. 4.2.

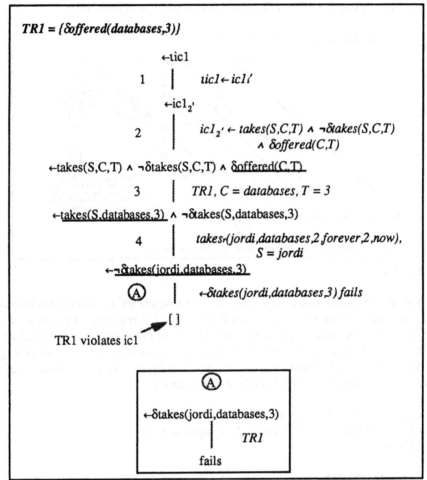

**Fig. 4.3.**

Steps 1 and 2 are SLDNF resolution steps where rules of A(D) act as input clauses. We may have several rules to resolve with, although only the failure branch that shows the violation of the integrity constraint is shown here.

Note that at steps 3 and 4 the predicate references to the transaction and to the database, respectively, and we go to the transaction or to the bt-ddb to find it, respectively.

At step A, the selected literal is: $\neg\delta takes(jordi,databases,3)$. In order to get a successful derivation, SLDNF search space must fail finitely for the subsidiary tree of: $\{\leftarrow\delta takes(jordi,databases,3)\}$.

Note that in the third step we have selected literal $\delta offered(C,T)$ instead of $takes(S,C,T)$. Given that in most real databases the number of facts is likely to be much greater than the number of events produced in a transition, it seems convenient to use a strategy of selecting first the events (once fully instantiated if they are negative).

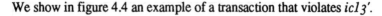

We show in figure 4.4 an example of a transaction that violates $ic13'$.

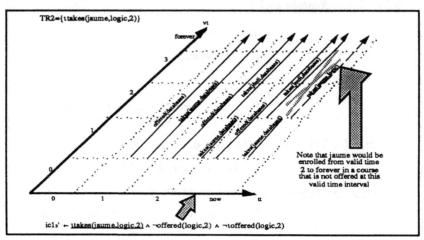

**Fig. 4.4.**

Note that transition rule $ic14' \leftarrow \iota takes(S,C,T) \wedge \delta offered(C,T)$ never holds because the bt-ddb was consistent at transaction time *now-1*, $ic2$ requires for a course to be offered it must have at least one student enrolled; if we delete a course $C$ at valid time $T$, for $ic2$ we must have one student enrolled in $C$ at valid time $T$ and that is $ic12'$. Therefore, we can eliminate $ic14'$ which is *mutually exclusive rule* with $ic24' \leftarrow \iota offered(C,T) \wedge \delta some\_enrol(C,T)$ and we finally obtain:

$ic12' \leftarrow takes(S,C,T) \wedge \neg \delta takes(S,C,T) \wedge \delta offered(C,T).$
$ic13' \leftarrow \iota takes(S,C,T) \wedge \neg offered(C,T) \wedge \neg \iota offered(C,T).$
$ic1' \leftarrow ic1_i' \quad i = 2,3$

## 4.3 Example with Ic4

Consider the integrity constraint:

$\qquad ic4 \leftarrow offered(C,T) \wedge \neg many\_students(C,T) \wedge many\_students(C,T1) \wedge T1 < T.$

The **transition rules** we obtain after replacing literals and distributing $\wedge$ over $\vee$ are:

$ic42' \leftarrow offered(C,T) \wedge \neg \delta offered(C,T) \wedge \neg many\_students(C,T) \wedge$
$\qquad \neg \iota many\_students(C,T) \wedge \iota many\_students(C,T1) \wedge T1 < T.$
$ic43' \leftarrow offered(C,T) \wedge \neg \delta offered(C,T) \wedge \delta many\_students(C,T) \wedge$
$\qquad many\_students(C,T1) \wedge \neg \delta many\_students(C,T1) \wedge T1 < T.$
$ic44' \leftarrow offered(C,T) \wedge \neg \delta offered(C,T) \wedge \delta many\_students(C,T) \wedge$
$\qquad \iota many\_students(C,T1) \wedge T1 < T.$
$ic45' \leftarrow \iota offered(C,T) \wedge \neg many\_students(C,T) \wedge \neg \iota many\_students(C,T) \wedge$
$\qquad many\_students(C,T1) \wedge \neg \delta many\_students(C,T1) \wedge T1 < T.$

$ic46' \leftarrow \iota offered(C,T) \wedge \neg many\_students(C,T) \wedge \neg \iota many\_students(C,T) \wedge$
$\quad \iota many\_students(C,T1) \wedge T1 < T.$

$ic47' \leftarrow \iota offered(C,T) \wedge \delta many\_students(C,T) \wedge many\_students(C,T1) \wedge$
$\quad \neg \delta many\_students(C,T1) \wedge T1 < T.$

$ic48' \leftarrow \iota offered(C,T) \wedge \delta many\_students(C,T) \wedge \iota many\_students(C,T1) \wedge T1 < T.$

$ic4' \leftarrow ic4_i' \quad i = 2,...,8$

where $\iota many\_students(C,T)$ and $\delta many\_students(C,T)$ are:

$\iota many\_students(C,T) \leftarrow many\_students_1'(C,T) \wedge \neg many\_students(C,T).$
$\iota many\_students(C,T) \leftarrow many\_students_2'(C,T) \wedge \neg many\_students(C,T).$
$\iota many\_students(C,T) \leftarrow many\_students_3'(C,T) \wedge \neg many\_students(C,T).$
$\iota many\_students(C,T) \leftarrow many\_students_4'(C,T) \wedge \neg many\_students(C,T).$
$\delta many\_students(C,T) \leftarrow many\_students(C,T) \wedge \neg many\_students_1'(C,T) \wedge$
$\qquad\qquad \neg many\_students_2'(C,T) \wedge \neg many\_students_3'(C,T) \wedge$
$\qquad\qquad \neg many\_students_4'(C,T).$

and where $many\_students_1'(C,T)$, $many\_students_2'(C,T)$,
$many\_students_3'(C,T)$ and $many\_students_4'(C,T)$ are:

$many\_students(C,T)_1' \leftarrow takes(S1,C,T) \wedge \neg \delta takes(S1,C,T) \wedge takes(S2,C,T) \wedge$
$\qquad\qquad \neg \delta takes(S2,C,T) \wedge S1 \neq S2.$

$many\_students(C,T)_2' \leftarrow takes(S1,C,T) \wedge \neg \delta takes(S1,C,T) \wedge \iota takes(S2,C,T) \wedge$
$\qquad\qquad S1 \neq S2.$

$many\_students(C,T)_3' \leftarrow \iota takes(S1,C,T) \wedge takes(S2,C,T) \wedge \neg \delta takes(S2,C,T) \wedge$
$\qquad\qquad S1 \neq S2.$

$many\_students(C,T)_4' \leftarrow \iota takes(S1,C,T) \wedge \iota takes(S2,C,T) \wedge S1 \neq S2.$

We show in figure 4.5 an example of a transaction that violates $ic43'$.

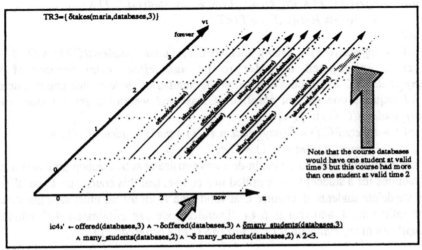

**Fig. 4.5.**

We show in figure 4.6 an example of a transaction that violates *ic45'*.

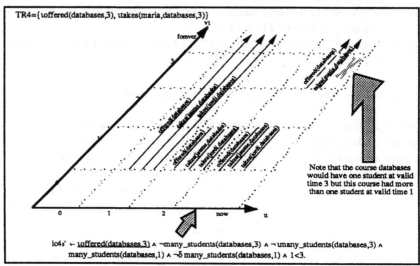

**Fig. 4.6.**

Note that integrity constraints *ic42'*, *ic44'*,*ic46'* ,*ic47'* and *ic48'* can be eliminated.

*ic42'* ← *offered(C,T)* ∧ ¬δ*offered(C,T)* ∧ ¬*many_students(C,T)* ∧
    ¬ι*many_students(C,T)* ∧ ι*many_students(C,T1)* ∧ *T1<T* .

and

*ic46'* ← ι*offered(C,T)* ∧ ¬*many_students(C,T)* ∧ ¬ι*many_students(C,T)* ∧
    ι*many_students(C,T1)* ∧ *T1<T*.

can be eliminated in order to be *inconsistent rules* because if we
ι*many_students(C,T1)* in a *T1 <T*, we ι*many_students(C,T)* so when one insert at
valid time *T1*, insert from *T1* to *forever*, including *T*.

*ic44'* ← *offered(C,T)* ∧ ¬δ*offered(C,T)* ∧ δ*many_students(C,T)* ∧
    ι*many_students(C,T1)* ∧ *T1<T* .

and

*ic48'* ← ι*offered(C,T)* ∧ δ*many_students(C,T)* ∧ ι*many_students(C,T1)* ∧ *T1<T* .

can be eliminated in order to be *null effect rules* because if we
ι*many_students(C,T1)*, it does not matter the number of students that one can delete
so *ic1* requires one student enrolled at least and we insert another one when
ι*many_students(C,T1)* in *T1<T* .

*ic47'* ← ι*offered(C,T)* ∧ δ*many_students(C,T)* ∧ *many_students(C,T1)* ∧
    ¬δ*many_students(C,T1)* ∧ *T1<T* .

can be eliminated because the bt-ddb was consistent at transaction time *now-1* and
*ic1* requires for a student to be enrolled in a course, that this course has to be offered
so if we delete students of a course *C* at valid time *T*, for *ic1* we must have this course
*C* at valid time *T* and that is *ic43'*. Therefore, we can eliminate *ic47'* which is
*mutually exclusive rule* with *ic14'* ← ι*takes(S,C,T)* ∧ δ*offered(C,T)*.

After this simplifications we finally obtain:

$ic43' \leftarrow offered(C,T) \land \neg \delta offered(C,T) \land \delta many\_students(C,T) \land$
$\qquad many\_students(C,T1) \land \neg \delta many\_students(C,T1) \land T1 < T.$
$ic45' \leftarrow \iota offered(C,T) \land \neg many\_students(C,T) \land \neg \iota many\_students(C,T) \land$
$\qquad many\_students(C,T1) \land \neg \delta many\_students(C,T1) \land T1 < T.$
$ic4' \leftarrow ic4_i' \qquad i = 3,5$

## 5 Comparison with Other Methods

Only a few methods for integrity checking in deductive databases incorporate time, as you can see in the bibliography of this research area in [9].

There are methods, such as Chomicki's method [5], [6] or Wüthrich's method [28], that use temporal logic to formulate integrity constraints. But these methods do not contain temporal information explicitly as in our case.

We could have chosen a logic-based Event Calculus, such as [10], [19], [24] or [27], to develop our method, but we think this choice is unimportant, considering that the main thing presented in this paper is a new integrity constraint checking approach for bt-ddb.

Plexousakis's method [18] formulates integrity constraints in a first order language provided by Telos [12], a language for knowledge representation. Telos adopts Allen's [1] interval based time model for representing historical information. The method consists in generating a parameterized simplified structure (PSS) for each literal of the integrity constraints and the deductive rules that can be affected by an update and it needs to construct a dependency graph for integrity constraint checking. The method for finding the simplified form is an extension of Nicolas's method [15], which includes temporal treatment.

Summarising, Plexousakis's method is focussed on temporal integrity constraint simplification with a large number of the thirteen relationships which can exist between two time intervals, defined by Allen [1]. Whereas in our case we do not have Allen's relationships. Furthermore, the method needs to use a meta-interpreter from Telos's language to parameterize a simplified structure. In contrast, we use only SLDNF proof procedure directly provided in a Prolog system.

## 6 Conclusions and Further Work

In this paper we have presented how and why to apply transition rules for integrity constraints checking in bt-ddbs. Given an update, the transition rules define predicate $p'$ in the updated bt-ddb in terms of transaction time point $now-1$ of the predicates appearing in the body of the rule, and the events that occur at transaction time point $now$. Event rules define explicitly the changes induced by the update on the derived predicates. We clarify that transition rules are important to recognise all the possible cases that produce violations of integrity constraints.

Our further work consists in completing our approach for integrity constraints checking in bt-ddbs with: updates of integrity constraints and deductive rules, recursive rules, simplifications of the event rules and more simplifications of transition rules to increase the efficiency incorporating related work in this area, for example [7].

Like other temporal deductive database systems as ChronoLog [3] and ChronoBase [23], we would try to incorporate our work in the FOLRE project [26].

## Acknowledgements

The authors would like to thank Antoni Olivé for the support he has given to this work and also P. Costa, D. Costal, E. Mayol, J. A. Pastor, C. Quer, M. R. Sancho, E. Teniente, T. Urpí and specially Michael Gertz for many useful comments and discussions.

This work has been partially supported by the CICYT PRONTIC program project TIC94-0512.

## References

1.    Allen, J.F. "Maintaining Knowledge about Temporal Intervals". In Communications of the ACM. Vol. 26. Num 11. 1983. pp 832-843.

2.    Apt, K.R.; Blair, H.A.; Walker, A. "Towards a Theory of Declarative Knowledge". In Foundations of Deductive Databases and Logic Programming (J.Minker ed.). Morgan Kaufmann. 1988. pp 89-148.

3.    Böhlen, M. "Managing Temporal Knowledge in Deductive Databases". PhD thesis, Swiss Federal Institute of Technology. Zürich, 1994.

4.    Bry, F.; Manthey, R.; Martens, R. "Integrity Verification in Knowledge Bases". ECRC Report D.2.1.a, München, April 1990, 26 p.

5.    Chomicki, J. "History-less Checking of Dynamic Integrity Constraints". In the 8th Int. Conf. on Data Engineering, IEEE Computer Society Press. Phoenix AZ, February, 1992. pp 557-564.

6.    Chomicki, J. "Efficient Checking Encoding of Temporal Integrity Constraints Using Bounded History Encoding". ACM Transactions on Database Systems. June, 1995. pp 149-186.

7.    Gertz, M.; Lipeck, U.W. ""Temporal" Integrity Constraints in Temporal Databases". Proc. of the International Workshop on Temporal Databases. Zürich. (Clifford/Tuzhilin Eds). Springer-Verlag, September, 1995. pp 77-92.

8.    Jensen, C.S.; Clifford, J.; Gadia, S.K.; Segev, A.; Snodgrass, R.T. "A Glossary of Temporal Database Concepts". Proc. SIGMOD-RECORD. Vol. 21. 1992.

9.    Kline, N. "An Update of the Temporal Database Bibliography ". Proc. SIGMOD-RECORD. Vol. 22. Num. 4. 1993.

10.   Kowalski, R.; Sergot, M. "A Logic-Based Calculus of Events" New Generation Computing. Vol 4, Num 1. February, 1986. pp 67-95. OHMSHA LTD and Springer-Verlag.

11.   Lloyd, J.W. "Foundations on Logic Programming". Second edition. Springer, 1987.

12.   Mylopoulos, J.; Borgida, A.; Jarke, M.; Koubarakis, M. "Telos: Representing Knowledge About Information Systems". ACM Transactions on information systems. Vol. 8. Num 4. 1990. pp 324-362.

13.   Martín, C.; Sistac, J. "Integrity Constraints Checking in Historical Deductive Databases". Proc. of the 5th. Int. Workshop on the Deductive Approach to Information Systems and Databases. Aiguablava, 1994. pp 299-324.

14.   Martín, C.; Sistac, J. "A Method for Integrity Constraint Checking in Temporal Deductive Databases". To appear in Proc. of the 3th. Int. Workshop on Temporal Representation and Reasoning. Florida, 1996.

15.   Nicolas, J.M. "Logic for Improving Integrity Checking in Deductive Databases". In Gallaire, H.; Minker, J. Eds. "Logic and databases". Plenum Press. 1978, pp 325-344.

16.   Olivé, A. "On the Design and Implementation of Information Systems from Deductive Conceptual Models". Proc. of the 15th. Int. Conf. on VLDB'89, pp 3-11.

17.   Olivé, A. "Integrity Constraints Checking in Deductive Databases". Proc. of the 17th. Int. Conf on VLDB'91. pp 513-523.

18.   Plexousakis, D. "Integrity Constraint and Rule Maintenance in Temporal Deductive Knowledge Bases". Proc. of the 19th. Int. Conf. on VLDB'93. pp 146-157.

19.   Sadri, F.; Kowalski, R. "Variants of the Event Calculus". Proc. of the 12th Int. Conf. on Logic Programming, 1995. pp 67-81.

20.   Sarda, N.L. "HSQL: A Historical Query Language". In [25], pp 110-140.

21.   Snodgrass, R.; Ahn, I. "Temporal Databases". IEEE Computer. Vol 19. Num 9. September, 1986.

22.   Sancho, M.R; Olivé, A. "Deriving Transactions Specifications from Deductive Conceptual Models of Information Systems". Proc. of CAiSE'94 conference. 1994, pp 311-324.

23.   Sripada, S.M.; Möller, P. "The Generalized ChronoBase Temporal Data Model". In K. Apt, F. Turini (eds). Meta-Logics and logic programming, MIT Press, 1995.

24.   Sripada, S.M. "Efficient Implementation of the Event Calculus for Temporal Deductive Databases". Proc. of the 12th Int. Conf. on Logic Programming, 1995. pp 99-113.

25.   Tansel, A.U.; Clifford, J.; Gadia, S.; Jajodia, S.; Segev, A.; Snodgrass, R. "Temporal Databases: Theory, Design and Implementation". Benjamin/Cummings. 1993.

26.   Urpí, T.; Teniente, E.; Pastor, J.A.; Mayol, E.; Martín, C. "FOLRE: Towards a System for the Integrated Treatment of Updates and Rule Enforcement in Deductive Databases". In Proc. of the Sixth ERCIM Database Research Group Workshop on Deductive and Interoperable Databases. Barcelona. Nov. 1994.

27.   Van Belleghem, K.; Denecker, M.; De Schreye, D. "Combining Situation Calculus and Event Calculus". Proc. of the 12th Int. Conf. on Logic Programming, 1995. pp 83-97.

28.   Wüthrich, B. "Large Deductive Databases with Constraints". PhD thesis, Swiss Federal Institute of Technology. Zürich, 1991.

# Invited Lecture

# Towards a Unified Agent Architecture that Combines Rationality with Reactivity

Robert Kowalski and Fariba Sadri

Department of Computing, Imperial College,
180 Queen's Gate, London SW7 2BZ, UK
(rak, fs)@doc.ic.ac.uk

Abstract. In this paper we analyse the differences between rational and reactive agent architectures, and propose a uniform agent architecture that aims to capture both so-called cases. For this purpose we employ a proof procedure, in control the choice behaviour, which combines definitions with integrity constraints. The proof procedure is general, and has been shown to subsume to unify abductive logic programming, constraint logic programming and semantic query optimisation. We also employ a resource-bounded formalisation of the proof procedure which allows an agent's reasoning to be interrupted and resumed, so that observations and actions can be performed.

## 1. Introduction

The traditional notion of a rational agent in Artificial Intelligence focuses on the agent's thinking process and downplays and ignores its interaction with the environment. This notion has been challenged in recent years by the contrary notion of a reactive agent that focuses on the agent's timely interaction with the environment and downplays or denies the role of thinking.

In this paper we propose an agent architecture that reconciles rationality with reactivity. Rationality is achieved by means of a proof procedure that employs backchaining in a knowledge base to reduce goals to subgoals. Reactivity is achieved by incorporating integrity constraints into the proof procedure and by formalising the proof procedure in such a way that it can be interrupted to make observations and perform actions.

The rest of the paper is structured as follows. Sections 2 and 3 discuss the notions of rational and reactive agents, respectively, and section 4 analyses their differences. Sections 5-9 develop the uniform architecture and the proof procedure that captures both types of agents as special cases.

## 2. From Knowledge based systems to rational agents

A traditional knowledge based system in Artificial Intelligence contains knowledge in symbolic often formal form, which can be both updated and queried. The only action such a system can perform is to return answers to queries.

# Towards a Unified Agent Architecture that Combines Rationality with Reactivity

Robert Kowalski and Fariba Sadri

Department of Computing, Imperial College
180 Queen's Gate, London SW7 2BZ, UK
{rak,fs}@doc.ic.ac.uk

**Abstract.** In this paper we analyse the differences between rational and reactive agent architectures, and propose a uniform agent architecture that aims to capture both as special cases. For this purpose we employ a proof procedure, to control the agent's behaviour, which combines definitions with integrity constraints. The proof procedure is general, and has been shown elsewhere to unify abductive logic programming, constraint logic programming and semantic query optimisation. We also employ a resource-bounded formalisation of the proof procedure which allows the agent's reasoning to be interrupted and resumed, so that observations and actions can be performed.

## 1 Introduction

The traditional notion of a rational agent in Artificial Intelligence focuses on the agent's thinking process and downplays or ignores its interaction with the environment. This notion has been challenged in recent years by the contrary notion of a reactive agent that focuses on the agent's timely interaction with the environment and downplays or denies the role of thinking.

In this paper we propose an agent architecture that reconciles rationality with reactivity. Rationality is achieved by means of a proof procedure that employs definitions in a knowledge base to reduce goals to subgoals. Reactivity is achieved by employing appropriate integrity constraints in the proof procedure and by formulating the proof procedure in such a way that it can be interrupted to make observations and perform actions.

The rest of the paper is structured as follows. Sections 2 and 3 discuss the notions of rational and reactive agents, respectively, and section 4 analyses their differences. Sections 5-9 develop the uniform architecture and the proof procedure that captures both types of agents as special cases.

## 2 From knowledge based systems to rational agents

A traditional knowledge based system in Artificial Intelligence contains knowledge in symbolic (often logical) form, which can be both updated and queried. The only action such a system can perform is to return answers to queries.

Moreover, it might expend an unlimited amount of resources to compute such answers.

Knowledge based systems differ from conventional database systems primarily in the richer forms of knowledge representation they employ. However, deductive databases, which represent knowledge in the form of both facts and rules, can be understood both as database systems and as knowledge based systems.

Traditional databases have many limitations. An important step towards removing these and towards enhancing their functionality is the extension to *active databases* e.g. [14, 15], which perform actions independently of users' queries. These actions are performed in response to events which occur externally in the environment or internally in the database. The actions serve a number of purposes, including view and integrity maintenance and communication with the environment.

Active databases typically achieve their added functionality through the use of a form of condition-action rules. We argue in this paper that such condition-action rules can be regarded as integrity constraints.

Databases which are both deductive and active can be understood as *agents*. The actions they perform can be understood as *goals*. These action goals arise either from higher level goals as the result of a goal-reduction process or from condition-action rules.

*Example 1.* The externally performed action *raise the alarm* might result from the higher-level internal goal *maintain security* by means of a rule

*maintain security* **if** *whenever there is an intruder raise the alarm*

which is "triggered" when an intruder is detected (by means of an update/observation/input to the knowledge base). □

Rational agents have both beliefs (or knowledge) and goals. Goals include actions which are output to the environment as well as higher-level goals which guide the agent's behaviour.

The behaviour of a rational agent can be specified (and implemented) by means of an abstract procedure which defines the agent's observation-thought-action cycle:

*to cycle at time $T$,*
 *i) observe any input at time $T$,*
 *ii) record any such input,*
*iii) (optionally) check inputs for satisfaction of integrity constraints,*
 *iv) solve (or re-solve) goals by constructing a plan, employing resources $R$,*
 *v) select a plan from among the alternatives,*
 *vi) execute any requisite atomic action (in the selected plan), at time $T + R + 1$,*
*vii) cycle at time $T + R + 2$.*

The amount of resources $R$ a traditional agent might expend on checking inputs and solving goals is unbounded. Traditionally, such an agent constructs a *plan*, consisting of an appropriate structure of atomic actions which completely and provably solves its higher-level goals. Only after having generated a complete plan, does the agent begin to execute it. Any observations made on later iterations of *cycle* which violate the agent's expectations require the agent to replan its earlier solution to its goals.

Critics (e.g. [1, 2]) of the traditional knowledge based approach argue that the lack of a bound on the resources $R$ renders the rational agent architecture unfeasible. They argue that rationality interferes with an agent's ability to react appropriately and in real time to changes that occur unpredictably in its environment.

## 3   (Generalised) Reactive agents

A reactive agent need have neither an explicit set of beliefs, stored in a knowledge base, nor an explicit representation of any goals. Reactivity can be achieved simply by means of an appropriate collection of stimulus-response, input-output or condition-action rules.

*Example 2.* The rule

**if** *there is an intruder* **then** *raise the alarm*

is triggered by an input observation of an intruder and immediately generates the action of raising an alarm as output to the environment. Such a rule needs no representation of its purpose, the goal towards which it is directed. In this example, there is no need for a representation of the world or even the internal state of the agent.                                                                        □

*Example 3.* The rules

**if** *clear ahead* **then** *move forward*
**if** *obstacle ahead* **then** *turn right*

similarly require no knowledge base, nor goal representation. Employed together as a pair, they achieve the implicit goals of movement and obstacle avoidance. Such rules, possibly sensitive to the contents of an updatable local state, are typical of the stimulus-response rules of Brook's subsumption architecture [1, 2].                                                                        □

*Example 4.* The rule

**if** *Agent requests do(self, Act, T2) at time T1*
      **and** *Agent is friendly*
      **and** *can do(self, Act, T2)*
      **and** $T1 < T2$
**then** *do(self, Act, T2)*

requires more powerful resources. It is triggered by an input request occurring at (*transaction*) time $T1$, but its remaining conditions are verified by consulting a knowledge base (or simply by looking up the value of variables in an internal state). However, the action itself cannot be performed immediately, but needs to become a *commitment*, which is executed later when the transaction time becomes equal to the *domain* time $T2$ of the action which is requested. Such condition-action rules are typical of the rules which govern the behaviour of agents in Shoham's AgentO architecture [12].                                    □

Condition-action rules can also be formulated in a modal language such as METATEM [6], which exploits Gabbay's separation theorem [5], stating that any temporal logic formula can be rewritten in a logically equivalent form:

**if** *formula about* **past then** *formula about* **future**.

*Example 5.* The execution of a METATEM rule, such as

**if yesterday** *Agent requests Act* **then sometime in the future** $do(Act)$

is similarly a process of matching conditions against information in an up-datable knowledge base and of creating commitments from the conclusions of the rule.                                                                             □

At an abstract level, all of these examples can be accommodated within a single condition-action rule production system interpreter:

*to cycle at time $T$,*
 *i) observe any input at time $T$,*
 *ii) (optionally) record any such input,*
*iii) match conditions of condition-action rules against inputs,*
*iv) (optionally) verify any remaining conditions of the rules using facts in the knowledge base,*
 *v) select an action to execute from the conclusions of competing rules (all of whose conditions are satisfied),*
*vi) execute any such action at time $T + n + 1$,*
*vii) cycle at time $T + n + 2$.*

Reactivity is achieved by limiting the amount of resources employed in steps (iii) and (iv) to some fixed small amount of time $n$. This is easy in cases, like examples 3.1 and 3.2, where there is no knowledge base and conditions are verified simply by matching them with the input. It is more difficult in cases, like example 3.3, where reasoning is needed to verify some of the conditions. One practical solution, employed in systems such as AgentO, is to restrict the form of the sentences in the knowledge base, so that conditions can be verified efficiently, within the restricted available time, $n$.

## 4  How to reconcile rationality with reactivity

In our characterisations of them, there are two main differences between rational and reactive agents:

- the form in which "knowledge" and "goals" are represented
- the amount of resources that may be consumed within a single cycle.

In a rational agent, goals are represented explicitly and knowledge is represented as goal reduction rules. Such goal reduction rules typically have the form *conclusion if conditions*, associated both with logic programs and with deduction rules in deductive databases. Backward reasoning is used to match goals to conclusions of rules, reducing them to subgoals which are the conditions of the rules. Actions are atomic goals to which no reduction rules apply.

In the traditional agent architecture, top-level goals are fully reduced to complete plans, consisting of atomic subgoals, before they are executed. This can take an unbounded amount of time.

In reactive agents, goals are achieved implicitly by condition-action rules, and efficiency is obtained by avoiding the overheads associated with goal reduction. By appropriate restrictions on the form of the knowledge base, if there is one, conditions can be verified efficiently, and a single iteration of the agent's cycle can be completed within a fixed, small amount of time, $n$.

To reconcile the differences between these two kinds of agent, we need therefore

1) to understand better the relationships between goals, goal-reduction rules and condition-action rules, and

2) to organise goal-reduction so that it can be interrupted after a fixed amount of time, $n$, to execute actions and to perform observations, and so that it can be resumed correctly on the next cycle.

For the first problem we will argue that condition-action rules can be interpreted as integrity constraints, and that there is a simple relationship between integrity constraints and goal-reduction rules, which facilitates employing them together in a single proof procedure.

For the second problem we will argue that the simple definition of the provability predicate *demo*, used in logic programming, can be extended to define an enhanced *demo* predicate which performs goal-reduction in the required manner.

## 5   Goals, integrity constraints and generalised logic programs

Database systems distinguish between two kinds of sentences: sentences which *define* the data and, accordingly belong to the database, and sentences (integrity constraints) which *constrain* the data and are not actually part of it. Typically, sentences that define the data have a simple syntax – variable-free atomic sentences in the case of relational databases; positive Horn clauses, usually without function symbols, in the case of deductive databases. However, sentences that constrain the data generally have a much richer syntax. In both relational and deductive databases, integrity constraints can be unrestricted sentences of first-order logic. In this respect, integrity constraints are like database queries, which can also be sentences of first-order logic.

The similarity between integrity constraints and queries is more than syntactic. It can be argued that they have the same semantics. However, many different semantics have been proposed for integrity constraints. These include proposals that they be consistent with the database (or the completion of the database), that they be theorems of the database (or its completion), or that they be epistemic (or metalevel) statements that "hold" of the database.

Recently, we have developed a proof procedure [3, 4, 9, 10, 13] for abductive logic programs with integrity constraints, in which we have found it useful to treat integrity constraints and queries identically. This requires that they have the same semantics. To a first approximation, the semantics we employ can be thought of as requiring that queries and integrity constraints be theorems of the completion of the knowledge base (i.e. database or program)[1].

The proof procedure, in standard logic programming fashion, uses definitions to reduce atomic goals to subgoals. These subgoals can themselves be formulae of full first-order logic. Subgoals, therefore, have the same syntax as queries and integrity constraints. This syntax is the key to the relationship between goals, goal-reduction rules and condition-action rules that we are looking for.

*Example 6.* Consider the (generalised) logic program

$maintain\text{-}security \leftarrow \forall T \ [intruder \ at \ time \ T \rightarrow do(self, raise\text{-}alarm, T)].$

Given the top-level goal (or integrity constraint)

$maintain\text{-}security$

the program reduces this to the (generalised) subgoal (or integrity constraint)

$\forall T \ [intruder \ at \ time \ T \rightarrow do(self, raise\text{-}alarm, T)].$ □

This example illustrates a general phenomenon: Given a set of goals $G$ and goal-reduction rules $Kb$, we can, in many cases, replace them by an equivalent set of condition-action rules $R$. The latter are equivalent to the former in the sense that the rules $R$ implicitly accomplish the goals $G$ in the manner prescribed by $Kb$. The condition-action rules $R$ can be viewed as a compiled form of $G$ and $Kb$. The process of generating $R$ from $G$ and $Kb$, called partial evaluation [11], is a powerful, but standard logic programming technique.

Not every knowledge base and initial set of goals can be reduced to a set of condition-action rules. The goals must be defined non-recursively, in particular.

We do not claim that every set of condition-action rules is the result of partially evaluating an explicit goal-reduction representation. It is quite possible that an agent might learn its condition-action rules directly, as the result of its interactions with the environment, without the mediation of any goal-reduction representation.

But if we accept that condition-action rules are just a special kind of integrity constraint (or generalised goal) and if an agent can reason with *both*

---

[1] More precisely, we require that they be true in all *intended* models of the knowledge base [10].

goal-reduction rules and integrity constraints, then there is no reason to require that condition-action rules be derived from "higher-level" explicit goal-reduction representations. Condition-action rules can join other (generalised) goals in the traditional rational agent architecture that recognises beliefs and goals as the two main components of an agent's state.

# 6   The proof procedure

We now outline a proof procedure based on [3, 4, 9, 10, 13], which reasons with two kinds of sentences:

i) *Definitions* in if-and-only-if form:

$$G \leftrightarrow D_1 \vee \ldots \vee D_n \qquad n \geq 0.$$

These are used for goal reduction. If $n=0$ the disjunction is equivalent *to false*.

ii) *Integrity constraints* in clausal form:

$$A_1 \vee \ldots \vee A_n \leftarrow B_1 \wedge \ldots \wedge B_m \qquad m, n \geq 0.$$

If $m=0$ the conjunction is equivalent to *true*. If $n=0$ the disjunction is equivalent to *false*.

The disjuncts $D_i$ of a definition are conjunctions

$$C_1 \wedge \ldots \wedge C_m \qquad m \geq 1$$

where each conjunct is either an atom (possibly *true*) or an implication with syntactic form (ii) identical to that of an integrity constraint. The $A_i$ and $B_i$, in the conclusion and conditions of implications (ii) are atomic formulae. As in N-Prolog [7], negative literals $\neg A$ are written as implications of the form

$$false \leftarrow A.$$

For simplicity, in this part of the paper, we ignore variables and quantifiers, restricting ourselves to the propositional case. A more complete account of similar proof procedures can be found in [3, 4, 9, 10, 13].

The inference rules of the proof procedure transform a *goal statement* which has the syntax

$$D_1 \vee \ldots \vee D_n$$

of the body of a definition into another goal statement, which has the same form. All integrity constraints are conjoined to every goal statement. By distributing disjunction over conjunction they become a conjunct of every disjunct of every goal statement. Thus, integrity constraints are treated as goals which are always present.

Goal statements have a procedural interpretation as an *or-and tree*. They can also be written in a logically equivalent *and-or tree* form (i.e. as a conjunction of disjunctions). In particular they can be put into a form where integrity constraints are written only once, conjoined to every goal statement.

Atomic subgoals of the form

$$do(self, Act, T)$$

are "solved" by executing them in step (vi)[2] of the agent cycle when the domain time $T$ becomes the current transaction time.

The proof procedure has four main inference rules:

i) **Goal reduction** uses a definition

$$G \leftrightarrow D_1 \vee ... \vee D_n$$

**case 1:** to replace a goal statement of the form[3]

$$(G \wedge G') \vee D \quad \text{by}$$
$$((D_1 \vee ... \vee D_n) \wedge G') \vee D$$

**case 2:** to replace a goal statement of the form

$$((D' \leftarrow G \wedge G') \wedge G'') \vee D \quad \text{by}$$
$$((D' \leftarrow D_1 \wedge G') \wedge ... \wedge (D' \leftarrow D_n \wedge G') \wedge G'') \vee D.$$

The second form of goal-reduction implicitly uses the equivalence

$$A \leftarrow (B \vee C) \quad \leftrightarrow \quad (A \leftarrow B) \wedge (A \leftarrow C).$$

ii) **Splitting** explicitly distributes $\vee$ over $\wedge$, replacing a formula of the form

$$(D \vee D') \wedge G \quad \text{by}$$
$$(D \wedge G) \vee (D' \wedge G).$$

iii) **Propagation** replaces a goal statement of the form

$$(G \wedge (D' \leftarrow G \wedge G') \wedge G'') \vee D \quad \text{by}$$
$$(G \wedge (D' \leftarrow G') \wedge G'') \vee D.$$

When the implication $D' \leftarrow G \wedge G'$ is an integrity constraint or an implication derived from an integrity constraint, propagation contributes to integrity verification[4].

---

[2] Note that the rational and reactive agents cycles differ primarily in steps (iii), (iv), (v).

[3] Here and elsewhere, we assume the commutativity and associativity of conjunction and disjunction. In particular, when we write a goal statement in the form $(G \wedge G') \vee D$, we intend that $G \wedge G'$ may be any disjunct in the goal statement and that $G$ may be any conjunct in the disjunct.

[4] In the propositional case, the implication $D' \leftarrow G \wedge G'$ is not needed in the derived goal statement, because it is "subsumed" by the derived implication $D' \leftarrow G'$. In the more general case, it needs to be retained when it is not subsumed.

iv) **Logical equivalence** replaces a formula by another formula which is both logically equivalent and more suitable for manipulation by the other inference rules. These include the following equivalences used as rewrite rules:

$$G \wedge true \; \leftrightarrow G$$
$$G \wedge false \leftrightarrow false$$
$$D \vee true \; \leftrightarrow true$$
$$D \vee false \leftrightarrow D.$$

The proof procedure was developed initially in an attempt to unify abductive logic programming, constraint logic programming and semantic query optimisation. For this purpose, definitions are used only for completely defined predicates. Incompletely defined predicates, such as abducibles, have to be treated differently. Technically the simplest, and most elegant way to deal with them is to approximate their definitions by means of integrity constraints, which are included conceptually, therefore, in every disjunct of every goal statement. These integrity constraints, in the simplest case, consist only of atoms or the negation of atoms.

Incompletely defined predicates include all input predicates, which describe observations, and all output predicates, which record the result of actions attempted by the agent. By recording observations in goal statements, the propagation inference rule implements the triggering of condition-action rules by the input as a special case. The verification of the remaining conditions of the condition-action rules is performed by other propagation steps or by case 2 of the goal-reduction rule.

We will see in section 8 that by recording the results of attempted actions in goal statements, propagation also eliminates any disjuncts of a goal statement which are incompatible with the results of the action.

## 7 Resource-bounded reasoning

The proof procedure just described combines the goal-reduction rules of a rational agent with the condition-action rules of a reactive agent. It combines them, moreover, as a special case of a general proof procedure which combines goal-directed, backward reasoning using definitions, with data-driven, forward reasoning using integrity constraints. This proof procedure provides us with a solution to the first of the two subproblems which we identified in section 4, of the problem of reconciling rationality with reactivity.

We still need a solution to the second subproblem, which is to control the reasoning process so that it functions correctly with bounded resources. For this purpose we employ a simple enhancement of the standard *demo* predicate. We intend the enhanced *demo* predicate to be invoked by the agent in place of steps (iii) and (iv) of the agent cycle.

The standard *demo* predicate for a propositional Horn clause language has a simple definition by means of a metalogic program:

$$demo(KB, G) \leftarrow demo(KB, G \leftarrow G') \wedge demo(KB, G')$$
$$demo(KB, G \wedge G') \leftarrow demo(KB, G) \wedge demo(KB, G')$$
$$demo(KB, true)$$

Here the same symbols, $\leftarrow$ and $\wedge$, are used for object level and metalevel implication and conjunction, respectively. $KB$ names a "knowledge base" of propositional Horn clauses, $G'$ names a conjunction of atoms and $G$ names an atom.
The first rule reduces $G$ to the subgoals $G'$, the second reduces the conjunction
of goals $G \wedge G'$ to separate subgoals $G, G'$, and the third asserts that an empty
set of goals is trivially solvable.

The simple $demo$ predicate above assumes that an unbounded amount of
resources is available for goal-reduction. Moreover, it returns no output. It simply
holds (at the metalevel) whenever the knowledge base solves the goal (at the
object level). Furthermore, it is restricted to goals which are conjunctions of
atoms. We need to remove all of these restrictions to obtain an enhanced $demo$
predicate that can be used to control the reasoning component of a resource-
bounded agent's cycle.

The following metalogic program defines the top-level of the enhanced $demo$
predicate we require. The new predicate $demo(KB, S, S', R)$ holds when the goal
statement $S$ can be reduced to the goal statement $S'$ in $R$ inference steps of the
proof procedure outlined in section 6.

$$demo(KB, S, S', R) \leftarrow step(KB, S, S'') \wedge demo(KB, S'', S', R - 1)$$
$$demo(KB, S, S, 0)$$

Here $step(KB, S, S'')$ holds when $S$ can be reduced to $S''$ in one inference step.
For example, the following two rules deal with case 1 of goal reduction and with
splitting, respectively:

$$step(KB, (G \wedge G') \vee D, (D' \wedge G') \vee D) \leftarrow (G \leftrightarrow D') \in KB$$
$$step(KB, ((D \vee D') \wedge G) \vee D'', (D \wedge G) \vee (D' \wedge G) \vee D'')$$

# 8 The cycle of an agent that combines rationality with reactivity

We can now reformulate the agent cycle in a uniform manner that includes both
the rational agent and the reactive agent as special cases:

*to cycle at time $T$,*
 *i) observe any input at time $T$,*
 *ii) record any such inputs,*
*iii) resume the proof procedure by first propagating the inputs,*
*iv) continue applying the proof procedure for a total of n inference steps,*
 *v) select, from among the alternatives, an atomic action whose domain time is
 compatible with the transaction time $T + n + 1$,*

*vi) execute any such action and record the results (success or failure),*
*vii) cycle at time $T + n + 2$.*

As mentioned in section 6, recording inputs and results of attempted actions is performed by adding to the current goal statement, atoms (in the case of observations and successful actions), or negations of atoms in the form

$$false \leftarrow do(self, act, t + n + 1)$$

(in the case of an action that fails at time $t + n + 1$).

The proof procedure is resumed at time $t$ in step (iii) by calling the enhanced *demo* predicate with arguments

$$demo(kb, s, s', n)$$

where $kb$ names the knowledge base, $s$ names the goal statement at time $t$, and $s'$ names the resulting goal statement at time $t + n$. For simplicity, we ignore the time taken to observe and record the input.

The goal statement $s'$ may contain one or more alternative actions that can be performed at time $t + n + 1$. This is the case whenever the goal statement has the form

$$(do(self, act, T) \land G) \lor D$$

where $T = t + n + 1$ is compatible with any constraints on $T$ in $G$. In step (v) the cycle commits to one of these actions (or more, if simultaneous execution of atomic actions is possible). Recording the result of any such attempted action by adding it to the goal statement $s'$ makes the result available for propagation on the next cycle. Such propagation will have the effect, if the action failed, of adding the implication $false \leftarrow T = t + n + 1$, i.e. $T \neq t + n + 1$ to the selected disjunct

$$do(self, act, T) \land G.$$

If the action succeeded it will have the effect of adding the implication $false \leftarrow T' = t + n + 1$, i.e. $T' \neq t + n + 1$ to any other disjunct which contains an action

$$do(self, act', T')$$

which is incompatible with $act$ because of an integrity constraint such as

$$\forall T[false \leftarrow do(self, act, T) \land do(self, act', T)].$$

## 9 Partial plans and scheduling

The feasibility of our proposed agent architecture depends in large measure on the form of the agent's goal-reduction rules and integrity constraints. The goal-reduction rules, in particular, need to construct partial plans in an incremental manner, so that execution can commence before all the atomic actions have been generated.

For this purpose, the goal-reduction rules have to provide greater detail about the beginning of a plan than they do about the end. This is illustrated by the following example of a rule which reduces the goal of moving from one place, $A$, to another place, $B$, to the subgoals of first taking a single step to a next location, $C$, and then moving from $C$ to $B$:

*Example 7.*

$$do(Agent, move(A, B), [T1, T2]) \leftarrow$$
$$next(A, C) \wedge clear(C, T) \wedge T1 \leq T \leq T2 \wedge$$
$$do(Agent, step(A, C), T) \wedge$$
$$do(Agent, move(C, B), [T, T2])$$

Here $T1$ and $T2$ are the earliest start time and the latest finish time for the action, $move(A, B)$, respectively.

Execution of actions generated by the rule above can commence at some time $T \geq T1$, after the first two conditions have been eliminated by goal reduction. The time $T$ for the execution of $step(A, C)$ must be early enough for the remainder of the partial plan, $move(C, B)$, to be completed before time $T2$.

We assume that such scheduling of actions is performed by a separate control layer which decides how to implement the non-determinism of the proof procedure and the selection step (v) of the agent cycle. The control layer will need to decide, therefore, not only when to attempt the atomic action $step(A, C)$, but also which location, C, from among the alternative next locations, to select. The control layer can use the same evaluation function both to guide the search strategy of the proof procedure and to select among alternative disjuncts of the current goal statement when commitments to actions need to be made.   □

## 10   Conclusion

In this paper we have outlined an attempt to reconcile the traditional notion of a rational agent with the contrary notion of a reactive agent. This work extends an earlier paper [8] with the same objectives. It also builds on recent developments of a proof procedure [3, 4, 9, 10, 13] which combines reasoning with both definitions and integrity constraints. Definitions are used to reduce goals to subgoals, in the manner of a rational agent. Integrity constraints are used to generate actions in response to updates from the environment, in the manner of a reactive agent.

A further key feature of the agent architecture is the resource-bounded formalisation of the proof procedure, which allows the agent's reasoning to be interrupted and resumed between one cycle and the next.

Future work includes further development of the temporal component of the object language, as well as applications of the single agent architecture to multi-agent systems.

**Acknowledgements**
The authors are grateful to Tze Ho Fung, Jacinto Davila, Francesca Toni and Gerhard Wetzel for discussions and their contributions to this work.

# References

1. Rodney A. Brooks. A robust layered control system for a mobile robot. *IEEE Journal of Robotics and Automation*, 2(1):14–23, 1986.
2. Rodney A. Brooks. Intelligence without reason. In J. Mylopolous and R. Reiter, editors, *Proceedings of IJCAI 91*, pages 569–595. Morgan Kaufmann Publishers, 1991.
3. Tze Ho Fung. A modified abductive framework. In N. Fuchs and G. Gottlob, editors, *Proceedings of Logic Programming Workshop*, 1994.
4. Tze Ho Fung. *Abduction by deduction*. PhD thesis, Imperial College, University of London, 1996.
5. Dov Gabbay. The declarative past and imperative future. In Howard Barringer, editor, *Proccedings of the Colloquium on Temporal Logic and Specifications, LNCS, Vol. 398*, pages 409–448. Springer-Verlag, 1989.
6. Dov Gabbay, Howard Barringer, Michael Fisher, Graham Gough, and Richard P. Owens. METATEM: A framework for programming in temporal logic. In *REX Workshop on Stepwise Refinement of Distributed Systems: Models, Formalisms, Correctness. Mook, Netherlands. LNCS Vol. 430*, pages 94–129. Springer-Verlag, 1989.
7. Dov Gabbay and Uwe Reyle. N-prolog: An extension of prolog with hypothetical implications I. *Journal of Logic Programming*, 1:319–355, 1984.
8. Robert A. Kowalski. Using meta-logic to reconcile reactive with rational agents. In K. Apt and F. Turini, editors, *Meta-Logic and Logic Programming*, pages 227–242. MIT Press, 1995.
9. Robert A. Kowalski, Francesca Toni, and Gerhard Wetzel. Towards a declarative and efficient glass-box clp language. In N. Fuchs and G. Gottlob, editors, *Proceedings of Logic Programming Workshop (WLP'94)*, 1994.
10. Robert A. Kowalski, Gerhard Wetzel, and Francesca Toni. A unifying framework for alp, clp and sqo. Technical report, Department of Computing, Imperial College, London, April 1996.
11. John W. Lloyd and John C. Shepherdson. Partial evaluation in logic programming. *Journal of Logic Programming*, 11:217–242, 1991.
12. Yoav Shoham. Agent-oriented programming. *AI Journal*, 60(1), pages 51–92, 1993.
13. Gerhard Wetzel, Robert A. Kowalski, and Francesca Toni. A theorem-proving approach to clp. In Geske U., Krall A., (eds), *Workshop Logische Programmierung*, volume 270 of *GMD-Studien*, pages 63–72. Bonn, Germany, 1995.
14. Jennifer Widom. Deductive and active databases: two paradigms or ends of a spectrum. In N.W. Paton and H. Williams, editors, *Rules in Database Systems: Proceedings of the 1st International Workshop*, pages 306–315. Springer-Verlag, 1994.
15. Carlo Zaniolo. A unified semantics for active and deductive databases. In N.W. Paton and H. Williams, editors, *Rules in Database Systems: Proceedings of the 1st International Workshop*, pages 271–287. Springer-Verlag, 1994.

Updates

# Updates

# Learning Query Rules for Optimizing Databases with Update Rules

D. Laurent, C. Vrain

LIFO  –  Université d'Orléans
BP 6759 - F-45067 Orléans Cedex 2 - FRANCE
e-mail: {laurent,vrain}@lifo.univ-orleans.fr

Abstract In this paper, we are interested in deductive database semantics and inductive logic programming. We focus on a particular approach to building Datalog¬ databases based on two kinds of rules, namely update rules and query rules. In our approach, every fact to be inserted or to be deleted is stored in the database, in order to handle updates over extensional or intensional predicates in a sound and deterministic way.

However, one important problem occurring is that the overhead incurred by the storage of inserted and deleted facts may be important, and so, the intensional database (i.e. the query rules) may enable us to derive contradiction with respect to the extensional database (i.e. the facts stored in the database together with the updates).

In order to cope with these difficulties, we study storage optimization and then, we propose to use inductive learning techniques in order to compute new query rules, so that the semantics of the resulting database remains the same as that of the original one and satisfies our optimization criteria.

## 1   Introduction

In this paper, we consider an approach, in Datalog¬ Databases containing two kinds of rules, namely update rules and query rules, and in which every insertion and every deletion over extensional or intensional facts are deterministic [[1]]. However, in this approach, more facts than in traditional approaches are stored. This is why we address the problem of optimizations. The main contribution in this respect is to use Inductive Logic Programming (ILP) in order to compute both the stored facts and the query rules in such a way that stored information is optimized, while preserving the semantics of the current database. We note that, in our approach, update rules express constraints that must always be satisfied during the lifetime of the database. This is why these rules are never changed.

In the remaining of this section, we roughly describe our approach to updates and we introduce some basic notions concerning ILP.

Database and Updates In our approach, a database is seen as a set of positive and negative facts and as two sets of rules, namely update rules and query rules. Semantically, update rules are of the form $l_0 \leftarrow l_1$, where $l_0$ and $l_1$ are literals, and query rules are standard Datalog¬ rules. Roughly speaking,

# Learning Query Rules for Optimizing Databases with Update Rules

D. Laurent, Ch. Vrain

LIFO – Université d'Orléans
BP 6759 - F-45067 Orléans Cedex 2 - FRANCE
email: {laurent,cv}@lifo.univ-orleans.fr

**Abstract.** In this paper, we are interested in coupling deductive database approaches and inductive logic programming. We focus on a particular approach to updating $Datalog^{neg}$ databases based on two kinds of rules, namely update rules and query rules. In this approach, every fact to be inserted or to be deleted is stored in the database, in order to handle updates over extensional or *intensional* predicates in a sound and deterministic way.
However, two important problems occur: first, the overhead incurred by the storage of inserted and deleted facts may be important, and, second, the intensional database (i.e., the query rules) may enable to derive contradictions with respect to the extensional database (i.e., the facts stored in the database together with the update rules).
In order to cope with these difficulties, we study storage optimization, and then, we propose to use Machine Learning techniques in order to compute new query rules, so that the semantics of the resulting database contains the semantics of the original one and satisfies our optimization criterion.

## 1  Introduction

In this paper, we consider an approach to $Datalog^{neg}$ databases containing two kinds of rules, namely update rules and query rules, and in which every insertion and every deletion over extensional or intensional facts are deterministic ([7]). However, in this approach, more facts than in traditional approaches are stored. This is why we address the problem of optimizations. The main contribution in this respect is to use Inductive Logic Programming (ILP) in order to change both the stored facts and the query rules in such a way that stored information is optimized, while preserving the semantics of the current database. We note that, in our approach, update rules express constraints that must always be satisfied during the lifetime of the database. This is why these rules are never changed.

In the remaining of this section, we roughly describe our approach to updates and we introduce some basic notions concerning ILP.

**Database and Updates** – In our approach, a database is seen as a set of positive and negative facts and as *two* sets of rules, namely *update rules* and *query rules*. Syntactically, update rules are of the form $L_0 \leftarrow L_1$ where $L_0$ and $L_1$ are literals, and query rules are standard $Datalog^{neg}$ rules. Roughly speaking, update rules are activated during update processing, whereas query rules are activated during query processing.

An update is seen as the insertion or deletion of a fact: when inserting a fact $f$, $f$ is stored and when deleting $f$, $\neg f$ is stored. Thus, both insertion and deletion require the storage of a ground literal in the database. Additionally, the update rules are activated to compute the *side effects* of this update.

**Running Example.** We consider the predicate symbols *move* and *win* with the following meaning: $move(a, b)$ means that one can move from $a$ to $b$ and $win(a)$ means that $a$ is a winning position. Let us consider the following update rules:

$$UR_1 : \quad \neg win(x) \leftarrow move(x, x)$$
$$UR_2 : \neg move(x, x) \leftarrow win(x)$$

Intuitively, rule $UR_1$ means that inserting a move from a position to itself entails that this position cannot be a winning one. Similarly, rule $UR_2$ means that inserting a winning position entails that a move from this position to itself must become false. An important aspect of update rules is that they act as *constraints*. In our example, rules $UR_1$ and $UR_2$ stipulate that one cannot have at the same time a winning position $a$ and a move from $a$ to itself.

Now given a database state (i.e., a set of ground literals) defined by:

$$\mathcal{L}_0 = \{move(a, b),\ move(b, c),\ move(a, d),\ win(a),\ win(e)\}$$

let us insert the fact $f = move(a, a)$. Clearly, the rule $UR_1$ applied to $f$ shows that $win(a)$ must become false. Therefore, in order to maintain consistency, the insertion requires to remove $win(a)$ from $\mathcal{L}_0$. As a consequence, the updated database state is defined by:

$$\mathcal{L}_1 = \{move(a, a),\ move(a, b),\ move(b, c),\ move(a, d),\ win(e)\}.$$

We note that, in our model, deletions are treated in a similar way as insertions: deleting $win(e)$ from $\mathcal{L}_1$ requires to store the literal $\neg win(e)$ in the database and to restore consistency. Since no update rule is triggered in this case, we just have to replace in $\mathcal{L}_1$ the positive literal $win(e)$ by its negation $\neg win(e)$. The database state after the deletion is:

$$\mathcal{L}_2 = \{move(a, a),\ move(a, b),\ move(b, c),\ move(a, d),\ \neg win(e)\}. \quad \Box$$

More generally, let $f$ be a fact, call $l$ the literal $f$ or $\neg f$ following that $f$ is inserted or deleted. Then, updates are performed as follows:

*Step* 1 : Place the literal $l$ in $\mathcal{L}$.

*Step* 2 : Remove from $\mathcal{L}$ every literal whose consequences through update rules generate a contradiction to $l$ or any of its consequences.

Now, given a database state $\mathcal{L}$, let us denote by $\xi_\mathcal{L}$ the set of all literals in $\mathcal{L}$ along with all literals that can be derived from those of $\mathcal{L}$ using the update rules. If the set $\xi_\mathcal{L}$ is consistent (i.e., does not contain a fact $f$ and its negation $\neg f$), then the database is said to be *consistent*.

In our running example, applying the update rules $UR_1$ and $UR_2$ to the set $\mathcal{L}_2 = \{move(a, a),\ move(a, b),\ move(b, c),\ move(a, d),\ \neg win(e)\}$ gives the following set: $\xi_{\mathcal{L}_2} = \mathcal{L}_2 \cup \{\neg win(a)\}$.

**Query Answering** – A query operation does not change the sets $\mathcal{L}$ or $\xi_{\mathcal{L}}$. It simply uses these sets in order to compute the answer. Actually, query processing in our model takes into account the fact that update rules are, in fact, constraints, all consequences of which must hold in the database until a new update. Thus, ground literals derived by query rules must not be in contradiction with those of $\xi_{\mathcal{L}}$. We cope with this problem by considering the literals of $\xi_{\mathcal{L}}$ as *exceptions* to query rule derivations.

**Running Example** (continued). Suppose that the database state is defined by:

$$\mathcal{L} = \{move(a,a),\ move(a,b),\ move(b,c),\ move(a,d),$$
$$move(c,e),\ move(e,c),\ win(c),\ \neg win(e)\}.$$

Assume moreover that we have the following query rule (along with the update rules $UR_1$ and $UR_2$ seen earlier):

$$QR:\ win(y) \leftarrow move(x,y),\ \neg win(x).$$

Since $\neg win(a)$ is in $\xi_{\mathcal{L}}$, the rule $QR$ applies showing that $win(a)$ should hold. This is clearly a contradiction and, as the elements of $\xi_{\mathcal{L}}$ are given priority over facts derived through query rules, we consider that $\neg win(a)$ holds. Thus, $\neg win(a)$ is an exception to the query rule $QR$. It can be seen that $win(b)$, $win(c)$, $win(d)$, $\neg win(a)$ and $\neg win(e)$ hold in the database.     □

It is important to note that, in our model, *two* kinds of negation are present: negation in update rules, which corresponds to classical negation, and negation in query rules, which corresponds to the negation of the well founded semantics. In this respect, we make the following assumption, in the spirit of [2], [5]: for every atom $A$ if $\neg A$ is derived through the update rules, then $\neg A$ still holds with respect to the query rules. This point has lead us to modify the operators of the well founded semantics (see Section 2.2); this is discussed in more details in [7].

Although our approach correctly solves the problem of deterministic updates in the presence of constraints, it has the following two drawbacks:

1. the storage of inserted and deleted facts implies an overhead, and
2. query rules may have so many exceptions that they become irrelevant.

In this paper, we address both problems in two directions. First, we address the problem of storage optimizations during update processing. Second, we propose to "learn" new query rules when they have too many exceptions. In this respect, it is important to recall that, since update rules act as constraints, update rules are considered *fixed*. Thus, update rules never change during the life of the database. Moreover, after learning new query rules, the resulting database is intended to:

– have a model containing the model of the original database,
– contain new query rules reflecting "better" the "past experience,"
– contain *fewer* exceptions than the original database.

**Running Example** (continued). Recall that $\mathcal{L}$ and $\xi_{\mathcal{L}}$ are defined by:

$$\mathcal{L} = \{move(a,a),\ move(a,b),\ move(b,c),\ move(a,d),$$
$$move(c,e),\ move(e,c),\ win(c),\neg win(e)\},$$
$$\xi_{\mathcal{L}} = \mathcal{L} \cup \{\neg move(c,c),\ \neg win(a)\}.$$

Assume that, instead of the query rule $QR$, we consider the following query rule:

$QR'$ :  $win(z) \leftarrow move(y, z), move(x, y), \neg win(x), x \neq z$.

Then, it can be seen that, applying $QR'$ only to the facts of $\xi_{\mathcal{L}}$ over the predicate $move$ allows to derive $win(b)$, $win(c)$, $win(d)$, $\neg win(a)$ and $\neg win(e)$. Thus, with this new rule at hand, the storage of $win(c)$ and of $\neg win(e)$ is not necessary. Note that this implies that the literal $\neg move(c, c)$ must now be stored in the database, since this literal is no longer deduced through the update rules. Thus, the new set $\mathcal{L}'$ of stored literals is $\mathcal{L}' = (\mathcal{L} \setminus \{win(c), \neg win(e)\}) \cup \{\neg move(c, c)\}$. We note that we have: $\xi_{\mathcal{L}'} \subseteq \xi_{\mathcal{L}}$.

As a consequence, considering $QR'$ instead of $QR$ better reflects the changes that have been performed on the database (through updates to which update rules are applied). Note that, by doing so, answers to queries are not changed and the set of exceptions $\xi_{\mathcal{L}}$ decreases.  $\square$

**Comparison to Other Works** – We first compare our update method with revision programming ([11]). In [11], a literal can be either "true" or "false" while, in our approach, it can also be "unknown". Moreover, the interpretation of deletion is different in the two approaches. Indeed, in our approach, "delete $l$" means that the negation of $l$ is true, i.e., deleting $l$ corresponds to the insertion of its negation into the database. In the approach of [11], "$out(l)$" means that $l$ is removed from the database and, in this context, as $l$ is not in the database, it is considered to be false.

In [9], it is shown that our approach can be related to default reasoning [18], and in [7], the relationship between our approach and that of extended logic programs ([6]) is considered.

On the other hand, the approach of [8], where two types of rules are used, general rules and exception rules, is closely related to our approach as we also use two types of rules. Update rules in our approach are less general than those proposed in [8], since they have exactly one literal in the body and one in the head. However, the objective of [8] is to study essentially queries, whereas our objective is to study database queries *and* updates. Regarding the interaction between the two types of rules there is an important difference. Namely, the derivations by the two types of rules are interleaved in [8] whereas they are completely separated in our approach. This results in different semantics; we refer to [7] for more details on this topic.

Now, comparing our approach with active databases, it turns out that update rules can be seen as particular cases of *event-condition-action* rules, or active rules ([1], [25]) where the "condition" part is omitted. Indeed, update rules are activated on an update request (the "event" part in active rules) and compute further updates (the "action" part in active rules). However, an important point in our approach is that update rules may concern extensional as well as *intensional* facts, which is not possible with active rules that concern *only* extensional predicates. For instance, in our running example, both update rules $UR_1$ and $UR_2$ deal with the intensional predicate $win$.

**Inductive Logic Programming** – For computing new query rules as suggested in our running example, we use Inductive Logic Programming (ILP).

Many works in the field of ILP are concerned with the problem of learning definitions of target predicates from positive and negative examples of these predicates. Two main approaches can be distinguished:

- interactive learning and theory revision: MIS [19], Clint [17], or KRT [26],
- empirical learning, such as FOIL [16] or Golem [15].

In the field of interactive learning, the examples of the target predicates are processed one after the other: each time an error occurs - a positive (respectively negative) example is not covered (respectively is covered) by the current program - the program is modified by means of generalization (respectively refinement) operators to recover from the error. Questions are generated by the system in order to determine the truth value of facts which are unknown and which are covered by generalization steps.

This kind of learning could seem well-suited to our problem: the set of rules is changed only when an error occurs and we can guess that the database will be only slightly changed[1]. However, we have discarded this solution since, for sake of efficiency, we do not modify the database each time it is updated. Rules are changed only when the number of exceptions is high enough to guess that the rules are no more relevant. Moreover, in these systems, the underlying logic is either a two-valued logic (as in MIS or in Clint) or a four-valued logic (as in KRT or in Clint), whereas our approach is based on the three-valued well founded semantics ([21]).

This explains why we prefer empirical learning systems that take as input a whole set of examples and use heuristics to guide the search of a "good" program. In our application, the model of the database provides us with positive and negative examples of the intensional predicates that must be learned. The other predicates compose a knowledge base that can be used to build the new definitions of the target predicates. Moreover, although many errors occur in the initial database, prior information can be extracted from the set of rules, as for instance the dependency graph between predicates. We present heuristics suggested by the initial set of rules, so that the learned set of rules preserves the "global" form of the initial one.

The paper is organized as follows: in Section 2, we first recall some basic notions concerning databases as defined in [7], and we study optimized databases. In Section 3, we first recall the basic features of the system MULT_ICN ([12, 14]) and then we see when to apply MULT_ICN so as to compute new query rules. In Section 4, we present the algorithms, and finally, Section 5 contains concluding remarks together with suggestions for further work. Due to lack of space, proofs are omitted, they can be found in [23].

---

[1] This is not always true, since for instance, the system Clint [17] recovers from incorrectly classified negative examples by deleting a rule and building a new one that could differ a lot from the original one.

# 2 Database and Update Semantics

## 2.1 Preliminaries

We assume the reader to be familiar with standard terminology of Logic Programming (see [3, 10, 20]), and we now recall the basic notions related to the so-called well founded semantics [21].

Given an alphabet $\mathbf{A}$, a *partial interpretation* of $\mathbf{A}$ is a consistent set of ground literals, i.e., a set of the form $Int = I \cup \neg.J$, where $I$ and $J$ are sets of facts such that $I \cap J = \emptyset$ and where $\neg.J$ denotes the set $\{\neg f \mid f \in J\}$. Moreover, given a literal $L$, we use the notation $-L$ to mean $\neg p(t_1, \ldots, t_n)$ if $L = p(t_1, \ldots, t_n)$ and to mean $p(t_1, \ldots, t_n)$ if $L = \neg p(t_1, \ldots, t_n)$. This notation is extended to partial interpretations as follows: let $Int = I \cup \neg.J$, then $-Int$ stands for $J \cup \neg.I$.

Given a program $\mathcal{P}$, we denote by $Inst(\mathcal{P})$ the variable-free program obtained by instantiating the rules in $\mathcal{P}$, using the constants of the underlying Herbrand universe.

The well founded semantics of a program $\mathcal{P}$ is defined by two operators, denoted by $T$ and $U$, which compute true facts and false facts, respectively. These operators are defined as follows: let $Int$ be a partial interpretation,

- $T(Int)$ is the set of the facts $f$ for which there exists in $Inst(\mathcal{P})$ a rule $f \leftarrow L_1, \ldots, L_k$ such that $L_i \in Int$, for every $i = 1, \ldots, k$.
- $U$ is the unfounded operator: $U(Int)$ is the union of all sets $Unf$ which satisfy the following: for every fact $f$ in $Unf$ and for every rule $f \leftarrow L_1, \ldots, L_k$ in $Inst(\mathcal{P})$, $\exists i \in \{1, \ldots, k\} : -L_i \in Int$ or $L_i \in Unf$.

As shown in [21], $T \cup \neg.U$ is a monotonic operator and its least fixed point is a partial interpretation, called the *well founded model* of $\mathcal{P}$. We denote this model by $\mathcal{M}(\mathcal{P}) = \mathcal{M}^+(\mathcal{P}) \cup \neg.\mathcal{M}^-(\mathcal{P})$; facts in $\mathcal{M}^+(\mathcal{P})$ are said to be *true* and facts in $\mathcal{M}^-(\mathcal{P})$ are said to be *false* (with respect to $\mathcal{P}$).

## 2.2 Databases and their Models

As mentioned in our introductory section, a database is composed by a consistent set of ground literals and by two sets of rules: a set of update rules and a set of query rules. Query rules are standard Datalog$^{neg}$ rules, whereas update rules are rules of the form $L_0 \leftarrow L_1$, where $L_0$ and $L_1$ are literals.

Given a set of update rules $UR$, we denote by $Inst(UR)$ the set of all instantiations of the rules of $UR$ and we consider two operators, $\xi$ and $\vartheta$, defined as follows: for every set of ground literals $Int$,

$$\xi(Int) = Int \cup \{head(r) \mid r \in Inst(UR) \wedge body(r) \in Int\}$$
$$\vartheta(Int) = Int \cup \{body(r) \mid r \in Inst(UR) \wedge head(r) \in Int\}.$$

Roughly, the operator $\xi$ can be seen as the immediate consequence operator associated with the rules in $UR$, whereas $\vartheta$ works on update rules in the "opposite direction", that is, from the head to the body.

As shown in [7], $\xi$ and $\vartheta$ are monotonic, and thus, each of the sequences:

$$\xi^0(Int) = Int \quad \text{and} \quad \xi^k(Int) = \xi(\xi^{k-1}(Int)), \quad \text{for every integer } k > 0,$$
$$\vartheta^0(Int) = Int \quad \text{and} \quad \vartheta^k(Int) = \vartheta(\vartheta^{k-1}(Int)), \quad \text{for every integer } k > 0,$$

has a limit, denoted by $lfp(\xi, Int)$ or $\xi_{Int}$ and by $lfp(\vartheta, Int)$ or $\vartheta_{Int}$, respectively.

**Definition 1.** A set $UR$ of update rules is *consistent* if for every ground literal $L$, the set $\xi_L$ is a partial interpretation. $\quad\square$

**Definition 2.** A *database* is a triple $\Delta = (\mathcal{L}, UR, QR)$ where:
- $\mathcal{L}$ is a partial interpretation,
- $UR$ is a consistent set of update rules,
- $QR$ is a set of usual Datalog$^{neg}$ rules. $\quad\square$

Similarly to standard Datalog databases ([3, 20]), a predicate $p$ is called *intensional* if there is a query rule in $QR$ whose head is over $p$. Any other predicate is called *extensional*. The sets of extensional predicates and of intensional predicates are denoted by E_PRED and I_PRED, respectively. We note that update rules are *not* considered here. In our Running Example, *move* is extensional (although occurring in the head of an update rule), and *win* is intensional. We now define when a database is consistent.

**Definition 3.** A database $\Delta = (\mathcal{L}, UR, QR)$ is said to be consistent if $\xi_{\mathcal{L}}$ is a partial interpretation. The set $\xi_{\mathcal{L}}$ is called *the exception set*. $\quad\square$

**Example 1.** Consider a database $\Delta = (\mathcal{L}, UR, QR)$ where $\mathcal{L} = \{a, b\}$ and where:

$$UR: \quad c \leftarrow \neg b \qquad e \leftarrow c \qquad \neg e \leftarrow a$$
$$QR: \quad d \leftarrow a, c \qquad e \leftarrow a, b$$

Then we have $\xi_{\mathcal{L}} = \{a, b, \neg e\}$, and so, $\Delta$ is consistent. $\quad\square$

As explained in the introductory section, the semantics of a consistent database $\Delta = (\mathcal{L}, UR, QR)$ is computed as follows:

1. compute first the exception set $\xi_{\mathcal{L}}$, then
2. apply the query rules to the result of step 1 above.

Step 2 is performed in our approach by using the well founded semantics. However, since this computation may lead to contradictions with respect to step 1, we define two operators $T^*$ and $U^*$ as follows ([7]): Let $\xi_{\mathcal{L}} = \xi_{\mathcal{L}}^+ \cup \neg.\xi_{\mathcal{L}}^-$, and let $T$ and $U$ be the well founded operators associated to the program consisting of the facts in $\xi_{\mathcal{L}}^+$ and of the rules in $QR$. For every partial interpretation $Int$, we define:

$$T^*(Int) = T(Int) \setminus \xi_{\mathcal{L}}^- \quad \text{and} \quad U^*(Int) = U(Int) \cup \xi_{\mathcal{L}}^-.$$

As shown in [7], $T^*$ and $U^*$ as defined above are monotonic and thus, the sequence $[M_i]_{i \geq 0}$ defined by:

$$M_0 = \emptyset, \text{ and } M_i = T^*(M_{i-1}) \cup \neg.U^*(M_{i-1}), \text{ for } i > 0$$

has a limit. This limit is a partial interpretation, which is called the *model of* $\Delta$, and is denoted by: $M(\Delta) = M^+(\Delta) \cup \neg.M^-(\Delta)$. Moreover, it is easily seen that $\xi_{\mathcal{L}} \subseteq M(\Delta)$.

**Example 1** (continued). Consider again the database $\Delta = (\mathcal{L}, UR, QR)$ where $\mathcal{L} = \{a, b\}$ and where:

$$UR: \quad c \leftarrow \neg b \qquad e \leftarrow c \qquad \neg e \leftarrow a$$
$$QR: \quad d \leftarrow a, c \qquad e \leftarrow a, b$$

Recalling that $\xi_{\mathcal{L}} = \{a, b, \neg e\}$, and applying $T^*$ and $U^*$ to $M_0 = \emptyset$, we find:

- $T^*(M_0) = \{a, b\} \setminus \{e\} = \{a, b\}$,
- $U^*(M_0) = \{c\} \cup \{e\} = \{c, e\}$.

Thus, $M_1 = \{a, b, \neg c, \neg e\}$, and the next step computes $M_2$ as follows:

- $T^*(M_1) = \{a, b, e\} \setminus \{e\} = \{a, b\}$,
- $U^*(M_1) = \{c, d\} \cup \{e\} = \{c, d, e\}$.

Thus, $M_2 = \{a, b, \neg c, \neg d, \neg e\}$, and the next step computes $M_3$ which is equal to $M_2$. As a consequence, the model of $\Delta$ is $M(\Delta) = \{a, b, \neg c, \neg d, \neg e\}$. □

Although in the example above every atom is either true, or false in $M(\Delta)$, it may happen, as in the standard well founded semantics, that the model of the database is *partial* (i.e., there are atoms that are neither true, nor false). We use the following terminology:

- facts in $M^+(\Delta)$ are *true* with respect to $\Delta$,
- facts in $M^-(\Delta)$ are *false* with respect to $\Delta$,
- facts that are neither true nor false are *unknown* with respect to $\Delta$.

## 2.3 Database Updates

In this paper, we consider that updating a database means inserting or deleting a fact, while leaving the database consistent. In our approach, insertions as well as deletions require to store a ground literal in the database: inserting $f$ (respectively deleting $f$) requires to store $f$ (respectively $\neg f$) in the database, and additionally, to remove from the database other literals whose consequences through update rules are in contradiction with $f$ (respectively $\neg f$) or with any of its consequences through update rules.

**Definition 4.** Let $\Delta = (\mathcal{L}, UR, QR)$ be a database and let $l$ be a literal. Define the *update of $l$ in* $\Delta$, denoted by $upd(l, \Delta)$, to be a database $(\mathcal{L}', UR, QR)$ defined by: $\mathcal{L}' = (\mathcal{L} \setminus lfp(\vartheta, -\xi_l)) \cup \{l\}$. □

**Example 1** (continued) Consider now the insertion of $e$ in the database $\Delta = (\mathcal{L}, UR, QR)$ where $\mathcal{L} = \{a, b\}$ and where:

$$UR: \quad c \leftarrow \neg b \qquad e \leftarrow c \qquad \neg e \leftarrow a$$
$$QR: \quad d \leftarrow a, c \qquad e \leftarrow a, b$$

We have $\xi_e = \{e\}$ and thus, $-\xi_e = \{\neg e\}$. As a consequence, $lfp(\vartheta, -\xi_e) = \{\neg e, a\}$. Therefore, $e$ and $a$ can not be present in the database at the same time. So, when inserting $e$, $a$ must be removed from $\mathcal{L}$. As a consequence, the set $\mathcal{L}'$ of the database $upd(e, \Delta)$ is: $\mathcal{L}' = \{b, e\}$.  □

It is important to note that, according to Definition 4, insertions and deletions of extensional facts as well as of *intensional* facts are performed in a deterministic manner. It is shown in [7] that every insertion or deletion is performed in a consistent manner, i.e., for every consistent database $\Delta$ and every literal $l$, $\Delta' = upd(l, \Delta)$ is consistent and $l$ is in $M(\Delta')$.

Since our approach requires to store inserted facts as well as deleted facts, this results in an overhead which should be minimized. To this end, we consider next the problem of storage optimization.

## 2.4   Optimized Databases

It has been shown in [9] that, when no update rules are present, the only interesting case of storage optimization is the following: when deleting a fact over an extensional predicate, the corresponding negative literal has not to be stored in the database.

In the presence of update rules, this case of optimization is not possible, as shown by the following example.

**Example 2.** Consider the database $\Delta = (\mathcal{L}, UR, QR)$ where $\mathcal{L} = \{a, b\}$ and where:

$$UR: \quad c \leftarrow \neg b$$
$$QR: \quad d \leftarrow a$$

Deleting $b$ from $\Delta$ gives the database $\Delta' = upd(\neg b, \Delta)$ defined by $(\mathcal{L}', UR, QR)$ where $\mathcal{L}' = \{a, \neg b\}$. Thus, we have:

$$\xi_{\mathcal{L}'} = \{a, c, \neg b\} \qquad \text{and} \qquad M(\Delta') = \{a, c, d, \neg b\}.$$

On the other hand, as $b$ is an extensional fact, we could think of optimizing the deletion by simply removing $b$ from $\mathcal{L}$ and not storing $\neg b$. In other words, we could think that the database $\Delta_1 = (\mathcal{L}_1, UR, QR)$, where $\mathcal{L}_1 = \{a\}$, is the optimized version of the updated database. However, we obtain:

$$\xi_{\mathcal{L}_1} = \{a\} \qquad \text{and} \qquad M(\Delta_1) = \{a, d, \neg b, \neg c\}.$$

Since $\Delta'$ and $\Delta_1$ do not have the same model, the storage of $\neg b$ when deleting $b$ cannot be avoided in this case.  □

On the other hand, it can be seen from Example 2 that update rules allow for some optimizations. Indeed, let us now consider the insertion of $c$ in $\Delta'$ : the resulting database $\Delta'' = upd(c, \Delta')$ is $(\mathcal{L}'', UR, QR)$ where $\mathcal{L}'' = \mathcal{L}' \cup \{c\} = \{a, c, \neg b\}$.

Since $c$ is in $\xi_{\mathcal{L}'}$, $\Delta''$ and $\Delta'$ have the same model. Thus, putting $c$ in $\mathcal{L}'$ has no influence on the result and so, $\Delta'$, which contains fewer facts than $\Delta''$, can be considered as the updated database. The following definition characterizes this situation.

**Definition 5.** Let $\Delta = (\mathcal{L}, UR, QR)$ be a consistent database. We say that $\Delta$ is an *optimized* database if, for every literal $l$ in $\mathcal{L}$, we have: $\vartheta_l \cap \mathcal{L} = \{l\}$.  □

We now define how to perform updates while keeping the database optimized.

**Definition 6.** Let $\Delta = (\mathcal{L}, UR, QR)$ be a database and let $l$ be a literal. The *optimized update of $l$ in $\Delta$*, denoted by $opt\text{-}upd(l, \Delta)$, is the database $(\mathcal{L}', UR, QR)$ where $\mathcal{L}'$ is defined by the following algorithm:

if $\vartheta_l \cap \mathcal{L} \neq \emptyset$ then set $\mathcal{L}'$ to $\mathcal{L}$
else 1. store $l$ in $\mathcal{L}$ and remove from $\mathcal{L}$ all literals of $lfp(\vartheta, -\xi_l)$
     2. remove from $\mathcal{L}$ all literals of $\xi_l \setminus \{l\}$.    □

As shown by the following proposition, processing updates according to Definition 6 gives an optimized database having the same exceptions – and thus the same model – as if the database were updated according to Definition 4.

**Proposition 7.** *Let $\Delta = (\mathcal{L}, UR, QR)$ be a consistent optimized database, let $l$ be a ground literal, and let $\Delta_1 = (\mathcal{L}_1, UR, QR)$ be the database $upd(l, \Delta)$. If $\Delta' = (\mathcal{L}', UR, QR)$ denotes the database $opt\text{-}upd(l, \Delta)$, then:*
1. $\Delta'$ *is optimized,*
2. $\mathcal{L}' \subseteq \mathcal{L}_1$,
3. $\xi_{\mathcal{L}'} = \xi_{\mathcal{L}_1}$,
4. $M(\Delta') = M(\Delta_1)$.    □

In the remaining of the paper, we shall assume that updates are performed according to Definition 6, i.e., for every $l$ in $\mathcal{L}$, $\vartheta_l \cap \mathcal{L} = \{l\}$.

## 3 Rule Learning

As has already been mentioned, our approach to database updating solves the important problem of non determinism of database updating, but at the cost of an overhead which should be minimized. We have previously coped with this problem by optimizing the storage of the literals in $\mathcal{L}$. On the other hand, query rules that define a set $P$ of predicates may have so many exceptions that they are "irrelevant." In this case, we propose to replace these rules by others having no exceptions. We have then to change the set $\mathcal{L}$ into a set $\mathcal{L}'$ satisfying the optimization criterion defined previously.

### 3.1 The Learning System MULT_ICN

**An Overview** – The system MULT_ICN [13, 14] is an empirical multiple predicate learning system based on three-valued semantics of negation that can be either Fitting semantics or the well founded one. Here, we consider only the well founded semantics, on which is based the approach to updates considered in this paper. As far as we know, there exist no other learning systems based on this semantics. The system MULT_ICN can be defined as follows:

- BASE is a set of extensional or intensional predicates, called basic predicates (basic predicates are not expected to be learned),
- BK is a set of rules and/or facts defining the predicates of BASE,
- TARG is the set of target predicates that must be learned (BASE $\cap$ TARG = $\emptyset$),

- $E = E^+ \cup \neg E^-$ is a partial interpretation over predicates of TARG, where $E^+$ and $E^-$ represent the positive and negative examples, respectively.

MULT_ICN learns a general logic program $\mathcal{P}$ defining predicates of TARG and satisfying the following conditions:

- $\mathcal{P}$ is a set of rules, $p(\mathbf{x}) \leftarrow l_1, \ldots, l_q$ where $p \in$ TARG and $l_k$ $(k = 1, \ldots, q)$ is:
  - either a literal over a predicate of TARG $\cup$ BASE containing only variables, among which at least one appears in the head of the rule or in a literal $l_j$, $j < k$,
  - or a literal $y_u = y_v$ or $y_u \neq y_v$ where $y_u$ and $y_v$ are variables that appear in the head of the rule or in a literal $l_j$, $j < k$.
- $\mathcal{P}$ is correct with respect to $E$, i.e.,
  - $\forall e \in E^+$, $e \in \mathcal{M}^+(\mathcal{P} \cup$ BK$)$, ($\mathcal{P}$ is *complete* with respect to $E^+$)
  - $\forall e \in E^-$, $e \in \mathcal{M}^-(\mathcal{P} \cup$ BK$)$, ($\mathcal{P}$ is *consistent* with respect to $E^-$).

**Running Example** (continued). In terms of Machine Learning, learning new rules defining the predicate *win* means that the target predicate is *win*. Here, *win* is defined on $\{a, b, c, d, e\}$ by the following examples:

$$E^+ = \{win(b),\ win(c),\ win(d)\} \quad \text{and} \quad E^- = \{win(a), win(e)\}.$$

Moreover, the basic predicate *move* is defined by: $move(a, a)$, $move(a, b)$, $move(b, c)$, $move(a, d)$, $move(c, e)$ and $move(e, c)$.

It can be seen that the following program is correct with respect to $E^+ \cup \neg E^-$ :

$$QR_0 : win(z) \leftarrow move(y, z), move(x, y), \neg win(x), x \neq z. \qquad \square$$

Let us notice that when the basic predicates are specified by a set BK of rules and/or facts, MULT_ICN computes the model $\mathcal{M}(\text{BK})$, which is the only necessary information about BK needed during the learning process. Note that this model may be either a total model or a *partial* model.

**Semantics Relative to an Interpretation** – Since basic predicates occur in the rules of the learned program, the semantics of this program must be computed with respect to $\mathcal{M}(\text{BK})$. To this end, we introduce the following definitions:

Given a program $\mathcal{P}$ defining a set $P$ of predicates, we define ([12, 14]) two operators $T_{\mathcal{P}}$ and $U_{\mathcal{P}}$ as follows: Let $Lit$ be a partial interpretation over predicates not in $P$ and let $T$ and $U$ be the operators of the well founded semantics associated to $\mathcal{P}$. Then, for every partial interpretation $Int$, define:

- $T_{\mathcal{P}}(Int) = T(Int \cup Lit)$,
- $U_{\mathcal{P}}(Int)$ as the greatest unfounded set of $P$ with respect to $Int \cup Lit$.

It is shown in [12] that $T_{\mathcal{P}}$ and $U_{\mathcal{P}}$ are monotonic; we denote by $\mathcal{M}(\mathcal{P}, Lit)$ the least fixed point of the operator $T_{\mathcal{P}} \cup \neg.U_{\mathcal{P}}$. $\mathcal{M}(\mathcal{P}, Lit)$ is called the *semantics of $\mathcal{P}$ with respect to $Lit$.*

As shown in [14], the semantics of $\mathcal{P}$ with respect to $\mathcal{M}(\text{BK})$ computes the semantics of the learned program $\mathcal{P}$ when applied to the semantics of the knowledge base. In other words, we have that:

$$\mathcal{M}(\mathcal{P}, \mathcal{M}(\text{BK})) \cup \mathcal{M}(\text{BK}) = \mathcal{M}(\mathcal{P} \cup \text{BK}).$$

**Building Rules** – As most empirical systems ([15, 16]), the process to build rules relies on the notion of extensional coverage, defined as follows:

**Definition 8.** Let $\mathcal{P}$ be a set of rules defining the target predicates, let $E$ be the set of examples, let BK be a set of rules and/or facts defining the basic predicates and let $e$ be a fact.

- $\mathcal{P}$ *extensionally covers* $e$ if there exists a rule $l \leftarrow l_1, \ldots, l_n$ in $Inst(\mathcal{P})$ such that $e = l$ and, for every $i = 1, \ldots, n$, $l_i \in E \cup \mathcal{M}(\text{BK})$.
- $\mathcal{P}$ *extensionally rejects* $e$ if, for all rules $l \leftarrow l_1, \ldots, l_n$ in $Inst(\mathcal{P})$ such that $e = l$, there exists a literal $l_i$ ($i = 1, \ldots, n$) satisfying $-l_i \in (E \cup \mathcal{M}(\text{BK}))$. □

The general algorithm of MULT_ICN can then be outlined as follows: *as long as some positive examples are not covered, build a rule that extensionally covers some positive examples and extensionally rejects all the negative ones.*

Let us now briefly describe how a rule is built. First, the system chooses a predicate $p$ among the target predicates for which uncovered positive examples remain. It considers the most general rule, that is to say $p(\mathbf{x}) \leftarrow$, and it specializes it by adding a literal, until all negative examples are rejected. Assuming that the clause that has already been built is $p(\mathbf{x}) \leftarrow L_1, \ldots, L_j$, the next literal is chosen among the set of all literals that satisfy the following properties:

– they are built over predicates of TARG $\cup$ BASE $\cup \{=\}$,
– they are composed only of variables,
– if $L_j$ is $x_u = x_v$ or $x_u \neq x_v$ then the variables $x_u$ and $x_v$ must appear either in the head of the clause or in literals $L_k$, for $k < j$.
– otherwise, at least one variable must appear either in the head of the clause or in a literal $L_k$, for $k < j$.

The "best" literal is chosen according to the number of positive examples that are covered by this literal and the number of negative examples that are rejected by it. It is important to note in this respect that this heuristic is all the more relevant that the number of examples is high.

The number of literals that are considered is very large, especially when the arities of predicates are high. We discuss at the end of Section 5 how we can use information from the initial database to reduce the search space.

**Running Example** (continued). To build $QR_0$, the system starts from the most general rule, $win(z) \leftarrow$. This rule is too general since it extensionally covers all the negative examples. Among all the possible literals $move(x, x)$, $\neg move(x, x)$, $move(x, y)$, ..., MULT_ICN selects the best one, $move(y, z)$, and studies the rule $win(z) \leftarrow move(y, z)$. This rule still covers the negative examples $win(a)$ and $win(e)$; it is specialized by adding $move(x, y)$ and then $\neg win(x)$. As it still covers the negative example $win(a)$, it is specialized by adding the literal $x \neq z$. This rule extensionally covers all the positive examples and rejects the negative ones. □

**Completeness and Consistency** – Suppose now that instead of building the rule $QR_0$, MULT_ICN builds the rule $QR_1$ that extensionally covers the positive examples and rejects all the negative examples. The learned program is:

$$QR_1: \quad win(y) \leftarrow move(x, y), \neg win(x), x \neq y$$

Although it extensionally covers all the positive examples and rejects the negative ones, its semantics is $\{\neg win(a), win(b), win(d)\}$. □

This example shows that the notion of extensional coverage is not sufficient to ensure the correction of the learned program. To deal with this problem, while building a set of clauses, MULT_ICN builds the set of recursive dependencies between examples, denoted by $\mathcal{P}_{rec}$. We do not give here the way it is built, but we just illustrate it with our Running Example.

**Running Example** (continued). When building the rule $QR_1$, MULT_ICN builds the following set of recursive dependencies:

$$\mathcal{P}_{rec}: \quad \begin{array}{ll} win(b) \leftarrow \neg win(a) & win(d) \leftarrow \neg win(a) \\ win(c) \leftarrow \neg win(e) & win(e) \leftarrow \neg win(c) \end{array}$$

The recursive dependency $win(b) \leftarrow \neg win(a)$ comes from the instantiated rule $win(b) \leftarrow move(a, b), \neg win(a), a \neq b$, and states that, to prove $win(b)$, it is sufficient to prove $\neg win(a)$. Similarly, the recursive dependency $win(e) \leftarrow \neg win(c)$ comes from the instantiated rule $win(e) \leftarrow move(c, e), \neg win(c), c \neq e$. This states that to correctly reject $win(e)$, it is necessary to prove $win(c)$. □

Using the set $\mathcal{P}_{rec}$, the system determines whether the learned program is complete and consistent with respect to the examples. As soon as a rule is built, the set of corresponding recursive dependencies is built and its *gain* is computed.

Assuming that $\mathcal{P}$ is the set of rules that have already been built and that $Uncov$ is the set of positive examples that are not yet covered by $\mathcal{P}$, then the gain of a rule is defined as the ratio of the number of positive examples that are extensionally covered by $\mathcal{P}$ to the number of positive examples that are proved by $\mathcal{P} \cup Uncov$. If this ratio is lower than an acceptability rate, fixed by the user before learning, the rule is not accepted and the system tries to build a new one.

The following basic theorem (proved in [14]) shows that the programs built by MULT_ICN are correct.

**Theorem 9.** *Let* TARG *be a set of target predicates, let $E$ be the set of examples, let* BASE *be a set of basic predicates (*BASE ∩ TARG $= \emptyset$*) defined by their semantics $\mathcal{M}(BK)$. A program $\mathcal{P}$ built by* MULT_ICN *and defining the predicates of* TARG *from predicates of* TARG ∪ BASE *satisfies the property:* $E \subseteq \mathcal{M}(\mathcal{P}, \mathcal{M}(BK))$. □

## 3.2 Triggering Rule Learning

As has been argued in our introductory section, given a consistent database $\Delta = (\mathcal{L}, UR, QR)$, the learning phase is not triggered at each update. As will be seen later on, the criterion of when to trigger the learning phase is based on the difference between the model $M(\Delta)$ of the database $\Delta$ and the semantics of the query rules with respect to the extensional literals of $M(\Delta)$. Actually, this criterion should be tested when $\mathcal{L}$ is considered to contain too many *intensional* literals.

The goal of the learning phase is to compute a new set of query rules which allows to store as few ground literals as possible.

In order to formalize the criteria to be considered in this respect, we first recall from [3, 20] that, given a set $R$ of query rules, the associated dependency graph $G(R)$ is defined as follows:

- the nodes of $G(R)$ are the predicate symbols,
- if there exists a rule $r$ in $R$ such that $p$ is the head of $r$ and $q$ appears in the body of $r$, then $G(R)$ contains an edge from $q$ to $p$.

**Definition 10.** Let $R$ be a set of query rules and let $G(R)$ be its associated graph. If $p$ is a predicate symbol, the strongly connected component of $p$, denoted by $\gamma(p)$, is the set of all predicate symbols $q$ which occur in a cycle of $G(R)$ containing $p$.

We denote by $\sigma(p)$ the set of nodes $q$ that do not belong to $\gamma(p)$ but that belong to a path from $q$ to $p$ in $G(R)$.   □

We note that, if $p$ and $q$ belong to the same strongly connected component, then $\sigma(p) = \sigma(q)$. Therefore, if $\pi$ is a strongly connected component of $G(R)$, then $\sigma(\pi)$ denotes $\sigma(p)$, where $p$ is any predicate of $\pi$.

Let $P$ be a set of intensional predicates which is the union of strongly connected components of $G(QR)$ and let $\overline{P}$ be the set of predicates not in $P$. Let $Lit$ be a set of literals and let $QR$ be a set of query rules. We denote by:

- $Lit_{|P}$ the set of the literals in $Lit$ that are over predicates in $P$,
- $QR_{|P}$ the set of the rules in $QR$ whose heads are over predicates in $P$,
- $M(\Delta)_{|\sigma(P)}$ the restriction of $M(\Delta)$ to literals over predicates in $\sigma(P)$,
- $\mathcal{M}(QR_{|P}, M(\Delta)_{|\sigma(P)})$ the semantics of $QR_{|P}$ with respect to $M(\Delta)_{|\sigma(P)}$.

Comparing the interpretations $M(\Delta)_{|P}$ and $\mathcal{M}(QR_{|P}, M(\Delta)_{|\sigma(P)})$, we call an *error* over a predicate $p$ in $P$ any ground literal $p(\alpha)$ or $\neg p(\alpha)$ in the symmetric difference $M(\Delta)_{|P} \div \mathcal{M}(QR_{|P}, M(\Delta)_{|\sigma(P)})$.

**Running Example** (continued). In the database $\Delta = (\mathcal{L}, UR, QR)$ considered in this example, $\mathcal{L}$ and $\xi_{\mathcal{L}}$ are defined by:

$$\mathcal{L} = \{move(a, a),\ move(a, b),\ move(b, c),\ move(a, d),$$
$$move(c, e),\ move(e, c),\ win(c), \neg win(e)\},$$
$$\xi_{\mathcal{L}} = \mathcal{L} \cup \{\neg move(c, c),\ \neg win(a)\},$$

and $QR$ consists of the following query rule:

$$win(y) \leftarrow move(x, y), \neg win(x).$$

If we compute the model of $\Delta$ (using the associated operators $T^*$ and $U^*$) then we get: $win(b)$, $win(c)$, $win(d)$, $\neg win(a)$ and $\neg win(e)$. On the other hand, according to Definition 10, for $P = \{win\}$, we have $\gamma(P) = \{win\}$, and $\sigma(P) = \{move\}$.

If we consider the program composed of the rule $QR$ and if we compute its well founded semantics with respect to $M(\Delta)_{|\{move\}}$, then all ground atoms built over the predicate $win$ are undefined, and thus, they all belong to $M(\Delta)_{|\{win\}} \div \mathcal{M}(QR_{|\{win\}}, M(\Delta)_{|\{move\}})$.

We propose to learn new query rules, defining $win$ from $move$ and $win$, that better fit the actual database. This will be performed in two steps:

1. *Learning step:* A new set of rules, denoted by $QR'$, is learned so that the model of the database $\widetilde{\Delta} = \big((\xi_{\mathcal{L}})_{|\{move\}}, \emptyset, QR'\big)$ contains the model of $\Delta$.

2. *Optimization step:* A new set $\mathcal{L}'$ such that $\mathcal{L}' \subseteq \xi_{\mathcal{L}}$ is computed so that the database $\Delta' = (\mathcal{L}', UR, QR')$ and the database $\widetilde{\Delta}$ have the same model.

In order to achieve the learning step, we apply the system MULT_ICN with

$$E^+ = \{win(b),\ win(c),\ win(d)\} \quad \text{and} \quad E^- = \{win(a), win(e)\}.$$

The basic predicate *move* is defined by the facts: $move(a,a)$, $move(a,b)$, $move(b,c)$, $move(a,d)$, $move(c,e)$ and $move(e,c)$. MULT_ICN outputs the following rule

$$QR' : win(z) \leftarrow move(y,z), move(x,y), \neg win(x), x \neq z.$$

The database $\widetilde{\Delta}$ is defined by the set $(\xi_{\mathcal{L}})_{|\{move\}} = \{move(a,a),\ move(a,b),\ move(b,c),\ move(a,d),\ move(c,e),\ move(e,c),\ \neg move(c,c)\}$ and by the query rule $QR'$.

In this case, $\Delta$ and $\widetilde{\Delta}$ have the same model. Thus, with the new rule $QR'$ at hand, the storage of $win(c)$ and of $\neg win(e)$ is not necessary.

Nevertheless, if we remove $win(c)$ and $\neg win(e)$ from the database, the literal $\neg move(c,c)$, that was in $\xi_{\mathcal{L}}$, can no longer be deduced using the update rules $UR_1$ and $UR_2$. Thus, $\neg move(c,c)$ must now be stored in the database, implying that, in this example, the set $(\xi_{\mathcal{L}})_{|\{move\}}$ cannot be optimized.

Thus, the database $\Delta'$ that we obtain is defined by the new set $\mathcal{L}' = (\mathcal{L} \setminus \{win(c), \neg win(e)\}) \cup \{\neg move(c,c)\}$, the update rules $UR_1$ and $UR_2$ and the query rule $QR'$. We note that, although the set $(\xi_{\mathcal{L}})_{|\{move\}}$ cannot be optimized, we have: $\xi_{\mathcal{L}'} \subset \xi_{\mathcal{L}}$. $\quad\Box$

## 4 Algorithms

In this section, we describe how MULT_ICN is applied during the learning step and then, we give the algorithm performing the optimization step. Finally, we give a general algorithm showing how the learning phase is triggered and then how the new database is computed.

### 4.1 Learning Step

Let us assume that the number of errors over predicates in the strongly connected component $P$ is considered too large. In this case, we apply MULT_ICN with BASE $= \sigma(P)$, $\mathcal{M}(\text{BK}) = M(\Delta)_{|\sigma(P)}$, TARG $= P$ and $E = M(\Delta)_{|P}$ as inputs. Let $QR'_P$ be the output of MULT_ICN, that is, a new set of query rules defining predicates of $P$. Then, let $QR'$ be obtained by replacing in $QR$ the rules of $QR_{|P}$ by those of $QR'_P$.

Consider now the database (with no update rules) $\widetilde{\Delta} = \big((\xi_{\mathcal{L}})_{|\overline{P}}, \emptyset, QR'\big)$, where $(\xi_{\mathcal{L}})_{|\overline{P}}$ is the set of ground literals over predicates not in $P$ that are derived from $\mathcal{L}$ through the update rules. Then, based on Theorem 9 and on the following lemma, it is shown in [23] that $M(\widetilde{\Delta})$ contains $M(\Delta)$.

**Lemma 11.** *Using the notations introduced previously, we have:*
$M(\Delta)_{|P} \subseteq \mathcal{M}(QR'_P, M(\Delta)_{|\sigma(P)}) \Longrightarrow M(\Delta) \subseteq M(\widetilde{\Delta})$.     □

## 4.2 Optimization Step

Assuming that $\widetilde{\Delta}$ has been computed, we give an algorithm for computing a new set of literals $\mathcal{L}'$ such that (1) $\mathcal{L}' \subseteq (\xi_{\mathcal{L}})_{|\overline{P}}$, (2) $(\xi_{\mathcal{L}'})_{|\overline{P}} = (\xi_{\mathcal{L}})_{|\overline{P}}$, and (3) for every $l$ in $\mathcal{L}'$, $\vartheta_l \cap \mathcal{L}' = \{l\}$.

In this algorithm, $\vartheta_{|\overline{P}}$ denotes the operator $\vartheta$ applied to those update rules $L_0 \leftarrow L_1$ in $UR$ such that $L_0$ and $L_1$ are over predicates in $\overline{P}$.

**Algorithm** *new_set*

---

Input: a set of ground literals $\mathcal{L} = \mathcal{L}_{|\overline{P}} \cup \mathcal{L}_{|P}$;
Output: a new set of ground literals $\mathcal{L}'$.
Method:
   $ToStudy := (\xi_{\mathcal{L}})_{|\overline{P}} \setminus \xi_{(\mathcal{L}_{|\overline{P}})}$ ;
   % Literals in $ToStudy$ cannot be derived from $\mathcal{L}_{|\overline{P}}$ %
   $ToKeep := ToStudy$ ;
   for every $l$ in $ToStudy$ do
      if $(lfp(\vartheta_{|\overline{P}}, l) \setminus \{l\}) \cap ToKeep \neq \emptyset$    then
            $ToKeep := ToKeep \setminus \{l\}$ ;
   % Literals in $ToKeep$ are not derived by any literal in $ToStudy$ %
   $\mathcal{L}' := \mathcal{L}_{|\overline{P}} \cup ToKeep$

---

**Example 4.1.** In order to illustrate the Algorithm *new_set*, let us consider the following (instantiated) update rules:

$$d \leftarrow a \qquad e \leftarrow a \qquad e \leftarrow b \qquad \neg i \leftarrow f \qquad f \leftarrow \neg i$$
$$f \leftarrow \neg c \qquad g \leftarrow d \qquad h \leftarrow e \qquad \neg c \leftarrow \neg i$$

Moreover, assume that $\mathcal{L} = \{a, b, \neg c\}$ and that $P = \{b, c, e, g\}$. Thus, $\mathcal{L}_{|\overline{P}} = \{a\}$, $\mathcal{L}_{|P} = \{b, \neg c\}$, and $\vartheta_{|\overline{P}}$ works with the following rules:

$$d \leftarrow a \qquad \neg i \leftarrow f \qquad f \leftarrow \neg i$$

We have $\xi_{\mathcal{L}} = \{a, b, \neg c, d, e, f, g, h, \neg i\}$, and so, $(\xi_{\mathcal{L}})_{|\overline{P}} = \{a, d, f, h, \neg i\}$ and $\xi_{(\mathcal{L}_{|\overline{P}})} = \{a, d, e, g, h\}$. Thus, $ToStudy$ and $ToKeep$ are set to $\{f, \neg i\}$.

Now, considering the elements of $ToStudy$ one by one and with respect to $\vartheta_{|\overline{P}}$, we find that:
(1) $\neg i$ is removed from $ToKeep$ because $lfp(\vartheta_{|\overline{P}}, \neg i) = \{\neg i, f\}$ and because $f$ is in $ToKeep$. Thus we obtain $ToKeep = \{f\}$.
(2) $f$ is not removed from $ToKeep$ because $lfp(\vartheta_{|\overline{P}}, f) = \{f, \neg i\}$, but now, $\neg i$ is not in $ToKeep$.

Thus, $\mathcal{L}' = \{a, \neg i\}$. Note that the resulting set depends on the order in which literals in $ToStudy$ are considered: if we had considered $f$ before $\neg i$, $f$ would have been removed from $ToKeep$. This situation occurs when there are cyclic derivations, in which case the algorithm selects *one* literal from every cycle.

We note moreover that $\vartheta_a = \{a\}$ and $\vartheta_{\neg i} = \{f, \neg c, \neg i\}$. Thus, $\mathcal{L}'$ satisfies the optimization of Definition 5. $\square$

Now, let $\Delta' = (\mathcal{L}', UR, QR')$ be the database obtained from $\Delta$ by replacing $\mathcal{L}$ by the output of Algorithm *new_set* applied to $\mathcal{L}$ and by replacing $QR = QR_{|\overline{P}} \cup QR_{|P}$ by $QR' = QR_{|\overline{P}} \cup QR'_{P}$. Then, based on Lemma 11, the following theorem holds:

**Theorem 12.** *If* $M(\Delta)_{|P} \subseteq \mathcal{M}(QR'_P, M(\Delta)_{|\sigma(P)})$, *then:*
1. $\mathcal{L}'_{|P} = \emptyset$,
2. *for every* $l$ *in* $\mathcal{L}'$, $\vartheta_l \cap \mathcal{L}' = \{l\}$,
3. $\xi_{\mathcal{L}'} \subseteq \xi_{\mathcal{L}}$,
4. $M(\Delta) \subseteq M(\Delta')$. $\square$

Summarizing the results obtained in this section, we have shown that if we can replace the query rules in $QR_{|P}$ by the query rules in $QR'_P$ then:

1. literals over $P$ have not to be stored in the database,
2. the database is still optimized,
3. the exception set decreases, and
4. the semantics of the original database is contained in the semantics of the new database.

## 4.3 A General Algorithm

The algorithm given below takes as input a consistent database $\Delta = (\mathcal{L}, UR, QR)$, and returns as output a consistent database $\Delta' = (\mathcal{L}', UR, QR')$, in which the set of stored literals and the query rules may have changed, whereas the update rules have not been changed.

We note that no user interaction is required during the computation, so it is up to the system to choose the predicates to be learned: denoting by $\epsilon(P)$ the ratio of the number of errors to the number of literals in $M(\Delta)_{|P}$, predicates in $P$ are learned only if $\epsilon(P)$ is greater than a fixed number, say $\varepsilon$.

**Algorithm** *learn_db*
___
(1) *Computation of the set of predicates to be learned*
      1.1. Compute $M(\Delta)$ ;
      1.2. Compute $\mathcal{M}(QR, M(\Delta)_{|\text{E\_PRED}})$ ;
      1.3. Let $P$ be the set of predicates over which an error occurs ;
      1.4. $\Gamma(P) := \{\gamma(p) \mid p \in P\}$ ;
      1.5. For every element $\pi$ of $\Gamma(P)$ do
            1.5.1. Compute $\mathcal{M}(QR_{|\pi}, M(\Delta)_{|\sigma(\pi)})$ ;
            1.5.2. Compute $\epsilon(\pi)$ ;
            1.5.3. Remove from $\Gamma(P)$ every $\pi$ such that $\epsilon(\pi) < \varepsilon$ ;

% $\Gamma(P)$ : strongly connected components whose predicates are to be learned. %
(2) *Learning phase*

    2.1. *Done* := $\emptyset$ ; $QR'$ := $QR$ ;

    2.2. For every $\pi$ in $\Gamma(P)$ do

        2.2.1. Apply MULT_ICN with TARG = $\pi$, BASE = $\sigma(\pi)$,

            $\mathcal{M}(\text{BK}) = M(\Delta)_{|\sigma(\pi)}$ and $E = M(\Delta)_{|\pi}$ as input ;

        2.2.2. If "success" then

            Replace the rules in $QR'_{|\pi}$ with the new rules ;

            *Done* := *Done* $\cup$ $\pi$ ;

    2.3. Apply Algorithm *new_set* with $\mathcal{L} = \mathcal{L}_{|\overline{Done}} \cup \mathcal{L}_{|Done}$ as input,

    and let $\mathcal{L}'$ be the output.

---

Let $\Delta' = (\mathcal{L}', UR, QR')$ be the database obtained by Algorithm *learn_db*. Based on theorems 9 and 12, we have the following theorem:

**Theorem 13.** *Let $\Delta = (\mathcal{L}, UR, QR)$ be a consistent database and let $\Delta' = (\mathcal{L}', UR, QR')$ be the database after the execution of learn_db with $\Delta$ as input. Then: $M(\Delta) \subseteq M(\Delta')$, $\xi_{\mathcal{L}'} \subseteq \xi_{\mathcal{L}}$, and, for every $l$ in $\xi_{\mathcal{L}'}$, $\vartheta_l \cap \mathcal{L}' = \{l\}$.*   □

It is important to note that Theorem 13 above implies that, if $M(\Delta)$ is *total* (i.e., no fact of the Herbrand base is unknown with respect to $\Delta$), then $\Delta$ and $\Delta'$ have the *same* model, in other words answers to queries remain the same. When the model of the database is not total, answers to queries after the learning phase contain the answers obtained before the learning phase.

Regarding the rules generated by the system, the implementation of MULT_ICN shows that the learned rules are generally understandable. For instance ([22]), a database with recursive query rules specifying the transitive closure of a relation and with stored facts limiting the accepted paths to those of length 2 has been given as input to MULT_ICN. The new rules learned by the system are actually the expected ones, i.e., they are not recursive and compute the paths of length at most two.

On the other hand, since in the learning phase (2) of the algorithm above, the new rules that define predicates in $\pi$ are built with predicates of $\sigma(\pi)$, the following result holds:

**Proposition 14.** *Let us call $G(QR)$ the dependency graph of the initial database and $G(QR')$ the dependency graph of the learned database. Then $G(QR')$ is a subgraph of the reflexive and transitive closure of $G(QR)$.*   □

We terminate this section by discussing possible improvements concerning the learning phase (2) of Algorithm *learn_db*. First, in order to reduce the size of the search space, predicates can be typed. Second, update rules enable us to determine parts of rules that should not be changed. Indeed, let us consider the update rule: $L_0 \leftarrow L_1$ and the query rule: $L'_0 \leftarrow -L'_1, \ldots$ If there exists a substitution $\sigma$ that satisfies $L'_0 = L_0.\sigma$ and $L'_1 = L_1.\sigma$, then the query rule will never generate exceptions. Therefore, it could be interesting to start learning new query rules with the rule $L'_0 \leftarrow -L'_1$ and, if necessary, to refine it.

# 5 Concluding Remarks and Further Work

We have considered a deductive database model with two kinds of rules which allows to perform insertions and deletions of extensional or intensional facts in a deterministic manner. In this approach, inserted and deleted facts are stored in the database, and using the update rules, they generate a set of ground literals that act as exceptions to query rules derivations. This results in an overhead with respect to traditional approaches and, moreover, query rules may have so many exceptions that they become irrelevant with respect to the stored literals.

We have addressed both of these problems: First we have proposed to perform updates in such a way that the set of stored literals be optimized with respect to update rules derivations. Second, we have shown that ILP techniques could be used to compute new query rules having less exceptions. Moreover, each time new query rules are placed in the database, the set of stored literals is changed so that it is still optimized with respect to update rules derivations.

It is important to recall that new query rules are not computed at each update, for efficiency reasons. Rather, new query rules are computed according to a criterion based on the notion of error. Moreover, during the learning phase, the dependency graph is taken into account so that the new rules are "as close as possible" to the original rules.

MULT_ICN and our approach to deductive databases have been implemented in Prolog, and an implementation of Algorithm *learn_db* presented in this paper is currently in progress. Moreover, in order to apply our approach to realistic applications, we focus on particular cases, when no update rules are present and/or when query rules are positive. Such particular cases are of practical interest and result in an efficient implementation generating understandable rules.

# References

1. Abiteboul S., Hull R., Vianu V.: Foundations of Databases. Addison Wesley (1995).
2. Alferes J.J., Pereira L.M.: On Logic of program semantics with two kinds of negation. Joint Intl. Conf. and Symp. of Logic Programming (1992).
3. Ceri S., Gottlob G., Tanca L.: Logic Programming and Databases. Surveys in Computer Science, Springer-Verlag (1990).
4. Fitting M.: A Kripke-Kleene semantics for logic programs. Journal of Logic Programming. 2(4) (1985) 295–312.
5. Gelfond M., Lifschitz, V.: Logic Programming with Classical Negation. Seventh Intl. Conf. of Logic Programming (1990).
6. Gelfond M., Lifschitz, V.: Representing Actions in Extended Logic Programming. Joint Intl. Conf. and Symp. of Logic Programming (1992).
7. Halfeld Ferrari Alves M., Laurent D., Spyratos N.: Update Rules in Datalog Programs. Intl. Conf. on Logic Programming and Non-Monotonic Reasoning, LPNMR, LNAI **928** Springer-Verlag (1995) 71–84.
8. Kowalski R.A., Sadri, F.: Logic Programs with Exceptions. Seventh Intl. Conf. of Logic Programming (1990).
9. Laurent D., Phan Luong V., Spyratos N.: Updating Intensional Predicates in Deductive Databases. 9th IEEE Intl. Conf. on Data Engineering, ICDE (1993) 14–21.

10. Lloyd J.W.: Foundations of Logic Programming. Springer-Verlag (1987).
11. Marek V.W., Truszcyński M.: Revision Programming, Database Updates and Integrity. Intl. Conf. on Database Theory, ICDT'95, LNCS **893** Springer-Verlag (1995).
12. Martin L., Vrain C.: ICN : a single predicate learner. Technical Report 95-3 LIFO, Université d'Orléans (1995).
13. Martin L., Vrain C.: Mult_ICN: an empirical multiple predicate learner. Fifth Intl. Workshop on Inductive Logic Programming, L. De Raedt (Ed.), Leuven (1995) 129-144.
14. Martin L., Vrain C.: A Three-Valued Framework for the Induction of General Logic Programs. Advances in Inductive Logic Programming. L. de Raedt (Ed.), IOS Press (1996) 219-235.
15. Muggleton S., Feng C.: Efficient Induction of Logic Programs. Inductive Logic programming A.P.I.C. Series **38**, S. Muggleton (Ed.), Academic Press (1992) 281-298.
16. Quinlan J.R.: Learning Logical Definitions from Relations. Machine Learning Journal **5** Kluwer Academic Publishers (1990) 239-266.
17. de Raedt L.: Interactive theory revision, an inductive logic programming approach. Academic Press Limited (1992).
18. Reiter R.: A Logic for Default Reasoning. Artificial Intelligence **13** (1980).
19. Shapiro E.Y.: Algorithmic Program Debugging. ACM Distinguished Dissertation, MIT Press (1982).
20. Ullman J.D.: Principles of Databases and Knowledge Base Systems. Vol. I-II Computer Science Press (1989).
21. Van Gelder A., Ross K.A., Schlipf J.S.: The well founded Semantics for General Logic Program. Journal of the ACM **38**(3) (1991) 620-650.
22. Vrain C., Laurent D.: Apprentissage de règles et Bases de données déductives (French). Technical Report 95-5, LIFO, Université d'Orléans (1995).
23. Vrain C., Laurent D.: Learning Query Rules for Optimizing Databases with Update Rules. Technical Report 95-19, LIFO, Université d'Orléans (1995).
24. Vrain C., Martin L.: Inductive learning of normal clauses. Machine Learning: ECML-94, *LNAI*, **784** F. Bergadano, L. De Raedt (Eds.), Springer Verlag (1994) 435-438.
25. Widom J., Ceri S.: Active Database Systems. Morgan Kaufmann (1996).
26. Wrobel S.: Concept Formation and Knowledge Revision. Kluwer Academic Publishers (1994).

# Active Databases

# Formal Characterization of Active Databases

Chitta Baral¹ and Jorge Lobo²

¹ Department of Computer Sci., Univ. of Texas at El Paso, El Paso, TX 79968, USA
² Department of EECS, Univ. of Illinois at Chicago, Chicago, IL 60607, USA

**Abstract.** In this paper we take a first step towards characterizing activity in Databases. Characterizing the activity of active databases allows
additional flexibility in weighing the effects of different priority criteria between triggered rules, different actions, and transactions, and
also in reasoning about effects of transactions and prove them without actually executing them. Our characterization is new in but different
from earlier researches by Zaniolo in terms of making a clear distinction
between syntax and syntactical execution of actions, and allowing concurrent actions. We use the above-mentioned [SS96] to characterize the
non-determinism that arises when several rules can fire at the same time
and the preference between them is not specified. We show through examples how our language allows us to express features of different active
database systems.

## 1  Introduction and motivation

The core concept that makes a database active is the concept of an active rule. An
active rule is generally composed of three parts: an event that causes the rule to
be triggered, a condition that is checked when the rule is triggered, and an action
that is executed if the condition is satisfied when the rule is triggered. Based on
this simple but powerful idea several database systems have been designed and
implemented [CF..., BW94, CP96, Hanc, PS96, SK96, Wi96]. Active rules
are used to perform activities such as integrity constraint and view maintenance,
monitor services and work-flow management.

Although there has been considerable research and development in this area (as
reflected in the report book edited by Widom and Ceri [WC96]), there has been
very little attention in the study of formal foundations. In the 'Conclusion' chapter
section of the 'Conclusion' chapter in [WC96], Widom and Ceri express this
sentiment by the following:

> Finally, two largely neglected and crucially important areas within the
> field of active-database systems are formal foundations and usability. Al-
> though some very preliminary work has been done in the area of formal
> foundations [PAT, Wi94, Zan93], there is no unifying theory under-
> lying active database systems... A formal foundation for active database

# Formal Characterization of Active Databases

Chitta Baral[1] and Jorge Lobo[2]

[1] Department of Computer Sc. Univ. of Texas at El Paso El Paso, TX, 79968, USA
[2] Department of EECS Univ. of Illinois at Chicago Chicago, IL 60607, USA

**Abstract.** In this paper we take a first step towards characterizing active databases. Declarative characterization of active databases allows additional flexibility in studying the effects of different priority criteria between fireable rules, different actions and event definitions, and also to make claims about effects of transaction and prove them without actually executing them. Our characterization is related but different from similar attempts by Zaniolo in terms of making a clear distinction between actual and hypothetical execution of actions and allowing non-determinism. We use the 'choice' construct [SZ90] to characterize the non-determinism that arises when several rules can fire at the same time and the preference between them is not specified. We show through examples how our language allows us to express features of different active database systems.

## 1 Introduction and motivation

The core concept that makes a database active is the concept of an active rule. An active rule is generally composed of three parts: an *event* that causes the rule to be triggered, a *condition* that is checked when the rule is triggered, and an *action* that is executed if the condition is satisfied when the rule is triggered. Based on this simple but powerful idea several database systems have been designed and implemented [CFPB96, DBC96, GJ96, Han96, PS96, SK96, Wid96]. Active rules are used to perform activities such as integrity constraint and view maintenance, monitor services and work-flow management.

Although there has been considerable research and development in this area (as reflected in the recent book edited by Widom and Ceri [WC96]), there has been very little activity in the study of formal foundations. In the 'Future Directions' section of the 'Conclusion' chapter in [WC96], Widom and Ceri express this sentiment by the following:

> Finally, two largely neglected and crucially important areas within the field of active database systems are *formal foundations* and *usability*. Although some very preliminary work has been done in the area of formal foundations [FMT94, Wid92, Zan93], there is no unifying theory underlying active database systems ... A formal foundation for active database

rule languages would provide a very important step in understanding and characterizing the commonalities and differences across systems.

In general, besides the informal definition of an active rule, there is no consensus about the definition of events, how to process rules when several of them are triggered simultaneously, and how to characterize the set of possible actions. The differences arise because the appropriate alternative is determined by the specific application and most of the options are reasonable. These dissimilarities among the systems make a formal or declarative characterization difficult, and at this point, the only characterization that exists for many of the systems is operational.

The goal of this paper is to take a first step towards a formal framework in which we can precisely describe several active database systems. We develop a language called $\mathcal{L}_{active}$ where we can write descriptions of active databases. Our language borrows from the action description language $\mathcal{L}_0$ [BGP96] which has a clear distinction between actual and hypothetical occurrences of actions. In it, the authors emphasize the hypothetical nature of the situation calculus and argue that the action occurrences in the situations $res(a_1, s_0)$ (i.e. the situation that results from the application of action $a_1$ to situation $s_0$) and $res(a_2, s_0)$ should be considered to be hypothetical, since only one action[3] could have really happened in the situation $s_0$. This distinction is overlooked in most formalization of database updates (such as [Rei94, MW88]).

In $\mathcal{L}_{active}$ we allow the description of actions and their effects, definition of events, and various modes of evaluations for the active rules. This gives us the flexibility to express different event definitions in different active database systems (for example, the definitions in Starburst [Wid96] and A-RDL[SK96]) in a single framework.

The semantics of $\mathcal{L}_{active}$ is based on the automata-based semantics of action description languages, and allows us to define an entailment relation between a database description and queries about the state of the database after the execution of a sequence of transactions. Because of its commonality with the recent works on action description languages our language can be easily extended to incorporate additional features such as concurrent actions [BG96] and deductive rules [KL94, Bar95, LR94].

We start with a presentation of the syntax and semantics of the language. We then present a translation that takes an active database description into a logic program. This translation provides us a vehicle to actually compute the entailment relation. We use the 'choice' construct to characterize the non-determinism and ideas from the situation calculus to characterize the dynamic nature of an

---

[3] We are assuming that our language does not allow concurrent execution of actions.

active database. We conclude the paper with some general remarks on how our language must be generalized to capture many other properties of active database systems.

## 2  Syntax of $\mathcal{L}_{active}$

The alphabet of $\mathcal{L}_{active}$ consists of five disjoint nonempty sets of symbols $\mathcal{F}$, $\mathcal{A}$, $\mathcal{S}$, $\mathcal{E}$, and $\mathcal{M}$ called *fluents*, *actions*, *actual situations*, *events*, and *modes*. Elements of $\mathcal{A}$ will be denoted by (possibly indexed) letters $a$. We will also assume that $\mathcal{S}$ contains situations $s_0, \ldots, s_n$ (for an arbitrary large number $n$) and a special symbol $s_{now}$. The symbols $s_0$ and $s_{now}$ are referred to as *initial* and *current* situations, respectively.

Fluents are data items that can change their values in the database and they can take different forms according to the kind of database being used. For example, in a relational database, fluent names are tuples that can appear in a relation. In an object oriented database it could be the name of an object attribute together with a value in the domain of that attribute. Variables can replace the attribute's value in a fluent name, and they will represent parameters that can be replaced by any value in the domain of the attribute. To minimize the introduction of new notation we will present our examples loosely based on the relation model. A *fluent literal* is a fluent possibly preceded by negation $\neg$. Fluent literals will be denoted by (possibly indexed) letters $f$ and $p$ (possibly preceded by $\neg$). $\neg\neg f$ will be equated with $f$. For any fluent $f$, $\neg f = f$, and $\overline{f} = \neg f$. Similar to fluent literals, an *event literal* is an event possibly preceded by negation $\neg$.

We denote sequences[4] of actions by the Greek letter $\alpha$ and its indexed versions. For an action $a$, $\alpha \circ a$, means the sequence of actions where $a$ follows $\alpha$. We also sometimes denote sequence of actions with the Prolog's notation for lists. For example, the list of actions $[a_1, a_2, \ldots, a_n]$, denotes the sequence of actions where $a_1$ is followed by $a_2$ and so on up to $a_n$.

There are six kinds of propositions in $\mathcal{L}_{active}$ called *causal (or effect) laws*, *executability conditions*, *fluent facts*, *user-dictated action occurrences*, *active rules*, and *event definitions*.

- A *causal law* is an expression of the form

$$a \text{ causes } f \text{ if } p_1, \ldots, p_n \tag{1}$$

---

[4] In this paper by sequence we mean a finite sequence, except when is explicitly specified.

where $a$ is an action, and $f, p_1, \ldots, p_n$ $(n \geq 0)$ are fluent literals. $p_1, \ldots, p_n$ are called *preconditions* of (1). We will read this law as "$f$ is guaranteed to be true after the execution of an action $a$ in any state of the world in which $p_1 \ldots p_n$ are true".

If $n = 0$, we write the effect law as

$$a \text{ causes } f \tag{1a}$$

*Example 1.* The actions common to most database systems are the SQL operations *insert*, *delete* and *update* which we refer to in the rest of the paper by *add*, *del* and *upd* respectively. Following are causal laws describing the effect of these actions.

$add(F)$ **causes** $F$

$del(F)$ **causes** $\neg F$

$upd(F, G)$ **causes** $G$

$upd(F, G)$ **causes** $\neg F$

Many other actions can be specified in $\mathcal{L}_{active}$. We will only remark that actions can have different effects based upon the preconditions of the action. For example, the following action keeps count of the resource allocated to systems $p$ and $q$.[5]

$balance\_load\_pq(N)$ **causes** $p(X)$ **if** $p(Y), q(Z), Y \geq Z, X = Y + N.$

$balance\_load\_pq(N)$ **causes** $q(X)$ **if** $p(Z), q(Y), Y > Z, X = Y + N.$ $\quad\square$

Two causal laws of the form

$a$ **causes** $f$ **if** $p_1, \ldots, p_n$ and
$a$ **causes** $\neg f$ **if** $q_1, \ldots, q_m$

are said to be *contradictory* if $\{p_1, \ldots, p_n\} \cap \{\overline{q_1}, \ldots, \overline{q_m}\} = \emptyset$.

- An *executability condition* is an expression of the form

$$\textbf{executable } a \textbf{ if } q_1, \ldots, q_k \tag{2}$$

where $a$ is an action name, and each of $q_1, \ldots, q_k$ $(k \geq 0)$ is a fluent literal. About this proposition we say that it stipulates that $a$ is executable in a situation where $q_1, \ldots, q_k$ are satisfied.

---

[5] Strictly speaking we will need to define $>$ and $=$ fluents, and the operation $+$, but to simplify the presentation we appeal to the intuition of the reader for the semantics of these predicates.

*Example 2.* Example of executability conditions for inserts, deletes and updates are:

**executable** $add(F)$ **if** $\neg F$

**executable** $del(F)$ **if** $F$

**executable** $upd(F,G)$ **if** $F, \neg G$

An executability condition for $balance\_load\_pq(N)$ could be dictated by a constant $\kappa$ that the total load must not surpass.

**executable** $balance\_load\_pq(N)$ **if** $p(X), q(Y), \kappa > X + Y + N.$ $\qquad$ $\Box$

- An atomic *fluent fact* is an expression of the form

$$f \text{ at } s_0 \qquad (3)$$

where $f$ is a fluent literal and $s_0$ is the initial situation. The intuitive reading of (3) is "$f$ is observed to be true in the initial situation".

- A *user-dictated occurrence fact* is an expression of the form

$$\alpha \text{ ordered\_at } s \qquad (4)$$

where $\alpha$ is a sequence of actions, and $s$ is a situation constant. It states that "the sequence $\alpha$ of actions was ordered by the user for execution in situation $s$" (we assume that actions in the sequence follow each other immediately). User-dictated facts can be thought to be transactions ordered by users of the database. The transaction is defined by $\alpha$. The situation $s$ determined when the transaction happens. It is assumed that situation $s_i$ precedes situation $s_{i+1}$.

- An *active rule* is an expression of the form

$$\mathbf{r} : e \text{ evaluated\_in\_mode } m \text{ under\_conditions } p_1, \ldots, p_n \text{ triggers } \alpha \qquad (5)$$

where $e$ is an event, $m$ is the evaluation mode of the active rule, and $\mathbf{r}$ is the name of the rule. The rule in eqn(5) intuitively states that the event $e$ under conditions $p_1, \ldots, p_n$ triggers $\alpha$. $\alpha$ is referred to as the trigger of this active rule. There are two possible modes of execution $m$, *ignore* and *reconsider*.[6] The modes designate at what points a rule is considered for evaluation. Rules with *ignore* mode are considered only at points where events are generated. If the mode is *reconsidered*, the rule can be triggered: 1) At every point where events are generated, and 2) After an active rule has been fired. Events are generated

---

[6] We anticipate adding other modes of executions to our language.

by two types of situations, the situation that results after the execution of $\alpha$ in a user-dictated fact, and the situation that results after the evaluation of the active rules. (Note that in the second case, the first rule is triggered at point where an event was generated, any rule can be considered for execution. Subsequent rules in the batch must be in *reconsider* mode.)

If $n = 0$ in (5) we write it as:

$$r : e \text{ evaluated\_in\_mode } m \text{ triggers } \alpha \tag{6}$$

*Example 3.* Let us consider the following example from Zaniolo [Zan96], where the database contains the relations:

$Dept(D\#, Dname, Div, Loc)$ and $Emp(E\#, Ename, Jobtitle, Sal, D\#)$

and there is an active rule which says: "When a tuple is deleted from a department, then delete all employees who were working in the deleted department."

We can represent the above rule in our syntax by the following active rule:

$r_1 : del_e(dept(D\#, Dname, Div, Loc))$ **evaluated\_in\_mode** *reconsider*
**triggers** $del\_all\_emps(D\#)$

In the above active rule we use the subscript $e$ to distinguish between events and actions that otherwise look similar.

To describe the effect of the action $del\_all\_emps(D\#)$ we will need the following causal law:

$del\_all\_emps(D\#)$ **causes** $\neg Emp(E\#, Ename, Jobtitle, Sal, D\#)$

In the sequel we will consider the possibility of having $del\_all\_emps(D\#)$ as a complex action defined in terms of the simple actions *add* and *del*. $\square$

Rule execution is driven by the events that take place in the life of the database. The kind of events that can trigger a rule significantly varies from active database to active database, but most of the events can be characterized in terms of (a) the changes that occur in the database during the execution of a sequence of actions, and (b) the sequence of actions itself. This sequence of actions could be a transaction that has been dictated to the database by a user (external actions) or a series of actions generated by the execution of the active rules (internal actions). In $\mathcal{L}_{active}$ events can be defined in terms of the current state of database, the current action to be executed, and the events that have occurred so far. Thus,

- An *event definition* is an expression of the form

$$e \textbf{ after } a \textbf{ if } q_1, \ldots, q_m, e_1, \ldots, e_n \tag{7}$$

where $e$ is an event, $e_i$'s are event literals, and $q_j$'s are fluent literals. It states that the execution of $a$ induces an event $e$, if $q_1, \ldots, q_m$ hold (before $a$ is executed) and $e_1, \ldots, e_n$ were induced (before $a$ is executed). If $n$ and $m$ are both 0, we will write

$$e \textbf{ after } a \tag{8}$$

This simple syntactic structure allows us to define many types of events. Take, for example, the events in Starburst [Wid96]. They are defined in terms of net effects of the transitions instead of the individual operations generating the transitions. Net effects are defined based on the following four premises.

1. If a tuple is first inserted and then updated, then this is considered an insertion of the updated tuple.

2. If a tuple is first updated and then deleted, then this is considered the deletion of the original tuple.

3. If a tuple is updated several times, this is considered an update to the newest value.

4. If a tuple is first inserted and then deleted the actions are ignored.

The four rules can be defined in $\mathcal{L}_{active}$ as

$add_e(H) \textbf{ after } upd(G, H) \textbf{ if } add_e(G)$

$del_e(G) \textbf{ after } del(F) \textbf{ if } upd_e(G, F)$

$upd_e(G, I) \textbf{ after } upd(H, I) \textbf{ if } upd_e(G, H)$

$add_e(F) \textbf{ after } del(G) \textbf{ if } add_e(F) \quad (F \neq G)$

Note that these are schemas of event definitions where $G$, $F$ and $H$ range over all the fluents. The inequality in the last line is part of the schema. There are other active database system that use more complicated rules to define net effects. For example, the A-RDL system [SK96] has seventeen rules. They can be easily encoded in $\mathcal{L}_{active}$ using seventeen event definitions.

There are other kinds of events that are not defined in terms of net effects, but in complicated semantic criteria. For example, we can define the event "sharp increase of an object value" if the value of a particular object in the database is updated to a value 10% higher than the current value. The definition of this event in $\mathcal{L}_{active}$ will be:

$sharp\_increase_e(A)$ **after** $upd(value(A,Y), value(A,Z))$ **if** $Z \geq Y + Y * 0.1$

From the syntax of the language and the above examples it is clear that our language allows us to easily express actions (and their effects) and event definitions beyond the commonly used *add*, *delete* and *update*.

A collection of causal laws, executability conditions, fluent facts, user-dictated action occurrences, active rules and event definitions is called an *active database description* of $\mathcal{L}_{active}$. We will only consider active database descriptions whose propositions do not mention the situation constant $s_{now}$, and which do not have contradictory causal laws.

# 3 Semantics of $\mathcal{L}_{active}$

In this section we introduce a semantics of our active database specification language $\mathcal{L}_{active}$. We assume that states of the database are determined by sets of fluents and that actions executed in a particular state can add and remove such fluents according to the causal laws. The set of all possible behaviors of a dynamic system, satisfying causal laws and executability conditions of a given active database description $D$, can then be described by a transition diagram with states labeled by sets of fluents and transitions labeled by actions. To interpret the facts from $D$ we need to select the initial situation or state together with a path in the diagram describing the actual behavior of the system. In the following subsections we describe an automaton by a partial function from action sequences to states.

## 3.1 States and Causal Interpretations

A *state* is a set of fluents. A *causal interpretation* is a partial function $\Psi$ from sequences of actions to states such that:

(1) The empty sequence [ ] belongs to the domain of $\Psi$ and

(2) $\Psi$ is prefix-closed.[7]

$\Psi([\ ])$ is called the initial state of $\Psi$. The partial function $\Psi$ serves as an interpretation of the causal laws and executability conditions of $D$.

Given a fluent $f$ and a state $\sigma$, we say that $f$ *holds* in $\sigma$ ($f$ is *true* in $\sigma$) if $f \in \sigma$; $\neg f$ *holds* in $\sigma$ ($f$ is *false* in $\sigma$) if $f \notin \sigma$. We say an action $a$ is executable in a

---

[7] By "prefix closed" we mean that for any sequence of actions $\alpha$ and action $a$, if $\alpha \circ a$ is in the domain of $\Psi$ then so is $\alpha$.

state $\sigma$ if there exists an executability condition of the form (2) with action $a$, such that the preconditions $q_1, \ldots, q_k$ hold in $\sigma$.

Now we define effects of actions determined by causal laws and executability conditions of an active database description $D$.

A fluent literal $f$ is an (immediate) *effect* of (executing) $a$ in $\sigma$ if there is an effect law $a$ **causes** $f$ **if** $p_1, \ldots, p_n$ in $D$ whose preconditions $p_1, \ldots, p_n$ hold in $\sigma$. Let

$E_a^+(\sigma) = \{f : f \in \mathcal{F}$ and $f$ is an effect of $a$ in $\sigma\}$,

$E_a^-(\sigma) = \{f : f \in \mathcal{F}$ and $\neg f$ is an effect of $a$ in $\sigma\}$ and

$Res(a, \sigma) = (\sigma \cup E_a^+(\sigma)) \setminus E_a^-(\sigma)$. $Res$ is referred to as the *transition function*.

The following definition captures the meaning of causal laws and executability conditions of $D$.

**Definition 1.** A causal interpretation $\Psi$ *satisfies* the causal laws and executability conditions of $D$ if for any sequence $\alpha \circ a$ from the language of $D$,

if $E_a^+(\Psi(\alpha)) \cap E_a^-(\Psi(\alpha)) = \emptyset$, $\Psi(\alpha)$ is defined and $a$ is executable in $\Psi(\alpha)$

then $\Psi(\alpha \circ a) = Res(a, \Psi(\alpha))$,

otherwise $\Psi(\alpha \circ a)$ is undefined.

We say $\Psi$ is a *causal model* of $D$ if it satisfies the causal laws and executability conditions of $D$. $\square$

It is easy to see that causal models of active database descriptions are uniquely determined by their initial values, i.e., for any causal models $\Psi_1$ and $\Psi_2$ of an active database description $D$, if $\Psi_1([\,]) = \Psi_2([\,])$ then $\Psi_1 = \Psi_2$.

## 3.2 Situation Assignments, Event Interpretations and Trigger Interpretations

**Definition 2.** Let $\Sigma$ be a mapping from $S$ to sequences of actions from the language of $D$. This mapping will be called a *situation assignment of $\mathcal{D}$* if it satisfies the following properties:

1. $\Sigma(s_0) = [\,]$;

2. For every $s \in S$, $\Sigma(s)$ is a prefix of $\Sigma(s_{now})$. □

Intuitively, the set of events that are induced by the execution of an action $a$, is determined by a finite sequence of actions that have occurred previously to $a$, the action $a$, and the current state of the database. More precisely, an *event interpretation* is a mapping $\Xi$ from the set of finite sequences of actions, and the set of states to the power set of events. For an event $e$, if $e \in \Xi(\alpha, \sigma)$, then we say that $e$ is induced by $\alpha$ in state $\sigma$. For an event literal $e'$ such that $e' = \neg e$, where $e$ is an event, we say $e'$ is induced by $\alpha$ in state $\sigma$ if $e \notin \Xi(\alpha, \sigma)$.

**Definition 3.** An event interpretation $\Xi$ is said to satisfy the event definitions of an active database description $D$ if

$\Xi([], \sigma) = \emptyset$, and

$\Xi(\alpha \circ a, \sigma) = \{e \; : \;$ there exists an event description of the form (7) such that $q_1, \ldots, q_m$ hold in $Res(\alpha, \sigma)$, and for all $e_i$, $1 \leq i \leq n$, $e_i$ is induced by $\alpha$ in the state $\sigma$.$\}$ □

Informally, the execution of active rules can be described by the following loop.

1. Events trigger a set of active rules. If the set if empty the loop terminates.

2. One of these rules is selected and executed.

3. Then, if there are *reconsider* rules in the set of triggered rules, we go to step 2.

4. If there are no *reconsider* rules, the events are re-evaluated (based on the actions executed by the triggered rules) and we go to step 1.

Thus, given an initial sequence of actions (that may generate events) and an initial state, a *trigger interpretation* will define the sequence of actions that are triggered by the active rules according to the steps in the loop. Precisely, a trigger interpretation $\mathcal{T}$ will be a function that maps a sequence of actions and a situation into a (not necessarily finite) sequence of actions.

**Definition 4.** A trigger interpretation $\mathcal{T}$ is said to satisfy the active rules of an active database description $D$ if, for any sequence of actions $\alpha$, and a state $\sigma$, if

$$\mathcal{T}(\alpha, \sigma) = \beta_{1,1}, \ldots, \beta_{1,k_1}, \ldots, \beta_{m,1}, \ldots, \beta_{m,k_m}, \ldots$$

then (with the denotation of $\alpha$ by $\alpha_0$ and $\beta_{j,1}, \ldots, \beta_{j,k_j}$ by $\alpha_j$)

1. there exists an active rule of the form (5) with event $e$, conditions $p_1, \ldots, p_n$, and trigger $\beta_{j,1}$ ($j \geq 1$), such that

   - $e$ is in $\Xi(\alpha_{j-1}, Res(\alpha_0 \circ \ldots \circ \alpha_{j-2}, \sigma))$,[8] and

   - $p_1, \ldots, p_n$, hold in $Res(\alpha_0 \circ \ldots \circ \alpha_{j-1}, \sigma)$.

2. there exists an active rule of the form (5) that has not been used in the triggering of $\beta_{j,1}, \ldots, \beta_{j,l-1}$, with mode *reconsider*, event $e$, conditions $p_1, \ldots, p_n$, and trigger $\beta_{j,l}$ ($j \geq 1, l \geq 2$), such that

   - $e$ is in $\Xi(\alpha_{j-1}, Res(\alpha_0 \circ \ldots \circ \alpha_{j-2}, \sigma))$, and

   - $p_1, \ldots, p_n$, hold in $Res(\alpha_0 \circ \ldots \circ \alpha_{j-1} \circ \beta_{j,1} \circ \ldots \circ \beta_{j,l-1}, \sigma)$ and

If $\mathcal{T}(\alpha, \sigma) = \beta_{1,1}, \ldots, \beta_{1,k_1}, \ldots, \beta_{m,1}, \ldots, \beta_{m,k_m}$, (i.e. $\mathcal{T}(\alpha, \sigma)$ is a finite sequence) then besides the above two conditions, the following condition is also satisfied:

"There does not exist an active rule of the form (5) with event $e$, and conditions $p_1, \ldots, p_n$, such that the conditions hold in $Res(\alpha_0 \circ \ldots \circ \alpha_m, \sigma)$ and $e$ is in $\Xi(\alpha_m, Res(\alpha_0 \circ \ldots \circ \alpha_{m-1}, \sigma))$." $\qquad \square$

**Definition 5.** An *interpretation* $M$ of $\mathcal{L}_{active}$ is a triplet $(\Psi, \Sigma, \Xi)$, where $\Psi$ is a causal model of $D$, $\Sigma$ is a situation assignment of $S$, and $\Xi$ is an event interpretation. We have the added restriction that $\Sigma(s_{now})$ belong to the domain of $\Psi$. $\qquad \square$

**Definition 6.** For any interpretation $M = (\Psi, \Sigma, \Xi)$

(1) ($f$ **at** $s_0$) is true in $M$ (or satisfied by $M$) if $f$ is true in $\Psi([])$;

(2) ($\alpha$ **ordered_at** $s_i$) is true in $M$ if $\Sigma(s_i)$ is finite and $\Sigma(s_{i+1}) = \Sigma(s_i) \circ \alpha \circ \mathcal{T}(\alpha, \Psi(\Sigma(s_i)))$. $\qquad \square$

**Definition 7.** An interpretation $M = (\Psi, \Sigma, \Xi)$ is said to be a model of an active database description $D$, if the following conditions are satisfied.

  - $\Psi$ is a causal model of $D$.

  - All fluent facts in $D$ are true in $M$.

  - All user dictated occurrences are true in $M$.

  - $\Xi$ satisfies the event definition in $D$.

---

[8] In this part and part 2 of the definition, when $j = 1$, $Res(\alpha_0 \circ \ldots \circ \alpha_{j-2}, \sigma)$ denotes $\sigma$.

and $\Sigma(s_{now})$ is the minimal sequence that satisfies the above four conditions. $\square$

$\Sigma(s_{now})$ will be called the *actual path* of $M$ and for simplicity will often be denoted by $\Sigma_{now}$.

The *query language* associated with $\mathcal{L}_{active}$ will consist of hypothetical facts of the form

$$f \textbf{ after } \alpha \textbf{ ordered\_at } s \tag{9}$$

and will be denoted by $\mathcal{L}_0^Q$.

When $s$ in (9) is $s_{now}$, we write the query as:

$$f \textbf{ after } \alpha \tag{10}$$

If $\alpha$ is an empty sequence of actions we write the query as:

$$\textbf{currently } f \tag{11}$$

**Definition 8.** We say a query $q$ of the form (9) [9] is true in a model $M$ of an active database description $D$ if $f$ is true in $\Psi(\Sigma(s) \circ \alpha \circ \mathcal{T}(\alpha, \Psi(\Sigma(s))))$. $\square$

The following definition describes the set of acceptable conclusions one can obtain from an active database description $D$.

**Definition 9.** An active database description $D$ *entails* a query $q$ (written as $D \models q$) iff $q$ is true in all models of $D$. The set of all facts entailed by $D$ will be denoted by $Cn(D)$.

We will say that the answer given by $D$ to a query $q$ is *yes*, if $D \models q$; *no*, if $D \models \neg q$; and *unknown* otherwise. $\square$

Queries of the form (11) allow us to reason about what is true (and what is false) in the current situation of the database. Notice that this situation might be different in different models of the database description because of the non-determinism created by the active rules. Queries of the form (10) allow us to

---

[9] We can extend the queries to allow a sequence of user dictated action sequences in the standard way. Syntactically, (9) will then be extended to the form:

$$f \textbf{ after } \alpha_1, \ldots, \alpha_n \textbf{ ordered\_at } s$$

do hypothetical reasoning from the current situation and queries of the form
(9) allow us to do counter-factual reasoning from the past situations. We may
want to know properties of the database if we were to execute the sequence of
actions $\alpha$ in situation $s$ instead of the sequence of actions in the user-dictated
facts that were specified in the database description. Notice too, that if $\alpha$ is the
empty sequence we are asking for properties of the database in real situations
that occurred in the past.

# 4  A Translation to Logic Programs

In this section we present a translation $\Pi_s$ of active database descriptions into
logic programs with situation calculus notation. For simplicity, we currently assume that all actions are executable in all situations and only try to capture what
is true in the current situation. In the sequel we will remove these restrictions.

The logic program $\Pi_s D$ where $D$ is the active database description uses terms
of five sorts. (We follow the convention of variables starting with capital letters
and constants starting with small letters.)

- *fluents*: Fluent constants are denoted by $f, f'$, and fluent variables are denoted by $F, F', \ldots$.

- *events*: Event constants are denoted by $e, e'$, event variables are denoted by
  $E, E'$ and by $not(e)$ we denote the negative event of $e$.

- *actions*: Action constants are denoted by $a, a_0, a_1$, etc, and action variables
  with $A, A'$.

- *situations*: $s_0, \ldots, s_n$ are situation constants, and all other situation constants are constructed by application of the function symbol $res$ to a situation constant and an action. For example, if $a$ denotes an action and
  $s$ denotes a situation constant then $res(a, s)$ denotes a situation constant.
  Intuitively the situation constant $res(a, s)$ refers to the situation obtained
  by executing action $a$ in situation $s$. For convenience, by $[a_1, \ldots, a_m]s_0$ we
  denote the situation $res(a_m, res(a_{m-1}, \ldots, res(a_1, s_0)) \ldots)$. We use the reversed version of the Prolog's notation for lists; i.e. we have $[a_1, \ldots, a_m]$ to
  be equivalent to $[[a_1, \ldots, a_{m-1}]|a_m]$.

- *rules*: Rule constants are denoted by $r, r'$, and rule variables are denoted by
  $R, R', \ldots$

The program $\Pi_s D$ consists of the translations of the individual active rules, the
initial state, the events occurring at the initial state, and certain other logic
programming rules. The various predicates that are used in the translation have
the following intuitive meaning.

- $actual(s)$: Intuitively, $actual(s)$ is true if $s$ is an actual situation where the sequence of actions in $s$ can either be ordered by a user or triggered by an active rule.

- $holds(f,s)$ and $hyp\_holds(f,s)$: Intuitively, $hyp\_holds(f,s)$ is true if $f$ holds in the situation (hypothetical or actual) $s$, and $holds(f,s)$ is true if $f$ holds in the actual situation $s$.

- We denote a sequence of actions by $\alpha$, $\beta$ and $\gamma$. Hence, $[\alpha]$, denotes a list of actions. We denote a sequence of lists of actions by $\Gamma$. For example, $\Gamma$ could be the sequence $[\alpha_1], \ldots, [\alpha_k]$. The list $[\Gamma]$ is a list of list of actions.

- $flatten$, $append$: These are auxiliary procedures to manipulate sequence of actions. Intuitively, $flatten([\Gamma], [\alpha])$ is true if $[\alpha]$ is a flattened list obtained from flattening $[\Gamma]$, which is a list of list of actions. Intuitively, $append([\alpha], [\beta], [\gamma])$ means that the list $[\gamma]$ is obtained by appending the list $[\beta]$ to the list $[\alpha]$. (To save space we do not explicitly give rules defining these predicates in our translation.)

- $unfold$: Intuitively, $unfold(s, [\Gamma], [\alpha], [\beta]s_0)$ is true if $[\beta]$ is the list of actions from the initial state that corresponds to the situation $s$ followed by the flattening of $[\Gamma]$, followed by $[\alpha]$.

- $event(e, [\beta], s)$: Intuitively, $event(e, [\beta], s)$ means that the event $e$ is induced by the list of actions $[\beta]$ in situation $s$. The rules that define $event$ are given in Step 5.

- $event\_pt, trigger\_pt$: Recall the definition of a trigger interpretation $\mathcal{T}$ satisfying active rules in Definition 4. There we had $\mathcal{T}(\alpha, \sigma) = \beta_{1,1}, \ldots, \beta_{1,k_1}, \ldots, \beta_{m,1}, \ldots, \beta_{m,k_m}$. In this sequence, events are generated after the execution of $\alpha$ and after the execution of $\beta_{i,k_i}$, for $i \geq 1$. However, active rules can be triggered after any $\beta_{i,j}$ or after $\alpha$. Suppose we have a situation $s$ whose corresponding state is $\sigma$, and let $\alpha = a_1, \ldots, a_n$.

The predicate $event\_pt$ describes situations where the active database computes events that have happened since the last such computation. In the above example such points are described by the fact

$event\_pt(s, [[a_1, \ldots, a_n]])$, and the facts

$event\_pt(s, [[a_1, \ldots, a_n], [\beta_{1,1}, \ldots, \beta_{1,k_1}], \ldots, [\beta_{i,1}, \ldots, \beta_{i,k_i}]])$,
where, $1 \leq i \leq m$.

The predicate $trigger\_pt$ describes situations where the active database triggers. In the above example such points are described by the fact

$trigger\_pt(s, [[a_1, \ldots, a_n]], [])$, the facts

$trigger\_pt(s, [[a_1, \ldots, a_n]], [\beta_{1,1}, \ldots, \beta_{1,j_1}])$, where $1 \leq j \leq k_1$, and the facts

$trigger\_pt(s, [[a_1, \ldots, a_n], [\beta_{1,1}, \ldots, \beta_{1,k_1}], \ldots, [\beta_{i,1}, \ldots, \beta_{i,k_i}]],$
$\quad\quad [\beta_{i+1,1}, \ldots, \beta_{i+1,j}]),$
where, $1 \le i \le m$ and $1 \le j \le k_{i+1}$.

- $p\_occurs(r, s, [\Gamma], [\alpha])$ and $occurs(r, s, [\Gamma], [\alpha])$: Intuitively, the predicate $p\_occurs(r, s, [\Gamma], [\alpha])$ is true if the rule $r$ can be fired in the situation $s$ followed by the flattening of $[\Gamma]$ followed by $[\alpha]$. But since there may be many such rules that can fired in this situation, and the semantics of active database system dictates that only one such rule should be actually fired,[10] we denote the firing of this particular rule by the atom $occurs(r, s, [\Gamma], [\alpha])$.

- $ab(f, a, s)$: Intuitively, $ab(f, a, s)$ is true if the execution of action $a$ in situation $s$ may change the value of $f$.

- $last(s), currently(f)$: Intuitively, $last(s)$ is true if $s$ is the situation where the active database system *terminates*, and $currently(f)$ is true if $f$ is true currently, i.e., at the end of the execution of all actions triggered by the active rules.

We now present the translation $\Pi_s D$.

**1. Translating active rules:**

For an active rule of the form (5) the program $\Pi_s D$ contains the following three rules:

(1.1) $p\_occurs(\mathbf{r}, S, [\Gamma\|[\beta]], []) \leftarrow event\_pt(S, [\Gamma\|[\beta]]), unfold(S, [\Gamma], [], [\gamma]s_0),$
$\quad\quad event(e, [\beta], [\gamma]s_0), unfold(S, [\Gamma\|[\beta]], [], [\gamma']s_0),$
$\quad\quad holds(p_1, [\gamma']s_0), \ldots, holds(p_n, [\gamma']s_0)$

(1.2) $mode(\mathbf{r}, m) \leftarrow$

(1.3) $trigger(\mathbf{r}, \alpha) \leftarrow$

**2. Translating Fluent facts:**

If $f$ is true in the initial state then $\Pi_s D$ contains the following rule.

(2.2) $hyp\_holds(f, s_0) \leftarrow$

Otherwise $\Pi_s D$ contains the rule:

(2.3) $hyp\_holds(\neg f, s_0) \leftarrow$

---

[10] Similar to actions, in this paper we assume that there is no concurrent executions of rules.

## 3. Translating user dictated occurrences:

For an user dictate occurrences of the form (4) the program contains the following rule:

   (3) $event\_pt(s, [[\alpha]]) \leftarrow$

## 4. Translating causal rules:

For each causal rule of the form (1) we have the following rules:

   (4.1) $hyp\_holds(f, res(a, S)) \leftarrow hyp\_holds(p_1, S), \ldots, hyp\_holds(p_n, S)$

   (4.2) $ab(f', a, S) \leftarrow hyp\_holds(p_1, S), \ldots, hyp\_holds(p_n, S)$

where $f$ is the fluent $g$ if $f = \neg g$, or the fluent literal $\neg g$ if $f = g$.

## 5. Translating event definitions

For each event definition of the form (7) we have the following rule:

   $(5.1) event(e, [\alpha | a], [\gamma] s_0) \leftarrow hyp\_holds(q_1, [\beta] s_0), \ldots,$
                    $hyp\_holds(q_m, [\beta] s_0),$
                    $event(e_1, \alpha, [\beta] s_0), \ldots, event(e_n, \alpha, [\beta] s_0),$
                    $append([\gamma], [\alpha], [\beta])$

To define the truth of event literals we have the following additional rule:

   $event(not(e), [\alpha], S) \leftarrow not\ event(e, [\alpha], S)$

## 6. Inertia axiom

   (6.1) $hyp\_holds(F, res(A, S)) \leftarrow hyp\_holds(F, S), not\ ab(F, A, S)$

## 7. Other Rules:

The other rules in $\Pi_s D$ are:

(7.1) Additional rules defining $p\_occurs$:

   (7.1.1) $p\_occurs(R, S, [\Gamma], [\gamma]) \leftarrow p\_occurs(R, S, [\Gamma], [\alpha]),$
                   $occurs(R', S, [\Gamma], [\alpha]), trigger(R', [\beta]),$
                   $not\ ab_p(R, S, [\Gamma], [\alpha], [\beta]), append([\alpha], [\beta], [\gamma])$

(7.1.2) $ab_p(R, S, [\Gamma], [\alpha], [\beta]) \leftarrow occurs(R, S, [\Gamma], [\alpha]), trigger(R, [\beta])$

(7.1.3) $ab_p(R, S, [\Gamma], [\alpha], [\beta]) \leftarrow not\ mode(R, reconsider)$

These three rules take care of the pre-selection of *reconsider* rules. *p_occurs* in (7.1.1) marks the rule $R$ as a potential rule to be triggered if it was already pre-selected by $p_o ccurs$ in a previous firing, but it has not been used or it is not a rule in *ignore* mode. These two conditions are verified by (7.1.2) and (7.1.3).

(7.2) Rules defining *occurs*:

(7.2.1) $occurs(R, S, [\Gamma], [\alpha]) \leftarrow p\_occurs(R, S, [\Gamma], [\alpha])$
$\qquad\qquad not\ notoccurs(R, S, [\Gamma], [\alpha])$

(7.2.2) $notoccurs(R, S, [\Gamma], [\alpha]) \leftarrow occurs(R', S, [\Gamma], [\alpha]), neq(R, R')$

The above two rules implement the *choice* operator which was first introduced in [SZ90]. Intuitively, they guarantee that among all the rules that may possibly be fired in a situation $S$, only one gets fired in each stable model of the program and there is one stable model corresponding to each of the rules that may be possibly fired.[11]

(7.3) Rules defining *trigger_pt* and *event_pt*:

(7.3.1) $trigger\_pt(S, [\Gamma], []) \leftarrow event\_pt(S, [\Gamma])$

(7.3.2) $trigger\_pt(S, [\Gamma], [\gamma]) \leftarrow trigger\_pt(S, [\Gamma], [\alpha']), occurs(R, S, [\Gamma], [\alpha']),$
$\qquad\qquad\qquad trigger(R, [\alpha]), append([\alpha'], [\alpha], [\gamma])$

(7.3.3) $exists(S, [\Gamma], [\beta]) \leftarrow p\_occurs(R, S, [\Gamma], [\beta])$

(7.3.4) $event\_pt(S, [\Gamma|[\beta]]) \leftarrow trigger\_pt(S, [\Gamma], [\beta]),$
$\qquad\qquad\qquad not\ exists(S, [\Gamma], [\beta])$

(7.4) Rules defining intermediate termination of triggering:

(7.4.1) $terminates(S, [\Gamma]) \leftarrow event\_pt(S, [\Gamma]), not\ exists(S, [\Gamma], [])$

(7.5) Defining *actual* and *holds*:

(7.5.1) $actual(s_0) \leftarrow$

(7.5.2) $actual([\gamma]s_0) \leftarrow trigger\_pt(S, [\Gamma], [\alpha]), unfold(S, [\Gamma], [\alpha], [\gamma]s_0)$

---

[11] $neq(X, Y)$ checks that $X$ and $Y$ do not unify.

(7.5.3) $holds(F, [\gamma]s_0) \leftarrow hyp\_holds(F, [\gamma]s_0), actual([\gamma]s_0)$

The above rules make a fluent literal to hold in an actual situation if it hypothetical holds in that situation.

(7.6) Rules defining *unfold*:

(7.6.1) $unfold(s_0, [], [], s_0) \leftarrow$

(7.6.2) $unfold(s_{i+1}, [], [], [\gamma]s_0) \leftarrow unfold(S_i, [], [], [\alpha]s_0), terminate(s_i, [\Gamma]),$
$\qquad flatten([\Gamma], [\beta]), append([\alpha], [\beta], [\gamma])$

(7.6.3) $unfold(S, [\Gamma], [\alpha], [\gamma]s_0) \leftarrow unfold(S, [], [], [\beta_1]s_0),$
$\qquad flatten([\Gamma|[\alpha]], \beta_2), append([\beta_1], [\beta_2], [\gamma])$

(7.7) Rules defining *last_sit* and *last*:

(7.7.1) $not\_last\_sit(S) \leftarrow event\_pt(S', [\Gamma])$

(7.7.2) $last\_sit(S) \leftarrow not\ not\_last\_sit(S)$

(7.7.3) $last([\gamma]s_0) \leftarrow last\_sit(S), terminates(S, [\Gamma]),$
$\qquad unfold(S, [\Gamma], [], [\gamma]s_0)$

The above two rules define the last situation.

(7.8) Defining *currently*

(7.8.1) $currently(F) \leftarrow last([\gamma]s_0), holds(F, [\gamma]s_0)$

The above rule defines which fluent literals are true after the active database system terminates.
**End of the Translation**

Notice that the programs generated by the translation are not locally stratified because of the rules in (7.2). However, these rules follow the construction pattern of the choice operator introduced in [SZ90] which has a well-understood semantics based on the stable models of Gelfond and Lifschitz. Thus, $\Pi_s D$ will always have stable models, and it is possible to show a direct correspondence between the models of $D$ and the stable models of $\Pi_s D$. This correspondence allows us to show the following proposition.

**Proposition 10.** *For an active database description $D$,*

$$D \models \mathbf{currently}\ f \quad iff \quad \Pi_s D \models currently(f).$$

## 4.1 Incorporating priorities

In the characterization of active database systems in the past section we did not prioritize between the active rules that are simultaneously triggered. We gave equal priority to all of them. However, many systems allow prioritizing between these rules. Several different prioritizing strategies (also referred to as conflict resolution strategies), such as priority, specificity, recency, etc. are used. We now briefly sketch how these strategies can be incorporated in the logic programming translations.

Consider a predicate *preferable* of arity two that defines a preference relation between two rules. For example, $preferable(R1, R2)$ means that the rule $R1$ is preferable to rule $R2$. At this point we do not worry about how the relation *preferable* is obtained. (It may be directly given or it may be defined in terms of other conflict resolution parameters such as how recently the rules were used.) We assume that the relation given by *preferable* is a partial order.

Using the relation *preferable* we can now define a predicate *pref_occurs* as follows:

$$not\_pref\_occurs(R, S, [\Gamma], [\alpha]) \leftarrow p\_occurs(R', S, [\Gamma], [\alpha]),$$
$$preferable(R', R), neq(R, R')$$

$$pref\_occurs(R, S, [\Gamma], [\alpha]) \leftarrow p\_occurs(R, S, [\Gamma], [\alpha]),$$
$$not\ not\_pref\_occurs(R, S, [\Gamma], [\alpha])$$

The predicate *occurs* is now defined in terms of *pref_occurs* instead of *p_occurs* in the following way:

$$occurs(R, S, [\Gamma], [\alpha]) \leftarrow pref\_occurs(R, S, [\Gamma], [\alpha]), not\ not\_occurs(R, S, [\Gamma], [\alpha])$$

$$not\_occurs(R, S, [\Gamma], [\alpha]) \leftarrow occurs(R', S, [\Gamma], [\alpha]), neq(R, R')$$

## 5 Final remarks and future work

In this paper we have presented a formal framework to describe active databases. Our framework allows the representation of actions and their effects, event definitions, active rules with different execution modes, and reasoning about the value of the database in both actual and hypothetical situations. We intend to substantially add to our framework. In particular we plan to

- extend $\mathcal{L}_{active}$ to allow specification of priorities between rules,

- consider additional execution modes for the active rules,

- allow concurrent and complex actions where a complex action is defined in terms of simple actions,

- allow temporal conditions, and

- compare the use of temporal conditions vs. complex events.

We have some ideas of how to do this based on previous work on concurrent and complex actions [BG96, LLL+94, BK93], and temporal conditions [MLLB96, SW95]. In general, we believe that the methodology of using a transition system or automata is a promising approach to formally describe the semantics of active databases.

# References

[Bar95]    C. Baral. Reasoning about Actions : Non-deterministic effects, Constraints and Qualification. In *Proc. of IJCAI 95*, pages 2017–2023, 1995.

[BG96]     C. Baral and M. Gelfond. Reasoning about effects of concurrent actions. *Journal of Logic Programming (to appear)*, 1996.

[BGP96]    C. Baral, M. Gelfond, and A. Provetti. Representing Actions: Laws, Observations and Hypothesis. *Journal of Logic Programming (to appear)*, 1996.

[BK93]     A. Bonner and M. Kifer. Transaction logic programming. In D. S. Warren, editor, *Logic Programming: Proc. of the 10th International Conf.*, pages 257–279, 1993.

[CFPB96]   S. Ceri, P. Fraternali, S. Paraboschi, and L. Branca. Active rule management in Chimera. In J. Widom and S Ceri, editors, *Active Database Systems*, pages 151–176. Morgan Kaufmann, 1996.

[DBC96]    U. Dayal, A. Buchmann, and S. Chakravarthy. The HiPAC Project. In J. Widom and S Ceri, editors, *Active Database Systems*, pages 177–206. Morgan Kaufmann, 1996.

[FMT94]    P. Fraternali, D. Montesi, and L. Tanca. Active database semantics. In *Proc. of the Fifth Australasian Database Conference*, 1994.

[GJ96]     N. Gehani and H. Jagadish. Active database facilities in Ode . In J. Widom and S Ceri, editors, *Active Database Systems*, pages 207–232. Morgan Kaufmann, 1996.

[Han96]    E. Hanson. The Ariel Project. In J. Widom and S Ceri, editors, *Active Database Systems*, pages 63–86. Morgan Kaufmann, 1996.

[KL94]     G. Kartha and V. Lifschitz. Actions with indirect effects: Preliminary report. In *KR 94*, pages 341–350, 1994.

[LLL+94]   Y. Lesperance, H. Levesque, F. Lin, D. Marcu, R. Reiter, and R. Scherl. A logical approach to high level robot programming – a progress report. In *Working notes of the 1994 AAAI fall symposium on Control of the Physical World by Intelligent Systems (to appear), New Orleans, LA*, November 1994.

[LR94]     F. Lin and R. Reiter. State constraints revisited. *Journal of Logic and Computation*, 4(5):655–678, October 1994.

[MLLB96]  G. Mendez, J Llopis, J. Lobo, and C. Baral. Temporal logic and reasoning about actions. In *Common Sense 96*, 1996.

[MW88]  S. Manchanda and D. S. Warren. A logic-based language for database updates. In J. Minker, editor, *Foundations of Deductive Databases and Logic Programming*, pages 363–394. Morgan Kaufmann, 1988.

[PS96]  S. Potamianos and M. Stonebraker. The POSTGRESS rule system. In J. Widom and S Ceri, editors, *Active Database Systems*, pages 43–62. Morgan Kaufmann, 1996.

[Rei94]  R. Reiter. On specifying database updates. *Journal of Logic Programming*, 19,20:1–39, 1994.

[SK96]  E. Simon and J. Kiernan. The A-RDL system. In J. Widom and S Ceri, editors, *Active Database Systems*, pages 111–150. Morgan Kaufmann, 1996.

[SW95]  P. Sistla and O. Wolfson. Temporal conditions and integrity constraint checking in active database systems. In *Proceedings of the 1995 ACM SIGMOD International Conference on Management of Data*, San Jose, CA, 1995. ACM Press.

[SZ90]  D. Sacca and C. Zaniolo. Stable models and non-determinism in logic programs with negation. In *Proceedings of PODS 1990*, pages 205–217, 1990.

[WC96]  J. Widom and S Ceri, editors. *Active Database Systems - Triggers and Rules for advanced database processing*. Morgan Kaufmann, 1996.

[Wid92]  J. Widom. A denotational semantics for starburst production rule language. *SIGMOD Record*, 21(3):4–9, 1992.

[Wid96]  J. Widom. The Starburst rule system. In J. Widom and S Ceri, editors, *Active Database Systems*, pages 87–110. Morgan Kaufmann, 1996.

[Zan93]  C. Zaniolo. A unified semantics for active and deductive databases. In *Proceedings of 1st international workshop on rules in database systems*, pages 271–287. Springer-Verlag, 1993.

[Zan96]  C. Zaniolo. Active database rules with transaction-conscious stable models semantics. In *Proceedings of DOOD 1996*, pages 55–72, 1996.

# Nested Transactions in a Logical Language for Active Rules

Bertram Ludäscher     Wolfgang May     Georg Lausen

Institut für Informatik, Universität Freiburg
Am Flughafen 17, 79110 Freiburg, Germany
{ludaesch,may,lausen}@informatik.uni-freiburg.de

**Abstract.** We present a formal, broad, structured transaction-oriented
overall for a rule-based active database system in [Lud, LHL96]. we
have proposed *Statelog* as a unified framework for active and deductive
rules. Following the need for a better structuring capabilities, we introduce procedures as a means to group semantically-related rules and to
encapsulate their behavior. If, at least to executing elementary updates,
procedures can be called, thereby defining (sub)transactions which may
contain complex computations. A Statelog procedure is a set of EGA-
style Datalog rules together with an insert/removing or insert/... System
... operational model and procedure rules induce bulk propagation of facts
and processing of results of computations. Thus, Statelog
programs specify a nested transaction model which allows a much more
structured and natural modeling of complex transactions than previous approaches. Two equivalent semantics for a Statelog program P are
given: (i) a fixpoint procedural style semantics by a computation into a
logic ... [Bad] and (ii) a model-theoretic (Kripke-style) semantics. While
(ii) serves as a conceptual model of active rule behavior and allows to
reason about properties of the specified transactions, (i) — together with
the appropriate execution model — yields an operational semantics and
can be used as an implementation of P.**

## 1 Introduction

The need for a logically defined and intuitive semantics has been recognized
as one of the major theoretical problems in the area of active databases. The
active database manifesto, for example, requires as an essential feature that
"... rule execution must have a clear semantics, ie must define when, how, and
on what database state conditions are tested, if assertions executed." [DGG95].
Nevertheless, researchers continue to complain about the unpredictable behavior
of active rules and the lack of a uniform and clear semantics."

To overcome these difficulties, it has been suggested to use the logical foundation of deductive databases — with certain extensions — as a declarative semantics for active rules [Zan93, Zan95, Zan95, LL34, HL95]. The main benefits

---

Supported by grant no. GRK 184/1-96 of the Deutsche Forschungsgemeinschaft

"The unstructured unpredictable, and often nondeterministic behavior of rule processing can become a nightmare for the database rule programmer" [AWH95]. See
also [WC94, WC95, FCW94, DHW95, FT96].

# Nested Transactions in a Logical Language for Active Rules

Bertram Ludäscher      Wolfgang May⋆      Georg Lausen

Institut für Informatik, Universität Freiburg
Am Flughafen 17, 79110 Freiburg, Germany
{ludaesch,may,lausen}@informatik.uni-freiburg.de

**Abstract.** We present a hierarchically structured transaction-oriented concept for a rule-based active database system. In [LL94, LHL95], we have proposed *Statelog* as a unified framework for active and deductive rules. Following the need for better structuring capabilities, we introduce *procedures* as a means to group semantically related rules and to encapsulate their behavior. In addition to executing elementary updates, procedures can be called, thereby defining (sub)transactions which may perform complex computations. A Statelog procedure is a set of ECA-style Datalog rules together with an import/export interface. System-immanent frame and procedure rules ensure both propagation of facts and processing of results of committed subtransactions. Thus, Statelog programs specify a nested transaction model which allows a much more structured and natural modeling of complex transactions than previous approaches. Two equivalent semantics for a Statelog program $P$ are given: (i) a logic programming style semantics by a compilation into a logic program, and (ii) a model-theoretic Kripke-style semantics. While (ii) serves as a *conceptual model* of active rule behavior and allows to reason about properties of the specified transactions, (i) – together with the appropriate execution model – yields an operational semantics and can be used as an implementation of $P$.

## 1  Introduction

The need for a logically defined and intuitive semantics has been recognized as one of the major theoretical problems in the area of active databases. The active database manifesto, for example, requires as an essential feature that *"... rule execution must have a clear semantics, ie must define when, how, and on what database state conditions are evaluated and actions executed"* [DGG95]. Nevertheless, researchers continue to complain about the unpredictable behavior of active rules and the lack of a uniform and clear semantics.[1]

To overcome these difficulties, it has been suggested to use the logical foundations of deductive databases – with certain extensions – as a declarative semantics for active rules [Zan93, ZS94, Zan95, LL94, LHL95]. The main benefits

---

⋆ Supported by grant no. GRK 184/1-96 of the Deutsche Forschungsgemeinschaft.

[1] *"The unstructured, unpredictable, and often nondeterministic behavior of rule processing can become a nightmare for the database rule programmer"* [AWH95]. See also [Wid94, WC96, PCFW95, DHW95, FT96].

of this approach are better understanding, maintainability and reasoning about rules when compared to the usual implementation-dependent operational semantics. However, as we will show in Section 2, the existing "mergers" of active and deductive rules are not sufficient to model complex (trans)actions in a natural way, since they (i) lack structuring capabilities, and (ii) do not encapsulate the effect of semantically related rules. In particular, they neglect the fact that complex database transactions can be adequately modeled by *nested transactions* where the parent transaction may consult the outcome of subtransactions in order to perform its own complex tasks. As a solution, we propose the extension of our declarative framework for active rules [LHL95] by the concept of update *procedures*. Procedures execute as (closed) *nested transactions* whereas previous rule based approaches were limited to flat transactions. A Statelog procedure consists of a set of ECA-style Datalog rules each of which defines either

- a non-state-changing *query*, ie a (potentially recursive) view, or
- an *action*, ie
  - a *primitive update* request (insert, delete, modify),
  - a *complex update* request (procedure call), or
  - an *external action* to be issued by the database system, or
- a transaction control predicate.

System-immanent *frame* and *procedure rules* provide a declarative specification of state transitions and integrity preserving policies within the logical language without bothering the user with those problems.

The paper is structured as follows. The remainder of this section is devoted to an introduction to (flat) Statelog. Section 2 introduces the main ideas of procedures and nested transactions and their realization in Statelog. In Section 3 the syntax of the language is defined, Section 4 provides some examples. A logic programming semantics for Statelog is presented in Section 5 using a compilation from Statelog to logic programs. Section 6 defines a model-theoretic Kripke-style semantics which provides the connection between the intuitive understanding of procedure calls and the underlying state-oriented conceptual model. We give an overview on related work in Section 7 and conclude in the last section.

## 1.1 Statelog: Datalog and States

In this section, we introduce the basic ideas underlying *flat Statelog*[2] [LHL95]. The extended framework with procedures and nested transactions is described in Section 2.

While for query processing a "one-state logic" like Datalog is sufficient, active state-changing rules require access to different states and delta relations. In Statelog, this is accomplished by *state terms* of the form $[S + k]$, where $S + k$ denotes the $k$-fold application of the unary function symbol "+1" to the *state variable* $S$. The domain of $S$ is $\mathbb{N}_0$, ie relations of a Statelog program evolve

---

[2] We refer to the language described in [LHL95] as *flat Statelog*, since the state space is $\mathbb{N}_0$, ie a flat structure. In contrast, *Statelog with procedures* uses a hierarchical state space to model the execution of nested transactions.

over the *linear state space* $\mathbb{N}_0$. $S$ may only occur in state terms. A Statelog *rule* is of the form

$$[S + k_0]H(\bar{X}) \leftarrow [S + k_1]B_1(\bar{X}_1), \ldots, [S + k_n]B_n(\bar{X}_n) \quad ,$$

where the head $H(\bar{X})$ is an atom, and $B_i(\bar{X}_i)$ are atoms or negated atoms. A rule is *progressive*, resp. *local*, if $k_0 \geq k_i$, resp. $k_0 = k_i$, for all $i \in \{1, \ldots, n\}$. Since past states cannot be changed, we require that all rules are progressive.

Here and in the sequel, we denote by $\bar{X}$ a vector $X_1, \ldots, X_m$ of arguments (variables or terms) of suitable arity; ground terms are denoted by lower case letters.

**State Transitions and Frame Rules.** The user is relieved from handling states explicitly and may define only actions (including change requests to EDB relations) and views by local rules. The actual state change from $[S]$ to $[S + 1]$ is specified by system-generated *frame and procedure rules* (Section 3.2). E.g. the following frame rules define the effect of insert and delete requests in flat Statelog:

$$[S + 1] \ R(X) \leftarrow [S] \ R(X), [S] \ \neg\textbf{del:}R(X).$$
$$[S + 1] \ R(X) \leftarrow [S] \ \textbf{ins:}R(X).$$

Here R is an EDB relation, while **del:**R, **ins:**R, **mod:**R denote user-definable *request relations* (also called *delta relations*, or *deltas*) which are used to issue update requests.

*Remark. Depending on the underlying assumptions about modifications, the modify request mod:$R(\bar{X}_{old}/\bar{X}_{new})$ is **not** always equivalent to del:$R(\bar{X}_{old}) \wedge$ ins:$R(\bar{X}_{new})$. In this paper, we confine ourselves to describe insert and delete requests only. A declarative semantics for modifications can be found in [LML96].*

**Execution Model.** In addition to EDB, IDB, and request relations, there are relations which model the interface to the external application domain: *External events* $\triangleright ev(\bar{x})$ occurring within a certain "atomic" time interval are mapped to the current state $[S]$. E.g. an external temporal event may be denoted as $\triangleright$daily(Date), or, raised by some monitoring device, it may specify an event from the real world like $\triangleright$runway_clear(R), etc. *External actions* $\triangleleft a(\bar{x})$ are requests to perform some action in the application domain (like $\triangleleft$move(Thing,From,To)). It is assumed that external actions issued by the database system have no side-effects on the state of the database.

Triggered by the occurrence of one or more external events $\triangleright ev_i$ in $[S]$, the corresponding rules become activated. According to the additional conditions given in the rule bodies, the database is queried and the actions specified in the rule heads are performed using frame rules (for *internal actions*, ie update requests) or signaled to the outside (external actions). In the subsequent state $[S + 1]$, $\triangleright ev_i$ is regarded as *consumed*. Thus, for a current database state $[S]D$ and a set of events, the logical semantics of a program $P$ yields a sequence of intermediate states, a set of external actions, and a new database state $[S_{final}]D$, see Fig. 1. In flat Statelog, a *transaction* beginning at $[S]$ *terminates* when there are no changes to successive states, ie when $[S_{final}]D = [S_{final} + 1]D$.

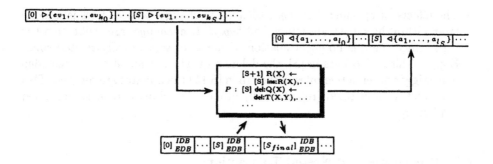

**Fig. 1.** Mapping of External Events to External Actions and Database States

## 2 Transaction-Oriented Hierarchical Structuring

The need for structuring capabilities and a more elaborated transaction model can be exemplified as follows (this example is adopted from [MW88, Che95]):

**Example 1 (To Hire or Not to Hire).** The employee Emp with salary Sal should be hired for department Dept provided the average salary *after* the update does not exceed a certain limit. This may be expressed in flat Statelog (or similarly in the related XY-Datalog approach [Zan93]) as follows:[3]

$[S]$ newemp(Emp,Sal,Dept), $[S+1]$ checksal(Dept) $\leftarrow$ $[S]$ ▷hire(Emp, Sal, Dept).
$[S]$ **ins:**empsal(Emp,Sal), **ins:**empdep(Emp,Dept) $\leftarrow$ $[S]$ newemp(Emp,Sal,Dept).
$[S+1]$ **del:**empsal(Emp,Sal),**del:**empdep(Emp,Dept) $\leftarrow$
    $[S]$ ▷hire(Emp,Sal,Dept), $[S+1]$ ¬check_ok.
$[S]$ check_ok $\leftarrow$ $[S]$ checksal(Dept), avg(Dept, Amt), Amt $<$ 50000.

When an external event ▷hire(Emp,Sal,Dept) occurs in the current state $[S]$, the new employee is preliminarily inserted and the new average salary is checked in $[S + 1]$ (rules 1 and 2). If it exceeds the admissible amount, the effect of the insert is undone (rule 3).

**Problems.** Although the above program specifies the desired transaction, there are some potential pitfalls and drawbacks with this "flat" approach:

- Undoing the effect of changes (here: the compensation of insertions by corresponding deletions) has to be programmed by the rule designer. However, it is often desirable to *automatically* propagate the failure of a subtransaction like checksal.
- There is no structure which allows grouping of semantically closely related rules. E.g. it is useful to view the insertion using newemp (rule 2) as an atomic subtransaction callable by the top-level transaction hire.

---

[3] It is assumed that the average avg(Dept,Amt) for each department is given by other rules. A conjunction $H_1, H_2 \leftarrow B$ in the head of a rule is equivalent to two rules $H_1 \leftarrow B$ and $H_2 \leftarrow B$, ie denotes simultaneous "execution".

- The effects of *ephemeral changes* [Zan95], ie changes whose effect is undone later within the same transaction, and *hypothetical changes* are visible to other rules, since there is no encapsulation of effects of semantically related rules. E.g., if ▷hire(...) occurs in [S], the delete requests **ins:empsal** and **ins:empdep** may trigger other active rules, although in [S+2] the updates are revoked. This may lead to unjustified (re)actions by other rules, similar to those described in [Zan95].

## 2.1 Procedures and Nested Transactions

In order to solve these problems, we propose the concept of Statelog *procedures*. A procedure $\pi$ is a set of *local* Statelog rules with an import/export interface describing which relations are visible and updatable by $\pi$. When $\pi$ is called at runtime, it defines a transaction $T_\pi$ by issuing primitive updates (through request relations) and/or calling other procedures which in turn define subtransactions etc. $T_\pi$ terminates either successfully, ie if commit is true in some state, or aborts. When $\pi$ calls another procedure $\rho$, a subtransaction $T_\rho$ is started whose results are either incorporated in $T_\pi$, if $T_\rho$ commits, or discarded otherwise. From the point of view of the calling transaction $T_\pi$, the subtransaction $T_\rho$ is atomic, therefore requests derived directly within $T_\pi$ and those submitted by $T_\rho$ should be indistinguishable. This is achieved by frame and procedure rules (Section 3.2).

The behavior of $\rho$ is *encapsulated*, since deltas defined by $T_\rho$ are only visible within $T_\rho$, but not in other (concurrent) transactions. Transactions execute in isolation and in an *all-or-nothing* manner, ie no results of $T_\rho$ will be visible in $T_\pi$ if $T_\rho$ aborts. Note that this does *not* mean that $T_\pi$ also aborts – on the contrary, $\pi$ can detect the failure of $T_\rho$ and issue alternative or compensating actions or retry the execution of $\rho$ later.

The way in which procedures execute (ie as nested transactions) induces a hierarchical structure of the state space. The model-theoretic foundation of this concept is given by Kripke structures with different accessibility relations, see Section 6. We represent this hierarchy by *transaction frames* and *complex state terms* which extend the flat state terms [S + k] of [LHL95].

The usual partitioning of the signature into base relations (EDB) and derived relations (IDB) is carried over to the hierarchical concept: base relations are passed from the current state to successor states (modulo the changes given by deltas) while IDB relations are not passed on but are rederived when needed. *All* user-defined changes to base relations have to be done via *requests*, ie by using request relations *ins:R, del:R, mod:R* (also called *delta relations*, or *deltas*).

*Protocol relations insd:R, deld:R, modd:R* (for *inserted, deleted, modified*, respectively) accumulate the *net effect* of user-defined requests and are automatically maintained by the system. Requested changes become effective in the transition to the successor state. Finally, there is a set $\Pi$ of procedure names and transaction control relations *BOT, EOT, abort* etc.

In this structured model, Example 1 can be specified as follows ($\pi \otimes \rho$ denotes sequential composition, ie first do $\pi$, then do $\rho^4$):

**Example 2 (To Hire or Not to Hire revisited).** The procedure hire defines an atomic transaction: First it calls newemp to insert the employee into the database, then it calls checksal to check the average salary. If this exceeds a certain amount, the transaction aborts. In the rules of hire it is specified that in this case hire should also abort, making no effects visible to its parent transaction.

**proc** hire(Emp,Sal,Dept); ∇empsal,empdep; △empsal,empdep;
   **initial:** newemp(Emp,Sal,Dept) ⊗ checksal(Dept) ← .
   **always:** abort ← **aborted:**checksal(Dept).
**endproc**
**proc** newemp(Emp,Sal,Dept); △empsal,empdep;
   **initial:** **ins:**empsal(Emp,Sal) ←.
           **ins:**empdep(Emp,Dept) ←.
**endproc**
**proc** checksal(Dept); ∇empdep,empsal;
   **initial:** abort ← avg(Dept,Amt), ¬Amt<50000.
**endproc**

The symbols "∇" and "△" denote import resp. export of relations (Section 2.3). The declarations initial, always (and final) specify when the corresponding rules should be executed, ie in the first state of the subtransaction, in every state, or in the last state, respectively; see Section 3.1 for details. hire may be called automatically from the top-level transaction using a rule of the form

$$\text{hire(Emp,Sal,Dept)} \leftarrow \triangleright\text{hire\_someone(Emp,Sal,Dept).}$$

Whenever the external event ▷hire_someone occurs, hire is executed as an atomic transaction. Fig. 3 depicts the state space which is created when hire(john,60000,d1) is called (and eventually aborted, since the average after the hypothetical update exceeds 50000).

## 2.2 Hierarchical State Space

In the hierarchical context, state terms are more complex and extend those of flat Statelog: every state term encodes the complete transaction hierarchy from the top-level transaction down to the current transaction. States on the same level are grouped into *(transaction) frames*. Given a set $\Pi$ of procedure names, the syntax of frame terms $\mathcal{F}(\Pi)$ and state terms $\mathcal{Z}(\Pi)$ over $\Pi$ is defined recursively:

1. $[\varepsilon]$ is a *frame term*.
2. $[F.n]$ is a *state term*, if $[F]$ is a frame term and $n \in \mathbb{N}_0$.
3. $[Z.\pi(\bar{x})]$ is a *frame term*, if $[Z]$ is a state term, $\pi \in \Pi$ is an $n$-ary procedure name, and $\bar{x}$ is a vector of $n$ terms from the underlying Herbrand universe.

---

[4] The symbol "⊗" is borrowed from [BK93], where it is called *serial conjunction*.

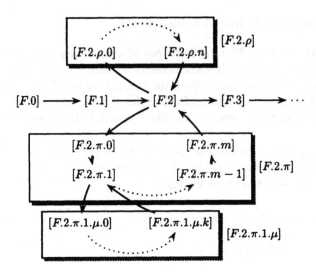

**Fig. 2.** States and Frames

With these, a hierarchically structured state space is constructed (Fig. 2): the *initial frame* $[\varepsilon]$ denotes the *top-level transaction*, its initial state is $[\varepsilon.0]$. Let $[Z]$ be the current state. Then for a procedure call $\pi(\bar{x})$ the frame of the subtransaction induced by the execution of $\pi(\bar{x})$ is $[F] = [Z.\pi(\bar{x})]$, the first state of the transaction is $[F.0] = [Z.\pi(\bar{x}).0]$. The successor state of $[F.n]$ (on the same level) is $[(F.n) + 1] := [F.(n + 1)]$. The grouping of states into frames is defined as

$$[F] := \{[F.n] \mid n \in \mathbb{N}_0\} \quad ,$$

which implies that every state $[F.n]$ belongs to exactly one frame $[F]$.

Using this representation, the frames $[Z.\pi(\bar{x})]$ and $[Z.\rho(\bar{y})]$ induced by *different* parallel procedure calls of $\pi$ and $\rho$ in the *same state* $[Z]$ can be uniquely identified (if the name of the procedure is the same, at least the parameters are different). Similarly, frames of transactions induced by the *same procedure call* from *different states*, $[Z_1.\pi(\bar{x})]$ and $[Z_2.\pi(\bar{x})]$, can also be distinguished.

## 2.3 Signatures and Visibility

When procedures execute in parallel or as nested transactions, the question arises which "versions" of relations should be visible within a transaction. In Statelog this issue is resolved using the hierarchical state space:

Assume two procedures $\pi$ and $\rho$ are called simultaneously in the same state, say $[F.2]$ (Fig. 2). This creates two different frames $[F.2.\pi]$ and $[F.2.\rho]$, thereby allowing $\pi$ and $\rho$ to maintain their own "view" of relations. Initially, ie in $[F.2.\pi.0]$ and $[F.2.\rho.0]$, $\pi$ and $\rho$ "see" the same versions of relations. $\pi$ and $\rho$ may update their versions subsequently and return the accumulated changes to $[F.2]$ as soon as they commit – here, in $[F.2.\pi.m]$ and $[F.2.\rho.n]$. For handling contradictory requests, conflict resolution policies can be specified by appropriate frame rules. Real parallelism is supported since frames maintain their own versions of relations, and simultaneously called procedures like $\pi$ and $\rho$ can execute independently and in parallel.

Given a frame $[F]$, we denote by $\Sigma_F$ the signatures visible in $[F]$. In particular, $\Sigma_F^{EDB}$ and $\Sigma_F^{IDB}$ denote base resp. derived relations visible in $[F]$. For the top-level frame $[\varepsilon]$ this induces signatures $\Sigma_\varepsilon^{EDB} := EDB$ and $\Sigma_\varepsilon^{IDB} := IDB$, where EDB and IDB denote the global database scheme.

The local signature $\Sigma_{F.n.\pi(\bar{x})}$ of a frame $[F.n.\pi(\bar{x})]$ is defined in terms of imported and private relations of the procedure $\pi$ which defines that frame:

Let $\Sigma_\pi^{Imp}$ and $\Sigma_\pi^{Exp}$ denote the signatures of *imported relations* and *exported relations* of $\pi$, respectively. All relation names occurring in $\pi$ but neither in $\Sigma_\pi^{Imp}$ nor in $\Sigma_\pi^{Exp}$ are assumed private and belong to the *private signature* of $\pi$ which is split into *private base relations* $\Sigma_\pi^{EDB}$ and *private derived relations* $\Sigma_\pi^{IDB}$.

$\Sigma^{EDB}$ and $\Sigma^{IDB}$ denote the union of all EDB/IDB relations used in procedures of a given program. Using private and imported relations, the visible relations of a frame are defined as follows:

**Definition 1 (Visible EDB/IDB Relations).** Let $[F'] := [F.n.\pi(\bar{x})]$ be the frame created by the procedure call $\pi(\bar{x})$ in $[F.n]$. Then the signature of *visible EDB/IDB relations* of the new frame $[F']$ is given by

$$\Sigma_{F'}^{EDB} := (\Sigma_F^{EDB} \cap \Sigma_\pi^{Imp}) \cup \Sigma_\pi^{EDB} , \qquad \Sigma_{F'}^{IDB} := (\Sigma_F^{IDB} \cap \Sigma_\pi^{Imp}) \cup \Sigma_\pi^{IDB} \qquad \square$$

Therefore, $[F']$ "sees" all imported EDB/IDB relations which are visible in the frame $[F]$ of the calling transaction and all private EDB/IDB relations of $\pi$.

EDB relations are imported by taking over their extensions from the calling state into the initial state of the subtransaction (rules $(D)$ in Section 3.2). In contrast, IDB relations are imported by including their defining rules into the rule set of the subtransaction frame (cf. Definition 5).

The export of an EDB relation is accomplished by "copying" the contents of the protocol relations of the final state of a subtransaction into the request relations of the parent transaction (rules $(E)$ in Section 3.2).[5]

User-defined rules may change EDB relations only through *request relations*. *Protocol relations* accumulate all non-revoked requests, ie the net effect of changes of a subtransaction is automatically maintained by the system. The extensions of the protocol relations are translated into requests for the calling transaction when the subtransaction commits.

**Definition 2 (Request and Protocol Relations).** Let $\Sigma_F^{EDB}$ be the signature of visible EDB relations in a frame $[F]$. Then the signatures $\Sigma_F^{Req}$ and $\Sigma_F^{Prot}$ of *request relations* and *protocol relations* of $[F]$ are defined as

$$\Sigma_F^{Req} := \{ins{:}R, del{:}R \mid R \in \Sigma_F^{EDB}\} , \quad \Sigma_F^{Prot} := \{insd{:}R, deld{:}R \mid R \in \Sigma_F^{EDB}\} \quad \square$$

---

[5] This provides a natural facility for implementing hypothetical updates: A procedure imports a relation *without exporting* it. Then it can operate on this relation without making changes visible to any other transaction.

Note that of the above-mentioned signatures, only $\Sigma_F^{IDB}$ and $\Sigma_F^{Req}$ are user-definable; the relations from $\Sigma_F^{EDB}$ and $\Sigma_F^{Prot}$ are maintained by the system.

The interface to the application domain is provided by sets $E$ of *external event names* and $A$ of *external action names*. These induce signatures for external events and actions:

**Definition 3 (External Events and Actions).** Given sets $E$ and $A$ of external events resp. actions, the signatures for external events and actions are

$$\Sigma^{Ev} := \{\triangleright e \mid e \in E\} \quad , \quad \Sigma^{Act} := \{\triangleleft a \mid a \in A\} \quad .$$

□

$\Sigma^{Ev}$ is visible (read-only) only within the distinguished procedure **main** (Section 3) defining the top-level transaction $[\varepsilon]$, while $\Sigma^{Act}$ is visible (write-only) in all frames.

Finally, the global signature contains additional relations for handling procedure calls and transaction management:

**Definition 4 (Transaction Management).** For a given set $\Pi$ of procedure names, the signature $\Sigma^{Proc} := \Pi$ is used to represent procedure calls. Transaction control is provided through the signature

$$\Sigma^{Subtr} := \{aborted{:}\pi, committed{:}\pi \mid \pi \in \Sigma^{Proc}\}$$

of relations indicating which subtransactions have committed or aborted, and through the 0-ary relations in

$$\Sigma^{Ctl} := \{BOT, running, EOT, alive, abort\} \quad .$$

□

All relations in $\Sigma^{Subtr}$ and $\Sigma^{Ctl}$ are globally visible (but in general have different extensions for each frame). $\Sigma^{Act}$ and $\Sigma^{Proc}$ are completely user-defined, abort is partly user-defined, the others are internally defined.

The signature $\Sigma$ comprises all previously mentioned signatures.

# 3 Syntax: Programs and Rules

In this section, we describe the syntax of user-defined rules and built-in frame and procedure rules. The logic programming semantics of programs is presented in Section 5.

## 3.1 User-Defined Rules

**Programs and Procedures.** A Statelog *program* is a finite set of Statelog procedures. There is a distinguished 0-ary procedure **main** (which is used to define the top-level transaction for the initial frame $[\varepsilon]$). An $n$-ary Statelog *procedure* $\pi$ is of the form

> **proc** $\pi(A_1, \ldots, A_n)$; $\nabla I_1, \ldots, I_k$; $\Delta O_1, \ldots, O_l$;
> **initial:** $P_{initial}(\pi)$; **always:** $P_{always}(\pi)$; **final:** $P_{final}(\pi)$
> **endproc**

where the arguments $A_i$ of $\pi$ are variables that may occur in the rules of $P_{...}(\pi)$. The relations $I_i \in \Sigma^{EDB} \cup \Sigma^{IDB}$ and $O_j \in \Sigma^{EDB}$ denote the imported, resp. exported relations[6]. The $P_{...}(\pi)$ are finite sets of Datalog rules (possibly with negation) of the following form:

$P_{initial}(\pi)$ is the set of *initial rules*. These are only enabled in the initial state of the transaction $T_\pi$ defined by $\pi$ and may be used for initialization purposes.

$P_{always}(\pi)$ is the set of *permanent rules*, applicable in all states of $T_\pi$.

$P_{final}(\pi)$ defines *final rules* which can be applied only in the last state of $T_\pi$. They have to be of the form "*abort ← ic-condition*" and may be used for integrity maintenance: if an inconsistency is detected (*ic-condition* becomes true), the current transaction is automatically aborted.

**Rules.** The user may define rules only through the sets $P_{...}(\pi)$ above, therefore, all user-definable rules have standard Datalog syntax. Depending on the relation symbol in the head of a rule, the following cases can be distinguished:

| | | |
|---|---|---|
| *Views:* | $V(\bar{X}) \leftarrow \ldots$ | for all $V \in \Sigma^{IDB}$ |
| *Change Requests:* | $ins{:}R(\bar{X}) \leftarrow \ldots$ | for all $R \in \Sigma^{EDB}$ |
| | $del{:}R(\bar{X}) \leftarrow \ldots$ | for all $R \in \Sigma^{EDB}$ |
| *Procedure Calls:* | $\pi(\bar{X}) \leftarrow \ldots$ | for all $\pi \in \Sigma^{Proc}$ |
| *External Actions:* | $\lhd A(\bar{X}) \leftarrow \ldots$ | for all $\lhd A \in \Sigma^{Act}$ |
| *Transaction Control:* | $abort \leftarrow \ldots$ | where $abort \in \Sigma^{Ctl}$ |

External events are allowed only in the body of rules of **main**, whereas actions may occur in all procedures, but are only allowed in rule heads. Since EDB relations are not directly user-definable by rules, all changes to base relations have to be accomplished through insert and delete requests. The materialization of these requests is implemented by frame rules which are described in the following section.

**Visibility.** Every procedure $\pi$ defines a set of *internal rules* $P(\pi)$ implementing the desired semantics of initial, always and final declarations. For every frame $[Z.\pi(\bar{x})]$ there is a set $P([Z.\pi(\bar{x})])$ of visible local rules, namely rules of $\pi$ and rules for imported IDB relations.

**Definition 5.** For a procedure $\pi$, the set of *internal rules* $P(\pi)$ is defined as

$$P(\pi) := \{h \leftarrow b, BOT \mid h \leftarrow b \in P_{initial}(\pi)\}$$
$$\cup \{h \leftarrow b, alive \mid h \leftarrow b \in P_{always}(\pi)\}$$
$$\cup \{h \leftarrow b, EOT \mid h \leftarrow b \in P_{final}(\pi)\}\,.$$

Using these, the set of *visible local rules* $P([F])$ of a frame is defined as

$$P([\varepsilon]) := P(\mathbf{main})$$
$$P([F.n.\pi(\bar{x})]) := P(\pi) \cup$$
$$\{h \leftarrow b \in P([F]) \mid h \in \Sigma^{IDB}_F \cap \Sigma^{Imp}_\pi\} \text{ for all } n \in \mathbb{N}_0, \pi \in \Sigma^{Proc} \quad {}_\Box$$

---

[6] W.l.o.g., we assume that relation names are unique, even when the arity is ignored.

The way IDB relations are treated reflects the intention that derived relations are imported by importing their defining rules, whereas EDB relations are imported by taking over their extensions into the initial state of a subtransaction.

## 3.2 System-Defined Rules

System-generated frame and procedure rules implement the intended semantics of request relations and procedure calls. All changes are encapsulated within the current transaction frame and invisible everywhere else until the transaction commits. State terms are used in the specification of transitions and transaction management. Let $[F]$ be the current frame. Then the following rules are visible (labels to the right of rules will be used in the compilation into a logic program in Section 5):

**Frame Rules.** Frame rules specify the correct handling of update requests and transitions. For all EDB relations $R$ visible in $F$, the following frame rules are also visible:

Updates on EDB relations are executed in the transition to the successor state. EDB relations are propagated to the successor state as long as EOT does not hold:

$$[Z+1]\ R(\bar{X}) \leftarrow [Z]\ ins{:}R(\bar{X}), \neg EOT. \qquad (B)$$
$$[Z+1]\ R(\bar{X}) \leftarrow [Z]\ R(\bar{X}), \neg del{:}R(\bar{X}), \neg EOT.$$

The non-revoked updates of $[F]$ are accumulated in protocol relations:

$$[Z+1]\ insd{:}R(\bar{X}) \leftarrow [Z]\ ins{:}R(\bar{X}), \neg EOT. \qquad (B)$$
$$[Z+1]\ insd{:}R(\bar{X}) \leftarrow [Z]\ insd{:}R(\bar{X}), \neg del{:}R(\bar{X}), \neg EOT.$$
$$[Z+1]\ deld{:}R(\bar{X}) \leftarrow [Z]\ del{:}R(\bar{X}), \neg EOT.$$
$$[Z+1]\ deld{:}R(\bar{X}) \leftarrow [Z]\ deld{:}R(\bar{X}), \neg ins{:}R(\bar{X}), \neg EOT.$$

While there are pending change requests, a transaction is running:

$$[Z]\ running \leftarrow [Z]\ ins{:}R(\bar{X}), \neg R(\bar{X}). \qquad (C)$$
$$[Z]\ running \leftarrow [Z]\ del{:}R(\bar{X}), R(\bar{X}).$$

A fixpoint is reached when there are no more changes, so EOT is signaled:

$$[Z]\ EOT \leftarrow [Z]\ BOT, \neg running.$$
$$[Z+1]\ EOT \leftarrow [Z]\ running, \neg abort, [Z+1]\ \neg running. \qquad (A)$$

The internal event abort terminates a transaction prematurely:

$$[Z]\ EOT \leftarrow [Z]\ abort. \qquad (A)$$

Apart from user-defined aborts, a transaction aborts if inconsistent requests are raised:

$$[Z]\ abort \leftarrow [Z]\ ins{:}R(\bar{X}), del{:}R(\bar{X}). \qquad (C)$$

States of a frame are *alive* if the transaction really uses them:

$$[Z]\ alive \leftarrow [Z]\ BOT.$$
$$[Z+1]\ alive \leftarrow [Z]\ running, \neg EOT. \qquad (A)$$

**Procedure Rules.** Procedure rules implement the semantics of procedure calls, ie the execution of subtransactions. For all procedures $\pi$, in a frame $[F]$ the following procedure rules are visible:

A procedure call creates the initial state of a new frame, signals BOT and initializes all imported relations:

$$[Z.\pi(\bar{X}).0] \; BOT \leftarrow [Z] \; \pi(\bar{X}). \tag{A}$$

$$\text{for all } R \in \Sigma_\pi^{Imp} \cap \Sigma_F^{EDB}: \quad [Z.\pi(\bar{X}).0] \; R(\bar{Y}) \leftarrow [Z] \; R(\bar{Y}), \pi(\bar{X}) . \tag{D}$$

The processing of the results is implemented by rules checking the successful termination of the subtransactions and evaluating their protocol relations: Since these contain the changes made by the subtransactions, their extensions are copied into the request relations of the parent transaction according to the export specification:

for all $R \in \Sigma_\pi^{Exp} \cap \Sigma_F^{EDB}$ :

$$[Z] \; ins{:}R(\bar{Y}) \leftarrow [Z] \; \pi(\bar{X}), [Z.\pi(\bar{X}).N] \; insd{:}R(\bar{Y}), EOT, \neg abort. \tag{E}$$
$$[Z] \; del{:}R(\bar{Y}) \leftarrow [Z] \; \pi(\bar{X}), [Z.\pi(\bar{X}).N] \; deld{:}R(\bar{Y}), EOT, \neg abort.$$

Thus, $[Z.\pi(\bar{x}).n] \; insd{:}R(\bar{y})$ and $[Z.\pi(\bar{x}).n] \; deld{:}R(\bar{y})$ with $[Z] \; \pi(\bar{x})$, $[Z.\pi(\bar{x}).n] \; EOT$, $\neg abort$ are equivalent to requests $[Z] \; ins{:}R(\bar{y})$ resp. $[Z] \; del{:}R(\bar{y})$ which are derived directly.

Parent transactions also perform some bookkeeping about committed and aborted subtransactions:

$$[Z] \; committed{:}\pi(\bar{X}) \leftarrow [Z] \; \pi(\bar{X}), [Z.\pi(\bar{X}).N] \; EOT, \neg abort.$$
$$[Z] \; aborted{:}\pi(\bar{X}) \quad \leftarrow [Z] \; \pi(\bar{X}), [Z.\pi(\bar{X}).N] \; EOT, abort. \tag{A}$$

The user can formulate application-specific aspects of transaction management, e.g. that the parent transaction should abort, if the child aborts:

$$abort \leftarrow \pi(\bar{X}), aborted{:}\pi(\bar{X}) .$$

## 3.3  Sequential Composition

To provide sequential execution of procedures as a built-in, the signature is extended with a connective "$\otimes$", which may be only used *in the head* of user-defined rules, e.g.

$$(A \otimes B) \leftarrow body .$$

means *first do A, then do B*, if *body* is true. $(A \otimes B)$ is compiled into two internal rules:

$$[Z] \; A, running \leftarrow [Z] \; (A \otimes B).$$
$$[Z + 1] \; B \leftarrow [Z] \; (A \otimes B), \neg abort.$$

The previous scheme generalizes to the polyadic case $A_1 \otimes \cdots \otimes A_k$ in the obvious way.

Sequential composition is not only useful to serialize the execution of procedures, but also for directly manipulating relations. E.g. the rule

$$del{:}R(\bar{X}) \otimes ins{:}R(\bar{X}) \leftarrow body \ .$$

generates exactly one intermediate state in which $\bar{X}$ is not in $R$. This can be useful in defining hypothetical updates, e.g. to test this intermediate state and see what would happen if $R(\bar{X})$ were deleted.

## 4 Examples

The hierarchical transaction model with import and export declarations allows a flexible treatment of several interesting features of databases, like for example the following:

- Static integrity constraints can be implemented by using the final rules for aborting transactions (Example 2).
- Checking the admissibility of changes and blocking inadmissible ones: for any fact $p(\bar{x})$ that should be guaranteed, derive $ins{:}p(\bar{x})$. Every request to delete it causes an inconsistency.
- Ephemeral updates: every transaction can try some updates, check their results and decide whether it should commit or abort (Example 2).
- Hypothetical updates: every transaction can work on relations which are imported but not exported without having any effect at commit-time. By this it can create a hypothetical scenario, check the outcome and report the consequences. This can be used to evaluate several alternatives in parallel.

**Example 3 (To Hire or Not to Hire: State Space and Database).**
The program given in Example 2 creates the frames and database states given in Fig. 3. Frames are presented by shadowed boxes, states are presented by ordinary boxes. In all states, the upper entry gives the state term, the data below the first horizontal line are facts which are derived by frame rules or local rules, and the data below the second line (if it exists) are facts which are derived from results of subtransactions.
In this example it is assumed that the average salary exceeds the admissible amount, so that the transaction hire(john,60000,d1) aborts, making no effects visible to its parent transaction.

**Example 4 (The Christmas-Problem).** Consider a relation empl(Employee, BirthDay, Salary) with the obvious meaning. We want to implement the following, informally given procedure: *Every employee shall be given a salary raise by 5% at his/her birthday; on Christmas every employee shall get an extra $1000.* This is accomplished in flat Statelog as follows [LHL95]:

$[S + 1]$ **mod:**empl(E,Bday,Sal$\leadsto$Sal1) $\leftarrow$
  $[S]$ $\triangleright$daily, date(Day), Day=Bday, empl(E,Bday,Sal), Sal1:= Sal*1.05).
$[S + 1]$ **mod:**empl(E,Bday,Sal$\leadsto$Sal1) $\leftarrow$
  $[S]$ $\triangleright$daily, date(Day), xmas(Day), empl(E,Bday,Sal), Sal1:= Sal+1000).

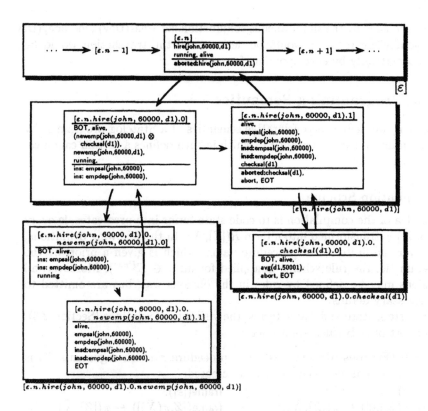

**Fig. 3.** Frames and Database States (cf. Example 2)

These rules work fine unless there is some employee whose birthday is on Christmas: Then two inconsistent modify-requests are generated, and the subsequent state is not well-defined. In a flat model, the problem could be solved by complete case splitting or by a rule using three states (however, this raises the problem that the intermediate state should not trigger other rules). In the structured model, the sequential composition inc_xmas ⊗ inc_bday is used by the top-level transaction incsal to specify the order of execution:

**proc main**; **always:** incsal(Day) ← ▷daily, date(Day). **endproc**

**proc** incsal(Day); ∇empl; ∆empl;
   **initial:** inc_xmas(Day) ⊗ inc_bday(Day) ←.
**endproc**

**proc** inc_xmas(Day); ∇empl; ∆empl;
   **initial: mod:**empl(E,Bday,Sal ⤳Sal1) ←
       xmas(Day),empl(E,Bday,Sal), Sal1:= Sal+1000.
**endproc**

**proc** inc_bday(Day); ∇empl; ∆empl;
   **initial: mod:**empl(E,Bday,Sal ⤳Sal1) ←
       Day=Bday, empl(E,Bday,Sal), Sal1:= Sal*1.05.
**endproc**

If "⊗" were replaced by the simultaneous conjunction inc_xmas(Day) , inc_bday(Day), then two conflicting requests would be derived and the transaction would be aborted automatically by corresponding frame rules.

# 5 Logic Programming Semantics

In this section, we define the declarative semantics of a Statelog program $P$ by a compilation into a logic program $P^*$, which in turn defines a certain canonical Herbrand-style model.

## 5.1 Compilation Scheme

The basic idea of the compilation is to code state terms into predicates, ie every term $[Z]R(\bar{X})$ is transformed into a term $R([Z], \bar{X})$. In the following definitions, $\pi$ ranges over the finite set of procedure names which is given a priori by the user program (ie, the rule scheme is applied for all $\pi \in \Sigma^{Proc}$). Moreover, all ∈-expressions may be defined by rules in the obvious way, but are omitted to avoid unnecessary details.

In a first step, state and frame terms, the visibility of relations (Section 2.3), and the import of IDB rules are defined:[7]

**Definition 6 (Frames and States).** If a procedure $\pi$ (with arguments $\bar{X}$) is called, a frame and all necessary states are created:

state($[\varepsilon.0]$).      frame($[\varepsilon]$).
state($[Z.\pi(\bar{X}).0]$) ← $\pi([Z], \bar{X})$.      frame($[Z.\pi(\bar{X})]$) ← $\pi([Z], \bar{X})$.
state($[Z + 1]$) ← state($[Z]$), alive($[Z]$).          □

**Definition 7 (Visible EDB).** The relation visible : $\mathcal{F} \times \Sigma^{EDB}$ defines $\Sigma_F^{EDB}$ (Definition 1), ie visible($[F], R$) means that $R$ is a visible EDB relation in frame $[F]$:

visible($[\varepsilon], R$) ← $R \in \Sigma_{main}^{EDB}$.
visible($[Z.\pi(\bar{X})], R$) ← frame($[Z.\pi(\bar{X})]$), $R \in \Sigma_\pi^{EDB}$.
visible($[F.N.\pi(\bar{X})], R$) ← frame($[F.N.\pi(\bar{X})]$), visible($[F], R$), $R \in \Sigma_\pi^{Imp}$.     □

**Definition 8 (Visible IDB).** The relation imports : $\mathcal{F} \times \Sigma^{IDB} \times \Sigma^{Proc}$ defines which IDB *rules* are visible in a frame, ie imports($[F], R, P$) means that in frame $[F]$ the IDB rules for $R$ from procedure $P$ are imported:

imports($[\varepsilon], R, \pi$) ← $R \in \Sigma_{main}^{IDB}$.
imports($[Z.\pi(\bar{X})], R, \pi$) ← frame($[Z.\pi(\bar{X})]$), $R \in \Sigma_\pi^{IDB}$.
imports($[F.N.\pi(\bar{X})], R, P$) ← frame($[F.N.\pi(\bar{X})]$), imports($[F], R, P$), $R \in \Sigma_\pi^{Imp}$ □

The main step consists of a compilation of the various rules from Section 3 (nesting of procedure calls, import of EDB/IDB relations, materialization of requests, etc.) into a logic program $P^*$. In particular, the restricted visibilities of relations have to be considered:

---

[7] Expressions of the form $[F.N]$ denote standard terms in the obvious way, ie $f_{[]}(f_{dot}(F, N))$.

**Definition 9 (Compilation $P \mapsto P^*$).** Apart from the preceding rules, the compiled program $P^*$ of a Statelog program $P$ contains the following rules:

1a. On the highest level the rules of the main part are activated:
for all rules $h(\bar{X}_0) \leftarrow b_1(\bar{X}_1), \ldots, b_n(\bar{X}_n) \in P(\boldsymbol{main})$:

$$h([\varepsilon.N], \bar{X}_0) \leftarrow b_1([\varepsilon.N], \bar{X}_1), \ldots, b_n([\varepsilon.N], \bar{X}_n), \text{state}([\varepsilon.N]).$$

1b. In every frame, the rules of the corresponding procedure are activated:
for every $\pi \in \Sigma^{Proc}$ and all rules $h(\bar{X}_0) \leftarrow b_1(\bar{X}_1), \ldots, b_n(\bar{X}_n) \in P(\pi)$:

$$h([Z.\pi(\bar{Y}_0).N], \bar{X}_0) \leftarrow b_1([Z.\pi(\bar{Y}_0).N], \bar{X}_1), \ldots, b_n([Z.\pi(\bar{Y}_0).N], \bar{X}_n),$$
$$\text{state}([Z.\pi(\bar{Y}_0).N]).$$

2. In all frames the appropriate defining rules of imported IDB relations are used: for every $\pi \in \Sigma^{Proc}$ and all rules $h(\bar{X}_0) \leftarrow b_1(\bar{X}_1), \ldots, b_n(\bar{X}_n) \in P(\pi)$:

$$h([F.N], \bar{X}_0) \leftarrow b_1([F.N], \bar{X}_1), \ldots, b_n([F.N], \bar{X}_n),$$
$$\text{state}([F.N]), \text{imports}([F], h, \pi).$$

3. The application of frame and procedure rules from Section 3.2 has to be restricted:

3a. In every state, all rules marked with $(A)$ are activated: for all such rules
$[Z_0] h(\bar{X}_0) \leftarrow [Z_1] b_1(\bar{X}_1), \ldots, [Z_n] b_n(\bar{X}_n)$ with state variable $Z$ in all $Z_i$:

$$h([Z_0], \bar{X}_0) \leftarrow b_1([Z_1], \bar{X}_1), \ldots, b_n([Z_n], \bar{X}_n), \text{state}([Z]).$$

3b. Frame rules marked with $(B)$ are restricted to visible EDB relations: for all such rules $[Z+1] h(\bar{X}_0) \leftarrow [Z] b_1(\bar{X}_1), \ldots, b_n(\bar{X}_n)$ with EDB relation $R$:
$$h([F.N+1], \bar{X}_0) \leftarrow b_1([F.N], \bar{X}_1), \ldots, b_n([F.N], \bar{X}_n),$$
$$\text{state}([F.N]), \text{visible}([F], R).$$

3c. Frame rules marked with $(C)$ are also restricted to visible EDB relations:
for all such rules $[Z] h \leftarrow [Z] b_1(\bar{X}_1), \ldots, b_n(\bar{X}_n)$ with EDB relation $R$:

$$h([F.N]) \leftarrow b_1([F.N], \bar{X}_1), \ldots, b_n([F.N], \bar{X}_n), \text{state}([F.N]), \text{visible}([F], R).$$

3d. Procedure rules marked with $(D)$ are restricted to imported EDB relations:
for all such rules $[Z.\pi(\bar{X}).0] R(\bar{Y}) \leftarrow [Z] R(\bar{Y}), \pi(\bar{X})$ with EDB relation $R$:

$$R([Z.\pi(\bar{X}).0], \bar{Y}) \leftarrow R([Z], \bar{Y}), \pi([Z], \bar{X}), \text{state}([Z]), R \in \Sigma_\pi^{Imp}.$$

3e. Procedure rules marked with $(E)$ are restricted to exported EDB relations:
for all such rules $[Z] h(\bar{Y}) \leftarrow [Z] \pi(\bar{X}), [Z.\pi(\bar{X}).N] b_1(\bar{Y}), \ldots, b_n(\bar{Y})$ with EDB relation $R$:

$$h([Z], \bar{Y}) \leftarrow \pi([Z], \bar{X}), b_1([Z.\pi(\bar{X}).N], \bar{Y}), \ldots, b_n([Z.\pi(\bar{X}).N], \bar{Y}),$$
$$\text{state}([Z.\pi(\bar{X}).N]), R \in \Sigma_\pi^{Exp}. \qquad \square$$

Note that the generated rules may be safely evaluated in a bottom-up style, since all rules are range-restricted provided the user-defined rules are range-restricted themselves.[8] Furthermore, by Definition 6 frames and states are only created when needed by the computation.

---

[8] A rule $r$ is *range-restricted* if every variable in $r$ occurs positively in the body of $r$.

## 5.2 Semantics and Termination

The semantics of a Statelog program $P$ depends on an $EDB$ and a set $EB$ of external events which have occurred in the current state and is given as a model $\mathcal{M}$.

Similar to [LHL95] one can find a syntactical condition which ensures that rules are *state-stratified* (ie, stratified within a state). Since all rules are progressive, this implies that $P^*$ is locally stratified and therefore has a unique *perfect model* [Prz88]. In case rules are not necessarily state-stratified, the *well-founded model* [VG89, VGRS91] provides a natural and generally accepted semantics. As it extends the perfect model semantics – ie coincides with the perfect model on locally stratified semantics – we use it as the canonical model $\mathcal{M}$:

**Definition 10 (Event Base).** The *event base* $EB := \{ ev(\bar{x}) \mid ev(\bar{x}) \text{ is signaled} \}$ is the set of all external events signaled in the current state.
□

**Definition 11 (Semantics of $P$).** The *semantics* $\mathcal{M}(P, EDB, EB)$ of a Statelog program $P$ w.r.t. a database $EDB$ and an event base $EB$ is the well-founded model of

$$P^* \cup \{\, r([\varepsilon.0], \bar{x}) \leftarrow . \mid r(\bar{x}) \in EDB \} \cup \{\, \triangleright ev([\varepsilon.0], \bar{x}) \leftarrow . \mid ev(\bar{x}) \in EB \}$$
□

Termination of rules can be guaranteed by enforcing that only finite models are actually generated:[9]

**Definition 12 (Termination).** Given an $EDB$ and an event base $EB$, a program $P$ *terminates* if there are only finitely many states in $\mathcal{M}(P, EDB, EB)$.
□

Since the chosen model-theoretic semantics $\mathcal{M}$ is deterministic, confluence is implied. Moreover, from the following lemma the uniqueness of the final state – if one exists – follows directly.

**Lemma 13.** *In every frame* $[F]$ *there is at most one state* $[F.m]$ *such that* $\mathcal{M}(P, EDB, EB^n) \models EOT([F.m])$. *In this case* $[F.m+1]$ *is an empty state, and there are no states* $[F.m']$ *with* $m' > m+1$.

*Proof.* Frame rules are deactivated when $EOT$ holds, thus EDB and protocol relations are empty in $[F.m+1]$. From $\mathcal{M} \models EOT([F.m])$ follows $\mathcal{M} \models \neg alive([F.m+1])$, disabling the local rules from $P([F])$ in $[F.m+1]$. Thus IDB and request relations are empty, no procedure is called in $[F.m+1]$, and no procedure return rule can insert any requests into $[F.m+1]$. Hence neither *running*, *BOT*, *EOT*, nor *alive* are derivable, so $[F.m+1]$ is really an empty state. Thus, $\mathcal{M} \models \neg state([F.m+2])$.

**Theorem 14.** *If a program $P$ terminates w.r.t. an $EDB$ and $EB$, there is a unique final state $[\varepsilon.m]$ such that* $\mathcal{M}(P, EDB, EB) \models EOT([\varepsilon.m])$.

---
[9] Another approach is to use a *finite representation* of infinite models, cf. [CI93].

In case of termination, the final state $[\varepsilon.m]$ represents the effect of executing the transaction given by $EB$ and $P$ on the database $EDB$: if $\mathcal{M} \models \neg abort([\varepsilon.m])$, then $[\varepsilon.m]$ is the new database state reached after executing this transaction. If $\mathcal{M} \models abort([\varepsilon.m])$, then the transaction aborts, and the database remains unchanged.

Note, that the converse of Theorem 14 does not hold, since EOT can be derived even if infinitely many states are nonempty. For example, the following program creates an infinitely deep nesting of procedure calls of $\pi$ but derives EOT on the top-level in the first state:

**proc main; initial:** $\pi \leftarrow .$ , abort$\leftarrow$. **endproc**
**proc** $\pi$; **initial:** $\pi \leftarrow$. **endproc**

There are different ways to enforce termination of rule processing, even though the problem of deciding whether a program $P$ terminates for all databases is undecidable in general. One way, similar to that of [Zan95], is to enforce termination at runtime by adjusting frame (and procedure) rules in such a way, that changes may not be revoked. In the presence of procedures, one has the additional requirement, that the *procedure call graph* induced by $P$ is acyclic (local rules may be recursive, of course).

Another approach, pursued in flat Statelog, is the class of $\Delta$-*monotone programs* which guarantees termination *at compile-time* [LHL95]. A similar notion can be defined for Statelog with procedures, but is beyond the scope of this paper.

# 6 Kripke-Style Semantics

In this section, a model-theoretic Kripke-style semantics is given, which interprets the state space as a suitable Kripke structure. It provides the connection between the intuitive understanding of procedure calls and the state-oriented model obtained by the logic programming semantics and can serve as a basis for formal verification. A class of Kripke structures appropriate to model nested transactions is defined together with the notion of a *minimal Kripke model* of a Statelog program w.r.t. an EDB and an EB. Then the equivalence of the Herbrand-style model (Section 5) and the minimal Kripke model is shown, showing the adequacy of the concept.

The Kripke-style semantics is presented in its two-valued version, thus covering all "well-behaved" computations, ie those where all states are completely defined. This is the case if and only if the well-founded model is total.

## 6.1 Statelog Kripke Structures

**Definition 15 (Statelog Kripke Structure).** A *Statelog Kripke structure* over a given Statelog signature $\Sigma$ is a tuple $\mathcal{K} = (\mathcal{G}, \mathcal{A}, \mathcal{Q}, \mathcal{R}, \mathcal{S}, \mathcal{U}, \mathcal{M}, \mathcal{P})$, (cf. Fig. 4) where

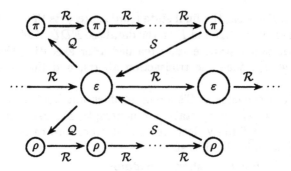

**Fig. 4.** Hierarchical Kripke Structure

$\mathcal{G}$ is a set of states,

$\mathcal{A}$ (actions) is a set of procedure names,

$\mathcal{Q}, \mathcal{S} \subseteq \mathcal{G} \times \mathcal{A} \times \mathcal{U}^\omega \times \mathcal{G}$, are two marked accessibility relations between states representing the procedure-call resp. -return relation: $\mathcal{Q}(g, \pi(\bar{x}), g')$ means that the first state of the subtransaction induced by a call of procedure $\pi$ with arguments $\bar{x}$ is $g'$. $\mathcal{S}(g', \pi(\bar{x}), g)$ means that $g'$ is the final state of the subtransaction induced by a call of procedure $\pi$ with arguments $\bar{x}$ in $g$. Thus, results of subtransactions have to be communicated along $\mathcal{S}$.

$\mathcal{R} \subseteq \mathcal{G} \times \mathcal{G}$ is another accessibility relation modeling the temporal successor relation. Let $\mathcal{R}^*$ denote the reflexive transitive closure of $\mathcal{R}$.

$\mathcal{U}$ is the universe of elements,

$\mathcal{M}$ is a function which maps every state to a first-order interpretation over $\Sigma$ with universe $\mathcal{U}$,

$\mathcal{P}$ is a function which maps every $g \in \mathcal{G}$ to a set of local rules (the rules visible in $g$).

□

To obtain a simpler notation, every state $g \in \mathcal{G}$ is identified with the corresponding first-order structure $\mathcal{M}(g)$.

**Definition 16.** A Statelog Kripke structure $\mathcal{K} = (\mathcal{G}, \mathcal{A}, \mathcal{Q}, \mathcal{R}, \mathcal{S}, \mathcal{U}, \mathcal{M}, \mathcal{P})$ over a signature $\Sigma$ is a *model* of a Statelog program $P$ over the same signature if

- $\mathcal{A}$ is the set $\Pi$ of procedure names occurring in $P$
- External actions are only present in the initial state on the highest hierarchical level: for all $g \in \mathcal{G}$ with $\mathcal{P}(g) \neq P(\boldsymbol{main})$ or $\exists g' : \mathcal{R}(g', g)$, $g|_{\Sigma^{Ev}} = \emptyset$.
- States with no temporal predecessor which are not targets of a procedure call, are initial states on the highest hierarchical level: for all $g \in \mathcal{G}$ with $\{h \mid \mathcal{R}(h, g)\} = \emptyset$ and $\{(h, a) \mid \mathcal{Q}(h, a, g)\} = \emptyset$ : $\mathcal{P}(g) = P(\boldsymbol{main})$ and there exists at least one state with this property.
- States which have no temporal predecessor or which are targets of a procedure call are beginnings of transactions and their protocol relations are empty: for all $g \in \mathcal{G}$ with $\{h \mid \mathcal{R}(h, g)\} = \emptyset$ or $\exists h, \pi, \bar{x} : \mathcal{Q}(h, \pi(\bar{x}), g)$: $g \models BOT$ and $g|_{\Sigma^{Prot}} = \emptyset$.
- Every $g \in \mathcal{G}$ is a model of the corresponding set of local rules: $g \models \mathcal{P}(g)$.

- $\mathcal{Q}$ represents exactly the procedure calls:
  for all $g \in \mathcal{G}$, $\pi \in \mathcal{A}$, $\bar{x} \in \mathcal{U}^\omega$: $g \models \pi(\bar{x})$ $\Leftrightarrow$ $\exists h : \mathcal{Q}(g, \pi(\bar{x}), h)$ .
- $\mathcal{S}$ represents exactly the return-from-subtransaction relation:
  for all $g, g', h' \in \mathcal{G}$, $\pi \in \mathcal{A}$, $\bar{x} \in \mathcal{U}^\omega$:

$$\mathcal{Q}(g, \pi(\bar{x}), g') \wedge \mathcal{R}^*(g', h') \wedge \mathcal{R}(h', h') \quad \Leftrightarrow \quad \mathcal{S}(h', \pi(\bar{x}), g) .$$

- The temporal accessibility relation $\mathcal{R}$ models the relationship between the EDB and request relations of one state and the EDB and protocol relations of the successor state: for all $g, h \in \mathcal{G}$:

$\mathcal{R}(g, h)$ $\Leftrightarrow$ $\mathcal{P}(g) = \mathcal{P}(h)$ and for all $R \in \Sigma^{EDB}$ :
$\quad h(R) = (g(R) \cup g(ins{:}R)) \setminus g(del{:}R)$ and $g(ins{:}R) \cap g(del{:}R) = \emptyset$ and
$\quad h(insd{:}R) = (g(insd{:}R) \cup g(ins{:}R)) \setminus g(del{:}R)$ and
$\quad h(deld{:}R) = (g(deld{:}R) \cup g(del{:}R)) \setminus g(ins{:}R)$ .

- The (marked) relation $\mathcal{Q}$ models the procedure calls:
  for all $g, g' \in \mathcal{G}$, $\pi \in \mathcal{A}$, $\bar{x} \in \mathcal{U}^\omega$:

$\mathcal{Q}(g, \pi(\bar{x}), g')$ $\Rightarrow$ $\mathcal{P}(g') = P(\pi) \cup \{h \leftarrow b \in \mathcal{P}(g) \mid h \in \Sigma^{IDB} \cap \Sigma^{Imp}_\pi\}$ and
$\quad\quad$ for all $R \in \Sigma^{EDB}$ : $g'(R) = g(R)$ if $R \in \Sigma^{Imp}_\pi$,
$\quad\quad\quad\quad\quad\quad\quad\quad\quad g'(R) = \emptyset$ if $R \notin \Sigma^{Imp}_\pi$ .

- The (marked) relation $\mathcal{S}$ models the feedback from subtransactions:
  for all $g \in \mathcal{G}$, $R \in \Sigma_{EDB}$, $\pi \in \mathcal{A}$:

$$g(ins{:}R) \supseteq \bigcup\nolimits_{\{g' \mid \exists \pi, \bar{x}: \mathcal{S}(g', \pi(\bar{x}), g) \wedge g' \not\models abort \wedge R \in \Sigma^{Exp}_\pi\}} g'(insd{:}R) \quad ,$$

$$g(del{:}R) \supseteq \bigcup\nolimits_{\{g' \mid \exists \pi, \bar{x}: \mathcal{S}(g', \pi(\bar{x}), g) \wedge g' \not\models abort \wedge R \in \Sigma^{Exp}_\pi\}} g'(deld{:}R) \quad ,$$

$$g(aborted{:}\pi) = \{\bar{x} \in \mathcal{U}^\omega \mid \exists g' : \mathcal{S}(g', \pi(\bar{x}), g) \wedge g' \models abort\} \quad ,$$

$$g(committed{:}\pi) = \{\bar{x} \in \mathcal{U}^\omega \mid \exists g' : \mathcal{S}(g', \pi(\bar{x}), g) \wedge g' \not\models abort\} \quad .$$

- All $\mathcal{M}(g)$ are minimal s.t. the above-mentioned conditions hold. $\quad\quad\quad$ □

**Definition 17.** Let $\mathcal{C}(g)$ be the subset of requests which are contributed to $g$ by subtransactions:

$$\mathcal{C}(g) := \{ins{:}R(\bar{x}) \mid \exists g' \in \mathcal{G}, \pi \in \mathcal{A}, \bar{y} \in \mathcal{U}^\omega :$$
$$\mathcal{S}(g', \pi(\bar{y}), g) \wedge R \in \Sigma^{Exp}_\pi \wedge g' \models insd{:}R(\bar{x}) \wedge \neg abort\} \cup$$
$$\{del{:}R(\bar{x}) \mid \exists g' \in \mathcal{G}, \pi \in \mathcal{A}, \bar{y} \in \mathcal{U}^\omega :$$
$$\mathcal{S}(g', \pi(\bar{y}), g) \wedge R \in \Sigma^{Exp}_\pi \wedge g' \models deld{:}R(\bar{x}) \wedge \neg abort\} \quad\quad □$$

**Lemma 18.** *The temporal successor relation $\mathcal{R}$ is deterministic:*

$$\text{for all } g, h, h' \in \mathcal{G}: \ \mathcal{R}(g, h) \wedge \mathcal{R}(g, h') \ \Rightarrow \ h = h' \quad .$$

**Definition 19.** A *computation path* in a Statelog Kripke structure $\mathcal{K}$ is a sequence $(g_1, g_2, \ldots)$ with $\mathcal{R}(g_i, g_{i+1})$ for all $i$. $\quad\quad\quad\quad\quad\quad\quad\quad$ □

Computation paths in the Kripke model correspond to frames in the Herbrand model. Since $\mathcal{R}$ is deterministic, in every model $\mathcal{K}$ of $P$, for every $g \in \mathcal{G}$ there is exactly one maximal (infinite, but possibly becoming stationary) computation path through $g$.

**Definition 20.** The non-extendable sequences in $\mathcal{R}^*$ are collected in a relation
$$\mathcal{R}^\wedge(g,h) :\Leftrightarrow \mathcal{R}^*(g,h) \wedge \neg\exists h' \neq h : \mathcal{R}(h,h') \quad,$$
and for $\pi \in \Sigma^{Proc}$, $\bar{x} \in \mathcal{U}^\omega$, $g \in \mathcal{G}$ such that $g \models \pi(\bar{x})$, let
$$(\pi(\bar{x}))(g) := h \in \mathcal{G} \text{ such that } \exists g' \in \mathcal{G} : \mathcal{Q}(g, \pi(\bar{x}), g') \wedge \mathcal{R}^\wedge(g', h)$$
denote the result of executing $\pi(\bar{x})$ in state $g$. □

Using this definition, $\mathcal{C}(g)$ can be characterized without explicitly mentioning $\mathcal{S}$:
$$\mathcal{C}(g) = \{ins\text{:}R(\bar{x}) \mid \exists \pi \in \mathcal{A}, \bar{y} \in \mathcal{U}^\omega :$$
$$g \models \pi(\bar{y}) \wedge R \in \Sigma_\pi^{Exp} \wedge (\pi(\bar{y}))(g) \models insd\text{:}R(\bar{x}) \wedge \neg abort\} \cup$$
$$\{del\text{:}R(\bar{x}) \mid \exists \pi \in \mathcal{A}, \bar{y} \in \mathcal{U}^\omega :$$
$$g \models \pi(\bar{y}) \wedge R \in \Sigma_\pi^{Exp} \wedge (\pi(\bar{y}))(g) \models deld\text{:}R(\bar{x}) \wedge \neg abort\} \quad.$$
In the following, for a set $\mathcal{I}$ of facts and a logic program $P$, let $\Phi_P(\mathcal{I})$ denote the set of true atoms in the well-founded model of $P \cup \mathcal{I}$.

**Theorem 21.** *For every Statelog program $P$, database $EDB$, and event base $EB$, there is a unique minimal Kripke model (ie with a minimal number of states) of $P$ with a distinguished initial state $g_0 \in \mathcal{G}$ such that $\mathcal{P}(g_0) = main$ and $\mathcal{M}(g_0) = \Phi_{main}(EDB \cup EB)$.*

Corresponding to Theorem 14, we have

**Theorem 22.** *If the minimal model $\mathcal{K}$ of a Statelog program $P$, a database $EDB$, and an event base $EB$ is finite and $\mathcal{R}$ has no cycles of length $> 1$, then there is a unique computation path $(g_0, g_1, \ldots, g_n, g_n, \ldots)$ with $g_n \models EOT$.*

## 6.2 Adequacy of Statelog Kripke Structures

**Theorem 23 (Adequacy).** *Statelog Kripke structures are an adequate model of the intended intuitive semantics of nested transactions:*

- *EDB relations are changed exactly via requests:*
  *for all $R \in \Sigma^{EDB}$, $\bar{x} \in \mathcal{U}^\omega$, $g, h \in \mathcal{G}$:*
  *if $(g,h) \in \mathcal{R}$ then $h \models R(\bar{x}) \Leftrightarrow (g \models R(\bar{x}) \wedge g \not\models del\text{:}R(\bar{x})) \vee g \models ins\text{:}R(\bar{x})$ .*
- *Every state contains all requests contributed by subtransactions:*
  *for all $g \in \mathcal{G}$: $g \supseteq \mathcal{C}(g)$ .*
- *IDB relations are derived locally by user-defined rules: for all $g \in \mathcal{G}$, $R \in \Sigma^{IDB}$, $\bar{x} \in \mathcal{U}^\omega$: $g \models R(\bar{x}) \Leftrightarrow R(\bar{x}) \in \Phi_{\mathcal{P}(g)}(g|_{\Sigma^{EDB}} \cup \mathcal{C}(g))$ .*
- *Requests are derived by user-defined rules or contributed by subtransactions:*
  *for all $g \in \mathcal{G}$, $R \in \Sigma^{IDB}$, $\bar{x} \in \mathcal{U}^\omega$:*
  *$g \models ins\text{:}R(\bar{x}) \Leftrightarrow ins\text{:}R(\bar{x}) \in \Phi_{\mathcal{P}(g)}(g|_{\Sigma^{EDB}} \cup \mathcal{C}(g))$ (Analogously for del:R).*
- *In all states the protocol relations contain all non-revoked changes of the corresponding subtransactions. For imported EDB relations, they subsume the differences between the EDB in the state where the subtransaction was initiated and the current state, while they represent exactly the EDB for non-imported relations: for all $g, h \in \mathcal{G}$:*
  *$(g,h) \in \mathcal{QR}^* \Rightarrow \forall R \in \Sigma^{EDB} \cap \Sigma_\pi^{Imp} : h(R) = (g(R) \cup h(insd\text{:}R)) \setminus h(deld\text{:}R)$*
  *and $\forall R \in \Sigma^{EDB} \setminus \Sigma_\pi^{Imp} : h(R) = h(insd\text{:}R)$ .*

## 6.3 Equivalence of Both Semantics

For every program $P$, database $EDB$ and event base $EB$, the Herbrand-style model of $P$, $\mathcal{M}(P, EDB, EB)$ can be split into states by its state term components and can be mapped bijectively to the minimal model $\mathcal{K}$ of $P$.

**Definition 24.** For a Statelog signature $\Sigma$, a Herbrand interpretation $\mathcal{H}$ over $\Sigma \cup \mathcal{Z}(\Sigma^{Proc})$ is contained in a Statelog Kripke structure $\mathcal{K} = (\mathcal{G}, \mathcal{A}, \mathcal{Q}, \mathcal{R}, \mathcal{S}, \mathcal{U}, \mathcal{M}, \mathcal{P})$ if $\mathcal{A} = \Sigma^{Proc}$, $\mathcal{U}$ is the underlying domain of $\mathcal{H}$, and there is a (partial) mapping $\eta : \mathcal{Z}(\Sigma^{Proc}) \to \mathcal{G}$ such that

- for all $[z] \in \mathcal{Z}(\Sigma^{Proc})$:
  if $\{(p, \bar{x}) \mid p \in \Sigma, \bar{x} \in \mathcal{U}^\omega, \mathcal{H} \models p([z], \bar{x})\} \neq \emptyset$ then $[z] \in \mathbf{dom}(\eta)$.
- for all $[z] \in \mathbf{dom}(\eta)$, $p \in \Sigma$, $\bar{x} \in \mathcal{U}^\omega$: $\eta([z]) \models p(\bar{x}) \Leftrightarrow \mathcal{H} \models p([z], \bar{x})$ .
- for all $[z] \in \mathbf{dom}(\eta)$: $\mathcal{H} \models \neg EOT([z]) \Leftrightarrow \mathcal{R}(\eta([z]), \eta([z+1]))$ .
- for all $[z] \in \mathbf{dom}(\eta)$: $\mathcal{H} \models EOT([z]) \Leftrightarrow \mathcal{R}(\eta([z]), \eta([z]))$ .
- for all $[z] \in \mathbf{dom}(\eta)$, $\pi \in \Sigma^{Proc}$, $\bar{x} \in \mathcal{U}^\omega$:
  $\mathcal{H} \models \pi([z], \bar{x}) \Leftrightarrow \mathcal{Q}(\eta([z]), \eta([z.\pi(\bar{x}).0]))$ .
- for all $[z] \in \mathbf{dom}(\eta)$, $\pi \in \Sigma^{Proc}$, $n \in \mathbb{N}_0$, $\bar{x} \in \mathcal{U}^\omega$:
  $(\mathcal{H} \models \pi([z], \bar{x}) \wedge \mathcal{H} \models EOT([z.\pi(\bar{x}).n])) \Leftrightarrow \mathcal{S}(\eta([z.\pi(\bar{x}).n]), \eta([z]))$ . $\qquad \square$

The following theorem states that the model obtained from the logic programming semantics is equivalent to the Kripke structure representing the model-theoretic semantics:

**Theorem 25.** *Let $P$ be a program, $EDB$ a database, and $EB$ an event base such that $\mathcal{M}(P, EDB, EB)$ is total. Then $\mathcal{M}(P, EDB, EB)$ is contained in the minimal Kripke model $\mathcal{K}$ of $P$ via a surjective mapping $\eta$.*

*Proof.* Set $\eta([\varepsilon.0]) := g_0$, $\eta([F.N+1]) := g$ such that $\mathcal{R}(\eta([F.N]), g)$ (well-defined by Lemma 18), $\eta([Z.\pi(\bar{x}).0]) := g$ such that $\mathcal{Q}(\eta([Z]), \pi(\bar{x}), g)$ for those $[Z]$ to be contained in $\mathbf{dom}(\eta)$ according to Definition 24.

In particular, the unique final state $[\varepsilon.m]$ of the Herbrand model $\mathcal{M}$ is the same as the stationary state of the unique computation path beginning in $g_0$ in the minimal Kripke Model $\mathcal{K}$. Thus, the logic programming semantics is also adequate w.r.t. the intuitive semantics.

# 7 Related Work

The idea of using state terms to refer to different states in logical rules has come up several times, e.g. in *XY-Datalog* [Zan93, ZAO93], to allow a unified semantics for active and deductive rules, and in [KLS92, LL94] as a means to specify updates in a declarative way. Flat Statelog [LHL95], XY-Datalog, and the temporal query languages $Datalog_{1S}$ and *Templog* [Cho90, AM89, Bau95] are closely related, since they all extend Datalog by a linear state space. In contrast, our present approach uses a branching hierarchical state space (similar to that of $Datalog_{nS}$ [CI93] which does not deal with active rules and procedures, however). The presented Kripke semantics extends that of [LS93] which is now a special case restricted to flat sequential computations.

[Zan95] proposes a "transaction-conscious" stable model semantics to cope with the problem that occurs when *ephemeral changes* (changes whose effect is undone within the same transaction) trigger active rules. Thus, to avoid unintended behavior, only durable changes should be visible to active rules. In our approach this problem is solved in a different way by the concept of "atomically executing" procedures which encapsulate their changes until the end of transaction. Thus, only the net effect of a subtransaction may trigger rules in the calling transaction.

*Transaction Logic* $\mathcal{T}_{\mathcal{R}}$ [BK93, BK94] deals, on a high level of abstraction, with the phenomenon of state changes in logic databases and employs a powerful model theory and proof theory. Primitive updates (so-called *elementary transitions*) are not part of $\mathcal{T}_{\mathcal{R}}$, but a parameter which is supplied by a transition oracle. In contrast, Statelog semantics provides a complete specification of changes from primitive updates to complex transactions and has a standard logic programming and Kripke-style semantics. Both languages can be combined by "plugging in" Statelog procedures in the transition oracle of $\mathcal{T}_{\mathcal{R}}$.

The concept of nested transactions in Statelog is similar to that of *HiPAC* [DBB+88, DBC96]. Statelog declarations *initial, always* and *final* allow execution of rules at specific points within a transaction and thus can be used in a similar way as *coupling modes* in HiPAC. E.g. integrity maintenance may be deferred until EOT by declaring the corresponding rules *final*.

The idea to structure rule sets using procedures or modules has already been introduced in the area of logic programming. E.g. [BMPT94, BT94] develop a modular design for logic programs including union, intersection, and encapsulation. However, they do not deal with active rules and state change, so their concept does not cover sequential composition, transactions etc.

[FT96] proposes *Extended ECA* rules as a common framework for a large number of existing active database systems and prototypes. In existing systems, the semantics of programs depends on the implicitly given operational semantics. These implicit assumptions are made apparent by encoding them in user-readable EECA rules. *Heraclitus[Alg, C]* [GHJ+93, GHJ96], is an extension of C which incorporates the relational algebra and elevates deltas to be "first-class citizens" of the database programming language. It allows to combine deltas and to express hypothetical updates, however no logical semantics is given.

Related to our work are approaches dealing with updates in deductive databases. Often, the rule semantics depends on a certain evaluation strategy, e.g. [Abi88, AV91, SK96] (bottom-up), or [MW88, Che95] (top-down), whereas e.g. [MBM95] is – like Statelog – independent of a certain strategy. However, these works do not cover the ECA-rule paradigm of active databases or the concept of nested transactions. Although Statelog allows a very intuitive "bottom-up reading" of rules (cf. Example 1), evaluation may also be done top-down due to the presence of explicit state terms $[S]$ and $[S + 1]$. This is in contrast to approaches like [Abi88, AV91] or [MW88, Che95], which refer to different states only *implicitly*. Thus their semantics is more tied to *either* bottom-up *or* top-down evaluation, respectively.

# 8 Conclusion

In recent work, the benefits of an integration of active and deductive rules have become apparent [Zan95, MZ95, LHL95]. First of all, a logical framework unambiguously specifies the semantics of rules – a necessary precondition to verify and reason about the behavior of rules. For example, the semantics of transactional events like abort and commit is completely specified in our logical framework. Moreover, properties like termination or expressive power can be investigated, as in [LHL95], *independent* of a given implementation. This complements work on termination and confluence of active rules which focuses more on specific systems like e.g. [AWH92, AWH95, BCP95, KU96].

In this paper, we have presented *Statelog*, based on a concept which integrates transaction-oriented programming of complex (trans)actions with logical foundations of deductive rules in a seamless way. This framework is an extension of flat Statelog [LL94, LHL95], and uses procedures as a means to structure rules and to encapsulate their behavior. Statelog programs have a declarative and deterministic semantics which is given (i) by a compilation into a standard logic programming semantics, which yields a (naive) implementation of the language, and (ii) by a Kripke-style semantics which describes a conceptual and implementation-independent model of active rule behavior. Procedures execute isolated and in an all-or-nothing style. The underlying nested transaction model facilitates parallel execution of concurrent transactions and allows to specify complex transactions in a natural way using subtransactions. We plan to extend the prototypical implementation of flat Statelog [Ham95] to the full language including procedures.

# References

[Abi88]   S. Abiteboul. Updates, a new frontier. In *ICDT*, Springer LNCS 326, pp. 1–18, 1988.

[AM89]    M. Abadi and Z. Manna. Temporal logic programming. *Journal of Symbolic Comp.*, 8(3), 1989.

[AV91]    S. Abiteboul and V. Vianu. Datalog extensions for database queries and updates. *JCSS*, 43, 1991.

[AWH92]   A. Aiken, J. Widom, and J. M. Hellerstein. Behavior of database production rules: Termination, confluence, and observable determinism. In *SIGMOD*, 1992.

[AWH95]   A. Aiken, J. Widom, and J. M. Hellerstein. Static analysis techniques for predicting the behavior of active database rules. *TODS*, 20(1):3–41, 1995.

[Bau95]   M. Baudinet. On the expressiveness of temporal logic programming. *Information and Computation*, 117(2), 1995.

[BCP95] E. Baralis, S. Ceri, and S. Paraboschi. Run-time detection of nonterminating active rule systems. In Ling et al. [LMV95].

[BK93] A. J. Bonner and M. Kifer. Transaction logic programming. In D. S. Warren, editor, *ICLP*. MIT Press, 1993.

[BK94] A. J. Bonner and M. Kifer. An overview of transaction logic. *Theoretical Comp. Sci.*, 133, 1994.

[BMPT94] A. Brogi, P. Mancarella, D. Pedreschi, and F. Turini. Modular logic programming. *ACM TOPLAS*, 16(4):1361–1398, July 1994.

[BT94] A. Brogi and F. Turini. Semantics of meta-logic in an algebra of programs. In *LICS*, pp. 262–270, Paris, France, July 1994.

[Che95] W. Chen. Programming with logical queries, bulk updates and hypothetical reasoning. In B. Thalheim, ed., *Proc. of the Workshop Semantics in Databases*, Prague, 1995. TU Cottbus.

[Cho90] J. Chomicki. Polynomial time query processing in temporal deductive databases. *PODS*, 1990.

[CI93] J. Chomicki and T. Imieliński. Finite representation of infinite query answers. *TODS* 18(2), 1993.

[DBB+88] U. Dayal, B. Blaustein, A. Buchmann, U. Chakravarthy, M. Hsu, R. Ledin, D. McCarthy, A. Rosenthal, S. Sarin, M. J. Carey, M. Livny, and R. Jauhari. The HiPAC project: Combining Active Databases and Timing Constraints. In *SIGMOD*, 1988.

[DBC96] U. Dayal, A. Buchmann, and S. Chakravarthy. The HiPAC Project. In J. Widom and S. Ceri, editors, *Active Database Systems: Triggers and Rules for Advanced Database Processing*, Morgan Kaufmann, 1996.

[DGG95] K. R. Dittrich, S. Gatziu, and A. Geppert. The active database management system manifesto: A rulebase of adbms features. In Sellis [Sel95].

[DHW95] U. Dayal, E. Hanson, and J. Widom. Active database systems. In W. Kim, ed., *Modern Database Systems: The Object Model, Interoperability, and Beyond*, Ch. 21. ACM Press, 1995.

[FT96] P. Fraternali and L. Tanca. A structured approach for the definition of the semantics of active databases. *TODS*, 1996. to appear.

[GHJ+93] S. Ghandeharizadeh, R. Hull, D. Jacobs *et al.* On implementing a language for specifying active database execution models. In *VLDB*, 1993.

[GHJ96] S. Ghandeharizadeh, R. Hull, and D. Jacobs. Heraclitus: Elevating deltas to be first-class citizens in a database programming language. *TODS*, 1996. To appear.

[Ham95] U. Hamann. Ein System zur Beschreibung und Ausführung von Änderungsoperationen in einer zustandsorientierten Erweiterung von Datalog. Master's thesis, Institut für Informatik, Universität Freiburg, 1995.

[KLS92] M. Kramer, G. Lausen, and G. Saake. Updates in a rule-based language for objects. *VLDB*, 1992.

[KU96] A. P. Karadimce and S. D. Urban. Refined triggering graphs: A logic-based approach to termination analysis in an active object-oriented database. In *12th ICDE*, 1996.

[LHL95] B. Ludäscher, U. Hamann, and G. Lausen. A logical framework for active rules. In *Proc. 7th Intl. Conf. on Management of Data (COMAD)*, Pune, 1995. Tata McGraw-Hill. ftp://ftp.informatik.uni-freiburg.de/documents/reports/report78/report78.ps.gz.

[LL94]    G. Lausen and B. Ludäscher. Updates by reasoning about states. In *2nd Intl. East-West Database Workshop*, Workshops in Computing, Klagenfurt, Austria, 1994. Springer.

[LML96]   B. Ludäscher, W. May, and G. Lausen. Nested Transactions in a Logical Language for Active Rules. Technical Report 80, Institut für Informatik, Universität Freiburg, 1996.

[LMV95]   T. W. Ling, A. O. Mendelzon, and L. Vieille, editors. *DOOD*, Springer LNCS 1013, 1995.

[LS93]    G. Lausen and G. Saake. A possible world semantics for updates by versioning. In *Proc. of 4th Workshop on Modelling Database Dynamics*, Volkse, 1993. Springer.

[MBM95]   D. Montesi, E. Bertino, and M. Martelli. Transactions and updates in deductive databases. Technical Report 2, Dipartimento di Scienze dell'Informazione, Università di Milano, 1995.

[MW88]    S. Manchanda and D. S. Warren. A logic-based language for database updates. In J. Minker, ed., *Foundations of Deductive Databases and Logic Programming*, pp. 363–394. 1988.

[MZ95]    I. Motakis and C. Zaniolo. Composite temporal events in active database rules: A logic-oriented approach. In *4th DOOD*, LNCS 1013, 1995.

[PCFW95]  N. W. Paton, J. Campin, A. A. A. Fernandes, and M. H. Williams. Formal specification of active database functionality: A survey. In Sellis [Sel95].

[Prz88]   T. C. Przymusinski. On the declarative semantics of deductive databases and logic programs. In J. Minker, ed., *Foundations of Deductive Databases and Logic Programming*, pp. 191 – 216. Morgan Kaufmann, 1988.

[Sel95]   T. K. Sellis, editor. *Proc. of the 2nd Intl. Workshop on Rules in Database Systems (RIDS)*, Athens, Greece, 1995, Springer LNCS 985.

[SK96]    E. Simon and J. Kiernan. The a-rdl system. In Widom and Ceri [WC96], Chapter 5.

[VG89]    A. Van Gelder. The alternating fixpoint of logic programs with negation. In *PODS*, 1989.

[VGRS91]  A. Van Gelder, K. Ross, and J. Schlipf. The well-founded semantics for general logic programs. *JACM*, 38(3):620 – 650, July 1991.

[WC96]    J. Widom and S. Ceri, editors. *Active Database Systems: Triggers and Rules for Advanced Database Processing*. Morgan Kaufmann, 1996.

[Wid94]   J. Widom. Active databases. In M. Stonebraker, ed. *Readings in Database Systems, 2nd edition*. Morgan Kaufmann, 1994. Introduction to Chapter 4.

[Zan93]   C. Zaniolo. A unified semantics for active and deductive databases. *Proc. of the 1st Intl. Workshop on Rules in Database Systems (RIDS)*, Edinburgh, 1993. Springer.

[Zan95]   C. Zaniolo. Active database rules with transaction conscious stable model semantics. In Ling et al. [LMV95].

[ZAO93]   C. Zaniolo, N. Arni, and K. Ong. Negation and Aggregates in Recursive Rules: the $\mathcal{LDL}++$ Approach. In S. Ceri, K. Tanaka, and S. Tsur, eds., *DOOD*, Springer LNCS 760, 1993.

[ZS94]    C. Zaniolo and R. Sadri. A simple model for active rules and their behavior in deductive databases. *Proc. 2nd ICLP Workshop on Deductive Databases and Logic Programming*, Santa Margherita Ligure, Italy, 1994.

# Panel Discussion

# Deductive Databases: Challenges, Opportunities and Future Directions

A Panel Discussion with the Participation of

*Arno Siebes, Shalom Tsur, Jeff Ullman,*
*Laurent Vieille, Carlo Zaniolo*

## Statement by C. Zaniolo (University of California, Los Angeles, USA)

This panel should focus on the many technical challenges and market opportunities that Deductive Databases have encountered and left unanswered during the last decade. In particular, there are the following issues:

- The lack of simple and effective solutions to problems such as non-stratified negation/aggregates, and support for updates or objects in logic, has reduced the effectiveness of deductive databases in application domains ranging from Bill-of-Materials to temporal queries, and from GIS applications to concrete-view maintenance. How much have these problems hampered the field in the past, and what is your forecast for the future?
- Many prototypes developed in the past lacked in functionality, robustness, availability and performance. How seriously have these problems impacted the deployment of the new technology, and will the situation change in the future?
- Many case-study applications have illustrated the benefits of the technology, but large commercial deployments have not materialized, yet. Which application areas are likely to provide the strongest market-pull in the future? Is there hope for some "killer application" to emerge ?

## Response by R. Ramakrishnan (Univ. of Wisconsin–Madison, USA)

Research over the past decade in the area of recursive query processing has brought us to the point where we can evaluate such queries with adequate efficiency. The question now is whether enough applications exist to justify further research and to support logic databases in the marketplace.

A number of research prototypes have used Prolog-influenced logic programming syntax, e.g., ADITI, CORAL, EKS, LDL, NAIL, XSB, to name some. These prototypes represent substantial achievements in terms of the techniques that were developed, and many of them continue to be developed and distributed. It is reasonable to ask whether any of these will lead to commercial products in the near future. (Indeed, EKS from ECRC formed the starting point for the Validity system, which is being developed at Groupe Bull.)

It is hard to predict the future of a technology that extends the commercial state of the art so significantly, and that currently does not have a "real-world" user base. The costs of building—and as we are finding out!—maintaining such systems are high and the pay-off depends largely on yet-to-be-gauged user needs.

For the record, here's what I think: *The field of logic and databases will have its greatest impact by influencing SQL and becoming a part of existing DBMS systems.* There is considerable evidence that this process has already begun:

1. The technology has found its way into several products already. For example, the Magic Sets technique was shown to be useful for dealing with non-recursive decision-support queries, and is now a part of several systems.
2. General recursive—not just transitive closure!—queries are supported in DB2 Version 2.1 today.
3. The current draft of the SQL3 standard contains SQL extensions to support general recursive queries as in DB2.

## Response by Arno Siebes (CWI, Amsterdam, The Netherlands)

I am a researcher in Data Mining and I am one of the founders of a company (Data Distilleries) that commercialises past and current research results. The question I want to discuss is: "are there similar possibilities for a Deductive Database researcher?" That is, are there market opportunities for Deductive Databases, and if so, what are they?

If *you* want to change *your* research prototype into a commercial product, these are two aspects of the same question: "why would a company want to buy a Deductive Database system?" In my experience the sole answer that companies accept is:"will it make money in the short term[1]?"

So, how do you prove that you can help them make money? Well, first of all *you* have to identify an application that you can do better than they do it now. Yes, you have to take a current application and you should not try to dream up something completely new.

For the sake of the argument let's assume that you picked computing the Bill-of-Materials. Then you have to make them agree on a pilot study. That is, together with one of their experts you use your system on one of their databases. And you have to make damn sure that this pilot study is a success.

And success means many things. First of all, their expert should be happy. So, don't be arrogant, don't say that your system is far superior to what they have been doing up to now and, most of all, don't tell him that with your system his job is gone. No, tell him that his problems are complex and that your system can help him to perform better. Don't get me wrong, in general this is simply true. It is most likely that your system is not the best thing since the invention of sliced bread.

---

[1] If you are lucky, they are willing to accept a not too long medium term. If you can only offer a vision in the long term, you're dead.

Why should you make the expert happy? Well, if you don't he will tell his boss that your system is lousy and you have lost. Because the second thing you have to do is to make the boss happy. That is, you should be able to demonstrate that your system made a significant difference. If the expert is happy, your in luck. Because, he will help you, he wants your tool.

Now for the good news. When you start this process, your tool may be buggy, they don't expect anything else from an academic. However, make sure that your interface looks nice. Remember, the expert must want to use your system, so it should appear to be usable by him.

Moreover, don't worry at all that there are all kinds of problems (such as non-stratified negation etc) that have not been solved yet. Most problems in business are pretty mundane and don't need any high-flying theory to be solved; common sense will do ok, in general.

After you have created the market pull in this way, you can worry about these problems. But now they are far easier to solve. You can earn money doing consultancy and (paid for) pilot studies. Moreover, you can get grants or investment money (remember, you created a market pull) to turn your prototype into a commercial product.

It is hard work, but it is fun, even if you never strike it rich.

## Response by Shalom Tsur (Argonne National Laboratories, USA)

Even though Deductive Database Technology has thus far not become the mainstream of database technology, many of the ideas that were conceived and implemented in the early DD prototypes have taken roots. As was already mentioned, such ideas as magic sets, general recursion and others are included in the latest versions of some of the commercial relational database products. As is often the case, evolution occurs in small steps and ideas, novel as they may be, are insufficient to scale such walls as the existing practices, the economical investment in existing systems and the renewed training effort required to take advantage of DD as a replacement technology.

Yet the ideas are too compelling to simply be forgotten. I believe that the commercial future of DD, which is a *sine qua non* for any further technological development, is guaranteed in an information world where change and its constant management become the norm rather than the exception. The constant need to respond to such changing patterns of fraudulent practices using credit cards or healthcare claims, the need to view constantly changing web information, the need to comply with constantly changing legislation, to name a few, will render the existing software development and maintenance practices uneconomical. The declarative method embedded in DD technology will thus become an economical necessity rather than a new toy for early adopters!

I do not believe that the open technological issues that were mentioned in Carlo's opening statement are the impediment to the development of DD technology; they will be reexamined when the commercial incentive exists.

While I cannot point to any "killer application," the use of DD as middleware between the management of structured, record-oriented data and unstructured, text-oriented data ("data glue") appears to be extremely promising. Again, the need to constantly review changing textual information is the driver in this case. The paper with B. Kero and myself in this volume recounts our early experience in this evolving type of application.

## Response by J. D. Ullman (Stanford University, California, USA)

I agree largely with Raghu, but would add that there has been a recent revision of the SQL3 recursion standard to include only linear recursion, but with stratified negation, and semi-naive evaluation. The new standard emphasizes the importance of the datalog approach and the ways it improves on the ad-hoc techniques that an earlier draft, which did not come from the datalog community.

The major problem we face is that much of the interest in DB's has shifted from structure, the kinds of things that logic expresses well, to abstract data types such as MPEG or JAVA, with their obvious power yet very little structure and a set of operators (e.g., play, rewind) that do not relate usefully to logic.

## Response by Laurent Vieille (Chief Architect, Validity Inc., France)

The commercial impact of Deductive Databases resides in Knowledge Independence. Traditional database management systems provide data independence (i.e., the ability to represent and manipulate data independently from the applications). Deductive-based systems are able to represent and manipulate knowledge, as represented by deduction and integrity rules.

Knowledge independence should not only be supported via deductive servers, or deductive repositories, but also via knowledge management tools. Advanced and powerful rule management tools are a necessary requirement, as indicated by early marketing studies. Such tools include explanation facilities, consistency checking, etc.

Applications which can benefit most from knowledge independence are applications with the following characteristics:

- Regulated Environment or complex policies;
- Frequently changing environment;
- Integration of large amount of data with rules;

Application areas having those characteristics can be found in:

- Electronic Mediation: rules to match demands and offerings, for promotional campaigns, for pricing;
- Customer Management Support: rules for the management of complex customer profiles, rules for the customization of the commercial offering;

- Concurrent Engineering: integrity rules for keeping the overall project coherent;
- Logistics (e.g., management of hazardous goods): integrity rules for regulation enforcement;

To summarize, the potential impact of deductive database technology goes well beyond the recursive extensions to SQL, even with the currently available research results. For instance, while SQL can actually be extended to a certain level, the nature of SQL does not support easily inference-based tools such as explanation or consistency checking tools.

Current research areas with potential impact include (not an exhaustive list!):

- Update and Transaction Languages;
- Proving consistency of transaction schemes with integrity rules;
- Pragmatic aspects of semantic query processing; etc.

# Semantics

# R-stable Models for Logic Programs

H. Jurkiewicz, and H. Verma

Free University of Brussels, VUB
Dept. of Computer Science
Pleinlaan 2, Brussels 1050, Belgium

Abstract. We propose a new semantics for general logic programs which
start from first principles of logic programming semantics. Our theory
makes precise our approach and is appropriate to some useful programs
which are not properly handled by existing semantics.

Keywords: logic programming, semantics

## 1. Introduction

The problem of defining semantics for general logic programs is a rapidly progressing area of research. Thus, there have recently emerged semantics such as the well-founded semantics [2], stable semantics [1], stable partial models [9], acceptable semantics [5], three-valued stable models [8], and regular models [11]. Each of these approaches suggests wave of associating models to a program. The various anomalies seem to differ slightly in their motivations, in that they have different expectations of models. In addition, there are some reasonable models of certain useful programs which are not delivered by some of the approaches.

This paper derives a unifying logic programming semantics from first principles. The paper is organized as follows: in Section 2, we define a new logic programming semantics, called simple models, which is based on "first principles", and show that it is consistent with most other semantics that have been proposed in the literature. In Section 4, we show how simple models can be obtained from so-called complete interpretations, which are possibly inconsistent interpretations that satisfy a stricter interpretation of the "negation-as-failure" principle. Section 4 introduces a proper restriction on simple models, called r-stable models. Intuitively, r-stable models are stable in that a further refinement of such a model (i.e. declaring an unaltered literal) does not result in an inconsistency. Finally, in Section 5, we discuss the relationship of r-stable semantics with other approaches.

acknowledges the support of the National Science Foundation, NFWO

# R-stable Models for Logic Programs

H. Jakobovits* and D. Vermeir

Free University of Brussels, VUB
Dept. of Computer Science
Pleinlaan 2, Brussels 1050, Belgium

**Abstract.** We propose a new semantics for general logic programs which stems from first principles of logic-programming semantics. Our theory unifies previous approaches and is applicable to some useful programs which are not properly handled by existing semantics.

**Keywords**: logic programming, semantics

## 1 Introduction

The problem of defining semantics for general logic programs is a rapidly progressing area of research. Thus, there have recently emerged semantics such as the well-founded semantics [2], stable semantics [1], stable partial models [9], acceptable semantics [6], three-valued stable models [8], and regular models [11]. Each of these approaches suggests ways of associating models to a program. The various approaches seem to differ slightly in their motivations, in that they have different expectations for models. In addition, there are some reasonable models of certain useful programs which are not delivered by some of the approaches. This paper derives a unifying logic-programming semantics from first principles.

The paper is organized as follows: in Section 2, we define a new logic-programming semantics, called *simple models*, which is based on "first principles", and show that it is consistent with most other semantics that have been proposed in the literature. In Section 3, we show how simple models can be obtained from so-called *complete interpretations*, which are possibly inconsistent interpretations that satisfy a strict interpretation of the "negation-as-failure" principle. Section 4 introduces a proper restriction on simple models, called *r-stable models*. Intuitively, r-stable models are stable in that a further refinement of such a model (i.e. deciding on undefined literals) does not result in an inconsistency. Finally, in Section 5, we discuss the relationship of r-stable semantics with other approaches.

---

* acknowledges the support of the National Science Foundation, NFWO

## 2  First Principles

**Definition 1.** A **logic program** $P$ is a countable set of rules of the form

$$p \leftarrow C$$

where $p$ is an atom and $C$ is a finite set of literals, i.e. atoms or negated atoms. The conclusion, $p$, is called the *head* and the set $C$ of subgoals is called the *body*. The arrow may be read "if".

The **Herbrand universe** of $P$ is the set of all possible ground (i.e. variable-free) terms that can be constructed using symbols from $P$. The **Herbrand base**, denoted $\mathcal{B}_P$, is the set of all possible ground atoms whose predicate symbols occur in the program and whose arguments are elements of the Herbrand universe.

An **interpretation** $I$ of $P$ is any set of literals from $\mathcal{B}_P \cup \neg\mathcal{B}_P$, where $\neg\mathcal{B}_P$ denotes the set $\{\neg p \mid p \in \mathcal{B}_P\}$. We use $I^+$ to denote the set of atoms in $I$. Similarly, $I^-$ is used to denote the set of atoms that occur negatively in $I$, i.e. $I^- = \{p \in \mathcal{B}_P \mid \neg p \in I\}$. $I$ is said to be **consistent** if $I^+ \cap I^- = \emptyset$. A **positive interpretation** of $P$ is any subset of $\mathcal{B}_P$.

Notice that we do not require $P$ to be finite. In this paper, we simply equate a traditional (finite) logic program with the set of ground instances of its rules.

In the logic programs of the form considered here, the heads of the rules are positive literals. There is no way, therefore, to prove that a negative literal holds. The accepted practice is thus to rely on the "closed-world assumption", which implies accepting the negation of a literal when the literal cannot be shown to hold. This well-known principle, known as "negation-as-failure" (naf), is widely recognized, but its exact implementation remains controversial. One of the requirements of any logic-program semantics, therefore, is to provide an implementation of naf. In most classical semantics this is achieved by means of the notion of unfoundedness, which was introduced in [2] as follows:

**Definition 2.** Let $P$ be a program and $I$ an interpretation of $P$. A set $U \subseteq \mathcal{B}_P$ of atoms is an **unfounded set** of $P$ with respect to $I$ if for each $p \in U$ and for each rule $p \leftarrow C$ in $P$, either

- $C \cup I$ is inconsistent, or
- $C \cap U \neq \emptyset$.

Intuitively, a set $U$ of literals is unfounded with respect to an interpretation $I$ if, for any $p \in U$, all rules that could motivate $p$ are disqualified, where a rule $p \leftarrow C$ may be disqualified either because it is "blocked" (i.e. the body of the rule is inconsistent with the interpretation $I$) or because it depends on another unfounded literal in $U$. Thus, if $U$ is unfounded with respect to $I$ then no literal in $U$ can be proven once one has accepted $I$.

Clearly, if $U_1$ and $U_2$ are unfounded w.r.t. an interpretation $I$, then so is their union $U_1 \cup U_2$. This motivates the following definition from [2]:

**Definition 3.** Let $I$ be an interpretation of a logic program $P$. The **greatest unfounded set** of $P$ with respect to $I$, denoted $\mathcal{U}_P(I)$ (or $\mathcal{U}(I)$ if $P$ is understood) is the union of all sets that are unfounded with respect to $I$.

The fundamental significance of the notion of unfoundedness is evident, since, as has been pointed out in [7], many recent approaches (including all those semantics which are included in the pure semantics, i.e. stable models, stable partial models, the well-founded (partial) model, three-valued stable models, and regular models) have required that $\mathcal{U}(I^+) = I^-$. However, we show by the following example that unfoundedness is insufficient to capture naf:

*Example 1.* Consider the following program:

$$p \leftarrow \neg p$$
$$q \leftarrow \neg p$$

The well-founded model (as defined in [2]) for this program is $I = \emptyset$. Notice that the literal $q$, which is not in $\mathcal{U}(I^+)$, cannot be proven since any proof of $q$ would require $\neg p$ to hold which, in turn, would imply $p$ and, thus, an inconsistency. The underivability of $q$ is captured in the suggested interpretation $\{\neg q\}$.

Thus, there may be positive literals which are not in $\mathcal{U}(I^+)$ and which cannot be proven. This motivates us to provide a semantics which extends the implementation of naf to include the negation of such literals.

The following definition will be useful in the definition of our semantics:

**Definition 4.** Let $P$ be a logic program and let $I$ be an interpretation of $P$.

- A literal $p$ is a **logical consequence** of $I$ with respect to $P$, denoted $I \vdash_P p$ (or $I \vdash p$ if P is understood) if either
  - $p \in I$, or
  - there exists a rule $p \leftarrow C$ in $P$ such that $I \vdash_P c$ for each $c \in C$.
- A set of literals $X$ is a logical consequence of $I$ if each of its elements is a logical consequence of $I$, in which case we write $I \vdash X$.
- The **deductive closure** of a set of literals $X$ with respect to $P$ is the set $\{p \mid X \vdash_P p\}$ and is denoted $X_P^*$ (or $X^*$ if P is understood).

We consider the following principles as criteria for an interpretation $I$ to be included in a semantics. The first requirement, which is universally accepted, is that $I$ be consistent and deductively closed. Second, as described in [9], $I$ should contain no assumption sets. This means that any set of positive literals $X \subseteq I^+$ must be derivable from $I \backslash X$. We express this as the condition $\neg I^- \vdash I^+$. Of course, there remains then to specify which negative literals are acceptable. Certainly, any $p \in \mathcal{U}(I^+)$ must be negated since there is no way to prove $p$ once one has accepted $I^+$. In order to include in our semantics the models such as that mentioned in the previous example, we relax the forementioned naf equality to the inequality $\mathcal{U}(I^+) \subseteq I^-$. Thus, we suggest the following axiomatic definition of our new semantics:

**Definition 5.** Let $P$ be a logic program and let $I$ be an interpretation. $I$ is called a **simple model** of $P$ if $I$ satisfies the following conditions:

1. $I$ is a **model**, i.e.

- $I$ is consistent.
- $I$ is deductively closed (in other words, $I$ satisfies the rules of $P$).
2. $I$ is **founded**, i.e.
    - $\neg I^- \vdash I^+$
3. $I$ respects the minimal requirement of **negation as failure**, i.e.
    - $\mathcal{U}(I^+) \subseteq I^-$

In order to show that most classical semantics satisfy the forementioned criteria, we refer to the pure semantics, which is defined in [7] as follows:

**Definition 6.** Let $P$ be a program and $J$ a positive interpretation of $P$. A set of atoms $A$ is an **assumption set** of $P$ with respect to $J$ if for each $p \in A$ and for each rule $p \leftarrow C$ in $P$, either

- $C \cup J$ is inconsistent, or
- $C \cap A \neq \emptyset$, or
- $C \not\subseteq J \cup \neg\mathcal{U}(J)$.

Clearly, if $A_1$ and $A_2$ are assumption sets w.r.t. an interpretation $J$, then so is their union $A_1 \cup A_2$. Thus, the **greatest assumption set** $\mathcal{A}(J)$ with respect to a positive interpretation $J$ is well-defined. An interpretation $I$ is a **pure model** of $P$ if $I^- = \mathcal{U}(I^+)$ and $\mathcal{A}(I^+) = \mathcal{B}_P \setminus I^+$, i.e. all atoms not in $I$ are assumptions.

**Theorem 7.** *Let $P$ be a logic program. An interpretation $I$ of $P$ is a pure model iff $I$ is a simple model and $I^- = \mathcal{U}(I^+)$.*

Theorems 2, 3 and 4 from [7] then imply:

**Corollary 8.** *Let $P$ be a logic program. All stable models, stable partial models, the well-founded (partial) model, three-valued stable models, and regular models of $P$ are simple models of $P$.*

*Example 2.* Consider again the program $P$ of example 1:

$$p \leftarrow \neg p$$
$$q \leftarrow \neg p$$

The simple models of $P$ are $\emptyset$ and $\{\neg q\}$.

*Example 3.* Consider the following program $P$:

$$p \leftarrow \neg p$$
$$q \leftarrow \neg p$$
$$r \leftarrow \neg q$$
$$s \leftarrow \neg r$$

It is easy to verify that the simple models of $P$ are $I_1 = \emptyset$, $I_2 = \{\neg s\}$, $I_3 = \{\neg r, s\}$, and $I_4 = \{\neg q, r, \neg s\}$. Notice that the empty set is the only model which is delivered by the pure semantics.

## 3  Reduced Models

As we mentioned in the previous section, the implementation of the negation-as-failure principle is not completely determined in the simple semantics since, in a simple model $I$, the set $\mathcal{U}(I^+)$ may be a strict subset of $I^-$. In this section we show that any simple model $I$ is generated by a so-called "complete" interpretation $J$ which does satisfy the equality $J^- = \mathcal{U}(J^+)$, but which is not necessarily consistent nor deductively closed. The transition from complete interpretations to simple models, which we call a "reduction", consists of the elimination of inconsistencies. Thus, the reduction of a complete interpretation is motivated by the requirement of consistency and deductive closure, but also results in the loss of the equality $J^- = \mathcal{U}(J^+)$.

**Definition 9.** An interpretation $J$ of a logic program $P$ is called a **complete interpretation** of $P$ if $J$ satisfies the following conditions:

1. $\mathcal{U}(J^+) = J^-$
2. $\neg J^- \vdash J^+$
3. $J$ is **total**, i.e. $J^+ \cup J^- = \mathcal{B}_P$.

**Definition 10.** An interpretation $I$ of a logic program $P$ is called a **reduced model** of $P$ if there is a complete interpretation $J$ of $P$ such that

$$I^+ = J^+ \setminus J^-$$
$$I^- = J^- \setminus J^+.$$

**Theorem 11.** *An interpretation $I$ of a logic program $P$ is a simple model iff it is a reduced model.*

*Example 4.* The simple model $I_3 = \{\neg r, s\}$ of the program in example 3 is a reduction of the complete interpretation $J = \{p, \neg p, q, \neg q, \neg r, s\}$.

*Example 5.* Consider the following program:

$$p \leftarrow \neg q$$
$$q \leftarrow \neg p$$

This program has three simple models. The simple model $\emptyset$ is a reduction of the complete interpretation $\{p, \neg p, q, \neg q\}$. The simple models $\{p, \neg q\}$ and $\{\neg p, q\}$ are reductions of themselves.

## 4  R-stable Models

In the previous sections we have defined a semantics which generates partial models for logic programs. Thus, our semantics differs from those approaches which define only total models. In those approaches, models contain truth values for all literals in the Herbrand base and there are, thus, no "undecided literals".

It is only natural now for us to investigate the stability of a partial model upon extension.

When a model $I$ is proposed, the so-called remainder program $P_I$ consists of rules which concern the remaining undecided literals and which take into account the truth values of the literals contained in the model. Thus, the remainder program $P_I$ does not refer to any literals from $I \cup \neg I$. A model $J$ of $P_I$ may then provide a possible "extension" of $I$ to $(I \cup J)^*$. However, $J$ may be incompatible with $I$ because $(I \cup J)^*$ might be inconsistent.

In this section, we examine a subclass of simple models that is "stable" under extension as described above, i.e. in order for $I$ to be a stable model, we demand that $(I \cup J)^*$ be consistent for any (stable) model $J$ of $P_I$.

The following definition uses a result due to Tarski in [10], which says that every monotonic function on a complete lattice has a least fixpoint.

**Definition 12.** Let $I$ be a simple model of a logic program $P$. The **remainder program** of $P$ with respect to $I$, denoted $P_I$, is defined as follows:

1. Let $R$ be the set of rules $p \leftarrow C$ which can be constructed using literals from $\mathcal{B}_P \cup \neg \mathcal{B}_P$. Let $\Phi_P$ be the least fixpoint of the following monotonic function:

$$\phi_P : R \rightarrow R$$
$$\phi_P(X) = P \cup X \cup \{p \leftarrow C \mid p \leftarrow C' \in X, q \in C', q \leftarrow D \in X, C = (C' \backslash q) \cup D\}.$$

2. From the program $\Phi_P$, delete all rules $p \leftarrow C$ such that
   - $C$ contains a positive literal, or
   - $p \in I^+ \cup I^-$, or
   - $C \cup I^+$ is inconsistent.

Intuitively, every rule is replaced by the corresponding derivations of a literal. Any remaining rule that contains a positive literal in the body can be deleted since either it is subsumed by new rules, or it does not correspond to a derivation (i.e. the head cannot be proven since its truth value depends on the truth value assigned to another positive literal). In particular, rules that represent endless loops are deleted. In addition, rules for $p \in I^+ \cup I^-$ are left out since we already decided on $p$. A remaining rule $q \leftarrow C$ is useless if $C \cup I^+$ is inconsistent (note that $C \subseteq \neg \mathcal{B}_P$), so we can remove it.

*Example 6.* Consider the following program $P$:

$$p \leftarrow q$$
$$q \leftarrow \neg p$$
$$r \leftarrow \neg q$$
$$s \leftarrow \neg r$$
$$s \leftarrow \neg s$$

It is easy to verify that $L = \{\neg r, s\}$ is a simple model of $P$. The remainder program $P_L$ consists of the following rules:

$$p \leftarrow \neg p$$
$$q \leftarrow \neg p$$

Stability of the deciding process is captured by the following recursive notion:

**Definition 13.** A simple model $I$ of a logic program $P$ is called **r-stable** if for any r-stable model $J$ of $P_I$, the set $(I \cup J)_P^*$ is consistent.

Notice that a base case for the recursion, which includes two possible situations, is included in definition 13. In the first situation, the simple model $I$ is empty, and is therefore trivially r-stable; indeed, when $I$ is empty, for any simple model $J$ of $P_I$, $(I \cup J)_P^* = J$ is consistent. In the second situation, $I$ is non-empty but there is no non-empty simple model $J$ of $P_I$. In this case, the only possible simple model of $P_I$ is $J = \emptyset$, and $(I \cup \emptyset)_P^* = I$ is consistent; therefore, $I$ is r-stable. Since $\mathcal{B}_{P_I} \subseteq \mathcal{B}_P$, we can show by standard techniques [4] that a base case is reached.

*Example 7.* Consider the simple model $I_3 = \{\neg r, s\}$ of the program $P$ in example 3:

$$p \leftarrow \neg p$$
$$q \leftarrow \neg p$$
$$r \leftarrow \neg q$$
$$s \leftarrow \neg r$$

It can easily be verified that $J = \{\neg q\}$ is a simple model of the remainder program $P_{I_3}$:

$$p \leftarrow \neg p$$
$$q \leftarrow \neg p$$

$J$ is r-stable since the remainder program $P_{I_3 J}$ contains only the rule

$$p \leftarrow \neg p$$

and, clearly, the only simple model of $P_{I_3 J}$ is $K = \emptyset$.

However, $(I_3 \cup J)_P^* = \{\neg r, s, \neg q, r\}$ is inconsistent; thus, the simple model $I_3 = \{\neg r, s\}$ of $P$ is not r-stable.

*Example 8.* Consider the simple model $I_4 = \{\neg q, r, \neg s\}$ of the program $P$ in example 3. The remainder program $P_{I_4}$ is the following:

$$p \leftarrow \neg p$$

The only simple model of $P_{I_4}$ is $J = \emptyset$, so $I_4$ is r-stable.

*Example 9.* Consider the following program $P$:

$$p \leftarrow \neg q$$
$$q \leftarrow \neg p$$
$$r \leftarrow p$$

The simple models of $P$ are $\emptyset$, $\{\neg r\}$, $\{\neg p, q, \neg r\}$ and $\{p, \neg q, r\}$. The r-stable models of $P$ are $\emptyset$, $\{\neg p, q, \neg r\}$ and $\{p, \neg q, r\}$. The simple model $\{\neg r\}$ is not r-stable. Indeed, the remainder program with respect to $\{\neg r\}$ is

$$p \leftarrow \neg q$$
$$q \leftarrow \neg p$$

which has, among its r-stable models, the model $\{p, \neg q\}$. This r-stable model is incompatible with $\{\neg r\}$, since $(\{p, \neg q\} \cup \{\neg r\})^*_P = \{p, \neg q, \neg r, r\}$ is inconsistent.

*Example 10.* The simple model $L = \{\neg r, s\}$ of the program $P$ in example 6 is not r-stable. The r-stable models are $\{\neg q, r\}$ and $\emptyset$. The unique pure model is the empty set.

*Example 11.* The simple models of the program in example 5 are all r-stable.

## 5  Relationships with Other Semantics

In this section we show that the inclusion relationships between the various semantics are as depicted in Fig. 1.

**Lemma 14.** *Let $I$ be a simple model of a logic program $P$. If $I^- = \mathcal{U}(I^+)$ then $I$ is r-stable.*

The following theorem is a consequence of Theorem 7 and Lemma 14:

**Theorem 15.** *Let $I$ be a pure model of a logic program $P$. Then $I$ is a r-stable model.*

**Corollary 16.** *Let $P$ be a logic program. All stable models, stable partial models, the well-founded (partial) model, three-valued stable models, and regular models of $P$ are r-stable models of $P$.*

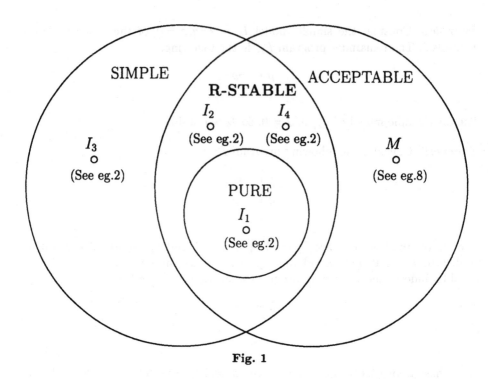

**Fig. 1**

Thus, all of these models are included in our semantics. Our examples showed that there are reasonable simple models which are not included in the fore-mentioned approaches. Notice that all of the r-stable models mentioned in our examples are delivered by the model-theoretic semantics associated with the acceptable semantics in [6]; however, we shall show in example 12 that the set of acceptable models is actually too large. The following definition is taken from [6]:

**Definition 17.** Let $P$ be a logic program and let $A$ and $B$ be subsets of $\neg\mathcal{B}_P$. Then $A$ **attacks** $B$ iff $A \vdash p$ for some $\neg p \in B$.

A is **acceptable** w.r.t. $B$ iff for any $X \subseteq \neg\mathcal{B}_P$ such that $X$ attacks $A\backslash B$, $X$ is not acceptable w.r.t. $A \cup B$.

A is an **acceptable extension** of $P$ iff $A$ is acceptable w.r.t. $\emptyset$.

In the following definition we show that the acceptable extensions can be used to define a model-theoretic semantics:

**Definition 18.** Let $I$ be an interpretation of a logic program $P$. $I$ is an **acceptable model** of $P$ iff there is an acceptable extension $A$ of $P$ such that $I = A^*$.

**Theorem 19.** &ndash; *Let $I$ be a simple model of a program $P$. Then $I$ is an acceptable model iff it is r-stable.*

&ndash; *Let $J$ be an acceptable model of a program $P$. Then $J$ is simple iff it is r-stable.*

The following example illustrates that acceptable models do not necessarily comply with the first principles of logic-programming semantics described in definition 5:

*Example 12.* Consider the program

$$p \leftarrow \neg p$$
$$q \leftarrow \neg p$$
$$r \leftarrow \neg q, \neg s$$
$$s \leftarrow$$

Clearly, $\emptyset$ is an acceptable extension. Its deductive closure is $M = \{s\}$. This model does not respect negation as failure (in the sense of Condition 3 in definition 5), since $\neg \mathcal{U}(M^+) = \{\neg r\} \not\subseteq M$. Therefore, $M$ is not a simple model.

Superfluous extensions such as the one in the above example can be avoided by considering only maximal acceptable extensions, as suggested for stable theories in [5]; however, the resulting semantics would then not include the well-founded model $\{s, \neg r\}$ of the above program, nor the model $\{p, \neg q\}$ of the following program:

$$p \leftarrow \neg q$$
$$q \leftarrow \neg p$$
$$r \leftarrow \neg s$$
$$s \leftarrow \neg r$$

The model $\{p, \neg q\}$ of this program reflects the ability to choose between the alternative literals $p, q$ and not to decide on either of the alternative literals $r, s$. Maximizing acceptable extensions thus implies losing the appeal of a single unifying definition covering all possibilities between well-founded and r-stable semantics.

In [3] we have defined a logic-programming semantics based on argumentation frameworks. The idea developed there is that every logic program can be associated with an argumentation framework $AF = (A, \rightsquigarrow)$, where $A$ is a set of arguments and $\rightsquigarrow$ is a binary relation on $A$ which represents attacks between arguments. Each argument in the framework is a derivation of a literal $p$. A derivation of $p$ attacks a derivation of $q$ if the derivation of $q$ relies on $\neg p$. This is reasonable since, if $p$ is true, a proof for $q$ that uses $\neg p$ is useless. Once a logic program is represented as an argumentation framework, any semantics for argumentation frameworks generates models for the logic program. The argumentation semantics which we have developed in [3] thus results in a logic-programming semantics, and the following theorem shows that the semantics derived from first principles of logic programming coincides with the semantics which results from argumentation theory.

**Theorem 20.** *Let P be a logic program.*

  – *An interpretation of P is a simple model iff it is a labelling-model, and*
  – *a simple model of P is r-stable iff it is robust,*

*where labelling-models and robustness are defined in [3].*

# References

1. Michael Gelfond and Vladimir Lifschitz. The stable model semantics for logic programming. In Robert A. Kowalski and Kenneth A. Bowen, editors, *Proceedings of the Fifth International Conference and Symposium on Logic Programming*, pages 1081–1086, Seattle, 1988. ALP, IEEE, The MIT Press.
2. A. Van Gelder, K. Ross, and J. S. Schlipf. Unfounded sets and well-founded semantics for general logic programs. In *Proceedings of the Seventh ACM Symposium on Principles of Database Systems*, pages 221–230, Austin, Texas, 1988. Association for Computing Machinery.
3. H. Jakobovits and D. Vermeir. Contradiction in argumentation frameworks. In *Proceedings of the IPMU conference*, 1996.
4. H. Jakobovits and D. Vermeir. Argumentation and logic-programming semantics. In preparation.
5. A.C. Kakas and P. Mancarella. Stable theories for logic programs. In *Proceedings of the International Symposium of Logic Programming*. 1991.
6. A. C. Kakas, P. Mancarella, and Phan Minh Dung. The acceptability semantics for logic programs. In P. Van Hentenrijck, editor, *Proceedings of the 11th International Conference on Logic Programming*, pages 504–519. MIT Press, 1994.
7. E. Laenens, D. Vermeir, and C. Zaniolo. Logic programming semantics made easy. In *Proceedings of the International Conference on Automata, Languages and Programming*, pages 499–508. 1992.
8. T. Przymusinski. Well-founded semantics coincides with three-valued stable semantics. *Fundamenta Informaticae*, 13:445–463, 1990.
9. D. Sacca and C. Zaniolo. Stable models and non-determinism for logic programs with negation. In *Proceedings of the 9th ACM SIGACT-SIGMOD-SIGART Symposium on Principles of Database Systems*. Association for Computing Machinery, 1990.
10. A. Tarski. A lattice theoretical fixpoint theorem and its application. *Pacific Journal of Mathematics*, (5):285–309, 1955.
11. Jia-Huai You and Li Yan Yuan. Three-valued formalization of logic programming: Is it needed? In *Proc. of the PODS'90 conference*, pages 172–182. 1990.

# The Expressive Power of Partial Models
# for Disjunctive Databases

## (Extended Abstract)

T. Eiter , N. Leone , D. Saccà

Christian Doppler Lab for Expert Systems,
Institut für Informationssysteme,
TU Wien, Paniglgasse 16, A-1040 Wien, Austria,
email: (eiter|leone)@dbai.tuwien.ac.at

ISI-CNR c/o DEIS-UNICAL

DEIS-UNICAL, Università della Calabria,
I-87030 Rende, Italy,
email: sacca@si.deis.unical.it

**Abstract.** We investigate the expressive power of partial model semantics for disjunctive deductive databases, in particular, partial stable,
regular model, maximal stable (M-stable), and least undefined (L-stable)
models, the semantics for function free disjunctive logic programs are considered, for which the expressiveness of queries based on possibility and
certainty inference is determined. The analyses have particular attention to the impact of syntactical restrictions on programs in the form of
limited use of disjunction and negation. It appears that the considered
semantics capture complexity classes up to the lower end of the polynomial
hierarchy. In particular, L-stable semantics has the highest expressive
power ($\Sigma_2^p$ resp $\Pi_2^p$). An interesting resulting this course is that, in
contrast with total stable models, negation is for partial stable models
more expressive than disjunction.

## 1. Introduction

In this paper, we study the expressive power of disjunctive deductive databases
and disjunctive datalog programs based on various partial model semantics. In
particular, we consider semantics based on

(P) partial stable models (also called 3-valued stable or P-stable models), which
have been proposed by Przymusinski [23]. Compared to total stable models,
partial stable models conservatively extend the class of programs for which an

* This work has been partially supported by the EC-US project "DEUS EX
MACHINA: Non Determinism in Deductive Databases" and by a MURST grant
(40% share) under the project "Sistemi formali e strumenti per basi di dati evolute".

# The Expressive Power of Partial Models for Disjunctive Deductive Databases[*]

(Extended Abstract)

T. Eiter[1]    N. Leone[1,2]    D. Saccà[3]

[1] Christian Doppler Lab for Expert Systems
Institut für Informationssysteme,
TU Wien, Paniglgasse 16, A-1040 Wien, Austria.
email: eiter@dbai.tuwien.ac.at, leone@dbai.tuwien.ac.at

[2] ISI–CNR c/o DEIS–UNICAL

[3] DEIS-UNICAL, Università della Calabria
I-87030 Rende, Italy
email: sacca@si.deis.unical.it

**Abstract.** We investigate the expressive power of partial model semantics for disjunctive deductive databases. In particular, partial stable, regular model, maximal stable (M-stable), and least undefined stable (L-stable) semantics for function-free disjunctive logic programs are considered, for which the expressiveness of queries based on possibility and certainty inference is determined. The analysis pays particular attention to the impact of syntactical restrictions on programs in the form of limited use of disjunction and negation. It appears that the considered semantics capture complexity classes at the lower end of the polynomial hierarchy. In particular, L-stable semantics has the highest expressive power ($\Sigma_3^P$ resp. $\Pi_3^P$). An interesting result in this course is that, in contrast with total stable models, negation is for partial stable models more expressive than disjunction.

## 1  Introduction

In this paper, we study the expressive power of disjunctive deductive databases, i.e., disjunctive datalog programs based on various partial model semantics. In particular, we consider semantics based on

(1) *partial stable models* (also called *3-valued stable* or *P-stable* models), which have been proposed by Przymusinski [23]. Compared to total stable models, partial stable models conservatively extend the class of programs for which an

---

[*] This work has been partially supported by the EC-US033 project "DEUS EX MACHINA: Non-Determinism in Deductive Databases" and by a MURST grant (40% share) under the project "Sistemi formali e strumenti per basi di dati evolute."

acceptable model exists; in particular, every disjunction-free (∨-free) program has some partial stable model, while it may lack a total stable model. Moreover, on the class of (disjunctive) stratified programs, partial stable models coincide with total stable models.

(2) *maximal stable* (*M-stable*) models [26, 14, 24], which are the partial stable models maximal under set inclusion (where a partial model is represented by the set of ground literals true in the model). On disjunction-free programs, M-stable models coincide with the preferred extensions of [10], the regular models of [31], the maximal stable classes of [4], and the M-stable models of [26, 24], as shown in [20, 14, 32].

(3) *regular models* [31], which are similar in spirit to M-stable models, but are based on a weaker concept of model than partial stability. As an advantage, every program admits a regular model. On the other hand, as discussed in [14], a drawback of regular models is that they do not obey to the CWA principle.

(4) *least undefined stable* (*L-stable*) models [14, 25, 24], which are the partial stable models with the minimal degree of undefinedness, i.e., no other partial stable model exists whose undefined atoms constitute a proper subset of the atoms that are undefined in an L-stable model. The relevance of L-stable models is confirmed by the fact that L-stable models differ from total stable models *only if* the program has no total stable model; thus, L-stable models can be considered as the best "approximation" of total stable models.

Objections to partial stable models came from the observation that every 3-valued model theoretic approach should meet the principle of *minimal undefinedness* [31], which prescribes that the *undefined* truth value should be used only when necessary (i.e., a "good" semantics should tend to minimize the set of undefined atoms). The attempt to minimize undefinedness in partial models led to the three notions of partial models above.

For each of the semantics mentioned, we analyze the expressive power of bound (Boolean) queries resorting to the common modalities of *possibility inference* –a literal is true if it is in some model– and *certainty inference* –a literal is true if it is in every model [1]. The main points of interest are:

- The expressive powers of the different partial vs total model semantics.
- The impact of minimizing undefinedness on expressive power.
- The impact of syntactical restrictions. In particular, the power of disjunction vs negation; the effect of stratified negation vs arbitrary negation; and, the effect of limited disjunction (in particular, *headcycle-free* disjunction [5]) vs unrestricted disjunction.

The main results on the expressiveness can be summarized as follows:

1. Partial stable models have the same expressive power as total stable models. Under possibility and certainty inference, they capture $\Sigma_2^P$ and $\Pi_2^P$, i.e., they can express precisely the database collections with complexity in $\Sigma_2^P$ and $\Pi_2^P$, respectively.

2. Under certainty inference, M-stable models and regular models are more powerful than the total stable models, as the former capture the class $\Pi_3^P$ while the latter capture $\Pi_2^P$; under possibility inference, both have the same power as total stable models and capture the class $\Sigma_2^P$.

3. L-stable models are always more expressive than total stable models, since, under possibility and certainty inference, they capture the classes $\Sigma_3^P$ and $\Pi_3^P$, respectively.

4. For partial models that minimize undefinedness (M-stable, L-stable, and regular models), negation is more expressive than disjunction under certainty inference and for L-stable models, also under possibility inference. Indeed, ∨-free programs with negation can express all of $\Sigma_2^P$ (or $\Pi_2^P$); however, only a fragment thereof can be expressed by ¬-free programs with disjunction. By contrast, under total model semantics ∨-free programs with negation can define only database collections in NP (or coNP), while ¬-free programs with disjunction can define database collections that are $\Sigma_2^P$-hard (or $\Pi_2^P$-hard) to recognize.

5. Allowing headcycle-free disjunction (on ¬-free programs) increases the expressibility to a strict fragment of NP (resp. coNP), which contrasts with the well-known fact that stratified negation (on ∨-free programs) does not increase the expressibility beyond polynomial time computability. Interestingly, the combination of headcycle-free disjunction and stratified negation captures NP (or coNP), for all variants of partial models that we consider.

Our study extends and complements the work in [24] on partial semantics for ∨-free programs, and the work in [12] on the expressiveness of total model semantics for disjunctive programs (for an overview in the field, cf. [18, 27]).

The analysis of the impact of syntactic restrictions carried out in this paper adds new insights to previous studies on complexity and expressiveness of restricted forms of disjunction (*headcycle-free* programs) [5, 6]. The results may support in choosing an appropriate fragment of the query language under a suitable semantics which fits the need in practice.

The more involved concepts of partial models that minimize undefinedness (M-stable, L-stable and regular models) provide expressive power of the third level of the polynomial hierarchy. Recall that the motivation for considering these concepts is due to the observation that in general, partial models may be "too much undefined". The expressiveness and complexity results tell us the computational effort we have to spend using these semantics, but also that we gain expressive power in a balanced way. Of course, the same classes of queries can be expressed by fragments of second-order logic [28], whose semantics is comparatively simple. However, our intent is to point out that we have equally powerful languages in the declarative, rule-based paradigm endowed with a naturally defined semantics. Rule-based languages seem to be more accessible to programmers than pure logic; moreover, partial model semantics has some (weak) modularity properties that allows to split a program into modules, cf. [13].

For space reasons, some proofs are omitted here. Proofs of all results are given in the full paper [14].

# 2 Partial Model Semantics

We review from [14, 23, 31] the basic definitions and characterizations of partial model semantics for disjunctive datalog programs.

## 2.1 Disjunctive Datalog Programs

A *rule* $r$ is a clause of the form

$$a_1 \vee \cdots \vee a_n \leftarrow b_1, \cdots, b_k, \neg b_{k+1}, \cdots, \neg b_m, \qquad n \geq 1, \ m \geq 0.$$

$a_1, \cdots, a_n, b_1, \cdots, b_m$ are atoms of the form $p(t_1, ..., t_n)$, where $p$ is a *predicate* of arity $n$ and the terms $t_1, ..., t_n$ are constants or variables. The disjunction $a_1 \vee \cdots \vee a_n$ is the *head* of $r$, while the conjunction $b_1, ..., b_k, \neg b_{k+1}, ..., \neg b_m$ is the *body* of $r$. We denote by $H(r)$ the set $\{a_1, ..., a_n\}$ of the head atoms, and by $B(r)$ the set $\{b_1, ..., b_k, \neg b_{k+1}, ..., \neg b_m\}$ of the body literals. Moreover, $B^+(r)$ and $B^-(r)$ denote the set of positive and negative literals occurring in $B(r)$, respectively.

A *disjunctive logic program* (simply *program* hereafter) is a finite set of rules. A $\neg$-free (resp. $\vee$-free) program is called *positive* (resp. *normal*). A term, (resp. an atom, a literal, a rule or a program) is *ground* if no variables occur in it. We often use upper-case letters, say $L$, to denote literals. Two literals are *complementary*, if they are of the form $p$ and $\neg p$, for some atom $p$. For a literal $L$, $\neg L$ denotes its complementary literal, and for a set $A$ of literals, $\neg.A = \{\neg L \mid L \in A\}$.

We denote by $U_{\mathcal{LP}}$, $B_{\mathcal{LP}}$, and $ground(\mathcal{LP})$ the Herbrand universe, the Herbrand base, and the instantiation of a program $\mathcal{LP}$, respectively.

An interpretation of $\mathcal{LP}$ is a consistent set of ground literals, i.e., a subset $I \subseteq B_{\mathcal{LP}} \cup \neg.B_{\mathcal{LP}}$ such that $I \cap \neg.I = \emptyset$; it is *total* if $\overline{I}$ is empty, and *partial* otherwise. By $I^+$ and $I^-$ we denote the set of positive and negative literals occurring in $I$, respectively, and by $\overline{I}$ the set $B_{\mathcal{LP}} - (I \cup \neg.I)$.

Following [23], we define a 3-valued logic with values $T$ *(True)*, $F$ *(False)*, and $U$ *(Undefined)*, ordered by $F < U < T$. Let $\mathcal{LP}$ be a program and $I$ an interpretation. The value of a ground literal $L$ in $I$, $value_I(L)$, is $T$ if $L \in I$, $F$ if $L \in \neg.I$, and $U$ otherwise (i.e., if $L \notin I \cup \neg.I$). For ground literals $L_1, ..., L_n$, the value of the conjunction $C$ of all $L_i$ is the minimum over the values of the $L_i$, i.e., $value_I(C) = min(\{value_I(L_i) \mid 1 \leq i \leq n\})$, while the value $value_I(D)$ of the disjunction $D$ of all $L_i$ is their maximum, i.e., $value_I(D) = max(\{value_I(L_i) \mid 1 \leq i \leq n\})$; if $n = 0$, then $value_I(C) = T$ and $value_I(D) = F$. Finally, a ground rule $r$ is *satisfied* by $I$ if $value_I(H(r)) \geq value_I(B(r))$.

An interpretation $M$ for $\mathcal{LP}$ is a *3-valued* model of $\mathcal{LP}$ if $M$ satisfies each rule in $ground(\mathcal{LP})$; if $M$ is total, it is a *total model*. A model $M_1 \neq M$ is *smaller than* $M$, denoted $M_1 \prec M$, iff $M_1^+ \subseteq M^+$ and $M_1^- \supseteq M^-$. A model $M$ is *minimal* iff there does not exist a smaller model $M_1$. Among total models, a model $M$ is *minimal* iff there exists no smaller total model $M_1$. We denote the set of the minimal total models by $MM^+(\mathcal{LP})$.

## 2.2 P-stable Models and Restricted P-stable Models

A *3-valued program* is a program $\mathcal{LP}$ where the constants $T$, $U$ and $F$ may occur in the body of rules from $\mathcal{LP}$. It is assumed that in every interpretation $I$, $T$ is true, $F$ is false, and $U$ is undefined.

Given an interpretation $I$ for a program $\mathcal{LP}$, the *GL-transformation* $\frac{\mathcal{LP}}{I}$ of $\mathcal{LP}$ w.r.t. $I$ is the positive 3-valued program obtained from $ground(\mathcal{LP})$ by replacing in the body of every rule all negative literals which are true (resp. undefined, false) w.r.t. $I$ by $T$ (resp. $U$, $F$). An interpretation $M$ for $\mathcal{LP}$ is a *3-valued model for* $\frac{\mathcal{LP}}{I}$ if it satisfies every rule in $\frac{\mathcal{LP}}{I}$. A 3-valued model $M$ for $\frac{\mathcal{LP}}{I}$ (resp. $\mathcal{LP}$) is *minimal* if there does not exist a 3-valued model $M_1 \neq M$ for $\frac{\mathcal{LP}}{I}$ (resp. $\mathcal{LP}$) such that $M_1^+ \subseteq M^+$ and $M_1^- \supseteq M^-$. In [23] it has been proven that $\frac{\mathcal{LP}}{I}$ has at least one minimal 3-valued model.

**Definition 1.** *[23, 14] Let $\mathcal{LP}$ be a program and $M$ be an interpretation. Then, $M$ is a P-stable (or 3-valued stable) model for $\mathcal{LP}$ iff $M$ is a minimal 3-valued model of $\frac{\mathcal{LP}}{M}$.* ∎

Notice that [13] provides an equivalent characterization of P-stable models in terms of unfounded sets.

*Example 1.* Consider the following program $\mathcal{LP}_1$:

$$a \vee b \leftarrow \qquad d \leftarrow \neg d, \ \neg b \qquad a \vee c \leftarrow \neg d$$

$M_1 = \{a, \ \neg b, \ \neg c\}$ *is a P-stable model for $\mathcal{LP}_1$. Indeed, $\frac{\mathcal{LP}_1}{M_1}$ is as follows:*

$$a \vee b \leftarrow \qquad d \leftarrow U, \ T \qquad a \vee c \leftarrow U$$

*and $M_1$ is a minimal 3-valued model of $\frac{\mathcal{LP}}{M_1}$. Similarly, $M_2 = \{b, \ c, \ \neg a, \ \neg d\}$ is a P-stable model for $\mathcal{LP}_1$, as it is a minimal 3-valued model of $\frac{\mathcal{LP}_1}{M_2}$, which is as follows:*

$$a \vee b \leftarrow \qquad d \leftarrow T, \ F \qquad a \vee c \leftarrow T$$

*However, $M_3 = \{a, \neg d\}$ is not a P-stable model of $\mathcal{LP}_1$.* ∎

As for normal (∨-free) logic programs [24], P-stable models are grouped into three main families: T-stable, M-stable, and L-stable models.

**Definition 2.** *[14, 25] A P-stable model $M$ is:*

(a) *T-stable (Total stable) if $M$ is a total interpretation;*
(b) *M-stable (Maximal stable) if there exists no P-stable model $N$ of $\mathcal{LP}$ such that $N \supset M$.*
(c) *L-stable (Least-undefined stable) if the set of its undefined atoms is minimal, i.e., there exists no P-stable model $N$ of $\mathcal{LP}$ such that $\overline{N} \supset \overline{M}$.* ∎

Note that the T-stable models coincide with the 2-valued (total disjunctive) stable models of [23].

*Example 2.* Consider the following program $\mathcal{LP}_2$.

$$a \leftarrow \neg b, \qquad b \leftarrow \neg a, \qquad c \vee d \leftarrow a, \qquad d \leftarrow c$$

The P-stable models of $\mathcal{LP}_2$ are: $M_1 = \{b, \neg a, \neg c, \neg d\}$, $M_2 = \{a, d, \neg b, \neg c\}$, and $M_3 = \{\neg c\}$. $M_1$ and $M_2$ are also M-stable models, while $M_3$ is not (as it is a subset of the P-stable model $M_1$, as well as of $M_2$). Both $M_1$ and $M_2$ are also L-stable models for $\mathcal{LP}_2$. Moreover, $M_1$ and $M_2$ are also T-stable models, as they are total interpretations. ∎

## 2.3 Regular Models

The notion of regular model is similar in spirit to M-stable models, but is based on a weaker concept of model than P-stable model.

A model $M$ for $\mathcal{LP}$ is *justified* (or *founded* [14]) iff $M^+ = N^+$ for some $N \in \mathrm{MM}^+(\mathcal{LP}(M))$, where the program $\mathcal{LP}(M)$ is obtained from $ground(\mathcal{LP})$ as follows: (i) remove all rules $r$ such that $B^-(r) \not\subseteq I^-$, and (ii) remove all negative literals from the remaining rules.

*Example 3.* Reconsider the program $\mathcal{LP}_1$ in Example 1. The interpretation $M_1 = \{a, \neg b, \neg c\}$ is founded. Indeed, $\mathcal{LP}_1(M_1)$ is the following program:

$$a \vee b \leftarrow$$

and $N = \{a, \neg b\}$ is a minimal total model $N$ of $\mathcal{LP}_1(M_1)$ such that $N^+ = M_1^+$. ∎

Foundedness basically states that every positive literal in an interpretation can be derived from the rules possibly using negative literals as additional axioms. Notice that the notion of foundedness is the underlying principle of total stable models [17]; in fact, a total interpretation of a program is a T-stable model precisely if it is founded.

**Definition 3.** *[31] Let $\mathcal{LP}$ be a logic program and $M$ an interpretation of it. Then, $M$ is a regular model of $\mathcal{LP}$ iff*

(a) $M$ is a founded 3-valued model of $\mathcal{LP}$, and
(b) $M$ is maximal w.r.t. inclusion, i.e., there exists no founded 3-valued model $N$ of $\mathcal{LP}$ with $N \supset M$.

Notice that every program has a regular model [31]. Thus, in contrast to the semantics from above, the regular model semantics assigns a model to every program.

*Example 4.* *[23] Let $\mathcal{LP}$ be the program below.*

$$work \lor sleep \lor tired \leftarrow$$
$$work \leftarrow \neg tired$$
$$sleep \leftarrow \neg work$$
$$tired \leftarrow \neg sleep$$

*It is easy to see that $\mathcal{LP}$ has no P-stable model (cf. [23]), and hence no M-stable, L-stable, and T-stable model. On the other hand, $\{work\}$, $\{sleep\}$, and $\{tired\}$ are (all the) regular models of $\mathcal{LP}$.* ∎

## 2.4 Relationships between Models

We briefly discuss some properties and relationships of the concepts of partial models from above; a more detailed account is given in [14]. We use $\mathcal{XS}_{\mathcal{LP}}$ as generic notation for the models of $\mathcal{LP}$, where $\mathcal{XS}_{\mathcal{LP}}$ is one of $\mathcal{PS}_{\mathcal{LP}}$, $\mathcal{MS}_{\mathcal{LP}}$, $\mathcal{LS}_{\mathcal{LP}}$, $\mathcal{TS}_{\mathcal{LP}}$, and $\mathcal{RS}_{\mathcal{LP}}$, and denotes the sets of P-stable, M-stable, L-stable, T-stable, and regular models of $\mathcal{LP}$, respectively. Whenever $\mathcal{LP}$ is understood from the context, we shall omit the subscript $\mathcal{LP}$.

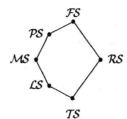

**Fig. 1.** Relation between partial model semantics

The inclusion order diagram for the different sets of models $\mathcal{XS}$ is displayed in Figure 1. There, $\mathcal{FS}$ denotes the set of founded 3-valued models of $\mathcal{LP}$.

Since the P-stable models and T-stable models are the 3-valued stable and 2-valued stable models, respectively, they coincide for locally stratified DLPs [23]. As a consequence,

**Proposition 4.** [14] *Let $\mathcal{LP}$ be a program. If $\mathcal{LP}$ is (locally) stratified, then $\mathcal{PS}_{\mathcal{LP}} = \mathcal{MS}_{\mathcal{LP}} = \mathcal{LS}_{\mathcal{LP}} = \mathcal{TS}_{\mathcal{LP}} = \mathcal{RS}_{\mathcal{LP}}$.*

Note that a (locally) stratified program has always P-stable models.

The concept of regular model is similar to M-stable model, but yet different [13]. However, if no disjunction occurs, the concepts coincide.

**Proposition 5.** [32] *Let $\mathcal{LP}$ be a normal program. Then, $\mathcal{MS} = \mathcal{RS}$.*

$\mathcal{MS}$ and $\mathcal{LS}$ on the one hand and $\mathcal{RS}$ on the other provide approximations of $\mathcal{TS}$. In fact, $\mathcal{LS}$ is accurate for the programs that are consistent under stable semantics.

**Proposition 6.** [14] *Let $\mathcal{LP}$ be a program. Then, $\mathcal{TS} \neq \emptyset$ implies $\mathcal{TS} = \mathcal{LS}$.*

## 2.5 Deterministic Semantics

Each set $\mathcal{XS}$ of models can be considered as the *intended models* of a program $\mathcal{LP}$. Although $\mathcal{XS}$ contains multiple models, a deterministic semantics can be enforced using two main approaches cf. [1, 24, 12]: the *possibility* (or *credulous, brave*) semantics, and the *certainty* (or *skeptical, cautious*) semantics.

**Definition 7.** *Let $\mathcal{LP}$ be a program and $A$ be a ground literal. Then*

(a) *$A$ is a $\exists_{\mathcal{XS}}$ (possible) inference of $\mathcal{LP}$, denoted $\mathcal{LP} \models_{\mathcal{XS}}^{\exists} A$, if $\exists M \in \mathcal{XS}$ such that $A \in M$ (i.e., $A$ is true in some model in $\mathcal{XS}$);*
(b) *$A$ is a $\forall_{\mathcal{XS}}$ (certain) inference of $\mathcal{LP}$, denoted $\mathcal{LP} \models_{\mathcal{XS}}^{\forall} A$, if $\forall M \in \mathcal{XS}$, $A \in M$ (i.e., $A$ is true in every model in $\mathcal{XS}$).* ∎

*Example 5. On program $\mathcal{LP}_2$ of Example 2 the various stable semantics coincide. Indeed, under P-stable, M-stable, L-stable and T-stable semantics, $\neg c$ is the only certain inference, and $a$, $\neg a$, $b$, $\neg b$, $\neg c$, $d$, and $\neg d$ are the possible inferences.*

*In Example 4, we have that work, sleep, and tired are $\exists_{\mathcal{RS}}$ inferences, while the set of $\forall_{\mathcal{RS}}$ inferences is empty.* ∎

# 3 Expressive Power

## 3.1 Preliminaries

In the context of deductive databases, programs as introduced above are known as disjunctive datalog ($DATALOG^{\vee,\neg}$) programs, i.e., the extension of datalog (with negation) [7, 21, 29] by disjunction [12]. Some of the predicate symbols correspond to database relations (the *extensional (EDB) predicates*), and are not allowed to occur in rule heads; the other predicate symbols are called *intensional (IDB) predicates*. Actual database relations are formed on a fixed countable domain $U$, from which also possible constants in a $DATALOG^{\vee,\neg}$ program are taken.

More formally, a $DATALOG^{\vee,\neg}$ program $\mathcal{LP}$ has associated a relational database scheme $\mathcal{DB}_{\mathcal{LP}} = \{r |\ r \text{ is an EDB predicate symbol of } \mathcal{LP}\}$; thus EDB predicate symbols are seen as relation symbols. A database $D$ on $\mathcal{DB}_{\mathcal{LP}}$ is a set of finite relations on $U$, one for each $r$ in $\mathcal{DB}_{\mathcal{LP}}$, denoted by $D(r)$; note that $D$ can be seen as a first-order structure whose universe consists of the constants occurring in $D$ (the *active domain* of $D$).[4] The set of all databases on $\mathcal{DB}_{\mathcal{LP}}$ is denoted by $\mathbf{D}_{\mathcal{LP}}$.

Given a database $D \in \mathbf{D}_{\mathcal{LP}}$, $\mathcal{LP}_D$ denotes the following program:

$$\mathcal{LP}_D = \mathcal{LP} \cup \{r(t) \leftarrow\ |r \in \mathcal{DB}_{\mathcal{LP}} \wedge t \in D(r)\}.$$

---

[4] We use here active domain semantics (cf. [2]), rather then a setting in which a (finite) universe of $D$ is explicitly provided [16, 8, 30]. Note that Fagin's Theorem and all other results to which we refer remain valid in this (narrower) context; conversely, the results of this paper can be extended to that setting.

**Definition 8.** *A (bound DATALOG$^{\vee,\neg}$) query $Q$ is a pair $\langle \mathcal{LP}, G \rangle$, where $\mathcal{LP}$ is a DATALOG$^{\vee,\neg}$ program and $G$ is a ground literal (the query goal). Given a database $D$ in $\mathbf{D}_{\mathcal{LP}}$ and a class of models $\mathcal{XS}$, the $\exists_{\mathcal{XS}}$ (resp., $\forall_{\mathcal{XS}}$) answer of $Q$ on $D$ is true if $G$ is a $\exists_{\mathcal{XS}}$ (resp., $\forall_{\mathcal{XS}}$) inference of $\mathcal{LP}_D$ and false otherwise. The set of all queries is denoted by $\mathbf{Q}$.* ∎

The constants occurring in $\mathcal{LP}_D$, $G$ define the active domain of query $Q = \langle \mathcal{LP}, G \rangle$ on the database $D$.

A bound query paired with an answer (i.e., inference) mode defines a Boolean $C$-generic query of [2], i.e., a map from $\mathbf{D}_{\mathcal{LP}}$ to $\{true, false\}$. As common, we focus in our analysis of the expressive power of a query language on generic queries, which are those mappings whose result is invariant under renaming the constants in $D$ with constants from $U$. Genericity of a bound query $\langle \mathcal{LP}, G \rangle$ is assured by excluding constants in $\mathcal{LP}$ and $G$. As discussed in [2, p. 421], this issue is not central, and we assume in the sequel that constants do not occur in queries.

**Definition 9.** *Let $Q = \langle \mathcal{LP}, G \rangle$ be a (constant-free) query. Then the database collection of $Q$ w.r.t. the set of models $\mathcal{XS}$ is:*

(a) under the possibility ($\exists_{\mathcal{XS}}$) variant of semantics, *the set of all databases $D$ in $\mathbf{D}_{\mathcal{LP}}$ for which the $\exists_{\mathcal{XS}}$-answer of $Q$ is true, which is denoted by $\mathcal{EXP}^{\exists}_{\mathcal{XS}}(Q)$;*
(b) under the certainty ($\forall_{\mathcal{XS}}$) variant of semantics, *the set of all databases $D$ in $\mathbf{D}_{\mathcal{LP}}$ for which the $\forall_{\mathcal{XS}}$-answer of $Q$ is true, which is denoted by $\mathcal{EXP}^{\forall}_{\mathcal{XS}}(Q)$.*

*The expressive power of $\mathbf{Q}$ under a type of semantics w.r.t $\mathcal{XS}$ is the family of the database collections of all queries $Q$, i.e., $\mathcal{EXP}^{\exists}_{\mathcal{XS}}[\mathbf{Q}] = \{\mathcal{EXP}^{\exists}_{\mathcal{XS}}(Q) | Q \in \mathbf{Q}, Q \text{ constant-free}\}$ and $\mathcal{EXP}^{\forall}_{\mathcal{XS}}[\mathbf{Q}] = \{\mathcal{EXP}^{\forall}_{\mathcal{XS}}(Q) | Q \in \mathbf{Q}, Q \text{ constant-free}\}$.* ∎

The expressive power of each semantics will be related to database complexity classes, which are as follows. Let $C$ be a Turing machine complexity class (e.g., P or NP), $\mathbf{R}$ be a relational database scheme, and $\mathbf{D}$ be a set of databases on $\mathbf{R}$.[5] Then, $\mathbf{D}$ is *$C$-recognizable* if the problem of deciding whether $D \in \mathbf{D}$ for a given database $D$ on $\mathbf{R}$ is in $C$. The *database complexity class DB-C* is the family of all $C$-recognizable database collections. If the expressive power of a given semantics coincides with some class *DB-C*, we say that the given semantics *captures $C$*.

Recall that the classes $\Sigma^P_k$, $\Pi^P_k$ of the polynomial hierarchy [28] are defined by $\Sigma^P_0 = \text{P}$, $\Sigma^P_{i+1} = \text{NP}^{\Sigma^P_i}$, and $\Pi^P_i = \text{co-}\Sigma^P_i$, for all $i \geq 0$. In particular, $\Pi^P_0 = \text{P}$, $\Sigma^P_1 = \text{NP}$, and $\Pi^P_1 = \text{coNP}$. By Fagin's Theorem [16, 28], complexity and second-order definability are linked as follows.

**Proposition 10.** *([16, 28]) A database collection $\mathbf{D}$ over a scheme $\mathbf{R}$ is in DB-$\Sigma^P_k$, $k \geq 1$, iff it is definable by a second-order formula $(\exists \mathbf{A}_1)(\forall \mathbf{A}_2)\cdots(Q_k \mathbf{A}_k)\phi$ on $\mathbf{R}$, where the $\mathbf{A}_i$ are lists of predicate variables preceded by alternating quantifiers and $\phi$ is first-order.* ∎

---

[5] As usual, adopting the data independence principle, it is assumed that $\mathbf{D}$ generic, i.e., it is closed under renamings of the constants in $U$.

## 3.2 The Power of $\mathcal{PS}$ Semantics

In [11], it was shown that $\exists_{\mathcal{PS}}$ and $\forall_{\mathcal{PS}}$ inference from propositional programs is complete for the complexity classes $\Sigma_2^P$ and $\Pi_2^P$, respectively. In this section, we complement these complexity results by capturing results for $\Sigma_2^P$ and $\Pi_2^P$.

**Lemma 11.** *Let $\mathcal{LP}$ be a ground program, and let $M$ be an interpretation. Deciding whether $M \in \mathcal{PS}$ is coNP-complete.*

**Lemma 12.** [12] *Every DB-$\Sigma_2^P$-recognizable database collection $\mathbf{D}$ can be defined by a (constant-free) query $Q = \langle \mathcal{LP}, G \rangle$ under $\exists_{TS}$ semantics, where $\mathcal{LP}$ is stratified and $G$ is an atom.*

By the coincidence of T-stable and P-stable models on stratified programs, we thus obtain the following results.

**Theorem 13.** $\mathcal{EXP}^{\exists}_{\mathcal{PS}}[\mathbf{Q}] = DB\text{-}\Sigma_2^P$.

**Proof.** We first prove that for any query $Q = \langle \mathcal{LP}, G \rangle$ in $\mathbf{Q}$, recognizing whether a database $D$ is in $\mathcal{EXP}^{\exists}_{\mathcal{PS}}(Q)$ is in $\Sigma_2^P$. $D$ is in $\mathcal{EXP}^{\exists}_{\mathcal{PS}}(Q)$ iff there exists a P-stable model $M$ of $\mathcal{LP}_D$ such that $G \in M$. To check this, we may guess an interpretation $M$ of $\mathcal{LP}_D$ and verify that: (i) $M$ is a P-stable model of $\mathcal{LP}_D$, and (ii) $G \in M$. By virtue of Lemma 11, (i) is done by a single call to an NP oracle (note that, since $Q$ is fixed, $ground(\mathcal{LP}_D)$ has size polynomial in $D$, and can be constructed in polynomial time), and (ii) is clearly polynomial. Hence, this problem is in $\Sigma_2^P$. Consequently, recognizing whether a database $D$ is in $\mathcal{EXP}^{\exists}_{\mathcal{PS}}(Q)$ is in $\Sigma_2^P$.

By Proposition 4 and Lemma 12, it follows immediately that every $\Sigma_2^P$-recognizable database collection $\mathbf{D}$ is in $\mathcal{EXP}^{\exists}_{\mathcal{PS}}[\mathbf{Q}]$. ∎

**Theorem 14.** $\mathcal{EXP}^{\forall}_{\mathcal{PS}}[\mathbf{Q}] = DB\text{-}\Pi_2^P$.

**Proof.** We first prove that for any query $Q = \langle \mathcal{LP}, G \rangle$ in $\mathbf{Q}$, recognizing whether a database $D$ is in $\mathcal{EXP}^{\forall}_{\mathcal{PS}}(Q)$ is in $\Pi_2^P$. Consider the complementary problem: Is $D$ *is not* in $\mathcal{EXP}^{\forall}_{\mathcal{PS}}(Q)$? Now, $D$ is not in $\mathcal{EXP}^{\forall}_{\mathcal{PS}}(Q)$ iff there exists a P-stable model $M$ of $\mathcal{LP}_D$ such that $G \notin M$. Following the line of the proof of Theorem 13, we can easily see that the latter problem is in $\Sigma_2^P$. Hence, deciding $D \in \mathcal{EXP}^{\forall}_{\mathcal{PS}}(Q)$ is in $\Pi_2^P$.

That every $\Pi_2^P$-recognizable database collection $\mathbf{D}$ is in $\mathcal{EXP}^{\forall}_{\mathcal{PS}}[\mathbf{Q}]$ is derived from Lemma 12 and Proposition 4. By these results, there exists a query $Q = \langle \mathcal{LP}, G \rangle$ with stratified $\mathcal{LP}$, whose $\exists_{\mathcal{PS}}$ answer is true on a database $D$ iff $D$ *is not* in $\mathbf{D}$. Let $Q' = \langle \mathcal{LP}', G' \rangle$ where $G'$ is a new propositional atom and $\mathcal{LP}' = \mathcal{LP} \cup \{G' \leftarrow \neg G\}$.

It is now easy to see that $G'$ is a $\forall_{\mathcal{PS}}$ inference of $\mathcal{LP}_D$ iff $G$ is not a $\exists_{\mathcal{PS}}$ inference of $\mathcal{LP}_D$, i.e., $D \in \mathbf{D}$. Consequently, $\mathcal{EXP}^{\forall}_{\mathcal{PS}}(Q') = \mathbf{D}$. ∎

It is worth noting that, under certainty semantics, the addition of disjunction increases the power of P-stable models by two levels in the polynomial hierarchy. Indeed, on normal programs $\forall_{\mathcal{PS}}$ semantics coincides with well-founded semantics, which expresses only a strict subset of the polynomial queries (cf. [2]).

## 3.3 The Power of $\mathcal{MS}$ Semantics

We next determine the expressive power of M-stable models, and start with the possibility semantics. As for normal programs [24], under the possibility semantics, the expressive power of M-stable models coincides with the expressive power of T-stable models.

**Theorem 15.** $\mathcal{EXP}_{\mathcal{MS}}^{\exists}[Q] = DB\text{-}\Sigma_2^P$.

In order to determine the expressive power of M-stable models under certainty semantics, we need to establish the complexity of recognizing M-stable models.

**Theorem 16.** *Let $\mathcal{LP}$ be a fixed program. Given a database $D$ on $\mathcal{DB}_{\mathcal{LP}}$ and an interpretation $M$ for $\mathcal{LP}_D$, deciding whether $M$ is an M-stable model for $\mathcal{LP}_D$ is $\Pi_2^P$-complete.*

**Proof.** (Sketch) We omit the membership part and consider the hardness part. Let $\mathcal{LP}$ be stratified and $\neg q$ be a ground literal where $q$ is an atom. Lemma 12 implies that deciding, given $D$, whether $\neg q$ is true in every T-stable model of $\mathcal{LP}_D$ is $\Pi_2^P$-hard (cf. also [12]). We reduce this problem in polynomial time to our problem. Let $\mathcal{LP}'$ be the program obtained from $\mathcal{LP}$ by the following steps:

(i) insert $\neg p$ in the body of each rule in $\mathcal{LP}$, where $p$ is a new propositional letter;

(ii) add the rules $p \leftarrow \neg q, \neg p$ and $q \leftarrow p$;

(iii) for each IDB predicate $s$ of $\mathcal{LP}$, add the rules
$$s(X_1, ..., X_n) \leftarrow \neg s(X_1, ..., X_n), \neg q \text{ and } s(X_1, ..., X_n) \leftarrow p.$$

Fix a database $D$ over $\mathcal{DB}_{\mathcal{LP}}$. Program $\mathcal{LP}'_D$ has a P-stable model on $D$, which is obtained if all ground atoms over IDB predicates are undefined. More precisely, let $A = \{r(t) \mid r \in \mathcal{DB}_{\mathcal{LP}}, t \in D(r)\}$ be the set of facts stored in the extensional database and $B$ the Herbrand Base $B_{\mathcal{LP}'_D}$ of $\mathcal{LP}'_D$ restricted to the database predicates (i.e., the predicates in $\mathcal{DB}_{\mathcal{LP}}$). Intuitively (and as easy to prove), $M = A \cup \neg.(B - A)$ is contained in every P-stable model of $\mathcal{LP}'_D$. In fact, it can be shown that $M$ itself is a P-stable model of $\mathcal{LP}'_D$.

On the other hand, it is immediate that $M$ is included in every P-stable model. It thus follows that $M$ is M-stable iff there exists no other P-stable model of $\mathcal{LP}'_D$. It can be shown that this is the case iff $\neg q$ is true in every T-stable model of $\mathcal{LP}'_D$. This implies that, given $M$ and $D$, deciding whether $M$ is an M-stable model of $\mathcal{LP}'_D$ is $\Pi_2^P$-hard. ∎

Thus, while recognizing P-stable models is in coNP, recognizing M-stable models is one level higher up in the polynomial hierarchy.

From this result, it is intuitive that the expressive power of certainty semantics using M-stable models is precisely one level higher up in the polynomial hierarchy than certainty semantics using P-stable models. This is actually the case.

**Theorem 17.** $\mathcal{EXP}^{\forall}_{\mathcal{MS}}[\mathbf{Q}] = DB\text{-}\Pi^P_3$.

**Proof.** (Sketch) Deciding whether there is any M-stable model $M$ of $\mathcal{LP}_D$ such that $G \notin \mathcal{LP}_D$ is in $\Sigma^P_3$; to solve that problem, guess an interpretation $M$ and use a $\Sigma^P_2$ oracle to check whether $M$ is not M-stable (cf. Theorem 16); if not (i.e., $M$ is M-stable), we check in polynomial time whether $G \in M$. It follows that recognizing whether a database $D$ is in $\mathcal{EXP}^{\forall}_{\mathcal{MS}}(\mathcal{Q})$ is in $\Pi^P_3$.

Let us now prove that every $\Pi^P_3$ recognizable database collection $\mathbf{D}$ on a database scheme $\mathcal{DB}$ is in $\mathcal{EXP}^{\forall}_{\mathcal{MS}}[\mathbf{Q}]$. By Proposition 10, $\mathbf{D}$ is definable by a second-order formula $(\forall \mathbf{A})\Psi$, where $\Psi$ is a $\Sigma^1_2$ formula over $\mathcal{DB}$ and $\mathbf{A} = a_1, \ldots, a_k$ is a list of predicate variables. Let $\mathcal{DB}'$ be $\mathcal{DB}$ extended with $\mathbf{A}$, and let $\mathbf{D}'$ be the collection of all databases $D' = (D, \mathbf{A})$ over $\mathcal{DB}'$ such that $D$ is from $\mathbf{D}$ and $D' \models \Psi.$[6] Clearly, a database $D$ on $\mathcal{DB}$ belongs to $\mathbf{D}$ iff every database $D' = (D, \mathbf{A})$ over $\mathcal{DB}'$ whose the relations $\mathbf{A}$ are drawn from the active domain of $D$ belongs to $\mathbf{D}'$. Note that by the results in [28], $\mathbf{D}'$ is $\Sigma^P_2$-recognizable. We use this to exhibit a query $Q1$ such that $\mathcal{EXP}^{\forall}_{\mathcal{MS}}(Q1)$ defines $\mathbf{D}$.

First, we show that there is a query $Q0 = \langle \mathcal{LP}0, G0 \rangle$ such that, given a database $D'$ on $\mathcal{DB}'$, the $\exists_{\mathcal{MS}}$ answer of $Q0$ is yes iff $D'$ belongs to $\mathbf{D}'$. $\mathcal{LP}0$ is program $\mathcal{LP}'$ from the proof of Theorem 16 and $G0 = \neg p$. Then, we use $Q0$ to construct a query $Q1 = \langle \mathcal{LP}1, G1 \rangle$ which defines $\mathbf{D}$. $\mathcal{LP}1$ results from $\mathcal{LP}0$ by adding the clause

$$a(X_1, \ldots, X_n) \vee \hat{a}(X_1, \ldots, X_n) \leftarrow$$

for each predicate $a$ from $\mathbf{A}$, where $\hat{a}$ is a new predicate of the same arity. These clauses simulate all possible choices for the predicates in $\mathbf{A}$, and generate all possible extensions $D' = (D, \mathbf{A})$ of $D$. By choosing $G1 = \neg p$, the $\forall_{\mathcal{MS}}$ answer of $Q1 = \langle \mathcal{LP}1, G1 \rangle$ is yes for database $D$ on $\mathcal{DB}$ iff $D$ belongs to $\mathbf{D}$, i.e., $\mathcal{EXP}^{\forall}_{\mathcal{MS}}(Q1) = \mathbf{D}$. ∎

Therefore, while the certainty variant of P-stable semantics has dual complexity compared to the possibility semantics, the certainty semantics based on M-stable models has higher complexity than the possibility semantics.

### 3.4 The Power of $\mathcal{LS}$ Semantics

The expressiveness of the $\forall_{\mathcal{LS}}$ semantics coincides with the expressiveness of the $\forall_{\mathcal{MS}}$ semantics. This is intuitive, since recognizing L-stable models has the same complexity as recognizing M-stable models.

**Theorem 18.** *Let $\mathcal{LP}$ be a fixed program. Give a database $D$ on $\mathcal{DB}_{\mathcal{LP}}$ and an interpretation $M$ for $\mathcal{LP}_D$, deciding whether $M$ is an L-stable model for $\mathcal{LP}_D$ is $\Pi^P_2$-complete.*

However, the query $Q1$ constructed in the proof of Theorem 17 does not serve to show that L-stable models can express all of $DB\text{-}\Pi^P_3$ under the certainty

---

[6] Here, the universe of $D'$ as a structure consists of the constants occurring in its relations.

semantics. The reason is that M-stable models $M_1$ and $M_2$ corresponding to different choices for the predicates $\mathbf{A}$, i.e., $M1 \not\subseteq M2 \not\subseteq M1$ may be comparable with respect to L-stability, e.g. $\overline{M_1} \subseteq \overline{M_2}$ is possible. A slight extension of the construction is sufficient to prove the expected result.

**Theorem 19.** $\mathcal{EXP}_{\mathcal{LS}}^{\forall}[\mathbf{Q}] = DB\text{-}\Pi_3^P$.

**Proof.** (Sketch) The membership part is analogous to the one of Theorem 17.

To prove that every $\Pi_3^P$-recognizable database collection $\mathbf{D}$ on a DB-scheme $\mathcal{DB}$ is in $\mathcal{EXP}_{\mathcal{MS}}^{\forall}[\mathbf{Q}]$, consider the query $Q1 = \langle \mathcal{LP}1, G1 \rangle$ in the proof of Theorem 17. Construct $\mathcal{LP}2$ from $\mathcal{LP}1$ by adding for the clauses $a(X_1, \ldots, X_n) \vee \hat{a}(X_1, \ldots, X_n) \leftarrow$ implementing the possible choices for $\mathbf{A}$, the following clauses:

$$\tilde{a}(X_1, \ldots, X_n) \leftarrow a(X_1, \ldots, X_n)$$
$$\hat{a}(X_1, \ldots, X_n) \leftarrow u$$
$$\tilde{a}(X_1, \ldots, X_n) \leftarrow u$$
$$u \leftarrow \neg u$$

These additional clauses serve to destroy the symmetry between the two possible choices for satisfying $a(X_1, \ldots, X_n) \vee \hat{a}(X_1, \ldots, X_n) \leftarrow$ in a P-stable model. After the addition of the above clauses, there are two P-stable models: $\{a(t), \tilde{a}(t)\}$ and $\{\neg a(t), \hat{a}(t)\}$, which are not comparable with respect to L-stability. By choosing $G2 = G1$, for any database $D$ the $\forall_{\mathcal{LS}}$ answer of the query $Q2 = \langle \mathcal{LP}2, G2 \rangle$ coincides with the $\forall_{\mathcal{MS}}$ answer of $Q1$. Consequently, $\mathbf{D} \in \mathcal{EXP}_{\mathcal{LS}}^{\forall}(Q2)$. ∎

Now let us consider possibility semantics. The expressiveness of $\exists_{\mathcal{MS}}$ semantics does not carry over to $\exists_{\mathcal{LS}}$ semantics. In fact, $\exists_{\mathcal{LS}}$ is more expressive than $\exists_{\mathcal{MS}}$. The reason is that it is not always possible to reach from an arbitrary P-stable model an L-stable model by successively adding literals. Thus, while in the case of M-stable models, possibility semantics only needs to inspect P-stability of a model, in the case of L-stable models the property of L-stability of P-stable models has to be taken into account.

**Theorem 20.** $\mathcal{EXP}_{\mathcal{LS}}^{\exists}[\mathbf{Q}] = DB\text{-}\Sigma_3^P$.

**Proof.** (Sketch) $D$ is in $\mathcal{EXP}_{\mathcal{LS}}^{\exists}(\mathcal{Q})$ iff there exists some L-stable model $M$ of $\mathcal{LP}_D$ such that $G$ belongs to $M$. A guess for $M$ can be verified in polynomial time with a single call to an $\Sigma_2^P$ oracle by Theorem 18. Thus, deciding whether $D \in \mathcal{EXP}_{\mathcal{LS}}^{\exists}(\mathcal{Q})$ is in $\Sigma_3^P$.

It remains to show that every $\Sigma_3^P$-recognizable database collection $\mathbf{D}$ on a database scheme $\mathcal{DB}$ is in $\mathcal{EXP}_{\mathcal{LS}}^{\exists}[\mathbf{Q}]$. Let $\mathbf{D}' = \overline{\mathbf{D}}$ be the complementary database collection on $\mathcal{DB}$, and consider the query $Q2 = \langle \mathcal{LP}2, G2 \rangle$ from the proof of Theorem 19, constructed for $\mathbf{D}'$ (which is in $\Pi_3^P$). Then, for any database $D$ on $\mathcal{DB}$, $D \notin \overline{\mathbf{D}}$ (i.e., $D \in \mathbf{D}$) iff $D \notin \mathcal{EXP}_{\mathcal{LS}}^{\forall}(Q2)$ iff $G2$ does not belong to some L-stable model $M$ of $\mathcal{LP}2_D$.

Construct $\mathcal{LP}3$ by adding the following clauses to $\mathcal{LP}2$:

$$a \vee b \leftarrow \neg p, \quad b \leftarrow p, \quad c \leftarrow \neg a, d, \quad d \leftarrow \neg d$$

Here, $a$, $b$, $c$ and $d$ are new propositional atoms. $\mathcal{LP}3_D$ has an L-stable model containing $\neg a$ iff $\mathcal{LP}2_D$ has some L-stable model not containing $\neg p$. It follows that for $G3 = \neg a$, the query $Q3 = \langle \mathcal{LP}3, G3 \rangle$ satisfies $\mathcal{EXP}^{\exists}_{\mathcal{LS}}(Q3) = \mathbf{D}$. ∎

## 3.5 The Power of $\mathcal{RS}$ Semantics

The definition of regular model is in the spirit of the definition of M-stable model (select the maximal models from a collection of models w.r.t. inclusion), but is based on a weaker notion of model. However, the expressive power of regular models is the same.

**Theorem 21.** $\mathcal{EXP}^{\exists}_{\mathcal{RS}}[\mathbf{Q}] = DB\text{-}\Sigma_2^P$.

Prior to the result on certainty expressibility, we note the complexity of recognizing regular models.

**Theorem 22.** *Let $\mathcal{LP}$ be a fixed program. Given a database $D$ on $\mathcal{DB}_{\mathcal{LP}}$, and an interpretation $M$ for $\mathcal{LP}_D$, deciding whether $M$ is a regular model for $\mathcal{LP}_D$ is $\Pi_2^P$-complete.*

**Theorem 23.** $\mathcal{EXP}^{\forall}_{\mathcal{RS}}[\mathbf{Q}] = DB\text{-}\Pi_3^P$.

**Proof.** (Sketch) The membership part is clear from Theorem 22. For the expressiveness part, use the query $Q1 = \langle \mathcal{LP}1, G1 \rangle$ in the proof of Theorem 17; the $\forall_{\mathcal{MS}}$ answer is identical to the $\forall_{\mathcal{RS}}$ answer. ∎

# 4 The Impact of Disjunction and Negation

The previous section gave a complete description of the expressive power and complexity of evaluating queries $Q = \langle \mathcal{LP}, G \rangle$ based on $DATALOG^{\vee, \neg}$ programs $\mathcal{LP}$ that resort to partial model semantics. An interesting issue is the impact of syntactical restrictions on the query programs $\mathcal{LP}$. In particular, comparing the power of disjunction with the power of negation is intriguing [12].

In an account of this issue, we focus here on the most powerful concepts of partial models, which are those that minimize undefinedness, and discuss queries whose programs make limited use of disjunction and negation. Starting from normal positive programs (i.e., pure datalog programs), we consider the effect of allowing the (combined) use of the following constructs:

- stratified negation ($\neg_s$)
- arbitrary negation ($\neg$)
- headcycle-free disjunction [5] ($\vee_h$)
- arbitrary disjunction ($\vee$)

Headcycle-free disjunction is a syntactical property of programs that gives no account to negation. A program $\mathcal{LP}$ is *headcycle-free* iff there are no two distinct atoms $a, b \in B_{\mathcal{LP}}$ such that $a$ and $b$ are on a negation-free cycle of the dependency graph of $ground(\mathcal{LP})$ (i.e., $a$ and $b$ mutually depend on each other without negation) and $a, b$ occur together in the head of some clause of $ground(\mathcal{LP})$. It is known that admitting headcycle-free disjunction besides full negation does not increase the complexity of T-stable models. The following proposition, which is implicit in [5], is straightforward from the fact that checking whether a total model of a positive headcycle-free program is minimal is polynomial [6].

**Proposition 24.** *(cf. [5, 6]) Let $\mathcal{LP}$ be a ground (i.e., propositional) headcycle-free program and let $M$ be an interpretation of it. Then, deciding if $M$ is a T-stable model of $\mathcal{LP}$ is polynomial.*

We say that a query $Q = \langle \mathcal{LP}, G \rangle$ uses *headcycle-free disjunction* iff $\mathcal{LP}$ is disjunctive and $\mathcal{LP}_D$ is headcycle-free for each $D$, and similarly that $Q$ is *(locally) stratified* iff $\mathcal{LP}_D$ is (locally) stratified for each $D$.

The expressive power of headcycle-free, stratified queries (that we denote by $Q_{\vee_h, \neg_s}$) has been investigated in [6] in a different setting. There, it is shown that every polynomial time computable output-query (a query that computes an output relation) can be "weakly expressed" in $Q_{\vee_h, \neg_s}$ using T-stable models, i.e., the query result is given by some T-stable model; if the input databases are ordered, it can be expressed in a stronger sense, i.e., the result is given by every T-stable model. Notice that such a notion of semantics is in general different from the usual notion of certainty or possibility inference. For bound (i.e., boolean) queries, weak expressibility coincides with possibility inference. Notice that the expressive power of headcycle-free stratified bound queries is higher than $DB$-P, and in fact $DB$-NP (see Figure 2).

By $Q_{np}$ we denote the set of queries $Q = \langle \mathcal{LP}, G \rangle$ such that $\mathcal{LP}$ is a normal positive program; for any combination $X$ of constructs from above, we denote by $Q_X$ the extension of $Q_{np}$ in $Q$ where the constructs in $X$ may be used in query programs. Note that the programs in $Q_\vee$ and $Q_{\vee_h}$ are $\neg$-free, while the programs in $Q_\neg$ and $Q_{\neg_s}$ are $\vee$-free.

The inclusion order diagrams of the resulting different fragments of $Q$, together with their expressive powers under $\exists_{\mathcal{XS}}$ and $\forall_{\mathcal{XS}}$ inference, where $\mathcal{XS}$ is from $\mathcal{LS}, \mathcal{MS}, \mathcal{RS}$, are displayed in Figure 2. Notice that different combinations $X$ may give rise to the same fragment (e.g., $X = \vee, \vee_h, \neg, \neg_s$ and $X' = \vee, \neg$); we have chosen for each fragment the smallest $X$ as a representative.

There are two main observations on the diagrams. First, the diagrams for $\exists_{\mathcal{LS}}$ inference differs from the diagram for $\exists_{\mathcal{MS}}$ and $\exists_{\mathcal{RS}}$ inference only on the three points along the right upper part of the outline (that is, on $Q_{\vee, \neg}$, $Q_{\vee_h, \neg}$, and $Q_\neg$). Coincidence on the remaining part is an immediate consequence of the coincidence of L-stable, M-stable and regular models on locally stratified programs (see Proposition 4), since in the respective fragments of $Q$ at most locally stratified negation can be used. Second, the diagram for $\forall_{\mathcal{LS}}$, $\forall_{\mathcal{MS}}$, and $\forall_{\mathcal{RS}}$ inference is the same and just symmetric to the diagram for $\exists_{\mathcal{LS}}$ inference.

For the fragments that allow at most locally stratified negation, this is an easy consequence of the facts that the concepts of models coincide to T-stable models, that always a T-stable model exists and that on any database $D$, the $\exists_{TS}$ answer of $\langle \mathcal{LP}, L \rangle$ is opposite to the $\forall_{TS}$ answer of $\langle \mathcal{LP}, \neg L \rangle$.

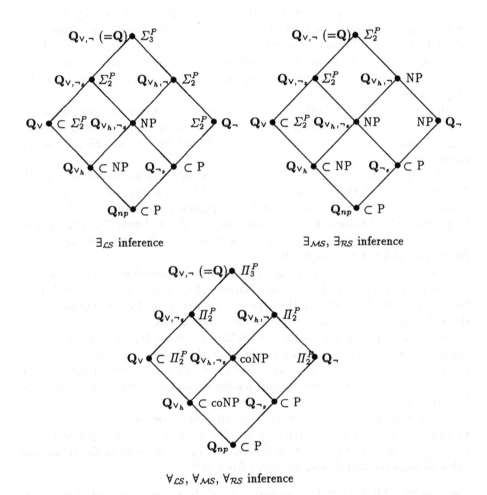

**Fig. 2.** Expressive power of queries based on partial models minimizing undefinedness (complexity class $C$ stands for $DB$-$C$)

Observe also that each of $DB$-$\Sigma_i^P$ and $DB$-$\Pi_i^P$ for $i = 1, 2, 3$ is expressed by at least one fragment. On the other hand, some fragments, namely $\mathbf{Q}_{\neg_s}$, $\mathbf{Q}_\mathsf{V}$ and the more restrictive fragments, allow to express only a strict subclass of the respective classes $DB$-$C$; however, they include queries that are hard for $C$.

An example of a nonexpressible query for all these fragments is the Even-

Constants query, which tells whether a given database $D$ on a fixed scheme $\mathcal{DB}$ contains an even number of constants. (See [14] for a proof.)

**Proposition 25.** *The Even-Constants query can not be expressed in* $\mathbf{Q}_\vee \cup \mathbf{Q}_{\neg_s}$ *using* $\exists_{\mathcal{XS}}$ *or* $\forall_{\mathcal{XS}}$ *inference, for any* $\mathcal{XS}$ *from* $\mathcal{PS}, \mathcal{TS}, \mathcal{MS}, \mathcal{LS}$, *and* $\mathcal{RS}$.

Let us verify the upper bounds for the expressive powers of the fragments. We first consider the fragments in which no negation or only stratified negation $\neg_s$ is allowed. Note that T-stable, L-stable, M-stable, and regular models coincide on the programs of such queries. Since each of these fragment expresses under $\exists_{\mathcal{TS}}$ inference just the complement of the queries under $\forall_{\mathcal{TS}}$ inference, we consider only $\exists$ inference in the sequel.

Restricting $\vee$ to $\vee_h$ besides restricting $\neg$ to $\neg_s$ leads to a decrease in expressive power. In fact, only queries in $DB$-NP can be expressed in $\mathbf{Q}_{\vee_h}$ using $\exists_{\mathcal{TS}}$ inference. On the other hand, if $\neg_s$ is allowed, then all of $DB$-NP can be expressed.

The expressive power of $\mathbf{Q}_{np}$ and $\mathbf{Q}_{\neg_s}$ has been studied extensively (see [21, 2]). Notice that on these fragments, $\exists_{\mathcal{TS}}$ coincides with $\forall_{\mathcal{TS}}$, since $\mathcal{TS}$ contains a single model. It is well-known that $\mathbf{Q}_{\neg_s}$ expresses a strict subset of $DB$-P (in fact, even a strict subset of the fixpoint-queries [22]), and that $\mathbf{Q}_{np}$ can express only monotonic queries (see [2] for monotonic queries). Thus, $\mathbf{Q}_{\vee_h}$ and $\mathbf{Q}_{\neg_s}$ allow for queries of different complexity.[7]

It remains to consider the fragments in which full negation $\neg$ is allowed. The results for the top elements in the diagrams $(\mathbf{Q}_{\vee,\neg})$ have been established in Section 3, while the results on the expressive power of $\mathbf{Q}_\neg$ for $\mathcal{LS}, \mathcal{MS}$ have been derived in [24]; by Proposition 5, they carry over to $\mathcal{RS}$.

In order to justify the results for the last fragment $\mathbf{Q}_{\vee_h,\neg}$ that we have to consider, it suffices to show that for each mode of inference, query-recognizability has the same upper bound as on $\mathbf{Q}_\neg$. The key result is that recognizing P-stable models of a program does not become harder if besides negation also headcycle-free disjunction is allowed.

For any program $\mathcal{LP}$ and interpretation $I$ of it, denote by $red(\mathcal{LP}, I)$ the program obtained from $ground(\mathcal{LP})$ as follows: (1) Remove every rule $r$ such that $H(r) \cap M^+ \neq \emptyset$ or $B^-(r)$ is false in $M$; (2) Remove from the remaining rules all negative literals and all atoms from $M^+$.

**Lemma 26.** [14] *Let* $\mathcal{LP}$ *be a program and* $M$ *be a founded model of* $P$. *Then,* $M$ *is a P-stable model of* $\mathcal{LP}$ *iff* $\overline{M} = N^+$ *for some* $N \in \mathrm{MM}^+(red(\mathcal{LP}, M))$.

Using this lemma, it is straightforward to generalize Proposition 24 to P-stable models. The lower complexity of recognizing T-stable and P-stable models

---

[7] In fact the expressive powers of $\mathbf{Q}_{\vee_h}$ and $\mathbf{Q}_{\neg_s}$ are incomparable: the collection of 3-colorable graphs can be defined in $\mathbf{Q}_{\vee_h}$ using $\exists$-inference, but not in $\mathbf{Q}_{\neg_s}$ (since $\mathbf{Q}_{\neg_s}$ resorts to a fragment of $L^\omega_{\infty,\omega}$, in which 3-colorability can not be defined [9]). On the other hand, e.g. a query whether two relations $R_1, R_2$ contain the same tuples is simple in $\mathbf{Q}_{\neg_s}$, while it is impossible in $\mathbf{Q}_{\vee_h}$ (the proof is easy with a weak monotonicity property of $DATALOG^\vee$ query programs from [12]).

entails also lower complexity for recognizing M-stable, L-stable models, and regular models (due to lower complexity of recognizing minimal models for headcycle-free, positive programs).

**Proposition 27.** *Let $\mathcal{LP}$ be a ground (i.e., propositional) headcycle-free program and let $M$ be an interpretation of it. Then, deciding if (i) $M \in \mathcal{PS}$ is polynomial; and (ii) $M \in \mathcal{XS}$ is in coNP, for $\mathcal{XS}$ from $\mathcal{LS}, \mathcal{MS}$, and $\mathcal{RS}$.*

**Proof.** *(i)*: By Lemma 26, $M$ is P-stable iff (1) $M$ is a model of $\mathcal{LP}$, (2) $M$ is founded (i.e., $M^+ = N_1^+$ for some $N_1 \in \mathrm{MM}^+(\mathcal{LP}(M))$), and (3) $\overline{M}^+ = N_2^+$ for some $N_2 \in \mathrm{MM}^+(red(\mathcal{LP}, M))$.

Notice that $\mathcal{LP}(M)$ and $red(\mathcal{LP}, M)$ are headcycle-free, positive, and polynomial-time constructible. It follows from Proposition 24 that the tests (2) and (3) can be performed in polynomial time.

*(ii)*: For $\mathcal{MS}$ and $\mathcal{LS}$, this follows easily from (i), and for $\mathcal{RS}$, from Proposition 24 and the fact that $\mathcal{LP}(M)$ is positive and headcycle-free. ∎

The data complexity of each query language $\mathbf{Q}_X$ in Figure 2 is completeness for the complexity class $C$ where $DB\text{-}C$ is the upper (resp. precise) bound for the expressiveness in the figure. (In case of $DB\text{-}P$, completeness is via logspace reductions.) The expression complexity of each fragment parallels the data complexity in the exponential analogue (EXPTIME, NEXP $= \Sigma_1^E$, NEXP$^{\mathrm{NP}} = \Sigma_2^E, \ldots$) of the class for the data complexity (P, NP $= \Sigma_1^P$, NP$^{\mathrm{NP}} = \Sigma_2^P, \ldots$).

# 5 Conclusion

Our results on the expressibility and complexity of partial model semantics in the general case, complemented by previously known results for total stable (T-stable) models [12, 11], are compactly represented in Table 1. Proofs for all results are in the full paper [14]. Each entry of a complexity class $C$ symbolizes $C$-completeness, and each entry $DB\text{-}C$ that $C$ is captured.

The high complexity of inference using L-stable models ($\Sigma_3^P$ resp. $\Pi_3^P$) is intuitively due to three sources of complexity that interact, in a sense, orthogonally: (1) the (possibly exponential) number of L-stable models; (2) the P-stability condition for a model; and, (3) the condition of minimal undefinedness. Similar intuitions underly the other kinds of models.

The results complement and extend previous results on disjunctive datalog and partial models for normal programs. They show that syntactic restrictions on query programs result in a broad spectrum of complexity classes that can be captured. In this context, interesting research issues remain to be addressed. One such issue are further syntactic restrictions and their effect on expressiveness and complexity. Another issue is to identify fragments of the language on which concepts of models coincide; in particular, fragments that extend locally stratified programs are interesting.

Certainty and possibility inference also appear in the context of incomplete information, cf. [15, 19, 2]. In a sense, models of a program can be seen as

| | P-Stable | T-Stable | M-Stable | L-stable | Regular |
|---|---|---|---|---|---|
| (a) Recognition and Existence for propositional (ground) programs | | | | | |
| Recognition | coNP | coNP | $\Pi_2^P$ | $\Pi_2^P$ | $\Pi_2^P$ |
| Existence | $\Sigma_2^P$ | $\Sigma_2^P$ | $\Sigma_2^P$ | $\Sigma_2^P$ | guaranteed |
| (b) Expressive Power | | | | | |
| Possibility | $DB\text{-}\Sigma_2^P$ | $DB\text{-}\Sigma_2^P$ | $DB\text{-}\Sigma_2^P$ | $DB\text{-}\Sigma_3^P$ | $DB\text{-}\Sigma_2^P$ |
| Certainty | $DB\text{-}\Pi_2^P$ | $DB\text{-}\Pi_2^P$ | $DB\text{-}\Pi_3^P$ | $DB\text{-}\Pi_3^P$ | $DB\text{-}\Pi_3^P$ |
| (c) Data Complexity | | | | | |
| Possibility | $\Sigma_2^P$ | $\Sigma_2^P$ | $\Sigma_2^P$ | $\Sigma_3^P$ | $\Sigma_2^P$ |
| Certainty | $\Pi_2^P$ | $\Pi_2^P$ | $\Pi_3^P$ | $\Pi_3^P$ | $\Pi_3^P$ |
| (d) Program Complexity | | | | | |
| Possibility | $NEXP^{NP}$ | $NEXP^{NP}$ | $NEXP^{NP}$ | $NEXP^{\Sigma_2^P}$ | $NEXP^{NP}$ |
| Certainty | $coNEXP^{NP}$ | $coNEXP^{NP}$ | $coNEXP^{\Sigma_2^P}$ | $coNEXP^{\Sigma_2^P}$ | $coNEXP^{\Sigma_2^P}$ |

**Table 1.** *Expressibility and complexity results on partial models*

"possible worlds", cf. [3, 19]. There might be interesting connections between partial models and this area, whose investigation remains for further work.

# References

1. A. Abiteboul, E. Simon, and V. Vianu. Non-Deterministic Languages to Express Deterministic Transformations. In *Proc. PODS-90*, pp. 218–229, 1990.
2. S. Abiteboul, R. Hull, and V. Vianu. *Foundations of Databases*. Addison-Wesley, 1995.
3. S. Abiteboul, P. Kanellakis, and G. Grahne. On the Representation and Querying of Sets of Possible Worlds. *Theoretical Computer Science*, 78:159–187, 1991.
4. C. Baral and V. Subrahmanian. Stable and Extension Class Theory for Logic Programs and Default Logic. *Journal of Automated Reasoning*, 8:345–366, 1992.
5. R. Ben-Eliyahu and R. Dechter. Propositional Semantics for Disjunctive Logic Programs. *Annals of Mathematics and Artificial Intelligence*, 12:53–87, 1994.
6. R. Ben-Eliyahu and L. Palopoli. Reasoning with Minimal Models: Efficient Algorithms and Applications. In *Proc. KR-94*, pp. 39–50, 1994.
7. S. Ceri, G. Gottlob, and L. Tanca. *Logic Programming and Databases*. 1990.
8. A. Chandra and D. Harel. Structure and Complexity of Relational Queries. *Journal of Computer and System Sciences*, 25:99–128, 1982.
9. A. Dawar. A Restricted Second Order Logic for Finite Structures. In D. Leivant, editor, *Proc. Intl Workshop LCC '94*, LNCS 960, 1995.
10. P. Dung. Negation as Hypotheses: An Abductive Foundation for Logic Programming. In *Proc. ICLP-91*, pp. 3–17. MIT Press, 1991.

11. T. Eiter and G. Gottlob. On the Computational Cost of Disjunctive Logic Programming: Propositional Case. *Annals of Mathematics and Artificial Intelligence*, 15(3/4):289–323, 1995.

12. T. Eiter, G. Gottlob, and H. Mannila. Adding Disjunction to Datalog. In *Proc. PODS-94*, pp. 267–278, May 1994.

13. T. Eiter, N. Leone, and D. Saccà. On the Partial Semantics for Disjunctive Deductive Databases. *Annals of Mathematics and Artificial Intelligence*, to appear, CD-TR 95/82, CD-Lab for Expert Systems, TU Vienna, August 1995.

14. T. Eiter, N. Leone, and D. Saccà. Expressive Power and Complexity of Partial Models for Disjunctive Deductive Databases. Technical Report CD-TR 95/83, Christian Doppler Laboratory for Expert Systems, TU Vienna, August 1995.

15. D. W. Etherington. *Reasoning with Incomplete Information*. Morgan Kaufmann Publishers, Inc., Los Altos, 1988.

16. R. Fagin. Generalized First-Order Spectra and Polynomial-Time Recognizable Sets. In R. M. Karp, editor, *Complexity of Computation*, pp. 43–74. AMS, 1974.

17. M. Gelfond and V. Lifschitz. The Stable Model Semantics for Logic Programming. In *Logic Programming: Proc. Fifth Intl Conference and Symposium*, pp. 1070–1080, MIT Press, 1988.

18. G. Gottlob. Complexity and Expressive Power of Disjunctive Logic Programming. In M. Bruynooghe, editor, *Proc. ILPS-94*, pp. 23–42, Ithaca NY, 1994. MIT Press.

19. G. Grahne. *The Problem of Incomplete Information in Relational Databases*, LNCS 554, 1991.

20. A. Kakas and P. Mancarella. Preferred Extensions are Partial Stable Models. *Journal of Logic Programming*, 14:341–348, 1992.

21. P. Kanellakis. Elements of Relational Database Theory. In J. van Leeuwen, editor, *Handbook of TCS (B)*, 1990.

22. P. Kolaitis. The Expressive Power of Stratified Logic Programs. *Information and Computation*, 90:50–66, 1991.

23. T. Przymusinski. Stable Semantics for Disjunctive Programs. *New Generation Computing*, 9:401–424, 1991.

24. D. Saccá. The Expressive Powers of Stable Models for Bound and Unbound DATALOG Queries. *Journal of Computer and System Sciences*. To appear.

25. D. Saccá, C. Zaniolo. Deterministic and Non-Deterministic Stable Models. submitted for publication to *Journal of Logic and Computation*, T.R. ISI-CNR, 1996.

26. D. Saccá, C. Zaniolo. Stable Models and Nondeterminism in Logic Programs with Negation. *Proc. ACM PODS*, 1990.

27. J. Schlipf. Complexity and Undecidability Results in Logic Programming. *Annals of Mathematics and Artificial Intelligence*, 15(3/4):257–288, 1995.

28. L. J. Stockmeyer. The Polynomial-Time Hierarchy. *Theoretical Computer Science*, 3:1–22, 1977.

29. J. D. Ullman. *Principles of Database and Knowledge Base Systems*. CS Press, 1989.

30. M. Vardi. Complexity of relational query languages. In *Proc. 14th ACM STOC*, pp. 137–146, 1982.

31. J.-H. You and L. Yuan. A Three-Valued Semantics for Deductive Databases and Logic Programs. *Journal of Computer and System Sciences*, 49:334–361, 1994.

32. J.-H. You and L. Yuan. On the Equivalence of Semantics for Normal Logic Programming. *Journal of Logic Programming*, 22(3):211–222, 1995.

# Stable Model Checking for Disjunctive Logic Programs *

N. Leone[1]    P. Rullo[2]    F. Scarcello[3]

[1] Information Systems Dep.,
Technical University of Vienna,
Paniglgasse 16, A-1040 Vienna, Austria.
email: leone@dbai.tuwien.ac.at

[2] DIMET
Università di Reggio Calabria
I-89100 Reggio Calabria, Italy
email: rullo@si.deis.unical.it

[3] DEIS
Università della Calabria
I-87030 Rende, Italy
email: frank@si.deis.unical.it

**Abstract.** The stable model semantics is the most widely acknowledged semantics for disjunctive logic programs.
The paper investigates computational aspects related to the stable model semantics of (function-free) disjunctive logic programs. In particular, an efficient algorithm for solving the (co-NP-hard decision) problem of checking if a model is stable is provided. The correctness of the proposed method is formally proven, and its computational complexity is analyzed. In general, the algorithm runs in polynomial space and single exponential time (in the worst case). However, the algorithm runs in polynomial time on the class of *head-cycle free programs* and, in case of general disjunctive logic programs, it limits the inefficient part of the computation *only* to the components of the program which are not head-cycle free. Some optimization techniques are also employed to reduce the amount of computation to be performed in practice.

## 1  Introduction

Disjunctive logic programming is nowadays widely recognized as a valuable tool for knowledge representation and commonsense reasoning having important applications in a variety of domains ranging from physical sciences, to artificial intelligence, to database applications, and to expert systems [1, 13, 10, 8]. An

* Work partially supported by *Christian Doppler Lab. for Expert Systems, Istituto per la Sistemistica e l'Informatica, ISI-CNR,* the EC-US project "DEUS EX MACHINA" and by a MURST grant (40% share) under the project "Sistemi formali e strumenti per basi di dati evolute".

important merit of disjunctive logic programming over normal (i.e., disjunction-free) logic programming is its capability to model incomplete knowledge [1, 13].

The most widely acknowledged semantics for disjunctive logic programming is the extension to the disjunctive case of the stable model semantics of Gelfond-Lifschitz [7]. According to this semantics [8, 15], a disjunctive program may have several alternative models (possibly none), each corresponding to a possible view of the reality.

The stable model semantics has a very high expressive power. Indeed, in [9, 4] it is proved that, under stable model semantics, (function-free) disjunctive logic programs capture the complexity class $\Sigma_2^P$ (i.e., they allow to express *every* property which is decidable in non-deterministic polynomial time with an oracle in NP). In [4], Eiter, Gottlob and Mannila show that the expressiveness of disjunctive logic programming has practical relevance, as concrete real world situations can be represented by stable model semantics for disjunctive programs, while they cannot be expressed by (disjunction-free) logic programs.

Another interesting aspect of stable model semantics for disjunctive programs is that it has strong connections to AI, since several non-monotonic logic languages can be equivalently translated into disjunctive programs under stable model semantics [6, 8, 16].

Even if much research work has been done on various aspects of disjunctive logic programming (e.g., semantics, complexity, expressive power, etc.), the important area concerning the computation of the semantics of disjunctive logic programs has not been investigated in depth.

The present paper is in this area and studies important aspects of the computation of the stable model semantics of disjunctive logic programs.

**Input:** A disjunctive logic program $\mathcal{P}$.
**Output:** The stable models of $\mathcal{P}$.
**begin**
  **for** each interpretation $I$ of $\mathcal{P}$ **do**
    Check the stability condition for $I$;
    **if** $I$ satisfies the stability condition
        **then output** *"I is a stable model of $\mathcal{P}$"*;
  **end_for**;
**end.**

**Fig. 1.** *Naive "Guess and Check" Algorithm for the Computation of Stable Models*

To introduce the problem of the computation of stable models, consider the naive algorithm shown in Figure 1. The algorithm, based on a trivial guess and check strategy, is highly inefficient and reveals the presence of two main sources of complexity in the computation of the stable models that interact, in a sense, orthogonally: (1) the exponential number of interpretations that are "candidates" for stable models, and (2) the check of the stability condition, which is well known to be a co-NP-hard decision problem[4] [14, 4, 5].

Thus, a method for the efficient computation of stable models, has to efficiently deal with both the above mentioned sources of complexity.

In this paper, we provide an efficient method for checking the stability condition (point (2) above); a technique to reduce the number of interpretations that are "candidates" for stable models is presented in a companion paper [12].

To check stable models efficiently, we resort to a recent characterization of stable models presented in [11], where the authors show that a model is stable if and only if it contains no unfounded set. Thus, to check if a model $M$ is stable, we verify that no subset of $M$ is an unfounded set (the notion of unfounded set, presented in [17] for normal programs, has been extended to disjunctive programs in [11]).

The correctness of the proposed method is formally proven, and its computational complexity is analyzed. In general, the algorithm runs in polynomial space and single exponential time (in the worst case). However, the algorithm runs in polynomial time on the class of *head-cycle free programs* [2, 3] and, in case of general disjunctive logic programs, it limits the inefficient part of the computation only to the components of the program which are not head-cycle free. Some relevant optimization techniques reduce the amount of computation to be performed in practice.

## 2 The Stable Model Semantics of Logic Programs

In this section we provide a short overview of the stable model semantics for function-free disjunctive logic programs. The reader is referred to [15, 8] for unexplained concepts.

A *term* is either a constant or a variable[5]. An *atom* is $a(t_1, ..., t_n)$, where $a$ is a *predicate* of arity $n$ and $t_1, ..., t_n$ are terms. A *literal* is either a *positive literal p* or a *negative literal ¬p*, where $p$ is an atom. We use an upper-case letter, say $L$, to denote either a positive or a negative literal. Two literals are *complementary* if they are of the form $p$ and $\neg p$, for some atom $p$. Given a literal $L$, $\neg.L$ denotes its complementary literal. Accordingly, given a set $A$ of literals, $\neg.A$ denotes the set $\{\neg.L \mid L \in A\}$.

A *(disjunctive) rule r* is a clause of the form

$$a_1 \vee \cdots \vee a_n \leftarrow b_1, \cdots, b_k, \neg b_{k+1}, \cdots, \neg b_m, \qquad n \geq 1, \ m \geq 0$$

where $a_1, \cdots, a_n, b_1, \cdots, b_m$ are atoms. The disjunction $a_1 \vee \cdots \vee a_n$ is the *head* of $r$, while the conjunction $b_1, ..., b_k, \neg b_{k+1}, ..., \neg b_m$ is the *body* of $r$. We denote by $H(r)$ the set $\{a_1, ..., a_n\}$ of the head atoms, and by $B(r)$ the set $\{b_1, ..., b_k, \neg b_{k+1}, ..., \neg b_m\}$ of the body literals. Moreover, $B^+(r)$ and $B^-(r)$ denote the set of positive and negative literals occurring in $B(r)$, respectively. A

---

[4] The mentioned complexity results refer to *data-complexity* [18] or to the computational complexity of the propositional case (i.e., for variable free programs).

[5] Note that function symbols are not considered in this paper.

*(disjunctive) program* is a finite set of rules. A term, an atom, a literal, a rule or program is *ground* if no variable appears in it. A ground program is also called *propositional* program.

Let $\mathcal{P}$ be a program. The *Herbrand Universe* $U_{\mathcal{P}}$ of $\mathcal{P}$ is the set of all constants appearing in $\mathcal{P}$. The *Herbrand Base* $B_{\mathcal{P}}$ for $\mathcal{P}$ is the set of all possible ground atoms constructible from the predicates appearing in the rules of $\mathcal{P}$ and the constants occurring in $U_{\mathcal{P}}$ (clearly, both $U_{\mathcal{P}}$ and $B_{\mathcal{P}}$ are finite). Given a rule $r$ occurring in a program $\mathcal{P}$, a *ground instance* of $r$ is a rule obtained from $r$ by replacing every variable $X$ in $r$ by $\sigma(X)$, where $\sigma$ is a mapping from the variables occurring in $r$ to the constants in $U_{\mathcal{P}}$. We denote by $ground(\mathcal{P})$ the (finite) set of the ground instances of the rules occurring in $\mathcal{P}$.

An *interpretation* for $\mathcal{P}$ is a consistent set of ground literals, that is, an interpretation is a subset $I$ of $B_{\mathcal{P}} \cup \neg.B_{\mathcal{P}}$ such that $I \cap \neg.I = \emptyset$. A ground literal $L$ is *true* (resp., *false*) w.r.t. $I$ if $L \in I$ (resp., $L \in \neg.I$). If a ground literal is neither true nor false w.r.t. $I$ then it is *undefined* w.r.t. $I$. We denote by $I^+$ and $I^-$, the set of positive and negative literals occurring in $I$, respectively. Moreover, $\bar{I}$ denotes the set of undefined literals w.r.t. $I$. The interpretation $I$ is *total* if $\bar{I}$ is empty (that is, $I^+ \cup \neg.I^- = B_{\mathcal{P}}$); otherwise, $I$ is *partial*.

Let $r$ be a ground rule in $ground(\mathcal{P})$. The head of $r$ is *true* w.r.t. $I$ if $H(r) \cap I \neq \emptyset$. The body of $r$ is *true* w.r.t. $I$ if $B(r) \subseteq I$ and is *false* if $B(r) \cap \neg.I \neq \emptyset$ (i.e., some literal in $B(r)$ is false w.r.t. $I$). Rule $r$ is *satisfied* (or *true*) w.r.t. $I$ if its head is true w.r.t. $I$ or its body is not true w.r.t. $I$.

A *model* for $\mathcal{P}$ is a total interpretation $M$ for $\mathcal{P}$ such that every rule $r \in ground(\mathcal{P})$ is true w.r.t. $M$. A model $M$ for $\mathcal{P}$ is *minimal* if no model $N$ for $\mathcal{P}$ exists such that $N^+$ is a proper subset of $M^+$. The set of all minimal models for $\mathcal{P}$ is denoted by $MM(\mathcal{P})$.

We point out that, according to the given definitions, we use the word "interpretation" to refer to a possibly partial interpretation, while a model is always a total interpretation.

Given a program $\mathcal{P}$ and a total interpretation $I$, the *Gelfond-Lifschitz transformation* ("GL transformation", for short) of $\mathcal{P}$ with respect to $I$, denoted $\mathcal{P}^I$, is the disjunctive positive program defined as follows:

$$\mathcal{P}^I = \{\, a_1 \vee \cdots \vee a_n \leftarrow b_1, \cdots, b_k \mid a_1 \vee \cdots \vee a_n \leftarrow b_1, \cdots, b_k, \neg b_{k+1}, \cdots, \neg b_m \text{ is}$$
$$\text{in } ground(\mathcal{P}) \text{ and } \neg b_i \in I, \text{ for all } k < i \leq m \}$$

(We note that, in the definition of GL transformation reported in [7, 15], Condition $\neg b_i \in I$ above is "$b_i \notin I$", since total interpretations are represented there by sets of atoms rather than sets of literals as in our case.)

**Definition 1.** [15] Let $I$ be a total interpretation for a program $\mathcal{P}$. $I$ is a *(disjunctive) stable model* for $\mathcal{P}$ if $I \in MM(\mathcal{P}^I)$ (that is $I$ is a minimal model of the positive program $\mathcal{P}^I$). The set of all stable models for $\mathcal{P}$ is denoted by $STM(\mathcal{P})$. □

*Example 1.* Let $P = \{a \vee b \leftarrow c; \quad b \leftarrow \neg a, \neg c; \quad a \vee c \leftarrow \neg b\}$. Consider $I = \{b, \neg a, \neg c\}$. Then, $P^I = \{a \vee b \leftarrow c; \quad b \leftarrow\}$.

It is easy to verify that $I$ is a minimal model for $P^I$; thus, $I$ is a stable model for $P$. □

Clearly, if $\mathcal{P}$ is positive then $\mathcal{P}^I$ coincides with $ground(\mathcal{P})$. It turns out that for a positive program minimal and stable models coincide.

## 3 Stable Models and Unfounded Sets

In this section we review from [11] the characterization of stable models in terms of unfounded sets.

**Definition 2.** [11] Let $I$ be an interpretation for $\mathcal{P}$. A set $X \subseteq B_P$ of ground atoms is an *unfounded set* for $\mathcal{P}$ w.r.t. $I$ if, for each $a \in X$ and for each rule $r \in ground(\mathcal{P})$ such that $a \in H(r)$, at least one of the following conditions hold:

1. $B(r) \cap \neg.I \neq \emptyset$, i.e., the body of $r$ is false w.r.t. $I$, or
2. $B^+(r) \cap X \neq \emptyset$, i.e., some positive body literal belongs to $X$, or
3. $(H(r) - X) \cap I \neq \emptyset$, i.e., an atom in the head of $r$, distinct from $a$ and other elements in $X$, is true w.r.t. $I$.

An unfounded set $X$ for $\mathcal{P}$ w.r.t. $I$ is *maximal* if no proper superset of $X$ is an unfounded set for $\mathcal{P}$ w.r.t. $I$. □

Informally, unfounded atoms are not derivable from the rules of $\mathcal{P}$ and thus, according to a closed world assumption principle, they are considered false.

*Example 2.* Consider the program $\mathcal{P} = \{a \vee b \leftarrow\}$ and let $I = \{b\}$ be a (partial) interpretation for it. The set $X = \{a\}$ is an unfounded set of $\mathcal{P}$ w.r.t. $I$. Indeed, the unique rule of $\mathcal{P}$ (with $a$ in the head) satisfies Condition 3 of Definition 2, as $(H(r) - X) \cap I = \{b\} \neq \emptyset$. The unfoundness of $a$ meets the intuition that, since $b$ is true, $a$ can not be derived from the program (and can therefore be assumed false).

Assume now that the interpretation $I$ for $\mathcal{P}$ is $I = \{a, b\}$. Then both sets $X = \{a\}$ and $Y = \{b\}$ are unfounded sets for $\mathcal{P}$ w.r.t. $I$. This intuitively means that the presence of either $a$ or $b$ is not justified in the interpretation (we should choose $a$ or $b$, but we can not accept both).

For the program $\mathcal{P} = \{ a \vee b \leftarrow ; a \leftarrow b ; b \leftarrow a \}$ and the interpretation $I = \{a, b\}$, the only unfounded set is $\emptyset$ (that is, no atom can be assumed false). □

It is worth pointing out that the above definition generalizes the one given for disjunction-free logic programs in [17], even if, unlike traditional logic programming, the union of two unfounded sets is not necessarily an unfounded set.

**Definition 3.** Let $I$ be a total interpretation for $\mathcal{P}$. $I$ is *unfounded-free* if no nonempty subset of $I$ is an unfounded set for $\mathcal{P}$ w.r.t. $I$. □

Now we can provide a useful characterization of stable models in terms of unfounded sets. In particular, we show that the unfounded-free condition exactly singles out the stable models. We wish to enphasize that, since for disjunction-free programs the definitions of stable model and unfounded set given in this paper coincide with the classical definitions given in [7] and [17], respectively, all the results below hold also for disjunction-free programs (under the classical definitions of stable model and unfounded set).

**Theorem 4.** [11] *Let M be a model for P. M is stable if and only if M is unfounded-free.*

An interesting problem is the determination of the exact computational complexity of checking the unfounded-free condition. Unfortunately, the next proposition shows that, unless P = NP, we can not efficiently test if $I$ is unfounded-free.

**Proposition 5.** [11] *Let P be a ground program and I be an interpretation for P. Deciding whether I is unfounded-free is co-NP-complete.*

# 4 An Algorithm for Checking Stable Models

Checking the stability condition is difficult in general. Indeed, it is well known that this is a co-NP-hard decision problem [14, 4, 5]. Interesting recent studies [2, 3], however, have proven that minimal model checking — the hardest part of stable model checking — can be efficiently performed for a relevant class of programs, called *head-cycle free* programs. We next provide an algorithm for checking stable models which runs in polynomial time for head-cycle free programs and, in case of general programs, limits the inefficient part of the computation only to the components of the program which are not head-cycle free.

The algorithm exploits the result of Theorem 4, and verifies unfounded freeness instead of checking the stability condition directly.

With every program $P$ we associate a directed graph $DG_P = (\mathcal{N}, E)$, called the *dependency graph* of $P$, in which (i) each predicate of $P$ is a node in $\mathcal{N}$, and (ii) there is an arc in $E$ directed from a node $a$ to a node $b$ iff there is a rule $r$ in $P$ such that $b$ and $a$ are the predicates of a positive literal appearing in $H(r)$ and $B(r)$, respectively.

Graph $DG_P$ singles out the dependencies of the head predicates of a rule $r$ from the positive predicates in its body[6].

*Example 3.* Consider the program $P_1$ consisting of the following rules[7]:

$$a \vee b \leftarrow \qquad\qquad c \leftarrow a \qquad\qquad c \leftarrow b$$

The dependency graph $DG_{P_1}$ of $P_1$ is depicted in Figure 2.a. (Note that since the sample programs are propositional the nodes of the sample graphs are atoms,

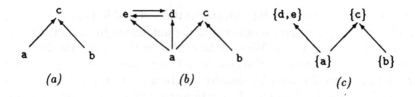

**Fig. 2.** Graphs $DG_{\mathcal{P}_1}$ (a), $DG_{\mathcal{P}_2}$ (b), and $\hat{D}G_{\mathcal{P}_2}$ (c)

as atoms coincide with predicates in this case.)

Consider now program $\mathcal{P}_2$ obtained by adding to $\mathcal{P}_1$ the rules below.

$$d \vee e \leftarrow a \qquad\qquad d \leftarrow e \qquad\qquad e \leftarrow d, \neg b$$

The dependency graph $DG_{\mathcal{P}_2}$ is reported in Figure 2.b.  □

The dependency graphs allow us to individuate head-cycle free programs [2, 3].

A program $\mathcal{P}$ is *head-cycle free* $(HCF)$ iff there is no clause $r$ in $\mathcal{P}$ such that two predicates occurring in the head of $r$ are in the same cycle of $DG_{\mathcal{P}}$.

*Example 4.* The dependency graphs of Figure 2 reveal that program $\mathcal{P}_1$ of Example 3 is HCF; while program $\mathcal{P}_2$ is not, as rule $d \vee e \leftarrow a$ contains in its head two predicates belonging to the same cycle of $DG_{\mathcal{P}_2}$.  □

Our method to test unfounded freeness of HCF programs is based on a transformation $\mathcal{R}_{\mathcal{P},I}$ which, given a set $X$ of ground atoms, derives the atoms in $X$ which satisfy at least one of the unfoundness conditions of Definition 2.

**Definition 6.** Let $\mathcal{P}$ be a program. Define $\mathcal{R}_{\mathcal{P},I}$ operator as follows:

$$\mathcal{R}_{\mathcal{P},I} : 2^{B_{\mathcal{P}}} \to 2^{B_{\mathcal{P}}}$$
$$X \;\mapsto\; \{A \in X \mid \forall r \in ground(\mathcal{P}) \text{ with } A \in H(r),$$
$$B(r) \cap (\neg.I \cup X) \neq \emptyset \text{ or } (H(r) - \{A\}) \cap I \neq \emptyset\}$$

□

It is easy to see that $\mathcal{R}_{\mathcal{P},I}$ is a monotonic operator. Moreover, given a set $X$ of ground atoms, it is soon recognized that the sequence $R_0 = X$, $R_n = \mathcal{R}_{\mathcal{P},I}(R_{n-1})$ is monotonically decreasing and finitely converges to a limit that we denote by $\mathcal{R}^{\omega}_{\mathcal{P},I}(X)$.

---

[6] Note that negative literals cause no arc in $DG_{\mathcal{P}}$.

[7] We point out again that we use propositional examples for simplicity; but the algorithm is defined for the general case of (function-free) programs with variables.

Intuitively, $\mathcal{R}_{\mathcal{P},I}(X)$ discards from $X$ only elements for which there exists some rule violating all unfoundness conditions for $\mathcal{P}$ w.r.t. $I$. Thus, $\mathcal{R}^{\omega}_{\mathcal{P},I}(X)$ contains the union of all unfounded sets for $\mathcal{P}$ w.r.t. $I$ included in $X$. As a consequence, if $\mathcal{R}^{\omega}_{\mathcal{P},I}(I^+)$ is the empty set for a total interpretation $I$, then $I$ is unfounded-free. This intuition is formalized by the following lemma and proposition.

**Lemma 7.** *Let $\mathcal{P}$ be a program and $I$ be a total interpretation for $\mathcal{P}$.*
*Every unfounded set for $\mathcal{P}$ w.r.t. $I$ which is contained in $I^+$ is also contained in $\mathcal{R}^{\omega}_{\mathcal{P},I}(I^+)$.*

**Proof.** Let $X \subseteq I^+$ be an unfounded set for $\mathcal{P}$ w.r.t. $I$. For each $A \in X$ and for each rule $r$ such that $A \in H(r)$, at least one of the following conditions holds: (i) $B(r) \cap (\neg.I \cup X) \neq \emptyset$ or (ii) $(H(r) - X) \cap I \neq \emptyset$. Hence, as $\{A\} \subseteq X$, $(H(r) - \{A\}) \cap I \neq \emptyset$ as well. Then, from definition of $\mathcal{R}_{\mathcal{P},I}$, $\mathcal{R}_{\mathcal{P},I}(X) = X$ holds and, since $\mathcal{R}_{\mathcal{P},I}$ is monotonic and $X \subseteq I^+$, $\mathcal{R}^{\omega}_{\mathcal{P},I}(I^+)$ must contain $X$ (we are done). □

**Proposition 8.** *Let $\mathcal{P}$ be a program and $I$ be a total interpretation for $\mathcal{P}$.*
*If $\mathcal{R}^{\omega}_{\mathcal{P},I}(I^+) = \emptyset$, then $I$ is unfounded-free.*

**Proof.** It follows immediately from Lemma 7. □
Therefore, $\mathcal{R}^{\omega}_{\mathcal{P},I}(I^+) = \emptyset$ is sufficient to guarantee that $I$ is unfounded-free.

*Example 5.* Consider again the (HCF) program $\mathcal{P}_1$ of Example 3 consisting of the rules:

$$r_1 : a \vee b \qquad\qquad r_2 : c \leftarrow a \qquad\qquad r_3 : c \leftarrow b$$

Given the total interpretation $I_1 = \{a, c, \neg b\}$, we have that:

$$R_0 = I_1^+ = \{a, c\}$$
$$R_1 = \mathcal{R}_{\mathcal{P}_1,I_1}(R_0) = \{c\}$$
$$R_2 = \mathcal{R}_{\mathcal{P}_1,I_1}(R_1) = \emptyset = \mathcal{R}^{\omega}_{\mathcal{P}_1,I_1}(I_1^+).$$

Indeed, $a$ is not in $\mathcal{R}_{\mathcal{P}_1,I_1}(R_0)$ because for rule $r_1$ both $B(r_1) \cap (\neg.I_1 \cup R_0) = \emptyset$ (as $B(r_1)$ is empty) and $(H(r_1) - \{a\}) \cap I_1 = \emptyset$ (as $H(r_1) - \{a\} = \{b\}$) hold. Atom $c$ is in $\mathcal{R}_{\mathcal{P}_1,I_1}(R_0)$, because both rules $r_2$ and $r_3$ with $c$ in the head verify the conditions required by the $\mathcal{R}_{\mathcal{P}_1,I_1}$ operator. In particular, $B(r_2) \cap R_0 = \{a\} \neq \emptyset$ and $B(r_3) \cap \neg.I_1 = \{b\} \neq \emptyset$. At the next step, $c$ is not in $\mathcal{R}_{\mathcal{P}_1,I_1}(R_1)$, as $B(r_2) \cap (\neg.I_1 \cup R_1) \neq \emptyset$ does not hold.

$I_1$ thus verifies the hypothesis of Proposition 8 and it is indeed easy to see that $I_1$ is unfounded-free.

For another example consider, on the same program $\mathcal{P}_1$, total interpretation $I_2 = \{a, b, c\}$, which is not unfounded free, as $\{a\}$ and $\{b\}$ are unfounded sets for $\mathcal{P}_1$ w.r.t. $I_2$. We have that:

$$R_0 = I_2^+ = \{a, b, c\}$$
$$R_1 = \mathcal{R}_{\mathcal{P}_1,I_2}(R_0) = \{a, b, c\} = \mathcal{R}^{\omega}_{\mathcal{P}_1,I_2}(I_2^+).$$

In this case, $\mathcal{R}^\omega_{\mathcal{P}_1,I_2}(I_2^+) \neq \emptyset$ and we can not apply Proposition 8, as it states a sufficient condition for unfounded freeness. However, we will see below (cf. Theorem 9) that, since $\mathcal{P}_1$ is HCF, condition $\mathcal{R}^\omega_{\mathcal{P}_1,I_2}(I_2^+) \neq \emptyset$ allows us to derive that $I_2$ is not unfounded free. □

Condition $\mathcal{R}^\omega_{\mathcal{P},I}(I^+) = \emptyset$ is thus sufficient for ensuring unfounded freeness (actually for HCF programs it is also necessary). Unfortunately, this condition is not necessary for unfounded freeness in the general case.

*Example 6.* Consider the (non-HCF) program $\mathcal{P}$ consisting of the following rules:

$$a \vee b \qquad\qquad a \leftarrow b \qquad\qquad b \leftarrow a$$

Given the total interpretation $I = \{a, b\}$, we have that $\mathcal{R}^\omega_{\mathcal{P},I}(I^+) = \{a,b\} \neq \emptyset$, while $I$ is unfounded free. □

Thus, condition $\mathcal{R}^\omega_{\mathcal{P},I}(I^+) = \emptyset$ is not in general necessary for an interpretation to be unfounded free. Nevertheless, we next prove that for HCF programs this condition is necessary for unfounded freeness (observe that the program $\mathcal{P}$ of Example 6, for which condition $\mathcal{R}^\omega_{\mathcal{P},I}(I^+) = \emptyset$ is not necessary for unfounded freeness, is not HCF).

The proof of the theorem refers to the notion of collapsed dependency graph which is the graph $\hat{D}G_\mathcal{P}$ obtained from $DG_\mathcal{P}$ by collapsing each (maximal) strongly connected component into a single node. Thus, every node of $\hat{D}G_\mathcal{P}$ is a set $Q$ of predicates. Moreover, given a set $Q$ of predicates and a set $J$ of atoms we denote by $\frac{J}{Q}$ the subset of $J$ whose predicates are from $Q$.

*Example 7.* The collapsed dependency graph $\hat{D}G_{\mathcal{P}_2}$ of $DG_{\mathcal{P}_2}$ is depicted in Figure 2.c. □

**Theorem 9.** *Let $\mathcal{P}$ be a HCF program and $I$ a total interpretation for it. Then $I$ is not unfounded free iff $\mathcal{R}^\omega_{\mathcal{P},I}(I^+) \neq \emptyset$.*

**Proof.** From Proposition 8 only $\Longleftarrow$ remains to be proven.

Suppose that $X = \mathcal{R}^\omega_{\mathcal{P},I}(I^+)$ is not empty. Take a node $Q$ of $\hat{D}G_\mathcal{P}$ such that: (a) some atom in $X$ has predicate in $Q$, and (b) there exists no other node $Q'$ of $\hat{D}G_\mathcal{P}$ containing a predicate of some atom in $X$ such that $Q$ is (transitively) reacheable from $Q'$ (i.e., with a directed path from $Q'$ to $Q$ in $\hat{D}G_\mathcal{P}$) [8]. Consider now set $\frac{X}{Q}$, we prove that $\frac{X}{Q}$ is an unfounded set for $\mathcal{P}$ w.r.t. $I$. Let $r$ be a rule in $ground(\mathcal{P})$ with an atom from $\frac{X}{Q}$ in the head. Since $\mathcal{R}_{\mathcal{P},I}(X) = X$, then $r$ satisfies at least one of the following conditions: (i) $B(r) \cap \neg.I \neq \emptyset$ or (ii) $B^+(r) \cap X \neq \emptyset$ or (iii) $(H(r) - \{A\}) \cap I \neq \emptyset$. Because of our choice of the node $Q$, no atom in the body of $r$ belongs to $X - \frac{X}{Q}$; thus condition (ii) yields $B^+(r) \cap \frac{X}{Q} \neq \emptyset$. Furthermore, condition (iii) entails $(H(r) - \frac{X}{Q}) \cap I \neq \emptyset$, because

---

[8] Note that the existence of such a node is guaranteed, because the collapsed graph has no cycle.

if $H(r)$ contained another element from $\frac{X}{Q}$, distinct from $A$, then $\mathcal{P}$ would not be head-cycle free, as the predicates of the elements in $\frac{X}{Q}$ belong to the same cycle of the dependency graph. Then $\frac{X}{Q}$ is an unfounded set for $\mathcal{P}$ w.r.t. $I$ and we are done. □

**Corollary 10.** *Let $\mathcal{P}$ be a HCF ground program and $M$ be a model for $\mathcal{P}$. Recognizing whether $M$ is a stable model is polynomial.*

**Proof.** It easy to see that $\mathcal{R}^\omega_{\mathcal{P},I}(I^+)$ is efficiently computable. Thus, the statement follows from Theorems 4 and 9. □

It is worth noting that, since stable and minimal models coincide for positive programs, condition $\mathcal{R}^\omega_{\mathcal{P},I}(I^+) = \emptyset$ can be also employed to check that a model of a positive HCF program is minimal. Thus, compared to the algorithm proposed in [3], Theorem 9 suggests an alternative simpler way for this check.

From the above results, if the program is head-cycle free we can efficiently check unfounded freeness by testing whether $\mathcal{R}^\omega_{\mathcal{P},I}(I^+) = \emptyset$. Unfortunately, as evidenced by Example 6, we cannot use this test for recognizing unfounded freeness in the general case and we should resort to an inefficient algorithm that blindly controls every element in the power set of $I^+$ to see if it is an unfounded set.

The complexity result of Proposition 5 indicates that we have no chance to find an efficient algorithm for checking unfounded freeness in the general case (unless P = NP). Nevertheless, we will introduce a couple of optimizations that, also for non-HCF programs, strongly improve the efficiency of the naive algorithm for the test of unfounded freeness.

The first optimization is a direct consequence of Lemma 7. Indeed, because of that result, we can limit our search of unfounded subsets of $I^+$ to the power set of $\mathcal{R}^\omega_{\mathcal{P},I}(I^+)$ (which may be sensibly smaller than the power set of $I^+$).

The second important optimization is supported by the proposition below, which shows that the test of unfounded freeness can be performed one component at a time. As a consequence: (a) the number of sets to be checked to verify the property is drastically pruned, and (b) the efficient technique suggested by Theorem 9 can be employed on the HCF components of $\mathcal{P}$ limiting the inefficient part of the computation only to the components which are not HCF.

Given a set $Q$ of predicates, we denote by $subp(Q)$ the *subprogram of $Q$* which is the set of the rules in $ground(\mathcal{P})$ with a head predicate from $Q$. (Note that the same rule may occur in the subprograms of two different (collapsed) nodes $Q_1$ and $Q_2$ of $\hat{DG}_\mathcal{P}$.)

**Proposition 11.** *Let $\mathcal{P}$ be a program, and $I$ a total interpretation for $\mathcal{P}$. Then, $I$ is not unfounded-free iff there exists a node $Q$ of $\hat{DG}_\mathcal{P}$ such that $\frac{I^+}{Q}$ contains a nonempty unfounded set for $subp(Q)$ w.r.t. $I$.*

**Proof.** ($\Longrightarrow$) Let $X$ be a non-empty unfounded set for $\mathcal{P}$ w.r.t. $I$, which is contained in $I^+$. Take a node $Q$ of $\hat{DG}_\mathcal{P}$ such that: (a) some atom in $X$ has predicate in $Q$, and (b) there exists no other node $Q'$ of $\hat{DG}_\mathcal{P}$ containing a predicate of some atom in $X$ such that $Q$ is (transitively) reacheable from $Q'$ (i.e., with a directed path from $Q'$ to $Q$ in $\hat{DG}_{\mathcal{P}}$). Note that the existence of such a node is guaranteed, because the collapsed graph has no cycle. Consider now set $\frac{X}{Q}$. We demonstrate that $\frac{X}{Q}$ is an unfounded set for $subp(Q)$ w.r.t. $I$. Let $r$ be a rule in $subp(Q)$ with an atom from $\frac{X}{Q}$ in the head. Since $\frac{X}{Q}$ is a subset of $X$, $subp(Q) \subseteq ground(\mathcal{P})$, and $X$ is an unfounded set for $\mathcal{P}$ w.r.t. $I$, then $r$ satisfies at least one of the following conditions: (1) $B(r) \cap \neg.I \neq \emptyset$, (2) $B^+(r) \cap X \neq \emptyset$, (3) $(H(r) - X) \cap I \neq \emptyset$. Now, Condition 1 is the same also for set $\frac{X}{Q}$. If (2) is satisfied, then $B^+(r) \cap \frac{X}{Q} \neq \emptyset$, as we chosen $Q$ as the lowest node of $\hat{DG}_{\mathcal{P}}$ with predicates appearing in $X$ (Condition (b) above). Finally, if (3) holds, then $(H(r) - \frac{X}{Q}) \cap I \neq \emptyset$, since $\frac{X}{Q} \subseteq X$. Therefore, $\frac{X}{Q}$ is a non-empty unfounded set for $subp(Q)$ w.r.t. $I$ contained in $\frac{I^+}{Q}$.

($\Longleftarrow$) Let $Q$ be a node of $\hat{DG}_{\mathcal{P}}$ such that $\frac{I^+}{Q}$ contains a non-empty unfounded set $X$ for $subp(Q)$ w.r.t. $I$. Then, $X$ is an unfounded set for $\mathcal{P}$ w.r.t. $I$ as well, since all rules in $ground(\mathcal{P})$ which have an atom from $X$ in the head occur also in $subp(Q)$ (by definition of $subp(Q)$) and, therefore, satisfy the unfoundness conditions also for $\mathcal{P}$. $\qquad\Box$

The results of Theorem 9 and Propositions 8 and 11 are all employed by the algorithm of Figure 3 for the efficient test of the unfounded-free property.

Informally, the algorithm processes one subprogram $subp(Q)$ at a time, as suggested by Proposition 11 (external **for** statement). In a first step we compute the fixpoint $X = \mathcal{R}^{\omega}_{subp(Q),I}(\frac{I^+}{Q})$ of $\mathcal{R}_{subp(Q),I}$ (in the **repeat-until** loop). If it is empty then, by virtue of Proposition 8, $\frac{I^+}{Q}$ contains no unfounded set, thus the computation of $subp(Q)$ terminates and the next subprogram is processed. Otherwise $(X \neq \emptyset)$, we check whether $subp(Q)$ is HCF, and, if so, the algorithm terminates returning $False$, as for HCF programs $\mathcal{R}^{\omega}_{subp(Q),I}(\frac{I^+}{Q}) \neq \emptyset$ is sufficient to guarantee that the interpretation is not unfounded-free (from Theorem 9). Finally, in the case that both $\mathcal{R}^{\omega}_{subp(Q),I}(\frac{I^+}{Q}) \neq \emptyset$ and $subp(Q)$ is not HCF, all subsets of $\mathcal{R}^{\omega}_{subp(Q),I}(\frac{I^+}{Q})$ are controlled (internal **for** statement) to see if one of them is an unfounded set.

It is worth noting that the algorithm performs a non-polynomial computation *only if* the program has a component that is not HCF for which, further, $\mathcal{R}^{\omega}_{subp(Q),I}(\frac{I^+}{Q}) \neq \emptyset$.

**Theorem 12.** *Given a program $\mathcal{P}$ and a total interpretation $I$ for $\mathcal{P}$, the algorithm of Figure 3 terminates in a finite amount of time returning the correct answer.*

**Proof.** The two **for** statements are performed on a finite number of elements and thus terminate in a finite amount of time. Moreover, the **repeat-until** statement also terminates finitely, since it computes a monotonically decreasing sequence (lower bounded by the empty set). The function thus ends in a finite amount of time.

**Input:** A disjunctive logic program P; a set of literals $I$.
**Output:** "Yes" if $I$ is a stable model, "No" otherwise.

**var** $X, Y, J$: SetOfLiterals;
    $Q$: SetOfPredicates;
**begin**
  **for** each node $Q$ of $\hat{D}G_P$
    $X := \frac{I^+}{Q}$;
    **repeat**    (* Computation of $\mathcal{R}^\omega_{subp(Q),I}(\frac{I^+}{Q})$ *)
        $J := X$;
        $X := \mathcal{R}_{subp(Q),I}(J)$
    **until** $J = X$;
    **if** $X \neq \emptyset$
      **then if** $subp(Q)$ is HCF
          **then output** "No";
          **else**   (* Computation of non-HCF components *)
             **for** each $Y \subseteq X$ **do**
               **if** $Y$ is an unfounded set for $subp(Q)$ w.r.t. $I$
                  **then output** "No";
             **end_for**;
  **end_for**;
  **output** "Yes";
**end**;

**Fig. 3.** The Algorithm for checking stable models

The correctness of the function is a consequence of the results of Proposition 8, Theorem 9, and Proposition 11, since the function implements the results of these statements (see the description above).     □

We close the section with some remarks on the efficiency of the algorithm of Figure 3.

The algorithm solves the decisional problem of checking unfounded freeness which, according to Proposition 5, is co-NP-hard. Thus, unless $\mathcal{P} = $ NP, exponential time is needed. Actually, the algorithm runs in single exponential time, as, in the worst case, all subsets of $I^+$ have to be analyzed to see if some of them is an unfounded set.

Nevertheless, there is a meaningful class of programs on which the algorithm terminates in polynomial time. In particular, HCF programs belong to this class which clearly contains also all normal logic programs (as an ∨-free program is HCF). Moreover, the algorithm runs polynomially also on the non-HCF programs for which $\mathcal{R}^\omega_{subp(Q),I}(\frac{I^+}{Q}) = \emptyset$ on every non-HCF component. We point out that, on programs out of this polynomial class, the inefficient part of the computation is limited to the subprograms which are not HCF. Thus, HCF components are solved in polynomial time, and, furthermore, the test for unfoundness is done on power sets of a sensibly smaller size in general. For instance, let $I$ be a total interpretation for a ground program $\mathcal{P}$. A naive algorithm for checking unfounded freeness of $I$ would generate all subsets of $I^+$ and verify if some of them is an unfounded set. Thus, this naive algorithm costs $O\left(|\mathcal{P}| \cdot 2^{|I^+|}\right)$, as it checks $2^{|I^+|}$ sets for unfoundness and each check can be clearly done in linear time in the size of $\mathcal{P}$[9]. Let $C(\mathcal{P})$ be the number of strongly connected components of $DG_\mathcal{P}$, that is, the number of nodes of $\hat{D}G_\mathcal{P}$ (note that $C(\mathcal{P})$ does not exceed the number of predicates of $\mathcal{P}$). To give an idea of the efficiency of the algorithm of Figure 3, suppose that, for each strongly connected component $Q$, we have that both $|\frac{I^+}{Q}| = \frac{|I^+|}{C(\mathcal{P})}$ (i.e., the atoms of $I^+$ are uniformly distributed on the components) and $|subp(Q)| = \frac{|\mathcal{P}|}{C(\mathcal{P})}$ hold. Then, the algorithm of Figure 3 processes a strongly connected component $Q$ in time:

- $O\left(|subp(Q)|^2\right) = O\left(\frac{|\mathcal{P}|}{C(\mathcal{P})}^2\right)$, if $subp(Q)$ is HCF (as $\mathcal{R}^\omega_{subp(Q),I}(\frac{I^+}{Q})$ is computed in quadratic time), and

- $O\left(|subp(Q)| \cdot 2^{|\frac{I^+}{Q}|}\right) = O\left(\frac{|\mathcal{P}|}{C(\mathcal{P})} \cdot 2^{\frac{|I^+|}{C(\mathcal{P})}}\right)$, if $Q$ is not HCF.

Therefore, the algorithm of Figure 3 runs in time

$$O\left(\frac{|\mathcal{P}|}{C(\mathcal{P})}^2 \cdot C_{hcf}(\mathcal{P}) + [C(\mathcal{P}) - C_{hcf}(\mathcal{P})] \cdot \frac{|\mathcal{P}|}{C(\mathcal{P})} \cdot 2^{\frac{|I^+|}{C(\mathcal{P})}}\right),$$

where $C_{hcf}(\mathcal{P})$ is the number of HCF components of $\mathcal{P}$. In particular, if the program $\mathcal{P}$ is head cycle free (i.e., $C_{hcf}(\mathcal{P}) = C(\mathcal{P})$), then the algorithm runs in time $O\left(\frac{|\mathcal{P}|^2}{C(\mathcal{P})}\right)$. If no component is HCF (i.e., $C_{hcf}(\mathcal{P}) = 0$), then the algorithm runs in time $O\left(|\mathcal{P}| \cdot 2^{\frac{|I^+|}{C(\mathcal{P})}}\right)$. Thus, even in this very bad case, a lot of useless computations are avoided (provided that $C(\mathcal{P}) > 1$) as the number of sets to be checked for unfoundness is $C(\mathcal{P}) \cdot 2^{\frac{|I^+|}{C(\mathcal{P})}}$ instead of the exponentially bigger $2^{|I^+|}$. (Actually, the size of the power sets to be tested for unfoundness is further reduced by the optimization suggested by Lemma 7, as the subsets of $\mathcal{R}^\omega_{subp(Q),I}(\frac{I^+}{Q})$ are checked in place of the subsets of $\frac{I^+}{Q}$).

Concerning space bounds, it is easy to see that the algorithm runs in polynomial space. Indeed, even if (in the worst case) the last **for** statement is executed on the power set of $I^+$, the elements of the power set do not need to be stored, as they can be generated when needed (following a straightforward enumeration policy).

# References

1. Baral, C., Gelfond, M., Logic Programming and Knowledge Representation *Journal of Logic Programming*, Vol. 19/20, May/July 1994, pp. 73–148.

---

[9] $|\mathcal{P}|$ and $|I^+|$ denote the size of $\mathcal{P}$ and $I^+$, respectively.

2. Ben-Eliyahu, R., Dechter, R., Propositional Semantics for Disjunctive Logic Programs, *Annals of Mathematics and Artificial Intelligence*, Vol. 12, 1994, pp. 53–87.
3. Ben-Eliyahu, R., Palopoli, L., Reasoning with Minimal Models: Efficient Algorithms and Applications, *Proc. Fourth International Conference on Principles of Knowledge Representation and Reasoning (KR-94)*, 1994, pp. 39–50.
4. Eiter, T., Gottlob, G., and Mannila, H., Adding Disjunction to Datalog, *Proceedings ACM PODS-94* , May 1994, pp. 267–278.
5. Eiter, T., Gottlob, G., On the Computational Cost of Disjunctive Logic Programming: Propositional Case, *Annals of Mathematics and Artificial Intelligence*, J. C. Baltzer AG, Science Publishers, Vol. 15, 1995, pp. 289–323.
6. Elkan, C., A rational Reconstruction of Nonmonotonic Truth Maintenance Systems, *Artificial Intelligence*, Vol. 43, 1990, pp. 219-234.
7. Gelfond, M., Lifschitz, V., The Stable Model Semantics for Logic Programming, *Proceedings Fifth Logic Programming Symposium*, MIT Press, Cambridge Mass., 1988, pp. 1070–1080.
8. Gelfond, M., Lifschitz, V., Classical Negation in Logic Programs and Disjunctive Databases, *New Generation Computing*, Vol. 9, 1991, pp. 365-385.
9. Gottlob, G., Complexity and Expressive Power of Disjunctive Logic Programming, In M. Bruynooghe, editor, *Proc. of the International Logic Programming Symposium (ILPS-'94)*, Ithaca NY, MIT Press, 1994, pp. 23–42.
10. IFIP-GI Workshop: *Disjunctive Logic Programming and Disjunctive Databases*, 13-th IFIP World Computer Congress,
11. Leone, N. , Rullo, P., Scarcello, F., Declarative and Fixpoint Characterizations of Disjunctive Stable Models, *Proceedings of International Logic Programming Symposium–ILPS'95*, Portland, Oregon, December 4–7, 1995.
12. Leone, N. , Rullo, P., Scarcello, F., On the Computation of Disjunctive Stable Models, *Proc. DEXA '96*, September 1996.
13. Lobo, J., Minker, J., Rajasekar, A., *Foundations of disjunctive logic programming*, The MIT Press, 1992.
14. Marek, W., Truszczyński, M., Autoepistemic Logic, *Journal of the ACM*, Vol. 38, No. 3, 1991, pp. 588–619.
15. Przymusinski, T., Stable Semantics for Disjunctive Programs, *New Generation Computing*, Vol. 9, 1991, pp. 401–424.
16. Sakama, C., Inoue, K., Embedding Circumscriptive Theories in General Disjunctive Programs, *Proc. LPNMR '95*, June 1995.
17. Van Gelder, A., Ross, K. A., Schlipf, J. S., The Well-Founded Semantics for General Logic Programs, *Journal of ACM*, Vol. 38, No. 3, 1991, pp. 620–650.
18. Vardi, M., Complexity of relational query languages, *Proceedings 14th ACM STOC*, 1982, pp. 137–146.

# Advanced Applications

# Analysis of Logic Based Systems

Danilo Boulanger*

C.N.CE Istituto del CNR, Via Santa Maria 36 I-56126 Pisa, Italy
e-mail: dinanzio@one-curce.cnr.it

Abstract. Model based analyses of declaring logic programs are discussed in detail. A model of a program captures its properties. Analyzing declaring models is, in principle, a flexible approach for verification and optimization of logic-based systems. A uniform implementation of these algorithms, which exploits deductive database technology is investigated. In particular, novel algorithms for generating finite models and for extracting properties from models are presented.

## 1  Introduction

Declarative use of logic-based systems is often considered as one of the major selling-point which significantly distinguishes logic-based systems from most of mainstream languages. Declarativeness significantly helps to develop applications involving a more concise and transparent semantics.

Applications with a declarative semantics are likely to be processed with research-based tools, which are aimed at checking and specifying "intended" properties of a program. The naturally suggests to exploit logic-based software as plug-in components in popular operating system environments since declarativeness helps to check and specialize such a component for particular requirements of the context in which it has to be plugged-in.

On the other hand, declarativeness is often in a striking contradiction with efficiency. This spoils the above observations. This problem and the above applecations of logic-based systems are the main motivation of this paper. Namely, the ultimate goal is a semantics-based tools which enable verification, specialization and optimization of declarative programs. However, what follows is only focused of developing analysis algorithms, which hopefully can be used as a component of such a tool. This only covers a part of the problem.

The aim of analysis algorithms which are discussed below is an investigating a program to suggest a more efficient its re-organization by transformation or introducing some additional constraints. In particular program points. This is typically done by "hand", when optimizing applications, which exploit deductive database and constraint solvers. Such analyses significantly deviate from those to be used in conventional compilers.

* A significant part of this research has been done at the CAD-FIRST, Berlin

# Analysis of Logic-Based Systems

Dmitri Boulanger*

CNUCE Istituto del CNR, via Santa Maria, 36 I-56126 Pisa, Italy
e-mail: dima@orione.cnuce.cnr.it

**Abstract.** Model based analyses of definite logic programs are discussed in detail. A model of a program captures its properties. Analyzing different models one obtains a flexible approach for verification and optimization of logic-based systems. A uniform implementation of the core algorithms, which exploits deductive database technology, is investigated. In particular, novel algorithms for generating large models and for extracting properties from models are presented.

## 1 Introduction

Declarativiness of logic-based systems is often considered as one of the major selling-point since it significantly distinguishes logic-based systems from most of mainstream languages. Declarativiness significantly helps to develop applications having a more clear and transparent semantics.

Applications with a declarative semantics are likely can be processed with *semantics*-based tools, which are aimed at checking and specializing "intended" properties of a program. This naturally suggests to exploit logic-based software as plug-in components in popular open system environments since declarativiness helps to check and specialize such a component for particular requirements of the socket in which it has to be plugged-in.

On the other hand, declarativiness is often in a striking contradiction with efficiency. This spoils the above observations. This problem and the above applications of logic-based systems are the main motivations of this paper. Namely, the ultimate goal is semantics-based tools which enable verification, specialization and optimization of declarative programs. However, what follows is only focused of developing analysis algorithms, which hopefully can be used as a component of such a toolkit. This only covers a part of the problem.

The aim of analysis algorithms, which are discussed below, is an investigating a program to suggest a more efficient its re-organization by transformation or introducing some additional constraints in particular program points. This is typically done by "hand" when optimizing applications, which exploit deductive databases and constraint solvers. Such analyses significantly deviate from those to be used in conventional compilers.

---

* A significant part of this research has been done at the GMD FIRST, Berlin.

An analysis of a program can be seen as obtaining some characterization of the set of *properties*, which is implied by chosen *semantics*. Thus, it relies on three issues — which semantics is applied, which properties to be derived and what does it mean "properties have been obtained". Indeed, one has to explain which programs he/she is talking about.

We deal with *definite (logic) programs* $P$ consisting of definite clauses

$$p_0(\bar{t}_0) \leftarrow p_1(\bar{t}_1), \ldots, p_n(\bar{t}_n)$$

with $p_i$ and $\bar{t}_i$, $i = 0, \ldots, n$, $n \geq 0$, predicates and tuples of terms, respectively. In most of the existing logic-based systems standard model based semantics of definite programs plays a crucial role. The above "abstracts" logic-based systems into definite programs.

Following Bossi [2], we mostly use the so-called $\mathcal{C}$-*semantics*. It associates each predicate $p$ in the program $P$ with the set of tuples

$$\mathcal{C}_p(P) =_{\mathsf{def}} \{\bar{t} \mid \{\overline{X}/\bar{t}\} \text{ is a } correct \text{ answer substitution for the query } \leftarrow p(\overline{X})\}$$

called *correct* answers for the predicate $p$. This is a "pure" declarative model based semantics since Lloyd [16] says that a tuple $\bar{t} \in \mathcal{C}_p(P)$ corresponds to the sentence $\forall : p(\bar{t})$, which is an "atomic" logical consequence of $P$. This is a "weakening" of the standard model based semantics, which associates the set of *all* logical consequences with a program.

Our choice of semantics is the result of a trade-off between efficiency, expressiveness and the above applications. The $\mathcal{C}$-semantics is enough for solving most of the above optimization problems since it expresses some "procedural" features of a program such as various variable dependencies combined with complex types. Moreover, it extends on programs, which are more complex than definite ones (see Section 2.2). In the context of logic-based systems, this is more important than capturing non-trivial "tricks" of the $SLD$-semantics such as definite freeness, which are not "understandable" in the $\mathcal{C}$-semantics.

Since the semantics is a *set of tuples of terms*, properties are defined as abstractions of tuples of terms. Namely, *the set of $\alpha$-properties*

$$\mathcal{P}^\alpha = \{\alpha(\bar{t}) \mid \bar{t} \text{ is a tuple of terms}\}$$

is induced by the mapping $\alpha$, called an *abstraction*, which satisfies: $\alpha(\bar{t}') = \alpha(\bar{t}'')$ for any tuples of terms $\bar{t}'$ and $\bar{t}''$, which are variants (renaming) of each other. This is a very general definition. It enables to treat various problem-specific analyses in a uniform way.

We mostly deal with **declarative analyses**. Such an analysis considers the set of correct answers as a semantics. Namely, given an abstraction $\alpha$, *the set of $\alpha$-properties of the correct answers* of the predicate $p$

$$\mathcal{C}_p^\alpha(P) =_{\mathsf{def}} \{\alpha(\bar{t}) \mid \bar{t} \in \mathcal{C}_p(P)\}$$

is considered as an **exact** analysis of the predicate $p$ with respect to the $\alpha$-properties. Typically it is *not* derivable. Therefore, a *safe declarative analysis* generates an approximation (a superset) of $\mathcal{C}_p^\alpha(P)$ for any predicate $p$ in $P$. Such analysis is more precise if it derives a more narrow approximation. These definitions are exploited throughout the paper.

Most of important declarative analyses can be explained as above. However, properties, which can be described as various aggregations of the set $\mathcal{C}(P)$, *cannot* be formalized with the above definitions in a straightforward way. Such analyses are out of the scope of this paper.

A declarative analysis can be seen as a **model based analysis**. Given an abstraction $\alpha$ and a program $P$, it consists of two steps:

1. Generation of a *model*[2] $M_P$ of a given definite program $P$
2. Obtaining an approximation of the set $\mathcal{C}_p^\alpha(P)$ of $\alpha$-properties of the correct answers of a predicate $p$ in $P$ using the above model $M_P$

Models to be generated at the first step are *(non-Herbrand) models of definite programs* in the standard sense of Lloyd [16]. A backbone of our approach is that any safe declarative analysis can be seen as an analysis of an appropriate model of a program. However, an important "pragmatic" restriction is applied — we only use *finite* models since this enables a very flexible and transparent implementation using deductive database systems.

The remaining part of the paper consists of two sections 2 and 3. Section 2 introduces the so-called $\alpha$-decoding algorithm. It corresponds to the second step of a model based analysis. In fact, it is a detailed explanation of the relation between a model and $\alpha$-properties of the $\mathcal{C}$-semantics of a program, which displays the most precise (non-improvable) model based analyses (see Proposition 1). Next, having this formalization, we explain our approach with several motivating examples. Finally, summarizing the introduced notions, we show the complete picture of the approach.

Section 3 mostly focuses on algorithms, which form the core of our approach. They are designed to be implemented using a deductive database technology. In particular, two novel techniques for model generation are explained in detail.

## 2 The $\alpha$-decoding Algorithm

### 2.1 Preliminaries

Following Lloyd [16], we use the standard notion of a first order language $\mathcal{L} = \langle \mathsf{F}, \mathsf{P}, \mathsf{V} \rangle$ with function symbols $\mathsf{F}$, predicates $\mathsf{P}$ and countable set of variables $\mathsf{V}$. Any such a language has at least one constant $c$. We write $f$, $g$ for function symbols, $p$, $q$ for predicates, $t$, $s$ for terms, and $\bar{t}$, $\bar{s}$ for tuples of terms. Variables appear in upper case. In particular, tuples consisting of pairwise distinct variables are written as $\overline{X}$ and $\overline{Y}$.

An *interpretation* $I = \langle J, \mathcal{H} \rangle$ of $\mathcal{L}$ consists of the *pre-interpretation* $J = \langle \mathsf{D}, \varPhi \rangle$ and of the *truth function* $\mathcal{H}$. The non-empty set $\mathsf{D} = \{d_1, \ldots, d_n, \ldots\}$ is the

---

[2] The Collins Gem English Dictionary says: "A model is a thing worthy of imitation."

*domain* of $J$. The set

$$\Phi = \{\varphi_f : \overline{D} \mapsto D \mid f \in \mathsf{F}\} \text{ with } \overline{D} =_{\text{def}} D \times \cdots \times D$$

is a set of *total* mappings assigned to the function symbols of the language. In other words, any function symbol $f \in \mathsf{F}$ of arity $n \geq 1$ is assigned the *function* $\varphi_f$, which is defined for any tuple $\overline{d} = \langle d_1, \ldots, d_n \rangle$ of domain elements $d_i \in D$, $i = 1, \ldots, n$. Also, any constant $c \in \mathsf{F}$ is assigned some domain element in $D$.

The truth function $\mathcal{H}$ is a possibly empty set of atoms $p(\overline{d})$ with $\overline{d} \in \overline{D}$. It indicates atoms $p(\overline{d})$ which are *true* in the interpretation $I$.

The pre-interpretation $J$ gives rise to the *evaluation* $\widetilde{J}$ of *ground* terms in $\mathcal{L}$, which is defined recursively as follows:

- $\widetilde{J}(f(\overline{t})) =_{\text{def}} \varphi_f(\widetilde{J}(t_1), \ldots, \widetilde{J}(t_n))$ for any function symbol $f/n \in \mathsf{F}$, $n \geq 0$ and for any tuple $\overline{t} = \langle t_1, \ldots, t_n \rangle$ of ground terms
- $\widetilde{J}(d) =_{\text{def}} d$ for any domain element $d \in D$

A *variable assignment* $\vartheta$ assigns each variable $X$ in $\mathsf{V}$ a domain element $\vartheta(X)$ in $D$. As usual, given a term $t$, $\vartheta(t)$ is obtained replacing each variable $X$ in $t$ with $\vartheta(X)$. Notice that given a tuple $\overline{t}$ of terms in $\mathcal{L}$, the above evaluation $\widetilde{J}$ is applicable on any tuple $\vartheta(\overline{t})$ with $\vartheta$ is variable assignment with respect to $J$.

Now the $J$-**representation** $\rho^J$ extends the evaluation $\widetilde{J}$ on *all* tuples $\overline{t} = \langle t_1, \ldots, t_n \rangle$, $n \geq 1$ of terms as follows: $\rho^J(\overline{t}) =_{\text{def}}$

$$\{\langle \widetilde{J}(\vartheta(t_1)), \ldots, \widetilde{J}(\vartheta(t_n)) \rangle \mid \vartheta \text{ is a variable assignment with respect to } J\}$$

A tuple of possibly non-ground terms is represented as a non-empty set of tuples of domain elements. Therefore, a set $D$ consisting of tuples of domain elements is a $J$-**representation set** of arity $n$, $n > 0$, iff

there exists a tuple of terms $\overline{t} = \langle t_1, \ldots, t_n \rangle$ such that $D = \rho^J(\overline{t})$

Note Lloyd [16] says that $D$ is the set of term assignments of $\overline{t}$ with respect to the pre-interpretation $J$.

All the above notions are standard. Below they are used very extensively. So, it is important to be fluent in the above definitions.

## 2.2 $J$-Models and $\alpha$-Properties

A *model* $M_T$ of a theory $T$ is an interpretation such that any sentence in $T$ is true in $M_T$. A theory $T$ is a *logical consequence* of $\widehat{T}$, iff any model of $\widehat{T}$ is a model of $T$. Theories having the same set of models are logically equivalent.

Any model $M_P$ of a program $P$ captures its properties. As it has been explained in Section 1, we are mostly interested in properties offered by the $\mathcal{C}$-semantics. The relation between $\alpha$-properties of the $\mathcal{C}$-semantics and a model of a program is quite transparent since it only relies on the standard notions in Section 2.1. However, we need a few definitions.

Assume an abstraction $\alpha$ and a pre-interpretation $J$ are given then: the $\alpha$-properties are said to be $J$-**derivable** iff

$- \rho^J(\bar{t}') = \rho^J(\bar{t}'')$ implies that $\alpha(\bar{t}') = \alpha(\bar{t}'')$ for any tuples of terms $\bar{t}'$ and $\bar{t}''$

This definition simply says that the abstraction $\alpha$ cannot be more fine-grained than the $J$-representation. This is **the correctness condition** ensuring existence of an algorithm for deriving the $\alpha$-properties from models having $J$ as a pre-interpretation. It is described below.

Let $M_P$ of a program $P$ be of the form $\langle J, \mathcal{H} \rangle$ with $J$ as a pre-interpretation and with $\mathcal{H}$ as a truth function. Below such models are called $J$-**models**. The set of domain tuples

$$\mathcal{H}_p =_{\text{def}} \{ \bar{d} \mid p(\bar{d}) \in \mathcal{H} \}$$

defines the $p$-restriction of $\mathcal{H}$ on the predicate $p$ (this is a technical definition). Given $J$-derivable $\alpha$-properties, the $\alpha$-**decoding** algorithm below generates an approximation of the set $C_p^\alpha(P)$ of $\alpha$-properties of the correct answers for a predicate $p$ in $P$:

1. construct all $J$-representation sets $D_k$, $k \in K$ such that $D_k \subseteq \mathcal{H}_p$
2. for each $k \in K$ find a tuple $\bar{t}_k$ such that $\rho^J(\bar{t}_k) = D_k$
3. report the set of $\alpha$-properties $\{ \alpha(\bar{t}_k) \mid k \in K \}$ as a result

Assume that $\bar{t} \in C_p(P)$ then: the sentence $\forall : p(\bar{t})$ is a logical consequence of $P$. This means that $M_P$ is a model of $\forall : p(\bar{t})$. Since the $J$-representation set $D = \rho^J(\bar{t})$ is the set of term assignments of $\bar{t}$ we have that $D \subseteq \mathcal{H}_p$. Indeed, recalling model-theoretic definition of the universal quantifier, one obtains that

the sentence $\forall : p(\bar{t})$ is true in the interpretation $\langle J, \mathcal{H} \rangle$ iff $\rho^J(\bar{t}) \subseteq \mathcal{H}_p$

Hence, step 1 discovers the above set $D$. Next, step 2 derives from this set some tuple of terms $\bar{s}$ such that $D = \rho^J(\bar{s})$. Since the abstraction $\alpha$ induces $J$-derivable properties, the tuple $\bar{s}$ satisfies $\alpha(\bar{s}) = \alpha(\bar{t})$. Hence, any property in the set $C_p^\alpha(P)$ is reported by step 3, i.e. the analysis is *safe*.

To investigate precision of the above approximation we slightly refine definition a model based analysis — a procedure is a $J$-**model based** $\alpha$-**analysis** iff given a program $P$, it derives an approximation of the set of $\alpha$-properties of the correct answers of any predicate in $P$ *only* using a $J$-model of $P$, i.e. as soon as a model is obtained, the program itself is thrown away.

Let A be a decoding algorithm which, given a $J$-model, derives from it a set of $\alpha$-properties. The algorithm A is *possibly more precise* than the $\alpha$-decoding iff there exists a $J$-model $M$ of a program $P$ such that A, being applied on $M$, reports a set of $\alpha$-properties for some predicate $p$ in $P$, which is *not* a superset of that obtained with the $\alpha$-decoding of $M$. With this definition, we have the following result:

**Proposition 1.** *Given a pre-interpretation $J$ and $\alpha$-properties, there is no (safe) $J$-model based $\alpha$-analysis iff at least one of the following conditions holds:*

- *the $\alpha$-properties are not $J$-derivable*
- *the decoding algorithm is possibly more precise than the $\alpha$-decoding.*

□

Hence, given a pre-interpretation $J$ and $J$-derivable $\alpha$-properties, a $J$-model based $\alpha$-analysis such that:

- it uses *least* $J$-models
- it exploits the $\alpha$-decoding of models

is not improvable in the class of $J$-model based $\alpha$-analyses. Such an improvement has to deal with programs themselves rather than only with their models (see Section 3.4 below).

Some logic-based system allow more complex programs than definite ones. The above only exploits *definition* of a model rather than specific features of definite programs. So, extending the $C$-semantics on arbitrary first order theories $T$ in the straightforward way:

$$C(T) =_{\text{def}} \{A \mid A \text{ is an atom such that } \forall: A \text{ is a logical consequence of } T \}$$

one obtains an approximation of the set $C^{\alpha}(T)$ of $\alpha$-properties of atomic logical consequences of $T$. However, computing models of programs such as normal programs or disjunctive programs needs complex algorithms of Bry [7, 8]. Also, some aspects of these programs might be missed since the $C$-semantics is weaker than the standard model model based one.

## 2.3 A Motivating Example

Below the well-known groundness analysis is exploited as an illustration of the intended use of the machinery introduced so far.

Let $J^{gi}$ be a pre-interpretation with the set $\{0, 1\}$ as a domain and with the following simple interpretation of function symbols:

- any constant $c$ has the image 1
- a tuple $\overline{d}$ of domain elements has the image 1 with respect to any appropriate function *iff* $\overline{d}$ only consists of 1's, i.e. iff it is of the form $\overline{1 \cdots 1}$
- a tuple $\overline{d}$ of domain elements has the image 0 with respect to any appropriate function *iff* $\overline{d}$ has occurrences of 0

This is a well-defined pre-interpretation since all function symbols in a language are assigned total functions. This is the only requirement which ensures that a pre-interpretation is well-defined (cf. Section 2.1). Note that the pre-interpretation $J^{gi}$ can be seen as language-independent since it does not know function symbols of a language. In fact, this exactly corresponds to abstract domains of Cousot and Cousot [10], which are typically program-independent.

---

[3] Denotations of pre-interpretations are consistent with those in [3, 4, 5, 6, 12].

Now consider the well-known naive reverse program $Rev =$

$$a_1: \; app([\,], L, L).$$
$$a_2: \; app([H|T], L, [H|R]) \leftarrow app(T, L, R).$$

$$r_1: \; rev([\,], [\,]).$$
$$r_2: \; rev([H|T], L) \leftarrow rev(T, R), app(R, [H], L).$$

Below we assume that clauses in a program have unique names, e.g. the above program consists of the clauses $a_1$, $a_2$, $r_1$ and $r_2$.

The sets

$$\mathcal{H}_{app} = \{\overline{000}, \overline{010}, \overline{100}, \overline{111}\} \text{ and } \mathcal{H}_{rev} = \{\overline{00}, \overline{11}\}$$

are the $app$ and $rev$ restrictions, respectively, of the truth function of the least $J^{gi}$-model of the program $Rev$, i.e. any $J^{gi}$-model of $Rev$ has the truth function consisting of supersets of the above sets.

Having the $LDL$-system [1], such a model generation is as follows. Given a program $P$ and a finite pre-interpretation $J$, one compiles $P$ into the $J$-**equivalent function-free** program $Q$ (i.e. $P$ and $Q$ have the same set of $J$-models). This can be done using the Gallagher's compiler [12]. Its modification is explained in Section 3.2. Next, the program $Q$ is arranged as an executable $LDL$-module. After a smart compile-time optimization an execution of $Q$ by the run-time $LDL$-engine generates the least $J$-model of $P$.

Least $J^{gi}$-models of definite programs have a simple and efficient decoding algorithm. Given a set $\mathcal{H}_p$ of domain tuples $\overline{d} = \langle d_1, \ldots, d_n \rangle$ of arity $n$, $n > 0$, which is the $p$-restriction of the truth function of a *least* $J^{gi}$-model, do:

1. assign to tuples in $\mathcal{H}_p = \{\overline{d}_k | k \in K\}$ distinct variables $U_k$, $k \in K$
2. construct a tuple $\langle t_1, \ldots, t_n \rangle$ of terms $t_i$, $i = 1, \ldots, n$ which satisfy:
   - $t_i$ is a ground term *iff* $d_i = 1$ for *any* tuple $\langle d_1, \ldots, d_i, \ldots, d_n \rangle$ in $\mathcal{H}_p$
   - $t_i$ is a non-ground term with occurrences of the variable $U_k$, which is assigned to the tuple $\overline{d}_k = \langle d_1, \ldots, d_i, \ldots, d_n \rangle$ in $\mathcal{H}_p$, iff $d_i = 0$

In the above example, with the variable assignment

$$\mathcal{H}_{app} = \{U_1 : \overline{000}, U_2 : \overline{010}, U_3 : \overline{100}, U_4 : \overline{111}\} \text{ and } \mathcal{H}_{rev} = \{U_1 : \overline{00}, U_2 : \overline{11}\}$$

one derives the tuples

$$\overline{t}_{app} = \langle [U_1, U_2], [U_1, U_3], [U_1, U_2, U_3] \rangle \text{ and } \overline{t}_{rev} = \langle [U_1], [U_1] \rangle$$

Note that $\rho^{gi}(\overline{t}_{app}) = \mathcal{H}_{app}$ and $\rho^{gi}(\overline{t}_{rev}) = \mathcal{H}_{rev}$. In general, given a $p$-restriction $\mathcal{H}_p$ of the truth function of a least $J^{gi}$-model of a definite program, there exists a tuple $\overline{t}_p$ such that $\rho^{gi}(\overline{t}_p) = \mathcal{H}_p$. In other words, a $p$-restriction of the truth function of a least $J^{gi}$-model of a definite program is a $J^{gi}$-representation set. The above decoding algorithm uncovers such a tuple of terms, which gives rise to the $J^{gi}$-representation set. This is a quite specific feature of the pre-interpretation $J^{gi}$, which does not hold for more complex pre-interpretations.

Given the $\alpha$-decoding algorithm, tuples of terms having the same $J^{gi}$-representation set might be considered as equivalent. This enables to simplify tuples of terms, which are obtained with the above decoding. For instance, dropping the variable $U_1$, which occurs in all terms in $\bar{t}_{app}$, and renaming the remaining variables, simplifies the above tuple $\bar{t}_{app}$ as $\langle [U_1], [U_2], [U_1, U_2] \rangle$.

The above tuples $\bar{t}_{app}$ and $\bar{t}_{rev}$ are the most general tuples, i.e. all other tuples, which form the complete decoding of the sets $\mathcal{H}_{app}$ and $\mathcal{H}_{rev}$, are obtained replacing variables with a constant in all possible ways. Namely, one generates the following two sets of tuples for $\mathcal{H}_{app}$ and $\mathcal{H}_{rev}$, respectively:

$$\begin{array}{ll} \langle [U_1], [U_2], [U_1, U_2] \rangle & \langle [U_1], [U_1] \rangle \\ \langle c, \ [U_2], [U_2] \rangle & \langle c, \ c \rangle \\ \langle [U_1], c, \ [U_1] \rangle & \\ \langle c, \ c, \ c \rangle & \end{array}$$

This can be done in a more systematic way:

- construct all subsets of $\mathcal{H}_p$ having the tuple $\overline{1 \ldots 1}$
- decode the obtained sets as it was explained above

Such a decoding gives rise to the most precise analysis since one could show that it exactly corresponds to the first two steps of the $\alpha$-decoding algorithm in Section 2.2 if it is applied on least $J^{gi}$-models.

Decoding of truth functions into tuples of terms does not care about properties to be derived. On the contrary, the final step of the $\alpha$-decoding only allows abstractions satisfying the correctness condition with respect to the used pre-interpretation. One could show that in our example properties such as definite groundness and variable dependencies, which are exactly those expressible in the abstract domain $PROP$ of Marriott and Søndergaard [18], are observable. Namely, the observable dependencies between non-ground terms in a tuple can be described as follows. Given a tuple of non-ground terms $\bar{t} = \langle t_1, \ldots, t_n \rangle$, $n \geq 1$, for a pair of non-empty sets $N', N'' \subseteq \{1, \ldots, n\}$ one observes variable dependencies which are expressible as

$$\cup_{i \in N'} var(t_i) \ = \ \cup_{j \in N'} var(t_j)$$

where the set of variables occurring in a term $t$ is written as $var(t)$. Hence, as an illustration, one observes the following properties of the correct answers of the predicates $app$ and $rev$ of the program $Rev$:

- $\langle t_1, t_2, t_3 \rangle$ is a correct answer for $app$ only if $var(t_1) \cup var(t_2) = var(t_3)$
- $\langle t_1, t_2 \rangle$ is a correct answer for $rev$ only if $var(t_1) = var(t_2)$

It is important to see that observing the above properties only needs most general tuples rather than all tuples of terms, which are required by the $\alpha$-decoding algorithm. Indeed, considering the above variable dependencies as an abstraction, say $\alpha$, one easily verifies that $\alpha(\bar{t}) = \alpha(\bar{t}.\theta)$ for any tuple of terms $\bar{t}$ and any substitution $\theta$. In other words, the $\alpha$-properties are downward closed.

However, this, again, thanks to specific features of the chosen abstraction *and* the pre-interpretation $J^{gi}$. In more complex situation this nice feature might be lost. Therefore, we have illustrated a more general technique.

The above illustrates a *deriving* properties, which is a typical goal of a static analysis. However, a lot of applications only needs a *verification* of *expected* properties. In our settings this problem is more simple since it needs not decoding of models. Let us illustrate this.

First of all, the least $J^{gi}$-model of the naive reverse program *Rev* enables to verify that the atoms $app([X],[],[])$ and $rev(X,[])$ are not correct answers of the program *Rev*. Indeed, the sets

$$\rho^{gi}(\langle[X],[],[]\rangle) = \{\overline{011},\overline{111}\} \quad \text{and} \quad \rho^{gi}(\langle X,[]\rangle) = \{\overline{01},\overline{11}\}$$

are not subsets of the *app* and *rev* restrictions of the truth function this model. Therefore, the sentences $\forall : app([X],[],[])$ and $\forall : rev(X,[])$ are not logical consequences of *Rev*, i.e. they are not correct answers.

A bit less trivial to show that the tuple $\langle t_1, t_2 \rangle$ is a correct answer of the predicate *rev* only if $var(t_1) = var(t_2)$. Assume that there exists a variable $X$ such that $X \in var(t_1)$ but $X \notin var(t_2)$ then: there exists a substitution $\theta$ such that the term $t_2.\theta$ is ground but the term $t_1.\theta$ contains the variable $X$. On the other hand, any instance of a correct answer is a correct answer. Therefore, the tuple $\langle t_1, t_2 \rangle.\theta$ is a correct answer. It is not difficult to see that the set

$$\rho^{gi}(\langle t_1, t_2 \rangle.\theta) = \{\overline{01},\overline{11}\}$$

is not a subset of the *rev*-restriction of the truth function of the least $J^{gi}$-model of the naive reverse program. So, the tuple $\langle t_1, t_2 \rangle.\theta$ is not a correct answer, i.e. we have a contradiction. Similar, assuming that there exists a variable $X$ such that $X \in var(t_2)$ but $X \notin var(t_1)$, one derives a contradiction. Applying this method, one could also verify that the tuple $\langle t_1, t_2, t_3 \rangle$ is a correct answer for the predicate *app* only if $var(t_1) \cup var(t_2) = var(t_3)$.

The main problem with the above method is ensuring that a hypothesis can be checked against the given $J$-model, i.e. one needs a proof that the corresponding properties are $J$-derivable.

## 2.4 Three Parts of Model based Analyses

Our approach exploits a trivial idea — take a database and store in it clever analyses. Given discussion in Section 2.3, the pre-interpretation $J^{giv}$ is a such a clever analysis. When an analysis is required, find it in the database and execute it. A database is organized as a collection of pre-interpretations. Model-based analysis algorithms provide a flexible and uniform way of querying such a database. The idea exactly fits mature deductive database systems[4]. However, such a technology needs a quite systematic organization.

---

[4] We use the *LDL*-system coupled with the DBMS Oracle.

The $\alpha$-decoding algorithm, which is a backbone notion of the approach, have been introduced in a "declarative form", i.e. it shows *what* should be implemented rather than *how*. This is important for the systematization of analyses in the database since it does not exploit features of particular pre-interpretations. Discussion in Section 2.3 illustrates that there are there important issues: the **model generation**, the **decoding of models** and the **granularity** of pre-interpretations.

A pre-interpretation $\hat{J}$ is a **refinement** of the pre-interpretation $J$, written $J \leq \hat{J}$, iff any properties, which are derivable with respect $J$ are also derivable with respect to $\hat{J}$. In other words, $\hat{J}$ is more precise than $J$ since $\hat{J}$ enables to observe more properties of tuples of terms. Pre-interpretations $J'$ and $J''$ have *the same granularity* iff $J' \leq J''$ and $J' \geq J''$. Given the correctness condition of the $\alpha$-decoding algorithm, an importance of a pre-interpretation in its granularity rather than in its structure (domain elements and functions), which only play the role of an implementation of granularities. Also, it is important to know that non-isomorphic pre-interpretations may have exactly the same sets of derivable properties, i.e. a granularity might have different implementations.

Given a class of pre-interpretations, which are allowed as entities of the database, one needs a language which describes granularities of these pre-interpretations. A crucial point is that such a class of pre-interpretations should be non-trivial to cover important applications. The language describing granularities enables to search subtable pre-interpretations in the database provided that required properties are explained in terms of this language. Also, having granularities, the database becomes a partially ordered set. This is exploited in the next section.

In this paper the notion of granularity is only illustrated by examples since it should be discussed separately. A more detailed discussion can be found in [3]. It is important to know that developing of granularities is a topic of algebraic specifications of Wirsing [20]. In fact, it is a problem of an enumeration of $J$-representation sets, which has been investigated by Mezei and Wright [19] and by Goguen [14]. Exploiting these results and the $LDL$-system, we have implemented a prototype fixpoint procedure for generating $J$-representation sets for a class of pre-interpretations.

Model generation is explained in the next section. It introduces two novel techniques: a model generation using a refinement chain and a model generation with indexing. Both of them are designed for constructing efficient model based analyses with the $LDL$-system. Refinement chains enable generation of large models. An importance of indexing in efficient decoding of models. Moreover, it might significantly increase precision of an approximation.

## 3 Model Generation

### 3.1 Programs in an Extended Language

First of all, let us explain a background of the compilation algorithm which, as it has already been mentioned in Section 2.3, rewrites a given program into the

$J$-equivalent function-free one. Recall that Maher [17] says that if $J$ is the Herbrand pre-interpretation, then the $J$-equivalence becomes logical equivalence, i.e. definite programs with the same set of Herbrand models are logically equivalent.

Let $P$ be a definite logic program in a language $\mathcal{L}$ and $J$ a finite pre-interpretation of $\mathcal{L}$ with D as a finite domain. Extending $\mathcal{L}$ with domain elements of D as constants, one obtains the *extended language* $\mathcal{L}_\mathsf{D} = \langle \mathsf{F} \cup \mathsf{D}, \mathsf{P}, \mathsf{V} \rangle$. It is a first order language, and, therefore, one may consider programs in $\mathcal{L}_\mathsf{D}$ and their $J$-models. In particular, our compiler takes a program in $\mathcal{L}$ and rewrites it into the $J$-equivalent program in $\mathcal{L}_\mathsf{D}$. In other words, the both programs being considered as programs in $\mathcal{L}_\mathsf{D}$ have the same set of $J$-models.

Let $C$ be a clause $p_0(\bar{t}_0) \leftarrow p_1(\bar{t}_1), \ldots, p_n(\bar{t}_n)$, $n \geq 0$ then: the $J$-representation of $C$ is the program (set)

$$\rho^J(C) =_{\text{def}} \{ p_0(\bar{d}_0) \leftarrow p_1(\bar{d}_1), \ldots, p_n(\bar{d}_n) \mid \langle \bar{d}_0, \bar{d}_1, \ldots, \bar{d}_n \rangle \in \rho^J((\bar{t}_0, \bar{t}_1, \ldots, \bar{t}_n)) \}$$

Similar, the set (ground function-free program in $\mathcal{L}_\mathsf{D}$)

$$\rho^J(P) =_{\text{def}} \bigcup_{C \in P} \rho^J(C)$$

is called a $J$-representation of the program $P$.

Let $\mathbf{I}^J$ be the set of interpretations of $\mathcal{L}$ having $J$ as a pre-interpretation. Given a program $P$ in $\mathcal{L}_\mathsf{D}$, for any $I$ of the form $\langle J, \mathcal{H} \rangle$ the operator

$$T_P^J : \mathbf{I}^J \to \mathbf{I}^J$$

is defined as follows: $T_P^J(I)$ is an interpretation with $J$ as a pre-interpretation and with the set

$$\mathcal{H} \cup \left\{ p_0(\bar{d}_0) \,\middle|\, \begin{array}{l} p_0(\bar{d}_0) \leftarrow p_1(\bar{d}_1), \ldots, p_n(\bar{d}_n) \in \rho^J(P), \; n \geq 0 \\ \text{and } \{ p_1(\bar{d}_1), \ldots, p_n(\bar{d}_n) \} \subseteq \mathcal{H} \end{array} \right\}$$

a truth function. This slightly reformulates Lloyd [16] and Maher [17]. Therefore, we have the following proposition.

**Proposition 2.** *An interpretation $I$ is a $J$-model of $P$ iff $T_P^J(I) = I$.* □

Hence, the set of fixpoints of the operator $T_P^J$ is the set of $J$-models of the program $P$. As usual, the least fixpoint of $T_P^J$ is the least $J$-model of $P$.

## 3.2 Least Model Generator

Let $P$ be a definite logic program in a language $\mathcal{L}$ and $J$ a finite pre-interpretation of $\mathcal{L}$ with D as a finite domain then: Proposition 2 enables to see an elimination of function symbols, which preserves $J$-equivalence, as a generation of the $J$-representation of a program. However, this is not acceptable because such a program typically has too much clauses. So, we use a bit more efficient rewriting.

Let $C$ be a clause. An atom $p(t_1, \ldots, t_n)$, $n \geq 1$ in $C$ is replaced by a function-free atom $p(s_1, \ldots, s_n)$ such that the terms $t_i$ and $s_i$, $i = 1, \ldots, n$ satisfy:

- $s_i = \tilde{J}(t_i)$ *iff* the term $t_i$ is ground
- $s_i$ is a fresh variable $Y_i$ *iff* the term $t_i$ is a non-ground non-variable term
- $s_i$ coincides with $t_i$ *iff* $t_i$ is a variable

A variable in $C$ with at least one occurrence as an argument of an atom is called a **surface** variable. Only surface variables are preserved by the above rewriting. Other variables having no such occurrence in $C$ are called **underground** variables. Let $\overline{X}$ be the surface variables occurring in replaced terms and $\overline{Y}$ be the new fresh variables, which has been introduced by the above rewriting then: a predicate $c(\overline{X}, \overline{Y})$, called the **derived constraint** of $C$, is added to the body as final step in compiling the clause $C$. So, introducing constraints drops *all* underground variables.

The above rewrites a program $P$ into the function-free program $Q$, which only consist of clauses having occurrences of variables and domain elements. As a final step of this rewriting, derived constraints in $Q$ have to be given definitions. Let $c(\overline{X}, \overline{Y})$ be such a constraint of a clause in $Q$ and $\bar{t} = \langle t_1, \ldots, t_m \rangle$, $m \geq 1$ the tuple of terms, which have been eliminated introducing the corresponding fresh variables $\overline{Y} = \langle Y_1, \ldots, Y_m \rangle$, i.e. the term $t_i$ in the original clause in $P$ has been replaced by the variable $Y_i$, $i = 1, \ldots, n$.

Consider the set

$$D_{\mathbf{c}} = \{ \tilde{J}(\vartheta(\langle \overline{X}, \bar{t} \rangle)) \mid \vartheta \text{ is a variable assignment} \}$$

called the **domain relation** of $\mathbf{c}$. The tuple $\langle \overline{X}, \overline{Y} \rangle$ is considered as attributes of this relation. Such a relation gives rise to the set of facts

$$\{ \mathbf{c}(\bar{d}) \mid \bar{d} \in D_{\mathbf{c}} \}$$

which can be added to the above compiled program. Taking into account the $T_P^J$-function and Proposition 2, observe that the constraint atoms in the compiled clauses, being unfolded with the above facts, produce a program, which is the $J$-representation of the "source" program $P$. Hence, our compilation algorithm preserves $J$-equivalence with respect to predicates in $P$.

Thus, given a definite program $P$ and a finite pre-interpretation $J$, our compiler generates the function-free program $Q$ and the database $db$ consisting of the domain relations of derived constraints in $Q$.

As an illustration, the above being applied on the program $Rev$ in Section 2.3 yields the program $Q =$

$$a_1 : app(1, L, L).$$
$$a_2 : app(Y_1, L, Y_2) \leftarrow app(T, L, R), c_{a_2}(T, R, Y_1, Y_2).$$

$$r_1 : rev(1, 1).$$
$$r_2 : rev(Y_1, L) \leftarrow rev(T, R), app(R, Y_2, L), c_{r_2}(T, Y_1, Y_2).$$

The variable $H$, which is an underground variable in $Rev$, has disappeared. The constraints $c_{a_2}$ and $c_{r_2}$ have domain relations, which are obtained as follows:

$$D_{a_2} = \{ \tilde{J}^{\mathfrak{g}^i}(\vartheta(\langle T, R, [H|T], [H|R] \rangle)) \mid \vartheta \text{ is a variable assignment} \}$$
$$D_{r_2} = \{ \tilde{J}^{\mathfrak{g}^i}(\vartheta(\langle T, [H|T], [H] \rangle)) \mid \vartheta \text{ is a variable assignment} \}$$

This results in the database *db* consisting of the following two relations:

$$c_{a_2}(0,0,0,0). \quad c_{r_2}(0,0,0).$$
$$c_{a_2}(0,1,0,0). \quad c_{r_2}(0,0,1).$$
$$c_{a_2}(1,0,0,0). \quad c_{r_2}(1,0,0).$$
$$c_{a_2}(0,1,0,1). \quad c_{r_2}(1,1,1).$$
$$c_{a_2}(1,0,1,0).$$
$$c_{a_2}(1,1,0,0).$$
$$c_{a_2}(1,1,1,1).$$

Considering this program as a definite program in a language consisting of constants 0 and 1, one observes that the least Herbrand model of this program, being restricted on the predicates *app* and *rev*, forms the sets

$$\mathcal{H}_{app} = \{\overline{000}, \overline{010}, \overline{100}, \overline{111}\} \text{ and } \mathcal{H}_{rev} = \{\overline{00}, \overline{11}\}$$

which have been already discussed in Section 2.3. Computing such a model with the *LDL*-system is straightforward. The database *db* is allocated as a in-memory *LDL*-database or, if a very large pre-interpretation is used, as a disk database. The *LDL*-compiler is smart enough to perform an optimization ensuring an efficient bottom-up fixpoint execution. It can be improved providing key and indexing declaration since the domain relations of constraints are allocated as a database. For large databases *db* such declarations are very important. The last thing which needs attention is the safety conditions, imposed by the *LDL*-system, e.g. the clause $a_1$ in the program $Q$ should be rewritten as

$$a_1 : app(1, L, L) \leftarrow dom(L), dom(L).$$

with additional database $\{dom(0), dom(1)\}$.

On the other hand, a simple analysis of the tuples

$$\langle T, R, [H|T], [H|R]\rangle \text{ and } \langle T, [H|T], [H]\rangle$$

which give rise to the above domain relations, enables to rewrite the above as

$$c_{a_2}(T, R, 0, 0). \quad c_{r_2}(0, 0, Y).$$
$$c_{a_2}(T, R, T, R). \quad c_{r_2}(1, Y, Y).$$

Similar optimization of constraint relation has been used by Gallagher [12]. It is more suitable for top-down execution with tabulation. However, it not that simple to use it for pre-interpretations with large domains in a uniform way.

## 3.3 Model Generation using a Refinement Chain

The above illustrates that computing of not very large models can be done with acceptable efficiency. An implementation of Gallagher [12] has shown that "small" pre-interpretations are those with about 5-6 domain elements. What follows is is aimed to compute models with more than 20 domain elements.

The main idea is that a large model should *not* be generated from "scratch", i.e. first, take a small pre-interpretation and generate the corresponding least model. Next, using the obtained model, generate a more precise model, etc. Namely, given a pre-interpretation $\widehat{J}$ having a large domain, $\widehat{J}$-model generation is supposed to be done with an appropriate refinement chain

$$J_0 \leq J_1 \leq \cdots \leq \widehat{J}$$

which starts with the small pre-interpretation $J_0$. It seems that for most of applications the pre-interpretation $J^{gi}$ is the best as the first element of such a refinement chain. Let us to show the mechanism, which makes use of the obtained least model to optimize generation of a more precise pre-interpretation.

Let $P$ be a program and $J$ a finite pre-interpretation. Consider the $J$-compiled program $Q$ and the corresponding database $db$, which are obtained as it has been explained in Section 3.2. It is important see that the program $Q$ itself nearly independent of the pre-interpretation $J$ since it only has occurrence of $J$-images of ground terms of $P$, which can be easily replaced if $J$ is changed.

Now take a clause $C$ in $Q$ having the form

$$p_0(\overline{s}_0) \leftarrow p_1(\overline{s}_1), \ldots, p_n(\overline{s}_n), \mathbf{c}(\overline{X}, \overline{Y})$$

with $\overline{s}_i$, $i = 0, \ldots, n$, $n \geq 0$, tuples consisting of variables and domain elements of $J$ and consider the set

$$\widetilde{D}_{\mathbf{c}} = \left\{ \vartheta(\langle \overline{X}, \overline{Y} \rangle) \;\middle|\; \begin{array}{l} \vartheta \text{ is a variable assignment such that it satisfies:} \\ \bullet \; \vartheta(\overline{s}_i) \in \mathcal{H}_{p_i} \text{ for all predicates } p_i \text{ in } C, i = 0, \ldots, n \\ \bullet \; \vartheta(\langle \overline{X}, \overline{Y} \rangle) \in D_{\mathbf{c}} \end{array} \right\}$$

where $D_{\mathbf{c}}$ is the domain relation of the above derived constraint $\mathbf{c}$. It is not difficult to see that

$$\widetilde{D}_{\mathbf{c}} \subseteq D_{\mathbf{c}}$$

On the other hand, taking the program $Q$ with the database $\widetilde{db}$, which is obtained from reduced domain relations $\widetilde{D}_{\mathbf{c}}$, and computing its least Herbrand model, one obtains exactly the same sets $\mathcal{H}_p$ for all predicates $p$ in $P$. In other words, replacing the database $db$ with the database $\widetilde{db}$ enables more efficient generation of the least $J$-model of $P$.

As an illustration of the above algorithm, the database $db$ in Section 3.2 reduces to the following database $\widetilde{db}$

$$
\begin{array}{ll}
c_{a_2}(0,0,0,0). & c_{r_2}(0,0,0). \\
c_{a_2}(1,0,0,0). & c_{r_2}(0,0,1). \\
c_{a_2}(1,0,1,0). & c_{r_2}(1,0,0). \\
c_{a_2}(1,1,1,1). & c_{r_2}(1,1,1). \\
c_{a_2}(1,1,0,0). &
\end{array}
$$

which corresponds to the domain relations $\widetilde{D}_{a_2}$ and $\widetilde{D}_{r_2}$.

A reduced $J$-database can be used to minimize a $\widehat{J}$-database if $J \leq \widehat{J}$. Let us illustrate this by an example, which exploits the pre-interpretation $J^{gi}$ as a "small" pre-interpretation. The "large" pre-interpretation $J^{giv}$ has the the set $\{v, 0, 1\}$ as a domain. Its set of functions is very similar to the one of $J^{gi}$ and it is defined as follows:

- any constant $c$ has the image 1
- a tuple $\overline{d}$ of domain elements has the image 1 with respect to any appropriate function *iff* $\overline{d}$ only consists of 1's, i.e. iff it is of the form $\overline{1 \cdots 1}$
- a tuple $\overline{d}$ of domain elements has the image 0 with respect to any appropriate function *iff* $\overline{d}$ has occurrences of 0 or/and occurrences of $v$

In other words, the domain element 0 of $J^{gi}$ has been split into $v$ and 0 in $J^{giv}$. However, the roles of $v$ and 0 in $J^{giv}$ are very different since the domain element $v$ does not appear as a target of any function. This significantly increases the expressive power. A detailed investigation of this effect can be found in [3].

Now consider the mapping

$$\kappa \colon \{v, 0, 1\} \to \{0, 1\}$$

such that

$$\kappa(v) = 0 \quad \kappa(0) = 0 \quad \kappa(1) = 1$$

It is a surjective homomorphism from the domain of $J^{giv}$ onto the domain of $J^{gi}$. In general, pre-interpretations, which are related with a surjective homomorphism, form a refinement chain, e.g. $J^{gi} \leq J^{giv}$.

Existence of surjective homomorphism is only a sufficient condition to have a refinement chain, i.e. refinement is more general notion since there exists pre-interpretations such that $J' \leq J''$ but there is no surjective homomorphism from $J''$ onto $J'$.

Now the above reduced domain relations $\tilde{D}_{a_2}$ and $\tilde{D}_{r_2}$, which are relations with respect to the pre-interpretation $J^{gi}$, can be used to filter out some domain tuples when generating the corresponding domain relations with respect to the pre-interpretation $J^{giv}$. Namely, this is done as follows:

$$D_{a_2} = \left\{ \overline{d} \;\middle|\; \begin{array}{l} \overline{d} = \tilde{J}^{giv}(\vartheta(\langle T, R, [H|T], [H|R]\rangle)) \text{ ssatisfies:} \\ \bullet\ \vartheta \text{ is a variable assignment w.r.t. } J^{giv} \\ \bullet\ \kappa(\overline{d}) \in \tilde{D}_{a_2} \end{array} \right\}$$

and

$$D_{r_2} = \left\{ \overline{d} \;\middle|\; \begin{array}{l} \overline{d} = \tilde{J}^{giv}(\vartheta(\langle T, [H|T], [H]\rangle)) \\ \bullet\ \vartheta \text{ is a variable assignment w.r.t. } J^{giv} \\ \bullet\ \kappa(\overline{d}) \in \tilde{D}_{r_2} \end{array} \right\}$$

where $\kappa(\langle d_1, \ldots, d_n\rangle) =_{\text{def}} \langle \kappa(d_1), \ldots, \kappa(d_n)\rangle$ with $d_i \in \{v, 0, 1\}$, $i = 1, \ldots, n$.

This results in the following $J^{giv}$-database $db$:

$$
\begin{array}{ll}
c_{a_2}(v, v, 0, 0). & c_{r_2}(v, 0, 0). \\
c_{a_2}(v, 0, 0, 0). & c_{r_2}(0, 0, 0). \\
c_{a_2}(0, v, 0, 0). & c_{r_2}(v, 0, 1). \\
c_{a_2}(0, 0, 0, 0). & c_{r_2}(0, 0, 1). \\
c_{a_2}(1, v, 0, 0). & c_{r_2}(1, 0, 0). \\
c_{a_2}(1, 0, 0, 0). & c_{r_2}(1, 1, 1). \\
c_{a_2}(1, v, 1, 0). & \\
c_{a_2}(1, 0, 1, 0). & \\
c_{a_2}(1, 1, 1, 1). &
\end{array}
$$

The above relation $c_{a_2}$ is much smaller than that generated as it was explained in Section 3.2.

Finally, computing the least $J^{giv}$-model of the program $Rev$, whose truth function consists of the set

$$
\mathcal{H}_{app} = \{\overline{1vv}, \overline{0v0}, \overline{1v0}, \overline{000}, \overline{010}, \overline{100}, \overline{111}\} \text{ and } \mathcal{H}_{rev} = \{\overline{00}, \overline{11}\}
$$

and using it to minimize the domain relations of the derived constraints, one obtains the following reduced $J^{giv}$-database $\widetilde{db}$:

$$
\begin{array}{ll}
c_{a_2}(0, 0, 0, 0). & c_{r_2}(0, 0, 0). \\
c_{a_2}(1, 0, 0, 0). & c_{r_2}(0, 0, 1). \\
c_{a_2}(1, 0, 1, 0). & c_{r_2}(1, 0, 0). \\
c_{a_2}(1, 1, 1, 1). & c_{r_2}(1, 1, 1).
\end{array}
$$

which looks exactly as the reduced database with respect to $J^{gi}$. However, it shows that the optimal computing of the least $J^{giv}$-model of $Rev$ needs not the domain element $v$ in the database of constraint relations. This information enables a significant effect when computing the next model in the refinement chain.

Thus, large models can be computed with acceptable efficiency. However, this needs a database of pre-interpretations to construct appropriate refinement chains. The above illustrates only the most simple way of using refinement chains. It has been already mentioned that surjective homomorphism are more restrictive than our definition of refinement. Therefore, there are algorithms which, exploiting our definition, enable more dramatic filtering when generating domain relations of derived constraints.

Our technology can be extended to optimize standard bottom-up fixpoint computations in the $LDL$-system. Namely, given a program, our analysis framework can be used as search procedure for an efficient finite refinement chain with last element as the standard model of this program. Doing this is a program-specific way, one might hope to obtain a very efficient algorithm. Indeed, such an algorithm would implement an important strategy of efficient processing of large sets of data: first process such sets with an efficient but imprecise algorithm; next, using these results process the sets again with a more precise algorithm, etc. Our technology hopefully enables a significant automation for re-organization of logic-based application following this recipe.

## 3.4 Model Generation with Indexing

Let $P$ be a program and $J$ a finite pre-interpretation. Consider again the $J$-complied program $Q$ which is obtained as it has been explained in Section 3.2. Recall that the programs $P$ and $Q$ consist of clauses with the same names, which establish bijection between clauses of $P$ and $Q$.

A clause $C$ in $Q$ having the form

$$c : p_0(\bar{s}_0) \leftarrow p_1(\bar{s}_1), \ldots, p_n(\bar{s}_n), c(\overline{X}, \overline{Y})$$

with c as its name and with $\bar{s}_i$, $i = 0, \ldots, n$, $n \geq 0$, tuples consisting of variables and domain elements of $J$ is re-compiled again as follows:

$$c : p_0(\bar{s}_0, c(Z_1, \ldots, Z_n)) \leftarrow p_1(\bar{s}_1, Z_1), \ldots, p_n(\bar{s}_n, Z_n), c(\overline{X}, \overline{Y})$$

Such a rewriting introduces fresh variables $Z_1, \ldots, Z_n$ for each atom in the body and creates the new term $c(Z_1, \ldots, Z_n)$ in the head. In particular, a fact of the form $c : p(\bar{s})$ rewrites as $c : p(\bar{s}, c)$. Typically such a program has an infinite least model. So, one needs a special mechanism to compute its fixpoint with the $LDL$-system. Before explaining such a mechanism, let us illustrate by an example what is the purpose of the above re-compilation.

Consider the program

$$P = \{\ c_1 : p(X, f(X, Y)).\quad c_2 : p(f(X, Y), Y).\ \}$$

The $p$-restriction of its least $J^{g^i}$-model is the set $\{\overline{00}, \overline{10}, \overline{01}, \overline{11}\}$. Applying the most precise decoding algorithm in Section 2.3, one obtains the tuple

$$\langle [U_1, U_2], [U_1, U_3] \rangle$$

showing that the least model does not capture any observable properties, i.e. we simply have no information.

Now if the program $P$ is compiled as above, we have the following

$$\{\overline{00\,c_1},\ \overline{00\,c_2},\ \overline{10\,c_1},\ \overline{01\,c_2},\ \overline{11\,c_1},\ \overline{11\,c_2}\ \}$$

as the $p$-restriction of the truth function of the least $J^{g^i}$-model of $P$. This enables splitting of the above set as follows:

$$c_1 : \{\overline{00},\ \overline{10},\ \overline{11}\ \} \text{ and } c_2 : \{\overline{00},\ \overline{01},\ \overline{11}\ \}$$

In other words, the last element in a tuple is used as its **index**, which enables splitting of the original model into two sets. Now decoding the above two sets, one obtains two tuples:

$$\langle [U_1], [U_1, U_2] \rangle \text{ and } \langle [U_1, U_2], [U_2] \rangle$$

which provide an *exact* analysis of $P$ showing that a tuple $\langle t_1, t_2 \rangle$ is a correct answers only if it satisfies *one* of the following conditions:

- $var(t_1) \subseteq var(t_2)$

– $var(t_1) \supseteq var(t_2)$

The correctness of the above analysis is explained in detail in [4]. It is important to see that the above "tricks" violate our definition of a model based analysis since the above re-compilation enforces a program to record operations of the fixpoint computation of its least model. Indeed, indices show which combinations of clauses have produced a domain tuple in the fixpoint.

Recall that our analysis with $J^{gi}$ is exactly the groundness analysis with the abstract domain $PROP$ of Marriott and Søndergaard [18]. This analysis has been investigated by Filé and Ranzato [11], who have explained that the so-called "lifting to power set" of the $PROP$ domain enables a strictly more precise analysis. The above is exactly this effect. However, in our setting it works for any finite pre-interpretation. Moreover, the power of the $LDL$-system enables a reasonable implementation, which is applicable for a large class of applications.

Let us show the basic elements of such an implementation. Let $p$ be a predicate in the re-compiled program and $\mathcal{H}_p$ the $p$-restriction of its least $J$-model. The standard fixpoint execution of this program might generate infinitely many tuples of the from $\langle \overline{d}, i \rangle$ with i as the index of domain tuple $\overline{d} \in \mathcal{H}_p$. An index i typically is a complex term indicating the combination of clauses, which have produced the domain tuple $\overline{d}$. As it is explained in [4], the above fixpoint computation stops when the following condition is detected.

Let i be an index in the current state of the computation. Consider the set

$$D_i = \{\overline{d} \mid \text{the tuple } \langle \overline{d}, i \rangle \text{ in the current state of the fixpoint computation}\}$$

Indices i' and i'' are *equivalent* with respect to the current state of the fixpoint computation iff $D_{i'} = D_{i''}$. The computation stops if its the new state is such that the set of tuples $\langle \overline{d}, i \rangle$, which is added to the previous state, satisfies:

– no new domain sub-tuple $\overline{d}$ is added to the previous state
– no index i, which is not equivalent with an old one with respect to the new state of the computation, is added to the previous state

The above has a simple and efficient implementation thanks to powerful set-handling facilities of the $LDL$-system.

Model generation with indexing significantly simplifies decoding of models since it typically suggests spiting of the truth functions into $J$-representation sets. As an illustration, model generation with indexing of the least $J^{giv}$-model of the predicate $app$ in the program $Rev$ needs 3 bottom-up iterations of the fixpoint computation. It generates 3 indices $a_1$, $a_2(a_1)$ and $a_2(a_2(a_1))$. The maximal depths of these indices indicates a number of iterations, which have been done to reach a fixpoint having the following configuration:

| | | |
|---|---|---|
| 1 | $a_1$ : | $\{\overline{1vv}, \overline{100}, \overline{111}\}$ |
| 2 | $a_2(a_1)$ : | $\{\overline{0v0}, \overline{1v0}, \overline{000}, \overline{010}, \overline{100}, \overline{111}\}$ |
| 3 | $a_2(a_2(a_1))$ : | $\{\overline{0v0}, \overline{1v0}, \overline{000}, \overline{010}, \overline{100}, \overline{111}\}$ |

It shows that the fixpoint actually has been reached in 2 iteration, i.e. the last third iteration only has detected this. Also, as it was explained, it associates a set of domain tuples with each index giving rise to the splitting of the *app*-restriction of the truth function of the least $J^{giv}$-model of the program *Rev* in Section 3.3 in two $J^{giv}$-representation sets. As a result, the following two tuples

$$\langle c, X_2, X_2 \rangle \text{ and } \langle [U_1,], X_2, [X_2, U_1] \rangle$$

are derived from the truth function. Observable properties are discussed in [3].

## 4    Conclusion

A model based approach for static analysis of logic-based applications with declarative semantics has been discussed. A theoretical background ensures that the approach is flexible and precise. However, its efficient implementation needs a full power of available deductive database systems such as *LDL*. The most important ideas for an efficient implementation have been illustrated.

Recently Gallagher [12] has introduced several model based analyses with a uniform and efficient prototype implementation. This has motivated an investigation of a more mature implementation technology based on deductive database systems.

An ultimate goal is deriving complex program-specific properties, which are important for a significant optimization and re-organization of declarative programs. Such properties are supposed to be used by a programmer as an interactive toolkit at the final stage of developing of a complex application exploiting deductive databases and constraint solvers. This means that rather complex problem-specific properties might be necessary. Therefore, derived properties are displayed as sample tuples of terms. This enables a programmer to observe properties, using *his* abstraction $\alpha$ provided that $\alpha$ satisfies the correctness condition with respect to the used pre-interpretation.

Our approach has an important feature, which distinguishes it from more conventional methods based on abstract interpretation approach of Cousot and Cousot [10]. Abstract interpretation relies on abstracting a *procedure*, which computes the so-called concrete semantics of a program. For instance, our groundness analysis in Section 2.3 is exactly that of Codish and Demoen [9], which is known as the most efficient one. In our settings, its correctness knows nothing about such "procedural" things as unification and operations on substitutions. Also, there is no difference between so-called top-down and bottom-up methods. Finally, we don't use the so-called lower bounds for generalizing intermediate results.

The so-called "generalized approach" of Giacobazzi, Debray and Levi [13] is a general abstract interpretation framework. It was also used as an important motivation since the used constraint systems have a transparent model based semantics. However, the way of exploiting them is different since we don't use explicitly fixpoint abstract computations. They are "hidden" inside a model generator.

All the above enables to focus on a uniform implementation of model generation, which is a bit more well-known problem in deductive database setting. Such an advantage has been illustrated introducing two novel techniques for model generation. They enable efficiency and precision of "power set" computations. However, this uniform implementation might be less efficient compared with particular analyses based on the abstract interpretation. The reason is that the abstract interpretation approach of Cousot and Cousot [10] enable the so-called weakening, which loosing precision gains efficiency. A similar technique in our settings for is a bit more difficult and needs more research.

## Acknowledgements

This research has been supported by the ERCIM Grant Nr.95-01.

# References

1. Arni,N., Ong,S., Tsur,S., Zaniolo,C., *LDL++: A Second Generation Deductive Database System*, Technical Report, MCC Corporation, 1993.
2. Bossi,A., Gabbrielli,M., Levi,G., Martelli,M., *The s-semantics Approach: Theory and Applications*, J. Logic Programming, **19-20**(1994), 149-197.
3. Boulanger,D., *Complete Analysis for Definite Logic Programs*, Proc. 11th Workshop Logische Programmierung, Technishe Universität Wien, GMD-Studien Nr.270, 1995, 101-110.
4. Boulanger,D., Bruynooghe,M., *Index-Driven Semantics of Logic Programs*, Technical Report CW211, K.U.Leuven, May,1995.
5. Boulanger,D., Bruynooghe,M., *A Systematic Construction of Abstract Domains*, Proc. 1st International Static Analysis Symposium, LNCS Vol.864, 1994, 61-77.
6. Boulanger,D., Bruynooghe,M., Denecker,M., *Abstracting s-semantics Using A Model-Theoretic Approach*, Proc. 6th Int. Symp. on PLILP, LNCS Vol.844, 1994, 432-446.
7. Bry,F., Manthey,R., *Proving Finite Satisfiability of Deductive Databases*, Proc. Conference Logic and Computer Science, 1987, Karlsruhe, LNCS, 1987.
8. Bry,F., Decker,H., Mathey,R., *A Uniform Approach to Constraint Satisfaction and Constraint Satisfiability in Deductive Databases*, Proc. Extended Database Technology 1988, Venice, LNCS, 1988.
9. Codish,M., Demoen,B., *Analyzing logic programs using "Prop"-ositional logic programs and a magic wand*, J. Logic Programming, **25**(1995), 249-274.
10. Cousot,P., Cousot,R., *Abstract Interpretation and Application to Logic Programs*, J. Logic Programming, **13**(1992), 103-179.
11. Filé,G., Ranzato,F., *Improving Abstract Interpretations by Systematic Lifting to the Powerset*, Proc. 1994 ISLP, 1994, 655-669.
12. Gallagher,J., Boulanger,D., Sağlam,H., *Practical Model-Based Static Analysis for Definite Logic Programs*, Proc. 1995 ISLP, 1995, 351-365.
13. Giacobazzi,R., Debray,S., Levi,G., *Generalized Semantics and Abstract Interpretation for Constraint Logic Programs*, J. Logic Programming, **25**(1995), 191-245.
14. Goguen,J., Thatcher,E., Waggner,E., Wright,J., *Initial Algebra Semantics and Continuous Algebras*, J. ACM, **24**(1977), 68-95.
15. Lassez,J.-L., Maher,M., Marriott,K., *Unification Revisited*, Foundations of Deductive Databases and Logic Programming, Morgan-Kaufmann, 1988, 587-625.
16. Lloyd,J., *Foundations of Logic Programming*, Springer, 1987.

17. Maher, M., *Equivalence of Logic Programs*, Foundations of Deductive Databases and Logic Programming, Morgan-Kaufmann, 1988, 627-658.
18. Marriott,K., Søndergaard,H., *Precise and Efficient Groundness Analysis for Logic Programs*, ACM Letters on Programming Languages, 2(1993), 181-196.
19. Mezei,J. Wright,J., *Algebraic Automata and Context-Free Sets*, Information and Control, **11**(1967), 3-29.
20. Wirsing,W., *Algebraic Specifications*, in: Handbook of Theoretical Computer Science, Vol.B Formal Models and Semantics, North Holland, 1990, 678-778.

# An Axiomatic Interpretation of Confidentiality Demands in Logic-Based Relational Databases

Adrian Spalka and Armin B. Cremers

Department of Computer Science III, University of Bonn
Roemerstrasse 164, D-53117 Bonn, Germany
E-mail: adrian/abc@cs.uni-bonn.de

**Abstract.** So-called logic-based relational database models based on Bell and La Padula's interpretation of mandatory security policies suffer from several semantic problems. We claim that the intention of these policies can be reduced to a single generic confidentiality demand. We interpret it in the context of a logic-based database as a definition of the intended model and state it as an axiom in addition to the axioms of a relational database. We then show that many security properties can already be proved from these few axioms. These properties characterise a mandatory preserving-policy conforming database with an unequivocal semantics of the data and a notion of category identical to that of relational databases.

## 1. Introduction

Security-level-based (mandatory) models of information flow were originally developed for information recorded on paper. Bell/La Padula (1973) present a formal interpretation of security-level-based mandatory security policies for operating systems. Although this interpretation relies on some assumptions valid for operating systems but not applicable to databases, it still has a decisive impact on the attempts undertaken during the eighties to devise a secure database model.

The introduction of the SeaView secure relational data model by Denning et al (1987) and Denning et al (1988) was regarded as a culminating point. However, the idea that the straight-forward view of the relational data model and of Bell and La Padula's interpretation yields a secure database turns out to be a too simple analysis. SeaView is largely security-level-based access classes, assigns from a purely syntactic consideration an access class to each attribute, tuple and relation name, and starts the Simple Security-Property and the *-Property as postulates. Contrary to the impression one might get at the first glance, SeaView's plain extension to the relational data model has led to severe semantic problems, which have already been observed by SeaView's inventors. Yet despite eight years of very intense research — there are countless works we can cite —, SeaView's then open problems remain open today. An estimation on the present state of research given by Winslett/Smith/Qian (1994) expresses also a disappointment.

1. Landwehr (1981) 249.

# An Axiomatic Interpretation of Confidentiality Demands in Logic-Based Relational Databases

Adrian Spalka and Armin B. Cremers
Department of Computer Science III, University of Bonn
Roemerstrasse 164, D–53117 Bonn, Germany
Email: adrian/abc@cs.uni–bonn.de

**Abstract.** Secure multilevel relational database models based on Bell and La Padula's interpretation of mandatory security policies suffer from severe semantic problems. We claim that the intention of these policies can be reduced to a single generic confidentiality demand. We interpret it in the context of a logic-based database as a distortion of the intended model and state it as an axiom in addition to the axioms of a relational database. We then show that many security properties can already be proved from these few axioms. These properties characterise a mandatory-security-policy-conforming database with an unequivocal semantics of the data and a notion of integrity identical to that of relational databases.

## 1 Introduction

Security-level-based mandatory controls of information dissemination were originally developed for information recorded on paper.[1] Bell/La Padula (1975) present a formal interpretation of security-level-based mandatory security policies for operating systems. Although this interpretation relies on some assumptions valid for operating systems but not applicable to databases, it still has a decisive impact on the attempts undertaken during the eighties to devise a secure database model.

The introduction of the SeaView secure relational data model by Denning et al (1987) and Denning et al (1988) was regarded as a culminating point. However, the idea that the straight *sum* of the relational data model and of Bell and La Padula's interpretation yields a secure database turns out to be a too simple analogy. SeaView interprets security levels as access classes, assigns from a purely syntactic consideration an access class to each attribute, tuple and relation name, and states the Simple-Security-Property and the *-Property as postulates. Contrary to the impression one might get at the first glance, SeaView's plain extension to the relational data model has led to severe semantic problems, which have already been observed by SeaView's inventors. Yet despite eight years of very intense research — there are countless works we can cite —, SeaView's then open problems remain open today. An estimation on the present state of research given by Winslett/Smith/Qian (1994) expresses also a disappointment:

---

1. Landwehr (1981):249.

Research into database security models is still in its infancy[2] We believe
that the current situation in the MLS community is analogous to the state of
research on null values in relational databases in the late 1970s. [3]

But, this notwithstanding, some representatives of the mainstream database security research community are still convinced that the SeaView secure relational
data model represents the right starting point.

We have good grounds to believe that this conviction is no longer tenable.
Firstly, we show in this work that a mandatory security policy uses security levels
only to express prohibitions of information dissemination, ie, confidentiality demands. If security levels are also to be used as access classes, then it must be explicitly shown that, in a given environment, this use is compatible with the intention of the prohibitions, which, eg, has indeed been done by Bell/La Padula
(1975) and Feiertag/Levitt/Robinson (1977) for operating systems. Secondly,
from a logical view, the extension of a predicate with new arguments creates a
new predicate the semantics of which, unless explicitly specified, remains undefined. And thirdly, Spalka (1996b) has shown that the Simple-Security-Property is
non-primitive, viz, it is not a postulate but a conclusion the validity of which relies
on the assumptions made about the underlying secure environment. The author
has also demonstrated that it contradicts the assumptions made by relational databases defined in the traditional set-orientated way. This result implies that the
accession of the Simple-Security-Property to relational databases definitely prevents the enforcement of confidentiality demands. Our further (presently unpub-
lished) studies have identified some more shortcomings all of which strengthen
our belief that SeaView is not well-defined.

We therefore propose in this work an axiomatic interpretation of security-
level-based mandatory security policies in logic-based relational databases that
establishes database properties as proofs from only a few — as we believe —
primitive assumptions. The advantage of this approach is that a critique of our
proposal can always be traced back to these assumptions, the necessity or appro-
priateness of which is, of course, supported only by our informal analysis.

A database is generally regarded as an image of a real-world section. In a
logic-based database, this image is assumed to be captured in the database's intended model. To keep matters simple in this work, we admit only ground atomic
formulae in confidentiality demands, ie, the objects a database tries to keep secret
are facts. We define the formal meaning of a confidentiality demand by character-
ising the difference between the intended model and one that can be said to satisfy the demand. This approach retains the original database, which corresponds
to the intended state of affairs, and yields a set of deliberately falsified individual
databases.

It is essential to realise that this step has not created a group of new alien
databases. They all still refer to the same real-world section: the original database
captures its intended image, and an individual, falsified one presents a distorted
image of it. To record the degree of the distortion we introduce a concept called
distortion-log.

---

2. Winslett/Smith/Qian (1994):627.
3. Winslett/Smith/Qian (1994):631.

Throughout the work we prove various properties of our assumptions, which represent a first characterisation of the axiomatic interpretation. Many results describe the effects of a distortion and give some guidance to its control.

One of the important properties of this interpretation of mandatory security policies is the independence of the database semantics from any particular confidentiality demands, ie, we guarantee that the addition or removal of confidentiality demands does not affect the semantics of the data nor the notion of integrity.

Although we discuss only briefly confidentiality enforcement methods in this work, we would like to conclude this part with a brief note on the general situation. When told to keep a thing secret from a person $A$, adults seem to need little advice on how to do it. Popular methods are: not to tell $A$ the whole truth, invent lies or avoid meeting $A$. In general, secrecy tries to exploit an assumed ignorance of the target-person. Yet, while some secrets are successfully concealed, some others are, in spite of all efforts, disclosed. If a secret is disclosed, one can ask whether the method has been inappropriate or whether the task itself has been not satisfiable — here it is already important to realise that either alternative can apply. In any case, once the disclosure is recognised, one can still look for another way to protect the corporate value, notwithstanding the lost data value. Difficult though the situation may be, it is definitely less dangerous than one that relies on a false sense of security, or one that keeps the secret while damaging other not less important values.

We would also like to mention two attempts to define non-multilevel secure databases from a logical perspective.

One of the first formal studies on confidentiality is Sicherman/de Jonge/van de Riet (1983). The authors consider the problem of confidentiality in a database, which acts like a question-answering system. The database is a collection of closed first-order formulae and its semantics is given by an extension to a maximally consistent set of formulae. The unit of protection is a formula and confidentiality is defined as non-derivability, ie, if a formula $A$ should be kept to be secret from a user, then he should be able to derive at most $A \vee B$, with some formula $B$, but not $A$ itself. The interface of the database can answer a user-question with 'Yes', 'No' or 'I know the correct answer, but I will not tell it'. The decision on the answer is made by a censor who takes the user-knowledge and the dialogue up to now into account. The censor, who never lies, gives the third answer if he arrives at the conclusion that the user will be able to deduct a secret with the help of a yes/no-answer. The authors demonstrate that this can still be of little avail since the user can make use of the censor's reasoning in his own one. One can moreover object that allowing the user to acquire knowledge of a secret up to a two-facts-disjunction is a quite weak form of secrecy. From our viewpoint, however, the main drawback of this interesting approach is that it prohibits updates of the database. In conclusion, the addition of a third answer is more difficult to handle than yes/no-answers. At the same time, the new attack-methods are hard to analyse in standard logic. Thus it seems that the benefits of an additional degree of freedom, viz a third answer, cannot compare with the increase of complexity in handling it.

In a database that is seen as a set of closed formulae with pure first-order logic semantics, Bonatti/Kraus/Subrahmanian (1992) define the confidentiality of a formula as non-derivability. The problem is that they do not make the closed world assumption — or any variant of it —, which, however, is made by most of the security-relevant applications, and they do not deal with integrity constraints nor with dynamic semantics.

The next section defines some basic set notions and logic-based databases. Section 3 formalises the intention of a security-level-based mandatory security policy in the original paper-based environment. Section 4 interprets a security-level-based mandatory security policy in a logic-based relational database, and presents an example of confidentiality enforcement. Lastly, the conclusion summarises the main results of this work and presents a brief outlook.

## 2  Basic notions

Let FS be an infinite and countable set of function symbols, PS a finite set of predicate symbols and $\rho$: FS $\cup$ PS $\to$ $N_0$ a function that assigns a rank to each symbol. Then B $=$ (FS, PS) is a database-signature (or a syntactical basis) if $\rho(\text{FS}) = 0$, ie, if FS comprises only constant symbols. Let VA be an infinite and countable set of variables. If $t \in$ FS or $t \in$ VA, then $t$ is a term (over B), $t \in$ TE. A term $t$ is ground, $t \in \text{TE}_G$, if $t \in$ FS. $\alpha \equiv p(t_1, ..., t_n)$ is an atomic formula (over B), $\alpha \in$ AF, if $p \in$ PS, $\rho(p) = n$ and $t_i \in$ TE for all $i = 1, ..., n$. $\alpha$ is ground or a fact, $\alpha \in \text{AF}_G$, if all $t_i$ are ground. The set of formulae or the language (over B), FO, is the smallest set such that: AF $\subset$ FO, $A, B \in$ FO $\Rightarrow A \vee B \in$ FO, $A \in$ FO $\Rightarrow \neg A \in$ FO, $A \in$ FO and $X \in$ VA $\Rightarrow$ $(\forall X: A) \in$ FO. A formula $A$ is closed, $A \in L$, if all its variables are quantified. We assume that $eq$ is a special predicate symbol of rank two the intended meaning of which is the canonical equality given by the extension of $L$. The equality theory for B, EQ, comprises the following formulae: $\forall X: eq(X, X)$, $\neg eq(c_1, c_2)$ for all distinct $c_1, c_2 \in$ FS, and $\forall X_1...X_k Y_1...Y_k: eq(X_1, Y_1) \wedge ... \wedge eq(X_k, Y_k) \to (p(X_1, ..., X_k) \to p(Y_1, ..., Y_k))$ for each $p \in$ PS such that $\rho(p) = k$.

Let $D$ be a non-empty set and $\omega$ a function on B such that there is a mapping $\omega(\text{FS})$: FS $\to D$, and for each $p \in$ PS such that $\rho(p) = k$ there is a mapping $\omega(p)$: $D^k \to \{\text{True, False}\}$. Then I $= (D, \omega)$ is an interpretation for B. I is a Herbrand interpretation if $D = \text{TE}_G$ and $\omega(\text{FS}) = \text{id}$. We consider only Herbrand interpretations. The truth value of a closed formula depends only on an interpretation. We therefore regard I as a mapping I: $L \to \{\text{True, False}\}$ and denote the truth value of $\varphi \in L$ with respect to I as $I(\varphi)$. Let $X \subset L$ then I is a model of $X$, $I \in \text{Mod}(X)$, if $\forall \varphi \in X: I(\varphi) = \text{True}$. The set $Y \subset L$ is a logical consequence of $X$, $X \vDash Y$, if $\text{Mod}(X) \subseteq \text{Mod}(Y)$.

Let $M$ be a finite set of facts. The definition of $p \in$ PS, $\rho(p) = n$, in $M$ is the set $\text{def}(p, M) = \{p(X_1, ..., X_n) \leftarrow eq(X_1, a_1) \wedge ... \wedge eq(X_n, a_n) \mid p(a_1, ..., a_n) \in M\}$. Suppose that $\text{def}(p, M) = \{\varphi_1, ..., \varphi_m\}$ and $\varphi_j \equiv p(...) \leftarrow E_j$ for all $j = 1, ..., m$, then $\text{comp}(p, M) \equiv \forall X_1...X_n: p(X_1, ..., X_n) \leftrightarrow E_1 \vee ... \vee E_m$ is the completion of

$p$ with respect to $M$, and comp($M$) = {comp($p$, $M$) | $p \in$ PS} $\cup$ EQ is the completion of $M$ (over B).

Let B be a signature, $C$ a finite set of closed formulae and $I$ a finite set of facts such that comp($I$) $\models C$, then $DB$ = (B, $C$, $I$) is a logic-based relational database with completion semantics. B defines the database language, $C$ is the set of integrity constraints, $I$ is a valid present state and the intended semantics of $I$ is defined by the (unique) Herbrand model M of comp($I$).

A transaction $T$ on $I$ is a tuple $T$ = ($T^-$, $T^+$) such that $T^-$, $T^+ \subset$ AF$_C$. The application of $T$ to $I$ yields the set $I'$ such that $I \setminus T^-$ = $I' \setminus T^+$. If $I'$ is valid, then $T$ is accepted and $I'$ becomes the present state of $DB$; otherwise $T$ is rejected. Let M' be the model of $I'$. The effect of $T$ on M is the partitioned set $\tau$ = $\delta \cup \iota$, $\tau \subseteq$ AF$_C$, such that M($\delta$) = True and M'($\delta$) = False, M($\iota$) = False and M'($\iota$) = True, and M($\alpha$) = M'($\alpha$) for any $\alpha \in$ AF$_C \setminus \tau$.

## 3 Security-level-based mandatory security policies

This section extracts the primitive intention of a security-level-based mandatory security policy from its original definition in a paper-based environment.

In the original paper-based environment, an instance of a security-level-based mandatory security policy can be represented as

$$MSP = (S, O, (SL, \leq), F)$$

such that:
- $S$ is a set of individuals who are called subjects and who represent the active units
- $O$ is a set of named documents which are called objects and which represent the protection units
- $SL$ is a set of security levels on which a partial order '$\leq$' is defined
- $F$: $S \cup O \rightarrow SL$ is a labelling-function that assigns a security level to each subject and object

Now two questions remain:
  i) Why is there a partial order on the set of security levels?
  ii) What is the purpose of assigning security levels to subjects and objects?
The answer to the first question is motivated in the following way. A security level $(l, C) \in SL$ is composed of a sensitivity level $l$ and a compartment-affiliation $C$ such that $l$ is an element of a totally ordered set and $C$ is a subset of a set of compartments. Then $(l_1, C_1) \leq (l_2, C_2) : \Leftrightarrow l_1 \leq l_2 \wedge C_1 \subseteq C_2$ defines a partial order on $SL$.

The labelling-function $F$ imposes this partial order on $S$ and $O$. This structure common to both sets, to answer the second question, is then used in the formulation of the following mandatory regulation:

> The dissemination of information of a particular security level (including sensitivity level and any compartments or caveats) to individuals lacking the appropriate clearances for that level is prohibited by law[4].

---

4. Landwehr (1981):249.

This statement unmistakably expresses that the basic and primitive intention of a mandatory security policy is the determination of confidentiality demands — and not that of access restrictions.

We therefore claim that the only and primitive relationship defined by a security-level-based mandatory security policy is the following one.

**Primitive Mandatory Requirement** Let $o \in O$ be an object and $s \in S$ a subject. Then $o$ should be kept secret from $s$ if $F(o) \leq F(s)$ does not hold.

On the basis of this requirement we can state the following lemma, which expresses the basic secrecy property of $MSP$.

**Lemma 1** Let $s_1, s_2 \in S$ such that $F(s_1) \geq F(s_2)$, and set $o \in \text{secret}(s)$ if $F(o) \leq F(s)$ does not hold. Then $\text{secret}(s_1) \subseteq \text{secret}(s_2)$.
*Proof* Follows immediately from the partial order properties of '$\leq$'. ∎

The only still undefined element is the semantics of the relationship $o \in \text{secret}(s)$ — this is not a deficiency but a degree of freedom that must be fixed in accordance with the structures and operations defined in a particular environment, eg an operating system or a database. Therefore, whenever an instance of a security-level-based mandatory security policy should be adapted to a new environment, the question we must ask in the first place is what is the intended meaning of the relationship $o \in \text{secret}(s)$ in this environment? This question can in turn be split into the following more precise questions:
- What are the protection objects?
- What are the subjects?
- When is information about an object disseminated to a subject?
- The dissemination of which kind of information is prohibited?

Not until after we have answered all these questions can we commence studying if and how the demanded prohibitions can be enforced.

# 4 An axiomatic approach to confidentiality in databases

This section presents an axiomatic interpretation of a security-level-based mandatory security policy in a logic-based relational database.

## 4.1 Preliminaries

Let $DB = (B, C, I)$ be a relational database with completion-based semantics the intended model of which is the Herbrand interpretation $M = (TE_C, \omega)$ for B and let $MSP = (S, O, (SL, \leq), F)$ be an instance of a security-level-based mandatory security policy, which expresses the primitive mandatory requirement.

**Assumption 1** An object, ie, the unit of protection is a fact[5] $a \in AF_C$ of the database language and the set of objects is the infinite set of facts $O = AF_C$.

This assumption implies that a confidentiality demand can be stated for any ground atomic formula independent of its present truth value in the intended database model. Informally, it allows us to express the wish to keep both the presence and the absence of a fact secret. In the traditional set-based view on relational databases, one can only assign a security level to an existing tuple, ie, only to presently true facts. This implies that in respect of the declaration of confidentiality demands, the expressive power of the logic-based view is greater than that of the set-based view on relational databases.

**Assumption 2** For a $s \in S$ set secret$(s) = \{o \in O \mid (F(o), F(s)) \notin \leq\} \subseteq O$.

We interpret the membership of an $o \in O$ in a set secret$(s)$, $s \in S$, as a confidentiality demand to keep $o$ secret from $s$. Spalka (1994) has shown that a confidentiality demand is as such ambiguous. To obtain a unique meaning it must comprise an explicit degree of confidentiality. In respect of the definitions give there, we consider in this work only facts at the degree G2, which expresses the intention to keep both the fact and its existence secret.

The formal implications of a confidentiality demand can be precisely described if we assume that M is the database's intended model and that for each subject there is a separate model, which represents a distortion of the intended model. Thus the intended model represents the intended image of a real-world section, and a subject's model represents a possibly distorted image of the same real-world section.

**Assumption 3** For each $s \in S$ there is a database $DB_s = (B_s, C_s, I_s)$ and a Herbrand interpretation $M_s = (TE_G, \omega_s)$ for $B_s$ that is a model of $DB_s$.

Since this assumption defines $DB_s$ as a database and $M_s$ as a model thereof without mentioning $DB$ or M, the properties and the behaviour of $DB_s$ is independent — or, which is the task of confidentiality enforcement methods, should look like being so — from that of $DB$. In particular, $M_s$ is the unique model of comp$(I_s)$, ie, there is no doubt about which data *belong* to a security level and which do not; and $C_s$ is the only instance to make a decision on the validity of $I_s$, ie, the question on how to interpret integrity at a security level receives a simple answer: do it in the standard way.

## 4.2 The primitive mandatory requirement

**Assumption 4** In a logic-based database, the intended meaning of the primitive mandatory requirement for a fact $a \in$ secret$(s)$ implies $M_s(a) = \neg M(a)$.

---

5. This corresponds to tuple-level labelling in the set-based view on relational databases. It does not restrict the expression of confidentiality demands; as Qian/Lunt (1992) have shown this assumption subsumes also relational databases that use element-level classification.

**Lemma 2** Let $s, s' \in S$. Suppose that $M_s(\alpha) = \neg M(\alpha)$. Then
$$F(s') \leq F(s) \Leftrightarrow M_{s'}(\alpha) = M_s(\alpha) = \neg M(\alpha)$$
*Proof* Follows immediately from Assumption 4 and Lemma 1. ∖

Now that secret(s) $\neq \emptyset \Rightarrow M_s \neq M$, we need to characterise the relationship between two interpretations. As we understand that M is the unique intended model and any $M_s$ is a distortion thereof, we believe that a $M_s$ is adequately characterised by its distortion with respect to M. We therefore introduce a construct we call the distortion-log.

**Distortion-log** Let $s \in S$. Then the distortion-log of $M_s$ with respect to M is
$$P_s = (A_s, X_s, Z_s)$$
such that:
- $P_s$ is a partition of $AF_G$
- $\forall \alpha \in A_s: M_s(\alpha) = M(\alpha)$
- $\forall \alpha \in X_s: M_s(\alpha) = \neg M(\alpha)$

- $\forall \alpha \in Z_s: \alpha \notin AF_G^{B_s}$

The set $A_s$ is the agreement-set of M and $M_s$; it comprises the facts which have the same truth value in both models. The set $X_s$ is the disagreement-set of M and $M_s$; it comprises the facts to which the models assign opposite truth values. And the set $Z_s$ is the defect of $M_s$ with respect to M; it comprises the facts interpreted by M but not by $M_s$. Thus $A_s$ represents the truthful part of $M_s$, and $X_s$ and $Z_s$ its falsified part.

The unique description of a $M_s$ is terms of its deviation from M also illustrates that a trusted user can never be confused with some *unsolicited* data about the intended state of affairs.

**Lemma 3** $B_s = B$ for all $s \in S$, ie $DB_s = (B, C_s, I_s)$ and $P_s = (A_s, X_s, \emptyset)$.
*Proof* Assumption 4 requires the truth value of a fact $\alpha \in$ secret(s) to be reversed in the subject's model $M_s$. For this to be possible, this fact must be interpreted by the subject's interpretation. By Assumption 2 secret(s) $\subseteq AF_G$ holds, ie, any fact over B can occur in a confidentiality demand. Thus $M_s$ must also interpret all facts over B. ∖

Since M and each $M_s$ interpret the same signature, B, any subject can query the database for the truth value of any fact — the question of whether the database responds with the fact's intended truth value, viz, that of the intended model, is partially answered by Assumption 4.

**Lemma 4** $M_s = M \Rightarrow$ secret(s) $= \emptyset$.
*Proof* Follows trivially from Assumption 4. ∖

Thus, if a subject's model is an undistorted copy of the intended model, then we know that no fact of the database should be kept secret from him. Ideally, we would like to replace the implication with an equivalence. But on the grounds of the preceding assumptions only, we cannot preclude that in the absence of confidentiality demands, there are some other reasons for distorting a subject's model. However, to indicate our belief that a distortion should be avoided unless explicitly requested, we state the missing implication in the following assumption.

**Assumption 5** $M_s = M \Leftarrow secret(s) = \emptyset$.

Note that the implication of Assumption 5 cannot be extended to the primitive one of Assumption 4. $M_s(a) = \neg M(a) \Rightarrow a \in secret(s)$ need not to hold in general, since to keep a fact secret we may be forced to lie as well about other facts, ie, to introduce distortions that are not backed by confidentiality demands. To state it as an assumption would preclude the use of aliases.

### 4.3 A first characterisation of the axiomatic interpretation

We now briefly state several useful properties of our so far developed notions.

**Lemma 5** $M_s = M$ is equivalent to $\exists a \in SL \forall b \in SL : b \leq a$ and $F(s) = a$.

This lemma states that there is no need to assume the existence of an upper bound of $(SL, \leq)$, or even to impose on $(SL, \leq)$ a lattice-structure, unless there exists an all-knowing subject.

**Lemma 6** For any $s, s' \in S$ such that $F(s') \leq F(s)$ the following condition holds $\forall a \in secret(s) : M_{s'}(a) = \neg M(a)$.

Lemma 6 shows that we do not violate any confidentiality demands if we allow a subject to look at models of subjects with a lower security level.[6] The converse does not hold in general since in a particular situation both $F(s') \leq F(s)$ and $secret(s') = secret(s)$ can be true. However, we must keep in mind that in concordance with all our assumptions the equality can always be transformed into a proper inclusion.

**Lemma 7** Let $s_1, s_2 \in S$, $M_{s_1}$ and $M_{s_2}$ be their interpretations, and $P_{s_1}$ and $P_{s_2}$ their distortion-logs. Suppose that $F(s_1) \geq F(s_2)$ then $A_{s_2} \subseteq A_{s_1}$.

Spalka (1996b) shows that the combination of the logic-based view of relational databases with the security-level-based mandatory security policy requirements creates an environment in which the Simple-Security-Property has no obvious meaning. Lemma 7 motivates and justifies its supersedure with the distortion-log.

---

6. We can restate Lemma 6 in the database terminology, ie, in terms of queries with range-restricted clauses submitted by subjects and answered with respect to models. This, however, does not enrich the idea of Lemma 6.

Given two subjects $s_1, s_2 \in S$ such that $F(s_1) \geq F(s_2)$, what can we say about their interpretations? We know that $M_{s_1}$ and $M_{s_2}$ interpret the same language. Since both positive and negative facts can occur in confidentiality demands, the sets of facts to which $M_{s_1}$ and $M_{s_2}$ assign the same truth value need not form any inclusion at all, either. But Lemma 7 shows that, analogous with the inclusion of object-sets implied by the Simple-Security-Property in environments in which sequences of object-sets have a free base[7], our interpretation of secrecy in logic-based databases implies an inclusion of the models' truthful parts.

We now investigate some consequences of Assumption 4 and present a method to bring it in line with the other assumptions.

The introduction of subjects and individual models requires us to denote a transaction as $T_{s,x} = (T^-, T^+)$, $s, x \in S$, to indicate that $T$ is submitted by $s$ and that $T$ should be applied to $DB_x$, ie, its effect $\tau$ is stated with respect to $M_x$.

Lemma 6 allows a subject to query the models of all subjects with lower security levels. To which models should a subject be allowed to apply a transaction? We think that the answer depends on the answer to the question if a subject can be assumed to know the contents of the delete and insert sets of a transaction he submits. The hardly surprising Yes implies the following lemma, which we can prove without contemplating any further on the meaning of 'knows'.

**Lemma 8** Let $T_{s,x}$ be an accepted transaction with a non-empty effect. Then the state $T_{s,x}$ yields does not violate Assumption 4 only if $F(x) \leq F(s)$.
*Proof* Suppose that $F(x) \leq F(s)$ does not hold. Then for any fact $\alpha \in \tau$ $\alpha \in \text{secret}(s)$ holds. By Lemma 2 for all $y \in S$ such that $F(y) \leq F(s)$ we have $M_x(\alpha) = \neg M_y(\alpha)$. Then Assumption 4 implies that $M(\alpha) = \neg M_y(\alpha)$. This, however, violates Assumption 4 since $\alpha \in \tau$ means that $s$ knows $M(\alpha)$. The other direction of the equivalence is trivial. ∎

We therefore assume that a transaction $T_{s,x}$ is only admitted to further processing if $F(x) \leq F(s)$. We assume in the following that this condition always holds.

Now suppose that the effect $\tau$ of an accepted $T_{s,s}$ comprises a secret, ie

$$\tau \cap \text{secret}(s) \neq \emptyset \qquad \text{(E1)}$$

This situation must be definitely prevented. From an informal viewpoint, the idea of a transaction expresses a reflection of some changes which already have happened in the real-world section in the database. So (E1) implies that

i) either the subject has come to know of the secret because the external security precautions have failed, which the database cannot reasonably assume,

ii) or the subject simply knows of the secret, which means that the respective confidentiality demand is nonsensical.

On the formal side, Lemma 8 illustrates the obvious contradiction incurred by the validity of (E1).

---

7. Let $M$ be a set. $\mathcal{B} \subseteq \mathcal{P}(M)$ is a base of a sequence $O_1, O_2, \ldots$ if $O_i \in \mathcal{B}$ for all $i$. A base $\mathcal{B}$ is free if it comprises all finite subsets of $M$.

An old idea though it is, a system of rights is treated only as an adjunct to a database product the manufacturer should supply. We believe that update rights must be included in a formal model. Restrictions on updates naturally correspond to a subject's limited powers to act on the real-world section. Moreover, a subject's powers are justified by an organisation's structure and security policy, by a subject's position and job tasks etc. Thus rights are well suited for the prevention of (E1) with respect to (i).

**Assumption 6** For each $s \in S$ there are sets $RD_s, RI_s \subseteq AF_G$ which informally represent a subject's powers in the real-world section. Formally, a transaction $T_{s,x}$ with the effect $\tau = \delta \cup \iota$ is rejected if $\delta \cap RD_s \neq \delta$ or $\iota \cap RI_s \neq \iota$ [8].

**Lemma 9** $secret(s) \cap (RD_s \cup RI_s) = \varnothing$, for any $s \in S$.
*Proof* Follows immediately from Lemma 8 and Assumption 6. ∖

**Corollary 1** $RD_s \subseteq A_s$ and $RI_s \subseteq A_s$, for any $s \in S$ and $M_s$.

In respect of the stating of confidentiality demands, Lemma 9 can be rewritten as $\alpha \in secret(s) \Rightarrow \alpha \notin (RD_s \cup RI_s)$, which illustrates that — just like in real life, too — we can only try to keep a fact secret if the respective subject is unable to alter it.

To solve the problem with (E1) indicated by (ii), we need to define what it means that a subjects knows of a fact and record the facts we suppose he knows. Motivated by the idea that a database is an image of a real-world section, and that a subject has some responsibilities within it, we call a fact $\alpha \in AF_G$ inspectable by $s \in S$ if $s$ can determine $M(\alpha)$, ie the intended truth value of $\alpha$, regardless of the value of $M_s(\alpha)$, ie, independently of what the database pretends to be $\alpha$'s truth value in front of $s$.

**Assumption 7** For each $s \in S$ there is a set $SK_s \subseteq AF_G$ which informally represents a subject's assumed special knowledge on the real-world section, ie, the inspectable facts. Formally, $\alpha \in SK_s \Rightarrow M_s(\alpha) = M(\alpha)$.

**Lemma 10** $secret(s) \cap SK_s = \varnothing$, for any $s \in S$.
*Proof* Follows immediately from Lemma 8 and Assumption 7. ∖

**Corollary 2** $SK_s \subseteq A_s$, for any $s \in S$ and $M_s$.

Analogously with Lemma 9, Lemma 10 expresses a trivial insight: do not try to

---

8. The setting of the insert rights requires in fact a deeper analysis of the database's modelling approach. For reasons of space, which by now become apparent, we only note that our assumption that the set of function symbols is infinite shows that a term is only a name that can be assigned to any real-world object and that the existence of an object with such a name is manifested in the database as a fact, ie, with the help of a predicate symbol.

keep a fact secret if the subject can find out its truth value without consulting the database.

We conclude this section with two properties we present here without a proof.

**Lemma 11 (Update truthfulness)** Let $T_{s,s}$ be a transaction such that the effect $\tau$ on $M_s$ yields $M_s'$. If $T_{s,s}$ is accepted, then the effect $\tau$ is also propagated to M, ie, the following condition holds: $\forall a \in \tau : M_s'(a) = M'(a)$.

**Corollary 3** Let $T_{s,s}$ be an accepted transaction, then for all $x \in S$ such that $F(s) \leq F(x)$ the effect of $T_{s,s}$ is also propagated to $M_x$.

**Lemma 12 (Subordinate validity)** Let $T_{s,s}$ be a transaction that yields $M'$. If $T_{s,s}$ is accepted, ie, if $M_s'$ is a model of $C_s$, then $M'$ is also a model of $C$.

**Corollary 4** Let $T_{s,s}$ be an accepted transaction, then for all $x \in S$ such that $F(s) \leq F(x)$ $M_x'$ is also a model of $C_x$.

Lemma 11 states that the database does not have the option of ignoring a subject's transaction — it either finds a reason to reject it or the changes must be reflected in the intended state of affairs represented by the model M.

Lemma 12 describes the following situation. Since $DB$ is the intended and undistorted image of the real-world section, it is also the definitive authority on the validity of any model that claims to be the intended one. Since by Lemma 11 $DB$ is forced to follow the changes of a subject's transaction, it must be careful not to let a $DB_s$ at a security level accept a transaction that would have to be rejected by $DB$.

## 4.4 An example of confidentiality enforcement

Both Lemma 11 and Lemma 12 are existential. They only say what should be prohibited but not how. At this point inventive confidentiality enforcement methods are needed. Spalka (1996a) presents a detailed study of some methods. Here, we illustrate our approach with the example of a database which has only range-restricted universally quantified integrity constraints.

Let $s \in S$, $DB_s = (B, C_s, I_s)$ and $M_s = (TE_G, \omega_s)$. Suppose that a subject who is authorised to do so intends to keep a fact $a$ secret from $s$, ie, to include $a$ in secret($s$). The following data-orientated method, which does not distort the integrity constraints but only the state's data, examines the satisfiability of a confidentiality demand and in case it is satisfiable yields the possible distortions.

If $a \in SK_s$, then the demand is immediately rejected on the grounds of Assumption 7. Otherwise, we examine the effects of setting $M_s(a) = \neg M(a)$ and moving $a$ out of $A_s$ and into $X_s$ with respect to the distortion-log of $s$. We are done if $M_s$ is still a model of $C_s$ and $RD_s = RI_s = \emptyset$.

Suppose that setting $M_s(a) = \neg M(a)$ invalidates a universally quantified, range-restricted constraint $\psi = \lambda_1 \vee ... \vee \lambda_n$ such that all links of the disjunction are literals. Let $\Pi = \{\pi_1, ..., \pi_m\}$ be the finite answer–set of $DB_s$ to $\leftarrow \neg \psi$. Then, for each $j = 1, ..., m$, $\psi \pi_j$ is a ground instance of $\psi$ that violates $\psi$, and each $\psi \pi_j$ comprises at least one distorted literal, ie, the truth value of which is reversed.

**Lemma 13** Let $\pi \in \Pi$. Then $K' = \{\lambda_1 \pi, ..., \lambda_n \pi\} \cap X_s \neq \varnothing$.

We call the set $K'$ the set of original candidates for a secret with respect to $\psi$ and $\pi$. Since a fact cannot be a candidate for a secret if the user can inspect it, we can immediately reduce $K'$ to $K = K' \backslash SK_s$.

The members of $K = \{\varepsilon_1, ..., \varepsilon_m, \eta_1, \eta_2, ...\}$, all of which are instances of the $\lambda_i$ and there is a $k$ such that $\alpha = \varepsilon_k$, can be split in two groups:

i) the secret facts $\varepsilon_i$ and
ii) the non-secret facts $\eta_j$
   The violation of $\psi$ has two reasons:
i) none of the $\varepsilon_i$ has in $M_s$ the same truth value as in $M$
ii) none of the $\eta_j$ has in $M_s$ a different truth value than in $M$.

We surely do not want to make $\psi \pi$ true by reversing an $\varepsilon_i$'s truth value in $M_s$ — it has been deliberately set so to keep it confidential. What we can do is to select an $\eta_j$ and reverse its truth value in $M_s$. We call such an $\eta_j$ an *alias* for the secret $\alpha$.

**Lemma 14** If $n = 0$, then the confidentiality demand cannot be enforced.
*Proof* With $K = \{\varepsilon_1, ..., \varepsilon_m\}$ we have no alias for $\alpha$, since $K$ contains only secrets. ◪

A fact $\eta$ qualifies as an alias for a secret with respect to a user $s$ if it satisfies the following *alias–conditions*:

i) $\eta$ is not confidential
ii) $\eta$ is not an alias
iii) $\eta$ is outside the powers of the user
iv) $\eta$ is not an element of the user's specific knowledge
v) The reversal of the truth value of $\eta_i$ in $M_s$ does not invalidate it.

Conditions (i) and (ii) ensure that an alias cannot reduce the disagreement-set. If $\eta$ is selected as an alias, then both subordinate validity and update truthfulness can be violated if a user is allowed to change it. Condition (iii) prevents it. Condition (iv) is necessary to ensure the truthfulness of the profile and condition (v) to ensure the profile's local validity.

The property of a fact being an alias for another secret fact must be recorded so that its truth value in a user's profile can be adjusted to that in the global model when it is no longer needed as an alias. The alias–relationship establishes a link between a user, a secret fact from the database and a fact from the user's profile. We can therefore administer it in a relation $alias(s, \alpha, \eta)$ with the meaning that $\eta$ is an alias for the facts $\alpha$ in the profile of the user $s$.

We now briefly sketch the dynamic considerations.

**Lemma 15** Suppose that no literal $\lambda_i\pi$ is confidential, ie all $\lambda_i\pi$ have the same truth value in M and $M_s$. Then $\psi$ respects the subordinate validity requirement.

**Lemma 16** Suppose that there is a literal $\lambda_i\pi$ that is an alias. Then $\psi$ respects the subordinate validity requirement.
*Proof* Let $\psi\pi = \varepsilon_1 \vee ... \vee \varepsilon_m \vee \eta \vee \mu_1 \vee ... \vee \mu_n$ such that
- all links of $\psi\pi$ are positive or negative ground literals
- all $\varepsilon_i$ are confidential
- $\eta$ is an alias
- all $\mu_j$ are not confidential

The existence of an alias in the still static consideration implies that:
- $M(\psi\pi) = M_s(\psi\pi) = $ True
- $M(\varepsilon_i) = $ True and $M_s(\varepsilon_i) = $ False for all $\varepsilon_i$
- $M(\eta) = $ False and $M_s(\eta) = $ True
- $M(\mu_j) = M_s(\mu_j) = $ False for all $\mu_j$

Firstly, according to our assumption, the user has no powers to alter the secret facts in his transaction. Secondly, an attempted alteration of the truth value of a $\mu_j$, ie, the deletion of a negative literal or the insertion of a positive one, cannot invalidate $\psi\pi$. Such a transaction even adds one more true link to it. The only remaining possibility, a change of the truth value of the alias $\eta$, will not be admitted. Thus the literal $\eta$ is a link that always remains true in the local evaluation of $\psi\pi$. ▨

The situation that threatens to disclose a secret can be characterised as follows. Suppose that the links of $\psi\pi = \varepsilon_1 \vee ... \vee \varepsilon_m \vee \mu_1 \vee ... \vee \mu_n$ are such that there is no alias among them. This has the following implications on the truth value of the links:
- $M(\psi\pi) = M_s(\psi\pi) = $ True
- $M(\varepsilon_i) = $ False and $M_s(\varepsilon_i) = $ True for all $\varepsilon_i$
- there is at least one $\mu_j$ such that $M(\mu_j) = M_s(\mu_j) = $ True

We see that the assessment of the truth value of $\psi\pi$ to True in M depends solely on the truth value of the non-secret links, whereas in $M_s$ it is also supported by the secret links. The user's attempt to make the facts $\mu_j$ false must be rejected — there is no way getting round that. The problem is to find a local explanation for the failure of the operation. The instance $\psi\pi$ is true in the profile, and we do not want to inform the user of its global evaluation. The idea is to show the user a different instance $\psi\sigma$ that turns from True to False in the profile with his transaction.

Let $\psi = \lambda_1 \vee ... \vee \lambda_m \vee \kappa_1 \vee ... \vee \kappa_n$ be an integrity constraint such that:
- There is a substitution $\pi$ such that $\psi\pi = \varepsilon_1 \vee ... \vee \varepsilon_m \vee \mu_1 \vee ... \vee \mu_n$
- $M'_s(\psi) = $ True

Let $\Theta = \{\sigma_1, \sigma_2, ...\}$ be the set of substitutions such that for each $\sigma_k \in \Theta$ the condition holds that for each $j = 1, ..., n$ $\kappa_j\sigma_k = \kappa_j\pi = \mu_j$. Then we must look for a substitution $\sigma_k \in \Theta$ such that each $\eta_i = \lambda_i \sigma_k$ satisfies the alias–conditions. If such a substitution exists, then each $\eta_i$ represents an alias for the corresponding secret fact $\varepsilon_i$. For each $\eta_i$ we then:

i) reverse its truth value in the profile, ie, set $M_s(\eta_i) = \neg M(\eta_i) =$ False

ii) register the distortion, ie, set $\eta_i \notin A_s$ and $\eta_i \in X_s$ in the distortion–log

iii) mark it as an alias for the secret $\varepsilon_i$, ie we create the entry alias($s, \varepsilon_i, \eta_i$)

**Lemma 17** $\psi$ respects the subordinate validity requirement.

*Proof* In this situation, the user's attempt to alter the truth value of the $\mu_j$ is rejected. The reason for it in the global database is the instance $\psi\pi$ with $\lambda_j\pi = \varepsilon_j$. The reason for it in the user's profile is the instance $\psi\sigma$ with $\lambda_j\sigma = \eta_j$. ⧫

We illustrate this procedure with a brief example.

Let $p$ be a two-place predicate and $p(a, b)$ a fact that should be kept secret from the user $s$. Suppose that $M(p(a, b)) =$ True and $M_s(p(a, b)) =$ False. Let moreover

$$\forall XYZ: \neg p(Z, X) \lor \neg p(Z, Y) \lor eq(X, Y) \tag{E2}$$

be the primary key integrity constraint for $p$. Suppose that $p(a, b)$ is the only $p$-fact in the database and that the user $s$ intends to insert $p(a, c)$. The substitution we should pay attention to is thus $\pi = \{X/b, Y/c, Z/a\}$. The figure below shows the evaluation of the truth value of (E2) in the global database and in the local profile before and after the intended insert operation.

| | $\neg p(Z, X) \lor \neg p(Z, Y) \lor eq(X, Y)$ | | | $\psi\pi$ | |
|--------|--------|--------|--------|--------|--------|
| M | False | True | False | True | OK |
| $M_s$ | True | True | False | True | |
| | INSERT $p(a, c)$ | | | | |
| M' | False | False | False | False | Danger! |
| $M_s'$ | True | False | False | True | |

We see that the database must reject the insert operation, yet the profile provides no explanation for that — a situation that must be avoided. The set of substitutions we should now consider is $\Theta = \{\sigma = \{X/t\} \mid t \in TE_G\}$. To reject the user's attempt to insert the fact $p(a, c)$, we must look for a $\sigma \in \Theta$ such that the fact $p(a, X)\sigma = p(a, b')$ satisfies the alias–conditions. Then we can set

$$M_s(p(a, b')) = \neg M(p(a, b')) = \text{True}$$

and mark it as an alias for $p(a, b)$, ie we create the entry alias($u, p(a, b), p(a, b')$). In this situation, the user's attempt to insert the fact $p(a, c)$ is rejected. The reason for it in the global database is the instance $\psi\pi$ with $\pi = \{X/b, Y/c, Z/a\}$. The reason for it in the user's profile is the instance $\psi\sigma$ with $\sigma = \{X/b', Y/c, Z/a\}$.

# 5 Conclusion

Section 3 extracts from security-level-based mandatory security policies their only genuine intention, the primitive mandatory requirement — which we have seen does not express a restriction of access. In section 4, given a logic-based database, we propose to interpret it as a reversal of truth values in the database's intended model, and add it as an axiom. We regard the intended model as the intended image of a real-world section and any model with an aberration in the truth value assignments as a distorted image of the same real-world section — this implies that confidentiality in databases is exclusively concerned with an innocuous distortion of truth values and the complete control of these distortions. The distortion-log, which describes the relation between the intended and any distorted model with respect to their disagreement in the truth value assignments.

Due to space limits, we only present a first characterisation of this axiomatic system, which already shows some useful properties. In particular we intend to continue this work with a more detailed presentation of dynamic semantics, ie, transaction properties, and a data-orientated, ie, alias-based confidentiality enforcement method.

Until now we have not been able to derive a contradiction from our axioms and, au fond, we hope that this remains the case.

# Acknowledgement

We would like thank the anonymous referees for their valuable comments, which have helped to improve this work.

# References

Bell, David Elliott, and Leonard J. La Padula. (1975) *Secure computer system: Unified exposition and multics interpretation.* MITRE Technical Report 2997. MITRE Corp, Bedford, MA.

Bonatti, Piero, Sarit Kraus and V.S. Subrahmanian. (1992) 'Declarative Foundations of Secure Deductive Databases'. Ed Joachim Biskup and Richard Hull. *4th International Conference on Database Theory – ICDT'92.* LNCS, vol 646. Berlin, Heidelberg: Springer-Verlag. pp 391–406. [Also in: *IEEE Transactions on Knowledge and Data Engineering* 7.3 (1995):406–422.]

Bonyun, David A. (1980) 'The Secure Relational Database Management System Kernel: Three Years After'. *1980 IEEE Symposium on Security and Privacy.* IEEE Computer Society Press. pp 34–37.

Bourbaki, Nicolas. (1968) *Theory of Sets.* Paris: Hermann.

Cremers, Armin B., Ulrike Griefahn and Ralf Hinze. (1994) *Deduktive Datenbanken.* Braunschweig: Vieweg.

Denning, Dorothy E., Teresa F. Lunt, Roger R. Schell, Mark Heckman and William R. Shockley. (1987) 'A Multilevel Relational Data Model'. *1987 IEEE Symposium on Security and Privacy.* IEEE Computer Society Press. pp 220–234.

—, —, —, William R. Shockley and Mark Heckman. (1988) 'The SeaView Security Model'. *1988 Symposium on Security and Privacy.* IEEE Computer Society Press. pp 218–233.

Feiertag, R.J., K.N. Levitt and L. Robinson. (1977) 'Proving multilevel security of a system design'. *6th ACM Symposium on Operating System Principles. ACM SIGOPS Operating System Review* 11.5:57–65.

Graubart, Richard D., and John P.L. Woodward. (1982) 'A Preliminary Naval Surveillance DBMS Security Model'. *1982 IEEE Symposium on Security and Privacy.* IEEE Computer Society Press. pp 21–37.

Landwehr, Carl E. (1981) 'Formal Models for Computer Security'. *ACM Computing Surveys* 13.3:247–278.

Qian, Xiaolei. (1994) 'Inference Channel-Free Integrity Constraints in Multilevel Relational Databases'. *1994 IEEE Symposium on Research in Security and Privacy.* IEEE Computer Society Press. pp 158–167.

— and Teresa F. Lunt. (1992) 'Tuple–level vs. element–level classification'. Ed Bhavani M. Thuraisingham and Carl E. Landwehr. Database Security VI. IFIP WG11.3 Workshop on Database Security 1993. Amsterdam: North-Holland, 1993. pp 301–315.

Sicherman, George L., Wiebren de Jonge and Reind P. van de Riet. (1983) 'Answering Queries Without Revealing Secrets'. *ACM Transactions on Database Systems* 8.1:41–59.

Spalka, Adrian. (1994) 'Secure Logic Databases Allowed to Reveal Indefinite Information on Secrets'. Ed Joachim Biskup, Matthew Morgenstern and Carl E. Landwehr. *Database Security VIII.* IFIP WG11.3 Working Conference on Database Security 1994. Amsterdam: North-Holland. pp 297–316.

—. (1996a) *A Study of the Extensibility of Logic-Based Databases with Confidentiality Capabilities.* PhD Thesis. Universtity of Bonn, Germany.

—. (1996b) 'The Non-Primitiveness of the Simple-Security Property and its Non-Applicability to Relational Databases'. *9th IEEE Computer Security Foundations Workshop 1996.* IEEE Computer Society Press.

Winslett, Marianne, Kenneth Smith and Xiaolei Qian. (1994) 'Formal Query Languages for Secure Relational Databases'. *ACM Transactions on Database Systems* 19.4:626–662.

# Query Evaluation

# Database Query Evaluation with the STARBASE Method

Pamela Phillip

University of Bristol, The Merchant Venturers Building, Woodland Road,
Bristol BS8 1UB, UK
email pip.bristol.ac.uk

**Abstract.** This paper presents STARBASE, a new method for database query evaluation which advances the state of the art in deductive database technology by providing an anytime method for searching the literals in the body of a rule so that the next literal to be processed is guaranteed to be one of the most instantiated ones. A prototype implementation of STARBASE applied is exhibited and its performance compared to XSB and Prolog for a range of examples. The prototype implementation is restricted to Datalog programs but can be extended to stratified programs. The main features of STARBASE which guarantee it to perform are (1) it focuses on data relevant to the query, (2) it avoids redundant computation and looping by storing partial results, and (3) it replaces subsumption checking with syntactic equality checking.

## 1. Introduction

Deductive databases integrate logic programming and databases. They extend conventional database systems by supporting complex queries, usually involving recursion. Datalog is the declarative language typically used by deductive databases. By using Datalog, a deductive database can between a set of facts (the Extensional Database or EDB) which are represented as predicates with constant arguments, together with a set of rules (the Intensional Database or IDB). Rules take the form of predicates, where $p$ is the head of the rule, and the list $q_1, q_2, \ldots, q_n$ is the body of the rule.

A rule can be interpreted (declaratively) as $p$ is true if $q_1$ and $q_2$ and ... and $q_n$ are true, each of $p$ and the $q_i$ are of the form $l(t_1, t_2, \ldots t_k)$, where $l$ is a predicate name of arity $a$ and each $t_i$ is either a constant or a variable.

The example in figure 1 shows a deductive database in which the EDB consists of seven facts, and the IDB contains three rules.

In a deductive database, queries are evaluated by using the rules to derive implicitly represented information from data stored explicitly as facts in the EDB. A major interest of deductive database research is the problem of finding efficient deductive retrieval methods. An ideal deductive query processor should have the following features:

- wide application domain (ideally it can evaluate programs, i.e. Datalog extended with function symbols, negation and non-ground tuples).

# Database Query Evaluation with the STARBASE Method

Estrella Pulido

University of Bristol, The Merchant Venturers Building, Woodland Road,
Bristol BS8 1UB, UK
e-mail: pulido@cs.bris.ac.uk

**Abstract.** This paper presents STARBASE, a new method for database query evaluation which advances the state of the art in deductive database technology by providing an automatic method for reordering the literals in the body of a rule so that the next literal to be processed is guaranteed to be one of the most instantiated ones. A prototype implementation of a STARBASE system is described and its performance compared to XSB and Prolog for a range of examples. The prototype implementation is restricted to Datalog programs, but can be extended to stratified programs. The main features of STARBASE which guarantee high performance are (1) it focuses on data relevant to the query, (2) it avoids redundant computation and looping by storing partial results, and (3) it replaces subsumption checking with syntactic equality checking.

## 1  Introduction

Deductive databases integrate logic programming and databases. They extend conventional database systems by supporting complex queries, usually involving recursion. Datalog is the declarative language typically used by deductive databases. By using Datalog, a deductive database can be seen as a set of *facts* (the Extensional Database or EDB) which are represented as predicates with constant arguments, together with a set of rules (the Intensional Database or IDB). Rules take the form p:-q$_1$,q$_2$,...,q$_n$, where $p$ is the *head* of the rule, and the list $q_1, q_2, \ldots, q_n$ is the *body* of the rule.

A rule can be interpreted declaratively as "p is true if q$_1$ and q$_2$ and ... and q$_n$ are true". Each of $p$ and the $q_i$'s are of the form $l(t_1, t_2, \ldots, t_n)$, where $l$ is a predicate name of arity $n$ and each $t_i$ is either a constant or a variable.

The example in figure 1 shows a deductive database in which the EDB consists of seven facts, and the IDB contains three rules.

In a deductive database, queries are evaluated by using the rules to derive implicitly represented information from data stored explicitly as facts in the EDB. A major interest of deductive database research is the problem of finding efficient deductive retrieval methods. An ideal deductive query processor should have the following features:

- wide application domain (ideally Horn clause programs, i.e. Datalog extended with function symbols, negation and non-ground tuples),

| EDB | likes(bill,cars). | friend(bill,ted). | dearer(4wds,cars). |
|-----|-------------------|-------------------|--------------------|
|     | likes(ted,bikes). | friend(ted,bill). | dearer(cars,mbks). |
|     |                   |                   | dearer(mbks,bikes). |
| **IDB** | buys(X,Y):-likes(X,Y). | | |
|     | buys(X,Y):-friend(X,Z),buys(Z,Y). | | |
|     | buys(X,Y):-buys(X,Z),dearer(Z,Y). | | |

**Fig. 1.** A deductive database

- high performance, and
- declarativeness (the system should be responsible for the efficient evaluation of the queries, and not the user).

Existing methods such as Magic Sets [2], SLD-AL Resolution [23], and SLG Resolution [3] have achieved the first two features in the list above, but at the expense of declarativeness. The reason is that in these methods, the user is responsible for determining an efficient ordering of literals in the body of rules, which is an indispensable requirement to prevent the generation of irrelevant facts when evaluating rules.

This paper presents STARBASE, a new method for database query evaluation based on graph traversal. It will show that STARBASE is comparable with the above-mentioned methods with respect to power and performance. It will also show that applicability is not sacrificed in STARBASE due to its automatic reordering of literals. The version of STARBASE described in this paper is a prototype which is restricted to Datalog but can be extended for full Horn clause programs with negation.

An additional contribution of this paper is to show that graph-based methods have been underestimated in the past and that they can compete with state-of-the-art methods.

The paper is organized as follows. Section 2 presents a brief review of existing database query evaluation methods. We describe the STARBASE system in section 3, and its formal properties in section 4. Performance results are reported in section 5. Indications of how the prototype implementation will be extended to Horn clause programs with negation are given in section 6. Finally, conclusions are presented in section 7.

## 2 Related work

Existing recursive query processing methods can be classified into three different categories: deductive database strategies, logic programming strategies, and graph traversal strategies.

The deductive database strategies can be classified into two categories: *evaluation strategies* and *optimization strategies*. The former includes methods such as Naive evaluation [22], Semi-naive evaluation [22], Henschen-Naqvi [7], and APEX [10]. Given a query and a database, these algorithms will produce the answer to the query. None of these methods is the ideal method we are looking for: either their application domain is too restricted, their efficiency too poor, or they present intrinsic difficulties for some cases.

The optimization strategies rewrite the rules to make their evaluation by a simple evaluation method more efficient. Examples of optimization strategies are Aho-Ullman [1], Static Filtering [8], Magic Sets [2], and Counting [2]. Among them, Magic Sets is the method with the widest domain of application. The Magic Sets method uses *sips* to establish the order in which body literals will be evaluated. For a single rule, different collections of sips can be associated and the choice between them is *a priori* free. In constrast, the graphs used in STARBASE to represent deduction rules have a one-to-one correspondence with the original rules. Furthermore, whereas the Magic Sets transformation assumes that the literals in the RHS of a rule form a single connected component, the STARBASE compilation technique can be applied to rules with multiple components.

Several deductive database systems such as CORAL [16] and LDL [21] implement the Magic Sets transformation. Both of them support some form of set-grouping and aggregation, i.e the ability to collect sets of tuples and to compute aggregate functions (sum, average, minimum, maximum, ...) over them.

The logic programming strategies include memoing top-down evaluation techniques such as OLDT Resolution [20], Extension tables [4], SLD-AL Resolution [23], SLG Resolution [3], and RQA/FQI [13]. These techniques are based on extending SLD Resolution. Unlike STARBASE, most tabling methods can handle negation and subgoals with function symbols, and their main achievement is that they prevent the interpreter from recomputing partial results, thus preventing looping and reducing redundant computation. In order to check whether a goal has been found earlier, tabling methods have to perform some form of subsumption check. It should be noted that, because of the cost of subsumption, systems implementing tabling methods such as XSB [18] use a variant test which succeeds for two goals if they are the same goal up to the renaming of variables. This test is quicker but fails to avoid redundant work in some cases.

By representing rules with a format where variables are not required, STARBASE replaces subsumption checking with syntactical equality checking. In the context of Datalog, there is no significant difference between the cost of subsumption and that of equality checking. However, if the scope of STARBASE can be extended beyond Datalog without the need of reintroducing variables (see section 6), STARBASE will be more efficient than existing tabling methods.

Like the Magic Sets strategy, existing tabling methods require sometimes considerable programmer intervention to establish the optimum runtime parameters and ordering of literals. In contrast, STARBASE provides a completely automated decision procedure for optimization.

The last group of query evaluation methods to be mentioned are methods based on graph traversal. They are the automaton-based strategies proposed by Grahne et al. [6] and by Wood [25]. As in STARBASE, these strategies view the database as a graph. However, these methods are more restricted than STARBASE in the kind of database and deduction rules that they can handle.

Other graph-based methods such as APEX and Static Filtering use graphs to represent rules. STARBASE differs from these strategies in that both the database and the deduction rules are viewed as graphs. Furthermore, in STAR-BASE, nodes in the graphs representing deduction rules correspond to variables and edges correspond to relations, whereas in *system graphs* (APEX and Static Filtering) nodes correspond to rules and relations, and edges are unlabelled. It is this mapping between nodes and variables and edges and relations in STAR-BASE which made it possible to define a decision procedure, based on a classical path-finding algorithm, for finding an efficient ordering of literals in the rule.

The lack of a decision procedure for determining the optimum ordering of literals in the body of rules is a major deficiency of methods such as Magic Sets and tabling strategies. The reason is that the wrong order in the evaluation of goals can cause a combinatorial explosion in the search space. Various methods have been proposed which attempt to solve the goal ordering problem in deductive databases. The method reported in [24] uses cost estimates to select from alternative orderings. Costs can be difficult to estimate because they usually involve the size of relations, which might be difficult to estimate accurately. However, cost metrics produce quite reasonable estimates and can be used in conjunction with other heuristics to produce a more accurate result.

In [22], an algorithm is proposed for reordering literals that uses the heuristic of favouring literals with the most bound arguments. This algorithm is also used in the method proposed by Morris [12] to construct a rule/goal graph when reordering of subgoals is permitted and there are forbidden binding patterns. For a given Datalog rule, the complexity of Ullman's method is $O(n^2)$, where $n$ is the length of the rule. In STARBASE, the method used to reorder subgoals in a rule is to find an Euler tour in the graph representing the rule. The complexity of this algorithm is $O(n)$, where $n$ is the length of the rule. For some rules, before an Euler tour can be found, some of the literals in the body of the rule have to be duplicated. Because of this, the complexity of the method used in STARBASE to reorder subgoals is, in the worst case, $O(n^2 \log n)$ [9].

The basic idea behind the STARBASE evaluation algorithm originated from the Chart Parsing algorithm, originally developed for processing sentences in natural language (NL) [5]. Two other methods based on parsing algorithms are Warren and Pereira's Earley Deduction proof procedure [14] which can be applied to any definite program (i.e. logic program without negation), and Rosenblueth's proof procedure [17]. As with tabling methods, the main difference between STARBASE and Earley Deduction is that the latter requires subsumption and in STARBASE this operation is replaced by equality checking. In contrast, Rosenblueth's method avoids subsumption, but applies to a class of programs and queries which is more restricted than Datalog, which is the application domain of STARBASE. In general, Earley Deduction and Rosenblueth's method attempt to build parsing insights into a logic programming framework, whereas STARBASE stays closer to the graph-based character of Chart Parsing.

# 3 The STARBASE system

The STARBASE system is implemented in two stages. At compile time, the Datalog rules are processed by the STARBASE rule compiler which transforms them into STARBASE productions.

At query time, the STARBASE evaluation algorithm answers queries on the database by viewing the EDB as a graph and traversing it in the way indicated by the STARBASE productions relevant to the query.

The main components of the system are described in detail in the following subsections. Prototypes of both the rule compiler and the query evaluator have been implemented in the C language.

## 3.1 Query evaluation in STARBASE

This section presents first, the basic algorithm for deduction from binary-chain programs, i.e. programs where rules are of the form

$$p(X_1, X_{n+1}) :- p_1(X_1, X_2), p_2(X_2, X_3), \ldots, p_{n-1}(X_{n-1}, X_n), p_n(X_n, X_{n+1})$$

where $n \geq 0$ and $X_1, \ldots, X_{n+1}$ are all distinct variables. Then, extensions to the basic algorithm are described which have the effect of increasing the scope to full Datalog.

In STARBASE, a database is viewed as a graph - the *database graph* - consisting of nodes and *hyperlinks*. A *hyperlink* of arity $n$ is a directed edge with a starting node, an ending node, and $n$-$2$ intermediate nodes. A hyperlink of arity 2 is equivalent to an edge in classical terminology.

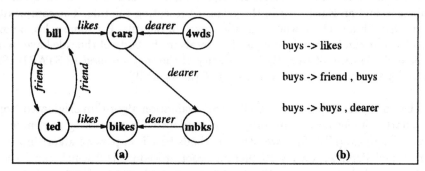

**Fig. 2.** (a) Database graph (b) STARBASE productions

Initially, the rules are transformed into STARBASE productions by dropping all variables and replacing the ":-" symbol with "→". The variables can be dropped because they are implicit in the binary-chain format of the rule. Figure 2 shows the database graph and the STARBASE productions for the example in figure 1.

In the process of answering a query, STARBASE builds a set of hyperlinks and a set of *edges*. They constitute what is called an "active chart". The hyperlinks of the database graph are treated by the STARBASE algorithm as pre-existing elements of the same chart. In this way, the "active chart" in STAR-BASE can be thought of as having two components: a permanent one which corresponds to the database graph, and a temporary one which consists of the edges and hyperlinks that are created when answering a query, and which are stored in tables.

*Edges* are directed binary links labelled with a tuple of the form $<head, body>$. The two components in an edge label have the following meaning:

> *head* is a predicate symbol which appears in the head of a STARBASE production,
>
> *body* is a list of predicate symbols which corresponds to (a part of) the body of a STARBASE production. The first element in the *body* is referred to as the *FEB*.

In what follows, we will represent an edge between nodes *start* and *finish* and labelled $<head, body>$ as the 4-tuple $<start, finish, head, body>$.

New edges and hyperlinks are created by applying the STARBASE *fundamental* and *top-down* rules which are formally described below.

**The fundamental rule.** Given an edge and a hyperlink, the fundamental rule creates a new edge as follows. The start point and the *head* are the same as in the original edge. The ending point is the end point of the hyperlink. The *body* is the *body* of the original edge with the FEB removed. The fundamental rule is illustrated in figure 3.

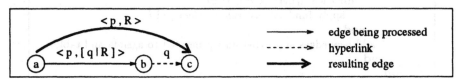

**Fig. 3.** The fundamental rule

**The top-down rule.** Given an edge, the top-down rule creates a new edge starting and ending at the ending point of the edge for each of the productions (if any) defining the predicate in the FEB of the edge. The top-down rule is illustrated in figure 4.

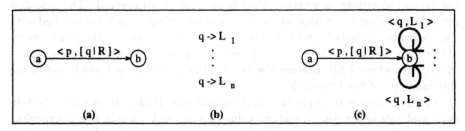

**Fig. 4.** (a) An edge with predicate $q$ as FEB (b) the set of productions defining $q$, (c) the result of applying the top-down rule to the edge.

**The STARBASE evaluation algorithm.** The STARBASE evaluation algorithm is summarised in figure 5. Initially, the evaluation algorithm creates an edge for each production defining the predicate in the query. These edges start and end at the node corresponding to one of the bound arguments in the query. They are placed in an agenda and stored in tables which index them according to appropriate criteria.

```
procedure solve(predicate,nodes)
  begin
    initialize agenda and tables;
    create initial edges and add them to the agenda and tables;
    while agenda is not empty do
      begin
        remove element elem from agenda;
        if elem is a hyperlink then
          begin
            if elem is a solution to the query then display it to user;
            E := set of edges resulting of applying
              the selection procedure to elem;
            for each edge a ∈ E do
              apply fundamental rule to a and elem
          end
        else /* elem is an edge */
          begin
            apply top-down rule to elem;
            H := set of hyperlinks resulting of applying
              the selection procedure to elem;
            for each hyperlink h ∈ H do
              apply fundamental rule to elem and h
          end
        add new edges and hyperlinks generated to agenda and tables;
      end
  end
```

**Fig. 5.** The STARBASE evaluation algorithm

The algorithm then enters the main cycle. On each cycle, an edge or hyperlink *elem* is taken off the agenda. Then the *selection* procedure selects either a set of hyperlinks from both the database graph and the tables, or a set of edges from the tables, according to whether *elem* is an edge or a hyperlink. The *selection* procedure applied to an edge will select those hyperlinks which are labelled with the predicate symbol of the FEB of the edge and which start at the ending point of the edge. Similarly, the *selection* procedure applied to a hyperlink will select those edges whose FEB matches the label of the hyperlink and which end at the starting node of the hyperlink.

The next step is to apply the fundamental rule. If *elem* is an edge, the fundamental rule is applied to each possible pair *(elem,h)*, where *h* is a hyperlink in the set of selected hyperlinks. If *elem* is a hyperlink, the fundamental rule is applied to each possible pair *(e, elem)*, where *e* is an edge in the set of selected edges. In addition, if the element being processed is an edge, the top-down rule is also applied.

When the removal of the FEB from the *body* of the original edge results in the empty list, a hyperlink is created instead of an edge. The label in this hyperlink will be the predicate symbol in the *head* component of the original edge.

The creation of a hyperlink with label *p* will fire the fundamental rule which will be applied to pairs consisting of the hyperlink and each of the existing edges that have *p* as the first element in the *body* component. Note that by triggering the fundamental rule with newly created hyperlinks as well as edges, *completeness* is ensured.

The evaluation process stops when the agenda is empty. The answers to the query will correspond to some of the hyperlinks generated during this process.

Figure 6 illustrates the edges and hyperlinks created by the algorithm when answering the query *buys(bill,X)* on a portion of the database in figure 2. The predicate names *buys, likes, friend,* and *dearer* have been abbreviated to *b, l, f,* and *d*, respectively. The hyperlink labelled *b* starting at node *bill* and ending at node *bikes* indicates that *bikes* is an answer to the query. Table 1 illustrates the sequence in which the edges and hyperlinks in figure 6 are generated by STARBASE.

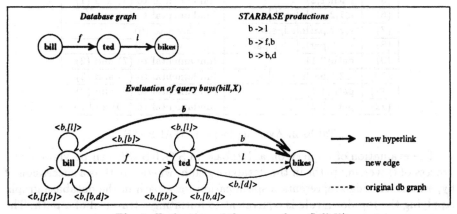

**Fig. 6.** Evaluation of the query *buys(bill, X)*

A new edge or hyperlink is created only if it is not syntactically equal to any other existing edge or hyperlink. This avoids redundant subcomputations and looping, thus ensuring *termination*. As an example of how equality checking prevents looping, consider an EDB containing two facts (1) edge(1,2) and (2) edge(2,1), and two STARBASE productions corresponding to the right-recursive version of the *path* relation (P1) *path → edge*, (P2) *path → edge, path*. Table 2 illustrates the set of edges and hyperlinks that are generated by STARBASE.

In this example equality checking avoids looping by preventing the creation of the edges and hyperlinks in table 3.

| No. | Edge/hyperlink | How generated |
|-----|----------------|---------------|
| (1) | f(bill,ted) | database hyperlink |
| (2) | l(ted,bikes) | database hyperlink |
| (3) | <bill,bill,b,[l]> | initialization |
| (4) | <bill,bill,b,[f,b]> | initialization |
| (5) | <bill,bill,b,[b,d]> | initialization |
| (6) | <bill,ted,b,[b]> | fundamental to (4) and (1) |
| (7) | <ted,ted,b,[l]> | top-down to (6) |
| (8) | <ted,ted,b,[f,b]> | top-down to (6) |
| (9) | <ted,ted,b,[b,d]> | top-down to (6) |
| (10) | b(ted,bikes) | fundamental to (7) and (2) |
| (11) | b(bill,bikes) | fundamental to (6) and (10) |
| (12) | <ted,bikes,b,[d]> | fundamental to (9) and (10) |

**Table 1.** Evaluation of the query $b(bill,X)$

| No. | Edge/hyperlink | How generated |
|-----|----------------|---------------|
| (1) | edge(1,2) | database hyperlink |
| (2) | edge(2,1) | database hyperlink |
| (3) | <1,1,path,[edge]> | initialization |
| (4) | <1,1,path,[edge,path]> | initialization |
| (5) | path(1,2) | fundamental to (3) and (1) |
| (6) | <1,2,path,[path]> | fundamental to (4) and (1) |
| (7) | <2,2,path,[edge]> | top-down to (6) |
| (8) | <2,2,path,[edge,path]> | top-down to (6) |
| (9) | path(2,1) | fundamental to (7) and (2) |
| (10) | <2,1,path,[path]> | fundamental to (8) and (2) |
| (11) | path(1,1) | fundamental to (6) and (9) |
| (12) | path(2,2) | fundamental to (10) and (5) |

**Table 2.** Avoiding loops in STARBASE

The evaluation of a query on a database in STARBASE can be viewed as a process of traversing paths in the database graph, where a path is a succession of hyperlinks. An edge represents a specification for a path in the database graph. Applying the top-down rule is equivalent to initiating a traversal of a path. The application of the fundamental rule to an edge and a hyperlink can be viewed as traversing the hyperlink in the way specified by the FEB of the edge.

Obviously the binary-chain form is quite restricted. As mentioned in section 2, two ways of using chart parsing for more general deduction are described in the literature. One of them is to put arguments back in literals and to modify Earley's parsing algorithm to work for literals with explicit variables. This is the approach taken by Warren and Pereira in Earley deduction [14]. Another approach [17] is to extend the chart parsing algorithm with unification and to define a class of programs that can be translated into binary-chain programs.

The STARBASE approach adopts a different strategy, namely, to drop arguments from literals and to use tags to represent variations in the pattern of arguments of literals. In addition, the fundamental and top-down rules are extended

| No. | Edge/hyperlink | How generated |
|-----|----------------|---------------|
| (11′) | <1,1,path,[edge]> | top-down to (10) |
| (12′) | <1,1,path,[edge,path]> | top-down to (10) |
| (13) | path(2,1) | fundamental to (10) and (11) |

**Table 3.** Edges and hyperlinks not created when avoiding loops

so that they can deal with these variations. The following section discusses all possible variations.

## 3.2  Rule compilation in STARBASE

The STARBASE rule compiler transforms a Datalog rule into a number of STARBASE productions. A minimum of $2^k - 1$ different STARBASE productions are generated from each Datalog rule, where $k$ is the arity of the head predicate of the Datalog rule. Each STARBASE production corresponds to one combination of arguments of the head predicate which will be bound at evaluation time.

Given a Datalog rule of the form $p\text{:-}q_1, \ldots, q_n$ and a binding pattern, the rule compiler generates a production of the form $p_i \rightarrow r_1, \ldots, r_m$, where $p_i$ is composed of the predicate symbol $p$, and a list of integers, and each $r_i$ (referred to as a *production element*) is composed of a predicate symbol and possibly a constraint and a list of tags.

In STARBASE, a graph, called the *rule graph*, is associated with each Datalog rule in the following way. The *head component* of the rule graph is composed of one hyperlink forming a single connected graph. In the body, however, each literal $p(t_1, \ldots, t_n)$ is modelled as a set of $n - 1$ simple edges (not hyperlinks) labelled $p_{12}$ to $p_{n-1n}$. Each edge $p_{ij}$ links nodes $v_i$ and $v_j$ corresponding to the terms $t_i$ and $t_j$ of the literal. The body of the rule may be composed of a number of disconnected subgraphs (the *body components*). Figure 7 shows the rule graph corresponding to the Datalog rule $a(X,E)\text{:-}r(Y,E),p(X,Y,Z),q(Z,c,E)$. It has a single body component.

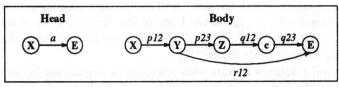

**Fig. 7.** Rule graph for rule $a(X,E)\text{:-}r(Y,E),p(X,Y,Z),q(Z,c,E)$

The order of production elements in the body of each STARBASE production will be determined by viewing each component in the rule graph as an undirected graph, and by finding a sequence of nodes and edges for each of these components which contains each edge at least once. Ideally, we would want the sequence to contain each edge exactly once. This kind of sequence is known in graph theory as a *postman trail* if the initial and final nodes are different, and as an *Euler tour* otherwise [11]. Several algorithms to find postman trails in a graph can be found in the literature. The one used in STARBASE is that proposed in [11].

There are some requirements that a graph has to satisfy so that an Euler tour or postman trail can be found for it. Although not every graph satisfies these requirements, it is always possible to transform a graph into an equivalent one which satisfies them. This is done by duplicating some of the edges in the graph. The STARBASE compiler fully automates a procedure which minimises the number of edges that have to be duplicated. Note that this transformation preserves the equivalence between Datalog rules and STARBASE productions because adding a copy of an existing edge to a rule graph is equivalent to adding a copy of a literal to the body of a rule.

The ordering achieved with the process described above corresponds to an ordering in the original Datalog rule which would guarantee that when a body literal is evaluated at least one of its arguments will be bound.

As illustrated in section 3.1, variables can be dropped from binary-chain rules because they are implicit in the format of the rule, i.e. because binary-chain rules satisfy the following requirements:

- All literals are binary.
- All arguments are variables.
- The last variable in every literal (except the last one in the body) is the first one in the literal that follows it.
- All variables in the body appear twice, except for the first argument of the first literal and the last argument of the last literal which appear once.
- The variables in the head literal correspond to the first argument of the first literal and the last argument of the last literal, respectively.

The goal of the compiler is to be able to drop all arguments from any Datalog rule. This is achieved by adding tags to the predicate symbols in the literals which indicate variations in the pattern of arguments of literals. The transformations performed by the compiler will be illustrated using the Datalog rule $a(X,E):-r(Y,E),p(X,Y,Z),q(Z,c,E)$.

The rule compiler starts the process of compiling a Datalog rule by dividing each n-ary literal $p(t_1,\ldots,t_n)$ in the body of the rule into a set of $n-1$ binary literals $p_{12}(t_1,t_2)$ to $p_{n-1n}(t_{n-1},t_n)$. The pair of integers added to the predicate symbol is an *index* tag. See figure 8(1).

The compiler handles literals with constants as arguments by adding a constraint tag to the corresponding predicate symbol which indicates whether its arguments are variables or constants. See figure 8(2).

Once the n-ary literals have been transformed into binary, the rule compiler divides the body literals into components and finds an Euler tour for each of these components. This process results in a rule consisting of a set of *pseudo-chains*, where a *pseudo-chain* is a subset of literals from the original rule which does not have any variable in common with literals in another *pseudo-chain*. See figure 8(3).

Because of the definition of an Euler tour, literals in each pseudo-chain are ordered in such a way that the last variable in a literal appears in the literal that follows it. Because literals are binary and because all arguments are variables, there is a limited choice for where the last variable $V$ in a literal $p$ may appear in the following literal $q$: it can appear either in the first place, in the second place, or it may not appear at all if $p$ is the last literal in a pseudo chain. In the first case, no tag needs to be added. If $V$ appears in the second place of $q$, the rule compiler will tag $q$ with the -1 tag. Finally, when $V$ does not appear in $q$ at all, the rule compiler tags $q$ with the * tag. See figure 8(4).

Variables that appear more or less frequently than required are dealt with by the rule compiler by adding a $/_L$ tag to the predicate symbol of the literal containing the first occurrence of the corresponding variable. List $L$ will contain the indices of the affected variables. In addition, a new element $s_i$ is added to the constraint of the predicate symbols of the literals containing the subsequent ocurrences. Integer $i$ is the index of the corresponding / tag. See figure 8(5).

Finally, the compiler specifies where the variables in the head literal appear in the body of the rule by adding a $@_L$ tag to the predicate symbol of literals containing the first occurrence of the variables in the head literal. Each pair $(i,j)$ in the list $L$ of a tag $@_L$ added to a predicate symbol $p$ indicates that argument $i$ of the literal with predicate symbol $p$ is the $j$-th argument of the head literal. See figure 8(6).

Variables in the resulting rule are not needed and can be dropped. In addition, consecutive elements corresponding to the same predicate symbol are merged into a single element. The result is a STARBASE production which the query processor will be able to handle. See figure 8(7).

---

**(1)** $r12(Y,E),p12(X,Y),p23(Y,Z),q12(Z,c),q23(c,E)$

**(2)** $r12(Y,E),p12(X,Y),p23(Y,Z),q12_{(\_,c)}(Z,D),q23_{(c,\_)}(D,E)$

**(3)** $p12(X,Y),p23(Y,Z),q12_{(\_,c)}(Z,D),q23_{(c,\_)}(D,E),r12(Y,E)$

**(4)** $p12(X,Y),p23(Y,Z),q12_{(\_,c)}(Z,D),q23_{(c,\_)}(D,E),r12^{-1}(Y,E)$

**(5)** $p12(X,Y),/_2p23(Y,Z),q12_{(\_,c)}(Z,D),q23_{(c,\_)}(D,E),r12^{-1}_{(s_1,\_)}(Y,E)$

**(6)** $@_{(1,1)}p12(X,Y),/_2p23(Y,Z),q12_{(\_,c)}(Z,D),@_{(3,2)}q23_{(c,\_)}(D,E),r12^{-1}_{(s_1,\_)}(Y,E)$

**(7)** $a \rightarrow /_2@_{(1,1)}p,@_{(3,2)}q_{(\_,c,\_)},r^{-1}_{(s_1,\_)}$

---

**Fig. 8.** Compiling rule $a(X,E):-r(Y,E),p(X,Y,Z),q(Z,c,E)$

## 4 Formal properties of the STARBASE evaluation algorithm

The STARBASE evaluation algorithm has the property of termination, and there is strong evidence that it also has the properties of soundness and completeness. The termination property is proved in [15] by proving that the number of edges and hyperlinks generated during evaluation is finite, and that a finite number of operations are performed on each of these edges or hyperlinks.

Soundness means that every answer found by an algorithm is correct, while an algorithm is complete if it finds all possible correct answers. These properties have not yet been proven for the STARBASE evaluation algorithm. However, as evidence for these properties, we can point to (1) the proofs for a related algorithm due to Rosenblueth [17], and (2) the following arguments for the possibility of establishing a correspondence between the STARBASE evaluation algorithm and deduction from definite-clause programs.

The STARBASE evaluation algorithm is sound if both the fundamental and the top-down rules are sound. This can be ensured by establishing a correspondence between an edge or hyperlink and a definite clause. A hyperlink $p(a_1, \ldots, a_n)$ corresponds to a clause of the form $p(a_1, \ldots, a_n) \leftarrow$. For a given edge $e$, the literals in the definite clause equivalent to $e$ can be obtained from the predicate symbols and tags in the elements of the *body* component of edge $e$.

Once this correspondence is established, the fundamental rule applied to an edge and a hyperlink can be proved to be equivalent to applying resolution to their associated clauses, and the top-down rule applied to an edge for a given production $p$ can be proved to be equivalent to instantiating the rule associated with $p$. Since both resolution and instantiation are sound, the soundness of the fundamental and top-down rules is guaranteed.

Intuitively, the completeness of the STARBASE evaluation algorithm is ensured by two facts: (1) that all edges and hyperlinks created during evaluation are stored, and (2) that the creation of any new hyperlink causes the fundamental rule to be fired with all appropriate existing edges.

The definitions and theorems required to prove the soundness and completeness of the STARBASE evaluation algorithm are enunciated in [15] and their complete proofs will be part of future work.

## 5   Performance evaluation

A preliminary performance evaluation was carried out using the prototype version of STARBASE and comparing it with XSB, a programming system which implements SLG Resolution, and, where applicable, Sicstus Prolog. The versions used were version 1.4.1 for XSB and version 2.1 for Sicstus Prolog. The evaluation was done using a range of representative examples based on the *path* relation and the *same generation* relation.

The execution times for the STARBASE prototype, although better than those of XSB in a few cases, are up to an order of magnitude slower. However, these do not give the best indication of the potential performance of STARBASE since the current prototype implementation contains several inefficiencies such as the data access and equality checking mechanisms. A much more promising indication of STARBASE's potential is given by the number of inferences since time and space costs are proportional to this measurement. For this reason, the number of inferences each of the above-mentioned systems performs for each of the test cases was analysed. In XSB, inferences are divided into two subsets: resolution steps and processing of intermediate results. These two subsets are equivalent in STARBASE to the number of edges and hyperlinks that are generated for a given query.

All tests were run on a 40MHz SPARCserver 10 with 128 Mbytes of main memory.

## 5.1 The *path* relation

**Benchmark.** Tests were performed using two versions of the IDB and three of the EDB as follows:

IDB1 - left recursion:      path(X,Y) :- path(X,Z), edge(Z,Y).
                              path(X,Y) :- edge(X,Y).
IDB2 - right recursion:    path(X,Y) :- edge(X,Z), path(Z,Y).
                              path(X,Y) :- edge(X,Y).

EDB1 - chain:              edge(1,2), edge(2,3), ..., edge(n-1,n)
EDB2 - cycle:              edge(1,2), edge(2,3), ..., edge(n,1)
EDB3 - binary tree:      edge(1,2), edge(1,3), ..., edge($2^{h-1}, 2^{h+1}$-1)

where $n$ represents the length of the chain or cycle, and $h$ represents the height of the binary tree.

The queries (Q1) path(1,X) and (Q2) path(X,1) were posed for each of the six combinations, the size of the EDB being varied in each case. The STARBASE productions corresponding to the different IDB and queries are illustrated in table 4. Two of the three productions associated with each Datalog rule are required for the examples. They correspond to two different binding patterns for the head literal and are distinguished by their heads ($p$ corresponds to the first argument being bound, whereas $p^{-1}$ corresponds to the second argument being bound).

| | Query Q1 | Query Q2 |
|---|---|---|
| IDB1 | $p \rightarrow p, e$ | $p^{-1} \rightarrow e^{-1}, p^{-1}$ |
| | $p \rightarrow e$ | $p^{-1} \rightarrow e^{-1}$ |
| IDB2 | $p \rightarrow e, p$ | $p^{-1} \rightarrow p^{-1}, e^{-1}$ |
| | $p \rightarrow e$ | $p^{-1} \rightarrow e^{-1}$ |

**Table 4.** STARBASE productions for the path example

**Resolution steps vs edges.** The number of resolution steps is computed in XSB by using the debugger provided. The debugger is set up so that only *call* ports print trace messages. Each procedure call corresponds to a resolution step. Consequently, the invocation identifier accompanying each procedure call can be used to compute the number of resolution steps performed for a given query.

In STARBASE, the number of edges is computed by having a counter which is incremented every time a new edge is taken from the agenda.

The results for one iteration are shown in tables 5 and 6. In these and subsequent tables, *mo* stands for memory overflow. Note that Prolog is only applicable in the cases shown.

| | | | Length | 8 | 32 | 128 | 512 | 2K |
|---|---|---|---|---|---|---|---|---|
| Q1 | Left | Chain | STARBASE | 9 | 33 | 129 | 513 | 2049 |
| | | | XSB | 9 | 33 | 129 | 513 | 2049 |
| | | Cycle | STARBASE | 10 | 34 | 130 | 514 | 2050 |
| | | | XSB | 10 | 34 | 130 | 514 | 2050 |
| | Right | Chain | STARBASE | 23 | 95 | 383 | 1535 | *mo* |
| | | | Prolog | 23 | 95 | 383 | 1535 | 6143 |
| | | | XSB | 23 | 95 | 383 | 1535 | 6143 |
| | | Cycle | STARBASE | 24 | 96 | 384 | 1536 | *mo* |
| | | | XSB | 24 | 96 | 384 | 1536 | 6144 |
| Q2 | Left | Chain | STARBASE | 23 | 95 | 383 | 1535 | *mo* |
| | | | XSB | 60 | 996 | 16260 | 261636 | *mo* |
| | | Cycle | STARBASE | 24 | 96 | 384 | 1536 | *mo* |
| | | | XSB | 132 | 2052 | 32772 | 524292 | *mo* |
| | Right | Chain | STARBASE | 9 | 33 | 129 | 513 | 2049 |
| | | | Prolog | 86 | 1490 | 24386 | 392450 | 6288386 |
| | | | XSB | 29 | 125 | 509 | 2045 | 8189 |
| | | Cycle | STARBASE | 10 | 34 | 130 | 514 | 2050 |
| | | | XSB | 34 | 125 | 514 | 2050 | 8194 |

**Table 5.** Path relation. Resolution steps vs edges. Chains and cycles.

| | | Height | 5 | 6 | 7 | 8 | 9 | 10 |
|---|---|---|---|---|---|---|---|---|
| Q1 | Left | STARBASE | 64 | 128 | 256 | 512 | 1024 | 2048 |
| | | XSB | 64 | 128 | 256 | 512 | 1024 | 2048 |
| | Right | STARBASE | 188 | 380 | 764 | 1532 | 3068 | 6140 |
| | | Prolog | 188 | 380 | 764 | 1532 | 3068 | 6140 |
| | | XSB | 188 | 380 | 764 | 1532 | 3068 | 6140 |
| Q2 | Left | STARBASE | 17 | 20 | 23 | 26 | 29 | 32 |
| | | XSB | 520 | 1288 | 3080 | 7176 | 16392 | 36872 |
| | Right | STARBASE | 7 | 8 | 9 | 10 | 11 | 12 |
| | | Prolog | 776 | 1928 | 4616 | 10760 | 24584 | 55304 |
| | | XSB | 248 | 504 | 1016 | 2040 | 4088 | 8184 |

**Table 6.** Path relation. Resolution steps vs edges. Binary trees.

**Intermediate results vs hyperlinks.** The number of returns in XSB is measured by using the XSB standard predicates *get_calls_for_table* and *get_returns_for_call*. The first of these predicates returns all the subgoals that have been stored for a given predicate. For a given stored subgoal, *get_returns_for_call* returns all found answers for that subgoal. A small program was written which, by using *findall*, collects all the stored subgoals for a predicate in a list $L$. The number of returns is obtained by adding the number of answers for each subgoal in list $L$.

In STARBASE, the number of hyperlinks is computed by having a counter which is incremented every time a new hyperlink is taken from the agenda.

The results for one iteration are shown in tables 7 and 8.

| | | | Length | 8 | 32 | 128 | 512 | 2K |
|---|---|---|---|---|---|---|---|---|
| Q1 | Left | Chain | STARBASE | 7 | 31 | 127 | 511 | 2047 |
| | | | XSB | 7 | 31 | 127 | 511 | 2047 |
| | | Cycle | STARBASE | 8 | 32 | 128 | 512 | 2048 |
| | | | XSB | 8 | 32 | 128 | 512 | 2048 |
| | Right | Chain | STARBASE | 28 | 496 | 8128 | 130816 | mo |
| | | | XSB | 28 | 496 | 8128 | 130816 | 2096128 |
| | | Cycle | STARBASE | 64 | 1024 | 16384 | 262144 | mo |
| | | | XSB | 64 | 1024 | 16384 | 262144 | mo |
| Q2 | Left | Chain | STARBASE | 28 | 496 | 8128 | 130816 | mo |
| | | | XSB | 35 | 527 | 8255 | 131327 | mo |
| | | Cycle | STARBASE | 64 | 1024 | 16384 | 262144 | mo |
| | | | XSB | 72 | 1056 | 16512 | 262656 | mo |
| | Right | Chain | STARBASE | 7 | 31 | 127 | 511 | 2047 |
| | | | XSB | 13 | 61 | 253 | 1021 | 4093 |
| | | Cycle | STARBASE | 8 | 32 | 128 | 512 | 2048 |
| | | | XSB | 16 | 64 | 256 | 1024 | 4096 |

**Table 7.** Path relation. Intermediate results vs hyperlinks. Chains and cycles.

| | | Height | 5 | 6 | 7 | 8 | 9 | 10 |
|---|---|---|---|---|---|---|---|---|
| Q1 | Left | STARBASE | 62 | 126 | 254 | 510 | 1022 | 2046 |
| | | XSB | 62 | 126 | 254 | 510 | 1022 | 2046 |
| | Right | STARBASE | 258 | 642 | 1538 | 3586 | 8194 | 18434 |
| | | XSB | 258 | 642 | 1538 | 3586 | 8194 | 18434 |
| Q2 | Left | STARBASE | 15 | 21 | 28 | 36 | 45 | 55 |
| | | XSB | 263 | 648 | 1545 | 3594 | 8203 | 18444 |
| | Right | STARBASE | 5 | 6 | 7 | 8 | 9 | 10 |
| | | XSB | 9 | 11 | 13 | 15 | 17 | 19 |

**Table 8.** Path relation. Intermediate results vs hyperlinks. Binary trees.

**Discussion.** As shown in tables 5-8, when the first argument in the query is bound, the number of resolution steps in XSB is equal to the number of edges in STARBASE. Similarly, the number of intermediate results in XSB is equal to the number of hyperlinks in STARBASE. However, when the second argument in the query is bound, the number of inferences performed in STARBASE is much lower than in XSB. This is because STARBASE uses the productions whose body elements are ordered in the most efficient way according to the query.

When the first argument in the query is bound, the number of resolution steps for Prolog is equal to the equivalent measure in STARBASE and XSB. However, when the second argument in the query is bound, the number of resolution steps performed in Prolog is greater than in XSB or STARBASE since redundant computation cannot be avoided in Prolog.

## 5.2 The *same generation* relation

**Benchmark.** For the same generation example, two versions of the IDB which differ in the ordering of their body literals were used with an EDB in the form of a 24x24x2 cylinder (i.e. a matrix of 24x24 nodes where each node except those in the last row has two offspring).

IDB1:      sg1(X,X) :- cyl(_,X).
               sg1(X,X) :- cyl(X,_).
               sg1(X,Y) :- cyl(X,Xp), sg1(Xp,Yp), cyl(Y,Yp).
IDB2:      sg2(X,X) :- cyl(_,X).
               sg2(X,X) :- cyl(X,_).
               sg2(X,Y) :- cyl(X,Xp), cyl(Y,Yp), sg2(Xp,Yp).

Two different queries were used for each version, namely one with the first argument bound (Query1) and one with the second argument bound (Query2). The STARBASE productions corresponding to relations *sg1* and *sg2* and both queries are illustrated in table 9. Two of the three productions associated with each Datalog rule are required for the examples. They correspond to two different binding patterns for the head literal and are distinguished by their heads (*sg1* and *sg2* correspond to the first argument being bound, whereas $sg1^{-1}$ and $sg2^{-1}$ correspond to the second argument being bound).

|  | Query Q1 | Query Q2 |
|---|---|---|
| sg1 | $sg1 \rightarrow cyl, sg1, cyl^{-1}$ | $sg1^{-1} \rightarrow cyl, sg1^{-1}, cyl^{-1}$ |
| sg2 | $sg2 \rightarrow cyl, sg2, cyl^{-1}$ | $sg2^{-1} \rightarrow cyl, sg2^{-1}, cyl^{-1}$ |

Table 9. STARBASE productions for the same generation example

**Number of inferences.** This section analyses the number of inferences performed by XSB and STARBASE for the *same generation* example. As with the *path* relation, they are divided into resolution steps (resp. edges) and intermediate results (resp. hyperlinks). The method used to perform the measurements is similar to the one used for the *path* relation. The only difference is that a predicate similar to the built-in predicate *findall* had to be implemented manually due to the limitations on the size of the buffer used by this predicate. The results for one iteration are shown in tables 10 and 11.

|  | Query 1 | | Query 2 | |
|---|---|---|---|---|
|  | sg1 | sg2 | sg1 | sg2 |
| STARBASE | 4974 | 4974 | 4974 | 4974 |
| XSB | 8076 | 401123 | 36689 | 386726 |

Table 10. Same generation example. Resolution steps vs edges.

|  | Query 1 | | Query 2 | |
|---|---|---|---|---|
|  | sg1 | sg2 | sg1 | sg2 |
| STARBASE | 4230 | 4230 | 4252 | 4252 |
| XSB | 3678 | 3678 | 8672 | 3678 |

Table 11. Same generation example. Intermediate results vs hyperlinks.

**Discussion.** The *same generation* example shows how STARBASE, in contrast to XSB, is not affected by the way in which the body literals are ordered in the Datalog rule. The reason is that the STARBASE productions generated for both relations *sg1* and *sg2* will be the same (see table 9). It also shows that in STARBASE there is very little variation in the number of inferences for Query 1 and Query 2. The reason is that in this case for both relations *sg1* and *sg2*, the STARBASE productions corresponding to arguments $X$ and $Y$ being bound differ only in that the hyperlink labelled *sg1* (resp. *sg2*) will be traversed in the reverse direction (see table 9).

STARBASE outperforms XSB for *sg2* since, due to its automatic reordering of literals, the number of edges generated is very low compared to the number of resolution steps that have to be performed in XSB.

# 6 Extensions to the STARBASE system

The STARBASE implementation described above can be extended to handle negation, subgoals with function symbols, non-ground tuples, and evaluable predicates. The following sections give some indications of how these extensions can be implemented.

## 6.1 Negation

Stratified negation is usually handled by dividing the predicate symbols into strata. This stratification specifies the order in which predicates have to be evaluated.

In STARBASE this can be implemented by labelling edges with an integer which would represent the stratum to which the predicate symbol in the *head* component belongs. An edge will be processed only if all edges in lower strata have been processed.

## 6.2 Subgoals with function symbols

STARBASE can deal with functions symbols as arguments for body literals by extending the format of productions to include function symbols in their bodies. When a function symbol appears in the body of a rule, the rule compiler will transform it into an equivalent predicate and process the rule graph in the usual way. As an example, the rule $a(X,Y):-p(X,f(Z)),q(Y,Z)$ will transformed into the STARBASE production $a \rightarrow p, f^{-1}, q$. The -1 tag applied to the function symbol $f$ indicates that the inverse function has to be evaluated.

The @ tag can be used for the case when the function symbol appears in the head of a rule. For example, the rule $p(f(X),Y):-q(X,Z),r(Z,Y)$ could be represented as the STARBASE production $p \rightarrow @_{(f(1),1)}q, @_{(2,2)}r$. The $@_{(f(1),1)}$ tag indicates that the result of applying function $f$ to the first argument of the hyperlink labelled $q$ will be the starting node (i.e. first) of the hyperlink $p$ that will be created by the evaluation algorithm.

### 6.3  Non-ground tuples

Non-ground tuples can be represented in STARBASE as productions with a single special predicate symbol *empty* in their bodies. The constraint accompanying this predicate symbol will indicate which are the arguments of the tuple. The symbol ∀ appearing in this constraint will stand for any node in the database graph. As examples, the tuples $p(X,X)$, $p(X,Y)$, $p(c,Y)$, and $p(X,c)$ would be represented in STARBASE as the following productions: $p \rightarrow empty_{(\forall, a_1)}$, $p \rightarrow empty_{(\forall, \forall)}$, $p \rightarrow empty_{(c, \forall)}$, and $p \rightarrow empty_{(\forall, c)}$, respectively.

### 6.4  Evaluable predicates

Built-in predicates such as arithmetic and comparison predicates can be treated in STARBASE as any other predicate as long as safety conditions are satisfied (i.e. they define finite relations).

## 7  Conclusions

This paper has described the STARBASE method for deductive query processing. Like Earley Deduction and Rosenblueth's method, STARBASE is developed from a parsing algorithm. However, by exploiting better the inherent efficiencies of graph traversal, STARBASE achieves a level of power and performance that places it amongst the leading methods in the field.

A major benefit which arises from the graphical approach taken in STARBASE is that it supports a decision procedure for rule optimisation. This is not the case for the other leading edge methods, which require sometimes considerable programmer intervention to establish an efficient ordering of literals.

A potential drawback of STARBASE is that tabling is not optional (as it is in the XSB system, for example). This means that the space complexity of STARBASE is higher for some types of problem than that of other methods. This could prove a major limitation on the application of STARBASE to large databases. In mitigation, it is likely that a mechanism can be devised for purging the tables of edges which can no longer contribute to new solutions. This idea is supported by the work presented in [19] about a modification of the bottom-up chart parser in which some edges can be disposed of as the chart is built.

The implementation of the STARBASE system described and evaluated in this paper is a prototype which works for all Datalog programs. It covers both the optimising rule compiler and the evaluation algorithm. The performance figures for the evaluation algorithm presented in the paper give a promising indication of STARBASE's potential. They are never worse than the corresponding figures for XSB, and are often considerably better.

Work is continuing on the STARBASE system with the immediate goals of (1) extending it to handle negation, subgoals with function symbols, non-ground tuples, evaluable predicates, and others, and (2) reengineering those parts of the system which are currently inefficient. Longer term goals include (1) a garbage collection mechanism to limit the space complexity of the system, and (2) parallelisation of the evaluation algorithm.

# References

1. A.V. Aho and J.D. Ullman. Universality of data retrieval languages. *Proc. Symp. Principles of Programming Languages*, 110–120, 1979.
2. C. Beeri and R. Ramakrishnan. On the power of magic. *JLP*, 10(10):255–299, 1991.
3. W. Chen and D.S. Warren. Query evaluation under the well founded semantics. *PODS'93*, 168–179.
4. S.W. Dietrich and D.S. Warren. Dynamic programming strategies for the evaluation of recursive queries. Technical Report 85/31, SUNY at Stony Brook, 1985.
5. G. Gazdar and C. Mellish. *Natural Language in Prolog. An Introduction to Computational Linguistics*. Addison-Wesley Publishing Company, 1989.
6. G. Grahne, S. Sippu, and E. Soisalon-Soininen. Efficient evaluation for a subset of recursive queries. *JLP*, 10:301–332, 1991.
7. L.J. Henschen and S.A. Naqvi. On compiling queries in recursive first-order databases. *Journal of the ACM*, 31(1):47–85, 1984.
8. M. Kifer and E. Lozinskii. Filtering data flow in deductive databases. *ICDT'86. LNCS 243*, 186–202.
9. J.V. Leeuwen. *Handbook of Theoretical Computer Science. Algorithms and Complexity*. Elsevier - The MIT Press, 1990.
10. E.L. Lozinskii. Evaluating queries in deductive databases by generating. *IJCAI'85*, 173–177.
11. E. Minieka. *Optimization Algorithms for Networks and Graphs*. Marcel Dekker, Inc., 1978.
12. K.A. Morris. An algorithm for ordering subgoals in NAIL! *PODS'88*, 82–88.
13. W. Nejdl. Recursive strategies for answering recursive queries - the RQA/FQI strategy. *VLDB'87*, 43–50.
14. F.C.N. Pereira and D.H.D. Warren. Parsing as deduction. *21st Annual Meeting of the Association for Computational Linguistics*, 137–144, 1983.
15. E. Pulido. *Recursive query processing in deductive databases using graph traversal and rule compilation techniques*. PhD thesis, University of Bristol, 1996.
16. R. Ramakrishnan, D. Srivastava, and S. Sudarshan. CORAL - control, relations and logic. *VLDB'92*, 238–250.
17. D.A. Rosenblueth. Chart parsers as proof procedures for fixed-mode logic programs. To be published in New Generation Computing.
18. K. Sagonas, T. Swift, and D.S. Warren. XSB as an efficient deductive database engine. *SIGMOD Record*, 23(2):442–453, 1994.
19. N.K. Simpkins and P. Hancox. Chart parsing in Prolog. *New Generation Computing*, 8:113–138, 1990.
20. H. Tamaki and T. Sato. OLD resolution with tabulation. *ICLP'86*, 84–98.
21. S. Tsur and C. Zaniolo. LDL: a logic-based data language. *VLDB'86*, 33–41.
22. J.D. Ullman. *Principles of Database and Knowledge-base Systems*. Computer Science Press, 1988.
23. L. Vieille. Recursive query processing: the power of logic. *Theoretical Computer Science*, 69:1–53, 1989.
24. D.H.D. Warren. Efficient processing of interactive relational database queries expressed in logic. *VLDB'81*, 272–281.
25. P.T. Wood. Queries on graphs. Technical Report CSRI-223, Computer Systems Research Institute. University of Toronto, December 1988.

# The Limits of Fixed-Order Computation

Konstantinos Sagonas, Terrance Swift, David S. Warren

Department of Computer Science
State University of New York at Stony Brook
Stony Brook, NY 11794-4400
{kostis,tswift,warren}@cs.sunysb.edu

**Abstract.** Fixed-order computation rules, used by Prolog and most deductive database systems, do not suffice to compute the well-founded semantics [19] because they cannot properly resolve loops through negation. This inadequacy is reflected both in formulations of SLS-resolution [8, 12] which is an ideal search strategy, and in more practical strategies like SLG [3], or Well-Founded Ordered Search [16]. Typically, these practical strategies combine an inexpensive fixed-order search with a relatively expensive dynamic search, such as an alternating fixpoint [18]. Restricting the search space of evaluation strategies by maximizing the use of fixed-order computation is of prime importance for efficient goal-directed evaluation of the well-founded semantics.

Towards this end, the theory of *modular stratification* [13], formulates a subset of normal logic programs whose literals can be statically reordered so that the program can be evaluated using a fixed-order computation rule. However, exploration of larger classes of stratified programs that can be evaluated in this manner has been left open in the literature, perhaps due to the lack of implementation methods that can benefit from such results. We address the limits of fixed-order computation by adapting results of Przymusinski [8] to formulate the class of *left-to-right dynamically stratified programs*. We show that this class properly includes other classes of fixed-order stratified programs. Furthermore, we introduce $SLG_{strat}$, a variant of SLG resolution that uses a fixed-order computation rule, and prove that it correctly evaluates ground left-to-right dynamically stratified programs. We outline how $SLG_{strat}$ can be used as a basis for restricting the space of possible SLG derivations and, finally, outline how these results are used in the abstract machine of XSB, and can be used in other methods such as Ordered Search of CORAL.

## 1 Introduction

It is known that the well-founded semantics (WFS) combines the features of both the *stable model* [5] and *partial Clark completion* [9] semantics and thus ensures a proper behavior under both positive and negative recursion. Also, it can be characterized as the only semantics which is both *rational* and *cumulative* [4]. As a result, the WFS provides a natural and intuitive semantics for the class of *all* normal logic programs. Furthermore, the WFS can be computed with polynomial data complexity for function-free programs, and as a result several practical evaluation strategies have been formulated for it. Despite all these properties, the WFS cannot be computed using a fixed computation rule. The reason is that an evaluation of a normal program may encounter a cycle through negation and mechanisms are needed to avoid or to break such cycles. The standard procedural semantics for the WFS is SLS-resolution [8, 12]. Unfortunately, SLS-resolution is not effective in general. As formulated by Przymusinski [8] SLS-resolution uses an oracle to select literals from lower dynamic strata, while Global SLS-resolution as formulated by Ross [12] requires a positivistic computation rule and that all negative literals are ideally evaluated in parallel. These departures from fixed computation are naturally reflected in more practical strategies for evaluating the WFS of normal logic programs [2, 3, 6, 16]. Typically, these strategies consist mainly of a phase that uses a fixed computation rule, followed by some other phase — usually more expensive — which, if necessary, alters that computation rule in order to try to avoid or break recursion through negation. In the case of the SLG resolution strategy of [3], tabling is the basis of the first of these phases while delay and simplification steps are used to break cycles through negation. In the Well-Founded Ordered Search of [16], magic templates with Ordered Search [10] are used for the first phase, while an alternating fixpoint similar to that of [18] is used for the second. The limitations of fixed-order computation[1] can be seen clearly in the following example.

*Example 1 [13].* Consider the following program and query p(a).

```
p(X) :- t(X,Y,Z), ¬p(Y), ¬p(Z).        t(a,b,a).
p(b).                                   t(a,a,b).
```

The rule instance p(a) :- t(a,Y,Z),¬p(Y),¬p(Z). cannot be evaluated using any fixed computation rule. After t(a,b,a) has been resolved against the first literal of that rule instance, the second literal must be chosen before the third to avoid the negative dependency through p(a); after t(a,a,b) has been used for resolution, the second literal should be skipped and the third literal must be resolved before it in order to properly fail for p(a). ∎

Fixed computation rules are important for efficient implementations of systems based on logic; for example most database optimizations rely on the presence of a fixed computation rule. More importantly, however, a break from a fixed computation rule subtly undermines the goal-orientation of techniques like tabling or magic templates since it may unnecessarily open up the search space by introducing subgoals that need not be *relevant* to proving a query. As a matter of fact, even the notion of goal-directedness is probably ill-defined in the absence of a fixed computation rule.

Given the importance of a fixed computation rule, it is natural to try to determine what its limits are and in what cases an evaluation has to break the fixed-order computation. The most notable attempt to address this problem is through the formalism of *modular stratification*. The salient feature of the modularly stratified class of programs, from the perspective of fixed computation rules, is that if a program is modularly stratified, then it is statically reorderable

---

[1] Without loss of generality, a fixed left-to-right computation rule can be used to exemplify the problems of all fixed computation rules, and so we will equate the left-to-right computation rule with general fixed rules throughout the paper. All results can be easily extended to any fixed computation rule.

so that it is modularly stratified for a fixed computation rule. This property has made modular stratification useful for deductive database systems based on magic-set evaluation (e.g. [11]). However, whether a program is modularly stratifiable at all is undecidable. Furthermore, programs which can be evaluated using a fixed computation rule may not be modularly stratified, as the program in the following example.

*Example 2.* The following program is neither *modularly,* nor *weakly stratified* [7].

$$
\begin{aligned}
&\text{s} :- \neg\text{s, p.} && \text{p} :- \text{q, } \neg\text{r, } \neg\text{s.} \\
&\text{s} :- \neg\text{p, } \neg\text{q, } \neg\text{r.} && \text{q} :- \text{r, } \neg\text{p.} \\
& && \text{r} :- \text{p, } \neg\text{q.}
\end{aligned}
$$

■

To our knowledge, the only stratification class that includes the program in Example 2 is *dynamic stratification* of [8] (also independently introduced by Bidoit and Froidevaux as *effective stratification* in [1]). From the perspective of the well-founded semantics, dynamic stratification is extremely powerful since all normal logic programs with two-valued well-founded models are dynamically stratified. The reason for the power of dynamic stratification is that components used in standard stratifications are determined statically, based on the syntactic form of the program, and more precisely, on the predicate dependency graph of the program. Therefore, these *components* do not depend in any way on the truth or falsity of the atoms appearing in the graph. This makes them very simple to use, but at the same time, limits their applicability to relatively narrow classes of programs. On the other hand, components of (left-to-right) dynamic stratification — as the name indicates — are generated dynamically. This process eliminates atom dependencies that can never be satisfied. Given the power of dynamic stratification, the goal of this paper is to study a restriction of this class to a fixed-order computation rule. We believe this restriction gives insight into the limits of fixed-order computations in general, and indicates useful features for effective evaluation methods for the well-founded semantics.

More specifically, the contributions of this paper are as follows.

1. We define a subclass of dynamically stratified programs, called *left-to-right dynamically stratified* (*LRD-stratified*) programs, and show that this class properly includes the class of left-to-right weakly stratified programs, and effectively includes all modularly stratified programs.

2. We introduce a variant of SLG resolution, called $SLG_{strat}$, which uses a fixed computation rule to evaluate ground LRD-stratified programs. $SLG_{strat}$ differs from SLG in that:

   (a) It suspends negative literals rather than delaying them.

   (b) It introduces the novel technique of *early completion* which uses information from *within* a dynamic stratum to break and sometimes avoid cycles through negation.

The structure of the rest of the paper is as follows. We define LRD-stratified programs in Section 2. We then introduce $SLG_{strat}$ in Section 3, and in Section 4 show the completeness of $SLG_{strat}$ for ground LRD-stratified programs. Section 5 addresses the issue of relevance and goal-orientation of evaluation strategies and sketches how $SLG_{strat}$ can be used as a basis to constrain the search space of possible derivations of full SLG. We conclude with a discussion of difficulties involved in formulating techniques for the open problem of evaluating non-ground LRD-stratified programs, and how these results are potentially applicable to other evaluation methods for stratified negation.

# 2 Left-to-Right Dynamically Stratified Programs

We assume the standard terminology of logic programming. The *Herbrand base* $H_P$ of a program $P$ is the set of all ground atoms. By a *3-valued interpretation* $I$ of a program $P$ we mean a pair $\langle T; F \rangle$, where $T$ and $F$ are subsets of the Herbrand base $H_P$ of $P$. The set $T$ contains all ground atoms that are true in $I$, the set $F$ contains all ground atoms that are false in $I$, and the truth value of the remaining atoms in $U = H_P - (T \cup F)$ is undefined. We usually require that the interpretation $I$ is *consistent*; i.e. that sets $T$ and $F$ are disjoint. If $A$ is a ground atom from $H_P$ then we write $val_I(A) = t$ ($val_I(A) = f$ or $val_I(A) = u$) if $A$ is true (false or undefined) in $I$, respectively. We call $val_I(A)$ the *truth value* of $A$ in $I$. A 3-valued interpretation of $P$ is called a 2-valued interpretation of $P$ if all ground atoms are either true or false in $I$, i.e. if $H_P = T \cup F$. A consistent 3-valued interpretation $M$ is a *3-valued model* of $P$ if $val_M(C) = t$, for every clause $C$ in $P$. If $M$ is 2-valued then it is called a *2-valued* or a *total model* of $P$. Any consistent 3-valued interpretation can be viewed as a function from the Herbrand base $H_P$ to the three-element set $\{f, u, t\}$, ordered by $f < u < t$.

## 2.1 Iterated Fixed Point under a Left-to-Right Computation Rule

We first adapt Przymusinski's definition of the iterated fixed point from [8] to a non-ideal left-to-right computation rule. Our main modification is the introduction of the notion of a *failing prefix* in defining the iterated fixed point operators $\mathcal{T}_I$ and $\mathcal{F}_I$ (Definition 1). Intuitively, $I$ represents facts currently known to be true or false and $\mathcal{T}_I(T)$ ($\mathcal{F}_I(F)$) contains facts not contained in $I$, whose truth (falsity) can be immediately derived from $P$ under the interpretation $I$, and assuming that all facts in $T$ are true (all facts in $F$ are false). The failing prefix constraint prevents false facts from inclusion in $\mathcal{F}_I(F)$, unless their falsity can be established by a left-to-right examination of the literals in clauses of $P$.

**Definition 1.** For sets $T$ and $F$ of ground atoms we define

$\mathcal{T}_I(T) = \{A : val_I(A) \neq t$ and there is a clause $B \leftarrow L_1, ..., L_n$ in $P$ and a ground substitution $\theta$ such that $A = B\theta$ and for every $1 \leq i \leq n$ either $L_i\theta$ is true in $I$, or $L_i\theta \in T\}$;

$\mathcal{F}_I(F) = \{A : val_I(A) \neq f$ and for every clause $B \leftarrow L_1, ..., L_n$ in $P$ and ground substitution $\theta$ such that $A = B\theta$ there exists a *failing prefix*: i.e. there is some $i$ ($1 \leq i \leq n$), such that $L_i\theta$ is false in $I$ or $L_i\theta \in F$, and for all $j$ ($1 \leq j \leq i-1$), $L_j\theta$ is true in $I\}$. $\square$

Even though the conditions $val_I(A) \neq t$ and $val_I(A) \neq f$ are inessential, they ensure that only *new* facts are included in $\mathcal{T}_I(T)$ and $\mathcal{F}_I(F)$, and will simplify the definition of dynamic strata below. Subsets $T_I$ and $F_I$ of the Herbrand base are obtained by iterating the operators $\mathcal{T}_I$ and $\mathcal{F}_I$ according to the following definition.

**Definition 2.** [8] Let $I = \langle T; F \rangle$ be an interpretation, we define

$$T_I^{\uparrow 0} = \emptyset \text{ and } F_I^{\downarrow 0} = H_P$$
$$T_I^{\uparrow n+1} = \mathcal{T}_I(T_I^{\uparrow n}) \text{ and } F_I^{\downarrow n+1} = \mathcal{F}_I(F_I^{\downarrow n})$$
$$T_I = \bigcup_{n < \omega} T_I^{\uparrow n} \text{ and } F_I = \bigcap_{n < \omega} F_I^{\downarrow n}$$

**Proposition 3.** [8] *The set $T_I$ is the least fixed point of the operator $\mathcal{T}_I$, and the set $F_I$ is the least fixed point of the operator $\mathcal{F}_I$.*

**Definition 4.** [8] Let $\mathcal{I}$ be the operator which assigns to every interpretation $I$ of $P$ a new interpretation $\mathcal{I}(I)$ defined by: $\mathcal{I}(I) = I \cup \langle T_I; F_I \rangle$. □

The operator $\mathcal{I}$ extends the interpretation $I$ to $\mathcal{I}(I)$ by adding to $I$ new atomic facts $T_I$ which can be derived from $P$ knowing $I$, and the negations of new atomic facts $F_I$ which can be assumed false in $P$ just by knowing $I$.

**Definition 5 Iterated Fixed Point.** [8] Let:

$$J_0 = \langle \emptyset; \emptyset \rangle;$$
$$J_{\alpha+1} = \mathcal{I}(J_\alpha), \text{ i.e. } J_{\alpha+1} = J_\alpha \cup \langle T_{J_\alpha}; F_{J_\alpha} \rangle;$$
$$J_\alpha = \bigcup_{\beta < \alpha} J_\beta, \text{ for limit } \alpha.$$

Let $J_{IF(P)}$ denote the fixed point interpretation $J_\delta$, where $\delta$ is the smallest countable ordinal such that both sets $T_{J_\delta}$ and $F_{J_\delta}$ are empty. We refer to $\delta$ as the *depth* of program $P$. □

$J_{IF(P)}$ is a consistent 3-valued interpretation of $P$. It can be proven that $J_{IF(P)}$ is the least fixed point of the operator $\mathcal{I}$. Note that $J_{IF(P)}$ is an informationally sound approximation of the well-founded model of $P$. Furthermore, as will soon be proven, $J_{IF(P)}$ is the well-founded model of $P$ if $P$ is left-to-right dynamically stratified. We introduce this class of programs in the following section.

## 2.2 Left-to-Right Dynamic Stratification

As observed in [8], the iterated fixed point induces a natural stratification on a program $P$.

**Definition 6 Dynamic Stratum under a Fixed-Order Computation Rule.** Let $\alpha$ be a countable ordinal. The $\alpha$'s *dynamic stratum* $S_\alpha$ of $P$ under a left-to-right computation rule is defined as

$$S_\alpha = \{A : A \in (T_{J_\alpha} \cup F_{J_\alpha})\}$$

for any $\alpha$ such that $T_{J_\alpha} \cup F_{J_\alpha}$ is not empty. Let $\delta$ be the minimal ordinal such that for all non-empty strata, $S_\alpha$, $\alpha < \delta$; then we call $\delta$ the *ultimate stratum* under a left-to-right computation rule, and

$$S_\delta = \{A : A \in H_P - \bigcup_{\alpha < \delta} S_\alpha\}$$

Conversely, let $A$ be a ground atom. The *dynamic stratum* of $A$ under a left-to-right computation rule is the unique ordinal number $\alpha$ such that $A \in (T_{J_\alpha} \cup F_{J_\alpha})$, and is $\delta$ otherwise. In general, for any possibly non-ground atom $A$ the *dynamic stratum* of $A$ is equal to:

$$stratum(A) = sup\{stratum(A\theta) : \theta \text{ is a ground substitution}\}$$

and let $str(\neg A) = min(\delta, str(A) + 1)$. □

The dynamic stratification of $P$ under a left-to-right computation rule is therefore a decomposition of the set of all atoms in $H_P$ into disjoint strata. The $\alpha$'s dynamic stratum of $P$ is defined at level $\alpha < \delta$ as the set of all atoms that were *newly added* to the interpretation $J_\alpha$ in order to obtain $J_{\alpha+1}$ (i.e. those atoms whose truth or falsity was determined at this very level). The ultimate stratum $S_\delta$ contains all the remaining atoms, i.e. all atoms whose truth value could not be determined when the fixed point was reached using a left-to-right computation rule. Some of the atoms in the ultimate stratum may be undefined in the well-founded model $M_P$ of $P$, or their truth value could be determined by using a non-fixed (possibly ideal) computation rule.

**Definition 7 Left-to-Right Dynamically Stratified Program.** A program $P$ is *left-to-right dynamically stratified* if its ultimate stratum $S_\delta$ is empty. □

**Theorem 8.** *Let $P$ be a left-to-right dynamically stratified program. Then the interpretation $J_{IF(P)}$ is a minimal 2-valued model of $P$.*

Since $J_{IF(P)}$ is the least fixed point of the operator $\mathcal{I}$, which itself is defined using least fixed points of the operators $T_I$ and $\mathcal{F}_I$, $J_{IF(P)}$ is an iterated fixed point model of $P$. It also coincides with the well-founded [19] and the unique stable model [5] of the program $P$.

## 2.3 Relationships between stratification classes

The power of dynamic stratification and of its restriction to dynamic stratification under a fixed computation rule, arises from the fact that components are determined dynamically rather than statically as they are in *weak* [7], or in *modular stratification* [13]. Another reason for the power of dynamic stratification is that it uses information from *within* the (dynamic) stratum to eliminate atom dependencies that can never be satisfied. In fact, a hierarchy of stratification classes can be defined as in the figure on the left where arrows indicate inclusion.

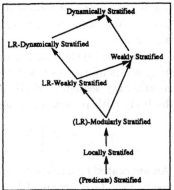

Most of the relationships between the stratification classes presented in the above figure are well-known in the literature. Theorem 9 substantiates the placement of LRD-stratification within the stratification hierarchy. The proof of Theorem 9, along with supporting definitions of the class of *left-to-right weakly stratified programs*, can be found in the full version of the paper.

**Theorem 9.** *The class of LRD-stratified programs properly includes the class of left-to-right weakly stratified, and (left-to-right) modularly stratified programs.*

# 3 Tabled Evaluation of LRD-stratified Programs

This section presents the formal definitions of $SLG_{strat}$, a resolution strategy based on tabling which will be shown to evaluate LRD-stratified programs using a left-to-right fixed-order computation rule. $SLG_{strat}$ is largely a restriction of SLG [3] and inherits most of its properties. Differences of $SLG_{strat}$ from SLG are noted as they occur. In particular, $SLG_{strat}$ adds a NEGATIVE SUSPENSION transformation and its necessary underpinnings along with an altered definition of when a set of subgoals is completely evaluated. The latter and the introduction of the NEGATIVE SUSPENSION transformation require a change of the COMPLETION transformation so that suspended computations are resumed.

## 3.1 An Example

To motivate the following sections that contain technical definitions of $SLG_{strat}$, we present the $SLG_{strat}$ evaluation of a query ?- q(a). against the following LRD-stratified program. Each program clause has been labeled for convenience of reference.

$$C_1 : \quad \text{q(X)} \; :- \; \text{t(X), } \neg\text{q(X)}. \qquad C_4 : \quad \text{p} \; :- \; \text{t(a), r.}$$
$$C_2 : \quad \text{q(a)} \; :- \; \neg\text{p, } \neg\text{r}. \qquad\qquad C_5 : \quad \text{r} \; :- \; \text{p, } \neg\text{r, } \neg\text{q}.$$
$$C_3 : \quad \text{t(a)}. \qquad\qquad\qquad\qquad C_6 : \quad \text{q} \; :- \; \text{q(X)}.$$

A *system* is a set of pairs of the form $(A : \rho)$, where $A$ is a subgoal and $\rho$ is a sequence of annotated rules for $A$. No two pairs in a system have the same (variant) subgoal. The sequence $\rho$ of annotated rules represents the history of the addition, suspension, and/or deletion of rules for subgoal $A$. The annotation of each rule in $\rho$ indicates where the rule is derived from and whether some rule is suspended or disposed. Intuitively, a rule is disposed when it no longer has anything to contribute to the derivation. In general, the sequence $\rho$ can be transfinite.

The initial system $S_0$ is empty. The query atom $q(a)$ is introduced as the first subgoal. Using the NEW SUBGOAL transformation, the initial sequence of $q(a)$ is an arbitrary sequence of all rules obtained by resolving $q(a) \leftarrow q(a)$ on $q(a)$ in the body with program clauses. After $q(a)$ is introduced the system is:

$$S_1 = \left\{ q(a) : \begin{bmatrix} 0 : \text{q(a)} \leftarrow \text{t(a), } \neg\text{q(a).} \; \langle C_1 \rangle \\ 1 : \text{q(a)} \leftarrow \neg\text{p, } \neg\text{r.} \qquad\quad \langle C_2 \rangle \end{bmatrix} \right\}$$

An annotated rule of the form $G\langle C \rangle$, where $C$ is (the label of) a program clause, means that $G$ is obtained by resolution with program clause $C$. The sequence of a subgoal is written as an array of pairs $\alpha : AG$ where $\alpha$ is an ordinal and $AG$ is an annotated rule. In general, the annotation in $AG$ indicates where the rule in $AG$ is derived from — either a program clause or an earlier rule in the sequence, and in the latter case, whether the earlier rule in the sequence is disposed. For each non-disposed rule in the sequence of a subgoal, its head captures variable bindings that have been accumulated, and its body contains literals that remain to be solved in order to derive answers for the subgoal. For a rule with a non-empty body, a literal is selected from the rule body by a computation rule. The atom of the selected literal is added as a new subgoal if it is not in the current system. In the example above, $t(a)$ is selected from the body of $q(a) \leftarrow t(a), \neg q(a)$ and is added as a new subgoal. Like $q(a)$, $t(a)$ has its own sequence of annotated rules obtained by resolution of $t(a) \leftarrow t(a)$ on $t(a)$ in the body with program clauses. So the system becomes:

$$S_2 = \left\{ q(a) : \begin{bmatrix} 0 : q(a) \leftarrow t(a), \neg q(a). & \langle C_1 \rangle \\ 1 : q(a) \leftarrow \neg p, \neg r. & \langle C_2 \rangle \end{bmatrix} \quad t(a) : \begin{bmatrix} 0 : t(a). & \langle C_3 \rangle \end{bmatrix} \right\}$$

A rule with an empty body is an *answer*, e.g., $t(a)$ in the above sequence for $t(a)$. Note that this subgoal has obtained all answers it will ever have; any other rules no longer have anything to contribute to the derivation. Subgoals that get their most general answer can be completed without taking into account possible dependencies that they might have. We call such subgoals *early completable* and the operation that is then performed *early completion* of subgoals. Early completion is a special case where a set of subgoals is completely evaluated and the COMPLETION transformation is applicable (see Definition 18).

Answers are returned to the appropriate selected literals through the POS-ITIVE RETURN transformation. By returning the newly derived answer, the sequence of $q(a)$ is extended as follows:

$$q(a) : \begin{bmatrix} 0 : q(a) \leftarrow t(a), \neg q(a). & \langle C_1 \rangle \\ 1 : q(a) \leftarrow \neg p, \neg r. & \langle C_2 \rangle \\ 2 : q(a) \leftarrow \neg q(a). & \langle 0, t(a) \rangle \end{bmatrix}$$

This last annotation indicates that $q(a) \leftarrow \neg q(a)$ is obtained from the rule corresponding to ordinal 0 by solving the selected atom using an answer $t(a)$. The selected literal of this sequence is negative. Its subgoal does not have any answers, and it is not yet known whether it will ever get any. Consequently, the selected negative literal cannot be resolved at this point. $SLG_{strat}$ *suspends* negative selected literals whose truth value is not known. This is done by employing the NEGATIVE SUSPENSION transformation. Doing so, the sequence of $q(a)$ is extended in two steps to that shown in system $S_9$ below.

Program clause resolution is then used to derive answers for $p$ which is the subgoal of the selected literal of the second suspended rule. After a sequence of NEW SUBGOAL, POSITIVE RETURN, and NEW SUBGOAL transformations the system is as follows:

$$S_9 = \left\{ q(a) : \begin{bmatrix} 0 : q(a) \leftarrow t(a), \neg q(a). & \langle C_1 \rangle \\ 1 : q(a) \leftarrow \neg p, \neg r. & \langle C_2 \rangle \\ 2 : q(a) \leftarrow \neg q(a). & \langle 0, t(a) \rangle \\ 3 : suspended & \langle 2 \rangle \\ 4 : suspended & \langle 1 \rangle \end{bmatrix} \quad \begin{array}{l} t(a) : \begin{bmatrix} 0 : t(a). & \langle C_3 \rangle \end{bmatrix} \\ p : \begin{bmatrix} 0 : p \leftarrow t(a), r. & \langle C_4 \rangle \\ 1 : p \leftarrow r. & \langle 0, t(a) \rangle \end{bmatrix} \\ r : \begin{bmatrix} 0 : r \leftarrow p, \neg r, \neg q. & \langle C_5 \rangle \end{bmatrix} \end{array} \right\}$$

Note that subgoals $p$ and $r$ form an *unfounded set* [19] and cannot get any answers. But they are not completed since they have rules in their sequences which have a selected literal and are not disposed. On the other hand, the literal ¬p cannot be unsuspended until the truth value of its subgoal is known. $SLG_{strat}$ handles this situation through the COMPLETION transformation that disposes all rules (that are not answers) of a set of mutually dependent subgoals when these subgoals have performed all possible operations. Applying the COMPLETION transformation to the set $\{p, r\}$ disposes all rules of these subgoals, and unsuspends rules of the system that are suspended on the completion of $p$ or $r$. The resulting system is the following:

$$
S_{10} = \left\{ q(a) : \begin{bmatrix} 0 : q(a) \leftarrow t(a),\ ¬q(a).\ \langle C_1 \rangle \\ 1 : q(a) \leftarrow ¬p,\ ¬r. \quad \langle C_2 \rangle \\ 2 : q(a) \leftarrow ¬q(a). \quad \langle 0, t(a) \rangle \\ 3 : suspended \quad \langle 2 \rangle \\ 4 : suspended \quad \langle 1 \rangle \\ 5 : unsuspended \quad \langle 1 \rangle \end{bmatrix} \quad \begin{array}{l} t(a) : \begin{bmatrix} 0 : t(a).\ \langle C_3 \rangle \end{bmatrix} \\ \\ p : \begin{bmatrix} 0 : p \leftarrow t(a),\ r.\ \langle C_4 \rangle \\ 1 : p \leftarrow r. \quad \langle 0, t(a) \rangle \\ 2 : disposed \quad \langle 1 \rangle \end{bmatrix} \\ \\ r : \begin{bmatrix} 0 : r \leftarrow p,\ ¬r,\ ¬q.\ \langle C_5 \rangle \\ 1 : disposed \quad \langle 0 \rangle \end{bmatrix} \end{array} \right\}
$$

Subgoals $p$ and $r$ are completed without any answers; by negation as failure literals ¬p and ¬r can be removed using two NEGATIVE RETURN transformations. Note that since the value of subgoal $r$ is known, a NEGATIVE SUSPENSION transformation is not needed. Like $t(a)$, subgoal $q(a)$ also got its most general answer. As a result, it is early completable. A COMPLETION transformation on $q(a)$ takes place and the resulting final system is as follows:

$$
S_{13} = \left\{ q(a) : \begin{bmatrix} 0 : q(a) \leftarrow t(a),\ ¬q(a).\ \langle C_1 \rangle \\ 1 : q(a) \leftarrow ¬p,\ ¬r. \quad \langle C_2 \rangle \\ 2 : q(a) \leftarrow ¬q(a). \quad \langle 0, t(a) \rangle \\ 3 : suspended \quad \langle 2 \rangle \\ 4 : suspended \quad \langle 1 \rangle \\ 5 : unsuspended \quad \langle 1 \rangle \\ 6 : q(a) \leftarrow ¬r. \quad \langle 1 \rangle \\ 7 : q(a) \quad \langle 6 \rangle \\ 8 : disposed \quad \langle 2 \rangle \end{bmatrix} \quad \begin{array}{l} t(a) : \begin{bmatrix} 0 : t(a).\ \langle C_3 \rangle \end{bmatrix} \\ \\ p : \begin{bmatrix} 0 : p \leftarrow t(a),\ r.\ \langle C_4 \rangle \\ 1 : p \leftarrow r. \quad \langle 0, t(a) \rangle \\ 2 : disposed \quad \langle 1 \rangle \end{bmatrix} \\ \\ r : \begin{bmatrix} 0 : r \leftarrow p,\ ¬r,\ ¬q.\ \langle C_5 \rangle \\ 1 : disposed \quad \langle 0 \rangle \end{bmatrix} \end{array} \right\}
$$

Note that all the subgoals of the final system are completed, and that the use of the NEGATIVE SUSPENSION transformation in conjunction with the *early completion* operation — which takes into account the truth value of subgoals in the system — avoided the loop through negation involving subgoal $q(a)$.

## 3.2 SLG Systems

A *subgoal* is an atom. In our tabling framework, two subgoals are considered the same if they are identical up to variable renaming. A *literal* is an atom, or the negation of an atom $A$ denoted as $¬A$.

SLG evaluations are modeled through sequences of *X-rules* associated with subgoals encountered in a system. The set of subgoals with their sequences of X-rules intuitively corresponds to the forest of trees representation commonly used by tabling methods [2].

**Definition 10 [3].** An *X-rule* $C$ is of the form:

$$H \leftarrow L_1, \ldots, L_n.$$

where $H$ is an atom, each $L_i(1 \leq i \leq n)$ is a literal, and $n \geq 0$. If $n = 0$, $C$ is called an *answer*.

A *computation rule* is an algorithm that selects from the body of an X-rule $C$ a literal $L$. $L$ is called the *selected literal* of $C$. If $L$ is an atom, it is also called the *selected atom* of $C$. □

X-rules are used to form X-elements which comprise the above-mentioned sequences.

**Definition 11 X-element.** Let $P$ be a finite program, $C$ be a rule in $P$, $G$ be an X-rule, $\alpha$ be an ordinal, and $H$ be an atom. Then an *X-element* is of the form $G\langle C\rangle$, $G\langle\alpha\rangle$, $G\langle\alpha, H\rangle$, $disposed\langle\alpha\rangle$, $suspended\langle\alpha\rangle$, or $unsuspended\langle\alpha\rangle$. □

**Definition 12 X-sequence.** [3] An *X-sequence* $\rho$ is a mapping from all ordinals that are smaller than some ordinal $\alpha$ to the set of X-elements. The ordinal $\alpha$ is the *length* of $\rho$. □

Each subgoal in a system has an associated X-sequence. The X-sequence captures the history of the addition/disposal of X-rules and, in $SLG_{strat}$, the suspension/unsuspension of X-rules for the subgoal during its partial deduction. Each X-element in the X-sequence indicates the origin of an X-rule — a rule in a program or an X-rule earlier in the X-sequence — along with whether an X-rule is disposed, suspended, or unsuspended.

More specifically, let $\rho$ be the X-sequence of a subgoal $A$. Let $\beta$ be an ordinal such that $\rho(\beta) = e$ for some X-element $e$, and $\alpha$ be an ordinal such that $\alpha < \beta$.

- If $e$ is of the form $G\langle C\rangle$, where $G$ is an X-rule and $C$ is a rule in a program, then $G$ is created by resolving $A \leftarrow A$ on $A$ in the body with $C$;
- If $e$ is of the form $G\langle\alpha\rangle$, where $G$ is an X-rule, then the X-rule corresponding to $\alpha$ in $\rho$ is disposed and replaced by $G$;
- If $e$ is of the form $G\langle\alpha, H\rangle$, where $G$ is an X-rule and $H$ is an atom, then $G$ is obtained by solving the selected atom of the X-rule corresponding to $\alpha$ in $\rho$ using an answer $H$;
- If $e$ is $disposed\langle\alpha\rangle$, then the X-rule corresponding to $\alpha$ in $\rho$ is simply disposed.
- If $e$ is $suspended\langle\alpha\rangle$, then the X-rule corresponding to $\alpha$ in $\rho$ is marked as suspended.
- If $e$ is $unsuspended\langle\alpha\rangle$, then the X-rule corresponding to $\alpha$ in $\rho$ is marked as unsuspended.

Intuitively, X-rules that are disposed from an X-sequence of a system do not appear in any future point in the sequence. Similarly, X-rules of a subgoal that are marked as suspended do not participate in the evaluation of the subgoal until they are marked as unsuspended.

We consider two main operations over X-sequences: concatenation and the least upper bound of an increasing chain of X-sequences. The former is used to extend the X-sequence of a subgoal, and the latter is needed for the transfinite definition of an $SLG_{strat}$ derivation that will be presented in Section 3.4.

**Definition 13.** Let $\rho_1$ and $\rho_2$ be X-sequences of length $\alpha_1$ and $\alpha_2$ respectively. The *concatenation* of $\rho_1$ with $\rho_2$, denoted by $\rho_1 \cdot \rho_2$, is an X-sequence of length $\alpha_1 + \alpha_2$ such that $(\rho_1 \cdot \rho_2)(i) = \rho_1(i)$ for every $i(0 \leq i < \alpha_1)$, and $(\rho_1 \cdot \rho_2)(\alpha_1 + j) = \rho_2(j)$ for every $j(0 \leq j < \alpha_2)$.

The X-sequence $\rho_1$ is said to be a *prefix* of $\rho_1 \cdot \rho_2$. If $\rho_2$ is a sequence of length 1 such that $\rho_2(0) = e$ for some X-element $e$, we also write $\rho_1 \cdot \rho_2$ as $\rho_1 \cdot e$. □

There is a natural prefix partial order over X-sequences. Let $\rho_1$ and $\rho_2$ be X-sequences. Then $\rho_1 \subseteq \rho_2$ if $\rho_1$ is a prefix of $\rho_2$. An X-sequence $\rho$ of length $\alpha$ can also be viewed as a set of pairs $\{\langle i, \rho(i)\rangle \mid 0 \le i < \alpha\}$, in which case the prefix relation reduces to the subset relation.

**Definition 14.** Let $\beta$ be an ordinal and $\rho_i (0 \le i < \beta)$ be an increasing chain of X-sequences (with respect to $\subseteq$), and let $\alpha$ be an ordinal such that the length of each $\rho_i (0 \le i < \beta)$ is less than $\alpha$. Then the least upper bound of the chain $\rho_i (0 \le i < \beta)$, denoted by $\bigcup\{\rho_i \mid 0 \le i < \beta\}$, exists since the length of each $\rho_i (0 \le i < \beta)$ is less than $\alpha$. It is the X-sequence that is the union of all $\rho_i (0 \le i < \beta)$ when an X-sequence is viewed as a set. □

Intermediate states of the evaluation of a query are represented by *systems*.

**Definition 15 System.** Let $P$ be a program, and $R$ be a computation rule. A *system* $S$ is a set of pairs of the form $(A : \rho)$, where $A$ is a subgoal and $\rho$ is its X-sequence, such that no two pairs in $S$ have the same subgoal. A subgoal $A$ is said to be *in* $S$ if $(A : \rho) \in S$ for some X-sequence $\rho$.

Let $(A : \rho) \in S$, where $A$ is a subgoal and $\rho$ is its X-sequence. Let $G$ be an X-rule and $\alpha$ be an ordinal. $G$ is said to be *the X-rule of A corresponding to $\alpha$ in $S$* if $\rho(\alpha)$ is either $G\langle C\rangle$, $G\langle i\rangle$, or $G\langle i, H\rangle$, where $C$ is a rule in $P$, $i < \alpha$, and $H$ is an atom.

Let $G$ be an X-rule of $A$ corresponding to $\alpha$ in $S$. Then

- $G$ is *disposed* if for some $j > \alpha$, $\rho(j)$ is either *disposed*$\langle\alpha\rangle$ or is $G'\langle\alpha\rangle$ for some X-rule $G'$;
- $G$ is an *answer of A* if $G$ is not disposed and has no literals in its body;
- $G$ is *suspended* on $B$ if $\neg B$ is the selected literal of $G$, $G$ is not disposed, and for some $j > \alpha$, $\rho(j)$ is *suspended*$\langle\alpha\rangle$, and there is no $k > j$ such that $\rho(k)$ is *unsuspended*$\langle\alpha\rangle$; we say that $G$ is *suspended* if there exists a subgoal $B$ such that $G$ is suspended on $B$.
- $G$ is an *active X-rule of A* if $G$ is not disposed or suspended and has a selected literal.

A subgoal $A$ in $S$ is *completed* if all X-rules of $A$ are either answers, or are disposed. □

## 3.3 Transformations of Systems of Subgoals

Starting with the empty system of subgoals, each transformation transforms one system into another. The initial X-sequence of a subgoal is obtained by resolution with rules in a program. Without loss of generality, we consider only *atomic queries* that contain a single atom.

**Definition 16 X-resolution.** Let $G$ be an X-rule, of the form $H \leftarrow L_1, \ldots, L_n$, and $L_i$ be the selected atom of $G$ for some $i(1 \le i \le n)$. Let $C$ be a rule and $C'$, of the form $H' \leftarrow L'_1, \ldots, L'_m$, be a variant of $C$ with variables renamed so that $G$ and $C'$ have no variables in common. Then $G$ is *X-resolvable* with $C$ if $L_i$ and $H'$ are unifiable. The X-rule:

$$(H \leftarrow L_1, \ldots, L_{i-1}, L'_1, \ldots, L'_m, L_{i+1}, \ldots, L_n)\theta$$

is the *X-resolvent* of $G$ with $C$, where $\theta$ is the mgu of $L_i$ and $H'$. □

The selected atom in the body of an X-rule can be solved by an answer; this process is called *answer resolution*. The selected negative literal in the body of an X-rule can be solved if the positive counterpart succeeds or fails, according to the following definition.

**Definition 17.** Let $S$ be a system. A subgoal $A$ in $S$ *succeeds* if $A$ has an answer of the form $A' \leftarrow$ where $A'$ is a variant of $A$, and *fails* if $A$ is completed in $S$ without any answers. If $A$ neither succeeds nor is completed in $S$, then we say that $A$ is *evolving* in $S$. □

Notice that a subgoal containing variables succeeds if it has any answer that does not bind any of its variables. As a special case, a ground subgoal succeeds if it has an answer. The COMPLETION transformation requires the notion of a set of subgoals that are completely evaluated so that their active and their suspended X-rules, can be disposed.

**Definition 18 Completely Evaluated.** Let $S$ be a system and $\Sigma$ be a non-empty set of subgoals in $S$, none of which is completed. $\Sigma$ is said to be *completely evaluated* iff for every subgoal $A \in \Sigma$, where $(A : \rho) \in S$ for some X-sequence $\rho$, either

- $A$ succeeds, or
- $A$ does not contain any suspended X-rule, and for every active X-rule $G$ of $A$ corresponding to some ordinal $\alpha$ in $S$, there exists an atom $A_1$ such that:
  - $A_1$ is the selected atom of $G$; and
  - $A_1$ is a subgoal in $S$ that is either completed or in $\Sigma$; and
  - for every atom $H$ that is the head of some answer of $A_1$ in $S$, there exists an ordinal $i > \alpha$ and an X-rule $G'$ such that $\rho(i) = G'\langle \alpha, H \rangle$.

For convenience, we call a subgoal $A$ *completely evaluated* iff there exists a set of subgoals $\Sigma$ that is completely evaluated, and $A \in \Sigma$. □

Note that according to this definition, any set $\{A\}$ consisting of a single subgoal $A$ that succeeds is a completely evaluated set of subgoals. This condition will be referred to as *early completion* of subgoals. Also note that in a completely evaluated set of subgoals, only those subgoals that succeed can contain X-rules that are suspended on the completion of another subgoal.

Let $P$ be a program, $R$ be an arbitrary but fixed computation rule, and $Q$ be an atomic query. The transformations of $SLG_{strat}$ are listed below:

- NEW SUBGOAL Let $A$ be a subgoal that is not in $S$ and that satisfies one of the following conditions:
  - $A$ is the initial atomic query $Q$; or
  - there is an active X-rule of some subgoal in $S$ whose selected literal is either $A$ or $\neg A$.

  Let $C_0, C_1, \ldots, C_{k-1}(k \geq 0)$ be all rules in program $P$ with which $A \leftarrow A$ is X-resolvable, and $G_i(0 \leq i < k)$ be the X-resolvent of $A \leftarrow A$ with $C_i$. Let $\rho$ be the X-sequence of length $k$ such that $\rho(i) = G_i\langle C_i \rangle (0 \leq i < k)$. Then

$$\frac{S}{S \cup \{(A : \rho)\}}$$

Remark: Repeated subgoals are not solved by resolution with program clauses.

- $\boxed{\text{POSITIVE RETURN}}$ Let $(A : \rho) \in S$, where $A$ is a subgoal and $\rho$ is its X-sequence. Let $G$ be an active X-rule of $A$ corresponding to an ordinal $\alpha$ in $S$. Let $A_1$ be the selected atom of $G$, and let $C$ be an answer of subgoal $A_1$ in $S$ that has $H$ in its head. If there is no ordinal $i > \alpha$ such that $\rho(i) = G_1\langle \alpha, H \rangle$ for some X-rule $G_1$, then

$$\frac{S}{S - \{(A : \rho)\} \cup \{(A : \rho \cdot (G_2\langle \alpha, H \rangle))\}}$$

where $G_2$ is the X-resolvent of $G$ with $C$.

Remark: $A_1$ may have multiple answers with the same atom $H$ in the head. Only one of them is used by POSITIVE RETURN to solve the selected atom $A_1$ in $G$. So, in particular, redundant answers are not used.

- $\boxed{\text{NEGATIVE RETURN}}$ Let $(A : \rho) \in S$, where $A$ is a subgoal and $\rho$ is its X-sequence. Let $G$ be an active X-rule of a subgoal $A$ corresponding to an ordinal $\alpha$ in $S$, and let $\neg A_1$ be the selected literal of $G$, where $A_1$ either succeeds or fails. Then

$$\frac{S}{S - \{(A : \rho)\} \cup \{(A : \rho \cdot disposed\langle \alpha \rangle)\}} \quad \text{if } A_1 \text{ succeeds}$$

$$\frac{S}{S - \{(A : \rho)\} \cup \{(A : \rho \cdot G'\langle \alpha \rangle)\}} \quad \text{if } A_1 \text{ fails}$$

where $G'$ is $G$ with the selected literal $\neg A_1$ deleted.

- $\boxed{\text{NEGATIVE SUSPENSION}}$ Let $(A : \rho) \in S$, where $A$ is a subgoal and $\rho$ is its X-sequence. Let $G$ be an active X-rule of subgoal $A$ corresponding to an ordinal $\alpha$ in $S$, and let $\neg A_1$ be the selected literal of $G$ such that $A_1$ is evolving in $S$. Then

$$\frac{S}{S - \{(A : \rho)\} \cup \{(A : \rho \cdot suspended\langle \alpha \rangle)\}}$$

Remark: Negative literals whose positive counterparts either are completed or succeed in $S$ are never suspended.

- $\boxed{\text{COMPLETION}}$ Let $\Sigma$ be a non-empty set of subgoals in $S$ that is completely evaluated, and let $\Xi$ be the set of subgoals in $S$ containing an X-rule that is suspended on a literal $\neg A_1$ where $A_1 \in \Sigma$. Then

$$\frac{S}{\begin{array}{c} \text{for every } B \in \Xi, \text{ replace } (B : \varrho) \in S \text{ with } (B : \varrho \cdot \varrho') \\ \text{and then} \\ \text{for every } A \in \Sigma, \text{ replace } (A : \rho) \in S \text{ with } (A : \rho \cdot \rho') \end{array}}$$

where

- $\varrho'$ is an arbitrary sequence of X-elements of the form $unsuspended\langle \alpha \rangle$, where $\alpha$ is an ordinal such that the X-rule of $B$ corresponding to $\alpha$ in $\varrho$ is an X-rule that is suspended on a literal $\neg A_1$ where $A_1 \in \Sigma$.
- $\rho'$ is an arbitrary sequence of X-elements of the form $disposed\langle \alpha \rangle$, where $\alpha$ is an ordinal such that the X-rule of $A$ corresponding to $\alpha$ in $\rho$ is an active X-rule.

Remark: COMPLETION does not depend upon any *a priori* stratification ordering of predicates or atoms. Instead, a set of subgoals is inspected and completed dynamically.

## 3.4   Derivation and $SLG_{strat}$ Resolution

**Definition 19.** Let $P$ be a finite program, $R$ be an arbitrary but fixed computation rule, and $Q$ be an atomic query. An $SLG_{strat}$ *derivation* for $Q$ (or *evaluation of* $Q$) is a sequence of systems $S_0, S_1, \ldots, S_\alpha$ such that:

- $S_0$ is the empty system $\emptyset$;
- for each successor ordinal $\beta + 1 \leq \alpha$, $S_{\beta+1}$ is obtained from $S_\beta$ by an application of one of the transformations, namely, NEW SUBGOAL, POSITIVE RETURN, NEGATIVE RETURN, NEGATIVE SUSPENSION, or COMPLETION;
- for each limit ordinal $\beta \leq \alpha$, $S_\beta$ is such that $(A : \rho) \in S_\beta$ if $A$ is a subgoal in $S_i$ for some $i < \beta$ and $\rho = \bigcup \{\rho' | (A : \rho') \in S_j \text{ and } j < \beta\}$.

If no transformation is applicable to $S_\alpha$, $S_\alpha$ is called a *final system* of $Q$.

$SLG_{strat}$ *resolution* is the process of constructing an $SLG_{strat}$ derivation for a query $Q$ with respect to a finite program $P$ under a computation rule $R$. □

To show that a final system always exists, we prove that each $SLG_{strat}$ derivation is a monotonically increasing sequence of systems with respect to some partial ordering and each system in an $SLG_{strat}$ derivation is bounded in size by some ordinal.

**Definition 20.** Let $P$ be a finite program, and $S_1$ and $S_2$ be systems. Then $S_1 \sqsubseteq S_2$ if for every $(A : \rho_1) \in S_1$, there exists $(A : \rho_2) \in S_2$ such that $\rho_1 \subseteq \rho_2$, i.e., $\rho_1$ is a prefix of $\rho_2$. □

The following proposition ensures that the addition of the *suspended* and *unsuspended* statuses in Definition 11, and the introduction of the NEGATIVE SUSPENSION transformation do not affect fundamental properties of SLG resolution.

**Proposition 21.** *Let $P$ be a finite program, $R$ be an arbitrary but fixed computation rule, and $Q$ be an atomic query. Then*

(a) *there exists some ordinal $\lambda$ such that for any system $S$ in any $SLG_{strat}$ derivation for $Q$, the length of the X-sequence of each subgoal in $S$ is bounded by $\lambda$;*

(b) *every $SLG_{strat}$ derivation of $Q$ is a monotonically increasing sequence of systems with respect to $\sqsubseteq$; and*

(c) *there exists some $SLG_{strat}$ derivation for $Q$, $S_0, S_1, \ldots, S_\alpha$, for some ordinal $\alpha$ such that $S_\alpha$ is a final system.*

Proposition 21 shows that some final system can be derived for an atomic query $Q$, given a finite program $P$ and an arbitrary but fixed computation rule $R$. As we will soon prove, it turns out that in our restriction of SLG resolution, for any final system $S$ for $Q$ either every subgoal in $S$ is completed, or no $SLG_{strat}$ transformation is applicable because some subgoals that are evolving in $S$ contain suspended X-rules (on subgoals that are also evolving in $S$). In the latter case, we say that the final system is *flummoxed*. Recall that non-succeeding subgoals cannot contain suspended X-rules in order to be completely evaluated; as a result the COMPLETION transformation cannot be applied to them. Note that a special instance of this occurs in non-ground programs where the final system may be flummoxed because some suspended X-rule of a subgoal in $S$ has a selected negative literal that is not ground and is evolving.

**Definition 22 Completed and Flummoxed System.** Let $S$ be a system. $S$ is *completed* if every subgoal in $S$ is completed, and is *flummoxed* if $S$ is final (i.e. no transformation is applicable to $S$) but not completed. □

**Lemma 23.** *Let $P$ be a finite program, $R$ be an arbitrary but fixed computation rule, and $Q$ be an atomic query. Then for every final system $S$ for $Q$, $S$ is either completed or flummoxed.*

### 3.5 Subgoal Dependencies

An SLG system $S$ induces a natural dependency relation between its subgoals. A subgoal $A$ *directly depends positively (negatively)* on a subgoal $B$ if $B$ ($\neg B$) is the selected literal of an active (suspended) rule of $A$. A subgoal $A$ *depends on* a subgoal $B$ if there is a sequence of subgoals $A_0, A_1, \ldots, A_n$, such that $A_0 = A$, $A_n = B$, and $A_i$ directly depends on $A_{i+1}$, for each $0 \leq i \leq n - 1$. We say that $A$ *depends positively on* $B$ if $A$ depends on $B$ through only positive direct dependencies, and we say that $A$ *depends negatively on* $B$ if $A$ depends on $B$ and at least one of the direct dependencies is negative. Finally, we say that a subgoal is *involved in a negative loop* if it depends negatively on itself.

The dependency relation outlined above can be extended to a *Subgoal Dependency Graph (SDG)* for a system $S$ whose vertices are non-completed subgoals in $S$ and whose labeled links are determined by the dependency relation. Using the $SDG$, we can identify sets of mutually dependent subgoals as *strongly connected components (SCCs)*. We can also speak of a *component graph* induced by a $SDG$ as a graph whose nodes are $SCCs$ in the $SDG$ such that two nodes in the component graphs have a link iff there is a link between elements of the corresponding $SCCs$.

The following theorem states that when a final system is flummoxed, then all its subgoals that are not completed depend (directly or indirectly) on some subgoal that is involved in a negative loop.

**Theorem 24.** *Let $P$ be a program, $R$ be an arbitrary but fixed computation rule, $Q$ be an atomic query, and $S$ be a flummoxed system in an arbitrary $SLG_{strat}$ derivation for $Q$. Then every subgoal in $S$ that is not completed depends negatively on a subgoal in $S$ that is not completely evaluated.*

### 3.6 Interpretation defined by an SLG system

Let $P$ be a program, $R$ be an arbitrary but fixed computation rule, and $S$ be a system in any SLG derivation for an atomic query. As observed in [3], SLG resolution can be viewed as program transformation technique that specializes a program with respect to a query. More specifically, SLG resolution tries to transform a system of subgoals, each having an associated sequence of X-rules, into one that contains only X-rules that are answers for the subgoals. Under this prism, for each subgoal $A$ in $S$, the multiset of X-rules of $A$ in $S$ that are not disposed constitutes the set of partial answers for $A$. The head of each X-rule contains relevant variable bindings that have been accumulated; while the remaining literals in the rule body are yet to be solved with respect to the original program $P$. Each SLG system $S$ represents a program $P_S$ containing partial answers for its subgoals. It is natural, therefore, to associate with every SLG system $S$ a 3-valued interpretation $I_S$ of $P_S$ that is constructed from $S$ according to the following definition.

**Definition 25.** [3] Let $P$ be a program, $R$ be an arbitrary but fixed computation rule, and $Q$ be an atomic query. Let $S$ be a system in an SLG derivation for $Q$. We associate with $S$ a pair $I_S = \langle T_S; F_S \rangle$, where $T_S$ and $F_S$ are subsets of the Herbrand base $H_P$ of $P$ constructed as follows:

- if a (possibly non-completed) subgoal $A$ in $S$ has an answer of the form $H \leftarrow$, then every ground instance $B$ of $H$ is true in $I_S$; that is, $B \in T_S$;
- if a subgoal $A$ in $S$ is completed and $B$ is a ground instance of $A$ such that $B$ is not an instance of any answer of $A$, then $B$ is false in $I_S$; that is, $B \in F_S$;
- no other element of $H_P$ is in $T_S \cup F_S$.                                            □

In general, the interpretation $I_S$ captures ground instances of subgoals that succeed or fail. For example, if a subgoal $A$ succeeds in $S$, then every ground instance of $A$ is in $T_S$, and if a subgoal $A$ fails, then $B \in F_S$ for every ground instance $B$ of $A$. As a special case, in ground programs, a ground atom $A \in T_S$ ($A \in F_S$) if and only if $A$ in $S$ and $A$ succeeds (fails) in $S$. From the correctness of our restriction of SLG resolution (to be presented as Theorem 30), and the way that the interpretation $I_S$ is constructed, it can be seen that the sets $T_S$ and $F_S$ are disjoint, and the following proposition is immediate:

**Proposition 26.** *Let $P$ be a program, $R$ be an arbitrary but fixed computation rule, and let $S$ be a system in an arbitrary $SLG_{strat}$ derivation for an atomic query $Q$. Then $I_S$ is a consistent interpretation of $P$.*

Since $I_S$ is a consistent interpretation of $P$, it can be viewed as valuation function of the elements of the Herbrand base $H_P$. In general, a ground instance of a subgoal $A$ that is in $S$ may be true, false, or undefined in $I_S$, while all other elements of $H_P$ that are not instances of subgoals in $S$ are undefined in $I_S$. If $B$ is a ground atom from $H_P$, we denote the truth value of $B$ in $I_S$ as $val_{I_S}(B)$.

We say that an interpretation $I' = \langle T'; F' \rangle$ *extends* an interpretation $I = \langle T; F \rangle$ if $T \subseteq T'$ and $F \subseteq F'$. We will denote this fact by $I \leq I'$. The following proposition states that each $SLG_{strat}$ transformation extends the interpretation of the system to which the transformation is applied.

**Proposition 27.** *Let $P$ be a program, $R$ be an arbitrary but fixed computation rule, $Q$ be an atomic query, and $S_0, S_1, \ldots, S_\alpha$ be any arbitrary $SLG_{strat}$ derivation for $Q$, where $\alpha$ is an ordinal. Then the sequence $\{I_{S_i}, i > 0\}$ is monotonically increasing, i.e. $I_{S_i} \leq I_{S_j}$ if $i \leq j$.*

# 4 Correctness of $SLG_{strat}$ for LRD-stratified Programs

Recall that for simplicity of presentation a left-to-right computation rule is used, and that the dynamic stratum of a ground atom is also defined under this left-to-right computation rule (Definition 6). All results of this section can be extended to any fixed-order computation rule.

**Lemma 28.** *Let $P$ be a ground LRD-stratified program, $Q$ be a ground atomic query, and $\mathcal{E}$ be an $SLG_{strat}$ derivation for $Q$ under a left-to-right computation rule. Then for any completely evaluated subgoal $A$ in a system $S$ in $\mathcal{E}$,*

$$val_{I_S}(A) = val_{M_P}(A)$$

*That is, the truth value of subgoal in $I_S$ is the value of the subgoal in $M_P$.*

The following lemma states that the $SLG_{strat}$ evaluation of ground LRD-stratified programs will never result in a flummoxed system.

**Lemma 29.** *Let $P$ be a ground LRD-stratified program, $Q$ be a ground atomic query, and $S_0, S_1, \ldots, S_\alpha$ be any $SLG_{strat}$ derivation for $Q$ under a left-to-right computation rule, such that $S_\alpha$ is a final system. Then $S_\alpha$ is completed.*

In order to prove correctness of $SLG_{strat}$ resolution, we will want to compare the interpretation of a system $S$ for a program $P$ and query $Q$ with the model $M_P$ for that program. In that case, we use the notation $M_P|_S$ to denote the restriction of $M_P$ to (ground) atoms which unify with subgoals in $S$.

**Theorem 30.** *Let $P$ be a ground LRD-stratified program and $Q$ be an atomic ground query. Then any $SLG_{strat}$ derivation for $Q$ under a left-to-right computation rule will produce a final system $S$ such that $I_S = M_P|_S$.*

## 5  Beyond LRD-stratified programs

Recall that dynamically stratified programs differ from most stratification formalisms in that their recursive components (consisting of ground atoms) are determined dynamically in the course of a transfinite fixpoint computation. This process eliminates all irrelevant dependencies between atoms; i.e. those dependencies that can never be satisfied. As a result, dynamic stratification is very powerful: every logic program has a two-valued well-founded model if and only if it is dynamically stratified. Otherwise, in a partial well-founded model, the undefined atoms may be designated as belonging to the *ultimate dynamic stratum*.

### 5.1  Goal-Orientation and Relevance

Since the well-founded semantics cannot be computed using a fixed computation rule, it is non-trivial to obtain an evaluation strategy that is completely goal-directed. In particular, it is difficult given a query $Q$ to guarantee that the computation rule will always select literals that are absolutely essential in order to prove or disprove $Q$. This ideal measure of relevance in computing the well-founded model is very strong, and, as it probably requires selecting literals based on knowing a priori their truth value, it is probably unobtainable for evaluation strategies whose computation rule is not guided by an oracle. Assuming that this requirement cannot be met in practice, it is then natural to ask how tight can be the relevance of an evaluation strategy for the well-founded semantics that uses a non-ideal (for example a mostly fixed-order) computation rule.

Restricting attention to the case where the evaluation encounters only ground subgoals, we describe the notion of *relevance of subgoals to a query* under a fixed computation rule (again, for simplicity of presentation we use a left-to-right computation rule). Let $Q$ be a ground query to a program $P$ and let $P$ contain a rule:

$$r : \; p(\bar{t}) :- l_1(\overline{t_1}), \ldots, l_n(\overline{t_n}).$$

where $l_i(\overline{t_i}) = (\neg)s_i(\overline{t_i})$. Then, the subgoal $s_i(\overline{b_i})$ of literal $l_i(\overline{b_i})$ is relevant to $Q$ if there is a ground instance

$$r' : \; p(\bar{a}) :- l_1(\overline{b_1}), \ldots, l_i(\overline{b_i}), \ldots$$

of (the head and the first $i$ body literals of) $r$ such that the head $p(\bar{a})$ is relevant to $Q$, and all instantiated literals $l_1(\overline{b_1}), \ldots, l_{i-1}(\overline{b_{i-1}})$ are either true or undefined in the well-founded model of $P$. We believe that even this criterion for relevance is still very strong for all normal logic programs and appears to be equally unobtainable by non-ideal evaluation strategies. Notice, however, that all subgoals encountered during the $SLG_{strat}$ evaluation of a query $Q$ against a left-to-right dynamically stratified program are relevant to $Q$. Further evidence for this can be obtained by noticing the similarity between the notion of *relevance* sketched above and the notion of the *failing rule prefix* of Definition 1. In other words, the class of programs that are fixed-order dynamically stratified can indeed be evaluated with the tightest possible relevance to the query using a fixed computation rule. This is yet another reason for our claim that fixed-order dynamic stratification can be considered as the limit of fixed-order computation.

It is now probably easy to see that the goal-directedness and strong relevance properties of $SLG_{strat}$ derivations make $SLG_{strat}$ more powerful than what was claimed in the previous section. More specifically, $SLG_{strat}$ can correctly process a query $Q$ to a program $P$ that is not LRD-stratified provided that subgoals belonging to the ultimate left-to-right dynamic stratum of $P$ are not relevant to $Q$. This is illustrated by the following examples.

*Example 3.* The following program is not LRD-stratified. As discussed in Example 1 the query p(a) cannot be evaluated using any fixed computation rule. Consequently, its $SLG_{strat}$ derivation using a left-to-right computation rule will result in a final system that is flummoxed.

```
p(X)  :- t(X,Y,Z), ¬p(Y), ¬p(Z).
p(b).
t(a,b,a). t(a,a,b). t(b,b,a).
```

Notice however, that $SLG_{strat}$ using a left-to-right computation rule suffices for the evaluation of query p(b), since subgoal $p(a)$ is not relevant to p(b). The encountered cycle through negation involving subgoal $p(b)$ is spurious and as such is eliminated by the *early completion* operation. ∎

*Example 4.* The definition of p/0 makes the following program non-stratified (and consequently non LRD-stratified).

```
a :- b.      b :- ¬a, p.
a.           p :- ¬p.
```

However, as subgoal $p$ is not relevant to queries ?- a. or ?- b. under a left-to-right computation rule, the rule for p/0 will not be examined, and $SLG_{strat}$ suffices for the evaluation of these queries. ∎

## 5.2 Towards Efficient Evaluation of the Well-Founded Semantics

By including the DELAYING, SIMPLIFICATION, and ANSWER COMPLETION transformations of SLG resolution, [2] $SLG_{strat}$ can be naturally extended to evaluate the well-founded semantics of all normal logic programs in a goal-oriented fashion. The resulting evaluation strategy, which we call $SLG_{RD}$ (*SLG with Reduced Delay*), is effective and inherits the properties of SLG resolution: it is sound and search space complete with respect to the well-founded partial model for all (non-floundering) queries, preserves all their three-valued stable models, and has polynomial data complexity for function-free programs.

However, through the introduction of the NEGATIVE SUSPENSION transformation, $SLG_{RD}$ significantly restricts the space of possible SLG derivations. SLG allows an arbitrary computation rule for selecting a literal from a rule body and an arbitrary control strategy for selecting transformations to apply. This flexibility, though theoretically appealing, may result in inefficient evaluation due to unnecessary use of the DELAYING (and as a result of the SIMPLIFICATION and the ANSWER COMPLETION) transformations. Unnecessarily DELAYING ground negative literals that the computation rule stumbles on, opens up the search space by expanding subgoals that may not be relevant to the query. Contrary to SLG evaluation, $SLG_{RD}$ suspends that computation path, and later applies the DELAYING transformation to these negative literals only if their subgoals have no left-to-right proof, i.e. only if their evaluation results in a flummoxed system. Specifically, the following theorem can be proven.

**Theorem 31.** *Let $\neg S$ be a selected literal in an $SLG_{RD}$ evaluation of a ground normal logic program $P$ under a left-to-right computation rule. Then the DELAYING transformation is applied to $\neg S$ if and only if $S$ belongs to the ultimate left-to-right dynamic stratum of $P$.*

This theorem can be seen as addressing the question of relevance in $SLG_{RD}$, our restriction of SLG resolution. In principle, if a rule instance is used in a left-to-right well-founded evaluation of a query, a literal of that rule should be relevant only if it is preceded by a sequence of literals that are true or undefined in the well-founded model. As discussed in the previous section, this criterion for relevance is very strong and appears unobtainable by practical strategies that mainly use a fixed computation rule. Theorem 31 thus states our approximation to this ideal measure of relevance by using the notion of the ultimate left-to-right dynamic stratum. The discussion of the previous section hints that this approximation is tight — possibly the tightest that can be achieved using a fixed computation rule.

# 6 Applicability of Results

The results of Section 4 show that $SLG_{strat}$ can form the basis of an engine to evaluate LRD-stratified programs, and the discussion of the previous section indicates that $SLG_{strat}$ can also be used as a basis to restrict the dynamic

---

[2] We do not repeat their definitions here; they can be included as presented in [3].

search in engines that evaluate the well-founded semantics. In fact, $SLG_{strat}$ has been implemented in the SLG-WAM of XSB [14]. The subset of transformations NEW SUBGOAL, POSITIVE RETURN, and COMPLETION (without the early completion of Section 3.3) suffices to evaluate definite programs. A detailed description of the their implementation, along with their integration with the SLD resolution of Prolog, is given in [17]. The addition to the SLG-WAM of NEGATIVE RETURN, NEGATIVE SUSPENSION and the *early completion* operation has been described in a companion paper ([15]) and this engine forms the basis of version 1.5 of XSB. Indeed, the performance results of [15] demonstrate that LRD-stratified programs besides being evaluatable using a fixed computation rule are also amenable to an efficient implementation. In fact, the introduction of the *early completion* mechanism can *reduce* the time and space needed for evaluation of even definite programs. Based on $SLG_{RD}$, i.e. using the DELAYING transformation to break the fixed-order search only whenever the evaluation encounters a flummoxed state, we continue our effort of extending the SLG-WAM to evaluate the well-founded semantics of all normal programs.

Despite the fact that our results have been presented using (variants of) SLG resolution, we believe that the underlying ideas are potentially applicable to deductive database systems whose engines have radically different designs from XSB. For example, CORAL [11] evaluates modularly stratified programs using Ordered Search [10]. Described simply, this technique keeps a tree of dependencies and restricts magic evaluation to magic facts that are in an SCC. Both Ordered Search and its extension Well-Founded Ordered Search as originally formulated do not contain a mechanism like early completion; a mechanism that usually eliminates many spurious negative cycles, thereby reducing the need for dynamic search. It appears possible to extend these strategies to include early completion by checking whether a given magic fact is subsumed by an answer fact.

# References

1. N. Bidoit and C. Froidevaux. Negation by default and unstratifiable logic programs. *Theoretical Comput. Sci.*, 78(1):85–112, January 1991.
2. R. Bol and L. Degerstedt. Tabulated resolution for well founded semantics. In D. Miller, editor, *Proceedings of the 1993 International Symposium on Logic Programming*, pages 199–219, Vancouver, October 1993. The MIT Press.
3. W. Chen and D. S. Warren. Tabled Evaluation with Delaying for General Logic Programs. *J. ACM*, 43(1):20–74, January 1996.
4. J. Dix. Classifying semantics of logic programs. In A. Nerode, W. Marek, and V. S. Subrahmanian, editors, *Logic Programming and Mon-Monotonic Reasoning, Proceedings of the first International Workshop*, pages 166–180, Washington D.C., July 1991. The MIT Press.
5. M. Gelfond and V. Lifschitz. The stable model semantics for logic programming. In R. A. Kowalski and K. A. Bowen, editors, *Proceedings of the Fifth International Conference and Symposium on Logic Programming*, pages 1081–1086, Seattle, August 1988. The MIT Press.
6. S. Morishita. An Extension of Van Gelder's Alternating Fixpoint to Magic Programs. *J. Comput. Syst. Sci.*, 52(3):506–521, June 1996.

7. H. Przymusinska and T. C. Przymusinski. Weakly Stratified Logic Programs. *Fundamenta Informaticae*, 13(1):51–65, March 1990.

8. T. C. Przymusinski. Every Logic Program has a Natural Stratification and an Iterated Least Fixed Point Model. In *Proceedings of the Eighth ACM Symposium on Principles of Database Systems*, pages 11–21, Philadelphia, Pennsylvania, March 1989. ACM.

9. T. C. Przymusinski. Well-Founded and Stationary Models of Logic Programs. *Annals of Mathematics and Artificial Intelligence*, 12:141–187, 1994.

10. R. Ramakrishnan, D. Srivastava, and S. Sudarshan. Controlling the search in bottom-up evaluation. In K. Apt, editor, *Proceedings of the Joint International Conference and Symposium on Logic Programming*, pages 273–287, Washington D.C., October 1992. The MIT Press.

11. R. Ramakrishnan, D. Srivastava, and S. Sudarshan. CORAL — Control, Relations, and Logic. In *Proceedings of the 18th Conference on Very Large Data Bases*, pages 238–249, Vancouver, Canada, August 1992.

12. K. A. Ross. A procedural semantics for well-founded negation in logic programs. *Journal of Logic Programming*, 13(1):1–22, May 1992.

13. K. A. Ross. Modular Stratification and Magic Sets for Datalog programs with Negation. *J. ACM*, 41(6):1216–1266, November 1994.

14. K. Sagonas, T. Swift, and D. S. Warren. XSB as an Efficient Deductive Database Engine. In *Proceedings of the ACM SIGMOD International Conference on the Management of Data*, pages 442–453, Minneapolis, Minnesota, May 1994.

15. K. Sagonas, T. Swift, and D. S. Warren. An Abstract Machine for Fixed-Order Dynamically Stratified Programs. In *Proceedings of the Thirteenth International Conference on Automated Deduction*, LNAI, New Brunswick, New Jersey, July 1996. Springer-Verlag. To appear.

16. P. J. Stuckey and S. Sudarshan. Well-Founded Ordered Search. In R. Shyamasundar, editor, *Proceedings of the 13th Conference on Foundations of Software Technology and Theoretical Computer Science*, number 761 in LNCS, pages 161–171, Bombay, India, December 1993. Springer-Verlag.

17. T. Swift and D. S. Warren. An abstract machine for SLG resolution: Definite Programs. In M. Bruynooghe, editor, *Proceedings of the 1994 International Symposium on Logic Programming*, pages 633–652, Ithaca, November 1994. The MIT Press.

18. A. Van Gelder. The Alternating Fixpoint of Logic Programs with Negation. In *Proceedings of the Eighth ACM Symposium on Principles of Database Systems*, pages 1–10, Philadelphia, Pennsylvania, March 1989. ACM.

19. A. Van Gelder, K. A. Ross, and J. S. Schlipf. The Well-Founded Semantics for General Logic Programs. *J. ACM*, 38(3):620–650, July 1991.

# Invited Lecture

# The $\mathcal{IQ}$ System* : A Deductive Database Information Lens for Reasoning about Textual Information

Bob Kero and Shalom Tsur

Argonne National Laboratory
Decision and Information Sciences Division
Argonne, Illinois, 60439
{bkero, tsur}@dis.anl.gov

**Abstract.** The $\mathcal{IQ}$ system, described in this paper, addresses two current problems in information retrieval (IR) from document repositories: (i) the "glut-of-information" that threatens to overwhelm the users of these systems and (ii) the loss of informational value as the documents are moved from their organizational setting into a machine-readable format. The answer to these problems discussed in the paper, proposes to restore much of this information by creating a context-base to store the additional recovered knowledge. The technology used is the $\mathcal{LDL}++$ deductive database: we demonstrate how to use the rule-extensions to declare levels of abstraction in the information that can be used to "zoom-in" or "pan-out" as required by the user (an "Information Lens"). The system takes extensive advantage of the World-Wide Web and enlists the capabilities of JAVA for information display. We discuss some of the performance issues that were experienced and conclude with a description of future R&D ideas along the lines started here.

## 1 Introduction

Many government agencies, private companies and other large organizations maintain or are developing an "Information Center" as part of their information infrastructure. The role of the Information Center within the organization is not unlike that of a library: to serve as a central repository for internal documentation and information received from external sources. The incoming information is archived and in addition, serves for day-to-day decision making purposes.

The rate of full-text information intake at the Department of Energy (DOE) Environment, Safety, and Health (ES&H) Information Center, as in most Information Centers, is constantly increasing. Most of this information is received in the form of scientific and technical documents on paper or in electronic format. In its present form, this ever-increasing flow poses a "glut-of-information" problem to the decision maker, who is forced to sift through it to select relevant pieces

---

* Work supported by the U.S. Department of Energy, Office of Information Management (EH-72), contract W-31-109-Eng-38.

of information. The fact that most decisions need to be taken in some limited time compounds the problem. Typically, it becomes impossible to review all of the potentially relevant documentation within the time frame allotted to decide. The present form of full-text searching support raises thus the serious concern that the quality of decision making may be impaired because decisions may be based on incomplete or random knowledge. This problem will be exacerbated as the present economic climate and tightening budget constraints force many organizations to do more with less.

Besides the information-glut problem, another factor that also contributes to the present unsatisfactory state of affairs is the *decontextualization* of the stored electronic full-text documents. This term deserves an explanation. Briefly, documents are created for a specific reason and within a specific context. The reason is often to meet a legislative or policy requirement, while the context is based on the organization(s) involved, people who created the document, time and place of authorship, and relationships to other documents and issues. For example, a DOE "Finding of No Significant Impact" document possesses at least one closely coupled specific relationship, lineage: child to parent, to its respective environmental assessment document. This type of additional knowledge, often vital to the decision-making process, is lost or made difficult to discern when each document's textual content is all that is preserved. Presently, the burden of remembering (or the cost of dynamically determining) contextual information is the sole responsibility of each user. This arrangement can quickly result in a heavy economical cost to the organization. Domain experts leverage their individual a priori knowledge of the corpus and its contents to better control their information searching and gathering. Novice users drown in what falsely looks like a predominately unrelated sea of documents. In either case, there is no capitalization upon an organizationally defined contextual understanding of the corpus, which would (1) increase searching efficiency, and (2) reduce uncertainty in the decision-making process for all classes of users. Instead, present technology normally allows the retrieval of the documents only if certain terms that appear in their text are used. The context is not an explicit part of the documentation; hence, it cannot be used in the search for relevant documentation. Consequently, the decision maker who must make decisions solely on the basis of document contents, without understanding their context, can be at a huge disadvantage.

The objectives of the $\mathcal{IQ}$ system are to effectively address these issues. The approach that we adopted was to *augment* the already existing information with contextual knowledge kept in a separate *context base*—a deductive database implemented in $\mathcal{LDL}++$ [AOTZ]. The responses to user queries, returned from IR engines containing documentation sources, are elaborated using the context base and distributed using the World-Wide Web (WWW) in the form of JAVA applets[2] [GM95]. Section 2.0 describes the evolution and architecture of the

---

[2] JAVA, is an architecturally neutral object-oriented programming language developed by Sun Microsystems, Inc. Applets, JAVA programs, can be transmitted over the Internet, run on multiple clients, and provide users with the multimedia richness of a CD-ROM.

$\mathcal{IQ}$ system. Section 3.0 describes the documentation reengineering process necessary to take advantage of this approach. This includes a reengineering of the existing stored documentation, and a means to encode future documentation to capture the contextual knowledge. Section 4.0 describes the technical considerations and experience gained thus far with the use of deductive database technology as embedded in this system. We conclude with some ideas for the next generation of the $\mathcal{IQ}$ system, briefly describe the cost-benefit considerations of the reengineering process and compare it with the conventional method of handling documentation.

## 2 The $\mathcal{IQ}$ Architecture

The overall goal of developing the $\mathcal{IQ}$ system is to create a tool to provide not only access, management, and storage of the information content found in the DOE ES&H Information Center, but also to the rich contextual tradition surrounding its uses in particular DOE communities-of-practice. Objectives of the system include providing a means to:

- retain the value of information content and its uses
- capture the rich contexts associated with information content as new information.
- coherently visualize large collections of information content through graphic abstractions and classifications
- contextually understand the relationships between hit list[3] elements and their associated documents
- interact with both document content and context
- allow for the definition and integration of future information contexts
- control the rate and amount of information content transmitted to a user

When the system is fully developed it will provide an effective means to manage the adaptation of the documents' content, its context, and its changing needs over time. Additionally, it will reduce the risk of decision making by providing accurate, timely and complete information to decision makers through a recontextualization process (i.e., the partial or full integration of information content and context). Finally, $\mathcal{IQ}$ will continually reduce the difficulty of managing and comprehending the accumulation of information content as it grows rapidly in volume and diversity.

The architecture of the $\mathcal{IQ}$ System, see Figure 1, is composed of three major pieces:

1. *The Document Repository.* This piece contains all of the document content found in the system.

---

[3] *Hit list* – a relevancy ranked list of document or document component identifiers (e.g., titles) corresponding to the textual content that the IR system deems pertinent to the users' query.

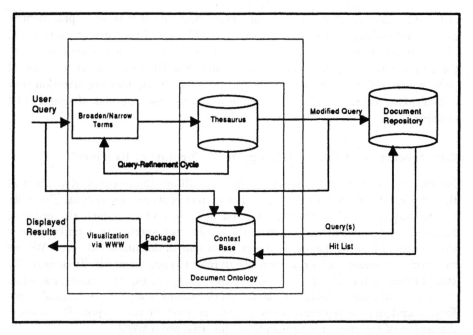

**Fig. 1.** $\mathcal{IQ}$ System Architecture

2. *The Document Ontology.* This piece contains knowledge pertaining to the relationships between pieces, whole, or classes of documents kept in the document repository, the linguistic knowledge describing and relating the uses of terminology found in those documents, and the rules governing the uses of all types of knowledge.

3. *The User Interface.* This piece allows users to access (e.g., query or view from different perspectives) the information in the document ontology and the document repository. Users can observe the results of their queries in various abstract graphical representations, instead of in hit lists, that will provide them with different contextual understandings. The interface visually abstracts the information using filters so users can reason with its specific contexts instead of just scanning or reading its actual text-level contents. This extensible set of information filters is used to constrain the information while the system's user controlled *information lens* is allowed to zoom in and out as to provide more or less detail.

The architecture of the $\mathcal{IQ}$ system is intrinsically connected to the use of information retrieval technologies, yet it is not tightly coupled to any particular product or method. Instead, the $\mathcal{IQ}$ system has been designed to augment current and future IR systems by building a uniform cap over them. Before providing an overview of the technology we will put the use of IR systems in a perspective. The advent of the World-Wide Web has brought a strong resurgence in the need to provide better techniques to access information. As enormous amounts of textual information continue to be loaded onto the WWW at unprecedented rates, a refocusing on the strengths and weaknesses of the current state of IR has occurred. At this time the field of IR is rapidly advancing. Innovations continue to be added to public domain and commercial IR systems at an accelerated pace, which makes choosing a specific product for a particular organization very difficult. Our approach should be seen as a way to lessen the risk of selecting IR systems.

## 2.1 Overview of the Technology for Information Retrieval

Information Retrieval technology is used to facilitate the retrieval of a subset of the relevant documents to a user, from a corpus of stored documents. Typically the assumption is that the corpus itself is large and can reach the order of hundreds of thousands of documents and the user specification pertains to a small subset of these, maybe on the order of tens of documents at most. We use the term "document" in a generic sense to refer to such magnetically or optically stored items as reports, manuals, newspapers, magazines, etc. Sometimes, when the documents are voluminous, the actual document is kept in its original paper format and only a reference to it is kept as part of the corpus. For a short discussion of the users requirements in this area see [Cro95].

The user specification is submitted to the system in form of a query, and the system's response is returned in the form of a hit list. In this paper we will distinguish between "traditional" methods for information retrieval and "knowledge intensive" methods. The former ones use the document texts, as they appear in the corpus, as the sole source of information for the resolution of the user's query; the later use additional information in the form of thesauri and other linguistic information to enhance and improve the query resolution process. Finally, we will discuss how the $\mathcal{IQ}$ system extends the abilities of current IR systems through a complementary design.

## 2.2 Traditional Methods for Full Text Searching

Traditional IR systems such as WAIS [WAI95] and Harvest [HAR95], store the full text of the document and group sets of documents in a corpus. These systems provide support for extensive indexing methods that allow for the retrieval of documents relevant to a user-posed query. User-queries are formulated as conjunctions, disjunctions and other Boolean expressions using terms being searched for in the corpus. The result of a query is in the form of a relevancy ranked hit-list.

The basic limitation of the traditional information retrieval methods is that, in order to access a document, its text must contain the *exact* terms that were used in the query. Thus, if a query uses the term "automobile," whereas the document contains the term "car," it will not be included in the hit list. This is also true for misspelled words, British vs. the American use of the language, the use of slang, etc. Another limitation is that all that is returned by a hit list, is the fact that a certain document contains a query term. Little is revealed about the distribution of the term throughout the document, or if the term was used in the title, body, or reference section of the document. This knowledge is often very important in assessing its relevance. The statistical measures typically employed contribute only very little in this respect since all they do are count occurrences but do not reveal anything about the whereabouts of the words in the text.

The measures of success typically used with IR technology include *precision* and *recall* which respectively, register the extent to which those documents appearing in the hit list should have been included and the extent to which all of the relevant documents have been hit. Over the years, the methods used for the resolution of user queries have continuously been refined to achieve high degrees of these measures.

## 2.3 Knowledge-Intensive Methods for Information Retrieval

Current commercial IR products such as Personal Librarian by Personal Library Software Corporation [PLS95] and RetrievalWare by Excalibur Technologies [EXC95], offer a range of knowledge-intensive capabilities. For example, RetrievalWare offers a high-end semantic network containing over 400,000 word meanings and over 1.6 million relationships to assist its users in query development and searching. The current $\mathcal{IQ}$ system has foregone the inclusion of general purpose dictionaries and thesauri and instead, has concentrated on the inclusion of one DOE domain specific dictionary/thesaurus on the order of 30,000 terms. This specialized dictionary/thesaurus consists of the approved vocabulary used throughout specific areas in DOE and contains many inter-term relationships including: broader term, more narrow term, related term, see also, see for, use in place of, used for. The vocabulary found in this resource permeates the ES&H corpuses of interest and therefore provides a valuable resource to the DOE ES&H Information Center's user base.

The following example provides a general understaing of how various inter-term relationships can be used in the query development and refinement process. Interaction with a thesaurus enables the *narrowing* or *broadening* of potential query terms. Thus the terms "Cardiologist," "Endocrinologist," and "Urologist," could be broadened to "Medical Doctor" and substituted in the query. Alternatively, a general term can be replaced with more specific instances. This process is driven by the structure and content of the thesaurus used.

## 2.4 Advancing the State of the Art

Traditionally, the user-system interaction is characterized by the following cyclic behavior:

**until** satisfied **do**
        send query to document source;
        receive hit list;
        read contents of each item on hit list;
        modify (or formulate new) query;
**od**

At each repetition of the cycle, the user scans the textual information in the hit list and based on this new input, decides whether to modify his/her query until the final hit list is deemed to be appropriate to his/her needs. This process, which is the textual equivalent of the "data mining" process in numerical databases, is tedious and as we already stated, is often an impediment in effective decision making. In contrast, the user interaction with the $\mathcal{IQ}$ system is of a very different nature. The user controls *two* cycles of interaction: one cycle to narrow or broaden the search terms used in each version of the query and the other cycle, using the context base, to observe the results at different levels of abstraction. This process can be likened to "zooming" and "panning" in and out of the information through an information lens. Only at the last stage, at the highest level of resolution, does the user actually access the textual information of the corpus. In some cases this last step may be entirely omitted! We expect the interaction with the meta information, rather than with the actual text to be vastly more efficient and to contribute in a significant way to the timeliness and quality of decision making. From the performance perspective, all of the visualization capabilities of the system are on the client side. Thus, the volume of information during each of the phases of the interaction is much smaller than the interaction with the document repository which necessitates the actual transfer of a set of documents from the server to the client.

# 3   Document Preparation

In this section we provide an overview of the mark up process and outline the steps that must be taken to transform existing and future corpuses of documentation into a format that lends itself to the $\mathcal{IQ}$ architecture.

## 3.1   Document Mark up

Organizations normally deal with diverse sets of documents which vary in size. When the size of documents grow beyond a few pages, the documents need to be decomposed in a way (e.g., logically by sections or paragraphs) suited to more efficient searching. For example, a user searching for a particular term would normally want to receive the immediate section of information surrounding the term, instead of the complete document the term was found in. To decompose a document into its component parts it is first necessary to identify the boundaries of each component. Since most documents are used in different ways and in different information systems throughout their life cycle, it is highly efficient to insert neutrally-formatted mark up (tags), based on each component's type, within the document to identify its components for future uses. After a document has been marked up, tools can be used to physically split and transform its content, based on the included tags, into the formats necessary to be used in commercial IR systems. Establishing a neutral approach allows for organizations to pay for the document preparation only once, even if information systems and their subsequent formats are changed in the future. The minimal cost of developing transformation filters from the neutral format to any new specific format would be the only future re investment ever needed. Documents that were produced using word processing systems (e.g., Microsoft Word), or other mark up languages (e.g., TeX), already contain an internal mark up. Native mark up formats can be used directly or can be transformed into an equivalent mark up language standard set of tags.

The mark up language of choice for the $\mathcal{IQ}$ system is the Standard Generalized Mark up Language[4] (SGML). One of the strengths of SGML relates to its ability to mark up a document in a neutral way, independent of the many ways the document can be processed in the future. [Smi92] The tagged documents must conform to a DTD[5]. An SGML parser (e.g., SGMLS) can be used to infer the structure of the document through the use of its included tags and check to see whether it is compatible with its declared DTD. The result of the document preparation process is a collection of document components, and a unique form of an enhanced parse tree used to preserve the logical structure and physical layout relationships between document components within a document.

It should be noted that the HyperText Mark up Language (HTML) is defined in an SGML DTD. In essence, HTML is a collection of styles (indicated by mark up tags) that define the components of a WWW document. The $\mathcal{IQ}$ system dynamically transforms the potentially more robust SGML marked up documents and document components into HTML for preview.

## 3.2 Document Preparation Process

Figure 2 graphically depicts the steps a document must go through to construct its enhanced parse tree.

**Step 1:** *Marking-up of the documentation.* During this step a document in ASCII format is marked-up using the SGML standard. Tags are assigned to each of the documents' components. This step, which clearly is the most labor-intensive in the process, can be performed either manually, meaning that the person(s) performing this task use a tool such as a general-purpose editor to scan the document, identify the components and insert the appropriate tags, or automatically, using a custom mark up tool or a commercial one such as Avalanche's FastTag, which identifies the components and attaches the tags to them.

**Step 2:** *Parsing of the marked up documents.* The tagged documents must conform to a DTD. A parser such as SGMLS infers the structure of the document

---

[4] *SGML* – an international electronic document exchange standard developed by the International Organization for Standardization (ISO)

[5] *Document Type Definition*— a specific set of document component types, their relationships, the tag set used for mark up, and a set of rules for which the presence (or absence) of document components at particular times could be checked.

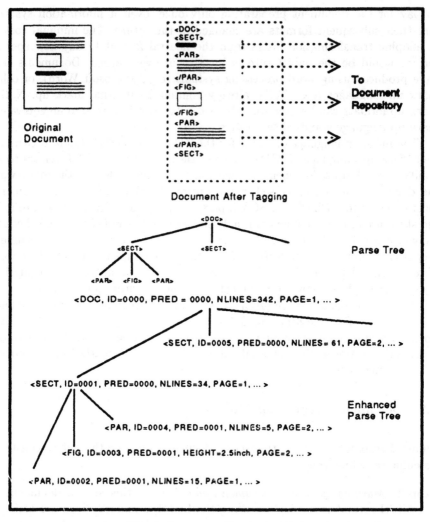

**Fig. 2.** Document Processing Steps

and checks to see whether it is compatible with the declared DTD. The result of this operation is the parse tree and the document components that
correspond to each of the nodes of this tree. Incompatible documents are
rejected.

**Step 3:** *Enhancement of the parsed document.* At this time each document component is assigned a unique id, and the same id is assigned to its corresponding tag instance in the parse tree. The tags are then enhanced with additional
information attributes. Attributes pertaining to a document include, but are
not limited to, the page number on where each document component starts,
the size of the component (e.g., in lines), a link between it and its parent

component, the type of the component, the offset from the top of the first page its starts on, and other ancillary information (e.g., titles or captions).

**Step 4:** *Splitting of the information.* Once enhanced, the textual parts and their attached id's are sent to a document repository (i.e., the IR engine) and the enhanced tags are sent to the context base. Thus, from the perspective of the repository, the input is still in its native format except that in actuality, each record in the repository is now a component of an original document. This fine granularity of information is of no consequence to the repository which should treat each of these records as if they were autonomous.

The information for the context base consists of tuples which can be stored in a standard, relational format. The context base can therefore be realized using an off-the-shelf relational database.

## 4 Context Base: the Role of Deductive Database Technology

In this section we discuss some of the details and the experience gained so far with the context base of the system. The purpose of the context base is, as we suggested, to store knowledge *about* the documentation as opposed to the knowledge contained in the documentation itself. We distinguish between *inter* and *intra-document* knowledge among documents. Intra-document knowledge pertains to relationships found within each of the documents as separate entities. For example, the relationships described between the various document components: paragraphs, sections, chapters etc. are part of the document's intra-document knowledge. This knowledge, which is extracted from the documents as parse-trees, is stored in an enhanced form in the context-base using the process described in the previous section. Thus, the requirement of efficient traversal of the forest of trees kept in the context base becomes of paramount importance in the implementation of the system and has, to a large extent, motivated us in the choice of deductive database (DD) technology for the project.

Inter-document knowledge pertains to relationships among separate documents in the document repositories. Typical relationships include common geographical sites or institutions at which documents originated, temporal relationships among documents and other relationships, of particular importance to individual users of the system. We elaborate on this subject later in this paper.

A third component of the context-base is the Thesaurus. As mentioned in Sec. 2, it is used to narrow or broaden the search terms presented to the document server. In our case the Data for the Thesaurus were given and these determined a set of relations such as broader_term, narrower_term, definition, citation, synonym, and scope. These relations can be queried to assist the user in the formulation of the right query to the document sources. Presently, the volume of the Thesaurus is on the order of 30,000 terms.

Another aspect that warrants in our view the use of DD technology is *Management of Change:* this problem needs to be examined from both the system administration perspective as well as the individual users'. The glut of information problem that we mentioned in the introduction forces the Information Center administration to regulate and control not only the intake of documents but also the outflow: documents that have become outdated or whose content is not relevant anymore to the present decision-making needs. The individual user typically responds to changing policies or other events and hence his/her needs rapidly change over time. As needs change, the capability to rapidly update and modify the views of the information presented to users must be available. We believe that DD technology can provide the flexibility combined with acceptable performance to accommodate this rapid change.

### 4.1 Logical Organization of the Context Base

Table 1 depicts the logical organization of the context base. It is divided into 5 sections:

1. Intra-document relations. This section contains the schema information for the `intra` relation containing the parse trees for the documents. Each component node has its own ID and the tree is represented by a parent-child relationship between nodes. `intra` contains also the additional information extracted during the parsing such as the physical layout of each node of the parse tree (page number, number of lines) used to generate the "display package" sent to the client viewer via a JAVA applet.
2. Inter-document relations. Presently, this section contains the `doc` relation which contains a record for each document with global information about it: origins, date of creation, title and other information.
3. Thesaurus information. This section contains the relation declarations required for the thesaurus. Some of these relations were mentioned earlier in this section.
4. Expanded information. The expanded information is required to augment the intra-document knowledge derived from the parse process. It contains derived, aggregate information about each of the documents. For example, for each node of the parse tree it contains the aggregate subtree size and range of node id's for the subtree of which the node is the root. This information, which is required for display purposes, can only be derived once the parse tree is materialized in the `intra` relation[6].
5. Display rules. Once the document information is collected and expanded, then a query form, compiled from the display rules, determines which portion of the information should be packaged and sent to the client for viewing. The portion is hit-dependent. We elaborate on this topic in the next section. Other rules are used to form query forms that can be invoked by the user to respectively request more or less information.

---

[6] In principle, this information could be collected "on the fly," during the parsing process. We do not however have any control over this process, nor do we know whether it is bottom-up. Therefore this option does not exist in our case.

| sec. | function | relations | size |
|---|---|---|---|
| 1 | intra-document | `intra` | ≈2000 records/doc |
| 2 | inter-document | `doc` | 1 record (≈200 bytes)/doc |
| 3 | thesaurus | `broader_term` `narrower_term` `definition` `citation` `synonym` `scope` | 30,000 terms |
| 4 | expanded | `stats` | one record for each `intra` record |
| 5 | display | `display rules` | 22 rules (incl. book and house-keeping rules) |

**Table 1.** Logical organization of the context base

## 4.2 Display and Interaction with Relevant Information

Figure 3 depicts the view of a document when seen by the user through a web browser[7]. In the lower part of this view a sequence of "thumb nails," each representing a page of the underlying document, can be seen. The thumb nails cannot be read but they contain sufficient information to form a birds'-eye (meta) view that reveals the informational outlines of the document and allows the user to form an opinion as to the actual relevance of the underlying information. The user can zoom in on the details by clicking on a thumbnail; thus causing the retrieval of the actual textual component containing the page. Each of the sections, graphs, tables and diagrams on a page can be discerned at the meta-level: sections of the document that were hit i.e., contain terms that were included in the user-query, have a different color which is determined by a relevance ranking formula. The user can, for example, easily observe the density of hits without having to retrieve the document itself.

Not all of the pages of the underlying document are represented at the same level. Portions of the document that are deemed irrelevant to the user-query are aggregated into "piles," represented by special, stack-like thumb nails. Clicking on a pile causes the pile to open and to display each of its included pages. Note that the structure is recursive: a pile can contain a set of pages and next-level piles which in turn, can be opened again.

Displaying an amount of information at the meta level, of interest to the user, is a critical issue. The options range between a "maximal" approach in which each page of the underlying document is represented by a thumbnail at the meta level when the document is hit anywhere, to a "minimal" approach in which only those pages in the document that were actually hit are represented. Both options are unsatisfactory: the maximal option is essentially that what the present generation of document retrieval systems offers. Thus, if the document

---

[7] In the actual display, the bars shown in different grey shades in the picture, are different colors, representing the relevancy of the documents in the query result.

379

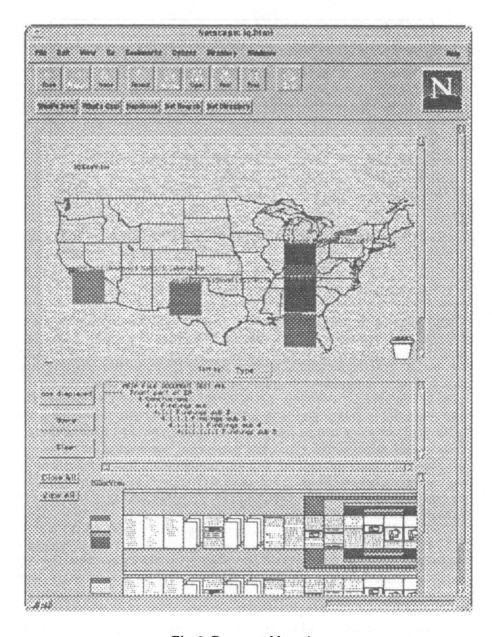

**Fig. 3.** Document Meta-view

has a volume of say 400 pages, then the user is forced to sift trough this volume of thumb nails to locate the information of interest. On the other hand, the minimal approach reveals only the immediate pages containing the hits which is too little. Normally, the immediate context around the hit is of importance to gain the right amount of information. The display rules in the context base derive this information from the intra-document data and knowledge of the hits. The hit-list of components, produced by a user-query and returned by the document retrieval system, is fed to the display query-form of the context base. The result is packaged and sent to the client for display by the browser.

Figure 4 depicts the parse tree of a document. This information is kept, as we mentioned, in the intra relation. For reasons of brevity the following description is a simplification of the operation of the real system. We have omitted many details that are not essential to the understanding of the principles involved.

Each of the nodes has its own id (tag) and represents a document component. As described in sec. 3, Nodes are typed, types being "paragraph," "section," "table," "figure," etc. A subset of the types is declared to be *stop_nodes*. A stop node, like stops in a zoom-lens, defines the next level of expansion or contraction of the information. Assume that the only stop type is "section" (a sub-section is also of type "section"). Thus, expanding a section reveals all of the components directly in this section and the headers of the next-level sections. In the Figure 4

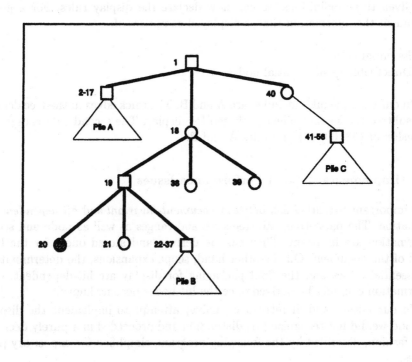

**Fig. 4.** Parse tree of a document

the squares denote stop nodes. In the example {1, 2, 19, 22, 41} are stop nodes and the other nodes are non-stop nodes. Hits are depicted by a filled node. In this example node 20 is hit. Note that, in general, hits can occur anywhere in the tree. A hit to an interior node means that the header title of the corresponding component was hit.

The *scope* of a stop node $N$ is the set of all non-stop nodes $\{N_1, N_2, \ldots\}$ such that,

1. there exists a path from each $N_i, i = 1, 2, \ldots$ to $N$, and,
2. the path does not include another stop-node $S, S \neq N$.

In our example, the scope of stop node 1 is {18, 38, 39, 40}.

An *expanded scope* is a scope containing node(s) that have been hit. In our example the scope of stop-node 19 is expanded and contains {19, 20, 21}. Note that the stop-node itself is included in the expansion.

A *pile* is a non-expanded scope. In the example we have included three piles. The root of each of these is labeled with the range of its id's. The root id of Pile A is 2 and its highest id is 17.

The *essential nodes* are the nodes in the expanded scopes and the nodes along the paths from roots of expanded scopes (subtrees) to the root of the tree. In our example the essential nodes are {1, 18, 19, 20, 21}.

Given these definitions we can now declare the display rules. For a given document the information that is displayed comprises of:

1. Essential nodes.
2. Direct siblings of essential nodes.

In our example piles included are A and B. The thick edges in the tree denote the subtree (nodes and piles) packaged for display. The second rule causes the inclusion of {38, 39, 40} and piles A and B.

## 4.3 Implementation and Performance Issues

It is important to distinguish between *document-invariant* and *hit-dependent* information. The parse-tree, sub-tree sizes and ranges as well as node and scope information are invariant. They can be derived and stored once, for the lifetime of the document. On the other hand, scope expansions, the determination of essential nodes and the final packaging for display are hit-dependent: this information can only be derived once the hit nodes become known.

In our initial (and in retrospect, naive) attempt to implement the display method we did not recognize this distinction and proceeded in a purely declarative fashion, described by the following program, simplified for expository purposes.

```
scope(X,Y) <-
        intra(X,_),
        stop_node(X),
        path(Y,X),
        ¬stop_node(Y).


expand(Z) <-
        hit(Y),
        scope(X,Y),
        scope(X,Z).


pile(X) <-
        scope(X,_),
        ¬expand(X).

essential(Z) <-
        path(Z,0),
        expand(Y),
        path(Y,Z).


display(X) <- essential(X).
display(X) <-
        essential(Y),
        intra(X,Y),
        pile(X).
```

The query ?display(X) produces the requisite information for the package but at a heavy cost since the document-invariant data are computed over and again. A cost-effective solution to the problem combines the declarative with a procedural method: the intermediate results, derived by each of the rules in the program above, are stored by updating auxiliary relations in the context base. For example, the result of the scope derivation is stored as,

```
store_scope <-
        scope(X,Y),
        +scope_rel(X,Y).
```

Where scope_rel(X,Y) is an extension to the database to store this intermediate result. The expand rule uses its result for its own derivation and each subsequent result is produced, in sequence, by a derivation from the intermediate data produced at the previous step. Note that within each step the order of derivation is still undefined and immaterial. The performance improvement over the naive method is more than an order of magnitude: for a document on the order of 1500 nodes the naive method requires approx. 360 seconds while the declarative/procedural method described here requires approx. 10 seconds.

## 4.4  Inter-Document Knowledge

Up to this point we have discussed the logical structure of a single document and its uses in the abstraction of the informational content of the document. Other useful knowledge can be found and utilized when the relationships among different documents are considered as well. The upper part of the view in Figure 3 shows how the result of a user query is geographically distributed: the documents in the hit list are superimposed on a US map and are clustered by their site of origin. The user observes for example, that a certain topic which was the intention of his/her query, generated a large volume of documentation at Argonne National Laboratory, Argonne, Illinois, without having to descend to the actual documentation level to reach this conclusion.

To offer the information in this form, documents are linked by their site of origin and this information is kept in the context base. The user can move from the geographical ("where") view to e.g., a temporal view where the result of his query is superimposed on a time line so that he/she can conclude *when* a certain topic was of interest. From each of these views the user can move to each of the individual documents as described in the previous sections. The user can thus explore the information from different angles and rapidly form an opinion.

We have assumed that the "where" and "when" views of information are generic and of use to a wide user population. These views are thus included as a part of the present $\mathcal{IQ}$ system. The templates (maps, time lines) required to display them are permanently kept at the client side and query results are superimposed so that only the essential information is sent from the server. Other views of the information may be user-specific or specific to certain sub-populations of the users. For example, a user may be interested in all the documentation of person(s) with whom he/she collaborated in the past on a specific topic (a "whom" view). To implement such views, the user needs the capability to declare a set of rules, extending the context base schema for this purpose, as well as the necessary client templates. This $\mathcal{IQ}$ capability will be the topic of research of the next prototype of the system. We believe that the declarative nature of deductive database technology makes it very suitable for supporting this extension requirement.

## 5  Conclusion

In this paper we have described the prototype of a system, intended to enhance the user benefit of information retrieval from existing systems. The system allows for the continuous utilization of existing information retrieval systems albeit, at the expense of reengineering the content of these systems, as described in Sec. 3. There exists therefore a trade-off between the initial investment required for document preparation and the continuous benefit of the added context knowledge produced by the process. Over time, as the added cost of document preparation decreases due to the introduction of automatic tagging methods, it is clear that the approach advocated here is advantageous compared with current practices.

From a systems' perspective, $\mathcal{IQ}$ is a form of middle ware, interspersed between the underlying IR systems and the user-clients. It is not geared towards any particular method and can thus be used simultaneously with a multitude of different retrieval technologies. The economy of implementation is further enhanced by its integration with standard web tools for the distribution and visualization of the results, such as JAVA. The system is still in its first phase of development and it is too early to draw definitive conclusions regarding the use of Deductive Database technology as the implementation tool. At this stage we have demonstrated the feasibility of the concept of an Information Lens. The objectives ahead include the extension of these ideas to include inter-document knowledge as previously discussed and, most importantly, the real test will come when the $\mathcal{IQ}$ system is applied to large volumes of prepared documentation. Performance and acceptable response times for user-interaction are key to the success and still remain to be shown. Our experience so far suggests that the right balance between the procedural and declarative components is critical to achieving an acceptable performance; the use of $\mathcal{LDL}++$ allows for a great deal of flexibility in this respect.

DD technology has been developed in the context of structured, relational data. This application area demonstrates that there is a significant degree of structure in textual data which lends itself to treatment by the traditional database methods, which hitherto has not been addressed by the IR research community. We expect and hope therefore that this paper will contribute towards the opening of a "new frontier" in database research that will look into the combined use of structured and non-structured data.

Lastly, the subject of interacting with information via WWW will play an increasing role in this research area. The difficulties in describing these forms of interaction using the traditional text-based medium, such as this paper, have become painfully obvious. The authors would like, therefore, to use this opportunity to exhort the community to regard the Web and all of the rich information exchange opportunities it affords, not only as a subject of research but also as a medium and tool for the publication of the results and the organization of future meetings in this area.

# References

[AOTZ] N. Arni, K. Ong, S. Tsur, and C. Zaniolo. $\mathcal{LDL}++$ : A second-generation deductive database system. Submitted for publication.

[Cro95] W. Bruce Croft. What Do People Want from Information Retrieval? (The Top 10 Research Issues for Companies that Use and Sell IR systems). *D-Lib Magazine*, November 1995.

[EXC95] http://www.excalib.com, 1995. Web Page, Excalibur Technologies, Inc.

[GM95] J. Gossling and H. McGilton. The JAVA Language: A White Paper. http://java.sun.com/whitepaper/java-whitepaper-1.html, 1995.

[HAR95] The harvest information discovery system. http://harvest.cs.colorado.edu, 1995. Web Page, Harvest Project, University of Colorado.

[PLS95] http://www.pls.com, 1995. Web Page, Personal Library Software Inc.

[Smi92]  Joan M. Smith. *SGML and Related Standards Document and Processing Languages*. Ellis Horwood Limited, 1992.

[WAI95]  Power tools for online publishing. http://www.wais.com, 1995. Web Page, WAIS Inc.

# Language Extensions

# Arithmetic and Aggregate Operators in Deductive Object-Oriented Databases

Gillian Dobbie[1] and Rodney Topor[2]

[1] Department of Computer Science
Victoria University of Wellington
PO Box 600
New Zealand
gill@comp.vuw.ac.nz
[2] School of Computing and
Information Technology
Griffith University
Nathan, Qld 4111
Australia
rwt@cit.gu.edu.au

**Abstract.** We extend our previous mathematical foundation for a deductive object-oriented language called Gulog to include arithmetic and aggregate operators. We describe the semantics of the extended language and present a corresponding query evaluation procedure.

## 1 Introduction

### 1.1 The problem

Arithmetic operators [3] and aggregate operators [14] have been added to realtional and deductive databases and logic programming in order to make the language more expressive. The semantics of these operators in logic programming is now understood [14]. This work has been broadened by Harel in his discussion of recursive languages, which are a generalization of languages with arithmetic [5]. However, it is not well-understood how arithmetic and aggregate operators interact with the features of deductive object-oriented languages. Mathematical foundations have been defined for deductive object-oriented languages [1, 7]. However, none of these include arithmetic and aggregate operators in their definitions. Some practical deductive object-oriented database systems like Coral++ [12], and LDL++ [15] do include arithmetic and aggregates operators, but the authors do not investigate how arithmetic and aggregate operators interact with the object-oriented features.

Previously, we provided a mathematical foundation for a range of deductive and object-oriented features by defining the semantics of a language called Gulog [4]. However, there are queries which are quite natural that cannot be expressed in Gulog. For example, it is not possible to count the number of students in a class, say COMP101, or count the number of students who have passed an exam, say the final exam for class COMP101. These kinds of queries are possible if we include arithmetic and aggregate operators in the language. In this paper we show

- how a deductive object-oriented database language can be extended to include arithmetic and aggregate operators
- how arithmetic and aggregate operators interact with other features in deductive object-oriented database languages
- what the meaning of queries and programs is in this language and
- how queries can be evaluated in deductive object-oriented databases?

### 1.2 Main results

We describe a mathematical foundation for a deductive object-oriented language with arithmetic and aggregate operators. We do this by extending the syntax and semantics of a language called

Gulog to include these operators. A naive extension can lead to ill-defined programs, so we first identify simple syntactic restrictions that ensure programs are simple, and hence have clear, intuitive meanings. We then extend the preferred model semantics of Gulog to allow for arithmetic and aggregate operators, and prove that every simple program has a unique preferred model and hence an unambiguous (and natural) meaning. Finally, we present a query evaluation procedure for simple programs. The procedure consists of a translation of a well-defined Gulog program with arithmetic and aggregate operators to a modularly stratified Datalog program with arithmetic and aggregate operators, followed by the application of a standard query evaluation procedure for modularly stratified Datalog programs. We prove that this procedure is sound with respect to the preferred model semantics for well-defined programs.

These results contribute to the theory of database languages that involve deductive, object-oriented and arithmetic components.

## 2 Technical details

Researchers have considered how arithmetic and aggregate operators interact with features of deductive databases. The most comprehensive coverage to date is [14]. There has been no work done specifically considering how these operators interact with features of object-oriented databases. This is the area covered we cover in this paper. Our work follows from that in the deductive database area.

In this section, we describe how Gulog can be extended in order to investigate the interaction of arithmetic and aggregate operators with features of object-oriented databases. In Section 2.1, we outline the syntax of a deductive object-oriented language with arithmetic and aggregate operators. Then, in Section 2.2, we describe a syntactic restriction which defines programs that have an intuitive meaning. We call these programs, simple programs. In Section 2.3, we provide a model semantics for simple programs based on preferred models and prove that every simple program has a unique preferred model. In Section 2.4, we discuss a query evaluation procedure for programs in this language, and prove that the procedure is sound with respect to the preferred model semantics. The query evaluation procedure that we describe involves translation. Although, a direct implementation is also possible. We present the translation to Datalog as a convenience, to allow us to build on correctness results for Datalog evaluation. To conclude, in Section 2.5, we describe the kinds of queries that cannot be expressed even when Gulog is extended with arithmetic and aggregate operators.

### 2.1 Syntax

In this section, we describe how arithmetic and aggregate operators can be included in Gulog [4]. In order to make the results clearer, we do not consider negation or multiple inheritance in this paper. The results can be straightforwardly extended to cover these concepts.

We start by illustrating the syntax of Gulog with an example.

*Example 1.* Clause 1 assigns the action *lower pressure* to a particular system failure (sf) if the pressure is high for that system failure.

$$\{x{:}sf\} \vdash x[action{\twoheadrightarrow}\text{``}lower\ pressure\text{''}] \leftarrow x[pressure \rightarrow high] \tag{1}$$

The variable typing $\{x{:}sf\}$ is separated from the rest of the clause by the symbol $\vdash$. Atom $\{x{:}sf\} \vdash x[action{\twoheadrightarrow}\text{``}lower\ pressure\text{''}]$ is the head of the clause. Atom $\{x{:}sf\} \vdash x[pressure \rightarrow high]$ is the body of the clause. The variable typing $\{x{:}sf\}$ tells us that in this clause the variable $x$ has type $sf$. The method atom $\{x{:}sf\} \vdash x[action{\twoheadrightarrow}\text{``}lower\ pressure\text{''}]$ describes a multi-valued method *action* that has a value *lower pressure* for an object $x$. The atom $\{x{:}sf\} \vdash x[pressure \rightarrow high]$ describes a functional method *pressure* that has a value *high* for an object $x$.

Method atoms may take arguments. In multi-valued method 2, we describe a method *failure* that acts on objects of type *reactor* with an argument of type *date* and returns a value of type *sf*.

$$\{x{:}reactor, y{:}sf, d{:}date\} \vdash x[failure@d{\twoheadrightarrow}y]. \tag{2}$$

In Gulog, the schema is separated from the program. The following example illustrates the kind of declarations allowed in the schema.

*Example 2.* Consider the following declarations.

$$r1{:}reactor \tag{3}$$
$$psf < sf \tag{4}$$
$$reactor[parts{\Rightarrow}part] \tag{5}$$
$$measurements(reactor, pressure\_sensor) \tag{6}$$

Object declaration 3 declares an object r1 is of type *reactor*. Type lattice declaration 4 declares that *psf* (pressure system failure) is a subtype of *sf* (system failure). Multi-valued method declaration 5 declares a 0-ary multi-valued method *parts*, which when applied to objects of type *reactor* returns values of type *part*. The signature of 0-ary multi-valued method *parts* is *reactor*$\Rightarrow$*part*. Finally predicate declaration 6 declares a 2-ary predicate *measurements* with signature *reactor* $\times$ *pressure_sensor*.

We now describe how Gulog can be extended to include arithmetic and aggregate operators. Arithmetic and aggregate atoms are allowed in the bodies of clauses. We illustrate the use of an aggregate atom in the following example. The syntax of aggregate atoms follows that introduced in [6].

*Example 3.* Clause 7 counts the number of failures that are recorded for each reactor and stores the reactor identifier and count in a relation *failure_count*.

$$\{x{:}reactor, y{:}date, z{:}sf, c{:}integer\} \vdash failure\_count(x, c) \leftarrow \tag{7}$$
$$group\_by(x[failure@y{\twoheadrightarrow}z], [x], c = count)$$

First, we illustrate the result of a query and then we describe the syntax of the clause. If the query $\{y{:}reactor, z{:}integer\} \vdash \leftarrow failure\_count(y, z)$ was applied to a database containing

$$r1[failure@12Sept95{\twoheadrightarrow}\text{"cooling system failure"}]$$
$$r2[failure@14Sept95{\twoheadrightarrow}\text{"system failure"}]$$
$$r1[failure@20Sept95{\twoheadrightarrow}\text{"condenser failure"}]$$

then the result would be $failure\_count(r1, 2), failure\_count(r2, 1)$.

In clause 7, the *group_by* atom in the body of the clause groups the *failure* method on the object $x$ to which it is applied and counts the number of *failures* for each $x$. The aggregate operator *count* does not take an argument as it is the count of the number of *failures* for each $x$.

Arithmetic operators are modeled as predicate atoms. There are built-in predicates for equality, arithmetic comparisons, and arithmetic operators that operate on integers. Aggregate operators are *sum*, *count*, *min*, *max* and *average*. An aggregate atom is defined as follows: $\Gamma \vdash group\_by(A, [x_1, \ldots, x_n], y = f(x_1, \ldots, x_p, z_1, \ldots, z_q))$ is an aggregate atom where $\Gamma$ is the variable typing for the variables in the atom, $A$ is an atom involving variables $(x_1, \ldots, x_n, z_1, \ldots, z_m)$, $x_1, \ldots, x_n$ are the *group_by* variables, $f$ is an aggregate operator, $(x_1, \ldots, x_p, z_1, \ldots, z_q)$ is a list of variables involving only some subset of the variables $(x_1, \ldots, x_n, z_1, \ldots, z_m)$. This list may be empty. Similarly, there may be no *group_by* variables. The variables $z_1, \ldots, z_m$ may not appear outside the aggregate atom. A ground instance of an aggregate atom is obtained by replacing the variables $x_1, \ldots, x_n, y$ by ground terms $x_{1_0}, \ldots, x_{n_0}, y_0$. The variables $z_1, \ldots, z_m$ are not instantiated in such a ground instance.

*Example 4.* In this example, we describe an aggregate atom and present a ground instance of that atom. Assume a set of declarations including *r1:reactor*.

The atom $A = \{y:integer, z:part\} \vdash group\_by(r1[parts \twoheadrightarrow z], [\,], y = count)$ gives the cardinality of the set of *parts* for reactor r1. The atom $group\_by(r1[parts \twoheadrightarrow z], [\,], 100 = count)$ is a ground instance of $A$. Note that variable $z$ is not instantiated in this ground instance of $A$.

**Definition 1.** Given a variable typing $\Gamma$, atom $\Gamma \vdash A$, and atoms, arithmetic atoms or aggregate atoms $\Gamma \vdash B_1, \ldots, \Gamma \vdash B_n$, $\Gamma \vdash A \leftarrow B_1 \wedge \cdots \wedge B_n$ is an *aggregate clause*. Atom $\Gamma \vdash A$ is the *head atom* of the clause. Atoms $\Gamma \vdash B_1, \ldots, \Gamma \vdash B_n$ are the *body atoms*.

An aggregate program is a set of aggregate clauses and is associated with a set of declarations.

**Definition 2.** An *aggregate program* with respect to a set of declarations $D$ is a finite set of aggregate clauses with respect to the set of declarations, $D$.

## 2.2 Simple programs

To ensure that programs have well-defined semantics, we impose restrictions that ensure they are "stratified", functional methods are single-valued, and the variables in arithmetic atoms will have a finite number of values assigned to them.

The following example illustrates a program that does not have a well-defined semantics.

*Example 5.* Assume appropriate declarations including *r1:reactor*, and consider the following program.

$$\{x:reactor, z:integer\} \vdash x[total \twoheadrightarrow z] \leftarrow group\_by(x[total \twoheadrightarrow z], [x], z = count)$$

This program is attempting to group a set of methods while generating new elements in those sets. We claim that this program does not have an intuitive meaning and so does not have well-defined semantics.

A program is inheritance-stratified if there are no cycles in the definition of a method or an aggregate atom. That is, no method depends on an inherited definition of the same method and no atom is defined in terms of itself in an aggregate atom.

**Definition 3.** An aggregate program $P$ with respect to a set of declarations $D$ is *inheritance-stratified* (or *i-stratified*) if there exists a mapping $\mu$ from the set of ground atoms to the set of non-negative integers such that, for every ground instance $C\theta$ of every clause $C$ in $P$ with respect to $D$, where $A$ is the head of the instance $C\theta$,

- $\mu(A') \leq \mu(A)$, where $A'$ is an atom or arithmetic atom in the body of the clause instance $C\theta$,
- $\mu(B') < \mu(A)$ for every ground instance $B'$ of $A'$, where $A'$ is the atom in a ground aggregation atom in $(\Gamma \vdash group\_by(A', [x_1, \ldots, x_n], y_0 = f(x_1, \ldots, x_p, z_1, \ldots, z_p)))\theta$ in the body of the ground clause $C\theta$,
- $\mu(B') < \mu(A)$ for every ground instance $C'\theta'$ that possibly overrides $C\theta$, where $B'$ is an atom or arithmetic atom in the body of $C'\theta'$, or for every ground instance $B'$ of $A'$ where $A'$ is the atom in a ground aggregation atom in $(\Gamma \vdash group\_by(A', [x_1, \ldots, x_n], y_0 = f(x_1, \ldots, x_p, z_1, \ldots, z_p)))\theta$ in the body of $C'\theta'$,
- $\mu(A') \leq \mu(A)$ for every ground instance $C'\theta'$ that possibly overrides $C\theta$, where $A'$ is the head of $C'\theta'$.

The second point in the above definition is the additional restriction required in the presence of aggregates.

*Example 6.* Consider again the declarations and program in example 5. The i-stratification of this program requires:

$$\mu(r1[total\twoheadrightarrow z_0]) < \mu(r1[total\twoheadrightarrow z_0])$$

As expected, this program is not i-stratified.

Again assume appropriate declarations including r1:*reactor*, and now consider the following program.

$$\{x{:}reactor, y{:}string, z{:}integer\} \vdash x[total\twoheadrightarrow z] \leftarrow$$
$$group\_by(x[action\twoheadrightarrow y], [x], z = count)$$

This program groups the *action* methods and gives information to method *total*. We claim that this program does have an intuitive meaning and also has a well-defined semantics. The i-stratification of this program requires:

$$\mu(r1[total\twoheadrightarrow z_0]) < \mu(r1[action\twoheadrightarrow y])$$

As expected, this program is i-stratified.

The class of simple aggregate programs is a generalization of the class of simple Gulog programs. It is necessary to extend the syntactic condition which ensures that functional methods are single-valued to ensure that a finite number of values will be assigned to variables in arithmetic atoms. Such an extension involves the definition of "finiteness dependency". The following definition and example are from [13].

**Definition 4.** A *finiteness dependency* on a predicate $R$ is a pair $S \rightarrow j$, where $j$ and each element of $S$ are argument positions of $R$. A database $B$ *satisfies* a finiteness dependency $S \rightarrow j$ for a predicate $R$ if, for every tuple $t$ in $R$, the set of tuples $\{s[j] \mid s \in R \text{ and } s[S] = t[S]\}$ is finite (where $t[S]$ is the projection of $t$ onto the positions in $S$.)

*Example 7.* The arithmetic relations $=$ and $+$ have the following finiteness dependencies.

$$= \{1\} \rightarrow 2, \{2\} \rightarrow 1$$
$$+ \{1,2\} \rightarrow 3, \{2,3\} \rightarrow 1, \{3,1\} \rightarrow 2$$

Consider $= \{1\} \rightarrow 2, \{2\} \rightarrow 1$. One way this can be read is that if the first argument of the $=$ predicate has a finite domain then the second argument has a finite domain. Similarly, if the second argument has a finite domain then the first argument has a finite domain. Comparison relations do not have any finiteness dependencies. Each (finite) $k$-ary base relation has $k$ dependencies $\emptyset \rightarrow j$, for $1 \leq j \leq k$.

In [2], Abiteboul and Hull showed that compile-time consistency checking to ensure that functional methods are single-valued is undecidable. To ensure that functional methods really are single-valued, we impose the following condition on programs. We extend this condition to ensure that there is a finite number of results for queries involving arithmetic atoms.

**Definition 5.** A variable $z$ is *restricted* with respect to the terms $\{t, t_1, \ldots, t_n\}$ in the conjunction $C$ if the following conditions hold.

- $C$ contains a method atom $t'[m'@t'_1, \ldots, t'_k \rightarrow z]$ and each variable in $t', t'_1, \ldots, t'_k$ either occurs in $t, t_1, \ldots, t_n$ or is itself restricted with respect to $\{t, t_1, \ldots, t_n\}$ in the remainder of $C$. For example, the variable $z$ is restricted with respect to $\{a, x\}$ in the conjunction $a[m'@x \rightarrow y] \wedge a[m''@y \rightarrow z]$.
- $C$ contains an arithmetic atom $p(t'_1, \ldots, t'_n)$, some $t'_j$ is $z$, $p$ has a finiteness dependency $S \rightarrow j$, and every variable in $\{t'_i \mid i \in S\}$ is restricted with respect to $\{t, t_1, \ldots, t_n, z\}$ in the remainder of $C$.

That is, a variable is restricted with respect to a set of terms in a conjunction if that variable will have a finite number of values assuming the set of terms has a finite domain.

We are now able to define the class of programs in which functional methods are single-valued and the variables in arithmetic atoms have a finite number of values. We call programs in this class well-defined programs.

**Definition 6.** An aggregate program $P$ with respect to a set of declarations $D$ is *well-defined* if the following conditions hold:

- For each clause $\Gamma \vdash t[m@t_1, \ldots, t_n \to t'] \leftarrow C$ in $P$ with respect to $D$, $t'$ is either an object symbol or is a variable that is restricted with respect to $\{t, t_1, \ldots, t_n\}$ in $C$.
- For each functional method $m$ with signature $\tau \times \tau_1 \times \cdots \times \tau_n \to \tau'$, and for each type $\sigma \leq \tau$, program $P$ with respect to $D$ does *not* contain two clauses

$$\Gamma \vdash t[m@t_1, \ldots, t_n \to s] \leftarrow C$$
$$\Gamma \vdash t'[m@t'_1, \ldots, t'_n \to s'] \leftarrow C'$$

such that $\Gamma \vdash t{:}\sigma$, $\Gamma \vdash t'{:}\sigma$, and atoms $t[m@t_1, \ldots, t_n \to x]$ and $t'[m@t'_1, \ldots, t'_n \to x']$ (where $x$ and $x'$ are new variables) are unifiable. This together with the first condition ensures that functional methods really are single-valued.
- For each clause $\Gamma \vdash A \leftarrow \cdots \wedge B \wedge \cdots$ where $B$ is an arithmetic atom, every variable $t_i$ in $B$ is restricted with respect to $\emptyset$ in the body of the clause.

The third point is the additional restriction required in the presence of arithmetic. It restricts the class of well-defined programs to those in which arithmetic atoms have a finite domain.

*Example 8.* This example presents two programs that aren't well-defined and one that is well-defined.

First, consider the aggregate clause:

$$\{x{:}integer, y{:}integer\} \vdash p(x, y) \leftarrow x + y = 5$$

We would not expect this clause to be well-defined because there are an infinite number of values that can be assigned to $x$ and $y$ to make the body of the clause true. Following our intuition, it is not suprising that $x$ and $y$ are not restricted with respect to $\emptyset$ in the body of this clause. Thus this program is not well-defined.

Secondly, consider the clause:

$$\{x{:}integer, y{:}integer\} \vdash o[m \to x] \leftarrow x + y = 5$$

Again, we would not expect this clause to be well-defined because there are an infinite number of values that can be assigned to $x$ and $y$ to make the body of the clause true. It is not suprising that $x$ is not restricted with respect to $\{o\}$ in the body of the clause.

Finally, consider the aggregate clause:

$$\{x{:}integer, y{:}integer\} \vdash p(x, y) \leftarrow x + y = 5 \wedge y = 3$$

We now find that $x$ and $y$ are restricted with respect to $\emptyset$ in the body of this clause. Thus this program is well-defined.

The following class of programs is particularly important because programs in this class have an intuitive meaning. That is, the interaction of the arithmetic and aggregate operators with other features of deductive object-oriented databases is well understood in this class of programs.

**Definition 7.** A program $P$ with respect to a set of declarations $D$ is called *simple* if $P$ with respect to $D$ is i-stratified and well-defined.

In the next section we show that every simple program has a unique preferred model that defines a natural semantics, and a simple evaluation procedure that is sound with respect to the resulting preferred model semantics.

## 2.3 Semantics

In this section, we describe the declarative semantics of programs. As in logic programming, the meaning of a program or database can be given by a preferred model. We first extend the definition of truth value to describe values for aggregate atoms.

**Definition 8.** Let $I$ be an interpretation, $L$ be an atom, and $\mathcal{T}$ a term assignment (with respect to $\Gamma$). Then an atom, arithmetic atom or aggregate atom, $A$, is given a *truth value* in $I$ (with respect to $\mathcal{T}$ and $\Gamma$) as follows:

- If $A$ is $\Gamma \vdash p(t_1, \ldots, t_n)$, and $t'_1, \ldots, t'_n$ are the term assignments of $t_1, \ldots, t_n$ (with respect to $\mathcal{T}$ and $\Gamma$), then $A$ is true in $I$ (with respect to $\mathcal{T}$ and $\Gamma$) if $p(t'_1, \ldots, t'_n) \in I$.

- If $A$ is $\Gamma \vdash t[m@t_1, \ldots, t_k \rightarrow t_n]$, and $t', t'_1, \ldots, t'_k, t'_n$ are the term assignments of $t, t_1, \ldots, t_k, t_n$ (with respect to $\mathcal{T}$ and $\Gamma$), then $A$ is true in $I$ (with respect to $\mathcal{T}$ and $\Gamma$) if $t'[m@t'_1, \ldots, t'_k \rightarrow t'_n] \in I$.

- If $A$ is $\Gamma \vdash t[m@t_1, \ldots, t_k \twoheadrightarrow s]$, and $t', t'_1, \ldots, t'_k, s'$ are the term assignments of $t, t_1, \ldots, t_k, s$ (with respect to $\mathcal{T}$ and $\Gamma$), then $A$ is true in $I$ (with respect to $\mathcal{T}$ and $\Gamma$) if $t'[m@t'_1, \ldots, t'_k \twoheadrightarrow s'] \in I$.

- If $A$ is $\Gamma \vdash group\_by(A'(t, t_1, \ldots, t_n), [t], y = f(t, t_1, \ldots, t_n))$ and $t', t'_1, \ldots, t'_n$ are the term assignments of $t, t_1, \ldots, t_n$ (with respect to $\mathcal{T}$ and $\Gamma$), then $A$ is true in $I$ (with respect to $\mathcal{T}$ and $\Gamma$) if $A'(t', t'_1, \ldots, t'_n) \in I$ and $f(S)$ is defined for the set $S = \{(t', t'_1, \ldots, t'_n) \mid A(t', t'_1, \ldots, t'_n) \in I\}$ and $y = f(S)$.

*Example 9.* Suppose $I = \{r1[parts \twoheadrightarrow valve], r1[parts \twoheadrightarrow heat\_exchanger]\}$. Then the following ground instance is true in $I$:

$$group\_by(r1[parts \twoheadrightarrow x], [\,], 2 = count).$$

A simple program may have more than one minimal model, so we define a priority relation that is used to identify preferred models of a program. As in [8], we can define a priority relationship between ground atoms (using possible overriding and aggregation), and use this to define a preference relationship between models. As in [8], we prefer models in which there are fewer occurrences of higher priority atoms. We say a model of a program $P$ with respect to a set of declarations $D$ is *preferred* if no models of $P$ are preferable to it.

**Definition 9.** Let $P$ be a program with respect to a set of declarations $D$. We define an *priority relation* $<_p$ based on $P$ between ground atoms with respect to $D$. We write $a \leq_p b$ to denote $a <_p b$ or $a = b$. We define the relation $<_p$ by the following rules, for every ground instance $C\theta$ of a clause $C$ in $P$ with respect to $D$:

- $A \leq_p A'$, where $A$ is the head of $C\theta$, and $A'$ is an atom or arithmetic atom in the body of $C\theta$,

- $A <_p B'$ for every ground instance $C'\theta'$ of $C'$ in $P$ with respect to $D$, that possibly overrides $C\theta$, where $A$ is the head of $C\theta$ and $B'$ is an atom or arithmetic atom in the body of $C'\theta'$,

- $A \leq_p A'$ for every ground instance $C'\theta'$ of $C'$ in $P$ with respect to $D$, that possibly overrides $C\theta$, where $A$ is the head of $C\theta$ and $A'$ is the head of $C'\theta'$, and

- $A <_p A'$ where $A$ is the head of $C$ and $A'$ is the ground instance of an atom in the ground aggregation atom in the body of $C$.

and for all ground atoms $A$, $B$, $C$ and $F$:

- if $A \leq_p B$ and $B \leq_p C$, then $A \leq_p C$,
- if $A \leq_p B$ and $B <_p C$ (respectively, $F <_p A$) then $A <_p C$ (respectively, $F <_p B$).

We use the definition in [4] for preferred models and depict that model $M_1$ is preferred over $M_2$ by $M_1 \ll M_2$. The following result holds.

**Theorem 10.** *Let $P$ be a simple program with respect to a set of declarations $D$. Then $P$ with respect to $D$ has exactly one preferred model, which we denote $M_P$. For every other model $M$, we have $M_P \ll M$.*

The proof of this theorem follows from that in [4], which in turn followed from Przymusinski's results for stratified logic programs.

## 2.4 Query evaluation

We now describe an evaluation procedure for a query in this language by translating the program and query to Datalog with aggregates. Because this language is a generalization of Gulog, we can simply extend the translation described for Gulog in Chapter 5 in [4]. In this translation, method atoms are translated to predicates, and overriding is dealt with by adding extra rules which indicate whether a definition from lower in the type hierarchy applies or not. To deal with inheritance, we also add extra rules that describe a type and its subtypes.

In the extended translation from a program written in the language described in this paper to Datalog, an aggregate atom $\Gamma \vdash group\_by(A, [x_1, \ldots, x_n], y = f(x_1, \ldots, x_p, z_1, \ldots, z_q))$ is translated to $\Gamma' \wedge group\_by(A', [x_1, \ldots, x_n], y = f(x_1, \ldots, x_p, z_1, \ldots, z_q))$, where $\Gamma'$ is the translation of $\Gamma$ and $A'$ is the translation of $A$. This extended translation treats aggregate atoms in a similar way to the way negative literals are treated in [4].

We now describe a query evaluation procedure that finds the computed answers for a query $Q$ and a program $P$ with respect to a set of declarations $D$. The computed answer is a set of substitutions. Suppose $\theta$ is a computed answer for a query $Q$ and a program $P$ with respect to a set of declarations $D$, we write $\theta$ is a computed answer for $P \cup \{Q\}$. In [4], we proved that if a simple Gulog program $P$ with respect to $D$ is i-stratified then $P$ with respect to $D$ is m-stratified. (m-stratification is like modular stratification.) Again in [4], we proved that if $P$ with respect to $D$ is m-stratified then its translation $P'$ is modularly stratified, and that the well-founded model of $P'$ is equivalent to the associated model of $P$ with respect to $D$. Ross proves, in [11], that any modularly stratified program can be rewritten as a left-to-right modularly stratified program. Lastly, Ramakrishnan et al. provide a procedure that evaluates programs with left-to-right modularly stratified negation and aggregation in [10] that is sound with respect to well-founded semantics.

The following soundness result then holds.

**Theorem 11.** *Let $P$ with respect to a set of declarations $D$ be a simple program, $M_P$ be the unique preferred model of $P$ with respect to $D$, $Q$ be a query, and $\theta$ be a computed answer for $P \cup \{Q\}$. Then $Q\theta$ is true in the unique preferred model $M_P$.*

## 2.5 Expressibility

It is important to realize not only what can be expressed but also what cannot be expressed in a language. We now discuss what can and cannot be expressed in Gulog with arithmetic and aggregate operators. The addition of arithmetic and aggregate operators to Gulog allows queries that involve counting to be expressed for a first time. With counting it is possible to express queries such as the one in the following example that determines if the size of a relation is even or odd.

*Example 10.* Let $p(0)$ represent true and $p(1)$ represent false. Consider a query that returns true if the size of a relation $q$ is even and false otherwise. This is expressed in the following clause:

$$\{x{:}integer, y{:}integer, z{:}integer\} \vdash p(x) \leftarrow$$
$$group\_by(q(z), [\,], y = count) \wedge x = y \bmod 2.$$

Some queries cannot be expressed even with arithmetic and aggregate operators. Consider a query whose input is a relation, $r$, which has $n$ tuples, and whose output is the cross product of $r$ with itself, $n$ times. As the width of the output relation depends on the data, it is not possible to express such queries in Gulog with arithmetic and aggregate operators.

# References

1. S. Abiteboul. Towards a deductive object oriented database language. *Data and Knowledge Engineering*, 5:263–287, 1990.
2. S. Abiteboul and R. Hull. Data-functions, datalog and negation. In *Proc. of the ACM SIGMOD International Conference on the Management of Data*, pages 143–153, 1988.
3. A. Chandra and D. Harel. Computable queries for relational data bases. *Journal of Computer and System Sciences*, pages 156–178, 1980.
4. G. Dobbie. *Foundations of Deductive Object-Oriented Database Systems*. Phd thesis, University of Melbourne, 1995.
5. D. Harel and T. Hirst. Completeness results for recursive data bases. In *Proceedings of the Twelfth ACM PODS Symposium on Principles of Database Systems*, 1993.
6. D. B. Kemp and P. J. Stuckey. Semantics of logic programs with aggregates. In V. Saraswat and K. Ueda, editors, *Proc. 1991 International Logic Programming Symposium*, pages 387–401, San Diego, USA, 1991.
7. M. Kifer, G. Lausen, and J. Wu. Logical foundations of object-oriented and frame-based languages. Technical Report 90/14 (revised), Department of Computer Science, State University of New York at Stony Brook, 1990. Further revised as Technical Report 93/06, April 1993.
8. T. C. Przymusinski. On the declarative semantics of deductive databases and logic programs. In J. Minker, editor, *Foundations of Deductive Databases and Logic Programming*, pages 193–216. Morgan Kaufmann, 1988. Further revised as [9].
9. T. C. Przymusinski. Every logic program has a natural stratification and an iterated fixed point model. In *Proceedings of the Eighth ACM PODS Symposium on Principles of Database Systems*, pages 11–21, 1989.
10. R. Ramakrishnan, D. Srivastava, and S. Sudarshan. Controlling the Search in Bottom-Up Evaluation. In *Proc. of the Joint Int. Conference and Symposium on Logic Programming*, pages 273–287, Washington DC, November 1992.
11. K. A. Ross. Modular stratification and magic sets for DATALOG programs with negation. In *Proc. of the ACM SIGMOD International Conference on the Management of Data*, pages 161–171, 1990.
12. D. Srivastava, R. Ramakrishnan, P. Seshadri, and S. Sudarshan. Coral++: Adding object-orientation to a logic database language. In *Proc. of the 19th VLDB Conference*, Dublin, Ireland, 1993.
13. R. W. Topor. Safe database queries with arithmetic relations. In *Proc. 14th Australian Computer Science Conference*, pages 02-1-02-13, 1991.
14. A. Van Gelder. Foundations of aggregation in deductive databases. In S. Ceri, K. Tanaka, and S. Tsur, editors, *Proceedings of the Third International Conference on Deductive and Object-Oriented Databases*, 1993.
15. C. Zaniolo, N. Arni, and K. Ong. Negation and aggregates in recursive rules: the LDL++ approach. In S. Ceri, K. Tanaka, and S. Tsur, editors, *Proceedings of the Third International Conference on Deductive and Object-Oriented Databases*, pages 204–221, Arizona, USA, 1993.

# Sequence Datalog: Declarative String Manipulation in Databases*

Anthony Bonner[1]                      Giansalvatore Mecca[2]
bonner@db.toronto.edu                  mecca@dia.uniroma3.it

1 Department of Computer Science - University of Toronto - Toronto, Ont. - Canada
2 D.I.A. - Università della Basilicata - via della Tecnica, 3 - 85100 Potenza, Italy

Abstract. We investigate logic based query languages for sequence databases, that is databases in which strings of symbols over a variable over a fixed alphabet can occur. We discuss different approaches to querying strings, including Prolog and Datalog with function symbols, and argue that all of them have important limitations. We then present an extension of Sequence Datalog, a logic for querying sequence databases, and show how this language can be used to perform structural recursion over sequences.

## 1 Introduction

In the last decade, new applications (e.g. CAD and CASE) have been a powerful driving force in the development of new database technology. New paradigms have arisen (e.g. object logical databases [4]) that provide greater flexibility than the traditional relational model. However, in some application areas, such as genome databases [14] and text databases [10], there is still a need for greater flexibility, both in data representation and manipulation. These applications are characterized by a need to store, manipulate and transform strings.

Strings are a particularly interesting domain for query languages. To comment to say, computations over strings can easily become infinite, even when the underlying alphabet is finite. This is because symbols are allowed to repeat, so the number of possible strings over any finite alphabet is infinite. The researcher thus faces an interesting challenge: on the one hand, the language should provide powerful primitives for restructuring strings; on the other hand, the expressive power of the language should be carefully limited to avoid infinite computations. In [21] we introduced a logic called Sequence Datalog for querying sequence databases. Sequence Datalog is a Horn-like logic with special interpreted function symbols that allow for structured recursion over strings. Sequence Datalog has both a clear declarative semantics and an operational semantics. The semantics are based on fixpoint theory, as in classical logic programming [19], and on a new notion of active domain, called the extended active domain, introduced to

*The first author was partially supported by an operating grant from the Natural Science and Engineering Research Council of Canada (NSERC). The second author was partially supported by 40% MURST, and Consiglio Nazionale delle Ricerche (CNR).

# Sequence Datalog: Declarative String Manipulation in Databases *

Anthony Bonner[1]
bonner@db.toronto.edu

Giansalvatore Mecca[2]
mecca@dis.uniroma1.it

[1] Department of Computer Science – University of Toronto – Toronto, Ont. – Canada
[2] D.I.F.A. – Università della Basilicata – via della Tecnica, 3 – 85100 Potenza, Italy

**Abstract.** We investigate logic-based query languages for sequence databases, that is, databases in which strings of symbols over a fixed alphabet can occur. We discuss different approaches to querying strings, including Prolog and Datalog with function symbols, and argue that all of them have important limitations. We then present the semantics of *Sequence Datalog*, a logic for querying sequence databases, and show how this language can be used to perform structural recursion over sequences.

## 1    Introduction

In the last decade, new applications (*e.g.* CAD and CASE) have been a powerful driving force in the development of new database technology. New paradigms have arisen (*e.g.* object oriented databases [4]) that provide greater flexibility than the traditional relational model. However, in some application areas, such as *genome databases* [14] and *text databases* [16], there is still a need for greater flexibility, both in data representation and manipulation. These applications are characterized by a need to store, manipulate and transform strings.

Strings are a particularly interesting domain for query languages. In contrast to sets, computations over strings can easily become infinite, even when the underlying alphabet is finite. This is because symbols are allowed to repeat; so the number of possible strings over any finite alphabet is infinite. The researcher thus faces an interesting challenge: on the one hand, the language should provide powerful primitives for restructuring strings; on the other hand, the expressive power of the language should be carefully limited, to avoid infinite computations.

In [21], we introduced a logic called *Sequence Datalog* for querying sequence databases. *Sequence Datalog* is a Horn-like logic with special, interpreted function symbols that allow for *structural recursion* over strings. Sequence Datalog has both a clear declarative semantics and an operational semantics. The semantics are based on fixpoint theory, as in classical logic programming [19], and on a new notion of active domain, called the *extended active domain*, introduced to

* The first author was partially supported by an operating grant from the Natural Sciences and Engineering Research Council of Canada (NSERC). The second author was partially supported by MURST and Consiglio Nazionale delle Ricerche (CNR).

allow for a bottom-up evaluation of rules. The language has considerable power to manipulate strings. In fact, Sequence Datalog with stratified negation can express any computable query on sequence databases [22].

In this paper, we discuss in detail the semantics of Sequence Datalog, comparing and contrasting it to traditional logic-based languages. Whereas [21] introduced semantics of Sequence Datalog informally, this paper provides the formal development. The paper is organized as follows. Section 2 discusses other approaches to string manipulation based on logic. Section 3 introduces Sequence Datalog, discussing its syntax and semantics. Section 4 provides preliminary definitions. finally, Section 5, develops the formal semantics of the language.

## 2 Background

In recent years, several query languages for sequence databases have been proposed in the literature. On one hand, there are languages based on functional and algebraic programming [13, 18]. In this context, some sophisticated and expressive languages have been proposed, and great care has been devoted to the development of *tractable* languages, that is, languages whose complexity is in PTIME.

On the other hand, there are languages based on predicate logic [24, 15, 17]. In this context, powerful logics for expressing string transformations have been proposed, but many of them suffer from the difficult trade-off between expressiveness, finiteness and effective computability. In some cases, a great part of the expressive power of the language has to be sacrificed to achieve finiteness. In other cases, both expressiveness and finiteness are achieved, but at expense of an effective procedure for evaluating queries, *i.e.*, at the expense of an operational semantics.

In [15, 27], for example, an *extended relational model* is defined, where each relation is a set of tuples of sequences over a fixed alphabet. A *sequence logic* [15] is then developed based on the notion of *rs-operations*. Each *rs-operation* is either a *merger* or an *extractor*. Intuitively, given a set of patterns, an associated *merger* uses the patterns to "combine" a set of sequences. Likewise, an *extractor* "retrieves" subsequences of a given sequence. The authors introduce the notion of a *generic a-transducer* as the computational counterpart of rs-operations. Based on their sequence logic, two languages for the extended relational model are defined, called the *s-calculus* and the *s-algebra*. The s-calculus allows for unsafe queries, that is, queries whose answers are not computable. A safe subset of the language is then defined and proven equivalent to the s-algebra. Unfortunately, this safe sublanguage cannot express many queries for which the length of the result depends on the database. These include natural queries such as the reverse and complement of a sequence.

This problem is partially solved by the *alignment logic* of [17], an elegant and expressive first-order logic for a relational model with sequences. The computational counterpart of the logic is the class of *multi-tape, nondeterministic, two-way, finite-state automata*, which are used to accept or reject tuples of sequences. In its full version, alignment logic has the power of recursively enumerable sets [23]. A subset of the language called *right restricted formulas* is then developed. For this sublanguage, the safety problem is shown to be decidable, and complexity results related to the polynomial-time hierarchy are presented. Unfortunately, the non-deterministic nature of the computational model makes the evaluation of queries problematic. In particular, because of existential quantification over the infinite universe of sequences, it is not easy to determine the maximum length of the sequences in a query answer, even when the query is known to be safe.

There is also the traditional logic-programming approach [19]. For example, in *Prolog* [12], lists can be used to represent strings, and the language provides a natural "head-tail" constructor for manipulating them. It is also well known [19] that this language is computationally complete on lists. However, the top-down evaluation strategy of Prolog is widely regarded as inadequate for database applications, since it implies a procedural, "tuple-at-a-time" mode of computation; whereas, a non-procedural, set-oriented evaluation strategy is considered an essential feature of database query languages. To solve this problem, one might consider adopting *Datalog* [10] and its bottom-up, set-oriented evaluation strategy, and enriching it with *function symbols* to model lists. Unfortunately, coupling function symbols with bottom-up evaluation can lead to extremely inefficient computations, as the next example shows.

*Example 1.* [**Complement of Binary Strings**] Let `list` be a unary predicate whose extent specifies a set of lists. Each list represents a string of binary symbols, that is, a string over the alphabet $\{0, 1\}$. For each of these lists, we want to construct the complementary list, that is, the list obtained by substituting each 0 by a 1, and each 1 by a 0. This can easily be done in Datalog with function symbols, [3] as follows:

```
r₁: answer(X)                    :- list(Y),
                                    complement(X, Y).

r₂: complement([ ], [ ])         :- true.
r₃: complement([H1|T1], [H2|T2]) :- compl(H1, H2),
                                     complement(T1, T2).

r₄: compl(0, 1)                  :- true.
r₅: compl(1, 0)                  :- true.
```

Rule $r_1$ states that a list, X, is in the query answer if it is the complement of a list, Y, in the relation `list`. The predicate `complement` is written using standard tail-recursion over lists. Unfortunately, this Prolog-like program does not work as well with a bottom-up evaluator as with a top-down evaluator. To see this, consider that when evaluated bottom-up, rules $r_2$ and $r_3$ start with the empty list and compute the complement of all possible lists of 0's and 1's, without bound.

---

[3] We use the binary function symbol `cons` to construct lists. We also adopt standard Prolog notation, so that [H|T] denotes the function term `cons(H,T)`, and [ ] is a constant symbol denoting the empty list.

This means two things. First, the program consisting of rules $r_1$ to $r_5$ has an infinite least fixpoint, even though the extent of predicate **answer** is finite. In addition, even if we prevented infinite computations (by, say, imposing an upper-bound on the length of the computed lists), the least fixpoint would still be very large and expensive to compute. In fact, if $l_{max}$ is the maximum length of a list in **list**, then the program computes the complement of all possible lists of 0's and 1's up to length $l_{max}$. The program therefore computes an exponential number of unnecessary intermediate results, while the natural algorithm for complement only requires linear time. This problem arises because, unlike Prolog, rules in Datalog are evaluated "from body to head," instead of "from head to body."

In the following sections, we introduce *Sequence Datalog* [21], a query language designed to overcome these limitations, by supporting a safe and efficient form of structural recursion over strings.

## 3  Overview of Sequence Datalog

We use a data model that is a simple extension of the relational model [15, 17]. In this model, we fix a finite set of symbols, $\Sigma$, called *the alphabet*. Database tuples may contain finite sequences of symbols over this alphabet, instead of just single symbols.

Within this model, we develop and investigate different forms of structural recursion over sequences, especially forms that guarantee terminating computations. At the same time, we wish to construct new sequences and restructure old ones. To meet these two goals, programs in *Sequence Datalog* have two kinds of *interpreted* function term: *indexed terms*, which extract subsequences; and *constructive terms*, which concatenate sequences. An indexed term has the form $s[n_1:n_2]$, and is interpreted as the subsequence of sequence $s$ from position $n_1$ to position $n_2$. Thus, $abcdef[2:5] = bcde$. A constructive term has the form $s_1 \bullet s_2$, and is interpreted as the concatenation of sequences $s_1$ and $s_2$. Thus, $abc \bullet def = abcdef$.

*Example 2.* [**Extracting Subsequences**] The following rule extracts all suffixes of all sequences in relation $r$:

$$suffix(X[N:end]) \leftarrow r(X).$$

This rule says that for each sequence $X$ in relation $r$, and for each integer $N$, the subsequence of $X$ extending from the $N^{th}$ element to the last element is a suffix of $X$. By convention, we interpret the keyword *end* as the last position in a sequence.

The semantics of Sequence Datalog is based on a fixpoint theory, as in classical Logic Programming [19]. Thus, each Sequence Datalog program $P$ has an associated "T-operator" that maps databases to databases. Each application of the operator may create new atomic formulas and new sequences. The operator is monotonic and continuous, and thus has a least fixpoint. If the least fixpoint is finite, then we say that the program has a *finite* semantics; otherwise, it has an *infinite* semantics. Because of the importance of finiteness and safety to database applications, the fixpoint semantics for Sequence Datalog involves certain subtleties that are absent in classical logic programming. Without this care, query answers can easily become infinite, as shown in Examples 1 and 3.

*Example 3.* [**Pattern Matching**] Suppose we are interested in sequences of the form $a^n b^n c^n$ in a unary relation $r$. In Sequence Datalog, the easiest way to retrieve all such sequences is with the following program, where $\epsilon$ is the empty sequence:

$$\gamma_1 : answer(X) \leftarrow r(X),$$
$$abc_n(X[1{:}N_1],\ X[N_1 + 1{:}N_2],\ X[N_2 + 1{:}end]).$$
$$\gamma_2 : abc_n(\epsilon, \epsilon, \epsilon) \leftarrow true.$$
$$\gamma_3 : abc_n(X, Y, Z) \leftarrow X[1] = a,\ Y[1] = b,\ Z[1] = c,$$
$$abc_n(X[2{:}end],\ Y[2{:}end],\ Z[2{:}end]).$$

For each sequence $X$ in $r$, the formula $answer(X)$ is true if it is possible to split $X$ into three parts such that $abc_n$ is true. Predicate $abc_n$ is true for triples of sequences of the form $(a^n, b^n, c^n)$. Unfortunately, if we evaluate the program over the entire universe of sequences, $\Sigma^*$, then the least fixpoint is infinite. In fact, there is an infinite number of sequence triples $(x, y, z)$ that satisfy rule $\gamma_3$, and the least fixpoint of the program contains an atom of the form $abc_n(x, y, z)$ for each of them.

The natural solution to these finiteness problems is to adopt an *active domain semantics*, so that rule evaluation is limited to sequences in the database. However, this must be done with some care if we are to support *structural recursion* over sequences, since in addition to the sequences in the database, we need access to their *subsequences*. For this purpose, we introduce a new active domain for sequence databases, called the *extended active domain*. This domain contains all the sequences occurring in the database, plus all their *subsequences*.[4] Substitutions range over this domain when rules are evaluated.[5]

*Example 4.* [**Pattern Matching (Continued)**] When evaluated over the extended active domain of the database, the rules in Example 3 have a finite fixpoint. In fact, rule $\gamma_3$ is evaluated only on triples of sequences belonging to the extended active domain of the database, that is sequences in the database or their contiguous subsequences. This has two effects: it allows structural recursion, and at the same time, it prevents infiniteness.

---

[4] In this paper, we use only *contiguous subsequences*, that is, subsequences specified by a start and end position in some other sequence. Thus, $bcd$ is a contiguous subsequence of $abcde$, but $bd$ is not.

[5] Note that the size of the extended active domain is at most quadratic in the size of the database domain. In fact, the number of different contiguous subsequences of a given sequence of length $k$ is at most $\binom{k+1}{2} + 1 = \frac{k(k+1)}{2} + 1$, where the extra "1" is for the empty sequence.

It is worth noting that in our semantics, the extended active domain is not fixed during query evaluation. Instead, whenever a new sequence is created (by the concatenation operator, •), the new sequence—and its subsequences—are added to the extended active domain. The fixpoint theory of Sequence Datalog, developed in Section 5, provides a declarative semantics for this apparently procedural notion. In general, the extended active domain of the least fixpoint may be larger than the extended active domain of the database. In the database, the domain consists of the sequences in the database and all their subsequences. In the least fixpoint, the domain consists of the sequences in the database and any new sequences created during rule evaluation, and all their subsequences.

*Example 5.* [**Concatenating Sequences**] The following rule concatenates all pairs of sequences from relation $r$:

$$answer(X \bullet Y) \leftarrow r(X), \ r(Y).$$

This rule takes any pair of sequences, $X$ and $Y$, in relation $r$, concatenates them, and puts the result in relation *answer*, thereby adding new sequences to the extended active domain. The extended active domain of the least fixpoint is therefore larger than the extended active domain of the database.

Observe that our semantics for sequence creation resembles the semantics of *value invention* in [2] in that sequences are added to the active domain as a side-effect of rule evaluation. In Sequence Datalog, however, the addition is purely declarative and deterministic, since the least fixpoint is unique.

Compared to Datalog with function symbols, or Prolog, several differences are apparent. The first is that Sequence Datalog has no uninterpreted function symbols, so that it is not possible to build arbitrarily nested structures. On the other hand, Sequence Datalog has a richer syntax than the $[Head|Tail]$ list constructor of Prolog. This richer syntax is motivated by a natural distinction between two types of recursion, one safe and the other unsafe. Recursion through construction of new sequences is *inherently unsafe* since it can create longer and longer sequences, which can make the active domain grow indefinitely. On the other hand, structural recursion over existing sequences is *inherently safe*, since it only creates shorter sequences, so that growth in the active domain is bounded. In fact, it is bounded by the set of all subsequences of the active domain, *i.e.*, by the extended active domain of the database. Typically, languages for list manipulation do not discriminate between these two types of recursion. Sequence Datalog does: constructive recursion is performed using constructive terms, of the form $X \bullet Y$, while structural recursion is performed using indexed terms, of the form $X[n_1:n_2]$. The next example illustrates both forms of recursion.

*Example 6.* [**Multiple Repeats**] Suppose we are interested in sequences of the form $Y^n$. The sequence *abcdabcdabcd* has this form, where $Y = abcd$ and $n = 3$.[6] Here are two straightforward ways of expressing this idea in Sequence Datalog:

---

[6] Repetitive patterns are of great importance in Molecular Biology [25].

$$rep_1(X, X) \qquad \leftarrow true.$$
$$rep_1(X, X[1{:}N])) \leftarrow rep_1(X[N+1{:}end], X[1{:}N]).$$

$$rep_2(X, X) \qquad \leftarrow true.$$
$$rep_2(X \bullet Y, X) \quad \leftarrow rep_2(Y, X).$$

The formulas $rep_1(X, Y)$ and $rep_2(X, Y)$ both mean that $X$ has the form $Y^n$ for some $n$. However, $rep_2$ has an infinite semantics, while $rep_1$ has a finite semantics. The rules for $rep_1$ do *not* create new sequences, since they do not use the concatenation operator, $\bullet$. Instead, these rules retrieve all sequences in the extended active domain that fit the pattern $Y^n$. To do this, they try to recursively "chop" an existing sequence, $X$, into identical pieces. We call this *structural recursion*. In contrast, the rules for $rep_2$ do create new sequences. They produce sequences of the form $Y^n$ by recursively concatenating each sequence, $Y$, in the domain with itself. We call this *constructive recursion*. Structural recursion is always safe, leading to a finite least fixpoint. In this example, constructive recursion is unsafe, leading to an infinite least fixpoint.

The clear distinction between recursion over existing sequences and recursion through creation of new sequences allows the programmer to avoid infinite computations in many cases, as the next example shows.

*Example 7.* [**Complement**] Suppose we are given a set of binary sequences and want to find the complement of all sequences in $r_1$. There are two ways of expressing this transformation in Sequence Datalog.

(*i*) The first approach uses tail recursion, as in Example 1. However, in Sequence Datalog, we can prevent infiniteness by using safe, structural recursion over one argument of a predicate to control constructive recursion over the other argument(s).

$$\gamma_1 : answer(Y) \qquad\qquad\qquad \leftarrow r_1(X), \; complement(X, Y).$$

$$\gamma_2 : complement(\epsilon, \epsilon) \qquad\quad \leftarrow true.$$
$$\gamma_3 : complement(X, \; Y \bullet Z) \leftarrow compl(X[1], \; Y),$$
$$\qquad\qquad\qquad\qquad\qquad\qquad complement(X[2{:}end], \; Z).$$

$$\gamma_4 : compl(0, 1) \qquad\qquad \leftarrow true.$$
$$\gamma_5 : compl(1, 0) \qquad\qquad \leftarrow true.$$

In this case, predicate *complement* constructs the complement of every sequence in the extended active domain of the database. Recursion starts with the empty sequence, and proceeds until the complement of every sequence in the extended active domain has been generated. Thus, unlike Example 1, recursion stops after a finite amount of time, since the active domain semantics prevents the generation of sequences of unbounded length.

(*ii*) Although they have a finite semantics, rules $\gamma_1$ to $\gamma_5$ are still highly inefficient, since they compute the complement of every sequence in the extended active domain of the database, not just the complement of sequences in relation $r_1$. This inefficiency can be avoided by expressing the query in another, more-efficient way, again using structural recursion.

$$\gamma_1' : answer(Y) \qquad\qquad\qquad \leftarrow r_1(X), \quad complement(X, Y).$$

$$\gamma_2' : complement(\epsilon, \epsilon) \qquad\qquad\qquad \leftarrow true.$$

$$\gamma_3' : complement(X[1{:}N+1], \ Z \bullet Y) \leftarrow r_1(X), \quad compl(X[N+1], \ Y),$$
$$complement(X[1{:}N], \ Z).$$

In these rules, each sequence in relation $r_1$ is scanned from beginning to end, and in the process, the complementary sequence is constructed one symbol at a time. Note that since the complement is generated only for sequences in relation $r_1$, rule evaluation requires only a linear number of database accesses (linear in the sum of the lengths of all sequences in $r_1$).

## 4 Preliminary Definitions

This section provides formal definitions for concepts used in the rest of the paper, including the concepts of *sequence database* and *sequence query*.

Let $\Sigma$ be a countable set of symbols, called the *alphabet*. $\Sigma^*$ denotes the set of all possible sequences over $\Sigma$, including the *empty sequence*, $\epsilon$. $\sigma_1 \sigma_2$ denotes the concatenation of two sequences, $\sigma_1, \sigma_2 \in \Sigma^*$. $\text{LEN}(\sigma)$ denotes the length of sequence $\sigma$, and $\sigma(i)$ denotes its $i$-th element. With an abuse of notation, we blur the distinction between elements of the alphabet and sequences of length 1.

We say that a sequence $\sigma'$ of length $k$ is a *contiguous subsequence* of sequence $\sigma$ if for some integer $i \geq 0$, $\sigma'(j) = \sigma(i+j)$ for $j = 1, \ldots, k$. Note that for each sequence of length $k$ over $\Sigma$, there are at most $\frac{k(k+1)}{2} + 1$ different contiguous subsequences (including the empty sequence). For example, the contiguous subsequences of the sequence $abc$ are: $\epsilon, a, b, c, ab, bc, abc$.

The data model for Sequence Datalog is an extension of the relational model in the spirit of [15, 17]. The model allows for tuples containing sequences of symbols, instead of just constant symbols. Formally, a *relation* of arity $k$ over $\Sigma$ is a finite subset of the $k$-fold cartesian product of $\Sigma^*$ with itself. A *sequence database* over $\Sigma$ (or simply *database*, for short) is a finite set of relations over $\Sigma$. We assign a distinct predicate symbol, $r$, of appropriate arity to each relation in a database. A *sequence query* is a partial mapping from the databases over $\Sigma$ to the relations over $\Sigma$. As usual, we assume fixed input and answer schema for queries [11].

## 5 Sequence Datalog: Syntax and Semantics

This section introduces the syntax and semantics of the language. We first discuss the syntax informally, and then present two different semantics; the first is a fixpoint semantics, and the second is a model-theoretic semantics. We show that the two semantics are equivalent.

## 5.1 Syntax

As mentioned in Section 3, *SequenceDatalog* has two interpreted function symbols for constructing complex terms—one for concatenating sequences, and one for extracting subsequences. Intuitively, if $X$ and $Y$ are sequences, then the term $X \bullet Y$ denotes the concatenation of sequences $X$ and $Y$. Likewise, if $I$ and $J$ are integers, then the term $X[I : J]$ denotes the subsequence of sequence $X$ extending from position $I$ to position $J$.

To be more precise, the language of terms includes four countable, disjoint sets: the set of non-negative integers, $0, 1, 2 \ldots$; a set of constant symbols, called the *alphabet* and denoted $\Sigma$; a set of variables, $R, S, T \ldots$, called *sequence variables* and denoted $V_\Sigma$; and another set of variables, $I, J, K \ldots$, called *index variables* and denoted $V_I$. A constant sequence (or *sequence*, for short) is an element of $\Sigma^*$. From these sets, we construct two kinds of term as follows:

- *index terms* are built from integers, index variables, and the special symbol *end*, by combining them recursively using the binary connectives $+$ and $-$. Thus, if $N$ and $M$ are index variables, then $3$, $N + 3$, $N - M$, $end - 5$ and $end - 5 + M$ are all index terms;
- *sequence terms* are built from constant sequences, sequence variables and index terms, by combining them recursively into *indexed terms* and *constructive terms*, as follows:
  - If $s$ is a sequence variable and $n_1, n_2$ are *index terms*, then $s[n_1{:}n_2]$ is an *indexed sequence term*. Here, $n_1$ and $n_2$ are called the *indexes* of $s$. For convenience, sequence terms of the form $s[n_i{:}n_i]$ are written $s[n_i]$.
  - If $s_1, s_2$ are *sequence terms*, then $s_1 \bullet s_2$ is a *constructive sequence term*. Thus, if $S_1$ and $S_2$ are sequence variables, and $N$ is an index variable, then $S_1[4]$, $S_1[1{:}N]$ and $ccgt \bullet S_1[1{:}end - 3] \bullet S_2$ are all sequence terms.

A term is *ground* if it contains no variables.

As in most logics, the language of formulas for *SequenceDatalog* includes a countable set of predicate symbols, $p, q, r, \ldots$, where each predicate symbol has an associated arity. If $p$ is a predicate symbol of arity $n$, and $s_1, \ldots, s_n$ are sequence terms, then $p(s_1, \ldots, s_n)$ is an atom. Moreover, if $s_1$ and $s_2$ are sequence terms, then the formulas $s_1 = s_2$ and $s_1 \neq s_2$ are also atoms. From atoms, we build *facts* and *clauses* in the usual way [19]. The head and body of a clause $\gamma$ are denoted HEAD($\gamma$) and BODY($\gamma$), respectively. A clause that contains a constructive term in its head is called a *constructive clause*. A Sequence Datalog *program* is a set of Sequence Datalog clauses in which constructive terms (terms of the form $s_1 \bullet s_2$) may appear in clause heads, but not in clause bodies.

## 5.2 Substitutions

A substitution $\theta$ is a mapping that associates a sequence with each sequence variable in $V_\Sigma$, and an integer with each index variable in $V_I$. Substitutions can be extended to partial mappings on sequence and index terms in a straightforward way. Because these terms are interpreted, the result of a substitution is either a sequence or an integer.

Intuitively, $\theta(s[n_1{:}n_2])$ is the contiguous subsequence of $\theta(s)$ extending from position $\theta(n_1)$ to position $\theta(n_2)$. Here, terms such as $s[n+1{:}n]$ are conveniently interpreted as the empty sequence, $\epsilon$. For example,

| $s$ | $\theta(s)$ |
|---|---|
| $uvwxy[3:6]$ | undefined |
| $uvwxy[3:5]$ | $wxy$ |
| $uvwxy[3:4]$ | $wx$ |
| $uvwxy[3:3]$ | $w$ |
| $uvwxy[3:2]$ | $\epsilon$ |
| $uvwxy[3:1]$ | undefined |

If the special index term *end* appears in the sequence term $s[n_1{:}n_2]$, then *end* is interpreted as the length of $\theta(s)$. Thus, $\theta(s[n{:}end])$ is a suffix of $\theta(s)$. Finally, $\theta(s_1 \bullet s_2)$ is interpreted as the concatenation of $\theta(s_1)$ and $\theta(s_2)$. The rest of this subsection makes these ideas precise.

**Definition 1. (Substitutions Based on a Domain)** Let $\mathcal{D}$ be a set of sequences and integers. A *substitution based on* $\mathcal{D}$ is a mapping that associates a sequence in $\mathcal{D}$ to every sequence variable, and an integer in $\mathcal{D}$ to every index variable.

Let $\theta$ be a substitution based on a domain. We extend $\theta$ from a total mapping on variables to a partial mapping on terms, as follows:

- if $s$ is a sequence in $\Sigma^*$ or an integer, then $\theta(s) = s$;
- in the context of the sequence term $S[n{:}end]$, we define $\theta(end) = \text{LEN}(\theta(S))$;
- if $n_1$ and $n_2$ are index terms, then $\theta(n_1 + n_2) = \theta(n_1) + \theta(n_2)$ and $\theta(n_1 - n_2) = \theta(n_1) - \theta(n_2)$;
- if $s$ is a sequence term of the form $S[n_1{:}n_2]$, then $\theta(s)$ is defined if and only if $1 \leq \theta(n_1) \leq \theta(n_2) + 1 \leq \text{LEN}(\theta(S)) + 1$, in which case
  - $\theta(s)$ is the contiguous subsequence of $\theta(S)$ extending from position $\theta(n_1)$ to $\theta(n_2)$ if $\theta(n_1) \leq \theta(n_2)$
  - $\theta(s) = \epsilon$ (the empty sequence) if $\theta(n_1) = \theta(n_2) + 1$
- if $s_1$ and $s_2$ are sequence terms, then $\theta(s_1 \bullet s_2) = \theta(s_1)\theta(s_2)$ if both $\theta(s_1)$ and $\theta(s_2)$ are defined; otherwise, $\theta(s_1 \bullet s_2)$ is *undefined*.

Substitutions can be extended to atoms, literals and clauses in the usual way. We need only add that $\theta(p(X_1, \ldots, X_n))$ is defined if and only if each $\theta(X_i)$ is defined. Likewise, $\theta(q_0 \leftarrow q_1, \ldots, q_k)$ is defined if and only if each $\theta(q_i)$ is defined.

## 5.3 Fixpoint Semantics

The semantics of clauses is defined in terms of a least fixpoint theory. As in classical logic programming [19], each Sequence Datalog program $P$ and database DB has an associated operator $T_{P,\text{DB}}$ that maps Herbrand interpretations to Herbrand interpretations. Each application of $T_{P,DB}$ may create new atoms, which may contain new sequences. As shown below, $T_{P,DB}$ is monotonic and continuous, and thus has a least fixpoint that can be computed in a bottom-up, iterative fashion.

The following items summarize the main ideas in the fixpoint semantics:

- The *extended active domain* of database DB is the union of the following three sets: (*i*) the *active domain* of the database, that is, the set of sequences occurring in DB; (*ii*) all contiguous subsequences of sequences in the active domain; and (*iii*) the set of integers $\{0, 1, 2, \ldots, l_{max} + 1\}$, where $l_{max}$ is the maximum length of a sequence in the active domain.
- The *least fixpoint* [19] of operator $T_{P,DB}$ is computed in a bottom-up fashion, by starting at the empty interpretation and applying $T_{P,DB}$ repeatedly until a fixpoint is reached. At each step, and for each ground instantiation of each clause in $P$, if each premise of the clause has been derived, then the head of the clause is added to the set of derived facts. Because $T_{P,DB}$ is continuous, this process is complete [19]; that is, any atom in the least fixpoint will eventually be derived.
- At each step, if a derived fact contains a new sequence (*i.e.*, a sequence not currently in the extended active domain), then it is added to the active domain. Thus, as the bottom-up computation proceeds, the active domain (and hence the extended active domain) may expand. At each step of the computation, substitutions range over the current value of the extended active domain.

Note that the least fixpoint can be an infinite set. In this case, we say that the semantics of $P$ over DB is *infinite*; otherwise, it is *finite*.

To develop the fixpoint semantics formally, we define the *Herbrand base* to be the set of ground atomic formulas built from predicate symbols in $\mathcal{P}$ and sequences in $\Sigma^*$. An *interpretation* of a program is a subset of the Herbrand base, and a *database* is a finite subset.

**Definition 2. (Extensions)** Given a set of sequences, *dom*, the *extension* of *dom*, written $dom^{ext}$, is the set of sequences and integers containing the following elements:

1. each element in *dom*;
2. for each sequence in *dom*, all its contiguous subsequences;
3. the set of integers $\{0, 1, 2, \ldots, l_{max} + 1\}$, where $l_{max}$ is the maximum length of a sequence in *dom*.

**Definition 3. (Extended Active Domain)** The *active domain* of an interpretation $I$, denoted $\mathcal{D}_I$, is the set of sequences occurring in $I$. The *extended active domain* of $I$, denoted $\mathcal{D}_I^{ext}$, is the extension of $\mathcal{D}_I$.

Note that active domains contain only sequences, while extended active domains contain integers as well. The following lemma states some basic results about extended active domains.

**Lemma 4.** *If $I_1 \subseteq I_2$ are two interpretations, then $\mathcal{D}_{I_1}^{ext} \subseteq \mathcal{D}_{I_2}^{ext}$. If $\mathcal{I}$ is a set of interpretations, then their union, $\bigcup \mathcal{I}$, is also an interpretation, and $\mathcal{D}_{\bigcup \mathcal{I}}^{ext} = \bigcup_{I \in \mathcal{I}} \mathcal{D}_I^{ext}$.*

Like any power set, the set of interpretations forms a complete lattice under subset, union and intersection. We define a T-operator on this lattice, and show that it is monotonic and continuous. In defining the operator, each database atom is treated as a clause with an empty body.

**Definition 5. (T-Operator)** The operator $T_{P,DB}$ associated with program $P$ and database DB maps interpretations to interpretations. In particular, if $I$ is an interpretation, then $T_{P,DB}(I)$ is the following interpretation:

$$\{\theta(\text{HEAD}(\gamma)) \mid \theta(\text{BODY}(\gamma)) \subseteq I \;\; \text{for some clause } \gamma \in P \cup DB$$
$$\text{and some substitution } \theta \text{ based on } \mathcal{D}_I^{ext} \text{ and defined at } \gamma\}$$

**Lemma 6. (Monotonicity)** *The operator $T_{P,DB}$ is monotonic; i.e., if $I_1 \subseteq I_2$ are two interpretations, then $T_{P,DB}(I_1) \subseteq T_{P,DB}(I_2)$.*

*Proof.* Follows immediately from Definition 5 and Lemma 4.

**Lemma 7. (Continuity)** *The operator $T_{P,DB}$ is continuous; i.e., if $I_1 \subseteq I_2 \subseteq I_3 \ldots$ is a (possibly infinite) increasing sequence of interpretations, then:*

$$T_{P,DB}\left(\bigcup_i I_i\right) \subseteq \bigcup_i T_{P,DB}(I_i)$$

*Proof.* Let $I = \bigcup_i I_i$ and let $\alpha$ be an atom in $T_{P,DB}(I)$. We must show that $\alpha$ is also in $\bigcup_i T_{P,DB}(I_i)$. By Definition 5, $\alpha = \theta(\text{HEAD}(\gamma))$ and $\theta(\text{BODY}(\gamma)) \subseteq I$, for some clause $\gamma$ in $P \cup DB$, and some substitution $\theta$ based on $\mathcal{D}_I^{ext}$. In addition, since the interpretations $I_i$ are increasing, their extended active domains $\mathcal{D}_{I_i}^{ext}$ are also increasing, by Lemma 4. With this in mind, we proceed in three steps.

- $\theta(\text{BODY}(\gamma))$ is a finite set of ground atomic formulas, and $\theta(\text{BODY}(\gamma)) \subseteq \bigcup_i I_i$. Thus $\theta(\text{BODY}(\gamma)) \subseteq I_{j_1}$ for some $j_1$, since the $I_i$ are increasing, and $\theta(\text{BODY}(\gamma))$ is finite.
- Let $\mathcal{V}$ be the set of variables in clause $\gamma$, and let $\theta(\mathcal{V})$ be the result of applying $\theta$ to each variable. Thus $\theta(\mathcal{V})$ is a finite subset of $\mathcal{D}_I^{ext}$, since $\theta$ is based on $\mathcal{D}_I^{ext}$. Thus $\theta(\mathcal{V}) \subseteq \bigcup_i \mathcal{D}_{I_i}^{ext}$ by Lemma 4. Thus $\theta(\mathcal{V}) \subseteq \mathcal{D}_{I_{j_2}}^{ext}$ for some $j_2$, since the $\mathcal{D}_{I_i}^{ext}$ are increasing, and $\theta(\mathcal{V})$ is finite.
- Let $j$ be the larger of $j_1$ and $j_2$. Then $\theta(\text{BODY}(\gamma)) \subseteq I_j$ and $\theta(\mathcal{V}) \subseteq \mathcal{D}_{I_j}^{ext}$. Let $\theta'$ be any substitution based on $\mathcal{D}_{I_j}^{ext}$ that agrees with $\theta$ on the variables in $\mathcal{V}$. Then $\theta'(\gamma) = \theta(\gamma)$. Thus $\theta'(\text{BODY}(\gamma)) \subseteq I_j$. Thus $\theta'(\text{HEAD}(\gamma)) \in T_{P,DB}(I_j)$ by Definition 5. Thus $\alpha \in T_{P,DB}(I_j)$. Thus $\alpha \in \bigcup_i T_{P,DB}(I_i)$.

Given a program $P$ and database DB, we define the following sequence of interpretations:

$$T_{P,DB} \uparrow 0 = \{\,\}$$
$$T_{P,DB} \uparrow (i+1) = T_{P,DB}(T_{P,DB} \uparrow i), \quad for\ i \geq 0$$
$$T_{P,DB} \uparrow \omega = \bigcup_{i=0}^{\infty} T_{P,DB} \uparrow i$$

Because $T_{P,DB}$ is monotonic and continuous, we can invoke the Knaster-Tarsky fixpoint theorem [19]. $T_{P,DB}$ thus has a least fixpoint, which is equal to $T_{P,DB} \uparrow \omega$. We say that $T_{P,DB} \uparrow \omega$ is the *fixpoint semantics* of program $P$ over database DB. Intuitively, $T_{P,DB} \uparrow \omega$ is the set of facts implied by program $P$ and database DB.

## 5.4 Model Theory

In this section we develop a model-theoretic semantics for Sequence Datalog programs, and show that it is equivalent to the fixpoint semantics developed above. Our notion of *model* is similar to the classical notion except that we restrict our attention to substitutions based on the extended active domain.

**Definition 8. (Models)** An interpretation $I$ is a *model* of a clause $\gamma$, written $I \models \gamma$, if and only if the following is true for each substitution $\theta$ based on $\mathcal{D}_I^{ext}$ and defined at $\gamma$:

$$if \quad \theta(\text{BODY}(\gamma)) \subseteq I \quad then \quad \theta(\text{HEAD}(\gamma)) \in I$$

An interpretation is a model of a Sequence Datalog program $P$ and a database DB if it is a model of each clause in $P \cup$ DB.

**Definition 9. (Entailment)** Let $P$ be a Sequence Datalog program, DB be a database, and $\alpha$ be a ground atomic formula. Then, $P$ and DB entail $\alpha$, written $P, \text{DB} \models \alpha$, if and only if every model of $P$ and DB is also a model of $\alpha$.

**Lemma 10.** *Let $P$ be a Sequence Datalog program, DB be a database, and $I$ be an interpretation. Then $I$ is a model of $P$ and DB if and only if it is a fixpoint of $T_{P,DB}$, i.e., if and only if $T_{P,DB}(I) \subseteq I$.*

*Proof.* To prove the *if* direction, suppose that $T_{P,DB}(I) \subseteq I$. Let $\gamma$ be any clause in $P \cup$ DB, and let $\theta$ be any substitution based on $\mathcal{D}_I^{ext}$ and defined at $\gamma$. If $\theta(\text{BODY}(\gamma)) \subseteq I$ then $\theta(\text{HEAD}(\gamma)) \in T_{P,DB}(I)$, by Definition 5. Thus $\theta(\text{HEAD}(\gamma)) \in I$, since $T_{P,DB}(I) \subseteq I$ by hypothesis. Thus, since $\theta$ is arbitrary, $I$ is a model of $\gamma$. Thus, since $\gamma$ is arbitrary, $I$ is a model of $P \cup$ DB.

To prove the *only if* direction, suppose that $I$ is a model of $P \cup$ DB. If $\alpha \in T_{P,DB}(I)$ then by Definition 5, $\alpha = \theta(\text{HEAD}(\gamma))$ for some clause $\gamma$ in $P \cup$ DB, and some substitution $\theta$ based on $\mathcal{D}_I^{ext}$. In addition $\theta(\text{BODY}(\gamma)) \subseteq I$. But $I$ is a model of $P \cup$ DB by hypothesis, and thus of $\gamma$. Hence $\theta(\text{HEAD}(\gamma)) \in I$, so $\alpha \in I$. Thus, any atom in $T_{P,DB}(I)$ is also in $I$. Thus $T_{P,DB}(I) \subseteq I$.

The following corollaries are immediate consequences of Lemma 10 and the fixpoint theory of Section 5.3. They show that the model-theoretic semantics and the fixpoint semantics for Sequence Datalog are equivalent.

**Corollary 11.** *A Sequence Datalog program P and a database* DB *have a unique minimal model, and it is identical to the least fixpoint of the operator* $T_{P,DB}$.

**Corollary 12.** *Let P be a Sequence Datalog program,* DB *be a database, and* $\alpha$ *be a ground atomic formula. Then* $P, \text{DB} \models \alpha$ *if and only if* $\alpha \in T_{P,DB} \uparrow \omega$.

**Acknowledgments** The authors would like to thank Paolo Atzeni and Victor Vianu for many comments on the subject of the paper.

# References

1. S. Abiteboul, R. Hull, and V. Vianu. *Foundations of databases.* Addison Wesley Publ. Co., Reading, Massachussetts, 1994.
2. S. Abiteboul and V. Vianu. Datalog extensions for database queries and updates. *Journal of Computing and System Sciences*, 43(1):62–124, August 1991.
3. K. Apt and M. H. Van Emden. Contributions to the theory of logic programming. *Journal of the ACM*, 29(3):841–862, 1982.
4. M. Atkinson, F. Bancilhon, D. DeWitt, K. Dittrich, D. Maier, and Z. Zdonik. The object-oriented database manifesto. In *First Intern. Conference on Deductive and Object Oriented Databases (DOOD'89), Kyoto, Japan*, pages 40–57, 1989.
5. P. Atzeni, editor. *LOGIDATA+: Deductive Databases with Complex Objects, Lecture Notes in Computer Science 701.* Springer-Verlag, 1993.
6. A. J. Bonner. Hypothetical Datalog: complexity and expressibility. *Theoretical Computer Science*, 76:3–51, 1990.
7. V. Breazu-Tannen, P. Buneman, and S. Naqvi. Structural recursion as a query language. In *Third Intern. Workshop on Database Programming Languages (DBPL'91)*, pages 9–19, 1991.
8. V. Breazu-Tannen, P. Buneman, and L. Wong. Naturally embedded query languages. In *Fourth International Conference on Data Base Theory, (ICDT'92), Lecture Notes in Computer Science*, pages 140–154, 1992.
9. S. Ceri, G. Gottlob, and L. Tanca. *Logic Programming and Data Bases.* Springer-Verlag, 1989.
10. S. Ceri, G. Gottlob, and L. Tanca. What you always wanted to know about Datalog (and never dared to ask). *IEEE Transactions on Knowledge and Data Engineering*, 1(1):146–166, March 1989.
11. A. K. Chandra and D. Harel. Computable queries for relational databases. *Journal of Computing and System Sciences*, 21:333–347, 1980.
12. W. Clocksin and C. Mellish. *Programming in Prolog.* Springer-Verlag, 1981.
13. L. S. Colby, E. L. Robertson, L. V. Saxton, and D. Van Gucht. A query language for list-based complex objects. In *Thirteenth ACM SIGMOD Intern. Symposium on Principles of Database Systems (PODS'94)*, pages 179–189, 1994.
14. Communications of the ACM. Special issue on the Human Genome project. vol. 34(11), November 1991.

15. S. Ginsburg and X. Wang. Pattern matching by RS-operations: towards a unified approach to querying sequence data. In *Eleventh ACM SIGACT SIGMOD SIGART Symp. on Principles of Database Systems (PODS'92)*, pages 293–300, 1992.

16. G. H. Gonnet. Text dominated databases: Theory, practice and experience. Tutorial presented at PODS, 1994.

17. G. Grahne, M. Nykanen, and E. Ukkonen. Reasoning about strings in databases. In *Thirteenth ACM SIGMOD Intern. Symposium on Principles of Database Systems (PODS'94)*, pages 303–312, 1994.

18. S. Grumbach and T. Milo. An algebra for POMSETS. In *Fifth International Conference on Data Base Theory, (ICDT'95), Prague, Lecture Notes in Computer Science*, pages 191–207, 1995.

19. J. W. Lloyd. *Foundations of Logic Programming*. Springer-Verlag, second edition, 1987.

20. G. Mecca and A. J. Bonner. Finite query languages for sequence databases. In *Fifth Intern. Workshop on Database Programming Languages (DBPL'95), Gubbio, Italy*, 1995.

21. G. Mecca and A. J. Bonner. Sequences, Datalog and Transducers. In *Fourteenth ACM SIGMOD Intern. Symposium on Principles of Database Systems (PODS'95), San Jose, California*, pages 23–35, 1995.

22. G. Mecca and A. J. Bonner. Sequences, Datalog and Negation. In preparation, 1996.

23. C. Papadimitriou. *Computational Complexity*. Addison-Wesley, 1994.

24. J. Richardson. Supporting lists in a data model (a timely approach). In *Eighteenth International Conference on Very Large Data Bases (VLDB'92), Vancouver, Canada*, pages 127–138, 1992.

25. D. B. Searls. String Variable Grammars: a logic grammar formalism for dna sequences. Technical report, University of Pennsylvania, School of Medicine, 1993.

26. D. Stott Parker, E. Simon, and P. Valduriez. SVP – a model capturing sets, streams and parallelism. In *Eighteenth International Conference on Very Large Data Bases (VLDB'92), Vancouver, Canada*, pages 115–126, 1992.

27. X. Wang. *Pattern matching by RS-operations: Towards a unified approach to querying sequence data*. PhD thesis, University of Southern California, 1992.

# Language Extensions for Semantic Integration of Deductive Databases*

P. Asirelli[1], C. Renso[2], F. Turini[2]

[1] IEI-CNR, Via S. Maria, Pisa, Italy. E-mail asirelli@iei.pi.cnr.it.
[2] Dipartimento di Informatica, Corso Italia, 40 - 56125 Pisa, Italy.
E-mail {renso,turini}@di.unipi.it.

Abstract. A language is a subject of semantic integration of deductive databases is proposed. The language allows one to construct a deductive system by extending a logic programming with a suite of operators for composing programs and manage passive datasets. The abstract semantics and implementation techniques of the extensions are discussed, and an example of integration of databases supporting libraries and departments is used to illustrate the usefulness of the approach.

## 1 Introduction

At present, in the database area, much attention is devoted to studying the possibility of integrating different databases or, in any case, databases which have been developed within other projects, and that may be resident at different sites [19]. This issue has been largely studied in the past dozen years, due to approaches such as federated databases, multidatabases, interoperable databases or mediators. Here, we focus on integration of deductive databases. The problem is twofold:

- at the lower level, how to enrich traditional databases with deductive capabilities;
- at the higher level, how to integrate deductive databases which have the same semantic domain, but possess different local models.

In the first case, one would like to integrate deductive databases (such as Datalog) with traditional databases. A successful approach to this problem was implemented for example in the CDD++ language[3]. Our proposal has not focus on this issue, although we intend to make use of such techniques. Our aim is to study the second issue, that is the problem of semantic integration of deductive databases. To illustrate the idea, we show a very simple case. Consider two crucial scenarios, each having a database which contains information about accommodations. They have the same semantic domain (accommodations) but they use different data representation, as we can see in the following example:

* Work partially supported by the EC-US Cooperative Activity Project and by CNR grant # 96.00055.07.

# Language Extensions for Semantic Integration of Deductive Databases*

P. Asirelli[1], C. Renso[2], F. Turini[2]

[1] IEI-CNR, Via S. Maria - Pisa, Italy. E-mail: asirelli@iei.pi.cnr.it,
[2] Dipartimento di Informatica, Corso Italia, 40 - 56125 Pisa, Italy.
E-mail: {renso,turini}@di.unipi.it

**Abstract.** A language in support of semantic integration of deductive databases is proposed. The language allows one to construct *mediators* by extending logic programming with a suite of operators for composing programs and message passing features. The abstract semantics and implementation techniques of the extensions are discussed, and an example of integration of databases supporting libraries and departments is used to illustrate the usefulness of the approach.

## 1   Introduction

At present, in the database area, much attention is devoted to studying the possibility of integrating different databases or, in any case, databases which have been developed within other projects, and that may be resident at different sites [19]. This issue has been largely studied in the past decades giving rise to approaches such as federated databases, multidatabases, interoperable databases or mediators. Here, we focus on integration of deductive databases. The problem is twofold:

- at the lower level, how to enrich traditional databases with deductive capabilities;
- at the higher level, how to integrate deductive databases which have the same semantic domain, but present different local models.

In the first case, one would like to integrate deductive databases (such as Datalog) with traditional databases. A successful approach to this problem was implemented, for example, in the $\mathcal{LDL} + +$ language [3]. Our proposal does not focus on this issue, although we intend to make use of such techniques. Our aim is to study the second issue, that is the problem of semantic integration of deductive databases. To illustrate the idea, we show a very simple case. Consider two travel agencies, each having a database which contains information about accommodations. They have the same semantic domain (accommodations) but they use different data representation, as we can see in the following example:

---

* Work partially supported by the EC-US Cooperative Activity Project and by CNR, grant #96.00069.02

**Agency A**
*lodging(excelsior, 4-star, rome, hotel, 500.000, 06/555175)*
*lodging(holiday-inn, 4-star, florence, hotel, 600.000, 055/555002)*
*lodging(solaria, 4-star, marilleva, apartments, 500.000, 0437/555789)*

:

**Agency B**
*hotel(miramonti, cortina, 600.000)*
*apartment(les alpes, m.d.campiglio, 1.000.000)*

:

In the first database the information is represented by means of the *lodging* predicate, where the first argument is the name of the accommodation, the second is the classification, the third is the location, the fourth is the kind of the accommodation and the last two arguments are the price in italian lire (per night the hotels and per week the apartments) and the telephone number, respectively. The database of the agency B represents accommodations in a different way. Each hotel is represented by the *hotel* predicate with three arguments, the first of which is the name, the second one the location and the last one the price (in italian lire). The apartments are represented with the *apartment* predicate. This is an example of schematic discrepancy, where the values of one database correspond to metadata (relations) in the other [12]. In an integrated environment, the user would like to access the information of both databases in a uniform way. For example, we would like to represent, somehow, the equivalence between the information on hotels of Agency A and Agency B, so that a user can ask information about hotels to both databases without having to know the local data representation of the agencies. On the other hand, we do not want to change the local databases. We aim at defining a *middle* layer between the data sources and the user level. This middle layer correspond to the concept of *mediator* (due to Wiederhold [23]) which can be regarded as a framework to perform semantic integration over multiple data sources and reasoning systems. Our approach aims at the definition of a *mediator* language for the semantic integration of different conceptual schema.

In the following, we refer to [21] where interoperability means *making information systems work together*. Interoperability can be intended at two levels of abstraction: *syntactic* (low level) and *semantic* (high level) one. In the syntactic the "meaning" of the terms is irrelevant. Examples of this kind of interoperation are different Unix systems which work together or cooperating SQL systems of different vendors. Semantic interoperation means integrating systems at a level which involves shared meaning, or semantics, of terms. In other words it is the process of specifying methods to resolve conflicts, pool information together, and define new compositional operations, based on existing operations, in the individual data sources. Ullman in [21] summarizes semantic interoperability in three broad approaches: *Point-to-point*, *Facilitator* and *Mediator* corresponding to different architectures.

The logic language we have in mind is an extension of Logic Programming with mechanisms to combine deductive databases according to the Mediator model. In particular, we will enrich Horn Clauses language by means of meta-features which make our language suitable to interoperability purposes [12]. We will give a formal declarative semantics of these mechanisms, based on the immediate consequences operator.

The plan of the paper follows. Section 2 introduces the syntax of the language and it provides an intuitive explanation of composition operators. Section 3 motivates our work by showing, as an example, the formalization of the problem of managing a library. In section 4 we give the denotational semantics via an extension of the immediate consequences operator. Section 5 shows the inference rules that describe the operational semantics of the language. Finally, in section 6 we make some comparisons of our language with other similar approaches in the literature and we discuss future work.

## 2  The Language

We consider a set of meta-level operations for composing definite logic programs, originally introduced in [6, 8, 2]: *Union* (∪), *Intersection* (∩), and *Constraint* (/). These operations define the following *language of program expressions*:

$$Pexp ::= Program \mid Pexp \cup Pexp \mid Pexp \cap Pexp \mid Pexp/Program$$

where *Program* is a named collection of clauses. Each set of clauses (program) is associated with a unique name by means of a global naming mechanism.

In the sequel we will abuse the notation and use a program identifier to directly denote the set of clauses associated with it.

The language of program expressions has been largely investigated both from the theoretical and from the application point of view (e.g. in [2, 6, 8, 10, 15]). In all these papers the language of program expressions has been employed as a meta-language for composing object programs written in a separate language, namely the language of definite programs. Other operators were introduced. For example, an *import* operator ◁ was introduced in [8] in order to handle modularization problems, and we expect that it may turn out useful in the future also in the context of mediator-based languages.

Here, we consider an extended object language in which program expressions may occur in object level programs. Namely, programs are extended definite programs that may contain meta-level calls to program expressions in clause bodies. More precisely, a program is a finite set of extended definite clauses of the form

$$A \leftarrow B_1, \ldots, B_n$$

where each $B_i$ is either an atomic formula or a meta-level formula of the form "$C$ in $Pexp$", where $C$ is an atomic formula and $Pexp$ a program expression. A goal like "$C$ in $Pexp$" introduces a form of message passing between object level program. The idea is that the program containing the goal "*C in Pexp*", sends the message $C$ to the "virtual" program denoted by "Pexp". As usual, logical variables act as input/output channels between programs.

We assume that the language in which programs are written is fixed. Namely, there is a fixed set of function and predicate symbols that include all function and predicate symbols used in the programs being considered. Moreover, program names and program composition operations are disjoint from all other constant and function symbols that may occur in programs. Notice also that in all expressions of the form "*A in Pexp*" occurring in the clause bodies of programs, the program expression *Pexp* is ground (i.e. it does not contain variables) by definition of program expression itself.

Below we will provide the language with a denotational semantics based on an extended immediate consequence operator. We will also describe an operational top-down semantics via an extension of SLD-resolution, and we will hint at methods for using the denotational semantics as a basis for an efficient bottom-up operational semantics based on techniques like the semi-naive computation strategy.

Here we give the operators an informal semantics by means of examples. Given a program expression E, we show a plain logic program that behaves as the program expression, i.e. it provides the same answers to the same queries, whatever is the operational semantics in use. Such a transformational approach, thoroughly described in [7, 2], is not practical in a database context, but it may be useful for an intuitive understanding of program expressions.

Consider the following plain programs

$P$:

$$arc(a, b) \leftarrow$$
$$arc(b, c) \leftarrow$$
$$arc(c, b) \leftarrow$$

$Q$:

$$arc(X, Y) \leftarrow arc(X, Z), arc(Z, Y)$$

$P$ describes a graph. $Q$ axiomatizes a general property of graphs. $P \cup Q$ behaves as a plain program containing the clauses of $P$ *and* the clauses of $Q$. As the example shows, union may be used to factor knowledge in different modules.

Intersection allows to combine knowledge by merging clauses with unifiable heads into clauses having the conjunctions of the bodies of the original clauses as body. The net effect is that the two plain programs act as sets of constraints one upon the other.

Consider the example

$P$:

$$likes(X, Y) \leftarrow sweet(Y)$$

$$hates(X, Y) \leftarrow bitter(Y)$$

$Q$:

$$likes(bob, Y) \leftarrow sour(Y)$$

Then the program expression $P \cap Q$ behaves as the plain logic program

$$likes(bob, Y) \leftarrow sweet(Y), sour(Y)$$

Notice that $P \cap Q$ does not say anything about hates, since nothing about hates is deducible from $Q$.

The constraint operator combines the features of union, intersection and a simple form of negation to provide an asymmetric composition between a program $P$ and a program $Q$. $Q$ acts as a set of constraints for $P$ as it is illustrated by the following example. Consider

$P$ :
$likes(X, Y) \leftarrow blond\_hair(Y)$
$green\_eyes(mary) \leftarrow$
$blond\_hair(mary) \leftarrow$
$blond\_hair(susan) \leftarrow$

$Q$ :
$likes(john, Y) \leftarrow green\_eyes(Y)$

The following plain program behaves as the program expression $P/Q$.

$$likes(X, Y) \leftarrow X \neq john, blond\_hair(Y)$$
$$likes(john, Y) \leftarrow green\_eyes(Y), blond\_hair(Y)$$
$$green\_eyes(mary) \leftarrow$$
$$blond\_hair(mary) \leftarrow$$
$$blond\_hair(susan) \leftarrow$$

Notice that the constraint is applied only to John while retaining the general knowledge about the rest of the people.

## 3  A Motivating Example

In the following we will show as an example a typical situation in which a library loans books to people of various departments. Each department has a database that contains information about its employees, and rules that state the local criteria for authorizing the loan of books from the library. The database of the library catalogues the publications, it contains information on users that have lost or destroyed books in the past, and rules that establish which kind of publications are loanable to users. The agreements between the library and the departments state that only authorized people can loan publications from the library, and that every employee is allowed to read the publications on the premises. Furthermore, special agreements between the library and each department are possible in order to grant longer periods of loan.

We will show a proposal for a formalization of this problems with the use of deductive databases for the representation of conceptual schemata, and mediators to allow the user to access, in a uniform way, the knowledge encoded in the various databases. Mediators are built using the language informally introduced in the previous section.

## 3.1 Architecture

The general architecture we refer to mirrors the architecture proposed by Ullman et al. in [18] where they propose the use of *wrappers* between information sources and the mediation layer. A *wrapper* can be defined as a component that converts data from each source to a *common model* , and provides a common query language for extracting information. A mediator combines, refines, integrates data from wrappers, providing applications with a "cleaner" view. The key point here is that wrapping does not affect the local models of the databases. It just builds a layer of information *above* the local databases. In the following, we show the proposed architecture, the entity-relationship schemata and the source code of the deductive databases, the common model obtained from wrappers, and some examples of mediators which use the composition operators to combine data from wrappers. We will see how the message passing mechanism can be used to implement wrappers and mediators.

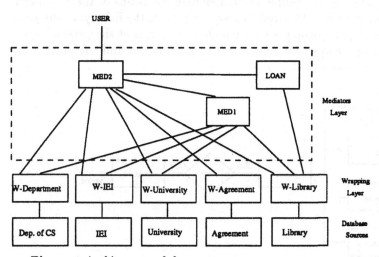

**Figure 1** Architecture of the system

The deductive databases represent the conceptual schema of the departments and of the library. The department of Computer Science, IEI (an Institute of the National Research Council), and the university have similar information but different ways of representing data. In other words, they have the same semantic domain, but different local schemata. Here the task of the wrapping phase is twofold: on one hand it translates the different models into a unique common model (which, in general, will be a superset of the various models) so that the wrapped version of each database represents its own information by means of a common model. On the other hand, wrapping transforms pieces of database information into a more compact form (as in the case of the Library database). In the mediator layer, we define two mediators and a set of constraint rules (Loan). The user can query Med-2 that exploits information from Med-1, the wrapped databases and the constraint rules.

## 3.2 Entity-Relationship Diagrams

Here, we present the design of the system, showing the local schemata of the databases and the schemata obtained from wrapping. In the schema integration phase each local model gives its contribution to the common model. We will explain this phase by means of an entity-relationship formalism, showing the diagrams both of the local models and of the models obtained by wrapping.

The department of Computer Science (fig. 2) represents people by means of four entities: *student, PhD student, researcher, professor*. Each entity is in relation with the entity *authorized* that represents people that are allowed to loan books from the library. Here the criterium is the following: each PhD student, researcher and professor is authorized to loan books, but not all the students are. In the IEI Institute (fig. 3), people are represented by means of the *researcher* entity. Each researcher is authorized to loan books from the library. In the University database (fig. 4), people are represented by means of the *person* entity, with *first name, last name*, the *department* they belong to and the *position* in the department as attributes.

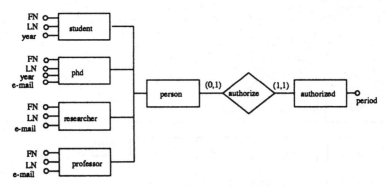

**Figure 2** Department of Computer Science local schema

**Figure 3** IEI local schema

**Figure 4** University local schema

The Library database (fig. 5) states that only books and journals are loanable publications. Each entity is identified by attributes such as *title, author, volume* and a special flag which represents the real availability of that publication in the library. Notice that proceedings of conferences are always available since they are not loanable. Furthermore, the library has a list of bad users, i.e. users who lost books in the past. The Agreements database (fig. 6) contains information about special agreements the library may have established with some departments. This situation is represented by means of the *special-agreement* entity, whose attributes specify the longer period of loan for a given department.

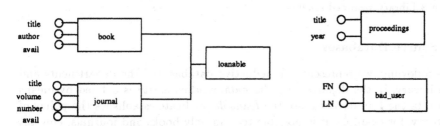

**Figure 5** Library local schema

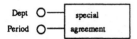

**Figure 6** Agreements local schema

Since the Department of CS, the University and IEI have the same semantic domain, we choose a common model that includes all the information of the local schemata we are interested in. In this example we represent people by means of *first* and *last name, department, position* and *year*, while we ignore e-mail. The diagram of the common model of the Department of CS, IEI and University is in figure 7. In the wrapped version of the Library (fig. 8), we represent each publication by means of the *publication* entity. It has attributes such as the type of publication (*book, journal ...*), *title, author, volume*. Again, we have the list of bad users.

**Figure 7** Common Model

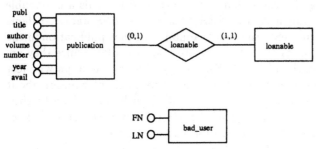

**Figure 8** Library wrapped schema

## 3.3   Source Databases

In the following, we represent the deductive databases of the departments and of the library. In the departments the *authorization* entity is defined by means of rules. In the Library database the *loanable* predicate establishes the policy of the library, for example: it is possible to loan only books and journals, and not proceedings. The Agreements database contains information about particular conditions, that is, it associates the longer loan period to each department that has a special agreement with the library,

### Department_of_CS

student(gianni, rossi, 3) ←
student(davide, verdi, 2) ←

⋮

phd(maria, gialli, 3, maria@cs) ←
researcher(giuseppe, bianchi, giuseppe@cs)←
professor(michele,neri, michele@cs)←

⋮

authorized(FN,LN, 3months) ← professor(FN, LN _)
authorized(FN,LN, 1month) ← researcher(FN, LN, _)

authorized(FN,LN, 1month) ← phd(FN, LN, _, _)
authorized(FN,LN, 1week) ← student(FN, LN, Year), Year ≥ 3


**IEI**

researcher(tommaso, rosi, tom@iei.cnr)←
researcher(luca, rossi, luca@iei.cnr)←
⋮

allow_loan(FN,LN, 3months) ← researcher(FN,LN, _)


## University

person(maria, gialli, cs, phd)←
person(susanna, monti, economy, professor)←
person(simone, verdi , literature, student) ←
⋮

authorized_for_loan(FN,LN, 1month) ← person(FN,LN, math, _)
authorized_for_loan(FN,LN, 1week) ← person(FN,LN, economy, professor)
authorized_for_loan(FN,LN, 1day) ← person(FN,LN, literature, professor)

## Library

book(sterling-shapiro, the-art-of-prolog, yes)←
book(ullman, database-and-knowledge-base-systems, yes)←
journal(communications-ACM, 10, 1, no)←
journal(communications-ACM,10, 2, yes)←
journal(ieee-computer,20, 1, no)←
journal(ieee-computer,20, 2, yes)←
proceedings(gulp, 1995)←
proceedings(vldb, 1994)←
⋮

loanable(Author, Title, nil, nil) ← book(Author, Title, Dept, Avail)
loanable(nil, Title, Vol, Num) ← journal(Title, Vol, Num, Avail)

bad_user(gianni, rossi)←
⋮


## Agreements

special_agreement(cs, 2months)←

special_agreement(math, 1month)←

$\vdots$

## Translated Databases

We choose a common model for databases that represent "similar" information by using different local schemata. Here, we represent people by the *person* predicate and the authorization by the *authorized_for_loan* predicate. The translation into a common model is done in a "dynamic" way by means of the message passing mechanism. We denote with the "W" prefix the wrapped databases. In this phase we deal with some kind of semantic heterogeneity. In the W-Department_of_CS, W-IEI and W-Library databases we solve a problem of semantic discrepancy between the local schemata and the chosen wrapped schemata. In the W-University database we just rearrange the attributes of the entity by selecting the attributes that represent information useful for mediators.

## W-Department_of_CS

person(FN, LN, student, Year, cs) ←
    student(FN, LN, Year) in Department_of_CS
person(FN, LN, professor, nil, cs) ←
    professor(FN,LN, Email) in Department_of_CS
person(FN, LN, researcher, nil, cs)←
    researcher(FN,LN, Email) in Department_of_CS
person(FN, LN, phd, Year, cs) ←
    phd(FN, LN, Year) in Department_of_CS

authorized_for_loan(FN,LN, Period) ←
    authorized(FN,LN, Period) in Department_of_CS

## W-IEI

person(FN, LN, research, nil, iei)←
    researcher(FN, LN, Email) in IEI

authorized_for_loan(FN, LN, Period) ←
    allow_loan(FN, LN, Period) in IEI

## W-University

person(FN, LN, Position, nil, Dept)←
    person(FN, LN, Dept, Position) in University

authorized_for_loan(FN,LN, Period) ←
              authorized_for_loan(FN,LN, Period) in University


## W-Library

publication(book, Author, Title, nil, nil, nil, Avail)←
              book(Author, Title, Avail) in Library
publication(journal, nil, Title, Vol, Num, nil, nil, Avail)←
              journal(Title, Vol, Num, Avail) in Library
publication(proceedings, nil, Title, nil, nil, Year, yes)←
              proceedings(Title, Year) in Library

loanable(Author, Title, Vol, Num) ←
              loanable(Author, Title, Vol,Num) in Library

bad_user(FN, LN)←
              bad_user(FN,LN) in Library


## W-Agreements

special_agreement(Dept, Period)←
              special_agreement(Dept, Period) in Agreements


## Mediators
Med-1 states the general loan regulation on the basis of information about publications that are in the Library database and by checking the authorization in all the departments. Loan contains a restricting rule which defines the *loan* predicate stating that the loan is possible only if a person is not a bad user and if the publication is really available in the library.

In Med-2 we find two rules. The first one deals with the loan of publications. The rule refines the information obtained by Med-1 by means of the constraint rule in Loan and by checking for special agreements. It replies to the user with the period for which the person is allowed to loan the book. The other rule is concerned with the use of a publication on the premises. Since the consultation of a publication on the premises does not require any authorization, all employees of the departments are allowed to consult publications if they are really available. The user can query Med-2 in order to loan or to use a given publication on the premises.

Notice that both mediators refer to the wrapped version of the databases in order to apply the operators correctly. Finally, a short remark on negation: in this example we use negation in the constraint rule although the abstract semantics is defined for positive programs. However, the negation used here is a shorthand for a check on a list of extensional atoms.

**Med-1**

loan(FN, LN,Author,Title, Vol, Num, Period) ←
       loanable(Author,Title, Vol, Num) in W-Library,
       authorized_for_loan(FN, LN, Period) in
              W-IEI ∪ W-Department_of_CS ∪ W-University


**Loan**

loan(FN, LN, Author, Title, Vol, Num, Period)←
           not bad_user(LN,FN) in W-Library,
           publication(Author,Title, Vol, Num, yes) in W-Library


**Med-2**

loan_to_user(FN,LN,Author,Title, Vol, Num, Period) ←
       loan(FN, LN, Author, Title, Vol, Num, Period1) in Med-1 / Loan
       person(FN, LN, Position, Year, Dept) in
            W-IEI ∪ W-Department_of_CS ∪ W-University
       special_agreement(Dept, Period2) in W-Agreements
       max_period(Period1, Period2, Period)

use(FN,LN,Author,Title, Vol, Num) ←
           person(FN, LN, Position, Year, Dept) in
           W-IEI ∪ W-Department_of_CS ∪ W-University
           publication(Author,Title, Vol, Num, yes) in W-Library

Notice that in Loan, the variable *Period* in the rule for loan does occur in the head, but it does not occur in the body. However, the clause is a constraint that will never be evaluated as it is. Later, the clause will be used in the constraint construction, and this apparent anomaly will disappear.


# 4 Denotational Semantics

We now define the denotational semantics of the language in a bottom-up style by extending the standard immediate consequence operator $(T_P)$ semantics for logic programs. The semantics we are going to give does not include the definition of the "message passing" mechanism. The introduction of the "in" feature makes the bottom-up definition much more complex. The reader can refer to [4, 9] for the formal definition.

Recall that, for a definite logic program $P$, the immediate consequence operator $T_P$ is a continuous mapping over Herbrand interpretations defined as follows [22]. For any Herbrand interpretation $I$:

$$A \in T_P(I) \Longleftrightarrow (\exists \mathbf{B} : A \leftarrow \mathbf{B} \in ground(P) \wedge \mathbf{B} \subseteq I)$$

where $\mathbf{B}$ is a (possibly empty) conjunction of atoms and $ground(P)$ denotes the ground (i.e. fully instantiated) version of program $P$.

Such an approach is motivated by the observation that the classical least model semantics is not compositional — it is not possible to obtain the least model of, say, the union of two programs $P$ and $Q$ by homomorphically composing the least models of $P$ and $Q$. In [6] it is shown that the $T_P$-based semantics is in fact both compositional and fully-abstract with respect to the repertoire of composition operations adopted in this paper.

In the definition of the constraint operator we will use the notation $E_{\pi(F)}$ with E program expression and F a program. The intuitive meaning is that $E_{\pi(F)}$ contains all the clauses of E which define predicate names which have also a definition in F. In the following we give the formal definition.

**Definition 1.** We give the definition by induction on the structure of E.

- E plain program, then $E_{\pi(F)}$ contains the clauses of E defining predicates that have a definition in F;
- $E = R \cup S$ then $E_{\pi(F)} = R_{\pi(F)} \cup S_{\pi(F)}$
- $E = R \cap S$ then $E_{\pi(F)} = R_{\pi(F)} \cap S_{\pi(F)}$
- $E = R / S$ then $E_{\pi(F)} = R_{\pi(F)}/S$

Finally, we denote with $E_{\pi(F)}-$ all the clauses of E which do not belong to $E_{\pi(F)}$

**Definition 2.** The semantics of program expressions is given as follows:

$$T_{(E \cup F)}(I) = T_E(I) \cup T_F(I)$$

The set of immediate consequences of the union of two program expressions is the set-theoretic union of the immediate consequences of the two expressions. (The symbol $\cup$ is used to denote both the program composition operation and the set-theoretic union.)

$$T_{(E \cap F)}(I) = T_E(I) \cap T_F(I)$$

Analogously, the set of immediate consequences of the intersection of two program expressions is the set-theoretic intersection of the immediate consequences of the two expressions.

$$T_{(E/F)}(I) = T_{E \cap F}(I) \cup T_{(E_{\pi(F)-})}(I) \cup (T_{E_{\pi(F)}}(I) \cap T_{(F,E)^c})(I))$$

The immediate consequences of a program expression $E$ constrained by a program $F$ is a combination of the union and intersection operator and a kind of *complement* of a program w.r.t. a program expression. Informally, consider the case in which $E$ is a plain program constrained by a set of clauses $F$. The resulting program is obtained by the union of two parts. One is the intersection of the two programs, that forces them to agree during the deduction. But intersection alone is not enough, because some clauses would be missing in the result. In particular, we miss all the clauses for predicates which are defined in $E$ and not constrained by $F$. These predicates are of two kinds: the ones which do not have a definition in $F$, and those which have a definition in $F$ that constrains only a subset of atoms potentially derivable in $E$. The complement of a program $F$ w.r.t a program expression $E$ is defined as follows:

$$T_{((F,E)^c)}(I) = \mathcal{B}_{E\pi(F)} \setminus T_F(\mathcal{B}_E)$$

Here we denote with $\mathcal{B}_E$ the Herbrand Base of the program $E$ and with $\mathcal{B}_{E\pi(F)}$ the set of atoms of the Herbrand Base of $E$ which have predicate names that have a definition in the program $F$. Therefore, the immediate consequences of the complement of a program $F$ w.r.t. a program expression $E$ is obtained by the set-difference of $\mathcal{B}_{E\pi(F)}$ and the heads of $F$ instantiated by the Herbrand base of $E$.

## 5 Operational semantics

We now present an operational semantics for the extended language by means of a set of inference rules. The operational characterization of the language is expressed by extending directly the standard notion of SLD refutation [1].

The standard notion of SLD refutation may be defined by means of inference rules of the form

$$\frac{Premise}{Conclusion}$$

with the meaning that *Conclusion* holds whenever *Premise* holds. We write $P \vdash_\vartheta G$ if there exists a top-down refutation for the goal $G$ in the program (expression) $P$ with computed substitution $\vartheta$.

Let us first present the rules that model the SLD refutation for definite programs.

$$\frac{}{P \vdash_\epsilon empty} \tag{1}$$

$$\frac{P \vdash_\vartheta G_1 \ \wedge \ P \vdash_\gamma G_2\vartheta}{P \vdash_{\vartheta\gamma} (G_1, G_2)} \tag{2}$$

$$\frac{P \vdash_\vartheta (H \leftarrow G) \ \wedge \ \gamma = mgu(A, H\vartheta) \ \wedge \ P \vdash_\delta G\vartheta\gamma}{P \vdash_{\vartheta\gamma\delta} A} \tag{3}$$

$$\frac{P \text{ is a program } \land \ A \leftarrow G \in P}{P \vdash_\epsilon (A \leftarrow G)} \tag{4}$$

Rule (1) states that the empty goal is solved in any program $P$ with the empty substitution $\epsilon$. Rule (2) deals with goal conjunction: A conjunction $(G_1, G_2)$ is solved in a program $P$ if both goals are solved in $P$. More precisely, rule (2) specifies a left-to-right order in the evaluation of conjunctive goals. First goal $G_1$ is solved with computed substitution $\vartheta$, and then goal $G_2$, suitably instantiated by $\vartheta$, is solved with computed substitution $\gamma$. (Notice that we might also write rule (2) without imposing the order of evaluation of conjuncts by employing a composition operator on substitutions, as defined for instance in [17].) Rule (3) states that an atomic goal $A$ is solved with computed substitution $\vartheta\gamma\delta$ if there is a clause $(H \leftarrow G)\vartheta$ in $P$ such that $A$ unifies with $H\vartheta$ via $\gamma$, and $G\vartheta\gamma$ is in turn solvable in $P$ with computed substitution $\delta$.

Notice that the substitution $\vartheta$ in $P \vdash_\vartheta (H \leftarrow G)$ in rule (3) is the empty substitution if $P$ is a program, as specified by rule (4). On the other hand, when $P$ is an arbitrary composition of programs the substitution $\vartheta$ in $P \vdash_\vartheta (H \leftarrow G)$ becomes relevant, as we shall see below.

The derivation relation $\vdash$ can be extended to deal with program compositions in a simple way. Namely, each composition operation is modeled by adding new inference rules defining whether some instance $(A \leftarrow G)\vartheta$ of a clause $A \leftarrow G$ belongs to the "virtual" program denoted by a program expression $E$, that is by proving $E \vdash_\vartheta (A \leftarrow G)$. From now onwards, we will say that $(A \leftarrow G)\vartheta$ belongs to $E$ as a shorthand for saying that the clause $(A \leftarrow G)\vartheta$ belongs to the virtual program: $\{(A \leftarrow G)\vartheta \ | \ E \vdash_\vartheta (A \leftarrow G)\}$.

We now present the inference rules modeling the composition operations.

$$\frac{P \vdash_\vartheta (A \leftarrow G)}{P \cup Q \vdash_\vartheta (A \leftarrow G)} \tag{5}$$

$$\frac{Q \vdash_\vartheta (A \leftarrow G)}{P \cup Q \vdash_\vartheta (A \leftarrow G)} \tag{6}$$

Rules (5) and (6) describe the union operation $\cup$. They state that a clause belongs to the program expression $P \cup Q$ if it belongs either to $P$ or to $Q$.

$$\frac{P \vdash_{\vartheta_1} (H_1 \leftarrow G_1) \ \land \ Q \vdash_{\vartheta_2} (H_2 \leftarrow G_2) \ \land \ \gamma = mgu(H_1\vartheta_1, H_2\vartheta_2)}{P \cap Q \vdash_{\vartheta_1\vartheta_2\gamma} (H_1 \leftarrow G_1, G_2)} \tag{7}$$

Rule (7) states that a clause $(x_1 \leftarrow y, z)\gamma$ belongs to the program expression $P \cap Q$ if there is a clause $x_1 \leftarrow y$ in $P$ and a clause $x_2 \leftarrow z$ in $Q$ such that $x_1$ and $x_2$ unify via $\gamma$. Here, the observation of rule 2 about the ordering of evaluation of conjuncts holds.

$$\frac{P_{\pi(Q)}- \cup (P_{\pi(Q)} \cap (Q,P)^c) \cup (P \cap Q) \vdash_{\vartheta} (A \leftarrow G)}{P/Q \vdash_{\vartheta} (A \leftarrow G)} \qquad (8)$$

In rule (8) we give the inference rule of the constraint operator which is a combination of union, intersection and complement.

$$\frac{P \vdash_{\vartheta} (p(\bar{x}) \leftarrow G), notunify(\bar{x}\vartheta, \bar{t}\gamma)}{(P, \_)^c \vdash_{\gamma} (p(\bar{t}) \leftarrow empty)} \qquad (9)$$

Rule (9) describes the top-down behavior of the complement operator. A unit clause $p(\bar{t}) \leftarrow empty$ belongs to the complement of a program expression P (w.r.t any other program) with computed substitution $\gamma$ if a clause $p(\bar{x}) \leftarrow G$ belongs to P with computed substitution $\vartheta$ and $\bar{x}\vartheta$ *does not unify* with $\bar{t}\gamma$. The key point here is the definition of the *notunify* predicate: it takes n-tuples of variables as arguments and it returns *true* if it does exists a bag of indices $\{a_1, \ldots, a_k\}, 1 \leq k \leq n$ such that $(x_{a_1}, \ldots, x_{a_k})\vartheta$ are ground, and exists at least one index $a_j$ such that $t_{a_j}\gamma \neq x_{a_j}\vartheta \wedge j \in \{1, \ldots, k\}$. If $\forall i \in [1, \ldots, n]$ $\bar{x}_i\vartheta$ is not ground then *notunify* returns *false*. It is worth noting that in the rule the second argument of the complement operator here is not used to perform the computation. In fact, while the second argument, in the bottom-up semantics defines the universe where values are chosen, in the top-down semantics, the arguments are already ground when this inference rules is applied.

$$\frac{Q \vdash_{\vartheta} A}{P \vdash_{\vartheta} (A \; in \; Q)} \qquad (10)$$

This rule defines the behavior of "*in*" formulae. Namely, solving an extended goal of the form "*A in Q*" simply amounts to solving $A$ in the program expression $Q$. We have proved in [9] that the top-down semantics in correct w.r.t the abstract semantics.

## 6 Conclusions

Our proposal aims at defining an interoperable language much in the spirit of others approaches developed in the last few years. In particular, we would like to mention here the HERMES [20] and the TSIMMIS [11] projects, and the SchemaLog [13] and IDL [12] languages. In the following we will try to point out some commonalities and differences between them and our proposal.

The mediator language of the HERMES project is a logical language enriched with mechanisms inherited from the Hybrid Knowledge Bases theory [14]. A mechanism somehow similar to our "message passing" *(domain call)* enables the mediator to extract information from a particular database. There, the mediator refers to databases which are really heterogeneous, in the sense that this mechanism allows the evaluation of queries in different domains, such as spatial, relational or text databases. The architecture of the HERMES system does not include any kind of wrapping, and the language does not offer composition operators.

In the TSIMMIS project, Ullman et al. [11] define a mediator language based on an object-oriented extension of SQL. This language is provided with a "message passing" mechanism to refer to the wrapped databases. Furthermore, it has higher order features, that allows one to deal with schematic discrepancies in a compact way. This is a feature shared also by IDL, a higher order logic language based on Horn clauses. This language allows variables ranging over data and metadata, the definition of a variable number of relations, depending on the state of the database, and views update capabilities.

SchemaLog is a logical language with higher order syntax which can be used in a federation of relational databases without wrapping. The main application fields of SchemaLog are database programming, schema browsing, schema integration and schema evolution.

It is worth noting that the common denominator of the languages mentioned above is that they are all defined starting from a logical language and by enriching it with meta or higher order features. This makes the languages suitable for dealing with interoperability. We have followed this common approach defining new mechanisms on top of logic programming and extending, in a conservative way, its formal semantics. Higher order syntax with variables ranging over data and metadata provides an elegant solution to the problem of schematic discrepancies. Our approach is different in that we concentrate on meta level composition of deductive databases, rather than on the use of meta features over terms and formulas.

The future developments of our research are in three main directions. The first one concerns an efficient implementation of the language. Our aim is to extend some of the classic query evaluation methods to the composition operators. In particular, we intend to study the possible extensions to the *seminaive* evaluation strategy and the *magic set* technique. Intuitively speaking, the seminaive evaluation technique consists in an efficient implementation of the immediate consequences operator (also called *naive* evaluation). The efficiency is obtained by focusing only on the new facts generated at each iteration, thereby avoiding recomputing the same facts in case of recursion. The idea underlying the magic set method is to combine bottom-up and top-down techniques in order to have a "goal-driven bottom-up" computation, in the sense that the bottom-up computation computes only the facts "relevant" to the query [16, 5]. We have encouraging preliminary results in this respect. The second direction is to study how to introduce update mechanisms in the language. The last direction is the study of techniques for introducing negation in the language. It seems that extending the Fitting operator could be a good starting point [2].

# Acknowledgments

We are grateful to Dr. Alessandra Raffaetá for helpful comments.

# References

1. K. R. Apt. Logic programming. In J. van Leeuwen, editor, *Handbook of Theoretical Computer Science*, pages 493–574. Elsevier, 1990. Vol. B.
2. D. Aquilino, P. Asirelli, C. Renso, and F. Turini. An operator for composing deductive databases with theories of constraints. In A. Nerode V. W. Marek, editor, *3rd International Conference on Logic Programming and Non Monotonic Reasoning*, volume 928, Lexington, KY, USA, June 1995. LNCS.
3. N. Arni, K. Ong, and C. Zaniolo. Negation and aggregates in recursive rules: the LDL++ approach. In *Proc. 3rd Int. Conference on Deductive and O-O DBs, DOOD93*, Phoenix, December, 6-8 1993.
4. P. Asirelli, C. Renso, and F. Turini. Semantic integration of deductive databases. Technical Report TR B4-17, IEI-CNR, June 1996.
5. C. Beeri and R. Ramakrishnan. On the power of magic. *Journal of Logic Programming*, 10(324), 1991.
6. A. Brogi. *Program Construction in Computational Logic*. PhD thesis, University of Pisa, March 1993.
7. A. Brogi, A. Chiarelli, V. Mazzotta, P. Mancarella, D. Pedreschi, C. Renso, and F. Turini. Implementations of program composition operations. In M. Hermenegildo and J. Penjam, editors, *Proceeding of the Sixth Int'l Symp. on Programming Language Implementation and Logic Programming*, volume 844 of *LNCS*. Springer-Verlag, Berlin, 1994.
8. A. Brogi, P. Mancarella, D. Pedreschi, and F. Turini. Modular Logic Programming. *ACM Transactions on Programming Languages and Systems*, 16(4):1361–1398, 1994.
9. A. Brogi, C. Renso, and F. Turini. Program composition and message passing in logic programming. technical report, University of Pisa, 1996.
10. A. Brogi and F. Turini. Fully abstract compositional semantics for an algebra of logic programs. *Theoretical Computer Science*, 150, 1995.
11. S. Chawathe, H. Garcia-Molina, J. Hammer, K. Ireland, Y. Papakonstantinou, J. Ullman, and J. Widom. The TSIMMIS project: Integration of heterogeneous information sources. In *Proceedings of IPSJ Conference*, Tokyo, Japan, October 1994.
12. R. Krishnamurthy, W. Litwin, and W. Kent. Language features for interoperability of databases with schematic discrepancies. In *ACM SIGMOD Conference*, volume 20. ACM, 1991.
13. L. Lakshmanan, F. Sadri, and I. Subramanian. Logic and algebraic languages for interoperability in multidatabase systems. Technical Report TR-DB-95-01, Department of Computer Science, Concordia University, 1995.
14. J. Lu, A. Nerode, and V.S. Subrahmanian. Hybrid knowledge bases. *IEEE Transactions on Knowledge and Data Engineering*, 1994.
15. P. Mancarella and D. Pedreschi. An algebra of logic programs. In R. A. Kowalski and K. A. Bowen, editors, *Proceedings Fifth International Conference on Logic Programming*, pages 1006–1023. The MIT Press, 1988.

16. P. Mascellani and D. Pedreschi. The declarative side of magic. submitted for publication, 1996.
17. C. Palamidessi. Algebraic properties of idempotent substitutions. In Springer-Verlag, editor, *Proc. of the 17th International Colloquium on Automata, Languages and Programming (ICALP)*, number 443 in Lecture Notes in Computer Science, pages 386–399, 1990.
18. Y. Papakostantinou, H. Garcia-Molina, and J. Ullman. Medmaker: A mediation system based on declarative specifications. In *ICDE*, 1996. to appear.
19. A. Silberschatz, M. Stonebraker, and J. Ullman. Database research: Achievements and oppurtunities into the 21st century. Technical report, NFS Report, 1995.
20. VS. Subrahmanian, S. Adali, A. Brink, JJ. Lu, A. Rajput, J. Rogers, R. Ross, and C. Ward. HERMES: A heterogeneous reasoning and mediator system. submitted for publication. Can be found in
http://www.cs.umd.edu/projects/hermes/overview/paper/index.html.
21. J. Ullman. High level interoperation. Slides.
22. M. H. van Emden and R. A. Kowalski. The semantics of predicate logic as a programming language. *Journal of the ACM*, 23(4):733–742, 1976.
23. G. Wiederhold. Mediators in the architecture of future information systems. *IEEE Computer*, 25:38–49, March 1992.

# Unification of Bounded Simple Set Terms in Deductive Databases *

Sergio Greco,[1] Cristinel Mateis[1] and Eugenio Spadafora[2]

[1] DEIS, Univ. della Calabria, 87030 Rende, Italy
{ greco, mateis }@si.deis.unical.it
[2] ISI-CNR, c/o DEIS - Univ. della Calabria, 87030 Rende, Italy
eugenio@si.deis.unical.it

**Abstract.** In this paper we consider the problem of unification of bounded simple set terms in the field of deductive databases. Simple set terms are of the form $\{e_1, \ldots, e_n\}$, where $e_i$ is a constant or a variable and are much used in deductive database systems such as $\mathcal{LDL}$ and Coral. In this paper we consider a restricted form of unification, called "weak unification", which is mainly used in the field of deductive databases where the database may contain both constants and variables and the program is "safe". The main results are: (a) the detailed complexity analysis of the weak unification problem by providing a formula for determining the number of weak unifiers, and (b) the invention of an optimal weak unification algorithm.

## 1 Introduction

Several recent papers [7, 22, 1, 2, 15] have addressed the problem of extending logic programs with sets in order to handle aggregation of objects. In this paper we shall refer to the extensions proposed by [7], that has been adopted in many systems (e.g., the logic language $\mathcal{LDL}$ [35, 28] and, in some form, the system Coral [30]). In this extension sets are defined either by enumerating their elements (*bounded set terms*) or by giving conditions for determining them (*grouping variables*).

A grouping variable is of the form $\langle Y \rangle$ and may only occur in the head of the rule. Thus, a rule may have the following form

$$p(x_1, \ldots, x_h, \langle Y \rangle) \leftarrow B_1, \ldots, B_n$$

where $B_1, \ldots, B_n$ are the goals of the rules, $p$ is the head predicate symbol with arity $h + 1$, $x_1, \ldots, x_h$ are terms, and $\langle Y \rangle$ is a grouping variable. Informally, the grouping variable $\langle Y \rangle$ will represent a set after suitable ground substitutions for the variable $Y$. For example, the grouping variable $\langle P\# \rangle$ in the following rule:

$$part\_set(S\#, \langle P\# \rangle) \leftarrow supplier(S\#, P\#)$$

* Work partially supported by a European Union grant under the EU-US project "DEUS EX MACHINA: non-determinism for deductive databases" and by a MURST project "Sistemi formali e strumenti per basi di dati evolute".

will collect into a set all the parts supplied by every supplier.

Bounded set terms are of the form $\{e_1, ..., e_n\}$, where $e_1, ..., e_n$ are (not necessarily ground) terms corresponding to the elements of the set. Bounded set terms as defined above are special cases of set terms as known in the literature [8, 10, 11, 12, 16, 18, 19, 21, 25, 26, 32, 33, 34, 37]. Indeed, the classical definition of set term assumes that enumeration of the elements in a set term can be partial, thus a set term may have the form $\{e\} \cup s$ so that it contains the element $e$ in addition to those in the set $s$ — moreover, to recursively decompose a set into strictly smaller sets, it may also be required that $e$ is not contained in $s$ and the notation $\{e \mid s\}$ is, then, used [16]. To distinguish from the general cases, we say that our set terms are *bounded* in the sense that their elements are fully enumerated. Despite their simplicity, bounded set terms are important as they occur very frequently in many application areas, such as databases and logic programming [28, 22, 20].

A crucial problem with bounded set terms is unification. This problem differs from first-order unification in that it must take into account *idempotency* (i.e., two elements in a set term may refer to the same object) and *commutativity* (i.e., the order of elements is immaterial) and, therefore, it could result in multiple incomparable matches[3] [32]. For example, given the two set terms $S = \{X, Y, a\}$ and $T = \{a, b\}$, we have three unifiers, namely, $\sigma_1 = \{X/a, Y/b\}$, $\sigma_2 = \{X/b, Y/a\}$, and $\sigma_3 = \{X/b, Y/b\}$.

The introduction of sets requires an ad-hoc resolution strategy for dealing with grouping variables as well as for unifying set-terms. In this paper we shall investigate the latter problem in a special case which we shall call weak unification. Weak unification of set terms is a restricted form of unification that can be used in the field of deductive databases for "safe queries" and databases containing both constants and variables. A variable appearing in a database fact is used to denotes any constant. To distinguish variables appearing in database facts from variables appearing in the program we shall use the terms *database variables* and *query variables*.

We point out that deductive database systems are mainly based on the bottom-up resolution strategy and that, for "safe queries" and ground database relations, matching is the only form of unification used [36]. However, recently there have been different proposals to introduce unground tuples in database relations (e.g., the system Coral [30] or constraint databases [17]). Thus, weak unification is an extension of matching for the case of databases with unground tuples. More specifically, in weak unification one of two bounded simple set terms contains only constants and database variables and we compute the part of the maximal general unifiers necessary to answer the query.

Consider for instance the two sets $S = \{X, a\}$ and $T = \{Y, Z\}$ where $Y$ and $Z$ are database variables and $X$ is a query variable. The two sets $S$ and $T$ have the following five unifiers: $\theta_1 = \{Z/a, X/Y\}$, $\theta_2 = \{Z/a, Y/X\}$, $\theta_3 = \{Y/a, X/Z\}$,

---

[3] A binary function symbol $f$ is said to be (i) *idempotent* if $f(a, f(a, s)) = f(a, s)$, (ii) *commutative* if $f(a, f(b, s)) = f(b, f(a, s))$, and, (iii) *associative* if $f(a, f(b, c)) = f(f(a, b), c)$.

$\theta_4 = \{Y/a, Z/X\}$ and $\theta_5 = \{X/a, Y/a, Z/a\}$. Moreover, (i) the unifier $\theta_5$ is not most general because it can be obtained by composition of $\theta_1$ with $\{Y/a\}$, (ii) the unifiers $\theta_2$ and $\theta_4$ can be derived, respectively, from $\theta_1$ and $\theta_3$ by renaming of variables (and vice versa). Thus, the two sets have four complete sets of mgu's and one of them consists of the mgu's $\theta_1$ and $\theta_3$. In weak unification we are interested only to know substitutions for the variable $X$ and therefore, we have two weak mgu's $\sigma_1 = \{X/Y\}$ and $\sigma_2 = \{X/Z\}$ which are equivalent since they both substitute the variable $X$ with a database variable, i.e., a variable denoting any value in the database. A complete set of weak mgu's for $S$ and $T$ contains either $\sigma_1$ or $\sigma_2$.

Although finding the matchers of two set terms is easy [5], the presence of variables in both sets makes the problem difficult. However, for the class of "safe queries" we do not need general unification since, under the bottom-up evaluation, one of the two terms contains only constants and database variables and to answer the query we are interested only to substitute query variables. Thus, in this paper we concentrate on the problem of weak unification of bounded simple set terms. In particular, we study the exact complexity of the problem by determining a tight time complexity lower bound for the problem and we present an optimal algorithm that performs weak unification of bounded simple set terms.

The problem of unifying commutative, idempotent terms has been deeply investigated by taking into account an additional property, *associativity*, [8, 12, 18, 25, 21, 32]. An excellent review of significant results in this area has been provided by Siekmann [32] (see also [21]); various complexity results are presented by Kapur and Narendran in [18]. In particular they prove that both unification and matching of terms with commutativity and idempotency are NP-hard; therefore the Set Term Unification Problem is NP-hard. Moreover, some algorithms have been proposed in the literature for unification with associativity and commutativity [26, 33, 25] as well as with associativity, commutativity and idempotency [26]; such algorithms cannot be extended to deal with commutativity and idempotency only.

A technique to extend the deductive database resolution strategy to deal with set terms, for the case of matching, has been proposed in [31] where the anomaly of the set term unification is removed at compilation time using rewriting techniques to transform set terms into 'standard' terms. This technique generates a number of rules that is exponential in the size of the rewritten terms. The case of set term matching has been studied in [5] where also an optimal matching algorithm is presented. Algorithms for the unification of bound simple set terms have been proposed in [34, 3]. An optimal algorithm for the unification of bounded set terms has been presented in [13]. Moreover, unification algorithms are too general and, consequently, inefficient for the case at hand.

The paper is organized as follows. In Section 2, we present basic (mainly, syntactic) definitions on set term unification. In Section 3 we formally introduce the problem of set term unification, giving suitable parameters for the characterization of the problem input and defining canonical unifiers, i.e., particular unifiers in a class of equivalent unifiers. In Section 4, we presents the complexity results. In Section 5, we present an optimal algorithm for unification of bounded simple set terms.

For space limitation, all proofs of our results are omitted or sketched. The complete proofs can be found in [14].

# 2 Basic Definitions

## 2.1 Unification of Standard Terms

A *(simple) term* can be either a variable or a constant. An atom is of the form $p(t_1, ..., t_n)$ where $p$ is a predicate symbol and $t_1, ..., t_n$ are terms. We assume that the set of variables is partitioned into the two subsets of database variables and query variables. Database variables appear as arguments in database tuples whereas query variables appear as arguments in logic programs.

A *substitution* is a finite set of pairs $\theta = \{X_1/t_1, ..., X_n/t_n\}$ where $X_1, ..., X_n$ are distinct variables and $t_1, ..., t_n$ are terms. Let $\theta = \{X_1/t_1, ..., X_n/t_n\}$ be a substitution and $T$ be a term, then $T\theta$ is the term obtained from $T$ by simultaneously replacing each occurrence of $X_i$ in $T$ by $t_i$ $(1 \leq i \leq n)$ — $T\theta$ is called an *instance* of $T$. Substitutions can be composed. Given two substitutions $\theta = \{X_1/t_1, ..., X_n/t_n\}$ and $\sigma = \{Y_1/s_1, ..., Y_m/s_m\}$ their *composition* $\theta\sigma$ is obtained from the set $\{X_1/t_1\sigma, ..., X_n/t_n\sigma, Y_1/s_1, ..., Y_m/s_m\}$ by deleting the pairs $X_i/t_i\sigma$ for which $X_i = t_i\sigma$ as well as the pairs $Y_i/s_i$ for which $Y_i \in \{X_1, ..., X_n\}$. Given two substitutions $\sigma$ and $\theta$, $\sigma$ is an *instance* of $\theta$, if there exists a substitution $\gamma$ such that $\sigma = \theta\gamma$. Moreover if both $\sigma$ is an instance of $\theta$ and $\theta$ is an instance of $\sigma$ then they are *equivalent*.

Let $S$ be a finite set of terms. A substitution $\theta$ is a *unifier* for $S$ if $S\theta$ is a singleton. We say that a set of terms $S$ *unify* if there exists a unifier $\theta$ for $S$. A unifier $\theta$ for $S$ is called a *most general unifier (mgu)* for $S$ if, for each unifier $\sigma$ of $S$, $\sigma$ is an instance of $\theta$. The mgu is unique modulo renaming of variables, thus all mgu's are equivalent. If $S$ contains only two terms and one of them is ground, a unifier $\theta$ for $S$ is called *matcher*; obviously, there exists at most one matcher and, therefore, at most one mgu. If the matcher exists then we say that the two terms *match*.

## 2.2 Unification of Set Terms

Let us now extend unification and matching of (bounded simple) set terms[4].

**Definition 1.** Let $S$ and $T$ be two set terms. A substitution $\theta$ for $\{S, T\}$ is a *unifier* if $S\theta = T\theta$; moreover, $\theta$ is a *maximal general unifier (mgu)* if there does not exist a unifier $\sigma$ such that $\theta$ is an instance of $\sigma$. Finally, if either $S$ or $T$ is ground then any unifier is called a *matcher*. □

---

[4] From now on we shall use set term to mean bounded simple set term.

We observe that it is not any more true that a *mgu* is unique modulo renaming of variables, thus not all mgu's are equivalent. For this reason, the mgu should here stand for maximal general unifier instead of most general unifier.

**Definition 2.** Let $S$ and $T$ be two set terms. A set $B$ of mgu's for $\{S, T\}$ is a *complete set (or base) of mgu's* if both no two mgu's in $B$ are equivalent and for each mgu $\theta$, there exists a (not necessarily distinct) mgu in $B$ that is equivalent to $\theta$.  □

Thus the set of all mgu's, for two set terms $S$ and $T$ can be partioned into equivalence classes using the equivalence relation for substitutions; the set of one representative for each class is a base of mgu's.

*Example 1.* Consider the two set terms $S = \{X, Y\}$ and $T = \{a, Z\}$. In this case we have 4 mgu's, namely $\theta_1 = \{X/a, Y/Z\}, \theta_2 = \{X/a, Z/Y\}), \theta_3 = \{X/Z, Y/a\}$ and $\theta_4 = \{Z/X, Y/a\})$. As $\theta_1$ is equivalent to $\theta_2$ and $\theta_3$ is equivalent to $\theta_4$, there are two equivalence classes and, therefore, 4 bases of mgu's, thus $\{\theta_1, \theta_3\}$, $\{\theta_1, \theta_4\}$, $\{\theta_2, \theta_3\}$ and $\{\theta_2, \theta_4\}$. Observe that the unifier $\{X/a, Y/a, Z/a\}$ is not an mgu.

Consider now the two set terms $S = \{X, Y\}$ and $T = \{a, b\}$. In this case we have two mgu's (matchers), namely $\theta_1 = \{X/a, Y/b\}$ and $\theta_2 = \{X/b, Y/a\}$, and the unique base $\{\theta_1, \theta_2\}$.  □

In the next section we formalize the set term unification problem giving a rather general format for input set terms, the parameters that characterize the input and output, and a general scheme for describing the algorithms.

## 3  The Set Term Unification Problem

We first present a simple sufficient and necessary condition for a successful unification of two set terms. Let $S$ be a set term, we denote with $var(S)$ and $ground(S)$ the sets of variables and constants in $S$, respectively.

**Proposition 3.** *Two set terms $S$ and $T$ unify if and only if*

1. $|var(S)| \geq |ground(T - S)|$;
2. $|var(T)| \geq |ground(S - T)|$; *and*
3. $|var(S \cup T)| \geq |ground(T - S) \cup ground(S - T)|$.  □

We point out that Proposition 3 is applied to sets containing only simple terms while the general problem of deciding whether two set terms are unifiable is NP-complete [18]. Proposition 3 can be easily tested in time linear in the size of $S$ and $T$ since we are assuming that sets are stored as ordered lists. We shall therefore assume that the two set terms have already passed this test. This implies that, in case both $S$ and $T$ are ground, then $S = T$, thus they trivially unify through the empty substitution. Observe that if two set terms $S$ and $T$ have a unifier they have also a weak unifier. Therefore, in order to only deal with the general case, we assume that one of the two sets contains only constants and database variables whereas the second set contains at most one query variable.

The set term weak unification problem consists to find the set of mgu's for the two sets $S$ and $T$ defined as follows:

$$S = \{ a_1, ..., a_{h_1}, X_1, ..., X_{k_1}, Z_1, ..., Z_m, c_1, ..., c_n \}$$
$$T = \{ b_1, ..., b_{h_2}, Y_1, ..., Y_{k_2}, Z_1, ..., Z_m, c_1, ..., c_n \}$$

where $a_1, ..., a_{h_1}, b_1, ..., b_{h_2}, c_1, ..., c_n$ are distinct constants and $X_1, ..., X_{k_1}, Y_1, ..., Y_{k_2}, Z_1, ..., Z_m$ are distinct variables.

*Notation.* We shall denote set of constants and variables as follows: $\mathbf{a} = \{a_1, ..., a_{h_1}\}$, $\mathbf{b} = \{b_1, ..., b_{h_2}\}$, $\mathbf{c} = \{c_1, ..., c_n\}$, are sets of distinct constants, and $\mathbf{X} = \{X_1, ..., X_{k_1}\}$, $\mathbf{Y} = \{Y_1, ..., Y_{k_2}\}$, $\mathbf{Z} = \{Z_1, ..., Z_m\}$ are sets of distinct variables. Therefore, the constants in $\mathbf{c}$ and the variables in $\mathbf{Z}$ occur in both set terms, the constants in $\mathbf{a}$ and the variables in $\mathbf{X}$ only occur in $S$, the constants in $\mathbf{b}$ and the variables in $\mathbf{Y}$ only occur in $T$. Thus, $S = \mathbf{a} \cup \mathbf{X} \cup \mathbf{Z} \cup \mathbf{c}$ and $T = \mathbf{b} \cup \mathbf{Y} \cup \mathbf{Z} \cup \mathbf{c}$. The size of the input is $|S \cup T| = (h_1 + h_2 + k_1 + k_2 + m + n)$.

Given a substitution $\theta$ we denote with $\theta_D$ the set of variables which are substituted in $\theta$ (domain) and with $\theta_R$ the set of terms used to substitute variables in $\theta$ (range).

We now formally introduce the concepts of weak unification and weak mgu for two set terms $S$ and $T$ defined as above and such that $T$ contains only constants or database variables.

**Definition 4.** Let $S$ and $T$ be two set terms such that $T$ contains only constants or database variables. A substitution $\theta$ is a weak unifier for $S$ and $T$ if

1. $\theta_D = \mathbf{X}$, $\theta_R \subseteq T$, and
2. there exists a substitution $\sigma$ such that $S \theta \sigma = T \sigma$.

Moreover, a weak unifier $\theta$ is a weak mgu if there does not exist a weak unifier $\sigma$ such that $\theta$ is an instance of $\sigma$. $\quad\square$

Thus, weak unifiers are substitutions where all query variables are substituted and such that they can be composed with other substitutions to obtain unifiers.

**Definition 5.** Two weak unifiers $\theta$ and $\sigma$ are equivalent if $\theta$ is an instance of $\sigma$ and $\sigma$ is an instance of $\theta$, that is, if $\theta$ can be derived from $\sigma$ by renaming of database variables and vice versa. $\quad\square$

*Example 2.* Consider the two sets $S = \{X_1, X_2, a\}$ and $T = \{Y_1, Y_2\}$. There are six weak mgu's $\theta_1 = \{X_1/Y_1, X_2/Y_1\}$, $\theta_2 = \{X_1/Y_1, X_2/a\}$, $\theta_3 = \{X_1/a, X_2/Y_1\}$, $\theta_4 = \{X_1/Y_2, X_2/Y_2\}$, $\theta_5 = \{X_1/Y_2, X_2/a\}$ and $\theta_6 = \{X_1/a, X_2/Y_2\}$. Moreover, $\theta_1$ is equivalent to $\theta_4$, $\theta_2$ is equivalent to $\theta_5$ and $\theta_3$ is equivalent to $\theta_6$. $\quad\square$

**Fact 1** *Two set terms $S$ and $T$ have a weak unifier if and only if they unify.* $\square$

**Definition 6.** Let $S$ and $T$ be two set terms such that $T$ contains only constants or database variables. A set $B$ of weak mgu's for $\{S, T\}$ is a *complete set (or base) of weak mgu's* if both no two weak mgu's in $B$ are equivalent and for each weak mgu $\theta$, there exists a (not necessarily distinct) weak mgu in $B$ that is equivalent to $\theta$. □

Thus, as for the mgu's, the set of all weak mgu's can be partioned into equivalence classes using the equivalence relation for substitutions; the set of one representative for each class is a base of weak mgu's. Obviously all sets have the same number of substitution; we shall denote this number by $|bwmgu(S,T)|$. Two bases are equal modulo renaming of variables. In the case of matching, the base of bwmgu is unique although it is not necessarily a singleton.

*Example 3.* Consider the two sets $S$ and $T$ of Example 2. Because the two sets have three classes of equivalent weak mgu's and each class of equivalence contains two weak mgu's, the two sets have $2^3$ complete sets of weak mgu's.

Consider now the two sets $S = \{X_1, X_2, a, c\}$ ad $T = \{Y_1, b, c\}$ where $Y_1$ is a database variables. The two sets have a unique base of weak mgu's containing the following weak mgu's: $\theta_1 = \{X_1/b, X_2/b\}$, $\theta_2 = \{X_1/b, X_2/a\}$, $\theta_3 = \{X_1/a, X_2/b\}$, $\theta_4 = \{X_1/b, X_2/c\}$ and $\theta_5 = \{X_1/c, X_2/b\}$. The set of unifiers for $S$ and $T$ are obtained by composition of the weak unifiers with the substitution $\{Y_1/a\}$. □

A base of weak mgu's for $\mathbf{S}$ and $\mathbf{T}$ will be denoted as $bwmgu(\mathbf{S}, \mathbf{T})$. The weak unification problem can be stated as follows:

**Input:** Two set terms $\mathbf{S}$ and $\mathbf{T}$ such that $\mathbf{T}$ contains only constants or database variables.

**Weak unification problem:** Find a base of weak mgu's for $\mathbf{S}$ and $\mathbf{T}$.

**Output:** $|bwmgu(\mathbf{S}, \mathbf{T})|$ weak mgu's, each of them with size $k_1$.

Therefore, the size of the output of the set term weak unification problem is bound by $|bwmgu(\mathbf{S}, \mathbf{T})|$ and the number of query variables in $\mathbf{S}$. Thus, an optimal algorithm must be linear in the size of all matchers.

We shall assume that a set term matching algorithm returns all matchers and every variable assignment requires constant space (a variable substitution can be implemented by means of pointers to ground terms). Therefore, there exists an immediate lower bound to the time complexity of the problem.

## 4 Complexity of the Set Term Weak Unification Problem

In order to express the exact complexity of the weak unification of two set terms, that is the size of a base of weak mgu's, we consider two special cases which we identify as Problem $P_1$ and Problem $P_2$ whereas the general case is identified as Problem $P_0$. Thus, the two set terms $\mathbf{S}$ and $\mathbf{T}$ in the problems $P_0$, $P_1$ and $P_2$ are defined as follows:

*Problem* $P_0$

$$S = a \cup X \cup Z \cup c$$
$$T = b \cup Y \cup Z \cup c$$

*Problem* $P_1$

$$S = X \cup Z \cup c$$
$$T = b \cup Y \cup Z \cup c$$

*Problem* $P_2$

$$S = X \cup c$$
$$T = Y \cup c$$

Observe that the three problems define a hierarchy where problem $P_2$ is a special case of problem $P_1$ which is a special case of problem $P_0$.

In the next subsections we compute the complexity of the general problem by computing first the special cases. We start by computing the complexity of problem $P_2$, then we shall compute the complexity of Problem $P_1$ and, finally, we shall compute the complexity of the general problem.

## 4.1  Problem $P_2$

We are given two set terms $S = X \cup c$ and $T = Y \cup c$. The problem consists to find a base $bwmgu_2(S, T)$ of weak mgu's for $S$ and $T$.

**Theorem 7.** *The size of a base of weak mgu's for $S = X \cup c$ and $T = Y \cup c$, denoted as $|bwmgu_2(|X|, |Y|, |c|)|$, is equal to 1 if $|X| \leq |Y|$ whereas if $|X| > |Y|$ is equal to*

$$\sum_{i=i_{min}}^{i_{max}} \binom{|X|}{i} \times max\left(1, \sum_{y_1=1}^{1} \sum_{y_2=y_1+1}^{i-|Y|+2} \cdots \sum_{y_{|Y|}=y_{|Y|-1}+1}^{i} \prod_{j=1}^{|Y|} j^{(y_{j+1}-y_j-1)}\right) \times |c|^{(|X|-i)}$$

*where $i_{min} = max(|X| \times ord(|c| = 0), |Y| \times ord(|c| > 0))$, $i_{max} = |X| \times ord(|Y| > 0)$ and $y_{|Y|+1} = i+1$.*

**Proof (sketch).** The index $i$ ranges between $i_{min}$ and $i_{max}$ and denotes the number of $X$-variables which are substituted by $Y$-terms. In the above formula we have that

1. $\binom{|X|}{i}$ denotes the number of possible subsets of $X$ with cardinality $i$,

2. The expression $\sum_{y_1=1}^{1} \sum_{y_2=y_1+1}^{i-|Y|+2} \cdots \sum_{y_{|Y|}=y_{|Y|-1}+1}^{i} \prod_{j=1}^{|Y|} j^{(y_{j+1}-y_j-1)}$ computes the number of substitutions of $X$-variables with $Y$-terms, and

3. The expression $|c|^{(|X|-i)}$ computes the number of substitutions of the remaining $X$-variables with terms in c. □

*Example 4.* Consider the two set terms $\mathbf{S} = \{X_1, X_2, X_3, c_1\}$ and $\mathbf{T} = \{Y_1, Y_2, c_1\}$. A base of weak mgu's contains the following six substitutions: $\theta_1 = \{X_1/Y_1, X_2/Y_1, X_3/Y_2\}$, $\theta_2 = \{X_1/Y_1, X_2/Y_2, X_3/Y_1\}$, $\theta_3 = \{X_1/Y_2, X_2/Y_1, X_3/Y_1\}$, $\theta_4 = \{X_1/Y_1, X_2/Y_2, X_3/c_1\}$, $\theta_5 = \{X_1/Y_1, X_2/c_1, X_3/Y_2\}$ and $\theta_6 = \{X_1/c_1, X_2/Y_2, X_3/Y_1\}$.

Consider now the two sets $\mathbf{S} = \{X_1, X_2, c_1\}$ and $\mathbf{T} = \{Y_1, Y_2, c_1\}$. They have two weak mgu's $\theta_1 = \{X_1/Y_1, X_2/Y_2\}$ and $\theta_2 = \{X_1/Y_2, X_2/Y_1\}$ which are equivalent and, therefore, a base of weak mgu's contains only one weak mgu. □

## 4.2 Problem $P_1$

We are given two set terms $\mathbf{S} = \mathbf{X} \cup \mathbf{Z} \cup \mathbf{c}$ and $\mathbf{T} = \mathbf{Y} \cup \mathbf{b} \cup \mathbf{Z} \cup \mathbf{c}$. The problem consists to find a base $bwmgu_2(\mathbf{S}, \mathbf{T})$ of weak mgu's for $\mathbf{S}$ and $\mathbf{T}$.

We first introduce a technical lemma which says that a weak mgu for two set terms can be obtained by composition of a substitution for a subset of $X$-variables and a weak mgu for two set terms having the form reported in sub-problem $P_2$.

**Lemma 8.** *A substitution $\theta$ for the two set terms $\mathbf{S} = \mathbf{X} \cup \mathbf{Z} \cup \mathbf{c}$ and $\mathbf{T} = \mathbf{Y} \cup \mathbf{b} \cup \mathbf{Z} \cup \mathbf{c}$ is a weak mgu if and only if*

1. *there exists a substitution for $\sigma$ such that $\sigma_D \subseteq \mathbf{X}$, $\sigma_R \subseteq \mathbf{b}$ and $|\sigma_D| = |\sigma_R|$.*
2. *there exists a weak mgu $\delta$ for $\mathbf{S}' = (\mathbf{X} - \sigma_D) \cup \mathbf{c}'$ and $\mathbf{T}' = \mathbf{Y}' \cup \mathbf{c}'$ where let $\mathbf{Z}'$ be any subset of $\mathbf{Z}$ such that $|\mathbf{Z}'| = |\mathbf{Z}| - (|\mathbf{b}| - |\sigma_R|)$, $\mathbf{Y}'$ is equal to $\mathbf{Y} \cup \mathbf{Z}'$ and $\mathbf{c}' = \mathbf{c} \cup \mathbf{b}$.*
3. *$\theta = \sigma \delta$.* □

Thus, $X$-variables in $\sigma_D$ are substituted by distinct $b$-terms and a weak unifier $\theta$ is obtained by composition of $\sigma$ with a weak unifier $\delta$ of the sub-problem derived by deletion of variables and terms used in the substitution $\sigma$.

**Theorem 9.** *The size of a base of weak mgu's for $\mathbf{S} = \mathbf{X} \cup \mathbf{Z} \cup \mathbf{c}$ and $\mathbf{T} = \mathbf{Y} \cup \mathbf{b} \cup \mathbf{Z} \cup \mathbf{c}$ is*

$$|bwmgu_1(|\mathbf{X}|, |\mathbf{Y}|, |\mathbf{Z}|, |\mathbf{b}|, |\mathbf{c}|)| = \sum_{i=i_{min}}^{i_{max}} \binom{|\mathbf{X}|}{|\mathbf{b}| - i} \times \binom{|\mathbf{b}|}{|\mathbf{b}| - i} \times (|\mathbf{b}| - i)! \times$$

$$|bwmgu_2(|\mathbf{X}| - (|\mathbf{b}| - i), |\mathbf{Y}| + |\mathbf{Z}| - i, |\mathbf{c}| + |\mathbf{b}|)|$$

*where $i_{min}$ and $i_{max}$ are as follows:*

$$i_{min} = max(|\mathbf{b}| - |\mathbf{X}|, min(|\mathbf{b}|, |\mathbf{Z}|, \lceil \tfrac{|\mathbf{Y}| + |\mathbf{Z}|}{2} \rceil))$$

$$i_{max} = \begin{cases} min(|\mathbf{Z}|, |\mathbf{b}|) & \text{if } |\mathbf{Y}| > 0 \text{ or } (|\mathbf{Y}| = 0 \text{ and } |\mathbf{Z}| > |\mathbf{b}|) \\ max(i_{min}, |\mathbf{Z}| - 1) & \text{if } |\mathbf{Y}| = 0 \text{ and } |\mathbf{Z}| \leq |\mathbf{b}| \end{cases}$$

**Proof (sketch).** For the computation of the number of weak mgu's we have used Lemma 1. Thus, we compute the number of weak mgu's for the Problem $P_1$ by using the results of Problem $P_2$. The above formula selects two subsets of $X$-variables and $b$-terms with cardinality $|b| - i$, computes the substitutions of $X$-variables with $b$-terms and, for each substitution computes the number of weak mgu's of the sub-problem obtained by deleting from $\mathbf{X}$ the selected variables and by adding to c the $b$-terms. More specifically

1. The cardinal number $|b| - i$ denotes the number of variables in $\mathbf{X}$ which are substituted by distinct terms in b,
2. The number of possible subsets of $\mathbf{X}$ and b with cardinality $|b| - i$ are equal to $\begin{pmatrix} |\mathbf{X}| \\ |b| - i \end{pmatrix}$ and $\begin{pmatrix} |b| \\ |b| - i \end{pmatrix}$, respectively,
3. The number of substitutions of $X$-variables with $b$-terms is equal to $(|b|-i)\,!$.
   □

*Example 5.* Consider the two set terms $\mathbf{S} = \{X_1, X_2, Z_1, c_1\}$ and $\mathbf{T} = \{Y_1, b_1, Z_1, c_1\}$. From the formula of Theorem 2 we derive that the size of every base of weak mgu's is equal to four. For instance, the substitutions $\theta_1 = \{X_1/b_1, X_2/Y_1\}$, $\theta_2 = \{X_1/Y_1, X_2/b_1\}$, $\theta_3 = \{X_1/c_1, X_2/Y_1\}$ and $\theta_4 = \{X_1/Y_1, X_2/c_1\}$ define a base of weak mgu's for $\mathbf{S}$ and $\mathbf{T}$. □

## 4.3   Problem $P_0$

We are given two set terms $\mathbf{S} = \mathbf{X} \cup \mathbf{a} \cup \mathbf{Z} \cup \mathbf{c}$ and $\mathbf{T} = \mathbf{Y} \cup \mathbf{b} \cup \mathbf{Z} \cup \mathbf{c}$. The problem consists to find a base $bwmgu_0(\mathbf{S}, \mathbf{T})$ of weak mgu's for $\mathbf{S}$ and $\mathbf{T}$.

**Lemma 10.** *A substitution $\theta$ for the two set terms $\mathbf{S} = \mathbf{X} \cup \mathbf{a} \cup \mathbf{Z} \cup \mathbf{c}$ and $\mathbf{T} = \mathbf{Y} \cup \mathbf{b} \cup \mathbf{Z} \cup \mathbf{c}$ is a weak mgu if and only if $\theta$ is a weak mgu for $\mathbf{S}' = \mathbf{X} \cup \mathbf{Z}' \cup \mathbf{c}'$ and $\mathbf{T}' = \mathbf{b} \cup \mathbf{Y}' \cup \mathbf{Z}' \cup \mathbf{c}'$ where $\mathbf{Y}'$ is any subset of $\mathbf{Y}$ such that $|\mathbf{Y}'| = max(|\mathbf{Y}| - |\mathbf{a}|, 0)$, $\mathbf{Z}'$ is any subset of $\mathbf{Z}$ such that $|\mathbf{Z}'| = min(|\mathbf{Y}| + |\mathbf{Z}| - |\mathbf{a}|, |\mathbf{Z}|)$ and $\mathbf{c}' = \mathbf{c} \cup \mathbf{a}$.* □

Thus, a weak mgu $\theta$ for $\mathbf{S}$ and $\mathbf{T}$ as defined in Problem $P_0$ can be found by selecting two subsets of variables $\mathbf{Y}'' \subseteq \mathbf{Y}$ and $\mathbf{Z}'' \subseteq \mathbf{Z}$ which are substituted by terms in a and by computing a weak mgu for the two sets $\mathbf{S}'$ and $\mathbf{T}'$ above defined. The sets $\mathbf{Y}'$ and $\mathbf{Z}'$ denote the set of variables in $\mathbf{Y}$ and $\mathbf{Z}$ which are not substituted by terms in a.

**Theorem 11.** *The size of a base of weak mgu's for $\mathbf{S} = \mathbf{X} \cup \mathbf{a} \cup \mathbf{Z} \cup \mathbf{c}$ and $\mathbf{T} = \mathbf{Y} \cup \mathbf{b} \cup \mathbf{Z} \cup \mathbf{c}$ is denoted $|bwmgu_0(|\mathbf{X}|, |\mathbf{Y}|, |\mathbf{Z}|, |\mathbf{a}|, |\mathbf{b}|, |\mathbf{c}|)|$ and is equal to*

$$|bwmgu_1(|\mathbf{X}|, max(|\mathbf{Y}| - |\mathbf{a}|, 0), min(|\mathbf{Y}| + |\mathbf{Z}| - |\mathbf{a}|, |\mathbf{Z}|), |\mathbf{b}|, |\mathbf{c}| + |\mathbf{a}|)|$$

**Proof. (sketch)** We fix a number of variables in $\mathbf{Y}$ and $\mathbf{Z}$ which could be used to match with the terms in a and then we use the result of sub-problem $P_1$ to the sets obtained by deleting from $\mathbf{Y}$ and $\mathbf{Z}$ the selected variables and by adding the terms in a to the set c. In particular

1. The number of $Y$-variables substituted by $a$-terms is equal to $min(|\mathbf{a}|, |\mathbf{Y}|)$. Thus, the number of remaining $Y$ variables is $|\mathbf{Y}| - min(|\mathbf{a}|, |\mathbf{Y}|) = max(|\mathbf{Y}| - |\mathbf{a}|, 0)$.

2. The number of $Z$-variables substituted by $a$-terms is equal to $|\mathbf{a}| - min(|\mathbf{a}|, |\mathbf{Y}|) = max(0, |\mathbf{a}| - |\mathbf{Y}|)$. Thus, the number of remaining $Z$ variables is $|\mathbf{Z}| - max(0, |\mathbf{a}| - |\mathbf{Y}|) = min(|\mathbf{Y}| + |\mathbf{Z}| - |\mathbf{a}|, |\mathbf{Z}|)$. □

*Example 6.* Consider the two set terms $\mathbf{S} = \{X_1, a_1, a_2, Z_1, c_1\}$ and $\mathbf{T} = \{Y_1, Y_2, b_1, Z_1, c_1\}$. The number of weak mgu's is $|bwmgu_0(1, 2, 1, 2, 1, 1)| = |bwmug_1(1, 0, 1, 1, 3)|$ which is equal to 4 (namely, $\theta_1 = \{X_1/b_1\}$, $\theta_2 = \{X_1/c_1\}$, $\theta_3 = \{X_1/a_1\}$ and $\theta_4 = \{X_1/a_2\}$) □

## 5  An Optimal Algorithm

In this section we present an optimal algorithm which computes a base of weak mgu's for the two sets $\mathbf{S}$ and $\mathbf{T}$ as defined in Problem $P_0$.

The algorithm uses an array of counters $L$ to keep track of how many times each term has been currently used in the assignments of the current substitution. In order to make this test in constant time, $L$ is defined of type *linked_array*, that is a dynamic array of counters such that some of the counters are organized as a doubly-linked list, say $list(L)$, using suitable indices to implement pointers — an extra entry in the array (with index 0) is used for pointing at the first and last elements of the list as well as for recording the number of its elements. For instance, the linked array represented in Figure 1, consisting of the counters $a - e$, stores the list $< b, e, d >$.

| | 0 | 1 | 2 | 3 | 4 | 5 |
|---|---|---|---|---|---|---|
| element | 3 | a | b | c | d | e |
| previous | 4 | / | 0 | / | 5 | 2 |
| next | 2 | / | 5 | / | 0 | 4 |

— **Fig. 1.** Example of linked array —

At the beginning all counters in $L$ are linked in $list(L)$. As soon as a counter $i$ becomes greater than 0, then $L[i]$ is removed from $list(L)$ using the function $remove(L, i)$, although the element can be still accessed in the array. Later on, if the counter $i$ is decremented to 0, it is appended in the list using the function $add(L, i)$. The functions $first(L)$ and $next(L, i)$ return, respectively, the index of the first element in $list(L)$ and the index of the element in $list(L)$ following $L[i]$ — the index 0 denotes the end of the list. The function $cardlist(L)$ returns the current number of elements in $list(L)$; this number is automatically updated in the entry 0 of the array while the list is modified. All the above functions can be easily implemented so that they work in constant time. The following Figure 2 reports the data structures used by our algorithm.

```
type Term_Type = (Y, Z, a, b, c);
     substitution = record
                          term : Term_Type;
                          index : Cardinal
                     end;
     unifier = array [integer range ⟨⟩] of substitution;
     linked_array = array [integer range ⟨⟩] of record
                          Counter, Pred, Next : cardinal;
                     end;
```

— **Fig. 2.** *Data structures* —

A weak unifier algorithm should return one substitution at a time; this requirement would imply the usage of search strategies such as backtracking that may reduce the readability of the algorithm. Therefore, we shall describe the algorithm by means of a set of coroutines so that no backtracking is needed. We first introduce two preliminary coroutines which are used by the weak unifier algorithm.

The first coroutine, called *Select_subset*, receives two linked arrays $X$ and $X_s$, three cardinal numbers $n$, $k$ and $j$ and returns the linked array $X_s$ with $k$ elements. The parameter $k$ denotes the number of elements to be inserted into $X_s$, the parameter $n$ contains a copy of the value of $k$ at the moment of the first activation and the parameter $j$ is only used to memorize the index of the last element selected—initially its value is zero. The function $cardlist(X[i..last(X)])$ returns the number of elements in the linked array $X$ between the positions $i$ and $last(X)$.

```
coroutine Select_Subset(X, X_s : linked_array; n, k, j : Cardinal);
var i : Cardinal;
begin
    if k = 0 then send(X_s)
    else begin
       i := next(X, j);
       while cardlist(X[i..last(X)]) ≥ k do begin
            remove(X, i);   insert(X_s, i);
            Select_Subset(X, X_s, n, k − 1, i);
            insert(X, i);   remove(X_s, i);
            i := next(X, i)
       end;
       if k = n then send("done")
    end
end  Select_Subset;
```

— **Fig. 3.** *Coroutine Select_Subset* —

The second coroutine we present generates all substitutions for a set of variables $X_s$ with terms in $U$. This coroutine, called *assign*, receives in input (1) a unifier $\theta$, (2) a linked array $U$ containing the list of terms used to substitute $X$-variables, (3) a linked array $X_s$ storing the list of $X$-variables which are substituted by $U$-terms, (4) a variable $i$ denoting the position of the current variable in $X_s$ to be substituted and (5) a flag $ty$ whose value can be either *set* or *multiset*. In particular, if the value of the parameter $ty$ is equal to *set* the variables in $X_s$ are substituted by distinct terms otherwise it is possible to substitute more variables with the same term.

```
coroutine assign(θ : unifier; Xₛ, U : linked_array;
                      i : Cardinal; ty : (set, multiset));
begin
        if i > last(Xₛ) then send(θ)
        else begin
                k := first(U);
                while k ≤ last(U) do begin
                        θ[i] := (U, k);
                        if ty = set then remove(U, k);
                        assign(θ, Xₛ, U, next(Xₛ, i), ty);
                        if ty = set then insert(U, k);
                        k := next(U, k)
                end
        end;
        if i = first(Xₛ) then send("done")
end assign;
```

— **Fig. 4.** *Coroutine assign* —

The implementation of our algorithm follows the formula computing the number of weak unifiers. It turns out that, when a weak mgu is requested, the coroutine will start and will fix the input parameters of the problem, namely, the cardinalities of the sets of variables and constants. Next, the algorithm fixs the parameters of the sub-problem $P_1$ and activates the coroutine $bwmgu_1$ which computes the weak unifiers for the case where the set of constant a is empty. Every weak unifier $\theta$ received from the coroutine $bwmgu_1$ is sent to the caller by using the command $send(\theta)$. The array $\theta$ represents variable substitutions through indices; in particular, $\theta[i] = (Y, j)$ will denote that the variable $X_i$ is substituted by the term $Y_j$. After all answers are returned, the coroutine indicates that there are no more answers and stops. All coroutines return a data structure of type *unifier* or a linked array or the string *"done"* which means that all answers have been computed. A parameter of the form $S[i..j]$ denotes the subarray of $S$ whose indexes are contained be in the range $i..j$.

```
coroutine Set_Term_Weak_Unification(S, T : set_term);
var θ  : unifier[1..k₁];
    X : linked_array [0 .. k₁];
    Y : linked_array [0 .. k₂];
    a : linked_array [0 .. h₁];
    b : linked_array [0 .. h₂];
    Z : linked_array [0 .. m];
    c : linked_array [0 .. n];
begin
    initialize(X, Y, Z, a, b, c);
    bwmgu₁(X, Y[1..(k₂ - h₁)], Z[1..min(m, m + k₂ - h₁)], b, (c ∪ a));
    receive(bwmgu₁, θ);
    while θ ≠ "done" do begin
        send(θ);
        receive(bwmgu₁, θ)
    end;
    send("done")
end Set_Term_Weak_Unification;
```

— **Fig. 5.** *Set_Term_Weak_Unification Algorithm* —

The coroutine $bwmgu_1$ computes the set of weak mgu's. Its implementation follows the formula determining the number of weak mgu's determined in Theorem 2. In particular, for all sub-sets $X_s \subseteq X$ and $b_s \subseteq b$ with cardinality $i$ $(i_{min} \leq i \leq i_{max})$, all matchers of $X_s$ and $b_s$ are computed and, next, for each matcher, all weak mgu's for the two sets $(X - X_s) \cup c \cup b$ and $Y \cup Z[1..m - i] \cup c \cup b$ are computed by the coroutine $bwmgu_2$.

```
coroutine bwmgu₁(X, Y, Z, b, c : linked_array);
var θ : unifier[1, .., k₁];
    Xₛ : linked_array[1, .., k₁];
    bₛ : linked_array[1, .., h₂];
    i, iₘᵢₙ, iₘₐₓ : Cardinal;
begin
    iₘᵢₙ = max(h₂ − k₁, min(h₂, m, ⌈(k₂+m)/2⌉))
    if k₂ = 0 and m ≤ h₂ then iₘₐₓ := max(iₘᵢₙ, m − 1)
                          else iₘₐₓ := min(m, h₂);
    for i := iₘᵢₙ to iₘₐₓ do begin
        Select_subset¹(X, Xₛ, h₂ − i, h₂ − i, 0);
        receive(Select_subset¹, Xₛ);
        while Xₛ ≠ "done" do begin
            Select_subset²(b, bₛ, h₂ − i, h₂ − i, 0);
            receive(Select_subset², bₛ);
            while bₛ ≠ "done" do begin
                assign¹(θ, Xₛ, bₛ, first(Xₛ), set);
                receive(assign¹, θ);
                while θ ≠ "done" do begin
                    bwmgu₂(X, (Y ∪ Z[1..m − i]), (c ∪ b), θ);
                    receive(bwmgu₂, θ);
                    while θ ≠ "done" do begin
                        send(θ);
                        receive(bwmgu₂, θ)
                    end;
                    receive(assign¹, θ)
                end;
                receive(Select_subset², bₛ)
            end;
            receive(Select_subset¹, Xₛ)
        end
    end;
    send("done")
end bwmgu₁;
```

— **Fig. 6.** *Coroutine bwmgu₁* —

In order to distinguish different activation of the coroutine *Select_subset* we have used index associated with the coroutine, thus, *Select_subset¹*, *Select_subset²*, *Select_subset³* and *Select_subset⁴* denote three different activations of the same coroutine.

The coroutine *bwmgu₂* computes the set of weak mgu's for two set terms as defined in Problem $P_2$. It's implementation, reported in Figure 7, follows the formula determining the number of weak mgu's determined in Theorem 7.

```
coroutine bwmgu₂(X, Y, c : linked_array; θ : unifier);
var X_s, X_r : linked_array[1, .., k₁];
     i, i_min, i_max, fx_s : Cardinal;
begin
   if k₂ ≥ k₁ then begin
      copy(Y[1..k₁], X, θ);
      send(θ);
   end
   else begin
      for i := max(k₁ × ord(n = 0), k₂ × ord(n > 0)) to k₁ × ord(k₂ > 0)
      do begin
         Select_subset³(X, X_s, i, i, 0);
         receive(Select_subset³, X_s);
         while X_s ≠ "done" do begin
            fx_s := first(X_s);
            θ[fx_s] := (Y, 1);
            remove(X_s, fx_s);
            Select_subset⁴(X_s, X_r, k₂ − 1, k₂ − 1, 0);
            receive(Select_subset⁴, X_r);
            while X_r ≠ "done" do begin
               copy(Y[2..k₂], X_r, θ);
               fill_Y(X_s, X_r, first(X_s), first(X_r), θ);
               receive(fill_Y, θ);
               while θ ≠ "done" do begin
                  assign²(θ, X, c, first(X), multiset);
                  receive(assign², θ);
                  while θ ≠ "done" do begin
                     send(θ);
                     receive(assign², θ)
                  end;
                  receive(fill_Y, θ)
               end;
               receive(Select_subset⁴, X_r)
            end;
            insert(X_s, fx_s);
            receive(Select_subset³, X_s)
         end
      end (* for *)
   end; (* else *)
   send("done")
end bwmgu₂;
```

— **Fig. 7.** *Coroutine bwmgu₂* —

The coroutine *fill_Y* assigns to a set of variables $X_s$ terms taken from a set of database variables $Y$. It receives (1) a linked array $X_s$ storing the set of variables to be substituted, (2) a linked array $X_r$ storing the set of variables which have been substituted in a precedent phase, (3) a cardinal $i$ denoting the current variable in $X_s$ to be substituted, (4) a cardinal $j$ which is used to determine the maximum $Y$-variable which can be used to substitute $X$ variables, and (5) the unifier $\theta$.

```
coroutine fill_Y(X_s, X_r : linked_array; i, j : cardinal; θ : unifier);
var l, k : cardinal;
begin
    if i > last(X_s) then send(θ)
    else begin
        while (j < i) and ( next(X_r, j) ≠ 0 ) do
            j := next(X_r, j);
        l := θ[j].index − ord((j > i) or ( next(X_r, j) ≠ 0 ));
        k := 1;
        while k ≤ l do begin
            θ[i] := (Y, k);
            fill_Y(X_s, X_r, next(X_s, i), j, θ);
            k := k + 1
        end
    end;
    if i = first(X_s) then send("done")
end  fill_Y;
```

— **Fig. 8.** *Coroutine fill_Y* —

Observe that the local variable $l$ denotes the index of the maximum $Y$-variable which can be used to substitute the variable $X_s[i]$.

It is easy to see that the algorithm determines a base of weak mgu's for **S** and **T** where substitutions are represented by means of indices. Moreover, the algorithm is also optimal since its complexity is linear in the size of the computed base of weak mgu's. The formal proof showing correctness, completeness and optimality of the algorithm can be found in complete version of the paper [14].

## 6   Conclusions

Sets have been recently introduced in deductive databases and constraint query languages to extend its expressive power. As a consequence, new types of terms (called *set terms*), may then occur as arguments of predicates and they have particular rules for unifications that reflect the idempotency and commutativity properties of sets. In this paper we have analyzed a restricted form of unification, called "weak unification", which is mainly used in the field of deductive databases where the database may contain both constants and variables and the program is "safe". In particular, we have presented the exact complexity of the weak unification problem by providing a formula for determining the number of weak unifiers, and an optimal algorithm for the computation of the complete set of weak unifiers.

# References

1. S. Abiteboul and S. Grumbach, COL: A logic-based language for complex objects, *Proc. EDBT*, pp. 271-293, 1988.
2. S. Abiteboul and P. Kanellekis, Object Identity as a Query language primitive, *Proc. ACM SIGMOD Conf. on Management of Data*, 1989.
3. P. Arenas-Sanchez, and A. Dovier, Minimal Set Unification, *Proc. GULP-PRODE'95 Joint Conf. on Declarative Programming*, 1995, pages 447-458.
4. N. Arni, S. Greco and D. Saccà, Set-Term Matching in Logic Programming, *Proc 4th Int. Conf. on Database Theory*, 1992, pages. 436-449.
5. N. Arni, S. Greco and D. Saccà, Matching of Bounded Set Terms in the Logic Language LDL++, *Journal of Logic Programming* (to appear).
6. F. Baader and W. Buttner, Unification in Commutative Idempotent Monoids, *Theoretical Computer Science*, No. 56, 1988, pages. 345-353.
7. C. Beeri, S. Naqvi, O. Shmueli and S. Tsur, Set Constructors in a Logic Database Language, *Journal of Logic Programming*, Vol. 10, No 3 & 4, Apr.May, 1991.
8. W. Buttner, Unification in the Data Structure Sets, *Proc. 8th Int. Conf. on Automated Deduction*, 1986, pages 470-488.
9. A. Dovier, E. G. Omodeo, E. Pontelli and G. F. Rossi, { log }: A Logic Programming Language with Finite Sets, *Proc. 8th Int. Conf. on Logic Programming*, 1991.
10. C. Dwork, P. C. Kanellakis, and J. C. Mitchell, On the Sequential Nature of Unification, *Proc. 8th Int. Conf. on Automated Deduction*, 1986, pages. 416-430.
11. C. Dwork, P. C. Kanellakis, and J. C. Mitchell, Parallel Algorithm for Term Matching, *Journal of Logic Programming*, Vol. 11, No 1, Jan. 1985, pages. 35-50.
12. F. Fages, Associative-Commutative Unification, *8th Int. Conf. on Automated Deduction*, 1986, 416-430.
13. S. Greco, *Optimal Unification of Bounded Set Terms*, Technical Report, 1996.
14. S. Greco, C. Mateis, E. Spadafora, Unification of Bounded Simple Set Terms in Deductive Databases, *Technical Report ISI-CNR*, 1996.
15. N. Immerman, S. Patnaik and D. Stemple, The Expressiveness of a Family of Finite Set Languages, *Proc. of the Tenth ACM Symposium on Principles of Database Systems*, pages 37-52, 1991.
16. Jayaraman, B.: Implementation of Subset-Equational Programs, Journal of Logic Programming, Vol. 12, 299-324, April 1992.
17. P. C. Kanellakis, G. M. Kuper, and P. Z. Revez: Constraint query languages, Proc. Int. Symp. on Princ. of Database Systems, 1990.
18. Kapur, D., Narendran, P.: NP-completeness of the Set Unification and Matching problems, Proc. 8th Int. Conf. on Automated Deduction, 489-495, 1986.
19. Kapur, D., Narendran, P.: Double-Exponential Complexity of Computing a Complete Set of AC-Unifiers. Proc. 8th Int. Conf. on Logic in Computer Science, 11-21, 1992.
20. Kifer, M., Lausen, G.: F-Logic: A Higher-Order Language for Reasoning About Objects, Inheritance and Scheme, Proc. ACM SIGMOD Conference, 134-146, 1989.
21. Knight, K.: Unification: A Multidisciplinary Survey, *ACM Comp. Surveys*, Vol. 21, No. 1, 1989, 93-124.

22. Kuper, G. M.: Logic Programming with Sets, J. of Computer and System Science, No. 41, 1990, 44-64.
23. Lassez, J., Maher, M.J., and Marriot, K.: Unification Revisited, in *Foundations of Deductive Databases and Logic Programming*, (Minker ed.), Morgan-Kaufman, 1988.
24. Ledermann, W., Vajda, S. (Eds): *Handbook of Applicable Mathematics*, Vol. 5, Part B, 1985.
25. C. Lincoln and J. Christian, Adventures in Associative-Commutative Unification, *Proc. 9th International Conference on Automated Deduction*, 1988, pages. 358-367.
26. M Livesey and J.H. Siekmann, Unification of A+C-Terms (Bags) and A+C+I-Terms (Sets), Tech. Report, 5/67, Facultat fur Informatik, Univ. Karlruhe, 1976.
27. C. Mateis, *Sets Unification: Theory and Algorithms*, Master degree's Thesis, 1996.
28. S. Naqvi and S. Tsur, *A logical Language for Data and Knowledge Bases*, Comp. Science Press, 1989.
29. M. S. Paterson, Linear Unification, *J. of Computer and System Science*, No. 16, 1978, 158-167.
30. R. Ramakrisnhan, D. Srivastava, and S. Sudanshan. CORAL — Control, Relations and Logic. In *Proc. of 18th VLDB Conference*, 1992.
31. O. Shmueli, S. Tsur and C. Zaniolo, Compilation of Set Terms in the Logic Data Language (LDL), *Journal of Logic Programming*, Vol. 12, No 1 & 2, Jan.Feb., 1992, pages 89-119.
32. J. Siekmann, Unification Theory, *Journal of Symbolic Computation*, No. 7, 1989, pages 207-274.
33. M.E. Stickel, A Unification Algorithm for Associative-Commutative Functions, *Journal of ACM* Vol. 28, No. 3, 1981, pages. 423-434.
34. F. Stolzenburg, An Algorithm for general Set Unification and its Complexity, *Proc. ICLP Workshop on Sets in Logic Programming* 1994.
35. S. Tsur and C. Zaniolo, LDL: A Logic Based Data Language *Proc. 12th Conference on Very Large Data Bases*, 1986.
36. J.K. Ullman, *Principles of Database and Knowledge-Base Systems*, Vol. 1, Computer Science Press, Rockville, Md., 1988.
37. R. M. Verma and I. V. Ramakrishnan, Tight Complexity Bound for Term Matching Problems, *Information and Computation*, No. 101, pages 33–69, 1992.

# Logic Constructs
# and
# Expressive Power

# Expressiveness of Semipositive Logic Programs with Value Invention *

Luca Cabibbo

Dipartimento di Discipline Scientifiche: Chimica e Informatica
Università degli Studi di Roma Tre
Via della Vasca Navale 84 — I-00146 Roma, Italy
cabibbo@inf.uniroma3.it

Abstract. We study the expressive power of the relational query language $\textsf{while}_{Q^{+}_N}{}^+$ of semipositive datalog programs extended with a
mechanism of safe value invention. We show a semantics for value invention based on the use of Skolem functor terms. We show that this
language expresses exactly the class of semicomputable queries, that is
the class of computable queries that are preserved under extensions.

## 1. Introduction

A theory of relational database queries has its origin in the definition by Chandra
and Harel [4] of the computable queries as a 'reasonable' class of mappings from
databases to databases. More precisely, the computable queries are the class of
partial recursive functions between finite relational structures that satisfy a criterion called generality. The notion of genericity formalizes the data-independence
principle in databases: it intuitively states that atomic values in instances have to
be considered as uninterpreted, and that the only significant relationships among
data are based on equality and non-equality of values.

Mathematical logic is a main foundation of several aspects of relational database theory. In particular, it provides the basis for many declarative query
languages. From the relational calculus to datalog, and their extensions and variants, logic-based query languages are usually obtained from suitable restrictions
of first-order logic, by specializing them to the context of the theory of queries,
that is, to remain in the realm of generic transformations and finite structures.
For instance, relational calculus is the class of function-free open formulae of the
first-order predicate calculus, and datalog is the language of function-free Horn
clauses. These languages often omit function symbols because their utilization
can lead to violation of the criterion of generality or to infiniteness. However,
the standard equality ($=$) and non-equal by ($\neq$) predicates are usually allowed
making their use safe by means of simple syntactical restrictions.

* This work was partially supported by Consiglio Nazionale delle Ricerche, by MURST,
within the Project "Basi di dati evolute: modelli, metodi e strumenti," and by Università di Roma Tre within the project "Sistemi Intelligenti."

# Expressiveness of Semipositive Logic Programs with Value Invention *

Luca Cabibbo

Dipartimento di Discipline Scientifiche: Chimica e Informatica
Università degli Studi di Roma Tre
Via della Vasca Navale 84 — I-00146 Roma, Italy
cabibbo@dis.uniroma1.it

**Abstract.** We study the expressive power of the relational query language WILOG$^{\frac{1}{2},\neg}$ of semipositive *datalog* programs extended with a mechanism of safe value invention. We adopt a semantics for value invention based on the use of Skolem functor terms. We show that this language expresses exactly the class of semimonotone queries, that is, the class of computable queries that are preserved under extensions.

## 1 Introduction

A theory of relational database queries has its origin in the definition by Chandra and Harel [6] of the *computable queries* as a 'reasonable' class of mappings from databases to databases. More precisely, the computable queries are the class of partial recursive functions between finite relational structures that satisfy a criterion called *genericity*. The notion of genericity formalizes the *data independence principle* in databases; it intuitively states that atomic values in instances have to be considered as uninterpreted, and that the only significant relationships among data are based on equality and non-equality of values.

Mathematical logic is a main foundation of several aspects of relational database theory. In particular, it provides the basis for many declarative query languages, from the relational calculus to *datalog*, and their extensions and variants. Logic-based query languages are usually obtained from suitable restrictions of first-order logic, by specializing them to the context of the theory of queries, that is, to remain in the realm of generic transformations and finite structures. For instance, relational calculus is the class of function-free open formulas of the first-order predicate calculus, and *datalog* is the language of function-free Horn clauses. These languages often omit function symbols, because their utilization can lead to violation of the criterion of genericity or to infiniteness. However, the standard equality ($=$) and non-equality ($\neq$) predicates are usually allowed, making their use safe by means of simple syntactical restrictions.

---

* This work was partially supported by *Consiglio Nazionale delle Ricerche*, by *MURST*, within the Project "Basi di dati evolute: modelli, metodi e strumenti," and by Università di Roma Tre, within the project "Sistemi intelligenti."

Languages based on first-order logic can be very expressive; however, the problem of logical implication of first-order formulas is not recursive. On the other hand, the basic relational calculus expresses LOGSPACE queries only, and the addition of an iterative construct (such as a fixpoint operator) does not lead beyond PSPACE queries [13, 21]. Such limitations are due to the fact that *datalog* and *fixpoint* queries may use only relations of fixed scheme and constants from the input database, hence their working space is polynomial in the size of the active domain of the input instance. Thus, in order to fulfill completeness as a query language, we need to restore a further mechanism from first-order logic, possibly preserving genericity and structure finiteness.

A way to overcome the PSPACE barrier consists in using constants outside the active domain of the input database; this approach has been pursued in [1], which introduced a mechanism of *value invention* in a rule-based language, with the purpose of allowing for new domain elements during computations. Since the presence of invented values in results of queries would violate the criterion of genericity (in fact, generic queries are domain-preserving mappings) generic computations should allow for value invention in temporary relations only.

Several semantics for value invention have been defined in the literature. The one proposed in [1] is pretty operational; in contrast, ILOG [11], another *datalog* extension, adopts a declarative semantics for value invention, using Skolem functor terms as suggested in previous proposals known as the 'alphabet logics' (e.g., [17]). This way, value invention in ILOG programs corresponds essentially to a limited use of function symbols in ordinary logic programs.

In [3] we have shown that wILOG⁻, (a syntactical subclass of ILOG with safe value invention and stratified negation) is a generic relational query language that expresses exactly the computable queries. We have also shown that, to obtain the whole expressiveness, the ability of using full stratified negation is not required; in fact, even the simpler class of wILOG⁻ programs made of (at most) two strata is a complete language. Furthermore, we showed that the language wILOG$^{\neq}$, in which the only form of negation allowed is non-equality, expresses the monotone queries, i.e., all the computable queries that satisfy the property of monotonicity.

In this paper we study the language wILOG$^{\frac{1}{2},\neg}$ of semipositive programs, in which negation can be applied to input relations only. We show that the language expresses a semantically meaningful class of generic queries, and precisely the computable queries that are preserved under extensions [2]. The property of being preserved under extensions corresponds to a weak form of monotonicity. Because *semi*positive wILOG expresses exactly the queries satisfying this property, we take the liberty to call them *semi*monotone.

All these results provide interesting counterpoints to results concerning stratified *datalog*⁻, highlighting the profound impact that value invention has in database manipulation.

The paper is organized as follows. We recall some preliminary definitions in Section 2. Section 3 introduces the family ILOG$^{(\neg)}$ of languages. Then, Section 4 is devoted to sketch completeness proofs from [3], concerning expressiveness of wILOG⁻ and wILOG$^{\neq}$. The expressive power of semipositive programs is characterized in Section 5. Section 6 proposes some concluding remarks. Because of space limitation, proofs are sketched. Details can be found in [4, 5].

## 2  Preliminaries

We assume the reader to be familiar with the *relational model*. We now briefly review the basic notions and notations.

We write $R(A_1 \ldots A_n)$ to indicate a *relation scheme* having name $R$ and attributes $\{A_1, \ldots, A_n\}$. The *arity* of $R$ is the number $\alpha(R)$ of its attributes. A *(database) scheme* $S$ is a finite set of relation schemes, each of them having a distinct name.

Let $\Delta$ be a countable set of *constants*, called the *domain*. We write $(A_1 : d_1, \ldots, A_n : d_n)$ to denote a tuple $t$ over the attributes $A_1 \ldots A_n$ such that $t(A_i) = d_i$, for $1 \leq i \leq n$. An *instance over a relation scheme* $R$ is a finite set of tuples over the attributes of $R$. An *instance* $\mathcal{I}$ *over a scheme* $S$ is a function mapping every relation name $R$ in $S$ to a relation instance over $R$. The *active domain* $adom(\mathcal{I})$ of an instance $\mathcal{I}$ is the set of all domain elements occurring in $\mathcal{I}$. We write $inst(S)$ to denote the set of all instances over a scheme $S$.

We now give an equivalent representation for instances, following the logic programming style. We assume the existence of a total order on the attribute names, and list sets of attributes according to the total order. This way, if the listing of attributes $A_1 \ldots A_n$ respects the total order, then we write $(d_1, \ldots, d_n)$ to represent a tuple $(A_1 : d_1, \ldots, A_n : d_n)$. A *fact over a relation scheme* $R$ is an expression of the form $R(d_1, \ldots, d_n)$, where $(d_1, \ldots, d_n)$ is a tuple over the attributes of $R$. An *instance over* $R$ is a finite set of facts over $R$. For a scheme $S$, an *instance over* $S$ is a finite set $\mathcal{I}$ that is the union of instances over the relations in $S$.

For a scheme $S$, we give to the set of instances over $S$ the structure of a *complete partially ordered set* [7] with respect to $\subseteq$, by extending $inst(S)$ with a conventional 'infinite' instance $\top_S$, in such a way that for any finite instance $\mathcal{I}$ over $S$ it is the case that $\mathcal{I} \subseteq \top_S$. This is especially useful in the context of r.e. queries, which can be partial functions, that is, possibly yielding as a result an *undefined instance*, i.e., the one we denoted $\top_S$.

Given schemes $S$ and $\mathcal{T}$, a *database mapping f from $S$ to $\mathcal{T}$*, denoted $f : S \rightarrow \mathcal{T}$, is a partial function from $inst(S)$ to $inst(\mathcal{T})$.

Let $C$ be a finite set of constants, out of the domain $\Delta$. A database mapping $f$ is *C-generic* if $f \cdot \rho = \rho \cdot f$ for any permutation $\rho$ over $\Delta$ (extended to instances in the natural way) that leaves $C$ fixed (i.e., $\rho(x) = x$ for any $x \in C$). A database mapping is *generic* if it is $C$-generic for some finite $C$. A *query from $S$ to $\mathcal{T}$* is a generic database mapping $f : S \rightarrow \mathcal{T}$.

The class $\mathcal{CQ}$ of *computable queries* [6] is the set of all queries $f$ such that the mapping $f$ is Turing computable.

The notion of *genericity* has been introduced to capture the fact that the only significant relationships among data are those based on (non-)equality of values, that is, values have to be considered as *uninterpreted*, apart from a finite set $C$ of domain elements, which may be fixed by the query. As a consequence of genericity, for a $C$-generic query $q$ and an input instance $\mathcal{I}$, $adom(q(\mathcal{I})) \subseteq adom(\mathcal{I}) \cup C$. This property states that queries are essentially *domain-preserving* database mappings.

We now recall the notions of monotonicity and preservation under extensions.

A query $q : \mathcal{S} \to \mathcal{T}$ is *monotone* if, for any pair of instances $\mathcal{I}, \mathcal{J}$ over $\mathcal{S}$, $\mathcal{I} \subseteq \mathcal{J}$ implies $q(\mathcal{I}) \subseteq q(\mathcal{J})$. Intuitively, the result of a monotone query does not decrease by adding new elements to the active domain of the input instance and tuples to the input relations.

Given a scheme $\mathcal{S} = \{R_1, \ldots, R_n\}$ and instances $\mathcal{I}, \mathcal{J}$ over $\mathcal{S}$, we say that $\mathcal{J}$ is an *extension of* $\mathcal{I}$ (written $\mathcal{I} \sqsubseteq \mathcal{J}$) if $adom(\mathcal{I}) \subseteq adom(\mathcal{J})$ and, for $1 \leq i \leq n$, $\mathcal{I}(R_i) = \mathcal{J}(R_i)|_{adom(\mathcal{I})}$, that is, the restriction of relation $\mathcal{J}(R_i)$ to the active domain of instance $\mathcal{I}$ coincides with $\mathcal{I}(R_i)$. A query $q : \mathcal{S} \to \mathcal{T}$ is *preserved under extensions* [2] if, for any pair of instances $\mathcal{I}, \mathcal{J}$ over $\mathcal{S}$, whenever $\mathcal{J}$ is an extension of $\mathcal{I}$, it is the case that $q(\mathcal{I}) \subseteq q(\mathcal{J})$. Intuitively, the result of a query preserved under extensions does not decrease by adding new elements to the input active domain and tuples containing at least a new element to the input relations.

Finally, we say that a database is *ordered* if it includes a binary relation (conventionally denoted *succ*) containing a successor relation on all the constants occurring in the active domain of the database. A database is *ordered with* min *and* max if it also contains two unary relations (denoted *min* and *max*) containing the minimum and maximum element according to the successor relation. A *query on an ordered database* is a query whose input scheme is an ordered database scheme and that ranges only over ordered instances.

# 3  The Language ILOG$^{(\neg)}$

In this section we briefly introduce the syntax and semantics of the language ILOG$^{(\neg)}$. The language was proposed by Hull and Yoshikawa; for a complete presentation we refer the reader to previous works of the authors [11, 12] and to [3]. We will not consider here the object-based characteristics of the language, which motivated its introduction; indeed, the focus of this paper is only in the relational setting.

The language is a variant of *datalog*, with stratified negation and a mechanism for value invention, which is indicated by the use of a distinguished symbol '*' in heads of clauses. We now highlight the main differences of the language with respect to *datalog*.

## 3.1  Syntax

Let a database scheme $\mathcal{S}$ be fixed. A *relation atom* is an expression of the form $R(t_1, \ldots, t_n)$, where $R$ is a relation with arity $n$ and $t_1, \ldots, t_n$ are terms (that is, constants from a domain $\Delta$ or variables from a set **Var**). An *invention atom* is an expression of the form $R(*, t_1, \ldots, t_n)$, where $R$ is a relation with arity $n + 1$, whose first attribute is conventionally called the *invention attribute name*, denoted ID, '*' is a special symbol called the *invention symbol*, and $t_1, \ldots, t_n$ are terms. Intuitively, the invention symbol and invention atoms are used to create new domain elements throughout the computation of the model of a program. A *positive literal* is a relation atom, and a *negative literal* $\neg L$ is the negation of a positive literal $L$; the *non-equality literal* $t_1 \neq t_2$ (where $t_1, t_2$ are terms) is also allowed in programs.

A *clause* $\gamma$ is an expression of the form

$$A \leftarrow L_1, \ldots, L_k.$$

where $A$ is either a relation or an invention atom (called the *head of* $\gamma$), and $L_1, \ldots, L_k$ (with $k \geq 0$) is a (possibly empty) finite set of literals (called the *body of* $\gamma$). Hereinafter we will consider *range-restricted* clauses only, in which every variable occurring either in the head or in a negative literal in the body, occurs in a positive relation literal in its body as well. A *rule* is a clause with a non-empty body. A *fact* is a clause with an empty body (that is, an atom $A$); a fact is *ground* if no variable occurs in it. A clause is an *invention* (*relation*, resp.) clause if its head is an invention (relation, resp.) atom.

The relation name occurring in the head of an invention clause is called an *invention relation*.

An ILOG$^{(\neg)}$ *program* is a finite set of clauses, with the condition that no invention relation occurs in the head of a relation clause. An ILOG$^\neg$ program is *stratified* if it satisfies the usual *stratification condition*. In the remainder of the work we will consider stratified ILOG$^\neg$ programs only.

A *positive* ILOG program is a program in which no negative literal occurs. An ILOG$^{\neq}$ program is a program in which the only negative literals allowed are non-equality literals.

For a program $\mathcal{P}$, denote $adom(\mathcal{P})$ the finite set of domain elements which explicitly occur in $\mathcal{P}$, and $sch(\mathcal{P})$ the database scheme made of the relation schemes occurring in $\mathcal{P}$. An *input-output scheme* (or, simply, *i-o scheme*) *for* $\mathcal{P}$ is a pair of schemes $(\mathcal{S}, \mathcal{T})$ such that *(i)* $\mathcal{S}$ and $\mathcal{T}$ are disjoint subsets of $sch(\mathcal{P})$, called the *input* and *output* scheme, respectively; and *(ii)* no relation name in $\mathcal{S}$ occurs in the head of a clause in $\mathcal{P}$. For a program $\mathcal{P}$ over i-o scheme $(\mathcal{S}, \mathcal{T})$, denoted $(\mathcal{P}, \mathcal{S}, \mathcal{T})$, relations in the input scheme play the role of *extensional* relations, relations in the output scheme that of *intensional* (or *target*) relations, whereas relations in $sch(\mathcal{P})$ but neither in $\mathcal{S}$ nor in $\mathcal{T}$ are viewed as *temporary* relations.

A *semipositive* ILOG$^{\frac{1}{2}, \neg}$ *program* is a program over an i-o scheme in which the negation is applied to input relations only (non-equality literals are still allowed).

### 3.2 Semantics

The semantics of ILOG$^{(\neg)}$ programs, as the ordinary semantics of stratified logic programs, is based on the notion of perfect model (minimal model for positive programs). The behaviour of the symbol '*', used for value invention in programs, can be specified following the so-called *functional approach*, according to which its meaning is completely characterized by means of Skolem functor terms. This way, value invention in ILOG programs corresponds essentially to a limited use of function symbols in logic programs.

Assume the existence of a countable set of *Skolem functor names*. For each different invention relation name $R$, with arity $n + 1$, there exists a distinct $n$-ary functor $f_R$, called the *Skolem functor associated with $R$*.

The semantics of an $ILOG^{(\neg)}$ program $(\mathcal{P}, \mathcal{S}, \mathcal{T})$ is a binary relation $\varphi_{\mathcal{P}} \subseteq inst(\mathcal{S}) \times inst(\mathcal{T})$, which is defined in terms of the following four-step process:

1. First, occurrences of the invention symbol '*' are replaced by appropriate Skolem functor terms, thus obtaining the *skolemization* $Skol(\mathcal{P})$ of $\mathcal{P}$, as follows. The head of each invention clause in $\mathcal{P}$, of the form $R(*, t_1, \ldots, t_n)$, is replaced by $R(f_R(t_1, \ldots, t_n), t_1, \ldots, t_n)$, where $f_R(t_1, \ldots, t_n)$ is the Skolem functor term built using the Skolem functor associated with $R$ and the terms already present in the head of the clause.

2. For an instance $\mathcal{I}$, consider its representation as a set of facts.

3. $Skol(\mathcal{P}) \cup \mathcal{I}$ is essentially a logic program with function symbols; a preferred model $\mathcal{M}_{Skol(\mathcal{P}) \cup \mathcal{I}}$ of $Skol(\mathcal{P}) \cup \mathcal{I}$ (minimal if $\mathcal{P}$ is either a positive ILOG or an $ILOG^{\neq}$ program, perfect if it is a stratified $ILOG^{\neg}$ program) can be found via a fixpoint computation; if $\mathcal{M}_{Skol(\mathcal{P}) \cup \mathcal{I}}$ is finite, call it the *model of $\mathcal{P}$ over $\mathcal{I}$*.

4. If the model of $\mathcal{P}$ over $\mathcal{I}$ is defined, it is something similar to a set of facts of the language, apart from the presence of (possibly nested) Skolem terms. In order to obtain an instance of the output scheme, we must coherently replace distinct functor terms by distinct new values (that is, values that do belong neither to $adom(\mathcal{I})$ nor to $adom(\mathcal{P})$), thus obtaining an instance $\mathcal{J}$ over $sch(\mathcal{P})$. Then, the *semantics* $\varphi_{\mathcal{P}}(\mathcal{I})$ of $(\mathcal{P}, \mathcal{S}, \mathcal{T})$ over $\mathcal{I}$ is the restriction of $\mathcal{J}$ to the relation names in $\mathcal{T}$. Otherwise (i.e., if $\mathcal{M}_{Skol(\mathcal{P}) \cup \mathcal{I}}$ is infinite), the *semantics* is *undefined*.

Note that the replacement of different Skolem functor terms by distinct new values (Step 4) is defined in a nondeterministic fashion; therefore, if Skolem functor terms appear in the model of $\mathcal{P}$ over $\mathcal{I}$, then the semantics of $\mathcal{P}$ might include several possible outcomes (related to the choice of new values), and (by considering *all* possible replacements) it is in general a binary relation rather than a function.

## 3.3 Safe Programs

Value invention is a too powerful mechanism for a relational query language. In particular, the semantics of an $ILOG^{(\neg)}$ program over an instance may lead to the introduction of new values, not in the active domain of the input database or of the program itself; this fact contrasts with the notion of genericity, and the semantics of ILOG$^{(\neg)}$ programs, in general, is not a query in the usual sense. However, it is possible to restrict the language, limiting the use of 'invention' in programs, to obtain a 'traditional' generic query language. We follow analogous definitions in [1].

A program $(\mathcal{P}, \mathcal{S}, \mathcal{T})$ is *safe* if, for any instance $\mathcal{I}$ of $\mathcal{S}$, the semantics $\varphi_{\mathcal{P}}(\mathcal{I})$ does not contain new invented values. Unfortunately, safety of ILOG$^{(\neg)}$ programs is an undecidable property (even limiting our attention to positive ILOG). The following two *syntactical* restrictions ensure safety of programs.

A program is *strongly safe* if no invention clause occurs in it. It is apparent that the language of strongly safe ILOG$^{(\neg)}$ programs, denoted sILOG$^{(\neg)}$, syntactically corresponds to stratified *datalog*$^{(\neg)}$.

Weak safety is defined relative to an i-o scheme, using the auxiliary notion of *invention-attribute set* [1, 3]. The idea is to avoid any mixing of values from the input active domain with invented values. Intuitively, a program is *weakly safe* if 'invented values' appear only in particular columns of the temporary relations in $sch(\mathcal{P})$. Because temporary relations do not contribute to the result of a program, the assignment of distinct new values has no influence on the possible outcomes, and thus it is not strictly necessary. The language of weakly safe ILOG$^{(\neg)}$ programs is denoted wILOG$^{(\neg)}$. Note that weak safety of a program can be checked in polynomial time in the size of the program.

## 3.4 Introductory Examples

The following examples show the main features of the language; these examples are interesting because they illustrate techniques that will be used to prove results of this paper.

*Example 1.* A *(total) enumeration of a finite set* $R$ is a listing of the elements of $R$ in any order, without repeats, and enclosed by brackets '[' and ']'. For example, if $R = \{a, b\}$, then the enumerations of $R$ are the lists [ab] and [ba].

A *partial enumeration of a finite set* $R$ is an enumeration of any (possibly empty) subset of $R$. In the previous case, the partial enumerations of $\{a, b\}$ are [], [a], [b], [ab], and [ba].

We now define an wILOG$^{\neq}$ program $\mathcal{P}_{code}$ that produces a representation of all the partial enumerations of a unary input relation $R$. Program $\mathcal{P}_{code}$ uses invention relations $list^{nil}(\text{ID})$ and $list^{cons}(\text{ID}, first, tail)$; values invented in these relations correspond to empty and non-empty lists, respectively; the target relation of the program is $list^{out}$, with the same scheme as $list^{cons}$. The program uses an auxiliary relation $misses(list, element)$ to denote which $R$'s elements a list is still missing to obtain a total enumeration. (In what follows, we will use a variable *Nil* in programs to highlight terms that are intended to unify with values corresponding to an empty list.)

$$list^{nil}(*) \qquad \leftarrow .$$
$$list^{cons}(*,\text{']'}, Nil) \leftarrow list^{nil}(Nil).$$
$$misses(RB, X) \quad \leftarrow list^{cons}(RB, \text{']'}, Nil), list^{nil}(Nil), R(X).$$
$$list^{cons}(*, X, L) \quad \leftarrow misses(L, X).$$
$$misses(L, Y) \qquad \leftarrow list^{cons}(L, X, L'), misses(L', Y), X \neq Y.$$
$$list^{out}(*, \text{'['}, L) \quad \leftarrow list^{cons}(L, X, L').$$

For an instance $\mathcal{I} = \{R(a), R(b)\}$, the model for $\mathcal{P}_{code}$ on $\mathcal{I}$ contains in $list^{out}$ (among others) the functor terms $f^{out}(\text{'['}, f^{cons}(a, f^{cons}(b, f^{cons}(\text{']'}, f^{nil}()))))$ and $f^{out}(\text{'['}, f^{cons}(b, f^{cons}(a, f^{cons}(\text{']'}, f^{nil}()))))$, where $f^{out}, f^{cons}$, and $f^{nil}$ are the Skolem functor names associated with $list^{out}, list^{cons}$, and $list^{nil}$, respectively. These terms are the representations for the total enumerations of relation $R$ in $\mathcal{I}$. The model also contains terms corresponding to the required other partial enumerations. □

The following example shows how to use semipositive negation to build total enumerations of a set $R$ in presence of an ordered database.

*Example 2.* Assume given an ordered database with $min$ and $max$, with a unary relation $R$ representing a finite subset of the active domain $\Delta$, and the conventional relations $succ, min$, and $max$ representing a *total order* on $\Delta$ (recall from Section 2 that $min$ and $max$ contains just the minimum and maximum element of $\Delta$, respectively, and $succ$ the successor relation on the element of $\Delta$ according to the total order). The following ILOG$^{\frac{1}{2}, \neg}$ program produces a representation of the total enumeration of $R$ that respects the total order. Relation $Represents$ indicates whether a list contains all the elements of $R$ up to a given one.

$$list^{nil}(*) \qquad \leftarrow .$$
$$list^{cons}(*, \text{']'}, Nil) \quad \leftarrow list^{nil}(Nil).$$
$$Represents(RB, X) \leftarrow list^{cons}(RB, \text{']'}, Nil), min(X), \neg R(X).$$
$$list^{cons}(*, X, RB) \quad \leftarrow list^{cons}(RB, \text{']'}, Nil), min(X), R(X).$$
$$Represents(LX, X) \leftarrow list^{cons}(RB, \text{']'}, Nil), min(X), R(X), list^{cons}(LX, X, RB).$$
$$Represents(LX, Y) \leftarrow Represents(LX, X), succ(X, Y), \neg R(Y).$$
$$list^{cons}(*, Y, L) \quad \leftarrow Represents(LX, X), succ(X, Y), R(Y).$$
$$Represents(LY, Y) \leftarrow Represents(LX, X), succ(X, Y), R(Y), list^{cons}(LY, Y, LX).$$
$$list^{out}(*, \text{'['}, LX) \quad \leftarrow Represents(LX, X), max(X).$$

Note that the foregoing program is semipositive (negation is applied to the input relation $R$ only). The strategy of computing the enumeration consists in iterating on the elements of the domain (using the relations defining the total order) and taking different actions whether the elements belong to the set or not. Semipositive negation allows to continue the iteration in case an element is missing from the relation $R$. □

## 3.5  Expressiveness of sILOG¬ and wILOG¬

We conclude the section by recalling known results concerning expressiveness of sILOG¬ and wILOG$^{(\neg)}$ as relational query languages.

Since strongly safe ILOG$^{(\neg)}$ corresponds syntactically to stratified *datalog*$^{(\neg)}$, it inherits a lot of well-known results. Among others, we recall that sILOG¬ expresses (total) queries in PTIME. Furthermore, it expresses the *fixpoint queries* if we drop the requirement of stratification and adopt the inflationary semantics for negation [1]. A result by Kolaitis [14] shows that the stratified semantics for sILOG¬ is weaker than the inflationary one. It is also known that the queries expressible in *datalog*$^{\neq}$ and semipositive *datalog*$^{\frac{1}{2},\neg}$ are monotone PTIME queries and PTIME queries preserved under extensions, respectively; however, these two languages fail to express exactly the two classes of queries [15, 2]. Finally, the language *datalog*$^{\frac{1}{2},\neg}$ expresses the PTIME queries on ordered databases with *min* and *max* [18].

On the other hand, wILOG$^{(\neg)}$ is much more expressive than sILOG$^{(\neg)}$, because of value invention. A result by Hull and Su [10] allows to infer that the language wILOG¬ expresses the computable queries. In [3], we strengthened this result, showing that the same expressive power can be achieved by means of the syntactically simpler language wILOG$^{1,\neg}$, obtained by limiting the use of negation to programs made of (at most) two strata, i.e., programs made of a positive stratum followed by a semipositive one. There, we also proved that the language wILOG$^{\neq}$, the programs in which the only form of negation allowed is non-equality, expresses the *monotone queries*, that is, the class of computable queries that satisfy the monotonicity property. The following section is devoted to outline the proof techniques used in [3].

## 4  Expressiveness of wILOG$^{1,\neg}$ and wILOG$^{\neq}$

In this section we highlight the crucial points in the characterization of the expressive power of the languages wILOG$^{1,\neg}$ and wILOG$^{\neq}$.

**Fact 1 [3].** wILOG$^{1,\neg}$ *expresses the computable queries.* wILOG$^{\neq}$ *expresses the monotone queries.*

The proofs of both the above propositions refer to suitable simulations of computations of an arbitrary (a monotone, respectively) computable query. We refer to *domain Turing Machines* [9] (*domTMs*) as the formalism to specify an effective algorithm for the computation of a query. The main point in using domTMs to implement queries is that, unlike conventional TMs, the alphabet to be used on a domTM tape includes a countable domain $\Delta$ of symbols. It also contains a finite set of 'working symbols,' corresponding to connectives likes parentheses and brackets. A domTM has a two-way infinite tape, and is equipped with a 'register,' which can be used to store a single letter of the alphabet. This register is used to express transitions that are (essentially) 'generic' and to keep finite the control of the machine. For, moves may only refer to a finite subset of the domain (corresponding to a set of interpreted domain elements) and to working symbols; in addition, it is possible to specify moves based on the (non-) equality between the content of the register and that of the tape cell under the head. The possible effect of a move, apart from changing the internal state of the machine, is to change the content of the register and that of the tape cell under the head, then to move the head.

Given an instance $\mathcal{I}$, an *enumeration of* $\mathcal{I}$ is a sequential representation of $\mathcal{I}$ on a domTM tape (where domain elements are separated by connectives, enclosing tuples within parentheses '(' and ')' and sets of tuples of different relations within brackets '[' and ']'). The difference between instances and enumerations is essentially that instances are *sets* of tuples, whereas enumerations are *sequences*. We denote by $enum(\mathcal{I})$ the set of all enumerations of an instance $\mathcal{I}$. For example, if $\mathcal{I}$ is the instance $\{R_1(a), R_2(a, b), R_2(b, c)\}$ over $\{R_1, R_2\}$, then the enumerations of $\mathcal{I}$ (assuming the listing of $R_1$ precedes that of $R_2$) are $e_1 = [(a)][(ab)(bc)]$ and $e_2 = [(a)][(bc)(ab)]$.

A result in [9] states that, for any computable query $q$, there exists an *order independent* domTM $M_q$ that computes the query; hence, order independent domTMs provide an effective way to implement queries. This means that, given an input instance $\mathcal{I}$, either $M_q$ does not halt on any enumeration of $\mathcal{I}$ (meaning that $q$ is undefined on input $\mathcal{I}$), or there exists an instance $\mathcal{J}$ such that, for any enumeration $e$ of $\mathcal{I}$, the computation of $M_q$ on $e$, denoted by $M_q(e)$, halts resulting in an output that is an enumeration of $\mathcal{J}$ (meaning that $q(\mathcal{I}) = \mathcal{J}$). For example, if $M_q(e_1) = [(c)(b)]$ and $M_q(e_2) = [(b)(c)]$, we assume $q(\mathcal{I}) = \{(b), (c)\}$.

Computations of a domTM $M_q$ can be simulated in $\text{wILOG}^{1,\neg}$ as follows:

1. Given an input instance $\mathcal{I}$, generate the family $enum(\mathcal{I})$ of all enumerations of $\mathcal{I}$, to be used as inputs for $M_q$. Note that, referring to an (essentially) deterministic language like $\text{wILOG}^{(\neg)}$, it is not possible to generate a *single* enumeration of $\mathcal{I}$, so that *all* of them must be generated.

2. Simulate the computation $M_q(e)$ for any enumeration $e \in enum(\mathcal{I})$; the various simulations are performed simultaneously and eventually result in an output enumeration for every enumeration of $\mathcal{I}$.

3. The various output enumerations are decoded into instances over the output scheme; denote the result of decoding an output enumeration $o$ by $decode(o)$. Then, take the union of such instances as the result of the overall process.

Following such approach, starting from $q$, and so from $M_q$, we proved in [3] that it is possible to build a $\text{wILOG}^{1,\neg}$ program $Q$ which computes the following query (on input instance $\mathcal{I}$):

$$\varphi_Q(\mathcal{I}) = \bigcup_{e \in enum(\mathcal{I})} decode(M_q(e)).$$

The hypothesis of order independence on $M_q$ guarantees that, for any enumeration $e$ of $\mathcal{I}$, $decode(M_q(e)) = q(\mathcal{I})$; hence, $\varphi_Q(\mathcal{I}) = q(\mathcal{I})$. In particular, we showed that:

1. All the enumerations of an instance can be computed by a two-strata ILOG¬ program $Q_{in}$, where each enumeration is represented by means of a different invented value (and its corresponding Skolem term).

2. The simulation of a domTM, starting from an enumeration and producing an output enumeration, can be done by an ILOG$^{\neq}$ (i.e., without negation) program $Q_{simu}$. Invented values are used to represent *strings* stored on the tape of the domTM. Termination and non-termination of a computation correspond to a finite or an infinite number of invented values, respectively, hence to a finite or an infinite model of the program.

3. The decoding phase can be done by an ILOG (i.e., positive) program $Q_{out}$.

It is worth noting that, during the simulation, the only phase that needs stratified negation is the construction of the enumerations of the input instance: the other two phases do not require negation at all.

With respect to the language wILOG$^{\neq}$, because the only negative literals allowed are non-equalities, it turns out that nonmonotonic queries can not be expressed. Interestingly, we have shown that the language expresses *all* the monotone queries. The sketch of the proof is as follows.

Let $q$ be a monotone query. Because it is computable, there exists an order independent domTM $M_q$ which implements $q$. For an input instance $\mathcal{I}$, to evaluate $q(\mathcal{I})$ we would like to simulate a computation of $M_q$ on an enumeration $e$ of $\mathcal{I}$. Because of genericity, we are forced to consider computations of $M_q$ on all enumerations of $\mathcal{I}$ rather than on a single one. Computing the enumerations of an instance is not a monotonic operation; however, it is possible to obtain the correct result even if we modify the strategy of computing the enumerations of $\mathcal{I}$ (recall that the other phases are not problematic for wILOG$^{\neq}$, because they do not involve negation).

The set $p\text{-}enum(\mathcal{I})$ of all *partial enumerations of* $\mathcal{I}$, is the set

$$p\text{-}enum(\mathcal{I}) = \bigcup_{\mathcal{J} \subseteq \mathcal{I}} enum(\mathcal{J}).$$

(For example, the set of the partial enumerations for an instance defined by the set of facts $\{R_1(a), R_2(a,b), R_2(b,c)\}$ includes, among others, [(a)][], [][(bc)], and [(a)][(bc)(ab)], the latter being a total enumeration.) Note that the computation of all the 'partial' enumerations of $\mathcal{I}$ is a monotonic operation (recall Example 1).

By simulating computations of $M_q$ on this set and taking the union of the results, we in turn evaluate a query $\tilde{Q}$ defined as:

$$\tilde{Q}(\mathcal{I}) = \bigcup_{e \in p\text{-}enum(\mathcal{I})} decode(M_q(e)) = \bigcup_{\mathcal{J} \subseteq \mathcal{I}} \bigcup_{e \in enum(\mathcal{J})} decode(M_q(e)) = \bigcup_{\mathcal{J} \subseteq \mathcal{I}} q(\mathcal{J}).$$

Because of the monotonicity of $q$, we have $q(\mathcal{J}) \subseteq q(\mathcal{I})$ for any $\mathcal{J} \subseteq \mathcal{I}$. As a consequence, $\widetilde{Q}(\mathcal{I}) = q(\mathcal{I})$.

For proving that wILOG$^{\neq}$ expresses the monotone queries, we have shown that the evaluation strategy $\widetilde{Q}$ for $q$ can be effectively implemented in wILOG$^{\neq}$, that is, that the computation of the partial enumerations of an instance can be performed in ILOG$^{\neq}$.

# 5 Expressiveness of Semipositive Programs

In this section we study the expressive power of the language wILOG$^{\frac{1}{2},\neg}$ of semipositive programs, that is, the class of programs in which negation can be applied to input relations only. This language is strictly more expressive than wILOG$^{\neq}$; indeed, wILOG$^{\frac{1}{2},\neg}$ allows to express non-monotone queries as well, e.g., the difference of two input relations. Hence, it is interesting to ask whether this language expresses the computable queries, as wILOG$^{1,\neg}$ does. We first give a negative answer to this question, by proving that queries defined by wILOG$^{\frac{1}{2},\neg}$ programs satisfy the property of being preserved under extensions, a weak form of monotonicity. Then, we strengthen the result by proving that semipositive wILOG$^{\frac{1}{2},\neg}$ expresses exactly this class of queries.

We need a few preliminary definitions. Given an instance $\mathcal{I}$ over a scheme $S = \{R_1, \ldots, R_n\}$, consider the *enriched scheme* $\overline{S} = \{R_1, \ldots, R_n, \overline{R_1}, \ldots, \overline{R_n}\}$ for $S$, and the *enriched instance* $\overline{\mathcal{I}}$ (over $\overline{S}$) for $\mathcal{I}$, defined in such a way that, for $1 \leq i \leq n$, relation $\overline{R_i}$ has the same scheme as $R_i$, $\overline{\mathcal{I}}(R_i) = \mathcal{I}(R_i)$, and $\overline{\mathcal{I}}(\overline{R_i})$ is the complement of $\mathcal{I}(R_i)$ wrt the active domain $adom(\mathcal{I})$, that is, $\overline{\mathcal{I}}(\overline{R_i}) = adom(\mathcal{I})^{\alpha(R_i)} - \mathcal{I}(R_i)$.

Given a wILOG$^{\frac{1}{2},\neg}$ program $\mathcal{P}$ over input scheme $S = \{R_1, \ldots, R_n\}$, we can easily eliminate negation from $\mathcal{P}$ by considering the program $\overline{\mathcal{P}}$ over the enriched input scheme $\overline{S}$ obtained from $\mathcal{P}$ by replacing each negative literal $\neg R_i(\ldots)$ by $\overline{R_i}(\ldots)$; call this program $\overline{\mathcal{P}}$ the *positivization of* $\mathcal{P}$. It turns out that, for any wILOG$^{\frac{1}{2},\neg}$ program $\mathcal{P}$, its positivization $\overline{\mathcal{P}}$ is a wILOG$^{\neq}$ program. Furthermore, for any input instance $\mathcal{I}$ for $\mathcal{P}$, if $\mathcal{P}$ is defined over $\mathcal{I}$, it is the case that $\mathcal{P}(\mathcal{I}) = \overline{\mathcal{P}}(\overline{\mathcal{I}})$, otherwise $\overline{\mathcal{P}}$ is undefined over $\overline{\mathcal{I}}$. It is this strict relationship between the languages wILOG$^{\frac{1}{2},\neg}$ and wILOG$^{\neq}$ that induces a limitation on the expressiveness of the former.

**Lemma 2.** *Let* $\mathcal{I}, \mathcal{J}$ *be instances over a scheme* $S$, *and* $\overline{\mathcal{I}}, \overline{\mathcal{J}}$ *their enriched instances. Then,* $\mathcal{J}$ *is an extension of* $\mathcal{I}$ *if and only if* $\overline{\mathcal{I}} \subseteq \overline{\mathcal{J}}$.

We introduced in Section 2 the notions of monotonicity and preservation under extensions. It should be noted that any r.e. monotone query $q$ satisfies the property of being *downward defined*, that is, if $q$ is defined over an input instance $\mathcal{I}$, it is so on any instance $\mathcal{J}$ contained in $\mathcal{I}$. Similarly, it can be proved that queries that are preserved under extensions satisfy the following property: A (partial) query $q : S \to \mathcal{T}$ is $\sqsubseteq$-*defined* if, for any pair of instances $\mathcal{I}, \mathcal{J}$ over

$\mathcal{S}, \mathcal{I} \sqsubseteq \mathcal{J}$ and $q$ defined over $\mathcal{J}$ imply that $q$ is defined over $\mathcal{I}$. Note that $\mathcal{I} \sqsubseteq \mathcal{J}$ implies $\mathcal{I} \subseteq \mathcal{J}$, but the converse does not hold in general; similarly, downward definedness implies $\sqsubseteq$-definedness, but the converse is not always implied.

Preservation under extensions is a weak form of monotonicity. In what follows, we shall however use a different terminology for this property, by calling *semimonotone* any query that is preserved under extensions. The next result, in conjunction with Theorem 5, motivates our choice for giving this name to the property.

**Lemma 3.** *Let* $\mathcal{P}$ *be a semipositive* $\mathrm{wILOG}^{\frac{1}{2},\neg}$ *program. Then, the semantics of* $\mathcal{P}$ *is a semimonotone query.*

*Proof.* Consider the positivization $\overline{\mathcal{P}}$ of $\mathcal{P}$ obtained by replacing negative literals. Let $\mathcal{I}, \mathcal{J}$ be instances over the input scheme of $\mathcal{P}$ such that $\mathcal{J}$ is an extension of $\mathcal{I}$, and $\overline{\mathcal{I}}, \overline{\mathcal{J}}$ the corresponding enriched instances. Because $\overline{\mathcal{P}}$ is a $\mathrm{wILOG}^{\neq}$ program, its semantics is a monotone query. Assume $\mathcal{P}$ defined on input $\mathcal{J}$; then, so it is $\overline{\mathcal{P}}$ on input $\overline{\mathcal{J}}$. Now, $\overline{\mathcal{I}} \subseteq \overline{\mathcal{J}}$, and by downward definition of $\overline{\mathcal{P}}$, the latter is defined on input $\overline{\mathcal{I}}$; moreover, because of its monotonicity, $\overline{\mathcal{P}}(\overline{\mathcal{I}}) \subseteq \overline{\mathcal{P}}(\overline{\mathcal{J}})$. Hence, $\mathcal{P}$ is defined on input $\mathcal{I}$ and $\mathcal{P}(\mathcal{I}) \subseteq \mathcal{P}(\mathcal{J})$. $\square$

For instance, a query which is not semimonotone is the one that computes the complement of the transitive closure $(CTC)$ of a binary relation. For, consider a scheme $G = \{N, E\}$, with $N$ unary (the nodes) and $E$ binary (the edges) for representing a directed graph. Consider instances $\mathcal{I}$ and $\mathcal{J}$ over $G$, where $\mathcal{I}(N) = \{(a)\}$ (a single node) and $\mathcal{I}(E) = \emptyset$ (no edges), and $\mathcal{J}(N) = \{(a),(b)\}$ and $\mathcal{J}(E) = \{(a,b),(b,a)\}$; $\mathcal{J}$ is an extension of $\mathcal{I}$ (indeed, $\overline{\mathcal{I}} \subseteq \overline{\mathcal{J}}$). Now, $CTC(\mathcal{I}) = \{(a,a)\}$, whereas $CTC(\mathcal{J}) = \emptyset$; hence, the query is not preserved under extensions.

As a consequence of Lemma 3, $CTC$ is not expressible in $\mathrm{wILOG}^{\frac{1}{2},\neg}$, that is, we have a query separating the class of semipositive programs from the computable queries.

**Lemma 4.** *The language* $\mathrm{wILOG}^{\frac{1}{2},\neg}$ *is strictly more expressive than* $\mathrm{wILOG}^{\neq}$. *The language* $\mathrm{wILOG}^{1,\neg}$ *is strictly more expressive than* $\mathrm{wILOG}^{\frac{1}{2},\neg}$.

Other simple queries belong to $\mathrm{wILOG}^{1,\neg} - \mathrm{wILOG}^{\frac{1}{2},\neg}$. Consider the following queries *min* and *max* defined over a scheme containing a binary relation *succ*, intuitively used to represent a successor relation over an ordered domain. The queries are defined as

$$min(succ) = \{x \mid \not\exists w : succ(w, x)\}$$
$$max(succ) = \{x \mid \not\exists w : succ(x, w)\}$$

It can be shown, by means of examples, that these queries are not semimonotone.

Again, it raises naturally the question of whether the language $\mathrm{wILOG}^{\frac{1}{2},\neg}$ expresses the semimonotone queries, or only part of them. The remainder of the section is devoted to show that $\mathrm{wILOG}^{\frac{1}{2},\neg}$ indeed expresses this class of queries.

**Theorem 5.** wILOG$^{\frac{1}{2},\neg}$ *expresses the semimonotone queries.*

*Proof. (Sketch).* The proof is similar in spirit to the ones concerning expressiveness of wILOG$^{1,\neg}$ and wILOG$^{\neq}$ [3], sketched in Section 4. Again, the simulation and decoding phases do not pose problems with respect to the language wILOG$^{\frac{1}{2},\neg}$, because they require no negation. Hence, we should concentrate on the enumeration phase; in this case, it requires a major modification with respect to the approaches followed for wILOG$^{1,\neg}$ and wILOG$^{\neq}$.

Consider a semimonotone query $q$. Let $M_q$ be an order independent domTM which implements $q$. For an input instance $\mathcal{I}$, our evaluation strategy can neither consider computation of $M_q$ on an enumeration $e$ of $\mathcal{I}$ (because of genericity) nor computations on all total enumerations of $\mathcal{I}$ (because the operation of computing the set $enum(\mathcal{I})$ is not preserved under extensions). Is there any suitable set of enumerations derivable from $\mathcal{I}$ such that: *(i)* this set is expressible by means of a semipositive program; and *(ii)* the union of results of computations of $M_q$ on this set yields $q(\mathcal{I})$? Fortunately, the answer is affirmative. To prove formally the result, we need some preliminary considerations and definitions.

Let $\mathcal{I}$ be an instance, and $D \subseteq adom(\mathcal{I})$ a subset of its active domain; denote $\mathcal{I}|_D$ the restriction of $\mathcal{I}$ to the domain $D$, that is, the instance obtained from $\mathcal{I}$ by considering only the facts involving constants in $D$ only. From the definition of extension, it follows that $\mathcal{I}|_D \sqsubseteq \mathcal{I}$. With respect to the active domain of $\mathcal{I}|_D$, note that in general only the inclusion $adom(\mathcal{I}|_D) \subseteq D$ holds, whereas the equality $adom(\mathcal{I}|_D) = D$ does not necessarily follow, because it is possible that $\mathcal{I}|_D$ does not include all elements from the domain $D$ on which it has been built.

Starting from an instance $\mathcal{I}$, by considering its restrictions to all subsets of its active domain, we obtain all instances for which $\mathcal{I}$ is an extension:

$$\{\mathcal{I}|_D \mid D \subseteq adom(\mathcal{I})\} = \{\mathcal{J} \mid \mathcal{J} \sqsubseteq \mathcal{I}\}.$$

Let $r\text{-}enum(\mathcal{I})$ be the set of enumerations of the instances obtained from $\mathcal{I}$ in such a way:

$$r\text{-}enum(\mathcal{I}) = \bigcup_{D \subseteq adom(\mathcal{I})} enum(\mathcal{I}|_D).$$

If we simulate computations of $M_q$ on this set, taking the union of the results, we in turn evaluate the following query:

$$\widehat{Q}(\mathcal{I}) = \bigcup_{e \in r\text{-}enum(\mathcal{I})} decode(M_q(e))$$

$$= \bigcup_{D \subseteq adom(\mathcal{I})} \bigcup_{e \in enum(\mathcal{I}|_D)} decode(M_q(e))$$

$$= \bigcup_{D \subseteq adom(\mathcal{I})} q(\mathcal{I}|_D) = \bigcup_{\mathcal{J} \sqsubseteq \mathcal{I}} q(\mathcal{J}).$$

Because $q$ is $\sqsubseteq$-defined, $\widehat{Q}$ is defined on input $\mathcal{I}$ whenever $q$ is; because of its semimonotonicity, $q(\mathcal{J}) \subseteq q(\mathcal{I})$ for any $\mathcal{J} \sqsubseteq \mathcal{I}$, hence $\widehat{Q}(\mathcal{I}) = q(\mathcal{I})$.

A wILOG$^{\frac{1}{2},\neg}$ program that computes $\widehat{Q}$ is composed of three parts, namely, $\widehat{Q}_{in}$, for the enumerating phase, and $Q_{simu}$ and $Q_{out}$, for the simulation and the decoding phases. As we already observed, we can use the programs $Q_{simu}$ and $Q_{out}$ described in [3], because the corresponding phases do not pose any problem with respect to the use of negation.

We now sketch how the ILOG$^{\frac{1}{2},\neg}$ program $\widehat{Q}_{in}$ works for doing suitable enumerations of the input instance. First, we define a unary relation $a\_dom$ to store the active domain of the input database. Then, we build all the partial enumerations of this set $a\_dom$. Any partial enumeration $d$ of $a\_dom$ is a total enumeration of a subset $D$ of $adom(\mathcal{I})$; besides, it naturally induces a total order on its elements (any enumeration being a list without repeats): while we build the enumerations, at the same time we define relations $min, max$, and $succ$ to make apparent the total orders associated with them. Starting from enumerations and using total orders, we iterate on their elements to build encoding of enumerations of the input relations, as in Example 2. More precisely, given a relation, we iterate on the possible tuples over it using $min, max$, and $succ$, and test membership in the input instance. If the tuple belongs to the input, we encode it and continue the iteration; if the tuple does not belong to the input (we use semipositive negation here) we simply skip it and continue the iteration. We then concatenate encodings of the input relations — it is possible to do it without resorting to negation anymore, as we did in [3].

Finally, we note that the program $\widehat{Q}$ defined by putting $\widehat{Q}_{in}$ together with the simulation and decoding programs $Q_{simu}$ and $Q_{out}$ from [3] is a wILOG$^{\frac{1}{2},\neg}$ program and indeed implements the computation strategy for $q$ described above.

$\square$

A comment on the different approaches to enumerate instances is useful here. We used the following enumerations with respect to the various languages: all total enumerations of the input instance, for wILOG$^{1,\neg}$; all partial enumerations of the input instance, for wILOG$^{\neq}$; all partial enumerations of the input active domain, for wILOG$^{\frac{1}{2},\neg}$. The latter approach, to lead to suitable enumerations of the input instance, requires the use of negation (semipositive, at least). In fact, wILOG$^{1,\neg}$ can build total enumerations of an instance following this strategy; on the other hand, wILOG$^{\neq}$ can not adopt this approach. Intuitively, having a total order at disposal is indeed useful to build enumerations of the input instance only if we can apply negation to the input relations.

The construction in Example 2, together with the proof of Theorem 5, suggest that it would be possible for a wILOG$^{\frac{1}{2},\neg}$ program to compute a total enumeration of an input instance if a total order (with $min$ and $max$) on the input domain were given. Indeed, this observation leads to the following result, showing that wILOG$^{\frac{1}{2},\neg}$ expresses the computable queries provided a total order is given.

**Corollary 6.** wILOG$^{\frac{1}{2},\neg}$ *expresses the computable queries on ordered databases with* min *and* max.

# 6 Discussion

In this paper we have studied the rule-based query language $wILOG^{\frac{1}{2},\neg}$ of semi-positive *datalog* programs with value invention. The semantics of value invention is based on a limited use of function symbols that preserves genericity. The main result is the characterization of the expressive power of the language as the class of semimonotone queries (Theorem 5). To the best of our knowledge, this is the first proposal of a language expressing exactly this class of queries.

A comparison between the expressiveness of the family $wILOG^{(\neg)}$ and that of stratified $datalog^{(\neg)}$ allows us to highlight the impact that value invention has in querying relational databases. Expressiveness of the two families of languages are very different: the former ranges over the computable queries, whereas the latter does not go beyond the PTIME queries. The hierarchy of $wILOG^{(\neg)}$ relative to the number of strata allowed collapses level '1' ($wILOG^{1,\neg}$); the same hierarchy referred to $datalog^{(\neg)}$ does not collapse [14]. Moreover, comparing the result in [14] with that in [1], it turns out that the stratified semantics for negation in $datalog^{(\neg)}$ is weaker than the inflationary one; in contrast, the two semantics for negation (though different) have been shown equally expressive in rule-based languages having a mechanism comparable to that of value invention [8].

Referring to languages with limited use of negation, it is known that the queries expressible in $datalog^{\neq}$ and semipositive $datalog^{\frac{1}{2},\neg}$ are monotone and semimonotone (preserved under extensions) PTIME queries, respectively. However, these two languages fail to express exactly the two classes of queries [15, 2]. In contrast, $wILOG^{\neq}$ and $wILOG^{\frac{1}{2},\neg}$ express *exactly* the classes of monotone and semimonotone computable queries, respectively.

The language $datalog^{\frac{1}{2},\neg}$ expresses the PTIME queries on ordered databases with *min* and *max* [18]. We obtained a similar result for the language $wILOG^{\frac{1}{2},\neg}$ with respect to the computable queries.

This work is clearly related to the original paper introducing ILOG [11]. However, there the focus is on query issues in the context of an object-based data model, whereas the main concern of this work is on the ability of expressing relational queries, especially with respect to a limited use of negation.

The idea of value invention originated from a proposal by Kuper and Vardi [16] to choose arbitrary symbolic *object names* to manage new complex object values defined in their logical queries.

The first completeness result for a *datalog* extension with value invention was shown by Abiteboul and Vianu [1]; the proof technique of building all enumerations of an input instance was also proposed there. Nevertheless, the connection between the family $ILOG^{(\neg)}$ and the *datalog* extensions proposed in [1] is looser than it might appear. Indeed, $datalog_{\infty}^{\neg}$ adopts the inflationary semantics for negation and a different semantics for value invention, making the language 'operational.' As a consequence, even the semantics of 'similar' $wILOG^{(\neg)}$ and $datalog_{\infty}^{\neg}$ programs with limited use of negation (i.e., semipositive, or no negation at all) can be different [11, Example 7.6].

Languages with value invention (or object creation) specify mappings such that new values (outside the input active domain) may appear in their result; this fact, in turn, implies a potential violation of the criterion of genericity. Because of the nondeterministic choice of new values, the semantics of such mappings define binary relations between databases, rather than functions. These mappings are called *database transformations*. Expressiveness of ILOG¬ as a database transformation languages has been formalized in [3, 5] as the class of *list-constructive transformations*, that is, 'generic' transformations in which new values in the result can be put in correspondence with nested lists constructed by means of input values. (List-constructive transformations have been introduced by Van den Bussche [19]; they are a subclass of the *constructive queries* of [20], the latter referring to 'hereditarely finite sets' rather than lists.) The results holding for ILOG¬ are the analogues of those proven for wILOG¬; more precisely, the class of two-strata programs expresses the list-constructive transformations, and ILOG$^{\neq}$ and ILOG$^{\frac{1}{2},\neg}$ express the class of monotone and semimonotone list-constructive transformations, respectively.

## Acknowledgements

The author would like to thank the anonymous referees for their detailed and helpful comments.

# References

1. S. Abiteboul and V. Vianu. Datalog extensions for database queries and updates. *Journal of Computer and System Science*, 43(1):62–124, August 1991.
2. F. Afrati, S. Cosmadakis, and M. Yannakakis. On Datalog vs. polynomial time. In *Tenth ACM SIGACT SIGMOD SIGART Symp. on Principles of Database Systems*, pages 13–25, 1991.
3. L. Cabibbo. On the power of stratified logic programs with value invention for expressing database transformations. In *ICDT'95 (Fifth International Conference on Data Base Theory), Prague, Lecture Notes in Computer Science 893*, pages 208–221, 1995.
4. L. Cabibbo. The expressive power of stratified logic programs with value invention. Technical Report n. RT-INF-11-1996, Dipartimento di Discipline Scientifiche, Università degli Studi di Roma Tre, 1996. Submitted to *Information and Computation*.
5. L. Cabibbo. *Querying and Updating Complex-Object Databases*. PhD thesis, Università degli Studi di Roma "La Sapienza", 1996.
6. A.K. Chandra and D. Harel. Computable queries for relational databases. *Journal of Computer and System Science*, 21:333–347, 1980.
7. C.A. Gunter and D.S. Scott. Semantic domains. In J. van Leeuwen, editor, *Handbook of Theoretical Computer Science*, volume B, pages 633–674. Elsevier Science Publishers (North-Holland), Amsterdam, 1990.
8. R. Hull and J. Su. Untyped sets, invention, and computable queries. In *Eigth ACM SIGACT SIGMOD SIGART Symp. on Principles of Database Systems*, pages 347–359, 1989.

9. R. Hull and J. Su. Algebraic and calculus query languages for recursively typed complex objects. *Journal of Computer and System Science*, 47(1):121–156, August 1993.

10. R. Hull and J. Su. Deductive query languages for recursively typed complex objects. Technical report, University of Southern California, 1993.

11. R. Hull and M. Yoshikawa. ILOG: Declarative creation and manipulation of object identifiers. In *Sixteenth International Conference on Very Large Data Bases, Brisbane*, pages 455–468, 1990.

12. R. Hull and M. Yoshikawa. On the equivalence of database restructurings involving object identifiers. In *Tenth ACM SIGACT SIGMOD SIGART Symp. on Principles of Database Systems*, pages 328–340, 1991.

13. N. Immerman. Relational queries computable in polynomial time. *Information and Control*, 68:86–104, 1986.

14. P.G. Kolaitis. The expressive power of stratified logic programs. *Information and Computation*, 90(1):50–66, January 1991.

15. P.G. Kolaitis and M. Vardi. On the expressive power of Datalog: Tools and a case study. In *Ninth ACM SIGACT SIGMOD SIGART Symp. on Principles of Database Systems*, pages 61–71, 1990.

16. G.M. Kuper and M.Y. Vardi. The logical data model. *ACM Trans. on Database Syst.*, 18(3):379–413, September 1993.

17. D. Maier. A logic for objects. In *Workshop on Foundations of Deductive Database and Logic Programming (Washington, D.C. 1986)*, pages 6–26, 1986.

18. C. Papadimitriou. A note on the expressive power of prolog. *Bulletin of the EATCS*, 26:21–23, 1985.

19. J. Van den Bussche. *Formal Aspects of Object Identity in Database Manipulation*. PhD thesis, University of Antwerp, 1993.

20. J. Van den Bussche, D. Van Gucht, M. Andries, and M. Gyssens. On the completeness of object-creating query languages. In *33rd Annual Symp. on Foundations of Computer Science*, pages 372–379, 1992.

21. M. Vardi. The complexity of relational query languages. In *Fourteenth ACM SIGACT Symp. on Theory of Computing*, pages 137–146, 1988.

# A More Expressive Deterministic Query Language With Efficient Symmetry-Based Choice Construct

by  F. Gire (*) and  H. K. Hoang  (*)

(*)  Université de Paris 1
Centre de Recherche en Informatique
90 rue de Tolbiac  75634 Paris cedex 13  France
gire@univ-paris1.fr    hoang@univ-paris1.fr ·
phone number: (16) 1 40 77 46 03
fax number: (16) 1 40 77 19 80

**Abstract.** In this paper, symmetry-based choice mechanisms are exploited to compute deterministic queries. We investigate a particular form of these choice mechanisms, called specified symmetry choice. This mechanism is efficient (i.e. computable in polynomial time) and can be added to Fixpoint Logic to give a language that is more powerful than the extension of Fixpoint with Counting.

## 1   Introduction

Non-deterministic mechanisms can sometimes be used to compute more efficiently deterministic queries. Such queries are computed by non-deterministic programs which happen to produce an unique output for each input. This property, called functionality, is crucial if one want to use non-deterministic programs to compute deterministic queries. Evidently,  if this property is checkable, it will be a promising approach to the problem of finding efficient languages, that are more powerful than known deterministic database languages, such as Fixpoint or Fixpoint+Counting. Unfortunately, it was shown that in general functionality is undecidable [AV1].

In this paper, we investigate an alternative approach to this problem, using restricted non-determinism. In [AV1] a choice operator W, called Witness, is introduced in the context of general non-determinism. We consider here choice operators which are *sound*, that is they produce always isomorphic results at any application. Requiring soundness is a reasonable way to use non-determinism. Actually one can consider isomorphic results as having the same sense. This restricted non determinism can therefore be used to express deterministic queries.

The notion of sound non determinism has been firstly considered in [GVdBG] under the term 'uniform semi-determinism'. The authors outlined the avantage of this form of non determinism by showing that counting queries can be expressed in an uniform semi-deterministical manner, i.e. sound in our term. The purpose of our paper is to show a restricted non deterministic mechanism with soundness property but having more expressive power, i.e. it can express other efficient deterministic queries than counting queries.

This sound non determinism is based on an extension of fixpoint computations with a non deterministic symmetry-based choice operation between usual deterministic steps. In our definition, an operation choice($\Phi$) , where $\Phi$ is a formula, is symmetry-based, if it returns an arbitrary element of the set of elements defined by $\Phi$ only when this set is consisting in symmetrical elements, i.e is an automorphism class. This extension allows to define queries up to isomorphism in general, and deterministic queries for the boolean case. Evidently, computations using this choice mechanism are practically unfeasible for arbitrary input databases because they involve an automorphism test at every choice step. These automorphism tests are feasible only for simple classes of structures. Our idea is to consider firstly this symmetry-based choice mechanism on such basic simple structures and show its avantage w.r.t. the expressive power, i.e. it can express efficiently more deterministic queries on these structures than known deterministic mechanism. Next, believing that many DB-PTIME queries on arbitrary input databases can in fact be reducible by some processus to queries on abstract structures of the above type, we introduce a so called logical reduction operator into the language to express these forms of reduction.

In this paper we consider as basic the class of structures that have FO-definable automorphism classes or FO-definable automorphisms.

We define a class $C_k$ of structures that have FO-definable automorphism classes. On input structures of this class the symmetry-based choice mechanism is efficient because the automorphism test at any choice step of the computation is reducible to a k-equivalence test between elements in a structure. We show that Fixpoint together with this choice mechanism expresses exactly all PTIME properties of $C_k$-databases . The class of k-rigid databases, on which it is known that Fixpoint=DB-PTIME (see [Daw]) is strictly included in this class.

The symmetry-based choice mechanism that uses FO-definable automorphisms, is called *specified symmetry-based* choice mechanism. In this proposal, the choice operator has the form choice($\Phi$,F), where the second argument F is a FO formula which is used to describe the intended automorphisms. The choice operation is trigged on a set defined by $\Phi$, only if the elements of this set satisfy the symmetries described by F. For example, let $F_T$ be the formula expressing, for any two given elements a and b, the mapping $f_{ab}$ corresponding to the transposition of a and b, then the choice operator choice($\Phi$,$F_T$) requires that the transposition of any two elements in $\Phi$ is an automorphism. The use of symmetries that are transpositions has been already investigated in [VdBG] in the form of the so-called *swap choice* . Our specified symmetry-based choice is more general in the sense that it takes into account general FO symmetries of the structure (not only transpositions).

The specified symmetry-based choice is efficient, since testing whether a given mapping is an automorphism is FO-definable and therefore in PTIME .

Our main result is that the language using this specified symmetry-based choice together with the logical reduction operator has an expressive power strictly greater that Fixpoint + Counting.

The paper is organized as follows. In section 2, we review some basic concepts and notations. In section 3, we present the general formalism of our non-deterministic mechanism, which is based on the introduction of an operator, called inflationary choice fixpoint operator. Section 4 defines the symmetry-based choice semantics of this operator. Section 5 studies the restriction of this mechanism on a class $C_k$ of databases. In Section 6 we present the specified symmetry-based choice and the result concerning its expressive power. Section 7 presents our main result which is obtained by an extension of the language with a so called logical reduction operator. Finally we draw some conclusions in Section 8.

## 2  Preliminaries

We review here the main definitions about queries and query languages. We use the relational model, and express queries using extensions of First-order logic.

A database schema is a finite set $\sigma$ of relation symbols of specified arities.

A database ( or finite structure) B over $\sigma$ is an interpretation of $\sigma$ over some finite universe U, denoted sometimes by dom(B), such that each relation symbol R of arity k in $\sigma$ is interpreted by a subset of $U^k$ , denoted by B(R). For each subset $\sigma'$ of $\sigma$, we denote by $B(\sigma')$ the sub-structure of B, limited to the sub-schema $\sigma'$.

Queries must be computable and generic. More precisely, let DB($\sigma$) be the set of all databases over $\sigma$ . A k-ary query on DB($\sigma$)  (see [CH1]) is a partial recursive function Q on DB($\sigma$) such that :
- for every B over $\sigma$, Q(B) is a k-ary relation on dom(B)
- Q is preserved under isomorphism, that is if h: A-> B is an isomorphism between the two structures A and B, then Q(B)= h(Q(A)).

A boolean query is a function Q : DB($\sigma$) -> {0,1} that is preserved under isomorphism.

The complexity of a query is defined with respect to the time/space used by a Turing machine to produce a standard encoding of the output relation starting from a standard encoding of the input database. DB-PTIME denotes the class of queries computable in polynomial time. Note that the above definition of the complexity of a query Q is not the usual one which is defined relatively to the decision problem (i.e. the input of the Turing machine is the encoding of an input Database I and a tuple b , and the output is *yes* if b is in Q(I) and *no* otherwise) but in  the case of PTIME the two notions coincide. In this paper, by "feasible queries" we mean queries of DB-PTIME.

Many query languages have been defined as extensions of first-order logic FO. A query in FO is defined as follows.
Consider a formula $\Psi(x_1,..,x_k)$ of FO over $\sigma$. Then $\Psi$ defines a query Q that maps each structure B over $\sigma$ to a k-ary relation Q(B) on U, defined by
$$\{ [a_1,..,a_k] \in U^k \mid B \models \Psi(a1,..,ak) \}.$$
FO is a too weak language to express main queries such as the transitive closure of a binary relation. Fixpoint queries have been introduced in [CH2] to remedy the expressive power of FO. The inflationary version of fixpoint logic, FO+IFP, is defined like first-order logic with the additional rule for the formulas construction:
if $\Psi(x_1,..,x_k,S)$ is a formula and S is a k-ary relation variable, then
IFP(S) $\Psi(x_1,..,x_k,S)$ is a formula.

A formula IFP(S) $\Psi(x_1,..x_k,S)$ as above defines for each structure B a relation of arity k, which is the limit of the following sequence :
$$I_0 (S) = B (S) , I_{i+1}(S) = I_i(S) \cup \{ \bar{a} \in U^k \mid I_i \models \Psi(\bar{a}) \}$$
where $I_i$, $0 \le i \le \omega$, coincides with B for each relation symbol different to S.

FO + IFP has been shown to define the fixpoint queries [GS] and to express exactly the DB-PTIME queries on ordered structures ([Imm],[Var]) .

## 3    Inflationary Choice Fixpoint Operator

As observed in [AV2] the computation of an usual fixpoint formula using k variables can be considered as a computation over the k-equivalence classes of tuples of the input structure. Two k-equivalent tuples (i.e satisfying by definition the same set of FO-formulas using at most k variables) can not be distinguished during this computation. This observation holds for all FO-based formulas using a fixed number of variables and it is known that FO-based formulas using a bounded number of variables can not express many low complexity queries such as the parity of a relation.

Non-determinism is introduced in query languages to overcome this limitation : this mechanism permits to distinguish the tuples of the database even with formulas using only a fixed number of variables. In [AV1], a non-deterministic extension of first-order logic is achieved by introducing the so-called "witness" operator. Informally, given a formula $\Phi(x)$, the witness operator Wx applied to $\Phi(x)$ chooses an arbitrary x that makes $\Phi$ true. The extension of inflationary fixpoint logic is obtained by adding to FO + W the usual inflationary fixpoint operator. This logic, noted by FO+IFP+W, is shown to capture exactly the class of NDB-PTIME queries, and therefore can express all DB-PTIME queries as well. As remarked in [AV1], FO+W alone seems unable to express more deterministic queries than FO, an inductive mechanism is needed , in addition to the W operator, to increase the expressive power (w.r.t deterministic queries). In our opinion it is because the computation can distinguish the tuples, by the witness operator, iteratively many times that it can express more queries than deterministic computations.

In this paper we use a non-deterministic formalism, based on the notion of "non-deterministic induction" which is motivated by the above tight connection between the choice and inductive mechanisms. We define a "non-deterministic " fixpoint operator, called inflationary choice fixpoint and denoted by $IFP_c$ as follows:

## Definition 1

Let $\Psi(\bar{x},S,T)$ , $\Phi(\bar{y},S,T)$ be FO formulas, containing the relation variables S,T whose arities match the free variables $\bar{x}$ and $\bar{y}$ , respectively. The formula
$$IFP_c[S,T] (\Psi,\Phi)$$
defines for each input structure A over $\sigma$ , a relation equal to the limit $I_\omega(S)$ of the sequence of structures computed as follows:

$$I_0(S) = \emptyset \quad I_0(T) = \emptyset$$

for each $i \geq 0$, there is two steps :

the *choice step* concerns the relation T:
$$I_i'(T) = \text{choice} (\Phi(I_i)) , \quad I_i'(S) = I_i(S) \tag{1}$$

where $\Phi(I_i) = \{ \bar{b} \mid I_i \models \Phi (\bar{b}) \}$

the *inductive step* concerns the relation S:
$$I_{i+1}(S) = I_i(S) \cup \{ \bar{a} \mid I_i' \models \Psi( \bar{a} ) \} , \quad I_{i+1}(T) = I_i'(T) \tag{2}$$

where $I_i'$ and $I_i$ are structures on $\sigma \cup \{S,T\}$ which coincide with A on $\sigma$.

◊

In this definition, the above set $\Phi(I_i)$ is called the choice set, and the operation choice($\Phi(I_i)$) in (1), chooses an arbitrary element of $\Phi(I_i)$.

So the computation can be seen as an alternation of the inductive step and the choice step. Remark that, during the computation, the relation T contains only one tuple which is the element chosen at each choice step.

*Example 1*

The formula $IFP_c[Succ,T] (\Psi,\Phi)$ computes non-deterministically a total order Succ on the input universe U , with

$$\Psi(x,y,Succ,T) = \quad [ (x=min) \wedge T(y) \wedge (\forall z \neg Succ(min,z))] \tag{1}$$
$$\vee [ T(y) \wedge ( \exists z\, Succ(z,x) \wedge (\forall z \neg Succ(x,z)) ] \tag{2}$$

$$\Phi(x) = \forall z \neg Succ(z,x) \tag{3}$$

At each choice step, (3) computes the set containing all elements that have not yet been ordered, the relation T contains only an arbitrary element of this set. In the inductive step that follows, this element is defined either as the first element (that is, we have Succ(min,y)) by (1) or as the successor of the last ordered element by (2). The above formulas use a fictitious constant symbol *min* of the language. However it is possible to avoid the use of such a constant symbol (*)
◊

We denote by $FO+IFP_c$ , the extension of first-order logic with the operator $IFP_c$.

It is not difficult to see that the non-deterministic computation defined by the operator $IFP_c$ is as powerful as the general non-deterministic computation defined by FO+IFP+W (cf Proposition 1 below) . Therefore, other efficient forms of non-deterministic induction are not more general than $IFP_c$, as for example the non deterministic mechanism based on an alternation of usual fixpoint computation mode and choice mode: such a mechanism can be defined by an operator $\mu_c$ , in a similar way as $IFP_c$ in Definition 1, except that the inductive step in the above definition is replaced by a fixpoint computation, i.e. :

$$I_{i+1}(S) = IFP(S) \; \Psi \; | \; I_{i'}$$

It is possible to simulate a formula of $FO + \mu_c$ by a formula of $FO + IFP_c$. Proposition 1 gives relationships between these different extensions of FO.

**Proposition 1 :**    a-    $FO + IFP_c = FO + IFP +W$

b-    $FO + \mu_c \subseteq FO + IFP_c$

In this paper we use $FO+ IFP_c$ to study symmetry-based non determinism. The reason of this choice will be explained in the next section.

# 4  Symmetry-Based Choice

In this section , we consider a non-deterministic mechanism in which the choice operation is trigged on a set of elements only if the elements in this set are all symmetric . This mechanism is called symmetry-based choice. Furthermore,we aim to define a choice mechanism which is sound, i.e all different possible sequences of computations are "equivalent ".

---

(*)  Succ can be also defined by the formula $IFP_c[Succ,T](\Psi,\Phi)$ with $\Psi(x,y) = T(x,y)$ and
$\Phi(x,y) = (\forall u \; \forall v \; \neg T(u,v)) \; \vee \; (\exists z \; T(z,x) \wedge (\forall z \; \neg Succ(z,y)))$

It is possible to define a symmetry-based choice version of FO + IFP + W by replacing the operator W by $W_{sym}$ which, applied on a formula $\Phi(x)$, returns one element only if the set of elements satisfying $\Phi$ are symmetric. However, this logic is not sound. In fact, in a formula of $FO+W_{sym}$ , which may have many occurrences of $W_{sym}$, we don't know in what order the corresponding choices will be executed. Two computations of a same $FO + W_{sym}$ formula may therefore not be isomorphic. The non-determinism, based on the $IFP_c$ operator, has the particular property that there is a priori an order in the execution of the different choices in a computation, which is the order corresponding to the iteration steps.

The symmetry-based version of inflationary choice fixpoint operator is denoted by $IFP_{c,s}$ whose definition is likely $IFP_c$ with the obvious symmetry restriction on the choice operation at each choice step, that is: in the choice step i, the choice operation returns an arbitrary element only if the choice set $\Phi(I_i)$ is an automorphism class of $I_i$ (otherwise the choice operation, choice($\Phi(I_i)$), does not return any element).

*Example 2*
Let us consider the formula $IFP_{c,s}[Succ,T](\Psi, \Phi)$ in which $\Psi$ is as in example 1 and $\Phi$ is the formula $\Phi(x) = R(x) \wedge (\forall z \neg Succ(z,x) )$ where R is an unary relation symbol. Let A be a structure on the schema $\sigma = \{R\}$.
During the computation for each structure $I_i$ on $\{R,Succ,T\}$ the choice set
$\Phi(I_i) = \{ a \mid I_i \models R(a) \wedge (\forall z \neg Succ(z,a) ) \}$
containing the elements of R which have not yet been ordered, is clearly an automorphism class of $I_i$.
Therefore the formula $IFP_{c,s}[Succ,T](\Psi, \Phi)$ defines as relation Succ a total order on the elements of R.
On the contrary if A is the following structure on the schema $\sigma = \{E,R\}$ where E is an additional binary relation symbol:   A = { E(a,b), E(a,c), R(a), R(b) }
then the choice set $\Phi(I_0)$ (where $I_0$ is the structure of Definition 1) is not an automorphism class. Therefore the choice step does not make any choice during the computation of $I_\omega(Succ)$ and so, on the structure A, $IFP_{c,s}[Succ,T](\Psi, \Phi)$ defines Succ as the empty relation.
$\Diamond$

For each schema $\sigma$, we define $FO+IFP_{c,s}(\sigma)$ the set of formulas of the form $IFP_{c,s}[S,T](\Psi, \Phi)$ where $\Psi$, $\Phi$ are FO formulas over $\sigma \cup \{S,T\}$.
The following proposition states that $FO+IFP_{c,s}(\sigma)$ is sound. This implies that bounded formulas of $FO+IFP_{c,s}(\sigma)$ express deterministic queries.

**Proposition 2:**
Let $\{I_0,I_1,...\}$ and $\{J_0,J_1,...\}$ be two sequences of computations of $IFP_{c,s}[S,T](\Psi, \Phi)$ on an input structure A over $\sigma$. Then for each i $\geq$ 0, $I_i$ is isomorphic to $J_i$. $\Diamond$

*proof:*

This can be shown by induction on the step i as follows. The base case is trivial, since $I_0 = J_0$. Now , for i>0, suppose that $I_i$ and $J_i$ are isomorphic, i.e for all formula $\Theta$ of $FO(\sigma \cup \{S,T\})$, $I_i \models \Theta$ iff $J_i \models \Theta$. It can be easily seen that if $\Phi(I_i)$ is an automorphism class of $I_i$, then so is $\Phi(J_i)$ for $J_i$.

We show at first that $I_i'$ and $J_i'$ are isomorphic. In fact, for all formula $\Theta$ of $FO(\sigma \cup \{S,T\})$, let $\Theta'(z)$ be the formula of $FO(\sigma \cup \{S\})$ constructed from $\Theta$ by replacing all occurrences of the atoms of the form $T(x)$ by $x=z$ , where z is a new variable . Suppose that $I_i'(T) = \{a\}$ and $J_i'(T) = \{b\}$ . If $I_i' \models \Theta$ then we have equivalently $I_i \models \Theta'(a)$ and because $I_i \models \Phi(a)$ we have $I_i \models \exists z \Phi(z) \wedge \Theta'(z)$. Since $I_i$ and $J_i$ are isomorphic, we also have $J_i \models \exists z \Phi(z) \wedge \Theta'(z)$, which implies that there is b' such that $J_i \models \Phi(b') \wedge \Theta'(b')$ . We deduce that b' is in the choice set $\Phi(J_i)$. So b and b' are equivalent on $J_i$ and we have $J_i \models \Theta'(b)$ or equivalently to $J_i' \models \Theta$. Thus we have shown that $I_i'$ and $J_i'$ are isomorphic. This implies that $I_{i+1}$ and $J_{i+1}$ are isomorphic too because the inductive step preserves the isomorphism of structures. $\Diamond$

*Remark :*

In the above symmetry-based choice mechanism the automorphism test in the choice step i is made locally w.r.t. the structure $I_i$ , without memory of the choices that were previously operated. A more restricted version of this symmetry based choice mechanism can be defined in order to take into account these previously operated choices. In this version the choice operation in the choice step i requires that the set $\Phi(I_i)$ is an automorphism class of $I_i^*$, where $I_i^*$ is an extension of $I_i$ in which the values of all preceding choices are stored. That is , $I_i^*$ is a structure on $\sigma \cup \{S, w_0, ... w_i\}$ , where $w_0, ... w_i$ are new constant symbols , such that for each $j \leq i$, $I_i^*(w_j) = I_j'(T)$ and $I_i^*$ coincides with $I_i$ on $\sigma \cup \{S\}$. The inflationary choice fixpoint operator using this restricted symmetry-based choice mechanism will be denoted by $IFP^*_{c,s}$ . This new symmetry-based choice however is a particular form of the former one.

## 5    Reduction to k-Equivalence Choice

The choice mechanism using $IFP_{c,s}$ involves automorphism tests and therefore is computationally intractable for arbitrary input databases. We propose here a feasible form of this symmetry-based choice by considering a class of databases on which this type of choice operation is efficiently computable: actually with input databases of this class the automorphism test at any choice step of the computation can be reduced to a k-equivalence test of tuples for some fixed k, which is known as checkable in polynomial time (see[AV2]).

**Definition 2:**

A structure is called k-reducible if for all m ≥ k, any m-equivalence class of m-tuples is an automorphism class (i.e for any m-equivalent tuples $(x_1,...,x_m)$ and $(y_1,...,y_m)$ there is an automorphism that maps $x_i$ to $y_i$ for $1 \leq i \leq m$ ) . $\Diamond$

For each k, let $C_k$ be the class of all k-reducible databases. It can be easily seen that the class of k-rigid databases (cf [Daw]), i.e databases in which each k-equivalence class is reduced to one element, is included in the class $C_k$.

*Example 3*

We give here an example of k-reducible structures which are not k-rigid. For any n, the class of all complete n-ary trees is 3-reducible. To see this, we remark at first that, any two vertices in a complete n-ary tree T are symmetric iff they have the same depth. On the other hand, for each d, there is a formula $F_d$ of FO with two variables and quantifier depth d that defines the vertices having the depth d in the tree ,

$$F_d(x) = \exists z(E(x,z) \, \exists x(E(z,x) \, \exists z(E(x,z) \, ... \, \exists x(E(z,x) \, \wedge \, \forall z \neg E(x,z))...)) \, ,$$

where $E(a,b)$ means that b is the parent of a.

So if two vertices x and y are 2-equivalent, they must have the same depth and are therefore symmetric. In general, for any m, the tuples of vertices $(a_1, .. ,a_m)$ and $(b_1, .. ,b_m)$ in a complete tree are symmetric iff, for all $1 \leq i \leq m$, $a_i$ and $b_i$ have the same depth, and for all $0 \leq i,j \leq m$ $a_i$ is an ancestor of $a_j$ iff $b_i$ is an ancestor of $b_j$. As the depth and the ancestor relation are definable by FO-formulas with at most 3 variables, it is easily seen that for any $m \geq 3$, $(a_1,... ,a_m) \equiv_m (b_1,...,b_m)$ implies $(a_1,...,a_m) \equiv_\infty (b_1,...,b_m)$.

The class of arbitrary trees is not k-reducible. In fact, the property of having the same depth is not sufficient to identify symmetric vertices. One needs also to take into account the number of childrens of the vertices. We think that if the above definition of k-reducible structures (which is relative to FO ) is extended to FO+Counting, then the class of arbitrary trees may be k-reducible for some k. We hope that the notion of k-reducibility or its extension can capture other more interesting classes of databases. ◊

The important property of k-reducibility is that it is preserved w.r.t. the choice operation. More precisely, we have the following proposition, which can be proved using the k-pebbles game technique (the proof is given in the Annex).

**Proposition 3:**

Let I be a structure over some signature $\Omega$, w be a constant symbol not in $\Omega$, c be any element of dom(I) and I' be an extension of I on $\Omega \cup \{w\}$ such that $I'(\Omega) = I$ and $I'(w) = c$.

If I is k-reducible then so is I'.

◊

By proposition 3 we deduce that, if the input structure A is k-reducible then for each i so is $I^*_i$, where $I^*_i$ is the structure defined in the remark of the section 4. So we deduce that $IFP^*_{c,s}$ is efficient on input structures of $C_k$, because the automorphism test at each step i can be reduced to a k-equivalence test.

Let us denote by $C_{|b}$ the set of boolean queries of a class of queries C.

**Theorem 1:**

On the class $C_k$, FO + IFP*$_{c,s}$ |b = DB-PTIME |b .

*Proof* :(sketch) The computation of each boolean formula of FO + IFP*$_{c,s}$ |b on an input of $C_k$ is evidently in PTIME. Now to prove the inverse inclusion we only have to prove that an order of the elements in the input structure can be simulated by a FO+IFP*$_{c,s}$ formula. This can be performed as follows :

Firstly, the k-equivalence classes of the structure are ordered in the manner of [AV2].

As each k-equivalence class is an automorphism class, an arbitrary element is chosen by the symmetry-based choice, in the first k-equivalence class containing elements that are not yet ordered. This element is inserted as successor of the last ordered element and the new k-equivalence classes will be computed and ordered again. The above computation is repeated until all elements of the input structure are ordered .

◊

# 6  Specified Symmetry-Based Choice

In this section we propose another efficient form of the symmetry-based choice by specifying the form of the symmetries required by the choice operation. As it will be seen in this section and the following, Counting can be expressed using a particular case of this mechanism.

Let us recall that in a general symmetry-based choice operation of the form choice($\Phi$) the automorphism test requires that for any two elements a and b in the choice set, defined by $\Phi$, there must exist an automorphism $f_{a \to b}$ that maps a to b. The type of the symmetry does not play any role in the choice operation (i.e. any mapping $f_{a \to b}$ which is an automorphism is accepted). We propose here a particular choice mechanism which is semantically richer than the general one in the sense that one can specify in each choice operation not only the choice set $\Phi$, but also the type F of the intended symmetry required between the elements of this set. That is, the choice operator will have now the form choice($\Phi$,F), where F is a set of mappings $f_{ab}$ for each pair of elements a and b of the choice set $\Phi$. "Automorphism test" has now a more specified sense, it means to test whether each given mapping $f_{ab}$ in F is an automorphism.

This form of choice mechanism is called specified symmetry-based choice. Contrary to the general one, specified symmetry-based choice is efficient, since testing whether a given mapping f is an automorphism is first-order definable and therefore in PTIME. We define below an inflationary choice fixpoint operator using this specified symmetry-based choice mechanism. For the sake of simplicity in the notations, we denote it by IFP$_{c,s}$ as in section 4 .

**Definition 3:**

Let $\Psi$, $\Phi$, F be FO formulas, containing the relation variables S,T such that the number of the free variables in $\Psi$ and $\Phi$ match the arities of S and T respectively, and the one of F equals to $(2* \text{arity}(T) + 2)$.
The formula

$$\text{IFP}_{c,s}[S,T]\ (\Psi,\Phi,F)$$

defines for each input structure A over $\sigma$, a relation equal to the limit $I_\omega(S)$ of the sequence of structures computed as follows:

$$I_0(S) = \varnothing \quad I_0(T) = \varnothing$$

for each $i \geq 0$, there is two steps :

the *choice step* concerns the relation T:
$$I_i'(T) = \text{choice}(\Phi(I_i),F(I_i)), \quad I'_i(S) = I_i(S) \tag{1}$$
the *inductive step* concerns the relation S:

$$I_{i+1}(S) = I_i(S) \cup \{\ \bar{a}\ \mid\ I_i' \models \Psi(\bar{a})\ \}, \quad I_{i+1}(T) = I'_i(T) \tag{2}$$

where $I_i'$ and $I_i$ are structures on $\sigma \cup \{S,T\}$ which coincide with A on $\sigma$.

The function $\text{choice}(\Phi(I),F(I))$ is defined as follows :

For any two elements $\bar{u}$, $\bar{v}$ let us denote by $F_{\bar{u}\ \bar{v}}$ the binary relation containing the tuples $(x,y)$ that satisfy $I \models F(\bar{u}, \bar{v}, x, y)$. The function $\text{choice}(\Phi(I), F(I))$ returns an arbitrary element in $\Phi(I)$ if, for any $\bar{a}$ and $\bar{b}$ in $\Phi(I)$, the mapping whose graph is $F_{\bar{a}\ \bar{b}}$ is an automorphism of I that maps $\bar{a}$ to $\bar{b}$ (otherwise the choice operation does not return any element).

$\Diamond$

The extension of FO with the specified symmetry-based choice fixpoint operator, defined as above, is denoted by $\text{FO}+\text{IFP}_{c,s}$.

*Example 4*

The choice operator using as F the formula :

$$F_T(u,v,x,y) = [(x=u \wedge y=v) \vee (x=v \wedge y=u)] \vee (x=y \wedge x\neq u \wedge x\neq v)$$

corresponds to the choice operation requiring that any two elements a and b of the choice set $\Phi(I)$ are symmetrical by transposition, i.e the transposition (a b) is in Aut(I). Consider a structure containing only one unary relation R. It is easy to see that the transposition of any two elements of R is an automorphism of this structure. So using the specified symmetry-based choice mechanism with the above formula $F_T$ we can generate a total order on R by the formula $\text{IFP}_{c,s}(\text{Succ},T)(\Psi,\Phi,F_T)$, where $\Psi$ and $\Phi$ are the formulas defined in the Example 2 of Section 3. By consequence FO + IFP$_{c,s}$ can express all counting queries over unary structures. For example, we can write a formula Even(R) of FO + IFP$_{c,s}$ which expresses that the cardinality of an unary relation R is even.

The following example illustrates a more significative application of the language.

*Example 5*

The query considered here is the PTIME property of graphs defined in [CFI]. The authors construct for any 3-regular graph G, a graph $\hat{X}(G)$ as follows:

+ each vertex u of G is replaced by a subgraph $X_3(u)$ . This subgraph has 3 pairs of vertices $(a_i, b_i)$ and a fixed number of middle vertices, with the property that for every even set of pairs, there is an automorphism of $X_3(u)$ that exchanges the vertices of exactly those pairs, but there is no such automorphism for an odd set of pairs.

+ To each edge (u,v) of u is associated one of the pairs $(a_i, b_i)$ from $X_3(u)$, call this pair $(a_{uv}, b_{uv})$. The pairs $(a_{uv}, b_{uv})$ and $(a_{vu}, b_{vu})$ of the two adjacent subgraphs $X_3(u), X_3(v)$ are then connected either in a straight way, by drawing the edges $(a_{uv}, a_{vu})$ and $(b_{uv}, b_{vu})$, or in a twist way, by drawing the edges $(a_{uv}, b_{vu})$ and $(b_{uv}, a_{vu})$.

Depending how the pairs between the subgraphs are connected, the graph $\hat{X}(G)$ is called twist or not. (For more description of these graphs, the reader is referred to [CFI] ). This property of graphs (twist or untwist) is polynomial time decidable, but it is shown that it can not be expressed by any formula of Fixpoint (+ Counting).

This property is efficiently expressed by symmetry-based choice. In fact, the graph $\hat{X}(G)$ has the following simple symmetries : consider a "cycle" of subgraphs $X_3(v_0),...,X_3(v_n)$ such that $X_3(v_m)$ is adjacent to $X_3(v_{m+1})$ for $0 \leq m < n$, and $X_3(v_n)$ is adjacent to $X_3(v_0)$. This cycle has the following property: let $f_m$, $0 \leq m \leq n$, be the automorphism of the subgraph $X_3(v_m)$ that exchanges the vertices of the two pairs participating to the connections between the subgraphs of the cycle, then the union $\cup f_m$, $0 \leq m \leq n$, is an automorphism of $\hat{X}(G)$. Using these symmetries, a choice mechanism allows us to generate a total order on the vertices of the graph $\hat{X}(G)$, and therefore to express all of its PTIME properties. This ordering on the vertices of $\hat{X}(G)$ is as follows:

As each pair in $\hat{X}(G)$ (following the construction in [CFI]) has an unique color, we suppose, for the sake of simplicity, that we have in the input an order $<_p$ between the pairs in $\hat{X}(G)$. The problem now is principally to order the vertices a,b in each pair (the ordering of the middle vertices in each subgraph will then immediately follows and therefore is omitted here).

To do this, we will iterate the three following steps:

step 1
   Compute a pair $(a_i, b_i)$ such that there is a definable symmetry between $a_i$ and $b_i$.
step 2
   Choose one of the vertices in $(a_i, b_i)$ (say $a_i$ ).
step 3
   Order $a_i < b_i$ and propagate the ordering in such a way that:
      If a pair is ordered then the pair connected to it is ordered too and
      if in a subgraph two pairs are ordered then the third one is ordered too.

Remark that the steps 1 and 3 are deterministic; only the step 2 is not deterministic.

As the computations of the steps 2 and 3 are obvious we detail only the computation of the step 1.

This step will compute a pair $(a_i, b_i)$ participating to a cycle of $\hat{X}(G)$ described as above, such that the pairs connecting the subgraphs of this cycle are all unordered. (As said before there is a definable symmetry of $\hat{X}(G)$ that maps $a_i$ to $b_i$ ). This cycle is computed as follows:

   Let $(x_1, y_1)$ be the first pair (w.r.t. the order $<_p$) of $\hat{X}(G)$ that is unordered (until the pairs in $\hat{X}(G)$ are not all ordered, there is always a such pair). We compute now a directed path containing only unordered pairs of $\hat{X}(G)$ by the following rules:

   + $(x_1, y_1)$ is the first pair of the path,

   + If the pair $(x_m, y_m)$ of a subgraph $X_3(u)$ is in the path and has not yet a successor then :
         a- if the pair $(x_{m+1}, y_{m+1})$ that is connected to $(x_m, y_m)$ is not yet in the path, then it is added to the path as successor of $(x_m, y_m)$; otherwise
         b- if not any other pair of $X_3(u)$ is in the path, then the first (according to $<_p$) of these other pairs that is unordered, is added to the path as successor of $(x_m, y_m)$,

   (Thus if a) and b) are not satisfied, then $(x_m, y_m)$ is the last pair of the path)

Following the ordering in step 3, if the pair is unordered then so is the pair connected to it, and if a subgraph contains an unordered pair then it must contain at least two such unordered pairs. From this remark one can easily verify that the so constructed path contains only unordered pairs. Furthermore this path reaches its last pair only if it returns to a subgraph through which it has already gone. As the length of the path is at most n where n is the number of pairs in $\hat{X}(G)$ , the path reaches its last pair after at most n iterations of the above induction rules. Let $(x_n, y_n)$ be this last pair and $(x_{m0}, y_{m0})$ be the pair of the path that belongs to the same subgraph as $(x_n, y_n)$. It can be easily seen that the subgraphs of $\hat{X}(G)$ that contain the pairs of the path from $(x_{m0}, y_{m0})$ to $(x_n, y_n)$ form the cycle of subgraphs that we require.

The ordering realized by iterating the above three steps can be seen as an alternation of a fixpoint mode (steps 1 and 3) and a choice mode (step 2). This form of computation can be defined by a formula using the fixpoint operator $\mu_c$ defined in section 3. By proposition 1 each formula of FO + $\mu_c$ can be simulated by a formula of FO+IFP$_{c,s}$. This is also true in the context of the symmetry-based choice. We conclude that the above ordering computation can be defined by a formula of FO + IFP$_{c,s}$.

Let us remark that the above computation uses the specified form of the symmetry-based choice: indeed at each choice step, the required symmetry between the elements of the choice set is definable by a formula $(\cup f_m)$.

◊

The following theorem is a direct consequence of Example 5 and is crucial for our main results.

**Theorem 2 :**

There is a PTIME property of structures, which is not definable by Fixpoint+Counting but can be expressed by a FO+IFP$_{c,s}$ formula. ◊

# 7 An Extension With Logical Reduction Operator

A real database may be arbitrary complex such that it may not have simple symmetries between its elements, as required in the previous section. However structures, having some specified symmetries, can be considered as particular views of some real database. Also a given input database can alternatively be considered as the collection of all of its particular abstract views . The reason for this approach is the fact that many queries may in fact be reduced to easier queries on such abstract views of the input structure. In this context, the language proposed in the previous section, can actually be more relevant to real database applications, if it is completed by an operator that can expres all of the above reductions. The language that we propose in this section is the extension of the one proposed in the previous section, and is based on the use of the so-called logical reduction operator.

Logical reductions between problems mean reductions that can be expressed in a logical language. The notion is derived from the idea of interpretations between theories and was used in [End] ,[Imm87] and [Daw] . In this section, we use this notion under the form of a constructor integrated in the language itself.

We begin the presentation of this reduction constructor by a simple example. Let R be an unary relation, the query " R has an even cardinality" can be expressed by the formula Even(R), as seen in the previous section. Let $G=(V,E)$ be a graph . The problem "G has an even number of edges" can be reduced to the first query, by interpreting G as an unary structure $\pi(G) =(B,R)$ over the domain of edges ,i.e. $B= V^2$ and with $R=\{ (x,y) \in B$ such that $G \models E(x,y) \}$ . Introducing a constructor I, we can express the second query by the formula

$$Even2 = I_{xy}(E(x,y); Even)$$

This formula is evaluated as follows :

$$G(V,E) \models Even2 \quad iff \quad \pi(G) (B,R) \models Even$$

The following definition of I generalizes the above notion :

**Definition 4 :**
Let L be a logic language, $\pi =< \varphi_1,..,\varphi_r>$ be a set of L-formulas over some schema $\sigma$ . Let $\Omega=(R_1,...R_r)$ be a schema, called the view schema, with $arity(R_i) = n_i$, $1\leq i\leq r$, such that, for each i, $arity(\varphi_i)=k_i n_i$, for some $k_i$, and let $\Psi$ be a L-sentence (i.e. a closed formula) over $\Omega$. For each structure A over $\sigma$ whose domain is U, we define a structure $\pi(A)$ over the schema $\Omega$ whose domain is $U^{k_1}\cup....\cup U^{k_r}$ ,s.t. for each i,

$$\pi(A)( R_i) = \{ \bar{a}_1.. \bar{a}_{ni} \mid \bar{a}_1,.., \bar{a}_{ni} \in U^{k_i} \text{ and } A \models \varphi_i ( \bar{a}_1,..., \bar{a}_{ni} ) \}$$

The formula $\Phi = I_{\bar{X}} (\varphi_1,...,\varphi_r ; \Psi)$ is evaluated as follows :

$$A \models \Phi \quad iff \quad \pi(A) \models \Psi$$

where $\bar{X}$ is the union of all free variables of $\varphi_1,..,\varphi_r$ .
◊

*Remark* : The above definition of I can be generalized in an obvious way to the case where $\pi$ is of the form $< \varphi_1(\bar{X}_1,\bar{Y}_1), ..,\varphi_r(\bar{X}_r,\bar{Y}_r) >$ with $|\bar{X}_i|=k_i. n_i$, for some $k_i$. The formula

$$\Phi(\bar{Y}) = I_{\bar{X}} ( \varphi_1(\bar{X}_1,\bar{Y}_1), ...,\varphi_r(\bar{X}_r,\bar{Y}_r) ; \Psi) \qquad (*)$$

where $\bar{Y}$ is the union of the free variables $\bar{Y}_1,..,\bar{Y}_r$ , is evaluated as follows :

$$A \models \Phi(\bar{Y}) \quad iff \quad \pi_{\bar{y}}(A) \models \Psi$$

where for each $\bar{Y}$ , $\pi_{\bar{y}}(A)$ is a structure defined likely $\pi(A)$ in the above definition, with

$$\pi_{\bar{y}}(A)( R_i) = \{ \bar{a}_1.. \bar{a}_{ni} \mid \bar{a}_1,..., \bar{a}_{ni} \in U^{ki} \text{ and } A \models \varphi_i ( \bar{a}_1,..., \bar{a}_{ni} , \bar{Y}_i ) \}$$

*Example 6:*

The set of vertices of a graph G that have an even in-degree can be expressed by the following formula :

$$\text{Even-in-Degree } (y) = I_x(E(x,y); \text{Even}) \qquad \lozenge$$

The logical reduction notion is particularly interesting in the context of symmetry based choice languages. In fact thanks to the logical reduction operator I we can express some queries on a structure A using symmetric properties of the structure $\pi(A)$. The latter structure is usually much simpler than the input structure in the sense that it may have FO-definable symmetries. Such a structure $\pi(A)$ is called a reduction or an abstract view of A. With this mechanism of reduction, one can look the complex input database in many possible abstract views and can extract from each of them the desired informations. These informations may be more difficult to extract directly from the input structure itself. An example of such information is the cardinality of a set of elements of an input structure. In this case, the abstraction consists to reduce this set to a pure set, on which one can use symmetry-based choice to count its elements. It should be remarked that the extension of FO + $\text{IFP}_{c,s}$ with the operator I is strictly necessary to express all counting queries for arbitrary input databases. To see it, let us consider a class C of structures such that any of them has no FO-definable symmetries. In this case $\text{FO+IFP}_{c,s}(C)$ coincides with FO+IFP(C), and therefore can not express, for instance, the even cardinality. So the extension of $\text{FO+IFP}_{c,s}$ with the operator I increases its expressive power . On the contrary, such an extension of FO+IFP does not increase its expressive power ( the reason is that a query on a structure A which can be expressed by a FO+IFP formula on an view structure $\pi(A)$ can also be expressed by a FO+IFP formula on the input A) .

The extension of $\text{FO+IFP}_{c,s}$ with the logical reduction operator I is formally defined as follows :

**Definition 5 :**

Let $\sigma$ be a schema, $\text{FO+IFP}_{c,s}+I$ ($\sigma$) is the set S($\sigma$) of formulas defined likely FO+IFP($\sigma$) with following additional rule for formula construction : If in (\*), for each i , $\varphi_i$ is in S($\sigma$), $\Psi$ is a sentence of $\text{FO+IFP}_{c,s}$ ($\Omega$) or S($\Omega$) for some $\Omega$, then the formula (\*) is in S($\sigma$).

*Remark :*

In a formula of $\text{FO+IFP}_{c,s}+I$, the $\text{FO+IFP}_{c,s}$ subformulas appear only in the boolean form. For this reason, the queries expressed by this language are strictly deterministic.

Let FO + IFP + C be the extension of Fixpoint with Counting (cf [GT]). We have the following Theorem:

**Theorem 3** :  $FO + IFP + C \subset FO + IFP_{c,s} + I \subseteq DB\text{-}PTIME$

*Proof* :

Since queries expressed by $FO + IFP_{c,s} + I$, as explained in the above remark, are deterministic and can be computed in polynomial time, the last inclusion is obvious. To show the first inclusion it is sufficient, by the theorem 2, to prove that each formula $\theta$ of $FO + IFP + C$ can be simulated by a formula of $FO+IFP_{c,s}+I$.

The simulation of a counting operation on a set defined by a subformula $\varphi$ of $\theta$ consists to reduce this set to a pure set, on which one can use symmerty-based choice to count its elements . More precisely, this simulation is realized as follows :

- Let Succ be a linear order on a set of elements U (that will be defined later), let R be an unary relation whose elements are not in U and E a relation containing only one element of U, then there is a sentence $\psi$ of $FO + IFP_{c,s}$ over the schema (Succ,R,E) expressing that the unique element of E is the Nth- element of U according to the relation Succ and N is the cardinality of R.

- Using the reduction operator, we can define , for each formula $\varphi(\bar{x})$ , a formula $\varphi*(z)$ expressing that z is the $N^{th}$- element of U w.r.t the order Succ and $N=Count(\bar{x}, \varphi(\bar{x}))$ . This reducing formula $\varphi*(z)$ expresses, for each z, the evaluation of the above sentence $\psi$ on a structure whose the relation R is the interpretation of the formula $\varphi(\bar{x})$, E is the interpretation of the formula $(x = z)$ and Succ is an ordering relation on U. This principle of simulation goes through for general count terms of the form $N = Count(\bar{x}, \varphi(y,\bar{x}))$, the corresponding formula that simulates it is denoted by $\varphi*(y,z)$ .

The simulation of the formula $\theta$ of $FO+IFP+C$ begins by generating, thanks to the choice mechanism using the symmetry $F_T$, an order Succ on the domain U of $(k+1)$-tuples, where k is the maximum $|\bar{x}|$ of all count terms of the form $Count(\bar{x}, \varphi(\bar{x}))$ in $\theta$. Then the simulation will compute the formula $\theta*$ which is the formula $\theta$ whose each occurrence of a count expression of the form $Count(\bar{x}, \varphi(y,\bar{x})) = N$ is replaced by the above subformula $\varphi*(y,z)$ and the quantifier on N by a corresponding quantifier on z .

◊

# 8 Conclusion

In this paper we have shown how restricted non deterministic mechanisms are useful to define a powerful but efficient deterministic query language. We think that the class of queries which can be expressed by this language is interesting because they take into account natural properties of structures (i.e. FO definable symmetries). It remains of course an open question whether taking into account these natural properties of structures is sufficient or not to characterize all DB-PTIME queries.

# References

[AV1]   S.Abiteboul and V.Vianu. Non-determinism in logic-based languages. Annals of Math. and Artif. Int., 3 :151-186, 1991.

[AV2]   S.Abiteboul and V.Vianu. Generic computation and its complexity. In Proc. 23rd ACM Symp. on the Theory of Computing, pages 209-219, 1991.

[CFI]   J. Cai, M. Furer, and N. Immerman. An optimal lower bound on the number of variables for graph identification. In Proc 30th IEEE Conf. on Foundations of Computer Science, pages 612-617, 1989.

[CH1]   A.Chandra and D.Harel. Computable queries for relational databases. Journal of Computer and System Sciences, 21(2) : 156-178, Oct. 1980.

[CH2]   A.Chandra and D.Harel. Structure and Complexity of relational queries. Journal of Computer and System Sciences, 25(1) : 99-128, Aug. 1982.

[Daw]   A. Dawar. Feasible Computation Through Model Theory. Ph.D Thesis. University of Pennsylvania, Philadelphia, 1993.

[End]   H. B. Enderton. A Mathematical Introduction to Logic. Academic Press, 1972

[GVdBG]  M.Gyssens, J. Van den Bussche, D. Van Gucht. Expressiveness of Efficient Semi-deterministic Choice Constructs ICALP 94, 820, 106-117.

[GS]   Y.Gurevich and S.Shelah. Fixed-point extensions of first order logic. In Pro 26th IEEE Symp. on Foundations of Computer Science, 210-214, 1983.

[GT]   S.Grumbach and C.Tollu. Query langugages with counters. In Proc. 4th Int. Conf. Database Theory, LNCS 646, 124-139. Springer-Verlag, 1992 .

[Imm82]N. Immermann. Upper and lower bounds for first-order definability. JCSS, 25:76-98,1982.

[Imm86]N. Immermann. Relational queries computable in polynomial time . Information and Control, 68:86-104, 1986.

[Imm87] N. Immermann. Languages that capture complexity classes. SIAM Journal on Computing,      16:760-778, 1987.

[KV]      Ph.G.Kolaitis and M.Y.Vardi. Fixpoint logic vs. infinitary logic in finite-model theory. In Proc. 7th IEEE Symp. on Logic in Computer Science, 46-57, 1992.

[Var]      M. Vardi. The complexity of relational query languages. In Proc. 14th ACM Symp. on the Theory of Computing, 137-146. 1982.

[VdBG]  J. Van den Bussche, D. Van Gucht. Semi-determinism . Proc. 11th ACM Sym. Principles of Database Systems, 191-201, 1992.

# Annex

## Proposition 3:

Let I be a structure over some signature $\Omega$, w be a constant symbol not in $\Omega$, c be any element of dom(I) and I' be an extension of I on $\Omega \cup \{w\}$  such that $I'(\Omega)=I$ and $I'(w)= c$.

If I is k-reducible then so is  I' .  $\Diamond$

*Proof:*

The proof is based on the k-pebbles game which characterizes the k-equivalence relation. We recall at first the definition of this game ( see also [Imm82 ] ,[KV]).

Assume that A and B are two structures over $\Omega$, and let $(a_1,...a_m)$ and $(b_1,...b_m)$ be (with $1 \leq m \leq k$) two m-tuples of A and B. Let $d_1,..d_l$ and $d_1',..d_l'$ be the interpretation of the constants of $\Omega$ on A and B respectively. The k-pebbles game between two players I and II on A and B and on the two tuples $(a_1,...a_m)$ , $(b_1,...b_m)$ behaves as follows. There are k pairs of pebbles $g_i$, $h_i$, $1 \leq i \leq k$. Initially, for each $1 \leq i \leq m$ , the pebbles $g_i$ and $h_i$ are placed on the elements $a_i$ and $b_i$ respectively. At each move r player I picks up one of the pebbles (which can be new or already used) and places it on an element of one of the structures (Say, he picks up $g_i$. He must then place it on an element of A). Player II then picks up the corresponding pebble (if player I chooses $g_i$ then player II must choose $h_i$) and places it on an element of the opposite structure ( B in this case). Player II has a winning strategy if he always find matching points to assure that, at any move r, the following mapping is a partial isomorphism :

$$f(r) : d_j \rightarrow d_j', \quad 1 \leq j \leq l$$
$$g_i(r) \rightarrow h_i(r) \ , \ 1 \leq i \leq k$$

where $g_i(r)$, $h_i(r)$ are the elements on which the pebbles $g_i$, $h_i$ are respectively sitting just after move r .

Fact : Player II has a winning strategy for the k-pebbles game on A,B beginning with the m first pairs $g_i,h_i$ on $a_i,b_i$  $1 \leq i \leq m$  respectively iff
A, $(a_1,..a_m) \equiv k$ B, $(b_1,..b_m)$ .

The proof of the proposition 3 is as follows :
Firstly, we will show that for all m-tuples $(a_1,....a_m),(b_1,...,b_m)$ with $m \geq k$ we have
if                    I', $(a_1,...,a_m)$ $\equiv m$ I', $(b_1,...,b_m)$         (1)
then                  I, $(a_1,...,a_m,c)$ $\equiv m+1$ I , $(b_1,...,b_m,c)$    (1')
where I, I' and c are as in proposition 3.

By the above fact, (1) means that player II has a winning strategy in the game on I' and its copy with m pairs of pebbles initially in the positions $g_i(0)=a_i$, $h_i(0)=b_i$, $1 \leq i \leq m$. That is, player II can assure, for all r, the following partial isomorphism :

$f_{I'}(r)$ :    c  $\rightarrow$  c    (interpretation of the constant w on I' and its copy)

$d_j \rightarrow d_j$ ,  $1 \leq j \leq l$ (for the interpretations of the other constant symbols in I' and its copy)

$g_i(r) \rightarrow h_i(r)$ , for $1 \leq i \leq m$

If in the first move, r=1, player I moves the pebble $g_i$ to the element c of I', then player II must move $h_i$ to the corresponding c of the copy of I' because  this is the only way to assure the above partial isomorphism. Since player II still has a winning strategy of the m-pebbles game, beginning with these new positions of the pebbles, we also have

$$I', (a_1,...,a_{i-1},c,a_{i+1},...,a_m) \equiv m \ I', (b_1,...,b_{i-1},c,b_{i+1},...,b_m)$$

which implies that

$$I, (a_1,...,a_{i-1},c,a_{i+1},...,a_m) \equiv m \ I, (b_1,...,b_{i-1},c,b_{i+1},...,b_m)$$

(because I is a substructure of I') and therefore

$$I,(a_1,..., a_{i-1},c,a_{i+1},...,a_m) \equiv m+1 \ I, (b_1,...,b_{i-1},c,b_{i+1},...,b_m) \qquad (2)$$

(because I is k-reducible and $k \leq m$ ) . Another consequence of (1) is that

$$I,(a_1,...,a_m) \equiv m+1 I , (b_1,...,b_m) \qquad (3)$$

(using as above the argument that I is a substructure of I' and  is k-reducible)

To obtain (1')  we show that player II has a winning strategy in the m+1-pebbles game on I and its copy with the pebbles initially in the positions $g_i(0)= a_i$, $h_i(0)= b_i$, $1 \leq i \leq m$, and $g_{m+1}(0)= c$, $h_{m+1}(0)=c$. That is we will show that player II can assure, for all r, that the mapping

$$f_I(r): \quad d_j \to d_j, \quad 1 \le j \le l \text{ (for the interpretations of the constant}$$
$$\text{symbols in I)}$$
$$g_i(r) \to h_i(r), \text{ for } 1 \le i \le m+1$$

is a partial isomorphism. This is true for r=0. In fact, the mapping $f_I(0)$ is exactly the preceding mapping $f_{I'}(0)$. Now, in the first move, r=1 :

+ if player I moves one of the (m+1)th pebbles, player II has a winning strategy, using (3) and the fact that he can consider the (m+1)th pebble as not already used.

+ If player I moves one of the j-th pebbles $1 \le j \le m$, say $g_1$ and he moves it from $a_1$ to $a_1'$, the player II has a winning strategy too. Indeed let us recall that from (2) we have:
I, $(c,a_2,...,a_m) \equiv m+1$ I, $(c,b_2,...,b_m)$ and therefore player II has a winning strategy in the (m+1)pebbles game beginning with m first pebbles on the points $(c,a_2,...,a_m)$ and $(c,b_2,...,b_m)$. In this game, suppose that in the first move player I picks up the pebble $g_{m+1}$ and put it on the above $a_1'$ and that player II answers by putting $h_{m+1}$ on $b_1'$. We know that player II still has a winning strategy from these new positions of the pebbles $(c,a_2,...,a_m, a_1')$ and $(c,b_2,...,b_m,b_1')$ or equivalently from the positions $(a_1',a_2...,a_m,c)$ and $(b_1',b_2,...,b_m,c)$ .
Returning now to our present game, we see that player II can answer by moving the pebble $h_1$ to the above $b_1'$. Evidently, he still has a winning strategy because the positions of the pebbles are now exactly the above positions. So, we have shown (1')

Let us now prove the k-reducibility property of I'.
Suppose we have (1). We have to prove $\quad$ I', $(a_1,...,a_m) \equiv \infty$ I', $(b_1,...,b_m)$ $\quad$ (1")
Using (1') and the fact that I is k-reducible we have :
$$\text{I, } (a_1,...,a_m,c) \equiv \infty \text{ I, } (b_1,...,b_m,c) \qquad (1''')$$
For any formula $\varphi(x_1,...x_m)$ of FO($\Omega \cup \{w\}$), let $\varphi'(x_1,...x_m,z)$ be the formula $\varphi$ in which each occurrence of the constant w is replaced by the new variable z. If I'$\models\varphi(a_1,...a_m)$ then equivalently I $\models \varphi'(a_1,...a_m,c)$. Now by (1'''), we deduce that II$\models\varphi'(b_1,...b_m,c)$ or equivalently I'$\models\varphi(b_1,...b_m)$. So we have shown (1").
$\lozenge$

# Author Index

# Springer-Verlag
# and the Environment

We at Springer-Verlag firmly believe that an international science publisher has a special obligation to the environment, and our corporate policies consistently reflect this conviction.

We also expect our business partners – paper mills, printers, packaging manufacturers, etc. – to commit themselves to using environmentally friendly materials and production processes.

The paper in this book is made from low- or no-chlorine pulp and is acid free, in conformance with international standards for paper permanency.

# Lecture Notes in Computer Science

For information about Vols. 1–1083

please contact your bookseller or Springer-Verlag